Interactive Computing Series

Microsoft® Office XP   Volume 1

Kenneth C. Laudon • Kenneth Rosenblatt

David Langley • Robin Pickering

Azimuth Interactive, Inc.

 **McGraw-Hill**
Irwin

Boston   Burr Ridge, IL   Dubuque, IA   Madison, WI   New York   San Francisco   St. Louis
Bangkok   Bogotá   Caracas   Kuala Lumpur   Lisbon   London   Madrid   Mexico City
Milan   Montreal   New Delhi   Santiago   Seoul   Singapore   Sydney   Taipei   Toronto

McGraw-Hill Higher Education

A Division of The McGraw-Hill Companies

MICROSOFT OFFICE XP VOLUME 1
Published by McGraw-Hill/Irwin, an imprint of The McGraw-Hill
Companies, Inc., 1221 Avenue of the Americas, New York, NY 10020.
Copyright 2002, by The McGraw-Hill Companies, Inc. All rights reserved.
No part of this publication may be reproduced or distributed in any form or
by any means, or stored in a database or retrieval system, without the prior
written consent of The McGraw-Hill Companies, Inc., including, but not
limited to, in any network or other electronic storage or transmission, or
broadcast for distance learning.

This book is printed on acid-free paper.

2 3 4 5 6 7 8 9 0 QPD/QPD 0 9 8 7 6 5 4 3 2

ISBN 0-07-247261-8

Publisher: *George Werthman*
Developmental editor I: *Sarah Wood*
Senior marketing manager: *Jeff Parr*
Senior project manager: *Pat Frederickson*
Senior production supervisor: *Michael R. McCormick*
Senior designer: *Pam Verros*
Supplement producer: *Mark Mattson*
Cover photograph: *Bill Brooks/© Masterfile*
Interior design: *Asylum Studios*
Cover designer: *JoAnne Schopler*
Compositor: *Azimuth Interactive, Inc.*
Typeface: *10/12 Times*
Printer: *Quebecor Printing Book Group/Dubuque*

Library of Congress Control Number: 2001096315

www.mhhe.com

InformationTechnology

Information Technology at McGraw-Hill/Irwin

At McGraw-Hill Higher Education, we publish instructional materials targeted at the higher education market. In an effort to expand the tools of higher learning, we publish texts, lab manuals, study guides, testing materials, software, and multimedia products.

At McGraw-Hill/Irwin (a division of McGraw-Hill Higher Education), we realize that technology has created and will continue to create new mediums for professors and students to use in managing resources and communicating information with one another. We strive to provide the most flexible and complete teaching and learning tools available as well as offer solutions to the changing world of teaching and learning.

MCGRAW-HILL/IRWIN IS DEDICATED TO PROVIDING THE TOOLS FOR TODAY'S INSTRUCTORS AND STUDENTS TO SUCCESSFULLY NAVIGATE THE WORLD OF INFORMATION TECHNOLOGY.

- **Seminar series**—Technology Connection seminar series offered across the country every year demonstrates the latest technology products and encourages collaboration among teaching professionals.

- **Osborne/McGraw-Hill**—This division of The McGraw-Hill Companies is known for its best-selling Internet titles: Harley Hahn's Internet & Web Yellow Pages, and the Internet Complete Reference. Osborne offers an additional resource for certification and has strategic publishing relationships with corporations such as Corel Corporation and America Online. For more information visit Osborne at www.osborne.com.

- **Digital solutions**—McGraw-Hill/Irwin is committed to publishing digital solutions. Taking your course online does not have to be a solitary venture, nor does it have to be a difficult one. We offer several solutions that will allow you to enjoy all the benefits of having course material online. For more information visit www.mhhe.com/solutions/index.mhtml.

- **Packaging options**—For more about our discount options, contact your local McGraw-Hill/Irwin Sales representative at 1-800-338-3987 or visit our Web site at www.mhhe.com/it.

Interactive Computing Series

GOALS/PHILOSOPHY

The *Interactive Computing Series* provides you with an illustrated interactive environment for learning software skills using Microsoft Office. The text uses both "hands-on" instruction, supplementary text, and independent exercises to enrich the learning experience.

APPROACH

The *Interactive Computing Series* is the visual interactive way to develop and apply software skills. This skills-based approach coupled with its highly visual, two-page spread design allows the student to focus on a single skill without having to turn the page. A Lesson Goal at the beginning of each lesson prepares the student to apply the skills with a real-world focus. The Quiz and Interactivity sections at the end of each lesson measure the student's understanding of the concepts and skills learned in the two-page spreads and reinforce the skills with additional exercises.

ABOUT THE BOOK

The **Interactive Computing Series** offers *two levels* of instruction. Each level builds upon the previous level.

Brief lab manual—covers the basics of the application, contains two to four chapters.

Introductory lab manual—includes the material in the Brief textbook plus two to four additional chapters. The Introductory lab manuals prepare students for the *Microsoft Office User Specialist Proficiency Exam (MOUS Certification)*.

Each lesson is divided into a number of Skills. Each **Skill** is first explained at the top of the page in the Concept. Each **Concept** is a concise description of why the Skill is useful and where it is commonly used. Each **Step (Do It!)** contains the instructions on how to complete the Skill. The appearance of the *MOUS Skill* icon on a Skill page indicates that the Skill contains instruction in at least one of the required MOUS objectives for the relevant exam. Though the icons appear in the Brief manuals as well as the Introductory manuals, only the Introductory manuals may be used in preparation for MOUS Certification.

Figure 1

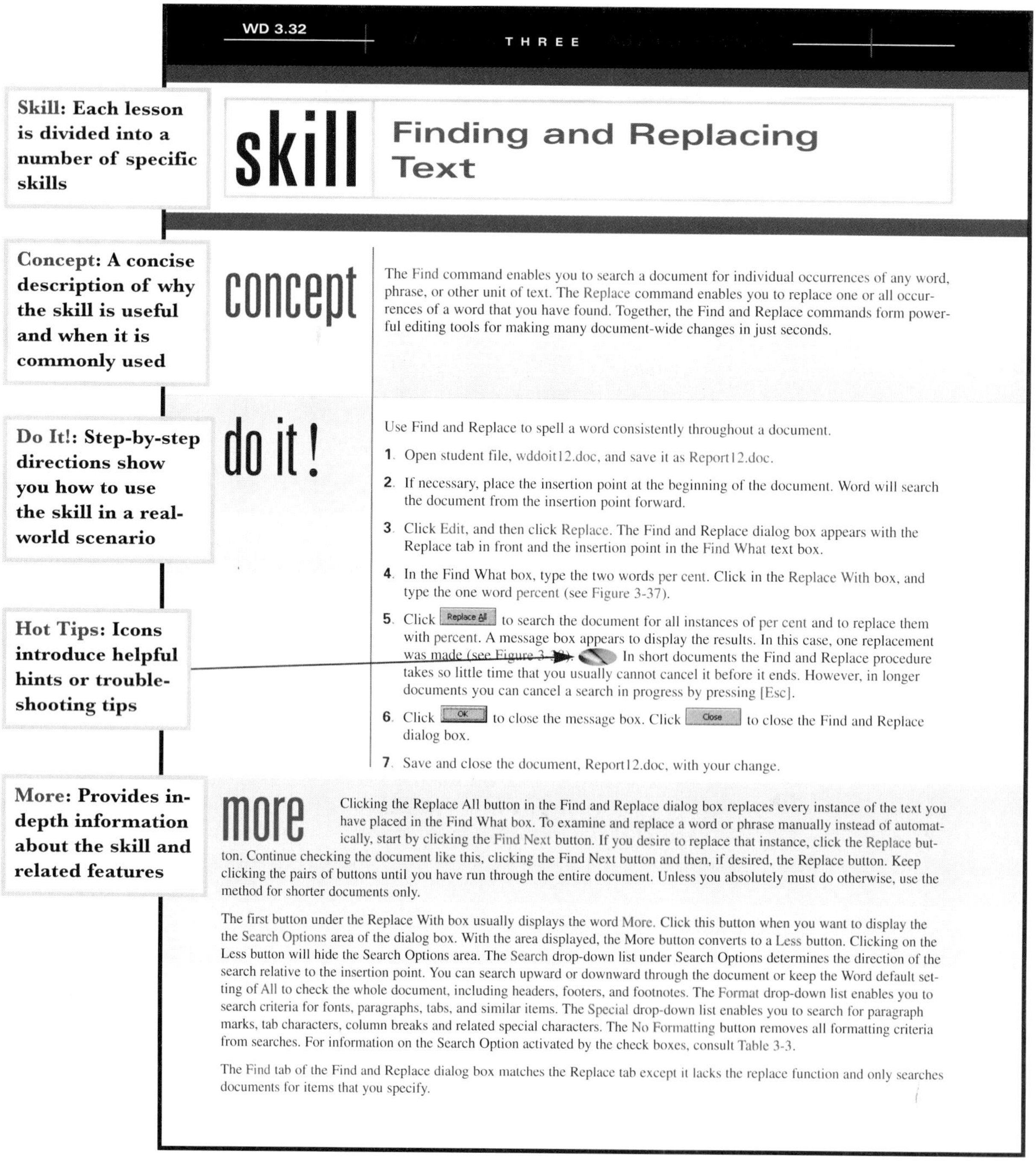

Skill: Each lesson is divided into a number of specific skills

skill — Finding and Replacing Text

Concept: A concise description of why the skill is useful and when it is commonly used

concept

The Find command enables you to search a document for individual occurrences of any word, phrase, or other unit of text. The Replace command enables you to replace one or all occurrences of a word that you have found. Together, the Find and Replace commands form powerful editing tools for making many document-wide changes in just seconds.

Do It!: Step-by-step directions show you how to use the skill in a real-world scenario

do it !

Use Find and Replace to spell a word consistently throughout a document.

1. Open student file, wddoit12.doc, and save it as Report12.doc.

2. If necessary, place the insertion point at the beginning of the document. Word will search the document from the insertion point forward.

3. Click Edit, and then click Replace. The Find and Replace dialog box appears with the Replace tab in front and the insertion point in the Find What text box.

4. In the Find What box, type the two words per cent. Click in the Replace With box, and type the one word percent (see Figure 3-37).

5. Click [Replace All] to search the document for all instances of per cent and to replace them with percent. A message box appears to display the results. In this case, one replacement was made (see Figure 3-▶). In short documents the Find and Replace procedure takes so little time that you usually cannot cancel it before it ends. However, in longer documents you can cancel a search in progress by pressing [Esc].

Hot Tips: Icons introduce helpful hints or trouble-shooting tips

6. Click [OK] to close the message box. Click [Close] to close the Find and Replace dialog box.

7. Save and close the document, Report12.doc, with your change.

More: Provides in-depth information about the skill and related features

more

Clicking the Replace All button in the Find and Replace dialog box replaces every instance of the text you have placed in the Find What box. To examine and replace a word or phrase manually instead of automatically, start by clicking the Find Next button. If you desire to replace that instance, click the Replace button. Continue checking the document like this, clicking the Find Next button and then, if desired, the Replace button. Keep clicking the pairs of buttons until you have run through the entire document. Unless you absolutely must do otherwise, use the method for shorter documents only.

The first button under the Replace With box usually displays the word More. Click this button when you want to display the the Search Options area of the dialog box. With the area displayed, the More button converts to a Less button. Clicking on the Less button will hide the Search Options area. The Search drop-down list under Search Options determines the direction of the search relative to the insertion point. You can search upward or downward through the document or keep the Word default setting of All to check the whole document, including headers, footers, and footnotes. The Format drop-down list enables you to search criteria for fonts, paragraphs, tabs, and similar items. The Special drop-down list enables you to search for paragraph marks, tab characters, column breaks and related special characters. The No Formatting button removes all formatting criteria from searches. For information on the Search Option activated by the check boxes, consult Table 3-3.

The Find tab of the Find and Replace dialog box matches the Replace tab except it lacks the replace function and only searches documents for items that you specify.

In the book, each skill is described in a two-page graphical spread (Figure 1). The left side of the two-page spread describes the skill, the concept, and the steps needed to perform the skill. The right side of the spread uses screen shots to show you how the screen should look at key stages.

Figure 1 (cont'd)

Figure 3-37 Find and Replace dialog box

Enter the word or phrase to search for and replace here

Enter the replacement word here

Use check boxes to activate search options

Click to determine direction of search

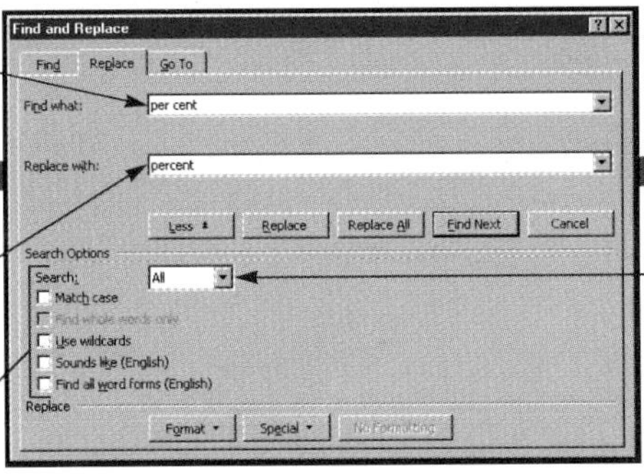

Figure 3-38 Report12.doc, after Find and Replace activity

Find and Replace makes one change in document

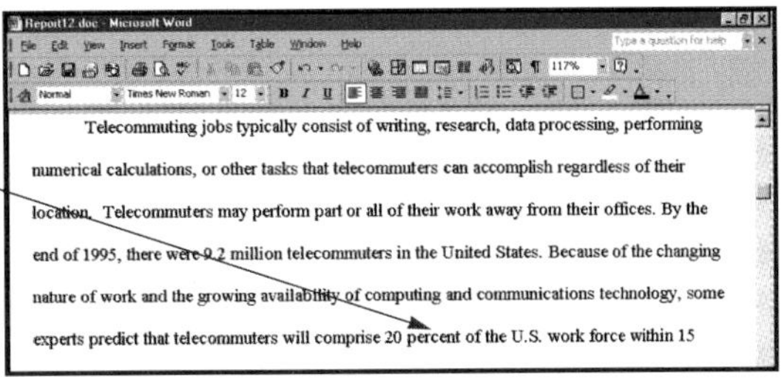

Telecommuting jobs typically consist of writing, research, data processing, performing numerical calculations, or other tasks that telecommuters can accomplish regardless of their location. Telecommuters may perform part or all of their work away from their offices. By the end of 1995, there were 9.2 million telecommuters in the United States. Because of the changing nature of work and the growing availability of computing and communications technology, some experts predict that telecommuters will comprise 20 percent of the U.S. work force within 15

Screen shots:
Show you what the screen should look like after following the Do It! steps

Table 3-3 Search Options

Option	Description
Match case	Finds those items in capitals and/or lowercase that exactly match contents of Find What box
Find whole words only	Finds only those items that are whole words, not parts of a larger word
Use wildcards	Searches for wildcards, special characters, or special search operators found in Find What box
Sounds like	Finds words that sound the same as in Find What box but are spelled differently
Find all word forms	Replaces all forms of the text in Find What box with proper forms of the word in the Replace with box; words in both boxes should be the same part of speech

Summary tables:
Give you a quick overview of shortcuts, toolbar icons, and options you can use to complete the skill

Practice

Open student file wdprac3-13.doc and save it as mywdprac3-13.doc. Following the instructions that appear at the beginning of the file, practice using the Find and Replace dialog box to search for and replace text. When you have completed the practice exercise, resave and close mywdprac3-13.doc.

Practice: Allows
you to practice the skill with a built-in exercise or directs you to a student file

END-OF-LESSON FEATURES

In the book, the learning in each lesson is reinforced at the end by a Quiz and a skills review called Interactivity, which provides step-by-step exercises and real-world problems for the students to solve independently.

The following is a list of supplemental material available with the Interactive Computing Series:

Skills Assessment

SimNet eXPert (Simulated Network Assessment Product)—SimNet provides a way for you to test students' software skills in a simulated environment. SimNet is available for Microsoft Office 97, Microsoft Office 2000, and Microsoft Office XP. SimNet provides flexibility for you in your course by offering:

• Pre-testing options
• Post-testing options
• Course placement testing
• Diagnostic capabilities to reinforce skills
• Proficiency testing to measure skills
• Web or LAN delivery of tests
• Computer based training materials (New for Office XP)
• MOUS preparation exams
• Learning verification reports
• Spanish Version

Instructor's Resource Kits

The Instructor's Resource Kit provides professors with all of the ancillary material needed to teach a course. McGraw-Hill/Irwin is dedicated to providing instructors with the most effective instruction resources available. Many of these resources are available at our Information Technology Supersite www.mhhe.com/it. Our Instructor's Kits are available on CD-ROM and contain the following:

Diploma by Brownstone—is the most flexible, powerful, and easy-to-use computerized testing system available in higher education. The diploma system allows professors to create an Exam as a printed version, as a LAN-based Online version, and as an Internet version. Diploma includes grade book features, which automate the entire testing process.

Instructor's Manual—Includes:
–Solutions to all lessons and end-of-unit material
–Teaching Tips
–Teaching Strategies
–Additional exercises

PowerPoint Slides—NEW to the *Interactive Computing Series*, all of the figures from the application textbooks are available in PowerPoint slides for presentation purposes.

Student Data Files—To use the *Interactive Computing Series*, students must have Student Data Files to complete practice and test sessions. The instructor and students using this text in classes are granted the right to post the student files on any network or stand-alone computer, or to distribute the files on individual diskettes. The student files may be downloaded from our IT Supersite at www.mhhe.com/it.

Series Web Site—Available at www.mhhe.com/cit/apps/laudon.

Digital Solutions

Pageout—is our Course Web site Development Center. Pageout offers a Syllabus page, Web site address, Online Learning Center Content, online exercises and quizzes, gradebook, discussion board, an area for students to build their own Web pages, and all the features of Pageout Lite. For more information please visit the Pageout Web site at www.mhla.net/pageout.

Digital Solutions (continued)

OLC/Series Web Sites—Online Learning Centers (OLCs)/Series Sites are accessible through our Supersite at www.mhhe.com/it. Our Online Learning Centers/Series Sites provide pedagogical features and supplements for our titles online. Students can point and click their way to key terms, learning objectives, chapter overviews, PowerPoint slides, exercises, and Web links.

The McGraw-Hill Learning Architecture (MHLA)—is a complete course delivery system. MHLA gives professors ownership in the way digital content is presented to the class through online quizzing, student collaboration, course administration, and content management. For a walk-through of MHLA visit the MHLA Web site at www.mhla.net.

Packaging Options—For more about our discount options, contact your local McGraw-Hill/Irwin Sales representative at 1-800-338-3987 or visit our Web site at www.mhhe.com/it.

Visit www.mhhe.com/it
THE ONLY SITE WITH ALL YOUR CIT AND MIS NEEDS.

acknowledgments

The *Interactive Computing Series* is a cooperative effort of many individuals, each contributing to an overall team effort. The Interactive Computing team is composed of instructional designers, writers, multimedia designers, graphic artists, and programmers. Our goal is to provide you and your instructor with the most powerful and enjoyable learning environment using both traditional text and new interactive multimedia techniques. Interactive Computing is tested rigorously in both CD-ROM and text formats prior to publication.

Our special thanks to George Werthman, our Publisher; Sarah Wood, our Developmental Editor; and Jeffrey Parr, Marketing Director for Computer Information Systems. They have provided exceptional market awareness and understanding, along with enthusiasm and support for the project, and have inspired us all to work closely together. In addition, Steven Schuetz provided valuable technical review of our interactive versions, and Charles Pelto contributed superb quality assurance.

The Azimuth team members who contributed to the textbooks and CD-ROM multimedia program are:

Ken Rosenblatt (Editorial Director, Writer)
Russell Polo (Technical Director)
Robin Pickering (Developmental Editor, Writer)
David Langley (Writer)
Chris Hahnenberger (Multimedia Designer)

contents

Office XP Volume 1

⑤ Skill covers at least one MOUS Certification Core objective.

ⓢ Skill covers at least one MOUS Certification Core objective.

⑤ Skill covers at least one MOUS Certification Core objective.

⑤ Skill covers at least one MOUS Certification Core objective.

⑤ Skill covers at least one MOUS Certification Core objective.

Office XP continued

⑤ Skill covers at least one MOUS Certification Core objective.

ⓢ Skill covers at least one MOUS Certification Core objective.

⑤ Skill covers at least one MOUS Certification Core objective.

Office XP **continued**

LESSON ONE

1

Introduction to Windows 2000

Windows 2000 is an operating system that controls the basic functions of your computer, such as loading and running programs, saving data, and displaying information on the screen. Operating system software is different from application software, such as a word processor or spreadsheet program, which you apply to letter writing or calculating data. Instead, operating system software provides the user interface—the visual display on the screen that you use to operate the computer by choosing which programs to run and how to organize your work. Windows 2000 offers a graphical user interface or GUI (pronounced "gooey") that presents you with pictorial representations of computer functions and data.

It is through these pictures, or icons, that you interact with the computer. Data files are represented by icons that look like pieces of paper, and can be organized into groups called folders, which look like manila folders. The My Computer icon, represented by a small desktop PC, allows you to organize these files and folders. Other icons allow you to run programs such as a word processor, a Web browser, or Windows' built-in file manager, Windows Explorer.

Windows 2000 is a powerful operating system that allows you to perform a variety of high-level tasks. Windows 2000 is actually the successor to the Windows NT 4.0 operating system, but it looks, acts, and responds in much the same manner as Windows 98. For instance, the GUI is very similar, using many of the same icons as Windows 98. It also includes integrated Web features. Thus, Windows 2000 gives you the ease of use of Windows 98, with the power, stability, and security previously provided by Windows NT. This makes Windows 2000 an ideal tool for operating a business whether it is run on a laptop computer, a desktop system, or a large business server.

Windows 2000 is easy to use and can be customized with the preferences and options that you desire. Built-in programs called Accessories can be used to help you with day-to-day tasks. Help offers fast tutorial and troubleshooting advice. This book will teach you about the basic elements of Windows 2000 and how to use them. You will learn file management, advanced Windows functions, Internet skills, and some of the other special features of Windows 2000.

skills

≶ **Examining the Desktop Icons**

≶ **Opening, Moving, and Resizing a Window**

≶ **Using the Start Menu**

≶ **Using the Taskbar**

≶ **Using Menus**

≶ **Using Dialog Boxes**

≶ **Getting Help**

≶ **Shutting Down Windows 2000**

skill Examining the Desktop Icons

concept

The screen you see when Windows 2000 completes the StartUp procedure is called the desktop. Do not be surprised if your desktop does not look exactly like the one pictured in Figure 1-1 as computer setups vary from machine to machine. (Throughout this book the appearance of your desktop and windows will depend on the software installed and the configuration of various settings of your computer.) Like the desk that you are sitting at, the Windows desktop is the workspace on which all actions are performed. On the left side of your screen you will see small pictures called icons. Icons are pictorial representations of a task, program, folder, or file. Each icon represents an application or utility that you can start. You use the mouse — a hand-controlled input device that, when connected to the computer and moved along a clean, flat surface, will move the graphical pointer around the screen — to double-click an icon to open an application or a file. The buttons on the mouse are used to give commands, and there are four basic ways you can use the mouse: pointing, clicking, double-clicking, and dragging.

do it !

Use the mouse to move the pointer ⬚ around the desktop to explore the desktop icons.

1. Using the mouse, move the pointer over various areas of the desktop to get a feel for how the pointer moves in relation to the motion of the mouse. Positioning the pointer over an item is called pointing.

2. Locate the My Computer icon on the desktop; it resembles a desktop PC. Place the pointer on the icon and click the left mouse button once. This will highlight the icon, indicating that it has been selected. Click a blank area of the screen to undo this selection. Note that primary mouse functions are done using the left button.

3. Double-clicking is done to open a program, file, or window. Open the My Computer window by placing the pointer on the My Computer icon and clicking the left mouse button twice quickly. The My Computer window, shown in Figure 1-2, will appear on the desktop.

4. To close the window you have just opened, position the pointer over the Close button ☒ in the upper-right corner and click the left mouse button.

5. Icons are not fixed on the desktop and can be moved by dragging. Move the pointer to the My Computer icon, then click and hold down the button. You have grabbed the icon.

6. With the mouse button held down, move the icon by dragging it to the center of your desktop. A faint image of the icon will appear to indicate the current position of the icon on the desktop. Let go of the mouse button to drop the icon into position. Then return the icon to its original position. ◀ If your mouse movements are running off the mouse pad, position the mouse pointer in the middle of the screen, and then pick up the mouse and place it in the middle of the mouse pad.

more

Windows 2000 allows you to change the way you work with icons so that the interface behaves more like a Web page. To make this change, click on the word Tools on the Menu bar in the My Computer window. This will cause a list of commands, called a menu, to appear. Click the Folder Options command on the

Tools menu to open the Folder Options dialog box. Whenever you see an ellipsis (three dots) following a command, it indicates that the command will open a dialog box revealing options for the execution of the command. The dialog box will open to a tab named General. In the bottom section of this dialog box, the default option is Double-click to open an item (single-click to select). This is the traditional way of interacting with Windows icons. If you select the first option in the section, Single-click to open an item (point to select), the operating system will switch to a Web-like environment where pointing and clicking are concerned.

Figure 1-1 The Windows desktop

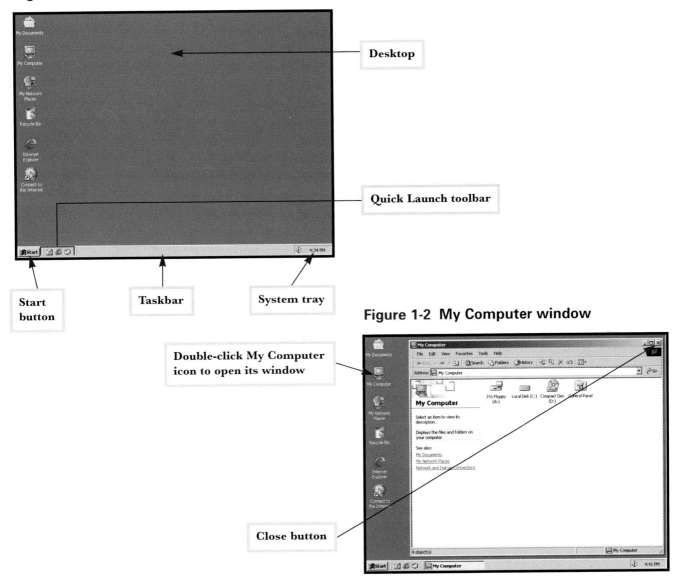

Desktop

Quick Launch toolbar

Start button

Taskbar

System tray

Figure 1-2 My Computer window

Double-click My Computer icon to open its window

Close button

Practice

Open the My Documents window by double-clicking its icon. Use the Close button to close the window.

skill Opening, Moving, and Resizing a Window

concept

As you saw in the previous Skill, icons are pictorial representations of different items on your computer, the most common of which are folders, files, and applications. When you double-click an icon to open it, its contents are revealed in a window or on-screen frame. It is in this window that you interact with a program or utility. Windows are flexible and can be moved, resized, reshaped, and even hidden.

do it !

Open the My Computer window, then resize, move, minimize, and close it.

1. Double-click the My Computer icon. The My Computer window will open, as shown in Figure 1-3.

2. You cannot resize or move a window that is maximized or fills the entire desktop. Look at the three sizing buttons at the right end of the window's title bar, the band at the top of the window that contains the name of the application (also see Table 1-1). The middle button's appearance will change depending on the window's state. If the Restore button 🗗 is visible, click it so the window will no longer be maximized. Once the window is restored to its previous size the button will change to the Maximize button 🗖.

3. Position the mouse pointer on the right edge of the window. This will change the pointer to a double arrow (↔) that is used to resize an object. In Windows 2000, the appearance of the mouse pointer changes to reflect its function during various tasks.

4. Click and hold the left mouse button, drag the edge of the window towards the center of the screen, and then let go of the mouse button to drop the side of the window into place. As you drag the mouse, the border of the window will move with the double arrow, toolbar buttons will disappear (don't worry, their respective commands can still be accessed through menus), and scroll bars (see More below) may appear. This action may be repeated on any of the window's four sides or at any corner. Resizing from the corner will alter both the height and width of the window.

5. Windows can be dragged and dropped just as icons can. Move the pointer over the title bar of the My Computer window, and then click and hold the left mouse button to grab the window.

6. With the mouse button depressed, drag the window to another area of the desktop.

(continued on WN 1.6)

Figure 1-3 Components of a window

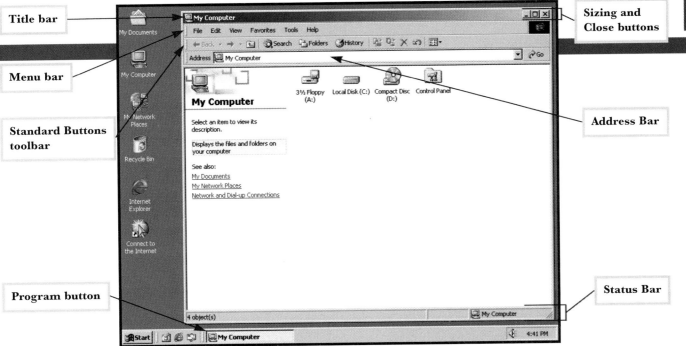

Title bar		Sizing and Close buttons
Menu bar		Address Bar
Standard Buttons toolbar		
Program button		Status Bar

Table 1-1 Sizing buttons

Sizing Button		Use
Maximize	▢	Enlarges the window so that it fills the entire screen, with the taskbar remaining visible
Restore	▣	Returns the window to its previous size
Minimize	_	Shrinks the window so it appears only as a program button on the taskbar
Close	✕	Closes a window or program

skill

Opening, Moving, and Resizing a Window (continued)

do it !

7. Click the Minimize button 🔲. The My Computer window will disappear from the desktop and be reduced to a program button on the taskbar, as shown in Figure 1-4. Clicking the Show Desktop button 🔲 minimizes all open windows. Clicking the button again opens all of the previously visible windows.

8. Click the My Computer program button to restore the window to its previous size.

9. Click File on the Menu bar. The File menu will appear as shown in Figure 1-5.

10. Position the pointer over the last command, Close, to highlight it, and then click the mouse button. The Close command will be executed, just as it would if you clicked the Close button ❎, and the window will disappear from the desktop.

more

When a window is too small to display all of its information, scroll bars (Figure 1-6) will appear on the right and/or bottom edges of the window. Scroll bars are context-sensitive objects and only appear when the situation is appropriate. The scroll bars are used to slide information inside the window so you can see additional contents of the window. If you need to scroll slowly, or only a short distance, click a scroll bar arrow located at the end of the scroll bar. The scroll bar box indicates where you are located in the window. Clicking above or below the scroll bar box moves the display in large increments. Dragging the scroll bar box allows you to control the slide of the window's information precisely.

In the above Skill you clicked the My Computer program button to unhide the window and make it active. An active window is identified by its highlighted title bar, and will be the frontmost window on your desktop if more than one program is running. You can also click the program button of a visible window to minimize it. Right-clicking a program button, clicking it with the right mouse button, will cause a pop-up menu to appear with commands that mirror those of the sizing buttons. These commands can also be found by clicking the Control icon, the icon at the left edge of the title bar representing the application, or by right-clicking the title bar. Right-clicking will usually cause a context-sensitive menu to appear. This menu will contain commands that relate to the task you are performing. Double-clicking the title bar will restore or maximize a window.

Figure 1-4   Minimized My Computer window

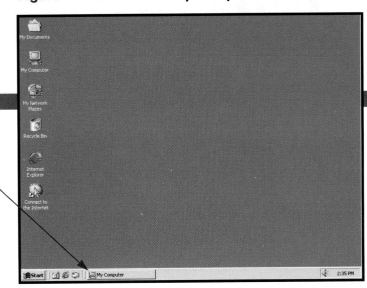

My Computer window
minimized to a program
button on the taskbar

Figure 1-5   Working with the File menu

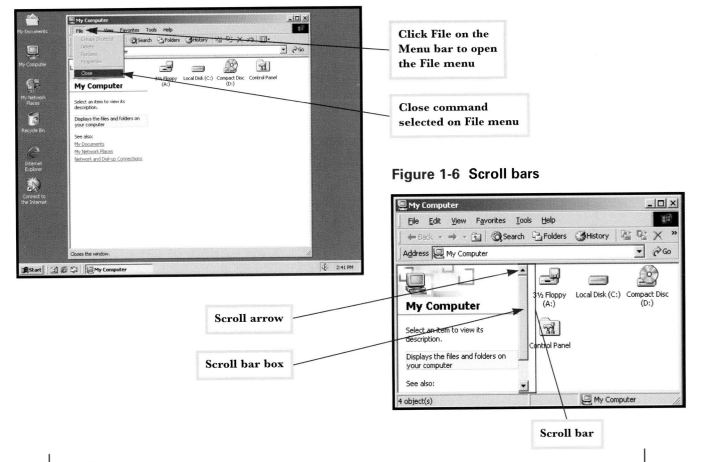

Click File on the
Menu bar to open
the File menu

Close command
selected on File menu

Figure 1-6   Scroll bars

Scroll arrow

Scroll bar box

Scroll bar

Practice

Open and maximize the My Documents window. Then restore the window and drag its right border
outward. Close the window when you are done.

skill | Using the Start Menu

concept

The Start button [🗿Start], located on the left side of the taskbar, provides a quick and easy way to open and organize the applications found on your computer. Clicking the Start button opens a special menu called the Start menu, shown expanded in Figure 1-7, that contains left-to-right lists of program groups. Items with an arrow ▶ next to them contain submenus. Pointing to an item highlights it; and a simple click will then open the program you wish to use.

do it !

Use the Start button to access the Start menu and start Windows Explorer, a file management utility that will be discussed in detail in Lesson 2 (if you do not see an item that is named in this Skill, click the double arrow at the bottom of the menu).

1. Click the Start button [🗿Start] on the taskbar, usually located at the bottom of your desktop. The Start menu will open. Do not be surprised if your Start menu does not match Figure 1-7 exactly. The appearance of your Start menu depends on the software installed and the shortcuts created on your computer.

2. Position the pointer over Programs (notice the little arrow) to bring up the Programs menu. The Programs menu contains a list of shortcuts to some of the applications found on your hard drive, as well as folders that hold groups of related shortcuts to other frequently used programs and utilities.

3. Guide the pointer to Accessories, which is likely located at the top of the Programs menu. The Accessories menu will appear alongside the Programs menu.

4. Move the mouse pointer over to the Accessories menu and click the program named Windows Explorer to launch it. Figure 1-8 displays an open Windows Explorer, with the My Documents folder selected. Notice that a program button displaying the name of the folder selected in Windows Explorer has appeared on the taskbar. ◖◗ The Start menu right-click pop-up menu has commands for quickly opening Windows Explorer and the Search feature.

5. Click the Close button [X] on the title bar to exit Windows Explorer.

more

Items on the Start menu and its submenus are really shortcuts to the actual folders and files that they represent.

The Documents menu contains a list of the files that have been opened most recently so that you can access your most recently and most often used data quickly.

On the Settings menu you will find folders that contain utilities for altering your computer's software and hardware settings. The way you interact with your desktop, the folders on it, the taskbar, and printers can all be altered through icons on the Settings menu.

One of the keys to using a computer is being able to locate the data you need. The Search menu offers you multiple ways in which to find information. You can search for files or folders on your computer, content on the World Wide Web, and people in locally stored address books and Internet directories.

Figure 1-7 Start menu

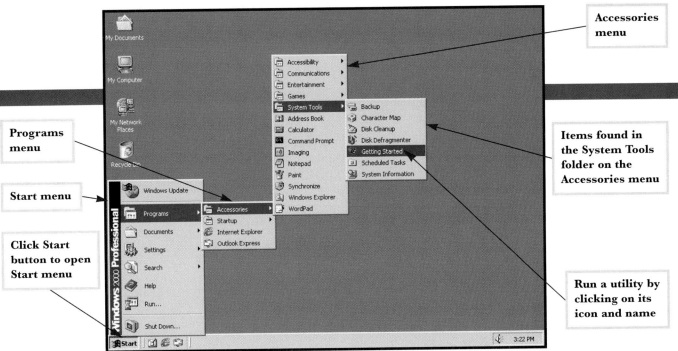

Accessories menu

Items found in the System Tools folder on the Accessories menu

Programs menu

Start menu

Click Start button to open Start menu

Run a utility by clicking on its icon and name

Figure 1-8 Windows Explorer

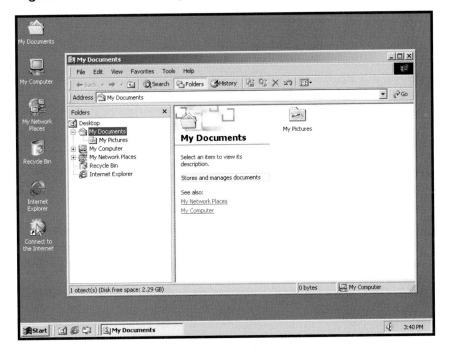

Practice

Use the Start button to open the Printers folder on the Settings menu. If your computer is hooked up to a printer or printers, the name(s) will appear in this window. Close the window from the title bar.

skill   Using the Taskbar

concept

The taskbar is your guide to the applications running on your system. Each open application creates its own program button on the taskbar, so switching between programs is as simple as the click of a button. While the taskbar is usually found at the bottom of the desktop, it is neither fixed in size nor location.

do it !

Use the taskbar to open two applications and switch between them. Then, move and resize the taskbar.

1. Click the Start button to open the Start menu, select Programs, select Accessories, and then click Windows Explorer.

2. Click the Start button, select Programs, select Accessories, and then click Calculator. The calculator will open and two windows will be on your desktop with their respective program buttons on the taskbar, as shown in Figure 1-9.

3. Click the Windows Explorer program button, which is labeled My Documents. The Windows Explorer window will become active, moving to the foreground of the desktop. Notice that its title bar is now blue, and its program button is indented. ⬭ You can move between open applications by holding [Alt] and then pressing [Tab]. Press [Tab] again to cycle through the list of all running applications. Release the [Alt] key when the correct icon is selected. Right-click the taskbar for more options. ⬎

4. Click the Calculator button to make the Calculator window active.

5. Position the mouse pointer on the top edge of the taskbar. The pointer will change to a vertical double arrow when it is in the correct spot.

6. Press and hold the mouse button and drag the top of the taskbar up, until it is three times its original height. The taskbar can be enlarged to up to half of your desktop.

7. Click a blank space on the taskbar, and then hold the mouse button down while dragging the taskbar to the right edge of your desktop, as shown in Figure 1-10. The taskbar can be placed on the top, bottom, left, or right of the desktop.

8. Drag the taskbar back to its original place on the desktop and then resize it so it is one program button high.

9. Click each application's Close button to remove the windows from the desktop.

more

Additional taskbar settings can be found in the Taskbar Properties dialog box, accessed by highlighting Settings on the Start menu and then clicking the Taskbar & Start Menu command on the Settings menu. When you open this dialog box you will see five options on the General tab. Those with a check mark are turned on. The Always on top option prevents any window from obscuring the taskbar. With Auto hide turned on, the taskbar will drop out of sight when it is not in use. Move the pointer to the bottom of the desktop to make it reappear. The relative size of your Start menu items is controlled with the Show small icons in Start menu. You can turn the taskbar clock on or off with the Show Clock command. The Use Personalized Menus command permits Windows to hide the menu items that you do not use frequently. When you do need to access a hidden item, click on the double arrow at the bottom of the menu to expand it to its full size.

Figure 1-9 Two open applications

Inactive application window

Active application window

Active program button

Inactive program button

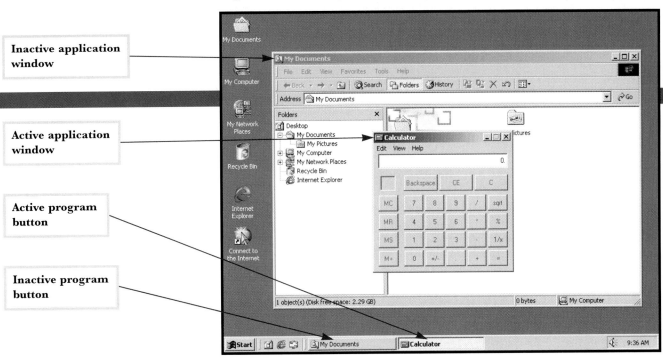

Figure 1-10 Resized and moved taskbar

Click and drag a blank space on the taskbar to move it

Click and drag the taskbar's edge to resize it

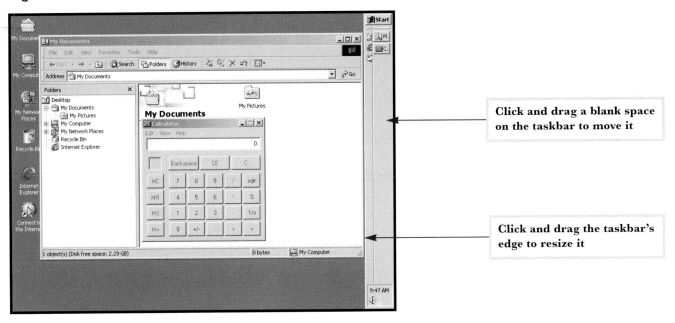

Practice

Turn on the Auto hide taskbar option. Then open Windows Explorer, My Computer, and Calculator. Practice moving among the open windows. If you do not like the Auto hide option, turn it off again.

skill | Using Menus

concept

A menu is a list of related operations, also known as commands, that you use to perform specific tasks. The menus that are available to you in any particular window are listed on the Menu bar, which is situated just below the window's title bar. Each Windows program has its own selection of menus, though many are similar. To access a menu, simply click on its menu title on the Menu bar. Some menu commands have shortcut buttons that allow you to execute them by clicking on a toolbar button. You will also find that many commands have keyboard shortcuts. If you prefer the keyboard to the mouse, Windows also provides a way to open all menus and choose any command without clicking.

do it !

Examine and use a typical menu in the My Computer window.

1. Double-click the My Computer icon to open its window..

2. Click View on the Menu bar to open the View menu, shown in Figure 1-11.

3. You will notice that in addition to commands, several symbols appear on the menu. A right-pointing triangle after a command indicates that the command has a submenu. Point to the Toolbars command with the mouse to reveal the Toolbars submenu.

4. Move the mouse pointer down to the Status Bar command. The Toolbars submenu closes. The check mark to the left of the Status Bar command indicates that the feature is currently turned on. A bullet next to a command tells you which command in a set is currently active. Only one command in a set such as the icon view commands may be active at a time.

5. Open the Toolbars submenu again. Then click the Standard Buttons command, which is turned on, to turn it off. The menu closes and the Standard Buttons toolbar disappears, as shown in Figure 1-12.

6. You can also use the keyboard to open a menu and execute a command. When you press the [Alt] key with the My Computer window active, one letter in each menu title is underlined. Pressing this letter will open the corresponding menu. Press [Alt], then press [V] to open the View menu.

7. Each command on a menu also has an underlined letter. Pressing this letter on the keyboard initiates the command. Press [T] to open the Toolbars submenu. Then Press [S] to execute the Standard Buttons command from the submenu, turning the Standard Buttons toolbar back on. Once a menu has been opened, you can use the arrow keys to move from command to command (up and down arrows) or from menu to menu (left and right arrows). Press [Enter] to execute a highlighted command.

more

Some commands have keyboard shortcuts that you can use to avoid opening menus altogether. You can learn many of these shortcuts simply by seeing them listed on a menu. For example, if you open the Edit menu in the My Computer window, you will see that the Select All command is followed by [Ctrl]+[A]. This means that you can use the Select All command by holding down the [Ctrl] key and pressing [A].

Figure 1-11 View menu

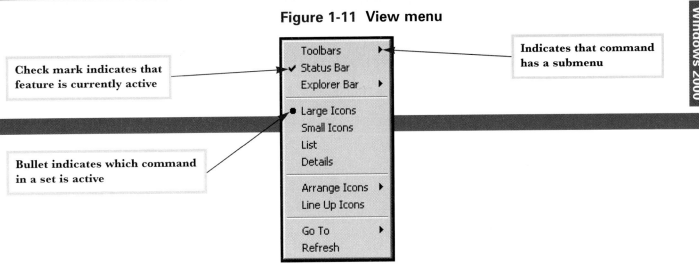

Check mark indicates that feature is currently active

Indicates that command has a submenu

Bullet indicates which command in a set is active

Figure 1-12 My Computer window without Standard Buttons

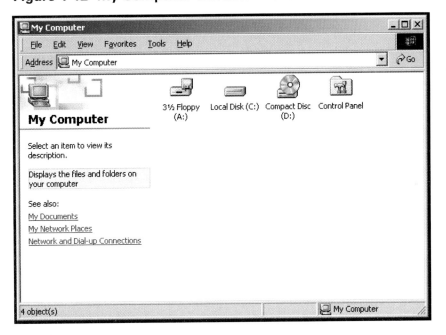

Practice

Open the My Computer window by double-clicking its icon. Then use the Close command on the File menu to close the window.

skill | Using Dialog Boxes

concept

Some commands require additional information before Windows will perform the operations that accompany them. In these cases, a dialog box will appear. Dialog boxes allow you to customize a command's options according to your needs or preferences. Commands that include a dialog box are followed on a menu by three dots, called an ellipsis.

do it !

Open the WordPad application, and then use the Print command to access and examine the Print dialog box.

1. Click [Start], highlight Programs, then highlight Accessories, and then click WordPad. WordPad, Windows 2000's built-in word processor, will open.

2. To add text to a WordPad document, you can simply begin typing. Type [Your Name]'s dialog box practice. Your document should look like Figure 1-13.

3. Open the File menu and click on the Print command. The Print dialog box will appear, as shown in Figure 1-14. The Print dialog box contains a number of common dialog box features, each connected to a specific printing option. Refer to the figure to gain an understanding of how each of these features works. When a dialog box has more than one option you can use the [Tab] key to cycle through the options.

4. Click the Cancel button [Cancel]. The dialog box closes without executing the Print command.

5. Close the WordPad window. Windows will ask you if you want to save changes to the document. Click [No].

more

Dialog boxes contain their own help tool. In the upper-right corner of a dialog box, you will find a button marked with a question mark. If you click on this button, a question mark will be attached to your mouse pointer. When you click on any dialog box feature with this pointer, a ScreenTip will appear that explains the feature (see Figure 1-15). Click the mouse button again to erase the ScreenTip and restore the pointer to its normal state.

Figure 1-13 WordPad document

Click Save button to save a WordPad document

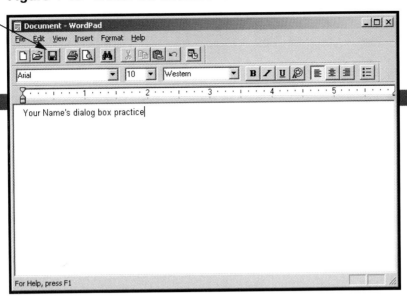

Figure 1-14 Dialog box features

Click tabs to access additional options

Click to get help on dialog box items

Use text box to enter a value

Click check box to activate associated option

Option buttons enable you to select one option in a set

Click up or down arrow to change value in spin box

Click to execute command

Click to perform operation without closing dialog box

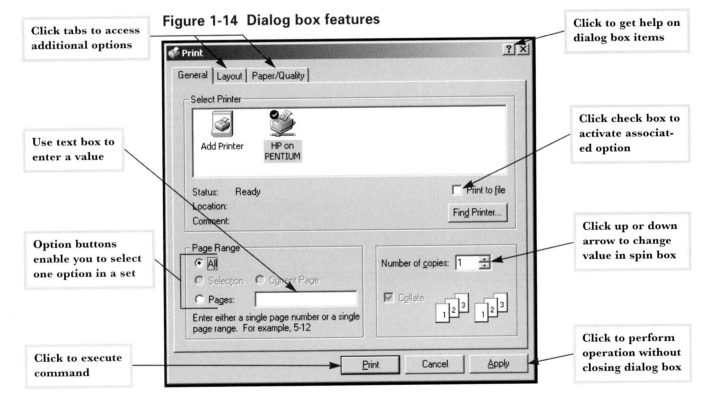

Practice

Find three other WordPad commands that use dialog boxes. View the features of each dialog box.

skill   Getting Help

concept

You might find that you need a little assistance along the way as you explore Windows 2000. The Help files provide you with an extensive list of topics that provide aid, troubleshooting advice, and tips and tricks. You can use Help while you work, and even print topics when it is inconvenient to use Help on the fly.

do it !

Use the Windows 2000 Help facility to learn about working with programs and word processing.

1. Click Start, then click Help on the Start menu. The Windows Help window will open with the Contents tab displayed, as shown in Figure 1-16. Each of the major help topics covered is listed next to a book icon. The Glossary and Reference help topics on the Contents tab are very useful for getting help on specific Windows 2000 features that are not covered by the other general help topics.

2. Position the pointer over Working with Programs in the Contents topics list. When you move the mouse pointer over the topic, the pointer will change to a hand, and the topic will be highlighted in blue and underlined, much like a Web page hyperlink.

3. Click Working with Programs. A list of subtopics will appear below it.

4. Click Start a Program. The help topic, including instructions, notes, and links to related topics, is loaded into the right half of the window for you to read (Figure 1-17).

5. Click the Index tab to bring it to the front of the left pane. The Index tab allows you to search the help files by keyword.

6. Type word processing. As you type, the list of topics will scroll to match your entry.

7. Click the subtopic WordPad to select it below the main topic word processing. Then click the Display button [Display] . Read the help text on Using WordPad that appears in the right frame.

8. Click [X] to exit Help.

more

The Windows 2000 Help facility is written in HTML (Hypertext Markup Language). This is the same language used to create Web pages. Help's interface is similar to that of the Windows 2000 system windows, such as My Computer, and the Web pages you view with a Web browser. Across the top of the Help window are five buttons. Clicking the Hide button shrinks the Help window to only its right frame, giving you more room to view other open windows. The Hide button changes to the Show button when the window is shrunk. The Back button takes you back to the topic you just viewed, while the Forward button takes you to the place you were before you clicked Back. The Options button offers you menu commands for the buttons, as well as others such as a print command and a stop command to interrupt long searches. The Web Help button gives you quick access to help on the Internet.

Figure 1-16 Windows Help facility

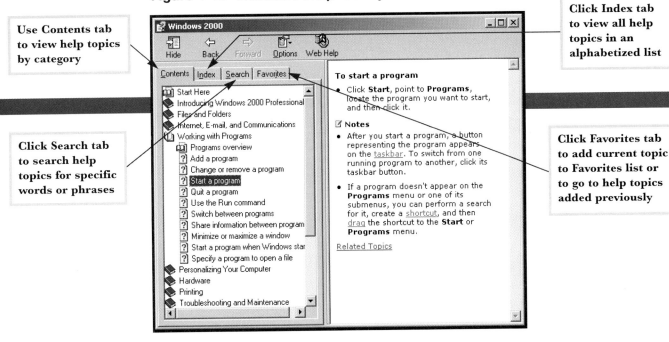

Use Contents tab to view help topics by category

Click Index tab to view all help topics in an alphabetized list

Click Search tab to search help topics for specific words or phrases

Click Favorites tab to add current topic to Favorites list or to go to help topics added previously

Figure 1-17 Help on WordPad

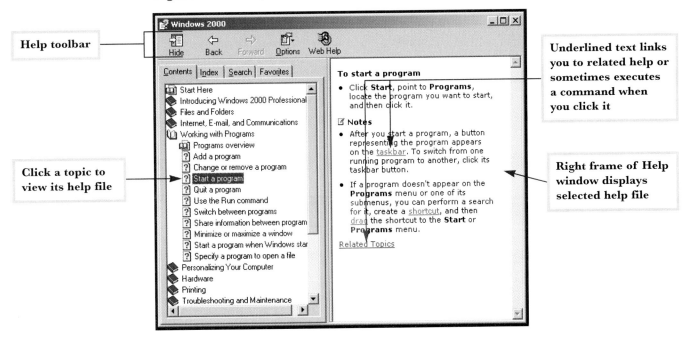

Help toolbar

Underlined text links you to related help or sometimes executes a command when you click it

Click a topic to view its help file

Right frame of Help window displays selected help file

Practice

Get help on printing a document using both the Contents tab and the Index tab. Close the Help facility when you are done.

skill | Shutting Down Windows 2000

concept

It is important to shut down Windows 2000 properly. Failure to do so can result in loss of unsaved data. When you go through the shutdown procedure, Windows 2000 checks all open files to see if any unsaved files exist. If any are found, you will be given the opportunity to save them. It also uses the shutdown procedure to copy the data it has logged while your system was running to your hard disk.

do it !

Shut down your computer to end your Windows 2000 session.

1. Click the Start button to open the Start menu.

2. Click Shut Down. A dialog box (Figure 1-18) will appear on your desktop.

3. A drop-down list in the center of the dialog box allows you to choose whether you want to log off the current user, shut down, or restart the computer. If the drop-down list box is set to Shut down, leave it as is. If not, click the arrow at the right end of the box, and then click Shut Down on the list that appears.

4. Click the OK button [OK]. Windows will go through its shutdown procedure. You can also access the Log Off and Shut Down commands by pressing [Ctrl]+[Alt]+[Delete] on the keyboard to open the Windows Security dialog box.

5. Turn off your computer when you see the message that reads: It is now safe to turn off your computer (see Figure 1-19).

more

Table 1-2 Shutdown Options	
Option	**Result**
Log off User	Ends the current session, but leaves the computer running so that another user may log on
Shut down	Prepares the computer to be turned off
Restart	Ends the current session, shuts down Windows 2000, and then starts Windows again

Figure 1-18 Shut Down Windows dialog box

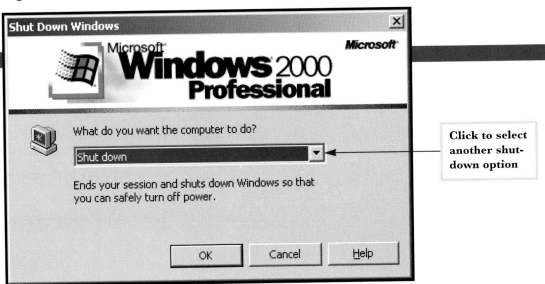

Click to select
another shut-
down option

Figure 1-19 Shut down confirmation

Practice

Make sure all files and applications on your computer are closed, and then restart your computer.

shortcuts

Function	Button/Mouse	Menu	Keyboard
Close window	☒	Click Control icon, click Close	[Alt]+[F4]
Maximize window	☐	Click Control icon, click Maximize	
Minimize window	▁ Or click program button on taskbar	Click Control icon, click Minimize	
Restore window	⧉	Click Control icon, click Restore	
Change active window	Click window, if visible, or click program button on taskbar		[Alt]+[Tab]
Get help on a specific item in a dialog box	?		[F1]

A. Identify Key Features

Name the items indicated by callouts in Figure 1-20.

Figure 1-20 Components of the Windows 2000 interface

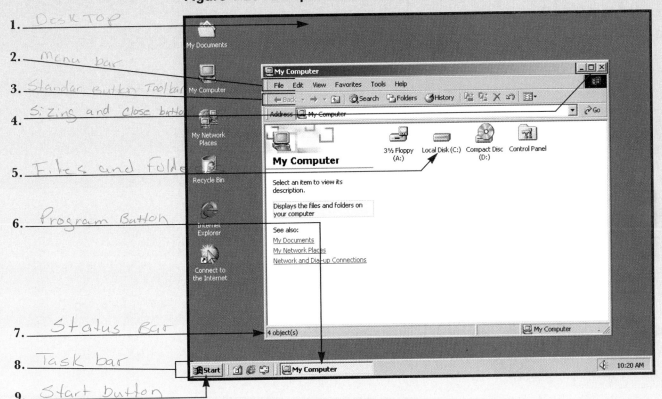

1. _Desktop_
2. _Menu bar_
3. _Standar Butten Toolbar_
4. _Sizing and close buttons_
5. _Files and folders_
6. _Program Button_
7. _Status Bar_
8. _Task bar_
9. _Start button_

B. Select the Best Answer

10. Traditional way of opening a file, program, or window

11. Returns a maximized window to its previous size

12. Appears when a window is too small to display its information

13. Where you provide additional information before a command is carried out

14. Organizes the help files in major categories represented by book icons

15. Where program buttons appear

16. Used to manipulate the pointer on the screen

17. Minimizes all open windows

18. Contains a list of related commands

a. Scroll Bar

b. Menu

c. Show Desktop button

d. Double-clicking

e. Restore button

f. Contents tab

g. Taskbar

h. Dialog box

i. Mouse

quiz (continued)

C. Complete the Statement

19. All of the following are basic ways you can use a mouse except:

a. Clicking

b. Dragging

c. Keying

d. Pointing

20. You can move a window:

a. When it is maximized

b. By dragging its title bar

c. When it is minimized

d. By using the double arrow pointer

21. To open a context-sensitive pop-up menu:

a. Click the mouse

b. Click the Start button

c. Double-click an icon

d. Right-click the mouse

22. To scroll through a window in large increments:

a. Click above or below the scroll bar box

b. Click a scroll bar arrow

c. Click the scroll bar box

d. Right-click the Control icon

23. To locate a help file by means of a scrolling list that matches a topic you enter, use the:

a. Contents tab

b. Index tab

c. Find tab

d. Explorer tab

24. To reposition the taskbar:

a. Open the Taskbar Properties dialog box

b. Select it and press the arrow keys

c. Drag it to a new location

d. Right-click it and choose the Move command

25. A standard menu contains a list of:

a. Related commands

b. Shutdown options

c. Help topics

d. Icons

26. Windows 2000's pictorial representation of a computer's functions and data is called:

a. An IBI or "ibbey" (Icon Based Interface)

b. A LUI or "louie" (Local User Interface)

c. A HUI or "huey" (HTML Unified Interface)

d. A GUI or "gooey" (Graphical User Interface)

27. An ellipsis after a command indicates that:

a. Windows is still working

b. The command is not available

c. The command has a keyboard shortcut

d. The command uses a dialog box

28. To open a menu, click on its title on the:

a. Menu bar

b. View menu

c. Standard Buttons toolbar

d. Keyboard

interactivity

Build Your Skills

1. Start Windows 2000 and work with the desktop icons:

   a. If it is not already running, turn on your computer.

   b. Use the mouse to point to the My Computer icon.

   c. Move the My Documents folder icon to the center of the desktop, and then back to its original position.

   d. Open the My Documents folder icon.

   e. Close the My Documents window.

2. Work with an open window:

   a. Open the My Computer window.

   b. Move the window so that its title bar touches the top of the screen.

   c. Maximize the window.

   d. Restore the window.

   e. Use the mouse to resize the window until it is shaped like a square.

3. Run multiple programs and use the taskbar:

   a. Open Windows Explorer and Calculator from the Start menu.

   b. In turn, make each of the three open windows the active window.

   c. Minimize all open windows.

   d. Move the taskbar to the top of the desktop.

   e. Make the taskbar twice its original size.

   f. Return the taskbar to its original location and size.

   g. Close all open windows and applications

4. Use the Windows 2000 help facility and then shut down Windows:

   a. Open Windows Help.

   b. Use the Contents tab to read about What's New in Windows 2000.

   c. Use the Index tab to get help on printing help topics.

   d. Close the Help facility.

   e. Shut down Windows 2000 properly and turn off your computer.

interactivity (continued)

Problem Solving Exercises

1. Using the skills you learned in Lesson 1 and your knowledge of the Windows 2000 operating system, arrange your desktop so that it resembles the one shown in Figure 1-21. Remember that computers can be configured in a number of different ways, and settings can be changed over time. Therefore, your setup, and the icons made available by it, may prevent you from replicating the figure exactly. Do not delete icons without consulting your instructor first.

Figure 1-21 Example of a Windows 2000 desktop

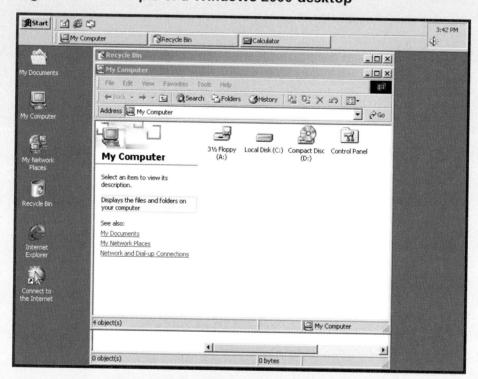

2. You have noticed an item on your Accessories menu named Notepad, but you are not sure what its function is. Use both the Contents and Index tabs in Windows 2000's Help facility to find out as much as you can about Notepad. Then use the Help facility to find out how to store the Notepad help topics you found on the Favorites tab. Once you have learned this procedure, add the most informative Notepad help topic to the Favorites tab.

3. You are working on a project that requires you to use two applications at the same time, Windows Explorer and Notepad. Open each application from the Start menu. Then resize and arrange the two open windows so that you can view them side by side on the desktop.

4. You are new to the Windows operating system, but you have used another operating system with a graphical user interface. You have decided to set up your desktop so that it resembles this system. Move all of your desktop icons to the right side of the desktop. Then move the taskbar so that it is anchored to the left side of the screen instead of to the bottom of it.

Managing Files with Windows Explorer

A file is a text document, picture, or any other collection of information that is stored under its own unique name. A folder, much like a paper folder, is a collection of files that can also house other folders. Your computer stores electronic files and folders as you might store paper ones in a filing cabinet. To make finding files and folders easier, you should group them in an organized and logical manner. The manner in which your files and folders are arranged is called a file hierarchy.

A file hierarchy, as shown in Figure 2-1, is similar to a family tree. The parent, child, and grandchild branches are represented by disk drives and folders. A file hierarchy depicts all the drives, applications, folders, and files on your computer. Placing similar files into well-named folders is the best way to create a meaningful file hierarchy. By viewing the higher levels of your file hierarchy, you will be able to get a sense of where files are stored without having to open each particular folder.

skills

⚡ **Viewing Folders with My Computer**

⚡ **Using Windows Explorer**

⚡ **Creating New Folders and Files**

⚡ **Moving and Copying Files and Folders**

⚡ **Creating Shortcuts**

⚡ **Using the Recycle Bin**

⚡ **Searching for Files or Folders**

My Computer and Windows Explorer are both file management tools. File management can be complex and even tricky at first. The key to understanding file management is being able to visualize and organize the placement of your files. Having to search through the entire file hierarchy every time you wish to locate an item can become time-consuming and frustrating. Learning how to manage your files effectively, by understanding My Computer and Windows Explorer, will help you to get the most out of your computer. My Computer and Windows Explorer are similar in function and in use. After a brief examination of My Computer we will concentrate on Windows Explorer, the more versatile file organizer.

Managing your files will often involve more than just organizing them. In this lesson, you will learn how to use the Recycle Bin to delete files and folders correctly. This will save you space on your hard drive and prevent you from disposing of important work accidentally. The lesson also introduces the Search command, which can help you locate a file when you lose track of it.

skill | Viewing Folders with My Computer

concept

My Computer is a tool that shows you the organization of the drives and configuration of folders on your computer. You can use My Computer to navigate through your system's files. Opening an icon in the My Computer window, usually for a drive or a folder, will show you that particular icon's contents. My Computer allows you to view the contents of your computer four different ways: by Large Icons, by Small Icons, in List form, or with Details. Once you open a drive or folder from the My Computer window, a fifth viewing option, Thumbnails, becomes available. How you view the contents of a drive or folder will depend on the information you require.

do it !

To get a better understanding of file management, explore your C: drive by viewing its contents with the different View options.

1. Open the My Computer window by double-clicking its icon on the desktop (usually located in the upper-left corner of the screen).

2. To toggle between views, you need to make sure the Standard Buttons toolbar is visible. Open the View menu and guide the pointer onto the Toolbar command. If there is no check mark beside the Standard Buttons command, point to it and click the left mouse button.

3. The My Computer window displays icons that represent your computer's disk drives and system control folders. Double-click the C: drive icon [Local Disk (C:)] to view the folders and files on your hard drive (your C: drive may have a different label than the one shown here). Figure 2-2 shows the C: drive window in Large Icons view. This view takes up window space, but offers a clear view of a window's contents. By default, Windows 2000 enables Web content in folders, meaning the folders are presented like Web pages with frames and graphics. Evidence of this appears on the left side of the window, where the selected drive is named and a pie chart graphic depicts the drive's storage capacity in percentages of free and used space.

4. To view the items as Small Icons, click the Views button on the right end of the Standard Buttons toolbar [▥▾]. A menu will appear, shown in Figure 2-3, allowing you to select your choice of views. The bullet marks the current view, Large Icons.

5. Click Small Icons on the Views button menu. The icons will become smaller, and they will be arranged alphabetically in rows. This view is useful when you have many icons to fit into one window.

(continued on WN 2.4)

Figure 2-1 Sample file hierarchy

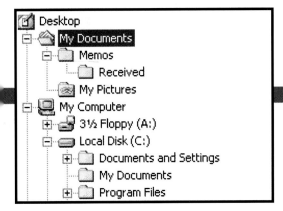

Figure 2-2 C: drive in Large Icons view

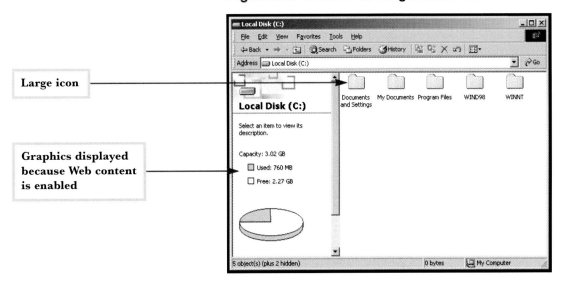

Figure 2-3 Views button menu

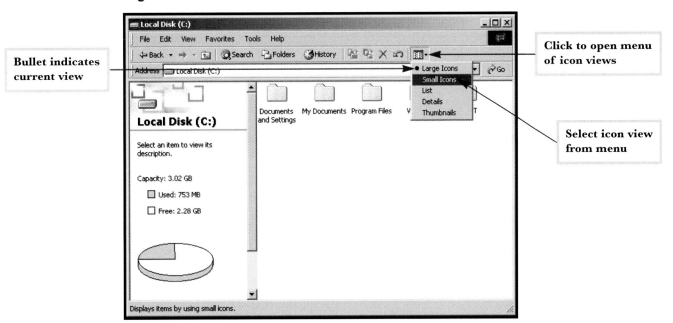

skill | Viewing Folders with My Computer (continued)

do it !

6. Click ▦▾ again, then select List. The icons will be put into List view. List view is similar to Small Icons except that icons are organized in columns.

7. Click ▦▾ again, then select Details. Figure 2-4 shows Details view, which will tell you the name of an item, its size if it is a file rather than folder, its type, and even the last time you modified it.

8. To return to the top level of the hierarchy, click the Up button ⊡. The Up button steps you up one level in the file structure, while the Back button ⟵Back returns you to the last file or folder you viewed regardless of its place in the hierarchy.

9. Right-click the title bar of the C: drive window, then select Close from the pop-up menu that appears to remove the window from the desktop.

more

As hard as you try, even with good file organization and file naming, it is impossible to remember what every file on your computer contains. Having Web content enabled in your folders can help relieve some of this frustration. Folders with Web content enabled allow you to see previews of file content, as well as get descriptions of hard drives and system folders. Compatible material includes Web pages, audio files, video files, and most graphic formats. When you select a file that can generate a preview, a small image of the file, called a thumbnail, will appear on the left side of the window, as shown in Figure 2-5. Thumbnails view allows you to view previews of all image files in a folder rather than file icons. Audio and video previews will contain controls for playing the particular file from the window without having to open another application.

The columns that are shown in Details view for a particular folder are determined by the Column Settings dialog box, which can be accessed by selecting the Choose Columns command from the View menu. The dialog box provides a list of column headings that are available for viewing and check boxes next to each heading to allow you to activate and deactivate the headings according to your needs and preferences. You can also alter the order in which the column headings appear, and specify their individual widths.

You can also customize the appearance of a folder by choosing the Customize This Folder command from the View menu. The command activates the Customize This Folder wizard, which will guide you through the steps required to choose or edit an HTML template for the active folder, change the folder's background picture and file name appearance, or add a comment to the folder. ⬤ The My Computer and Control Panel windows are always displayed as Web pages. The Customize This Folder wizard is not available for these folders.

The number and type of drives installed in a computer can vary greatly, but the configuration you have seen represented in this book is quite common. The drive designated with the letter A is almost always a 3½ inch floppy disk drive. The drive designated with the letter C is generally the computer's main hard drive. The D designation us usually assigned to the computer's CD-ROM drive. Traditionally, the letter B is reserved for a second floppy drive.

Figure 2-4   C: drive in Details view

Selected drive, folder, file, or Web address displayed in Address Bar

Click here to arrange window contents by date last modified

Click here to sort window contents by file format

Click here to arrange folders and files alphabetically by name

Click here to sort files by size

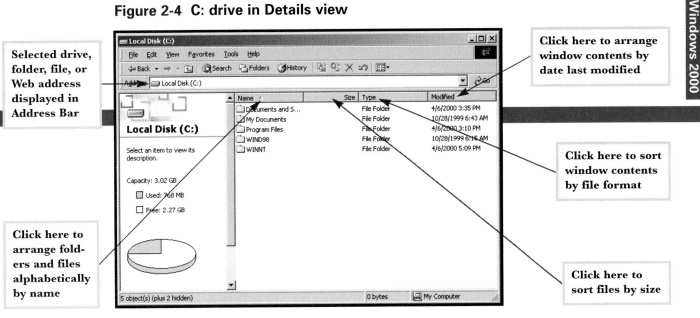

Figure 2-5   Preview of a bitmap image file

Details of selected file

Preview of selected file

Selected file

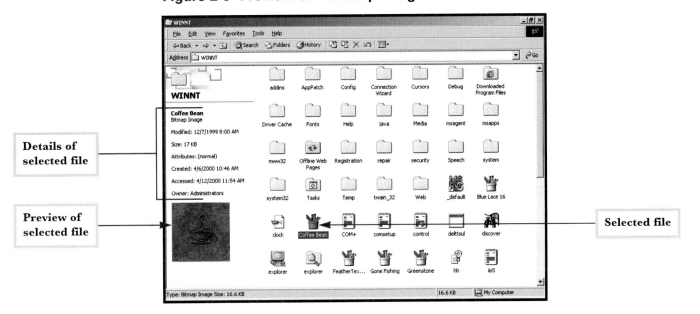

Practice

Open My Computer, double-click the Control Panel folder, then use the Views button to display the items in each of the available views. Leave the window in the view you like best. Close the window when you are finished.

skill | Using Windows Explorer

concept

Windows Explorer, found on the Accessories menu in Windows 2000, is similar to My Computer. Both are file management tools that allow you to view the contents of your computer. But, Windows Explorer is more powerful and provides you with more options than My Computer. Windows Explorer displays itself as the two-paneled window you see in Figure 2-6, allowing you to work with more than one drive, folder, or file at a time. The left panel, which usually consists of the Folders Explorer bar, shows all the folders and disk drives on your computer. The right panel, the contents panel, is a display of the items located within the folder or drive that is selected in the Folders Explorer bar. This two-paneled window creates a more detailed view of a specific folder and makes for easier file manipulation, especially copying and moving.

do it !

Use Windows Explorer to examine folders on your computer.

1. Click [Start], highlight Programs, highlight Accessories, and then click Windows Explorer on the Accessories menu. Windows Explorer will open with the contents of your computer shown in the left panel, and the My Documents folder selected. If you do not see the Folders Explorer Bar on the left, click the Folders button [Folders] on the Standard Buttons toolbar.

2. Click the plus symbol [+] next to My Computer in the Folders Explorer Bar (left panel). The [+] next to an item in this panel indicates that the item can be expanded to reveal its contents. You should now see the same drives and folders you saw previously in the My Computer window listed below My Computer in the left panel. Notice that the [+] you clicked has now changed to a [−]. This symbol indicates that a drive or folder is already expanded. Clicking the [−] collapses a drive or folder's contents back into the parent drive or folder. If a folder contains files but no subfolders, a plus sign will not appear next to it.

3. Click the [+] next to your C: drive in the Folders Explorer Bar to expand the drive, revealing its top level contents. The list of items you see in the left panel will differ from computer to computer depending on the files that have been installed and the way they have been configured.

4. Click the WINNT folder in the left panel. Now that the folder is selected, its contents, including subfolders and files, are displayed in the right panel (you may receive a message that explains the contents of the folder — if so, click the Show Files link that appears in the message).

5. Double-click the Media folder in the right panel to open the folder. (You could have also expanded the WINNT folder in the left panel, and then clicked the Media folder there to display its contents in the right panel.) Notice that the WINNT folder is now expanded in the Explorer Bar and the Media folder is shown with an open folder icon. The files inside the Media folder are sound files that were installed automatically with Windows 2000.

6. Press [Ctrl]+[A]. All of the items in the right panel will be selected, as shown in Figure 2-7. (Pressing [Ctrl]+[A] is the keyboard shortcut for the Select All command on the Edit menu.)

(continued on WN 2.8)

Figure 2-6 Windows Explorer

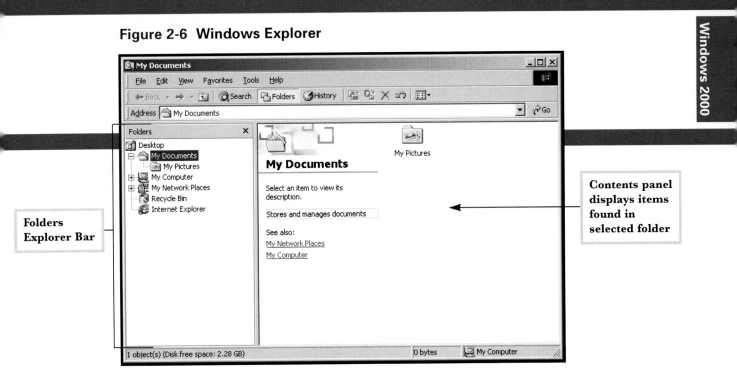

Folders Explorer Bar

Contents panel displays items found in selected folder

Figure 2-7 Media folder with all items selected

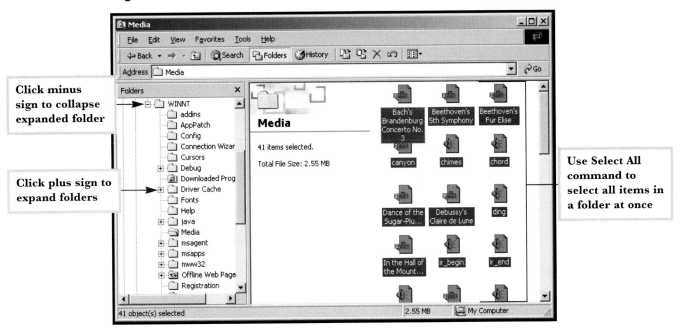

Click minus sign to collapse expanded folder

Click plus sign to expand folders

Use Select All command to select all items in a folder at once

skill Using Windows Explorer (continued)

do it !

7. Switch to Small Icons view, and then press [End] on the keyboard. The last file in the Windows folder will be selected. Since this is a sound file, audio controls appear in the window, allowing you to play the sound directly from Windows Explorer.

8. Press [Home] to select the first item listed in the Media folder.

9. Press [R] to select the first item in the folder that begins with the letter R. This is useful if you know the name of a file or folder and want to jump to it quickly.

10. Press [R] again to move to the next item in the list that begins with the letter R. Continuing to press [R] will cycle you through all the items in the folder that begin with R. Stop when you return to the first R item in the list.

11. With the first file that begins with R selected (most likely this will be recycle), hold [Ctrl] then click the file named chord. Holding the Control key down while you click allows you to select multiple, nonconsecutive files or folders.

12. Click the recycle sound file icon again to select it and deselect the chord file.

13. Hold [Shift], then click the first file listed. All of the files between the two you clicked will be highlighted, as shown in Figure 2-8. Holding the Shift key while you click allows you to select all of the items between the first and last selected.

14. Click a blank area to the right of the file names in the right panel to deselect all of the currently selected items. Leave Windows Explorer open for use in the next Skill.

more

Windows Explorer is a unique tool. As you saw in the Skill above, its two-paneled structure allows you to view all the folders on a specified drive, while working within a particular folder. One of the more powerful features of Windows Explorer is the left panel. The left panel, called the Explorer Bar, can be set to view one of four folders. By default, Windows Explorer opens in Folders view, which allows you to view any folders, files or utilities found on your computer or your network. The Search Explorer Bar, shown in Figure 2-9, allows you to activate Windows 2000's Search facility and locate files or folders directly in the Windows Explorer window. The Search Bar also contains a link that permits you to load an Internet search engine into Windows Explorer's left panel. If you would like to see a list of the locations you have visited recently, including local and network drives and Web sites, select the History Explorer Bar. Clicking the address or name of the place you want to view will load the site into the contents panel. You can choose to view items in the History Explorer Bar by date, site name, frequency of visits, or order visited today. The Favorites Explorer Bar allows you to store the places you visit most frequently so you can access them with a simple click. This feature is especially helpful with Web sites, which often have long, cumbersome addresses that are difficult to remember. You can close the active Explorer Bar by clicking the close button on its title bar, or by selecting the None command from the Explorer Bar submenu on the View menu. You can resize the panels of Windows Explorer. Place the pointer on the bar that divides the window (it will change to ◄─►), then drag to the left or right to resize the bar.

Figure 2-8 Selecting multiple folders

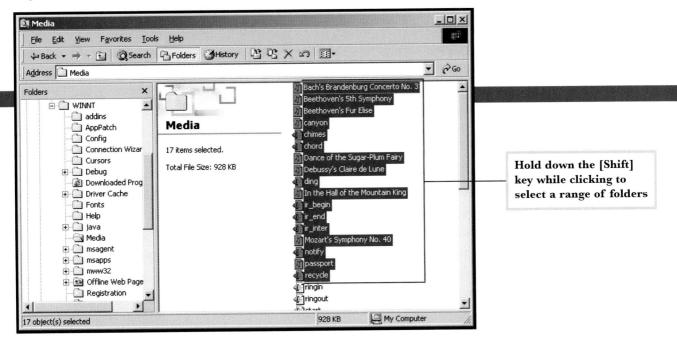

Hold down the [Shift] key while clicking to select a range of folders

Figure 2-9 Search Explorer Bar

Open View menu to select a different Explorer Bar, or click buttons on toolbar

Enter search criteria here

Click to load Internet search engine

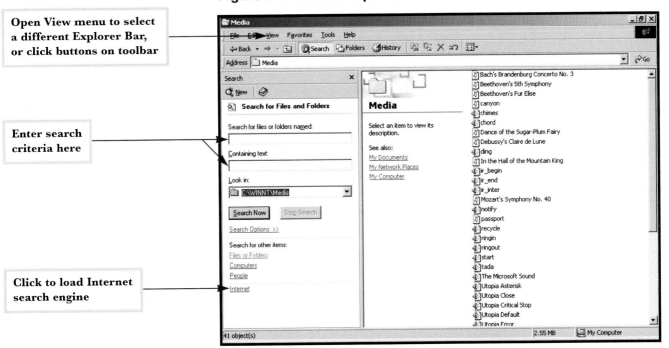

Practice

Expand the WINNT folder and select the Fonts folder in the Folders Explorer Bar. The files for all of the fonts installed on your computer will appear in the contents panel. Use the keyboard to select the font called Verdana.

skill
Creating New Folders and Files

concept

Creating folders is necessary when you want to store related files in a single location on a drive. Creating, naming, and placing folders properly in your hierarchy makes your work easier and more efficient. While most files are created in the program they will be used with, you can also make new, blank files right in the folder where they will be stored.

do it !

Create a new folder on your C: drive, and then create another folder within that folder. Finally, create two new files in the folder that you made.

1. Expand the C: drive, and then click its icon in the left panel of Windows Explorer to view the items on your main hard drive in the contents panel on the right.

2. Click File on the menu bar. The File menu will open.

3. Guide the pointer to New, then click Folder on the submenu that appears. A folder with the default name New Folder will appear in the contents panel with its name highlighted, ready to be changed.

4. Type My Student Files, then press [Enter] to give the folder a unique name so you can find it again. Notice that the new folder also appears in the left panel.

5. Click the new folder's icon in the left panel of Windows Explorer to select it and reveal its contents. The right panel should be blank since this folder is empty.

6. Click File, point to New, then select Folder to create a new folder within your My Student Files folder.

7. Type Alice, then press [Enter] to name the new folder. The folder will be in the contents panel and a plus will appear next to My Student Files (Figure 2-10) in the left panel to indicate that at least one folder is nested within the parent folder.

8. Click the plus ➕ next to the My Student Files folder in the Folders Explorer Bar to expand the folder and reveal the Alice folder nested inside.

9. Click File, select New, and then click WordPad Document on the menu that appears. A new file with the default name New WordPad Document will appear.

10. Type Letter.txt to rename the new file. Press [Enter] to confirm the file name. Creating a new file this way makes a blank document with a specific file format in the location you specify. The .txt at the end of the file name is an extension that tells the computer to associate the file with a particular program. By default, Windows 2000 associates the .txt extension with the Notepad program, but since this file was created as a WordPad document, it will open in WordPad when double-clicked. Folder and file names can be up to 215 characters long so you can name your data accurately. The only characters you are not allowed to use are: \ / : * ? " < > |.

11. Repeat the above step to create a WordPad document named To Do List.txt. Your window should look similar to the one shown in Figure 2-11.

(continued on WN 2.12)

Figure 2-10 Creating a new folder

Name of selected folder

Alice folder created inside My Student Files folder

Plus sign indicates that folder may now be expanded to reveal nested folders

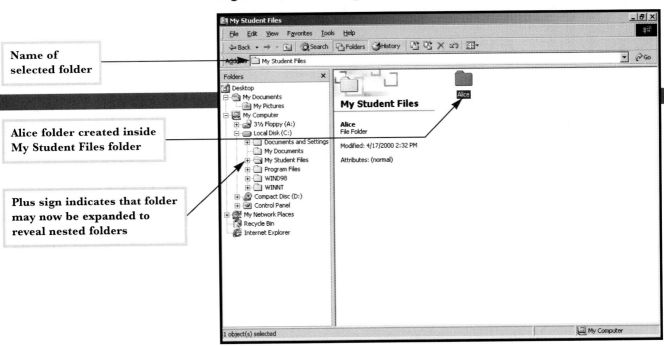

Figure 2-11 File hierarchy including new folder and files

New files in My Student Files folder

Parent folder

Child folder nested inside parent folder

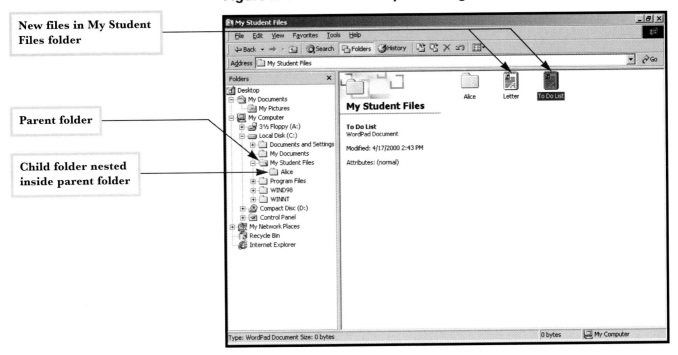

skill Creating New Folders and Files (continued)

more New folders and files can also be created by right-clicking. Once a parent folder is selected, right-click a blank space in the right panel. A pop-up menu will appear, as shown in Figure 2-12. Highlight the New command on this shortcut menu, and a submenu will appear. By choosing the appropriate command from the submenu, you can make a folder or file just as you would using the File menu.

If you right-click a file or folder you will be given a different pop-up menu. Figure 2-13 shows the menu that appears when you right-click on a file. The Open command opens the file with the application associated with the file's extension. The Open with... command allows you to choose a different application with which to open the file. The Print command lets you create a hard copy of the file without having to open the application with which it was created first. You can also use commands on the pop-up menu to cut, copy, delete, or create a shortcut to the file or folder you right-clicked. The Rename command allows you to change the name of the file or folder. Selecting a file or folder, pausing, and then clicking it again will also let you rename an item, as will selecting it and pressing [F2].

The pop-up menu that appears when you right-click a folder differs slightly from the file menu. It includes commands for opening the folder in Windows Explorer and setting network sharing options.

You can set options for each folder on your computer that control the way the folders appear and the way in which you interact with them. To do this, select a folder, open the Tools menu from the Menu bar, and then click the Folder Options command. The Folder Options dialog box, shown opened to the General tab in Figure 2-14, will appear. On the General tab, the Active Desktop section lets you determine whether Web content will be enabled on the desktop. The Web View section controls whether Web content is enabled in folders. The Browse Folders section is responsible for whether each folder you open appears in the same window or in a separate window. Finally, you can use the Click items as follows section to set your icon selecting and opening preferences: select by pointing/open by single-clicking (Web style) or select by single-clicking/open by double-clicking (traditional Windows style).

The View tab in the Folder Options dialog box contains advanced folder settings such as the option to display entire file paths in the Address Bar and the option to hide file extensions for known file types. The File Types tab is where associations between file types (extensions) and applications are set. The Offline Files tab allows you to make network files accessible when you are not connected to your network.

Figure 2-12 Right-click pop-up menu and submenu

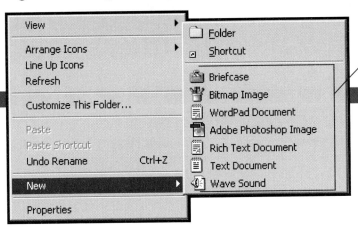

Select object to create from New submenu

Figure 2-13 Right-clicking a file

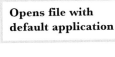

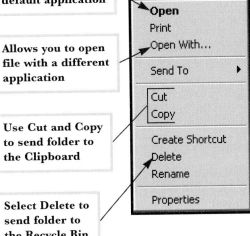

Opens file with default application

Allows you to open file with a different application

Use Cut and Copy to send folder to the Clipboard

Select Delete to send folder to the Recycle Bin

Figure 2-14 Folder Options dialog box

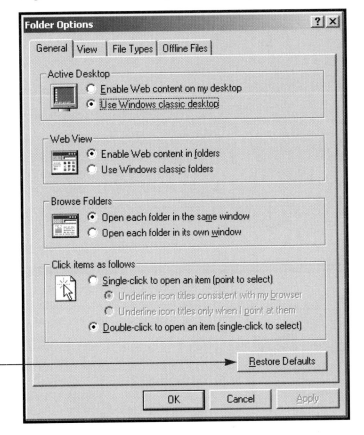

Click to restore Windows 2000's original settings

Practice

Create a folder inside the My Documents folder called Practice. Then create a new WordPad file called Prac2-3.txt inside this folder.

skill | Moving and Copying Files and Folders

concept

There are times when you will want to move and/or copy folders or files. Moving an item to group it with other files or folders that contain similar data can increase the overall efficiency of your work. Moving a folder changes its location and alters your file hierarchy accordingly. Copying a file or folder can be done to place a duplicate in another place on your system.

do it !

Move the Letter and To Do List files into the Alice folder, and then make a copy of the Alice folder inside the My Student Files folder.

1. Open Windows Explorer using the Start menu if it is not already open.

2. Click your My Student Files folder in the left panel to select it (expand My Computer and the C: drive if necessary). The contents of the My Student Files folder, the Alice folder, Letter.txt, and To Do List.txt, will appear in the contents panel.

3. Click the ⊞ next to the My Student Files folder so you can see the Alice folder in the left panel of Windows Explorer.

4. Hold down [Ctrl], while you click Letter.txt and To Do List.txt to select both files.

5. Drag the selected files from the right panel to the Alice folder in the left panel to move them. When you begin to drag, a faint outline of the files will follow the pointer. In certain areas, the pointer may become a circle with a line through it, indicating that you cannot drop your files at that particular location. You will know that the files are in the correct position when the Alice folder is highlighted, as shown in Figure 2-15. As soon as this occurs, release the mouse button to drop the files into the folder.

6. Click the Alice folder in the right panel to select it.

7. Click Edit to open the Edit menu, then select the Copy command to place a copy of the Alice folder on the Clipboard. The Clipboard is a temporary storage area in your computer's memory that holds copied or cut items until they are replaced on the Clipboard by another item or the computer is shut down.

8. Click Edit, then select Paste from the menu. A copy of the Alice folder will appear in the My Student Files folder as shown in Figure 2-16. ◆ Windows 2000 will not allow you to place two files with the same name in the same folder. If you attempt to do so, you will be asked if you want to overwrite the first file with the second. You may have files with the same name in different folders.

more

There are many ways to move and copy items in Windows 2000. Dragging and dropping files and folders from panel to panel in the Windows Explorer is one of the easiest ways to manage the information stored on your computer. Moving and copying can also be accomplished by dragging almost any item from your desktop to another system window or vice-versa. You can also move and copy with toolbar buttons. First, select the item you wish to move or copy. Then, click either the Move To 🗐 or Copy To 🗐 button on the Standard Buttons toolbar. In both cases, the Browse for Folder dialog box will appear, allowing you to choose a destination for the item to be moved or copied. Moving or cutting an item removes it from its original location. Copying leaves the original item in its original location.

Figure 2-15 Moving files

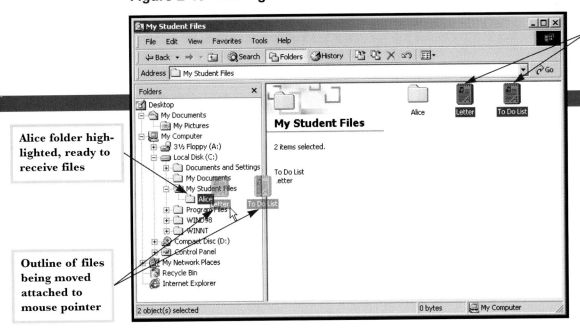

Selected files being moved

Alice folder highlighted, ready to receive files

Outline of files being moved attached to mouse pointer

Figure 2-16 Copying a folder

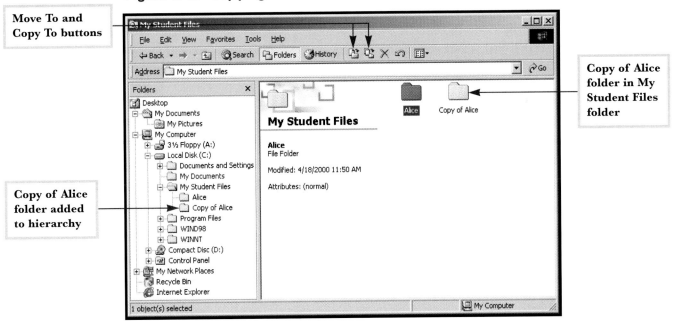

Move To and Copy To buttons

Copy of Alice folder in My Student Files folder

Copy of Alice folder added to hierarchy

Practice

Make a copy of Prac2-3.txt in the My Documents folder. Rename the copied file Prac2-4.txt. Then move Prac2-4.txt back to the Practice folder using the Cut command.

skill | Creating Shortcuts

concept

Shortcuts are icons that give you direct access to frequently used items so that you do not have to open applications or folders in order to work with the item. Shortcuts can be created for programs, folders, files, Internet addresses, or even devices like printers. You can place shortcuts directly on the desktop or Start menu, or anywhere else you find convenient.

do it !

Create a shortcut to the My Student Files folder on the desktop, rename it, and then change its icon.

1. Open Windows Explorer if it is not already running on your desktop.

2. If the Explorer window is maximized, click the Restore button so you can see a few inches of the desktop. You may have to resize the window so more of the desktop is visible.

3. Expand the appropriate icons so that the My Student Files folder is visible in the Folders Explorer Bar (left panel) of Windows Explorer. Place the mouse pointer over the folder's icon.

4. Right-drag (drag while holding down the right mouse button) the My Student Files folder to a blank space on your desktop. As the folder is dragged, a dimmed representation of it will move with the pointer. When you release the mouse button you will see the pop-up menu shown in Figure 2-17.

5. Click Create Shortcut(s) Here. A new folder named Shortcut to My Student Files will be created. The small arrow in the corner of the icon denotes that the folder is a shortcut, allowing you to access the My Student Files folder from the desktop without actually storing the folder on the desktop.

6. Right-click the Shortcut to My Student Files folder. A pop-up menu with commands relating to the folder will appear.

7. Click Rename. The folder's name will be highlighted so you can edit it.

8. Type To Be Deleted, then press [Enter] to rename the folder. Figure 2-18 displays the shortcut with its new name.

(continued on WN 2.18)

Figure 2-17 Right-dragging to create a shortcut

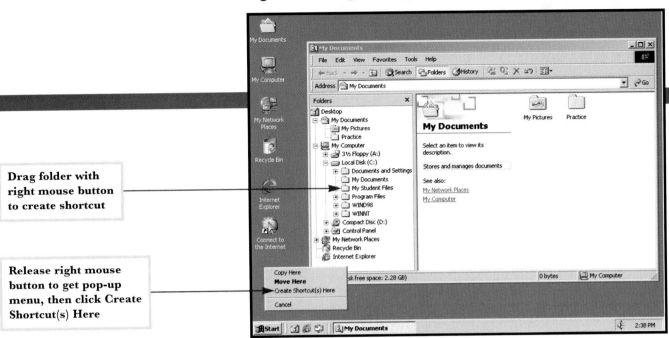

Drag folder with right mouse button to create shortcut

Release right mouse button to get pop-up menu, then click Create Shortcut(s) Here

Figure 2-18 Renamed shortcut folder on desktop

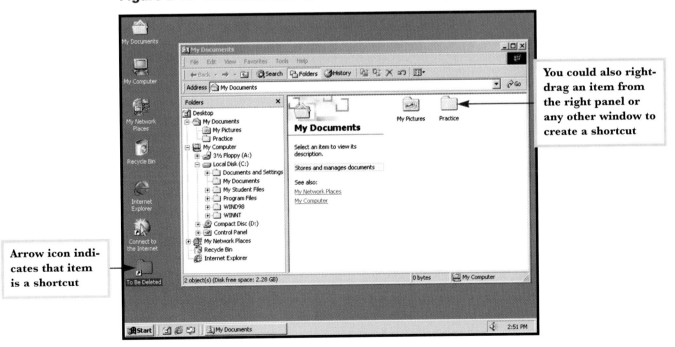

You could also right-drag an item from the right panel or any other window to create a shortcut

Arrow icon indicates that item is a shortcut

skill Creating Shortcuts (continued)

9. Right-click the To Be Deleted folder, then select Properties from the pop-up menu. A dialog box (Figure 2-19) titled To Be Deleted Properties will open to the Shortcut tab. This tab contains data relating to the selected folder's shortcut properties.

10. Click the Change Icon button Change Icon... . Figure 2-20 shows the Change Icon dialog box that will open.

11. Click and drag the horizontal scroll bar box to the right until the tree icon ♈ is visible.

12. Click the tree to select it.

13. Click OK . The Change Icon dialog box will close, returning you to the To Be Deleted Properties dialog box. The preview icon in the upper-left corner of the Shortcut tab will change to reflect your selection.

14. Click OK . The To Be Deleted Properties dialog box will close and the folder icon will be replaced with the tree icon, as shown in Figure 2-21. You do not have to be working in Windows Explorer in order to create a shortcut. You can also create shortcuts from the My Computer window or any standard folder window.

more
Shortcuts can be made for many items stored on your computer, including files, folders, and drives that you access over a network. For example, you can make a shortcut to a frequently used folder that you access over a network for quick access to those files. Shortcuts do not have to be placed on the desktop either. You can create a folder of shortcuts to your favorite programs and place it on your C: drive, or even the Start menu.

As you have seen, many tasks can be accomplished using drag and drop techniques. One of the more powerful Windows 2000 features allows you to drag files to program icons. Doing so will open the file with the program whose icon you drop it on, assuming the file and application are compatible. For example, you can create a shortcut to your word processing program and place it on the desktop. Then, you can drag word processing files to that shortcut to open them. This also works with printers.

In the above exercise you changed the name and icon for the shortcut you created without altering the folder that the shortcut points to. While a shortcut points to a specific item, that object can be renamed without effecting the shortcut. However, target objects that are moved to another folder or drive will cause the shortcut to malfunction. If a target item is moved, Windows 2000 has the ability to find it, or you can specify the new path manually. Since shortcuts are icons that point to the actual file, folder, or program that they represent, deleting a shortcut will not affect the target item.

You can also create a shortcut by right-clicking an item and then choosing Create Shortcut from the pop-up menu that appears. The shortcut will be created in the same folder as the original item. You can then move the shortcut to the desired location. If you drag a shortcut to the Start button, the Start menu will open. You can drop the shortcut on the Start menu or any of its submenus.

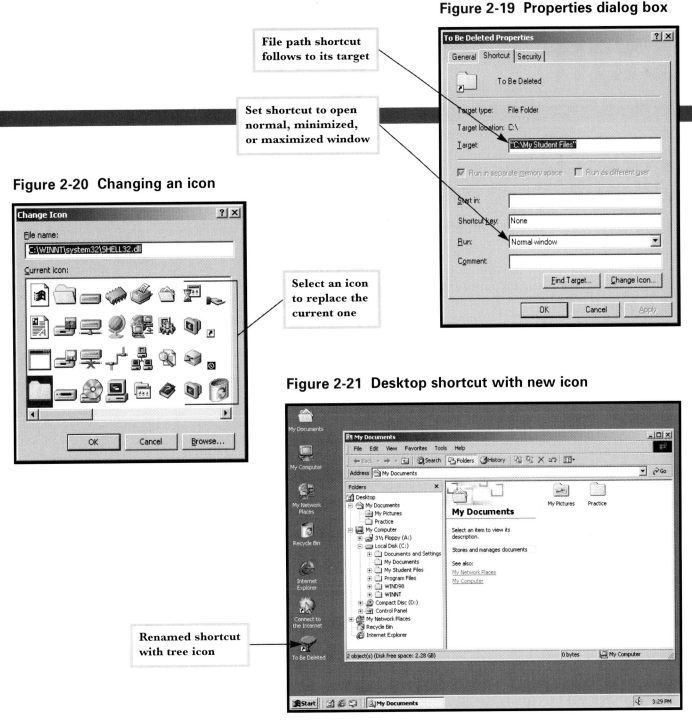

Figure 2-19 Properties dialog box

File path shortcut follows to its target

Set shortcut to open normal, minimized, or maximized window

Figure 2-20 Changing an icon

Select an icon to replace the current one

Figure 2-21 Desktop shortcut with new icon

Renamed shortcut with tree icon

Practice

Place a shortcut to the Practice folder on your desktop.

skill | Using the Recycle Bin

concept

The Recycle Bin is a storage place for files that have been deleted. Files that you no longer need should be deleted in order to save disk space and maximize the efficiency of your computer. If you decide that you need a file again, or have accidentally deleted a file, you can rescue it from the Recycle Bin. If you know you will never need a file again, you can delete the file permanently.

do it !

Send the Copy of Alice and To Be Deleted folders to the Recycle Bin. Then rescue To Be Deleted from the Recycle Bin. Finally, delete both items from your hard drive permanently.

1. Open Windows Explorer from the Start menu.

2. Expand the necessary icons, and then click the My Student Files folder in the left panel to select it.

3. Click the Copy of Alice folder in the right panel, then click the Delete button ☒ on the Standard Buttons toolbar. The Confirm Folder Delete dialog box (Figure 2-22) will appear, asking you if are sure you want to move the folder to the Recycle Bin.

4. Click [Yes]. The dialog box will close and the folder will be moved to the Recycle Bin. Notice the change in the Recycle Bin icon 🗑 when it is not empty.

5. Click the Close button ☒ to exit Windows Explorer.

6. Click and drag the To Be Deleted shortcut from the desktop to the Recycle Bin 🗑. When the Recycle Bin becomes highlighted, release the mouse button. The shortcut is deposited in the Recycle Bin.

7. Double-click the Recycle Bin icon. The Recycle Bin window will open. Figure 2-23 shows the inside of the Recycle Bin displaying all the files and folders you have sent there.

8. Drag the To Be Deleted shortcut from the Recycle Bin window to an empty space on the desktop. The shortcut appears on the desktop, and is now an accessible item that can be used. Items still in the Recycle Bin cannot be opened.

9. Right-click the To Be Deleted shortcut and choose the Delete command from the pop-up menu to send the folder back into the Recycle Bin.

10. Click [Yes] to confirm the operation.

11. Click the Empty Recycle Bin button [Empty Recycle Bin] (if not visible, click File, then click Empty Recycle Bin). The Confirm Multiple File Delete dialog box will appear.

12. Click [Yes] to delete the folders from your hard drive permanently.

13. Click ☒ to shut the Recycle Bin window. Note that you can also empty the Recycle Bin by right-clicking it and then choosing the Empty Recycle Bin command. Files can be erased immediately without being stored in the Recycle Bin. Right-click the Recycle Bin, then select Properties. On the View tab, uncheck the Display delete confirmation dialog command. This enables you to delete files in one step.

Table 2-1　Ways to delete or restore a selected file

To Delete	To Restore
Click Delete button on toolbar	Click Undo button [⟲] on toolbar
Right-click and select Delete from pop-up menu	Right-click file in Recycle Bin and select Restore
Drag file to Recycle Bin	Drag file from Recycle Bin to any location
Press [Delete]	Go to File menu in Recycle Bin and select Restore or click [Restore].

Figure 2-22　Confirm Folder Delete dialog box

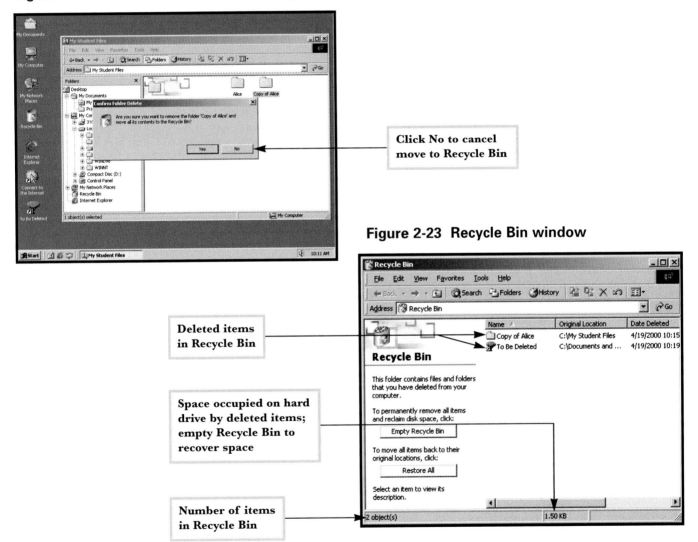

Click No to cancel
move to Recycle Bin

Figure 2-23　Recycle Bin window

Deleted items
in Recycle Bin

Space occupied on hard
drive by deleted items;
empty Recycle Bin to
recover space

Number of items
in Recycle Bin

Practice

Move the Practice shortcut you created in the last skill to the Recycle Bin. Then move the shortcut out of the Recycle Bin and back to the desktop. Delete the shortcut a second time using a different technique. This time, delete the shortcut permanently.

skill | Searching for Files or Folders

concept

Managing your files effectively includes knowing how to locate an item when you need it. The Search command on the Start menu is a tool that allows you to search your computer for files and folders when you do not know exactly where they are stored. You can also access the Search facility when working in Windows Explorer or My Computer by clicking the Search button [🔍 Search] to activate the Search Explorer Bar. The Search menu and Search Explorer Bar also provide direct links facilities for Web page and people directory searches. You can even search for other computers located on your network.

do it !

Use the Search command to locate the Discover Windows 2000 tour.

1. Click [🔲 Start], highlight Search, and then click For Files or Folders. The Search Results window, shown maximized in Figure 2-24, will open. The left side of the window contains the Search Explorer Bar. Near the top of the Explorer Bar is a text box in which you can enter the name, or a portion of the name, of the file or folder you wish to locate.

2. Type discover in the Search for files or folders named: text box. The Look in box should show your main hard drive. If not, click the arrow at the right edge of the box and select your main hard drive from the drop-down list.

3. Click the Search Now button [Search Now]. Windows will begin to search your computer's hard drive for any files or folders named discover. When the search is complete, the results will be displayed in the lower portion of the right panel (Figure 2-25). When your search is successful, you can open or run the item you have found by double-clicking it directly in the Search Results window. In this particular case, the item you have found is actually a shortcut and you would be prompted to insert your Windows 2000 CD-ROM in order to run the tour.

4. Close the Search Results window.

more

When you do not know the exact name of the file or folder you are looking for, you can use the wildcard character * in your search request. For example, if you search for all files or folders named J*, the search will return all files and folders whose names begin with the letter J. You can also use the Search Explorer Bar's Search Options feature when you do not know the file or folder name, or when you need to refine your search. When you click the Search Options link, the Search Options box opens in the Explorer Bar. The box contains four options: Date, Type, Size, and Advanced Options. Click the check box next to an option to use it. The Search Options box will expand to accommodate controls for the option you selected. For example, the Date option (Figure 2-26) allows you to search for files or folders that were last modified, created, or last accessed on a particular date or in a specific time frame. Setting such criteria can help narrow your search down to the items that will most likely satisfy your request.

Figure 2-24 Search Results window

Enter name of
desired file or
folder

Click to select
location to be
searched

Enter text con-
tained in desired
file or folder

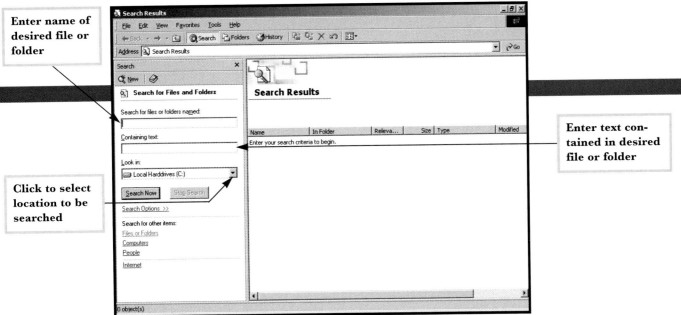

Figure 2-25 Results of search for discover

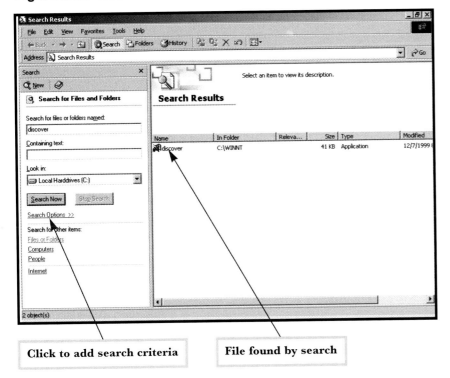

Click to add search criteria

File found by search

Figure 2-26 Date Search option

Practice

Use the Search command to locate your computer's Desktop folder.

shortcuts

Function	Button/Mouse	Menu	Keyboard
Large Icons view	Click button, the click Large Icons	Click View, then click Large Icons	[Alt]+[V], [G]
Small Icons view	Click button, then click Small Icons	Click View, then click Small Icons	[Alt]+[V], [M]
List view	Click button, then click List	Click View, then click List	[Alt]+[V], [L]
Details view	Click button, then click Details	Click View, then click Details	[Alt]+[V], [D]
Thumbnails view	Click button, then click Thumbnails	Click View, then click Thumbnails	[Alt]+[V], [H]
Move up one level in file hierarchy		Click Go, then highlight Go To, then click Up One Level	[Alt]+[V], [O], [U]
Move selected item to another folder		Click Edit, then click Move to Folder	[Alt]+[E], [V]
Copy selected item to another folder		Click Edit, then click Copy to Folder	[Alt]+[E], [F]
Cut selection		Click Edit, then click Cut	[Ctrl]+[X]
Copy selection to Clipboard		Click Edit, then click Copy	[Ctrl]+[C]
Paste selection to Clipboard		Click Edit, then click Paste	[Ctrl]+[V]
Delete selection	☒	Click File, then click Delete	[Delete]
Undo last action	↺	Click Edit, then click Undo	[Ctrl]+[Z]
Back	⇐ Back	Click View, highlight Go To, then click Back	[Alt]+[Left Arrow]
Forward	⇒	Click View, highlight Go To, then click Forward	[Alt]+[Right Arrow]

A. Identify Key Features

Name the items indicated by callouts in Figure 2-27.

Figure 2-27 Standard Buttons toolbar

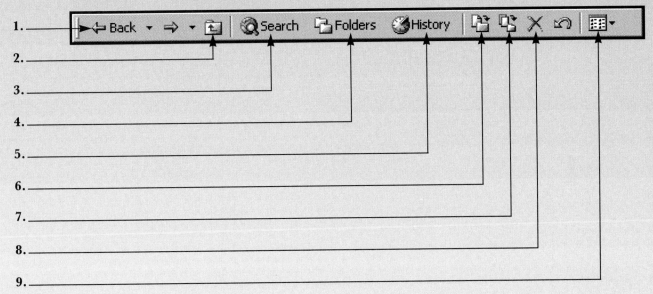

1. _____

2. _____

3. _____

4. _____

5. _____

6. _____

7. _____

8. _____

9. _____

B. Select the Best Answer

10. Right side of the Exploring window

11. One of the five Explorer Bars

12. Allows you to relocate a selected file or folder

13. Storage place for deleted items

14. Its keyboard shortcut is [Ctrl]+[A]

15. An icon that gives you direct access to a frequently used item

16. Tool that allows you to view, open, and organize the contents of your hard drive

a. My Computer

b. Shortcut

c. Contents panel

d. Select All command

e. Folders

f. Move To button

g. Recycle Bin

quiz (continued)

C. Complete the Statement

17. A small arrow attached to the bottom-left corner of an icon signifies:

a. A selected icon

b. An expanded folder

c. A shortcut

d. A restored file

18. The temporary storage device that holds cut and copied items is called the:

a. Recycle Bin

b. Explorer window

c. My Computer window

d. Clipboard

19. Clicking the Views button:

a. Automatically puts the icons in List view

b. Automatically puts the icons in Large Icons view

c. Opens the Views drop-down menu

d. Cycles to the next view on the Views menu

20. To view information about the icons listed in a window, put the icons in:

a. Details view

b. List view

c. The Recycle Bin

d. The Windows folder

21. A plus sign next to a folder or drive in the Folders Explorer Bar indicates that it can be

a. Collapsed

b. Expanded

c. Moved

d. Deleted

22. A file in the Recycle Bin:

a. Has been deleted permanently

b. Can be opened by double-clicking it

c. Can be restored by dragging it to a new location

d. Must be copied and pasted to be restored

23. To find a folder by searching for its file type or file size, click the:

a. Name & Location tab

b. Search Options link

c. Find Now button

d. Find Now tab

24. The powerful two-paneled tool that allows you to work with more than one drive, file, or folder is:

a. My Computer

b. Windows Explorer

c. The Recycle Bin

d. The Create Shortcut dialog box

interactivity

Build Your Skills

1. View the folders and files on your hard drive:

   a. Use My Computer to display the contents of your hard drive (C:).

   b. Put the contents of your hard drive in Small Icons view.

   c. Change to List view using the Menu bar.

   d. Return to the top level of the file hierarchy.

   e. Close the My Computer window without using the Close button.

2. Use Windows Explorer to view and select items on your hard drive:

   a. Open Windows Explorer.

   b. Expand My Computer, your C: drive, and then the Program Files folder.

   c. Select the Internet Explorer folder so that its contents are displayed in the right panel.

   d. Select all of the items in the contents panel.

   e. Select the PLUGINS folder in the contents panel without using the mouse.

   f. Select every other item in the contents panel.

   g. Select the last four items in the contents panel.

3. Create a new folder and a new file, then copy the file to another folder:

   a. Create a new folder on your C: drive (not in the Internet Explorer folder) called TYS.

   b. Make a copy of the folder.

   c. Create a new WordPad document called TYS2.txt in the original TYS folder.

   d. Place a copy of TYS2.txt in the My Documents folder.

4. Create a shortcut and practice using the Recycle Bin:

   a. Place a shortcut to the original TYS folder on your desktop.

   b. Send the Copy of TYS folder to the Recycle Bin without dragging it.

   c. Drag the Copy of TYS2.txt that you placed in the My Documents folder to the Recycle Bin.

   d. Empty the Recycle Bin.

5. Create a new shortcut and then use the Search feature to locate it on your hard drive:

   a. Place a shortcut to your C: drive on the desktop.

   b. Practice using the Search feature by locating the shortcut you just created.

   c. Open the shortcut from the Search Results window.

   d. Close all windows and delete the shortcut you created in step a.

interactivity (continued)

Problem Solving Exercises

1. You have been running a successful guitar instruction business for several years now. Since your business continues to grow, you have decided to start managing it with a computer running Windows 2000. The first step of this project is to set up your hard drive with a system of useful folders. Start with a main folder called Business. Within the Business folder you should place a folder for each day of the week that you teach, Monday through Friday. Eventually, each of these folders will contain a folder for each student who has a lesson on that day. For now, each day of the week folder should hold a new WordPad document called [Insert day] Schedule.txt. Back inside the Business folder, create one text document with the name Student List.txt and another called Master Schedule.txt. Finally, place a shortcut to Master Schedule.txt inside each day of the week folder.

2. Your supervisor has asked you to be in charge of the New Media department's new multimedia software and documentation. Create a folder on your C: drive named New Media. Create two folders inside the New Media folder named Programs and Documentation. Open the Documentation folder and place a new WordPad document named Tech Support.txt inside the folder. Copy the document to your My Documents folder. Then rename the Programs folder you created Software.

3. Before you install Windows 2000 throughout your office, you want to review the software's end user license agreement, but you are not sure where to find it. Use Windows 2000's Search facility to look for a file named eula on your local hard disk. If you find it successfully, double-click the file in the Search Results window to open it. Then close the file and create a shortcut to it on your desktop.

4. Your senior project will involve writing a report on four influential American public figures of the twentieth century. To start, create a folder on your C: drive named Senior_Project. Inside the Senior_Project folder, create four subfolders with the last names of four famous figures (e.g., Roosevelt, Frost, Steinem, and King). In each of the four subfolders, create and place a WordPad document named after the person for whom you named its related subfolder (e.g., Roosevelt.txt, Frost.txt, Steinem.txt, and King.txt). Create a subfolder in the My Documents folder called My_Senior_Project. Copy the four .txt files from the Senior_Project folder to the My_Senior_Project folder.

3

Working with Internet Explorer

Microsoft Internet Explorer is a software application that gives you the tools you need to take full advantage of the World Wide Web. Its integration with the Windows 2000 operating system makes it easy to browse the Web whether you want to find a local take-out restaurant, e-mail your sister to tell her about your new job, or find a message board relating to mandolins.

skills

- ⚡ **Introduction to the Internet**
- ⚡ **Opening Internet Explorer**
- ⚡ **Navigating the Web**
- ⚡ **Searching the Internet**
- ⚡ **Creating Favorites**
- ⚡ **Managing Favorites**
- ⚡ **Printing a Web Page**

One of the most used facets of the Internet is the World Wide Web. It has increasingly become a key element of business, culture, community, and politics. You have already seen the browser window, as it is the same one used for My Computer and the Windows Explorer. The function of a browser is just that: it lets you browse, or surf, and view the pages that make up the Web. The World Wide Web is like a long hyper-text document consisting of millions of pages that contain text, pictures, movies, and sounds. Among these pages you can find everything from information on NASA's latest launch to samples from your favorite musical artist's new CD.

When using Internet Explorer, most Web browsing can be done through a series of mouse clicks. Web pages are made up of hypermedia, which are words and pictures that are linked to other places on the Web and will transport you there when they are clicked. Internet Explorer also has toolbars that contain buttons to help you move through all the interesting material you will encounter on your journey across the Web.

As you wander around the Web you will encounter pages that you will want to return to later. To go to any page, all you need to do is remember the address (each Web page has its own), and then enter it into the text box provided on Internet Explorer's Address Bar. If you will want to visit a page often there is even a way to create direct links, or shortcuts, to your favorite Web sites. This is a good idea if a site's content changes frequently, such as that of a news service. The nature of the Web allows for frequent updating of a page's data. As you go through this book, keep in mind that a page's look or contents may have changed since the authors visited it. Some references may no longer be accurate when compared with what you view on your computer.

skill | Introduction to the Internet

concept

The Internet is an extended worldwide computer network that is composed of numerous smaller networks. In the late 1960s, the U.S. Defense Department's Advanced Research Projects Agency (ARPA) created a network of computers designed to withstand severe localized damage, such as that of a nuclear attack. Each computer on the ARPA network was connected to every other machine in such a way as to form a web. Each chunk of data sent from one machine to another was formatted as a packet, which also contained the address of where the packet originated and where it was headed. The web configuration and packet format enabled data to be rerouted if a node along its path in the network should be rendered inoperable. The packet-switching technology developed for ARPAnet became the foundation of today's Internet.

In the early 1980s, the National Science Foundation founded NSFnet, five supercomputing centers connected together on a network. Soon, other government agencies and educational institutions connected to NSFnet as well, adding information and infrastructure upon which an ever-larger network began to grow.

As more scientists, students, and computer enthusiasts became familiar with the Internet, more people began to log on from a variety of locations. Figure 3-1 illustrates the phenomenal growth of Internet use. Soon, new software was developed to facilitate access to the Internet. Along with e-mail and newsgroups, two major uses of the Internet, the World Wide Web began to rise in popularity in the first half of the 1990s. The WWW is made possible by hypermedia and hypertext, objects such as pictures or lines of text that, when clicked, instruct the browser to go to another location on the Web. This allows for a nonlinear presentation of information, making the WWW, in effect, one huge hypermedia document made up of millions of individual files, each with their own address on the Web. The address at which a document is located on the Internet is called a Uniform Resource Locator or URL. A URL consists of three parts: the protocol (such as http or ftp), the location of the server on the Internet (domain), and sometimes the path to the requested data on the server's drive.

The Web works on a client–server model (Figure 3-2). The server, which is the computer containing the requested data, sends information to the client, the computer which receives it. The transfer of data between server and client follows a standardized protocol, or information exchange process. The Web standard is HTTP (HyperText Transfer Protocol), which allows all kinds of computers to understand and reliably translate hypertext Web files. Internet Explorer is a Web browser, which, like all Web software, conforms to HTTP standards. Web browsers are programs that allow a computer to translate the hypertext and display it. All Web browsers can read the text of all Web pages because these pages are written with a platform-independent language called Hypertext Markup Language, or HTML. HTML documents consist of the text that will appear on the page, formatting instructions, and references to other files such as graphics that will be displayed on the page. The World Wide Web has become the most popular feature of the Internet, providing access to an almost unimaginable diversity of information.

Figure 3-1 The growth of the Internet

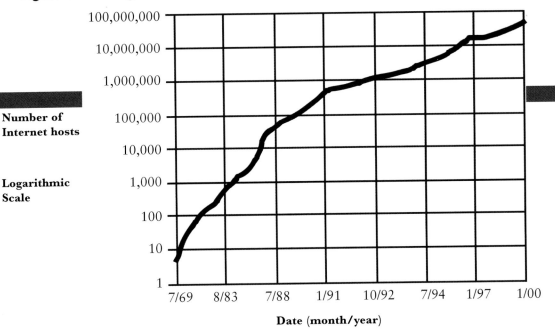

Number of
Internet hosts

Logarithmic
Scale

Date (month/year)

Figure 3-2 Clients and servers on the World Wide Web

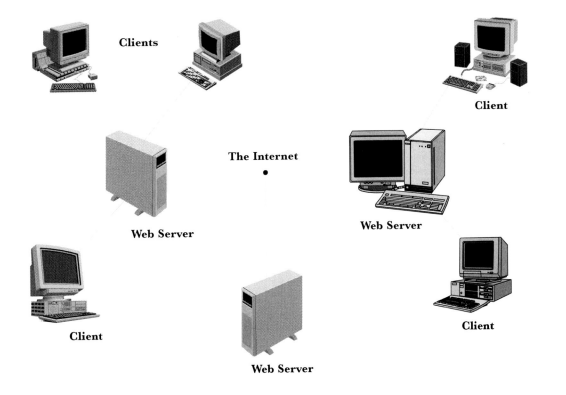

skill | Opening Internet Explorer

concept

Before you can begin surfing the Web with Internet Explorer (IE), you must open the application. You can do this in a variety of ways, including using the Start menu, the Quick Launch toolbar, or a desktop icon. This skill assumes that you have a valid Internet connection and that your Web browser has been configured correctly. If this is not so, begin by double-clicking the Connect to the Internet icon 🔌 on your desktop to launch the Internet Connection Wizard (also available on the Start menu: Programs/Accessories/Communications) which will guide you through the steps necessary to set up your Internet account and browser. Once you have run the Wizard, its shortcut icon will be removed from the desktop.

do it !

Open Internet Explorer and then guide the pointer over the various parts of the window to become familiar with its interface.

1. Click the Internet Explorer quick launch icon 🌐, located next to the Start button, to open the Internet Explorer window. Assuming that your connection to the Internet is valid, Internet Explorer will open. A page will appear in the browser window, which is shown maximized in Figure 3-3. This is called the browser's home page, and refers to the document that loads automatically when the application is launched. IE's default home page is the Microsoft Network's (MSN) home page, http://www.msn.com. (In this instance, the term home page refers to the main page of Microsoft's Web site.) Since Windows allows for customization, your browser window may be different than the ones shown, and your startup procedure may vary slightly from the one demonstrated here. For example, you may have to through a dial-up procedure if you are connecting to the Internet with a modem.

2. Internet Explorer's browser window resembles the standard Windows 2000 system window with which you are already familiar. You will notice the most change in the Standard Buttons toolbar. Table 3-1 explains some of the features of this toolbar and how they allow you to use IE most effectively.

more

Changing your browser's home page is a relatively simple procedure. Open the Tools menu from Internet Explorer's Menu bar and click the Internet Options command. The Internet Options dialog box will open to the General tab. The top section of the General tab is titled Home page, and it contains a text entry box that holds the Web address for your browser's current home page. This address will be selected automatically when the dialog box opens. You can type any Web address to replace the one that is already there. Then click [OK] to confirm the adjustment and close the dialog box. The next time you open your browser or click on the Home button, the Web page whose address you provided will appear in your browser window. 🖱️ To restore your browser's original home page setting, open the Internet Options dialog box from the View menu. Then click the Use Default button in the Home page section of the General tab.

If you have difficulty remembering the functions of the different toolbar buttons, you can customize the Standard Buttons toolbar so that it displays text labels for all buttons. To do this, right-click the toolbar, and then click the Customize command on the menu that appears. Near the bottom of the Customize Toolbar dialog box is a drop-down list box labeled Text Options that allows you to choose text labels for all button, selected buttons, or no text labels. The main part of this dialog box permits you to change which buttons actually appear on the toolbar.

Figure 3-3 Internet Explorer opened to MSN home page

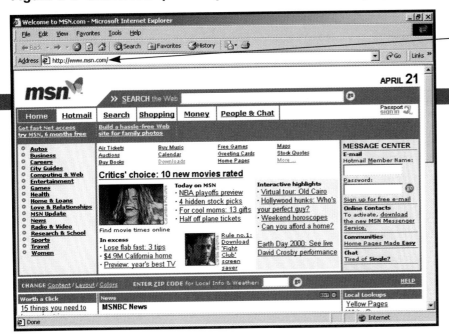

Address (URL) of current
Web page displayed in
Address Bar text box

Table 3-1 IE Standard Buttons toolbar

Button	Function
⊗	Stops the loading of a page into the browser window
↻	Reloads the current page; especially useful for pages that update frequently
🔍 Search ⭐ Favorites 🕐 History	Activates the corresponding Explorer bar in the browser window
🏠	Loads the browser's home page into the browser window; the home page can be set on the General tab of the Internet Options dialog box
✉▾	Opens a menu of commands related to working with e-mail
🖨	Instructs a printer properly connected to your computer to print a copy of the current page

Practice

Change your browser's home page to the following address: http://www.theglobe.com

skill | Navigating the Web

concept

Since information on the Web is not presented in a strictly linear fashion, it is possible to follow links in any order you like, examining whatever you wish in more detail. This is often referred to as browsing or surfing. Most Web browsing with Internet Explorer is done using a few basic actions and controls.

do it !

Practice moving around the Web using hyperlinks, navigation buttons, and the Address Bar.

1. From the MSN home page, you can gain access to news, free e-mail, reference materials, online shopping, and much more. Clickable words and images on the page are called hyperlinks. Position the pointer over the Hotmail link. The pointer will appear as a hand with a pointing finger 🖑 when over the link, indicating that it is an active link. The underlined text may also change color to red.

2. With the pointer still over Hotmail, click the left mouse button. The Microsoft Windows icon at the right end of the Menu bar will animate to indicate that the page you have requested is loading. The page should appear in the browser window momentarily, as shown in Figure 3-4.

3. Locate and click the Terms of Service link. You will be transported to a page that explains the terms of service for Hotmail®, Microsoft's free Web-based e-mail service. Notice that since you started following links, the Back button on the Standard Buttons toolbar has become active. Use the scroll bar to read text that is not visible.

4. Click the Back button ⟵Back to go back to the previously viewed page, the main Hotmail page.

5. Click the Forward button ⟶. The Terms of Service page reappears in the window. The Forward button only becomes active once the Back button has been clicked, and reverses the Back command.

6. Position the pointer in the Address Bar text box, and then click once. The URL (Uniform Resource Locator) of the current page will be selected.

7. Type http://www.altavista.com to enter this address manually, then press [Enter]. The home page of the AltaVista search engine, shown in Figure 3-5, will appear.

8. Click the Home button 🏠 to go back to your browser's home page. ⬛ Clicking the History button 🕒History on the toolbar opens the History Explorer Bar on the left side of the browser window. The History Bar lists all of the pages you have visited recently as hyperlinks so you can revisit them with a single click.

more

The Forward and Back buttons both have small black downward-pointing arrows on their right edges. These arrows indicate that the button has a drop-down menu associated with it. If you click the arrow with the left mouse button, a list of recently visited pages appears below the button with the most recent at the top. Using this list allows you to quickly go back to a previously visited page without having to click the Back button repeatedly. In the same way, the Forward button's drop-down list shows sites that can be visited by clicking the Forward button. Right-clicking the Back or Forward button will also bring up these menus.

Figure 3-4 Microsoft's Hotmail® page

Back button now available

Spinning icon indicates activity

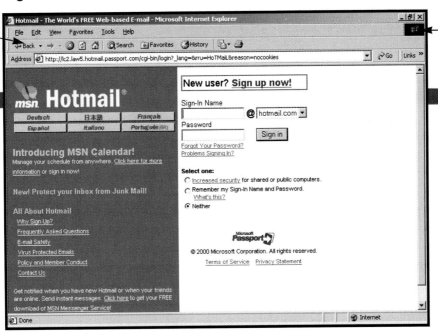

Figure 3-5 Using the Address Bar to enter a URL

Click current address to select it; then type address of page you want to visit

Click Address drop-down arrow to see list of URLs entered recently

Press [Enter] or click Go button to go to address displayed in Address Bar text box

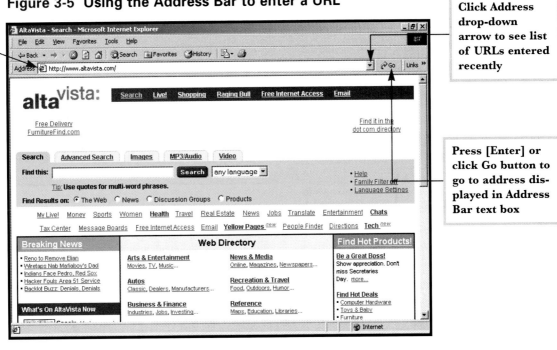

Practice

Visit the Web page found at http://www.usps.gov. Then use the toolbar to return to your browser's home page.

skill | Searching the Internet

concept

There is an inordinate amount of information on the Internet. Being able to find what you want will help make your experience surfing the Web more productive and enjoyable. With Internet Explorer's Search Explorer Bar, you can retrieve and display a list of Web sites related to your topic of interest, and then load the actual Web pages into the same window. This convenience prevents you from having to navigate back to your search page each time you want to follow a different link.

do it !

Use the Search Explorer Bar to find a Web site that offers used car listings.

1. Click the Search button [🔍 Search]. The Search Explorer Bar (Figure 3-6) will appear in the browser window. Notice that Internet Explorer's Search Bar differs from the one you saw in Windows Explorer. This one is configured for Internet searches rather than for finding files or folders, though a link for searching for files or folders is still provided.

2. The default search category is Find a Web page, and the Find a Web page containing: text-entry box is ready to receive your search query. Type "used cars" (include the quotes). Enclosing the phrase in quotation marks instructs the search engine to treat the words you enter as a single unit and only search for pages that contain used and cars next to each other in that order. If the keywords are not enclosed in quotation marks, the search will return any pages that simply contains either word.

3. Click the Search button [Search]. The MSN search engine lists links to the 10 Web pages that will most likely satisfy your needs, determined by factors such as proximity of the words to each other and to the top of the page. If you point to a link, you will receive a ScreenTip that includes a description of the page and its URL. ⬛ Most search engines are only case sensitive with uppercase letters. For example, a search for Bugs Bunny will return sites relating to the cartoon character, while a search on bugs bunny will result in a list of sites on insects and rabbits as well.

4. Click a link from the list of results to visit that page. The site will load in the right panel, while the search engine remains in the left panel so that you can select another link, as shown in Figure 3-7.

5. To view the page in the entire window, click the Search button again to hide the Explorer Bar. The current search will remain in the Search Bar until you close Internet Explorer or click the Search button again to begin a new search.

more

Once you click a link in Internet Explorer, the link will change color so that you know you have already visited it. This is very helpful when you are working with a list of links such as that in the Search Explorer Bar. Most searches will return more than 10 results. If the first ten do not satisfy your needs, you will find a link below them that allows you to view the next set of links that match your search criteria. If you still aren't successful, you can try using a different search engine by clicking the Next button [🔍 Next ▾] near the top of the Explorer Bar. If you want to choose a specific search engine, click the arrow on the right end of the Next button to open a menu of search engines. Clicking the New button [🔍 New] reloads the basic Search Explorer Bar (Figure 3-6) so you can choose a new category of search. Clicking the Customize button [Customize] allows you to choose which engines and directories will be used for each search category and the order in which they will be activated by the Next button.

Figure 3-6 Internet Explorer's Search Explorer Bar

Select a search category

Enter search words here

Click button to begin search

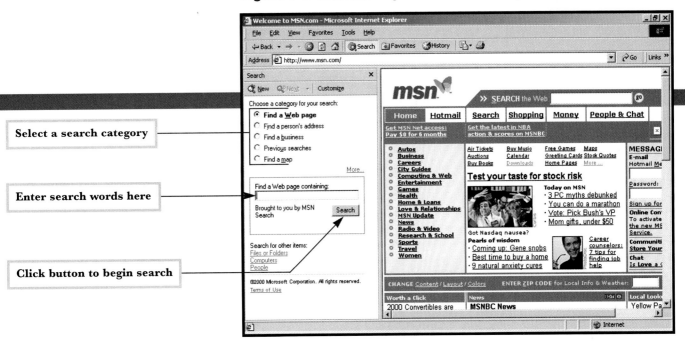

Figure 3-7 Using search results

Click to select a different search engine

List of links found as result of search

Right panel displays selected Web page while search results remain in Explorer Bar

Visited link changes color

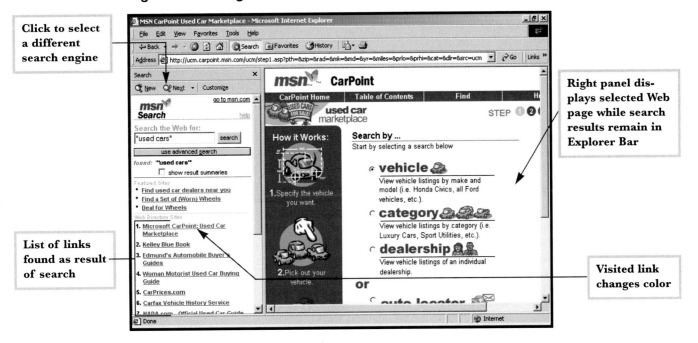

Practice

Use the Search Explorer Bar to find Web pages that will allow you to consult airline flight schedules. Then follow one of the links produced by your search.

skill | Creating Favorites

concept

Internet Explorer allows you to make direct links, or shortcuts, to your favorite Internet sites so that you may revisit them easily without having to remember long URLs. This is also known as bookmarking. The Favorites menu offers several options for adding, organizing, and managing your favorites. Shortcuts to frequently visited sites may also be placed on the Links toolbar, on the desktop, or in a folder on your hard drive.

do it !

Create a Favorite for a search engine, search for a site that contains a local weather forecast, and then place a shortcut to that site on the Links toolbar.

1. Click the Address text box to select its contents.

2. Type www.excite.com to replace the current URL, then press [Enter]. Internet Explorer automatically adds the protocol http://, and the Excite search engine/Web guide loads into the window.

3. Open the Favorites menu from the Menu bar, then click Add to Favorites. The Add Favorite dialog box will appear, as shown in Figure 3-8.

4. Click [OK] to create the favorite with the default settings and close the dialog box. The shortcut to the Excite page will be added to your Favorites list.

5. Open the Favorites menu to see that your shortcut is there. Then click the Favorites menu title again to close the menu.

6. Click in Excite's search text-entry box to place an insertion point there.

7. Type +weather +[the name of your city]. This instructs the search engine to look for sites that contain both of the words. If the plus signs had been omitted, sites containing either of the words, but not necessarily both, would be found.

8. Click [Search] to initiate the search (if a dialog box appears, click Yes to proceed).

9. Look through the list of matches, using the vertical scroll bar to advance the page as you go. Visit the sites that appear relevant to the original search objective by clicking their hyperlinks. Look for a site with a good local forecast. Use the Back button to return to the search results page to view additional found sites. When you find a site you like, stay there.

10. Assuming your Links toolbar is just visible at the right end of the Address Bar, drag the Links toolbar straight down so that it occupies its own row.

11. Click and hold the IE page icon 🛋 in the Address text box, and then drag it down to the Links toolbar. As you drag, the pointer will appear as an arrow with the shortcut arrow icon attached. A marker will appear in the Links toolbar indicating the place where the new Favorite will be created (only when you are between buttons or at the ends of the toolbar). When you release the mouse button a button for the current site will appear on the Links toolbar (Figure 3-9). A Favorite will also be added to the Links folder on the Favorites menu. ◖ You can drag any link on a page to create a shortcut just as you would to create it with the IE page icon. Dragging a link to the Links toolbar, for example, will create a shortcut for that link rather than the currently displayed Web page.

more

The Favorites that you create will not only appear on the Favorites menu in the Internet Explorer window, but everywhere the Favorites folder is accessible. This can include the Start menu and the Favorites menu in any system window. The Favorites that you create will be also be added to the Favorites Explorer Bar, which can be left open while you browse the Web for quick access to your shortcuts.

Figure 3-8 Add Favorite dialog box

Default favorite name taken from page title

Click to create favorite on different level of Favorites hierarchy

Figure 3-9 Adding a favorite to the Links toolbar

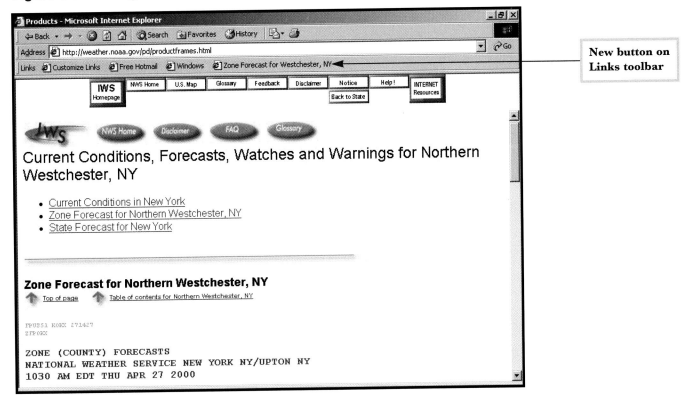

New button on Links toolbar

Practice

Add www.amazon.com to your Favorites folder. Then add www.usps.gov to your Links toolbar.

skill | Managing Favorites

concept

Without sufficient attention to organization, a long list of Favorites can be difficult to manage. By editing and grouping Favorites, you can make them much easier to use. Internet Explorer allows you to create or delete folders on the Favorites menu, redistribute Favorites among the folders, and rename Favorites and the folders that hold them.

do it !

Create a new folder that will store your personal Favorites, move a Favorite into that folder, and then rename the Favorite.

1. Click Favorites on the Menu bar, then click the Organize Favorites command. The Organize Favorites dialog box will open, as shown in Figure 3-10.

2. Click the Create Folder button [Create Folder]. A new folder will be created in the Organize Favorites dialog box with its default name selected, ready to be changed.

3. Type Search Engines, then press [Enter]. The name of the folder will change, and the folder will remain selected.

4. Click the favorite you created for the Excite page in the last skill to select it. Notice that its properties are displayed in the bottom-right corner of the dialog box.

5. Click the Move to Folder button [Move to Folder...]. The Browse for Folder dialog box will open.

6. Click the Search Engines folder you created to select it as the destination folder to which you will move the Excite favorite. When you select the folder it will be highlighted and appear as an open folder, as shown in Figure 3-11.

7. Click the OK button [OK]. The Browse for Folder dialog box closes, and the selected favorite is moved.

8. Click the Search Engine folder to show its contents in the dialog box.

9. Click the Excite Favorite to select it.

10. Click the Rename button [Rename]. The Favorite's name will be highlighted.

11. Type Excite.com, then press [Enter] to rename the Favorite, as shown in Figure 3-12. Close the Organize Favorites dialog box. You can use the drag-and-drop technique to move Favorites from folder to folder inside in the Organize Favorites dialog box. Right-clicking an item will allow you to rename it.

more

In the previous Skill you created a Favorite on the top level of the Favorites hierarchy. The Favorites folder is the default location for creating shortcuts. If you click the Create In button the dialog box will expand, showing you a pane in which the current Favorites hierarchy is displayed. This pane is similar to the Browse for Folder dialog box pictured in Figure 3-11. From this additional pane you can select the folder in which you wish to create the new Favorite, thereby eliminating the process of moving it later.

Figure 3-10 Organize Favorites dialog box

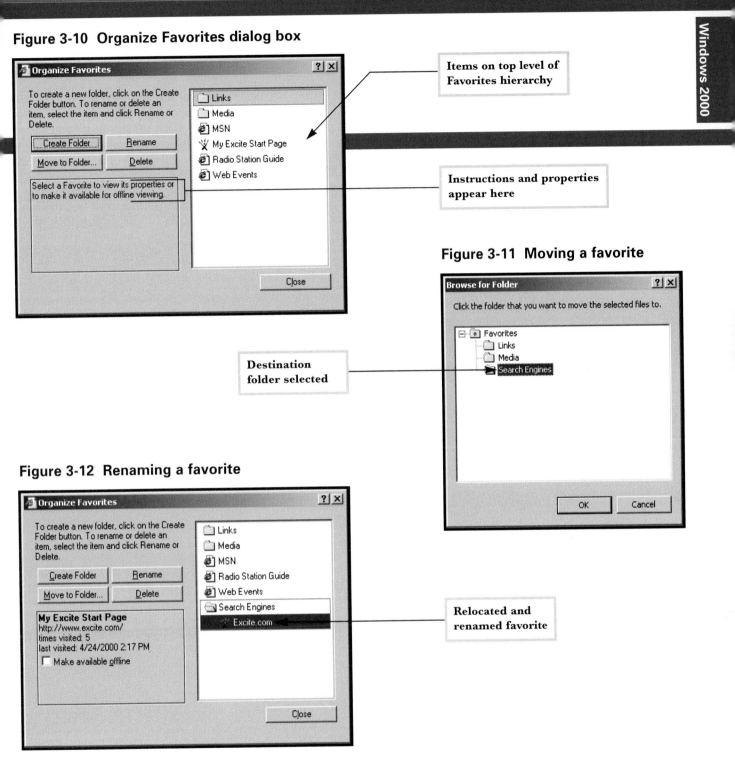

Items on top level of Favorites hierarchy

Instructions and properties appear here

Figure 3-11 Moving a favorite

Destination folder selected

Figure 3-12 Renaming a favorite

Relocated and renamed favorite

Practice

Create a new Favorites folder called Online Shopping. Then move the Amazon.com Favorite you created in the previous Practice exercise into this new folder.

skill | Printing a Web Page

concept

In general, Web pages are designed primarily for on-screen viewing. However, there may be occasions when you want to print a paper copy of a particular page. In fact, most online shopping sites suggest that you print your transaction page when you have completed a purchase so you can keep it for your records. In addition, many software and hardware manufacturers provide installation instructions online that you can print and then follow as you install new software.

do it !

Use Internet Explorer's Print command to print a paper copy of a Web page.

1. Use the Favorite you created earlier to go to www.excite.com.

2. Click File to open the File menu, then click the Print command. The Print dialog box, shown in Figure 3-13, appears with the General tab in front.

3. If your computer is connected to more than one printer, you can select the icon for the printer you wish to use in the Select Printer section of the dialog box.

4. When the correct printer is selected, click [Print] to print the Web page with the default settings. Your printer should print one copy of the page, but it might require more than one piece of paper to do so since Web pages are not necessarily designed to fit on standard paper sizes.

more

Even though Web pages are designed for the screen rather than paper, you do have some control over how a page will appear when you print it. Before you print, open the File menu and choose the Page Setup command. The Page Setup dialog box will open, as shown in Figure 3-14. In the Paper section of the dialog box, you can select the size of the paper you are printing on and how it is being fed into the machine. These options are also available on the Paper Quality tab in the Print dialog box. In the Headers and Footers section, you can specify text that will appear at the top and bottom of the printed page. The Orientation section determines whether the page will be printed like a traditional document (Portrait), or so that its left to right length is greater than its top to bottom length (Landscape). Page orientation can also be controlled from the Layout tab in the Print dialog box. Finally, you can set the distance for all four of the page's margins in the Margins section.

Some Web pages are divided into separate components known as frames. When you print a page that uses frames, the Print frames section of the Print dialog box (Figure 3-13) will be active. From here you can choose to print the page exactly as it appears on your screen, print a single frame that you select, or print each frame individually. Just below the Print frames section are two check boxes. The first instructs your printer to print all documents that are linked to the one you are currently printing while the second simply adds a table of these links to the end of the printout. These items are also available on the Print dialog box's Options tab. The Print dialog box's Collate option allows you to print complete sets of a document in page order when you are printing more than one copy of a multiple page document.

You can bypass the Print dialog box by clicking on the Print button on the Standard Buttons toolbar. Your document will be printed using the current print settings.

Figure 3-13 Print dialog box

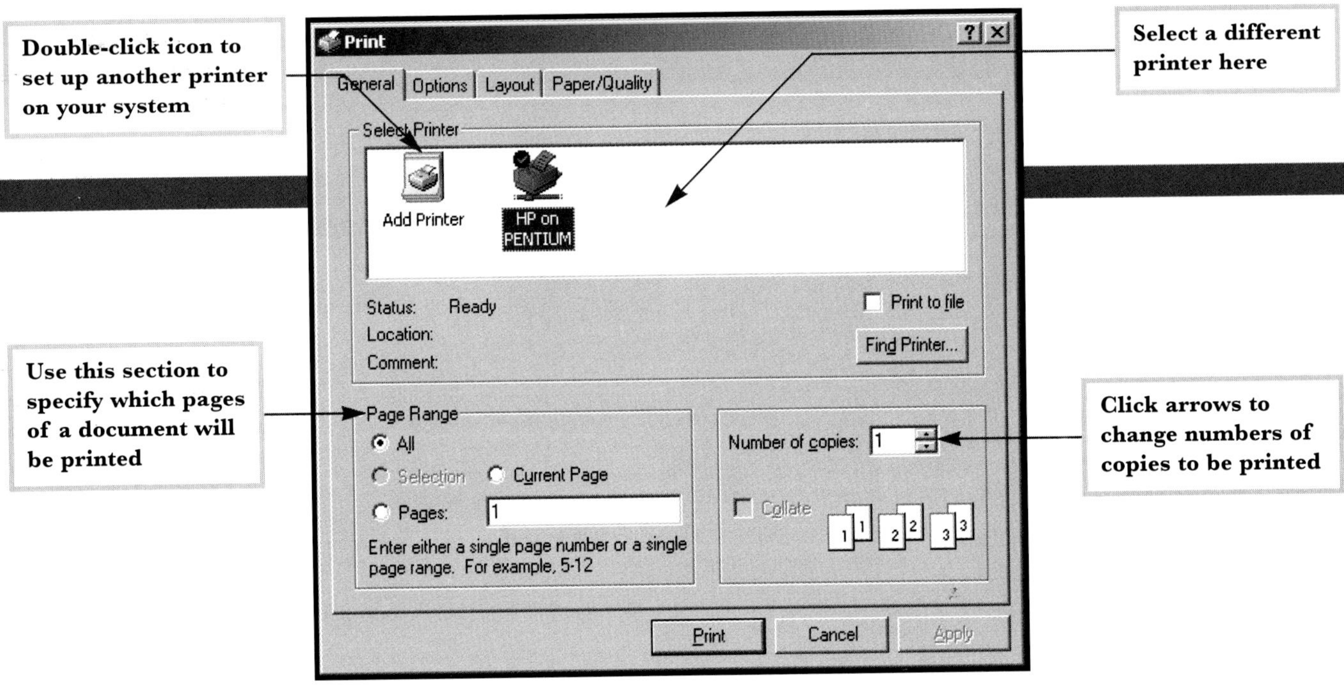

Double-click icon to set up another printer on your system

Select a different printer here

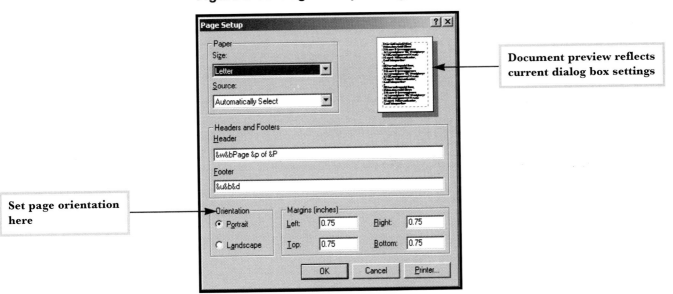

Use this section to specify which pages of a document will be printed

Click arrows to change numbers of copies to be printed

Figure 3-14 Page Setup dialog box

Document preview reflects current dialog box settings

Set page orientation here

![mouse] **Practice**

Print a copy of your browser's home page with the Orientation set to Landscape.

shortcuts

Function	Button/Mouse	Menu	Keyboard
Stop loading page		Click View, then click Stop	[Esc]
Refresh page		Click View, then click Refresh	[F5]
Go to browser's home page		Click View, point to Go To, then click Home Page	[Alt]+[Home]
Expand window to full		Click View, then click Full Screen	[F11]
Access e-mail from IE (start Outlook Express)		Click Tools, then click Mail and News	[Alt], [T], [M]
Print current page		Click File, then click Print (for dialog box)	[Ctrl]+[P] (for dialog box)
Open new browser window		Click File, point to New, then click Window	[Ctrl]+[N]
Open new page click Back		Click File, then click Open	[Ctrl]+[O]
Browse backward	⇐ Back	Click View, point to Go To, then click Back	[Alt]+[←]
Browse forward	⇒	Click View, point to Go To, then click Forward	[Alt]+[→]

A. Identify Key Features

Name the items indicated by callouts in Figure 3-15.

Figure 3-15 Internet Explorer's Standard Buttons toolbar

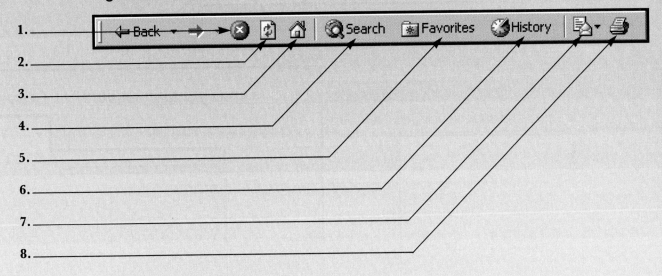

1. _____
2. _____
3. _____
4. _____
5. _____
6. _____
7. _____
8. _____

B. Select the Best Answer

9. Click this to go to your browser's home page

10. Dialog box that allows you to create shortcuts to pages you visit frequently

11. Language used to write Web pages

12. Protocol used to transfer data over the Web

13. Dialog box that allows you to relocate a Favorite

14. A subset of the Internet that allows users to publish documents on remote servers

15. An individual component of a Web page that can be printed independently

16. A Page Setup option

17. Reloads the current page in the browser window

18. Allows you to create buttons for your Favorites

a. Refresh button

b. World Wide Web

c. Home button

d. Links toolbar

e. Orientation

f. HTTP

g. Browse for Folder

h. HTML

i. Add Favorite dialog box

j. Frame

quiz (continued)

C. Complete the Statement

19. A document's address on the Web is also known as its:

a. EARL

b. IRL

c. URL

d. HTTP

20. To help you find documents on the Web, you should use:

a. IE's Search Explorer Bar

b. Windows 2000's help facility

c. Outlook Express

d. IE's Favorites Explorer Bar

21. All of the following are popular search engines except:

a. AltaVista

b. MSN Search

c. Outlook

d. Excite

22. The Web runs on a:

a. Linear platform

b. Decreasing number of hosts

c. Government-regulated network

d. Client–server model

23. You can create a favorite for the current page by dragging and dropping the:

a. Favorites button

b. IE page icon

c. Favorites Explorer Bar

d. Current URL

24. Clicking on the Print button causes your document to be printed without:

a. Margins

b. Headers and Footers

c. The appearance of the Print dialog box

d. Frames

25. To change your browser's home page, choose the Internet Options command from the:

a. Tools menu

b. File menu

c. Home page dialog box

d. Favorites menu

26. The mouse pointer changes to a hand with a pointing finger to indicate that:

a. The page you requested has finished loading

b. The link you are pointing to is a Favorite

c. You must wait until the page finishes loading

d. You are pointing to an active link

interactivity

Build Your Skills

1. Open Internet Explorer and practice navigating the Web:

    a. Launch Internet Explorer.

    b. If your browser is not set to open to www.msn.com, go there now.

    c. Look for a link to microsoft.com and click it to go to Microsoft's home page.

    d. Click the Privacy Policy link near the bottom of the page.

    e. Go back to Microsoft's home page.

    f. Return to the Privacy Policy page.

2. Visit a Web page whose address you have entered manually:

    a. Use the Address Bar to visit http://www.cnn.com.

    b. Stop the page before it finishes loading.

    c. Refresh the page.

3. Use the Search Explorer Bar to find Web sites about your hometown and store them as Favorites:

    a. Activate the Search Explorer Bar.

    b. Conduct a search for Web pages that relate to your hometown.

    c. Follow the links generated by the search until you have found two or three that you like.

    d. Add these sites to your Favorites list.

4. Create a new Favorites folder and move existing Favorites into it:

    a. Open the Organize Favorites dialog box.

    b. Create a new folder named [Your Hometown] Links.

    c. Move the Favorites you created in the previous step into the new folder.

    d. Rename the new folder so that its name is just that of your hometown and doesn't include the word Links.

5. Print a Web page with Landscape orientation:

    a. Direct your Web browser to one of the hometown Favorites you created above.

    b. Open the Page Setup dialog box from the File menu.

    c. Change the page orientation from Portrait to Landscape, then click OK.

    d. Open the Print dialog box.

    e. Print 2 copies of the current page.

interactivity (continued)

Problem Solving Exercises

1. Search the Web for information on guitars and guitar instruction. Use at least three different search engines to conduct your search. When you find helpful sites, be sure to bookmark them in appropriately named folders. Create at least four different folders to house favorites for the sites you find. Some categories you might use are: Guitar Sales, Online Instruction, and Chords and Tablature.

2. As a sales representative, you fit the title of "business traveler" perfectly. Fortunately, the World Wide Web can do wonders for your travel expenses. Various Web sites can now assist you in finding the cheapest air fares and hotel rooms available. Use the skills you have learned in this lesson to find at least three such sites on the Web. Add each site to your Favorites list. Then create a new Favorites folder named Travel Savings and move the Favorites you have added into the new folder.

3. As the Director of Human Resources at a large accounting firm, it is important for you to stay on top of the issues that affect the workforce. Chief among these is health insurance. Your approach to this topic is twofold. You like to keep one eye on what the insurance companies are saying about themselves, and the other on what the watchdogs are saying about the insurance companies. Use your Web skills to find the Web sites of major health care providers. Store the home pages of these sites in a Favorites folder named Health Care Providers. Then focus your Web search on pages that provide reviews of, or news about, particular health care companies. Organize these pages in a Favorites folder named Health Care Reviews. Print the page that offers the best summary of current health insurance issues.

4. Your department is in the market for a new color laser printer. You have been chosen to research the purchase and recommend a printer to your boss. Use your Web skills to find out as much as you can about four top of the line color laser printers. You should search for the Web sites of companies that actually manufacture and sell the printers as well as independent reviews of printers. When you find a page on a manufacturer's site, save it as a Favorite in a folder named Laser Printers. When you find a page that review the performance of a particular printer or printers, save it as a Favorite in a folder named Printer Reviews. After studying the four candidates you have found, select the printer that you think will best suit your department's needs (a high output rate, low maintenance, network ready, reliable service program). Create a button for the Web page of the printer you have chosen on the Links toolbar.

Introduction to Word

Microsoft Word 2002 is the latest edition of Microsoft's powerful word processing software application. It is designed to make the creation of professional-quality documents fast and easy. Word processing software allows you to type the text of a document electronically and edit, move, and stylize that text, even after it has been written. Word processors provide enormous flexibility in how the finished product will appear.

Word's capabilities are not limited to text. As features have been added through the various generations of the program, it has gained the capacity to serve as a desktop publishing tool. Among many other features, Word will let you:

* Starting Word
* Exploring the Word Screen
* Creating a Document and Entering Text
* Saving and Closing a Document
* Opening an Existing Document
* Deleting and Inserting Text
* Formatting Text
* Previewing and Printing a Document

◉ Copy, move, and change the appearance of text within a document

◉ Share text and other page elements among documents

◉ Create documents using ready-made templates

◉ Add page numbers and footnotes to documents automatically

◉ Find and correct spelling and grammar errors automatically

◉ Insert tables, charts, and pictures in your documents

◉ Request help while you are using the program

◉ Search for specific instances of text and formatting within a document

◉ See how your document will appear on paper before printing it

While you work on a document, it is stored in your computer's temporary memory. In order to keep a document permanently so you can work with it again, Word enables you to save it as a file on a storage device such as a floppy disk or hard disk drive. You can use Word to create everything from a one-page business letter to a book containing thousands of pages.

Lesson Goal:

Create a cover letter that will accompany a résumé a student is sending in order to apply for a job.

skill | Starting Word

concept

The first step in using the Microsoft Word program, or application, is launching it. The Windows operating system provides a number of ways to launch programs. When you install Word (or Microsoft Office, the suite of programs of which Word is a part), a shortcut to the program is placed on the Windows Start menu automatically. You can also open Word by locating and running its executable file, named Winword.exe, through My Computer or Windows Explorer.

do it !

Use the Start menu to launch the Microsoft Word application.

1. Turn on your computer and monitor and make sure that any peripheral devices such as your mouse are connected properly. When your edition of the Windows operating system finishes loading, the Windows desktop should appear on your screen (you may be asked to provide a user name and password before Windows finishes loading).

2. Click the Start button [🏁Start] on the Windows taskbar at the bottom of your screen. The Windows Start menu will appear.

3. Move the mouse pointer ↖ up the Start menu to the Programs folder. The Programs submenu will open beside the Start menu.

4. Move the mouse pointer over to the Programs submenu from the Start menu, and point to Microsoft Word. The program name will be highlighted, as shown in Figure 1-1. Newer editions of the Windows operating system such as Windows Me use personalized menus, which means that only the items you use most frequently are displayed on a menu when it first opens. If Personalized menus are active on your computer and you do not see Microsoft Word listed on the Programs menu, click the double arrow at the bottom of the menu to display the rest of the program listings.

5. Click the left mouse button once. Word will open with a blank document in the window (see Figure 1-2). If your copy of Word has been used previously, the appearance of the application window may differ from the one shown in the figure.

more

Do not be alarmed if your desktop or Start menu do not match the descriptions above or the figures on the next page exactly. With several different versions of Windows and countless software applications available, variances in system configuration are more than likely. Windows itself is highly customizable, so the location or appearance of items such as the taskbar and the desktop are also subject to change. Furthermore, you can customize the way in which you interact with the operating system. For example, you can alter the functionality of the mouse so that tasks that normally require a double-click only require a single click. For the purposes of this book, the term click means to press and release the left mouse button quickly. When instructed to double-click, you should press and release the left mouse button twice in rapid succession. A right-click instruction requires you to press and release the right mouse button once. Finally, click and drag means to press and hold the left mouse button down, move the mouse as instructed, and then release the mouse button to complete the action.

Word 2002

Figure 1-1 Opening Word from the Start menu

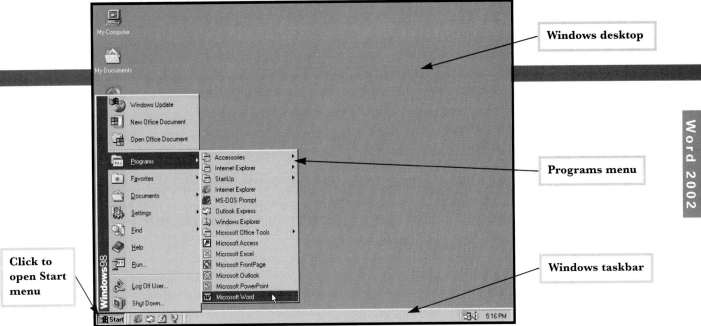

Windows desktop

Programs menu

Click to open Start menu

Windows taskbar

Figure 1-2 Word application window

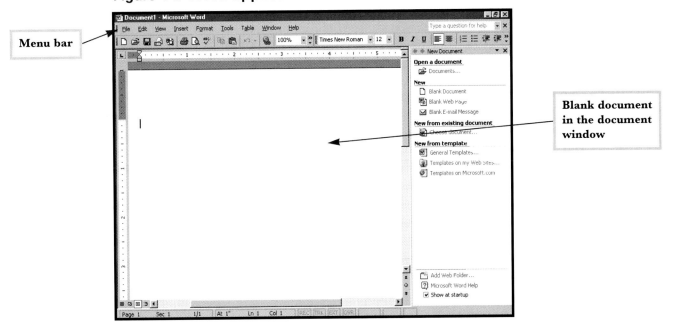

Menu bar

Blank document in the document window

Practice

Click the File menu title on the Menu bar. The File menu will drop down below its menu title. Move the mouse pointer down the File menu and click the Exit command to close the Word application. If you do not see the Exit command, click the double arrow at the bottom of the menu to expand the menu. When you have successfully exited Word, use the Start menu to open the application again.

skill | Exploring the Word Screen

concept

The Word application window consists of many features that are common to all applications running under the Windows operating system. These include a Title bar, a Menu bar, document and window control buttons, and toolbars. In addition to these items, Word has many unique features that are designed to make document production fast, flexible, and convenient. The main components of the Word window are shown in Figure 1-3 and are described below. Figure 1-3 displays Word in a maximized window set to Print Layout View with the Task Pane open. If your screen does not look like the figure, you can click View on the Menu bar to access commands that will allow you to switch to Print Layout View, activate the Task Pane, and set the Zoom level to 100%.

The Title bar shows the name of the active document and the name of the application. New documents are named Document1, Document2, etc., until they are saved with a new name.

The Menu bar displays the titles of the menus containing Word commands. Clicking one of these titles will make its menu appear, listing the commands from which you can choose. Word 2002 uses personalized menus by default, so only a few commands may appear when you first open a menu. These are the commands that have been deemed most popular by the designers of the software. If you do not click one of the available commands, the menu will expand after a few seconds to reveal more commands. You can expedite this expansion by clicking the double arrow at the bottom of the menu or by clicking the menu title again. Alternatively, double-click the menu title to open the full menu right away. As you use Word more and more, the program learns which commands you use most often. These commands will then be the first to appear when you open a menu.

The Standard toolbar contains buttons that serve as shortcuts to commonly used commands. When you rest the mouse pointer over a button, a ScreenTip that describes the button's function appears. The Formatting toolbar contains the Font and Font Size boxes along with many other options for formatting text and inserted objects. Overall, Word provides numerous other toolbars to help you complete your tasks. Some of these toolbars will appear automatically when you execute certain commands. You can activate any toolbar manually by opening the View menu, highlighting the Toolbars command, and then clicking the name of the toolbar you want to display on the Toolbars submenu. You hide an active toolbar by clicking its name again on the submenu. You may also click and drag toolbars to change their order, or click and drag them to other locations in the window.

In Print Layout View, the document window includes both a horizontal ruler and a vertical ruler. The rulers enable you to keep track of your position on the page and view and change the locations of items such as page margins, indents, tabs, columns, and table gridlines.

The insertion point is the blinking vertical bar that marks the place where text will appear when it is entered, or where an object will be placed when it is inserted.

The document window is the open space in which your document appears. When the mouse pointer is within the borders of the document it changes from the standard pointing arrow to an I-beam $\mathbb{I}$ so you can position it in text more accurately.

The Task Pane, which occupies the right side of the application window in the default setup, is a new feature. It helps you organize your most important Word tasks in a single location. The content of the Task Pane changes depending on the actions you are performing. For example, there are different Task Panes for searching, formatting, and opening documents.

In the current view, a vertical scroll bar appears on the right side of the document window, and a horizontal scroll bar is found at the bottom of the window. The position of the scroll bar boxes within the scroll bars indicates where the visible text is located in relation to the portions of the document that are not currently visible on the screen. Clicking the scroll arrows at the ends of the scroll bars advances the document in small increments. Clicking in the scroll bar itself, above or below the scroll bar box, advances the document in larger increments. You can also click and drag the scroll box within the scroll bar to move substantial distances in a document (such as several pages at once).

The Status bar at the bottom of the application window provides feedback about your current activity in Word. The left most section tells you what page and section of your document is currently displayed in the document window. It also indicates the total number of pages in the document. The next section shows the distance the insertion point is from the top of the page and its position on the page in terms of Line and Column number. The third portion of the Status bar is reserved for showing whether certain Word modes such as Overtype and Track Changes are active.

Figure 1-3 Components of the Word application window

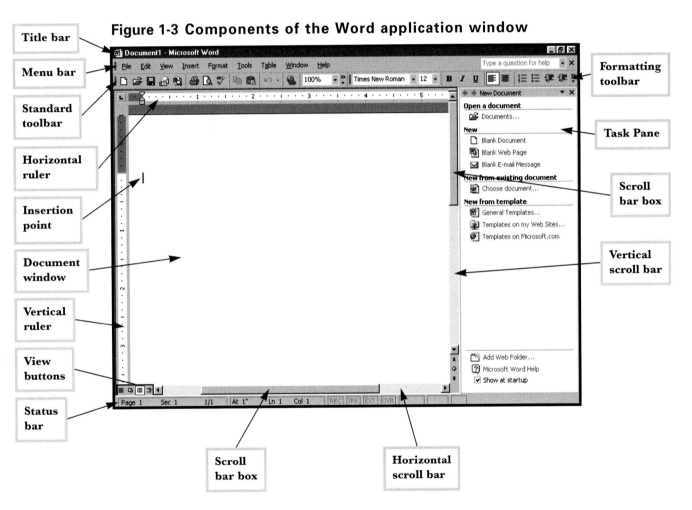

Practice

As shown in the figure above, the Standard and Formatting toolbars are arranged in a single row by default. This setting gives you more screen space for your document, but limits the number of buttons you can see on each of the toolbars. The double arrow pointing to the right at the end of the toolbar indicates that more buttons are available. The downward-pointing arrow indicates that a menu will appear if you click the arrows. Click a set of arrows and then click Show Buttons on Two Rows. The Formatting toolbar will move below the Standard toolbar so you have a better view of both toolbars.

skill | Creating a Document and Entering Text

concept

Data that you enter in Word becomes part of an electronic file also known as a document. You must have a document open in order to begin word processing. When you open the Word application, a new blank document appears in the document window automatically. In Print Layout View, the document is designed to look like an actual piece of paper.

do it !

Type a name and address in a new Word document to begin a letter.

1. Assuming you have already opened Word, a new document should be in the document window with Document1 in the Title bar. You can also create a new document when Word is running by clicking the New Blank Document button ◻ on the Standard toolbar.

2. Use the keyboard to type the following text, pressing [Enter] after each line as indicated:

   Sabrina Lee [Enter]
   12 Oakleigh Ave. [Enter]
   Indianapolis, IN 46202 [Enter]

3. The text will appear at the insertion point as you are typing it. When you are finished, your document should look like Figure 1-4.

4. Leave the document open for use in the next Skill.

more

In this exercise, you pressed [Enter] after each line of text to begin a new one because an address consists of short, distinct lines. When typing a document that does not require abbreviated lines, you do not have to press [Enter] to begin a new line. Word uses a feature known as Word Wrap to continue the text on the next line when you run out of space on the current line. When a word is too long to fit on the current line, it is placed at the beginning of the line below, allowing you to type without interruptions or guesswork.

You may have noticed that some words have wavy red lines or purple dots beneath them. The wavy red lines indicate that Word's Automatic Spell Checking feature is active, and the underlined words are not recognized by Word's dictionary. You will learn how to spell check later in this book. Purple dots below a word or phrase indicate a Smart Tag. In this example, Word has recognized "12 Oakleigh Ave." as an address. If you place the I-beam mouse pointer over the purple underline, a Smart Tag button ⓘ will appear. When you click the Smart Tag button, a menu containing commands related specifically to working with addresses will appear. Smart Tags will appear in a variety of circumstances, including when you type names, dates, Web addresses, and e-mail addresses. In each case, you can access a context-sensitive menu by clicking the smart tag button, giving you control over operations in Word that usually involve using another program such as an address book or e-mail client.

In addition to launching Word or clicking a toolbar button, you can create a new document by clicking Blank Document in the New section of the New Document Task Pane (see Figure 1-5). From the Task Pane, you can also create new documents from existing ones and new documents from templates. For now, you will learn to use general blank documents. Other types of documents and methods of document creation will be covered in later lessons. Some commands have shortcut key combinations associated with them. Pressing these key combinations on the keyboard is the same as executing the command from a toolbar or from the Task Pane. For example, the keyboard shortcut [Ctrl]+[N] creates a new document (the Ctrl key must remain pressed while you press N). ◣▬▶ If your Task Pane is hidden, clicking the New command on the File menu will open the New Document Task Pane.

Figure 1-4 Entering Text in Word

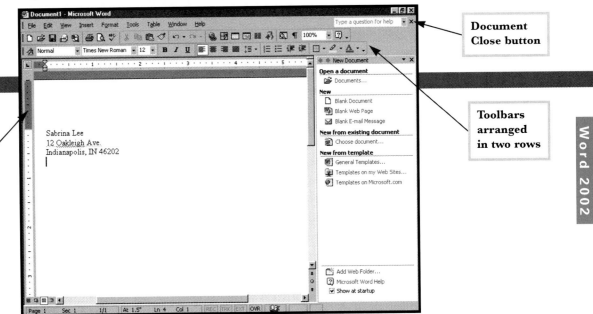

Document Close button

Toolbars arranged in two rows

Gray portion of vertical ruler indicates document's top margin

Figure 1-5 New Document Task Pane

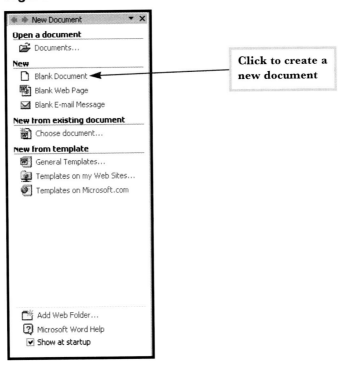

Click to create a new document

Practice

Click the New Blank Document button on the Standard toolbar. A new document will open in its own Word window. Type your name and address in the new document as if you were writing a letter. When you are done, click the Document Close button ☒ (the lower of the two buttons marked with an X) on the right end of the Menu bar to remove this practice document from the screen. When Word asks if you would like to save the document, click the button labeled No.

skill
Saving and Closing a Document

concept

It is essential to save documents by giving them unique names and locations on a storage device such as a floppy disk or hard disk. Otherwise, your work will be lost when you exit Word. It is also a good idea to save documents periodically as you work on them to minimize the amount of data lost due to power or computer failures. Closing a document removes it from the screen and "files it away," if you choose to save it, so you can retrieve it and continue working with it later. You can close individual documents and still leave Word running so you can work on other documents.

do it !

Save the name and address you typed in the previous Skill as a file and then close the file.

1. You should still have the name and address you typed in the previous Skill on your screen. Click File, then click Save As to open the Save As dialog box. When you are saving a document for the first time, the Save As dialog box will appear regardless of whether you have chosen the Save command or the Save As command. The Save As dialog box allows you to provide a file with a particular file name and select the location where the file will be saved. Once a file has been saved, the Save and Save As commands have different functions. Using the Save command or the Save button on the Standard toolbar will overwrite the old version of the file with the current version, without opening a dialog box. Using the Save As command will open the Save As dialog box, allowing you to save another version of the file with either a new file name, a new storage location, or both.

2. When the Save As dialog box opens, Word provides a suggested file name based on the initial text you have typed in the document. This default name is highlighted in the File name box, so you can replace it simply by typing a new name. Type Address.doc to replace the default file name. .doc is the file extension for Word documents. A file extension identifies a file as a certain type and associates the file with a specific program.

3. Word's default storage location is your computer's My Documents folder, which you can see selected near the top of the dialog box in the Save in drop-down list box. You can select a different location by clicking the Save in box to open its drop-down list, or by clicking one of the buttons on the Places bar on the left side of the dialog box. (For example, if you are to save your files on a floppy disk instead of the hard drive, insert the disk, open the Save in drop-down list, and click 3½ Floppy (A:) before continuing.) You also can create new folders for your documents. Click the Create New Folder button to the right of the Save in box. The New Folder dialog box appears, as shown in Figure 1-6.

4. Type Word Files in the Name text box as the name of the new folder, and then click the OK button OK . The folder is created and selected immediately in the Save in box. The dialog box should now look like Figure 1-7. The folder you just created is a subfolder of the My Documents folder, since that folder was selected in the Save in box when you clicked the Create New Folder button.

5. Click the Save button Save in the bottom-right corner of the dialog box to save the Address.doc file in the Word Files folder. The dialog box will close and the document remains on the screen. Notice that the file name you provided in the Save As dialog box now appears in the Title bar.

6. Click the Close button ☒ on the right end of the Menu bar to close the active document, Address.doc, but leave the Word application running.

more If you modify a document and do not save the changes before you close it, Word will open a dialog box that asks you if you want to save the changes. If you do not save, any changes you have made since the last time you saved the document will be lost when the document closes.

You have probably noticed that there are two similar-looking Close buttons in the upper-right corner of the Word window. The lower Close button ☒ (as it appears with the mouse pointer resting over it), which sits by itself on the right end of the Menu bar, is used for closing the active document. The upper Close button ☒, located on the Title bar, closes the application itself. If you have documents with unsaved changes open when you click the application Close button, you will be prompted to save the changes. Next to the application Close button are two buttons that help you control the size of the application window. Clicking the Minimize button ⬛ hides the window from view, leaving only its program button on the taskbar. The middle button changes depending on the current size of the window. When the window is maximized, you will see the Restore button 🗗 which reduces the window to its last smaller size. When the window is reduced, you will see the Maximize button 🗖, which increases the size of the window so that it fills the screen. You can also access window control commands by clicking the Word Control menu icon 🗔 on the left end of the Title bar.

Word 2002

Figure 1-6 New Folder dialog box

Type name for new folder here

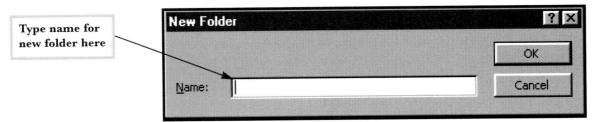

Figure 1-7 Save As dialog box

Places bar: click a location to select it in the Save in box

You may save a file without using a file extension, but never use an extension other than the correct one

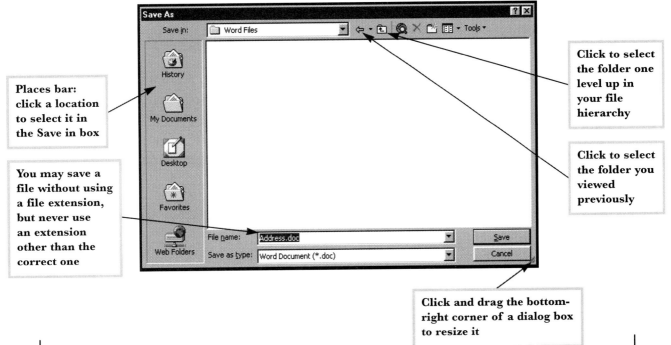

Click to select the folder one level up in your file hierarchy

Click to select the folder you viewed previously

Click and drag the bottom-right corner of a dialog box to resize it

Practice

Open a new document and type a short paragraph about how learning Word will be helpful to you. When you are finished writing, save the document in your Word Files folder using the file name Saving and Closing.doc. Then close the document but leave Word open.

skill | Opening an Existing Document

concept

To view or edit a document that has been saved and closed previously, you must open the document from the location in which it was stored. Since Word documents are associated with the Word application by the .doc file extension in their file names, you can double-click a Word document in My Computer or Windows Explorer and Word will launch automatically. However, if you are already working in Word, you can open Word files from directly within the application. If the Student Files that accompany this book have been distributed to you on a floppy disk, make sure you have inserted the disk in your floppy drive for this Skill.

do it !

Open an existing Word document that was previously saved on a floppy disk or hard disk.

1. With the Word application running, click the Open button 📂 on the Standard toolbar. The Open dialog box will appear. The Open dialog is constructed very similarly to the Save As dialog box you saw in the previous Skill. 👁 You also can access the Open dialog box by clicking File on the Menu bar and then clicking the Open command on the File menu.

2. Click the Look in drop-down list box. A list of locations available on your computer will appear, as shown in Figure 1-8.

3. If your Student Files are stored on a floppy disk, click 3½ Floppy (A:) on the drop-down list to select your floppy disk drive. If your Student Files are stored on a local or network drive, ask your instructor for the name of the location you should select.

4. If your Student Files are stored in a folder on your floppy disk or hard disk, you will need to double-click that folder to display its contents in the dialog box's Contents window. Otherwise, you should already see a list of files in the Contents window. Click the file named wddoit1-5.doc to select it. 👁 It is possible that your computer is set to hide file extensions of known file types, in which case you will see a file named wddoit1-5.

5. Click the Open button [Open ▾] in the bottom-right corner of the dialog box. The Word file wddoit1-5 will appear in the document window.

6. Click ☒ on the right end of the Menu bar to close the document.

more

Word can open a variety of file types in addition to the standard Word document (.doc). Which files appear in the Open dialog box depends on the setting in the Files of type box. To ensure that you are seeing all the files that are stored in the selected directory, click the Files of type box and select the All Files (*.*) setting. If you only want to view Word documents, select the Word Documents (*.doc) setting.

If you click the arrow on the right edge of the Open button in the Open dialog box, a menu appears that offers commands for opening a document in a specific manner. If you select Open Read-Only, Word will not allow any permanent changes to be made to the document during that particular work session unless you use Save As to save the document as a new file. Otherwise, you can edit the text on your screen and print, but you will not be able to save the changes. The Open as Copy command creates a new copy of your document, allowing you to keep the old version and edit the new one. The Open in Browser command becomes active when you have selected an HTML document in the Contents window. Executing this command enables you to view the document with your default Web browser instead of Word. Finally, use the Open and Repair command to open and recover a document that has been damaged by a program, system, or power failure.

👁 Files that you have worked with recently appear at the bottom of the File menu and on the Task Pane so you can open them without having to go through the Open dialog box (see Figure 1-9).

Figure 1-8 Open dialog box

Look in drop-down list box

Click a drive, folder, or other location to view its contents

Click Views button to change the manner in which files are listed

Click to choose a different file type to display

Click arrow to reveal additional Open options

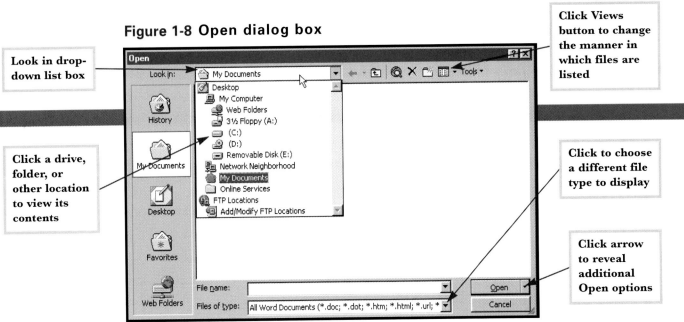

Word 2002

Figure 1-9 Opening recent documents

Names of recent files appear as commands; click file name to open file

Recent files also appear on Task Pane; click file name to open

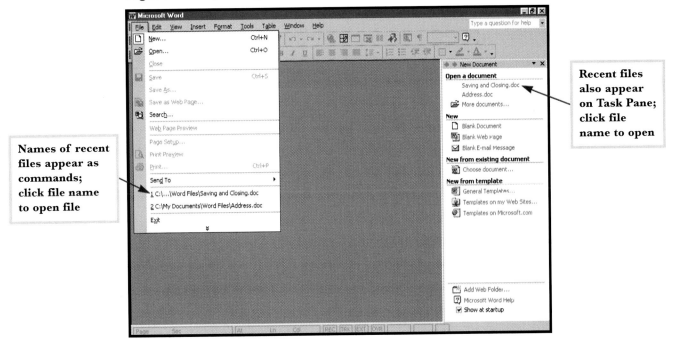

Practice

To practice opening a document, open the Student File named wdprac1-5.doc. Type a few sentences explaining the steps you used to open the file. Then use the Save As command to save the file in your Word Files folder using the name mywdprac1-5.doc (to change the file name in the Save As dialog box, you do not need to delete the entire name and then type the new one; simply click in front of the original name and type my). Close the file and leave Word running when you are done.

skill | Deleting and Inserting Text

 MOUS skill

concept

One of the fundamental advantages of word processing is the ease with which it enables you to change content that has been entered previously. Word makes it easy to edit, replace, or delete unwanted or inaccurate text. Editing skills are crucial for updating older documents and making revisions that will turn your rough drafts into final drafts.

do it !

Modify text in an existing document.

1. Open the Student File wddoit1-6.doc. In the Open dialog box, you can open a file by double-clicking it instead of clicking it once and then clicking the Open button.

2. Move the I-beam mouse pointer to the immediate right of the abbreviation Ave. in the second line of the address at the top of the document. Click to place the insertion point at the end of the line.

3. Press [Backspace] on the keyboard once to erase the period.

4. Type nue to complete the word Avenue.

5. Click between the two and the three in the date January 23, 2002 to place the insertion point between the two numbers.

6. Press the [Delete] key on the keyboard to erase the number three.

7. Type the number 4 on the keyboard to complete the date change. The document should now look like the one shown in Figure 1-10.

8. Save the file in your Word Files folder using the file name Deleting and Inserting.doc.

9. Close the file.

   If you make a mistake while working in Word, you can reverse your last action by clicking the Undo button 🔄 on the Standard toolbar. Click the arrow next to the Undo button to open a menu that lists all of your previous actions, allowing you to undo multiple actions at once (see Figure 1-11).

more

As you just saw, the [Backspace] key (some keyboards spell it Back Space and some only use a left-pointing arrow) erases the character immediately to the left of the insertion point. The [Delete] key erases the character to the right of the insertion point. Word inserts text at the insertion point; that is, it moves nearby text to the right instead of typing over it. To type over existing text so that it disappears instead of moving, double-click the Overtype button OVR on the Status bar to enter Overtype mode. Just remember that any text to the right of the insertion point will be deleted as you type. Double-click the Overtype button again to deactivate Overtype mode.

You can move the insertion point one character at a time to the left or right and one line at a time up or down with the arrow keys on the keyboard. This is especially helpful when you are moving the insertion point only a short distance. Additional ways to move the insertion point using the keyboard are shown in Table 1-1. If you will be using the [Home], [End], [Pg Up], and [Pg Dn] keys on the numeric keypad, as required for some of the movement techniques described in the table, make sure that Num Lock is disabled. Many keyboards now include separate keys for these functions.

Figure 1-10 Document after editing

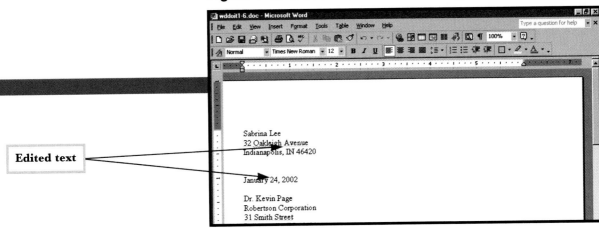

Edited text

Figure 1-11 Undoing multiple actions

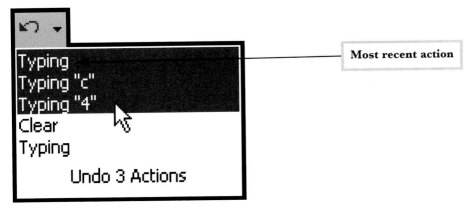

Most recent action

Table 1-1 Moving the insertion point with the keyboard

To Move the Insertion Point	Press
Left or right one word	[Ctrl]+[←] or [Ctrl]+[→]
Up or down one paragraph	[Ctrl]+[↑] or [Ctrl]+[↓]
Up or down one screen	[Pg Up] or [Pg Dn]
To the beginning or end of a line	[Home] or [End]
To the beginning or end of a document	[Ctrl]+[Home] or [Ctrl]+[End]

Practice

To practice inserting and deleting text, open the Student File wdprac1-6.doc and follow the instructions given in the file. When you are finished, save the file in your Word Files folder as mywdprac1-6.doc and close the file.

skill Formatting Text

concept

Word enables you to easily change the font (typeface), font size, text style, and text alignment in a document, as well as many other text and document characteristics. Formatting text serves to improve the presentation of your document. You can format text for both stylistic and organizational purposes.

do it !

Apply bold formatting to text in a letter and change the font size of the document.

1. Open the Student File wddoit1-7.doc.

2. Select Assistant to the Director of Public Relations in the first paragraph of the letter by clicking before the A and dragging (moving the mouse with the left mouse button held down) to the end of Relations (release the mouse button). Do not select the period. The selected text will be white on a black background.

3. Click the Bold button **B** on the Formatting toolbar. The letters in the job title will be set in a heavier text style.

4. Cancel the selection of the text by clicking once anywhere in the document window.

5. Select the entire document by clicking before the S in Sabrina at the top of the letter and dragging down to the last line (release the mouse button after the period in enc.). You also can select an entire document by pressing the keyboard shortcut [Ctrl]+[A].

6. Click the Font Size arrow 12 ▼ on the Formatting toolbar. A list of font sizes will appear. Click 10, as shown in Figure 1-12. The document text decreases in size.

7. Click the Font arrow Times New Roman ▼ , and then click the font named Arial on the drop-down list (you may have to scroll up the list of fonts). The typeface of the document changes to the Arial font.

8. Deselect the text as you did above and scroll to the top of the document.

9. Save the document in your Word Files folder as Formatting Text.doc and close it.

more

The Formatting toolbar allows you to change numerous text attributes. Font, or typeface, refers to the actual shape of each individual character as it appears on the screen or in a printed document. Font size is usually measured in points, with 72 points being equivalent to one inch. As an example, the text in a newspaper is generally 10-point type. Other Formatting toolbar options include Italic **I** , Underline **U** , Font Color **A** ▼ , and Highlight ▼ . The Font Color and Highlight buttons are always loaded with a color, which is indicated as part of the button icon. Clicking the buttons applies the formatting with the loaded color. Clicking the arrow next to the buttons opens a color palette, enabling you to select a different color. Another formatting option, Alignment, refers to the manner in which text follows the margins of your document (see Figure 1-13). Like the Italic, Underline, and Bold buttons, the Alignment buttons are toggle buttons, meaning you can apply and remove their formatting by clicking the same button.

Knowing how to format text for maximum effect is an essential skill that will make your documents appear crisp and professional. Notice how formatting is used on this page: different fonts and font sizes are used for headings and subject matter and important terms are colored for added emphasis. As you saw above, you must select items before you can format them. Note that you also can select an entire document by opening the Edit menu and clicking the Select All command. You can align an entire paragraph simply by placing the insertion point inside the paragraph before clicking the desired alignment button.

Figure 1-12 Changing font size

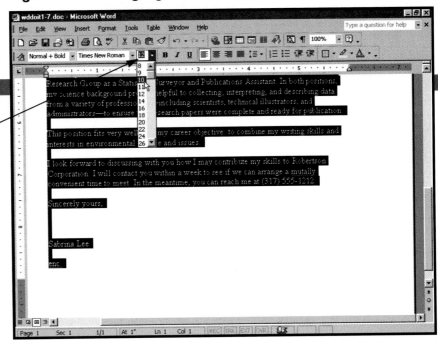

You also may click in the Font Size box, type a font size, and press [Enter] to apply it

Figure 1-13 Text alignment

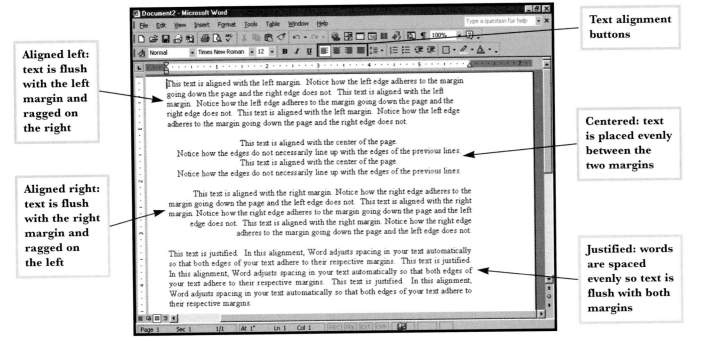

Aligned left: text is flush with the left margin and ragged on the right

Aligned right: text is flush with the right margin and ragged on the left

Text alignment buttons

Centered: text is placed evenly between the two margins

Justified: words are spaced evenly so text is flush with both margins

Practice

To practice formatting text, open the Student File wdprac1-7.doc and follow the instructions given in the file. When you have completed the exercise, save the file in your Word Files folder as mywdprac1-7.doc. Then close the file.

skill Previewing and Printing a Document

MOUS Skill

concept

While today's classrooms and offices are relying more and more on electronic documents, many people still prefer to work with hard copies (paper printouts) out of their documents. If your computer is properly connected to a printer, you can print a paper copy of a document with a click of a button. Or, if you desire more flexibility in printing, Word provides comprehensive printing options, including a Print Preview that allows you to see the document as it will appear when printed.

do it !

Preview and print a document.

1. Open the Student File wddoit1-8.doc and type your name at the top of the document.

2. Click the Print Preview button 🔍 on the Standard toolbar. The open document will appear in Preview mode. The reduced size of the document allows you to view how your text is arranged on the page.

3. Move the mouse pointer over the upper-left corner of the document. The pointer should appear as the Magnifier tool, as shown in Figure 1-14. If the Magnifier tool is not present, click the Magnifier button 🔍 on the Print Preview toolbar.

4. Click the upper-left corner of the document with the Magnifier tool. The preview will zoom in to 100% so you can see the document at its normal size. Notice that the Magnifier tool now contains a minus symbol instead of a plus symbol. Click again to zoom back out.

5. Click the Close button Close on the Print Preview toolbar to return to the regular document window.

6. Click File on the Menu bar, then click the Print command. The Print dialog box appears, as shown in Figure 1-15.

7. Click the OK button OK to print the document with the default print settings. Clicking the Print button 🖨 on the Standard toolbar skips the dialog box and prints using the default print settings automatically.

8. Close the document. You do not need to save it.

more

For more precise control over your view in Print Preview mode, click the Zoom box arrow 42% ▾ to open a list of magnification percentages. Then click a percentage on the drop-down list. The percentages are based on 100% being the actual size of the document. To select a Zoom percentage that is not on the list, click the current value in the Zoom box, type a new percentage, and press [Enter] on the keyboard.

To edit a document while in Print Preview mode, click the Magnifier button 🔍 to toggle it off. The mouse pointer will change to an I-beam. You then can enter and edit text as you normally would.

While Print Layout View affords you many of the same advantages as Print Preview mode, Print Preview includes some very useful and unique features. For example, you can choose to view multiple pages of a document on the same screen by clicking the Multiple Pages button 🔡 on the Print Preview toolbar. You also can reduce by one the number of pages in a document by clicking the Shrink to Fit button 📄 so that a small portion of text is not left alone on one page. Word accomplishes this reduction by decreasing the font sizes used in the document.

Figure 1-14 Print Preview mode

Print Preview toolbar

Magnifier tool

Click to obtain context-sensitive pointer that allows you to get help on features by clicking them

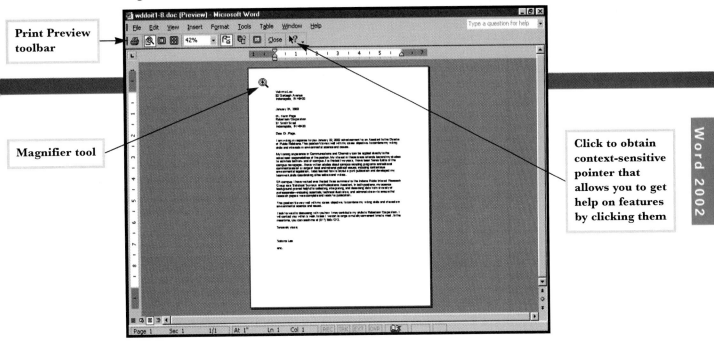

Word 2002

Figure 1-15 Print dialog box

Click to select a different printer

Click to specify a range of pages to print

Click to increase number of copies printed

Click to select odd or even pages only

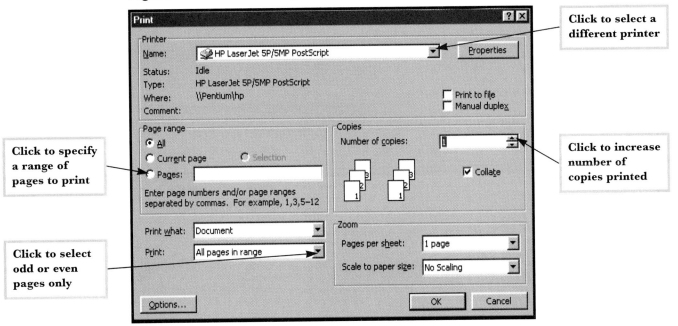

Practice

To practice previewing and printing a document, open the Student File wdprac1-8.doc. Type your name below the title of the document, and then preview and print the file as instructed. When you have completed the exercise, close the file. You do not have to save the file.

shortcuts

Function	Button/Mouse	Menu	Keyboard
Create new document	▯	Click File, then click New	[Ctrl]+[N]
Close active document	✕	Click File, then click Close	[Ctrl]+[W]
Save document for the first time	🖫	Click File, then click Save or Save As	[Ctrl]+[S]
Save changes to existing document	🖫	Click File, then click Save	[Ctrl]+[S]
Save document with new name and/or location		Click File, then click Save As	[Alt]+[F], [A]
Open existing document	📂	Click File, then click Open	[Ctrl]+[O]
Undo most recent action	↩▾	Click Edit, then click Undo	[Ctrl]+[Z]
Bold text	**B**	Click Format, then click Font; choose Bold, then click OK	[Ctrl]+[B]
Italicize text	*I*	Click Format, then click Font; choose Italic, then click OK	[Ctrl]+[I]
Underline text	U̲	Click Format, then click Font; choose Underline, then click OK	[Ctrl]+[U]
Align text left	≣	Click Format, then click Paragraph	[Ctrl]+[L]
Align text right	≣	Click Format, then click Paragraph	[Ctrl]+[R]
Center text	≣	Click Format, then click Paragraph	[Ctrl]+[E]
Justify text	≣	Click Format, then click Paragraph	[Ctrl]+[J]
Select All		Click Edit, then click Select All	[Ctrl]+[A]
Print active document	🖨 (skips dialog box)	Click File, then click Print	[Ctrl]+[P]
Exit Word	✕	Click File, then click Exit	[Alt]+[F4]

A. Identify Key Features

Name the items indicated by callouts in Figure 1-16.

Figure 1-16 Elements of the Word screen

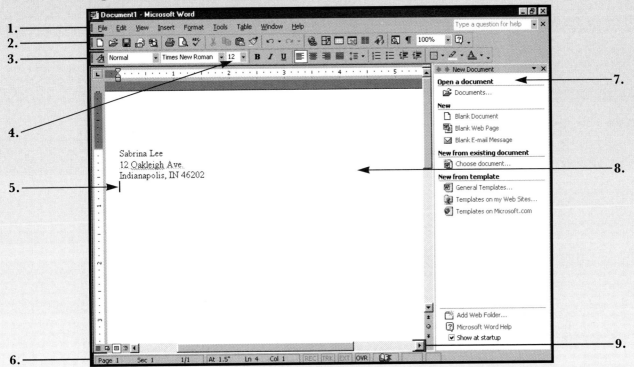

B. Select the Best Answer

10. The exact location where text appears when entered

11. The shape of characters such as letters and numbers

12. Reduces a window to a button on the Windows taskbar

13. The way in which text relates to the page's margins

14. A window that contains options for executing a command

15. Allows you to see how your document will appear when printed

16. The unit of measurement for font size

17. New feature that organizes numerous important features in one location

a. Alignment

b. Print Preview

c. Task Pane

d. Insertion point

e. Dialog box

f. Points

g. Minimize button

h. Font

quiz (continued)

C. Complete the Statement

18. In order to apply bold formatting to a section of existing text, you must first:

a. Click one of the Formatting buttons

b. Save the document

c. Select the text to be formatted

d. Click the Start button

19. Clicking the 🖫 button:

a. Ejects the floppy disk

b. Saves the active document

c. Searches your hard drive for a file

d. Selects the active line or paragraph

20. Clicking the 🔍 button on the Standard toolbar:

a. Searches the document for spelling errors

b. Magnifies the document

c. Opens Print Preview mode

d. Opens the Task Pane

21. The file extension for Word documents is:

a. .txt

b. .htm

c. .doc

d. .mp3

22. Examples of text formatting do not include:

a. Font size

b. Justification

c. Text style

d. File extensions

23. The icon that appears when Word recognizes text you have entered and can provide related commands is a:

a. Shortcut

b. ScreenTip

c. SmartTag

d. Task Pane

24. Text that is justified is:

a. Grammatically correct

b. Adjusted to meet both margins

c. Bold

d. Only visible in Print Preview

25. A button that turns a feature both on and off is called a:

a. Drop-down list

b. SmartTag

c. Toggle button

d. Scroll bar box

26. The Status bar provides all of the following information except:

a. Number of misspelled words in the document

b. Status of Overtype mode

c. Number of pages in the document

d. Position of the insertion point in the document

interactivity

Build Your Skills

1. Identify a job that interests you and determine what the employer is looking for in a prospective employee:

   a. Go to the classified section of a newspaper or to a Web site that lists jobs and find a specific job listing that you think might suit you (Web sites you may try: www.careerbuilder.com, www.monster.com, www.jobs.com).

   b. Think about what skills and experience might be necessary to apply for the job you have found. Determine how your own skills and experience relate to the qualifications that the job would require.

2. Open Word and write a brief letter applying for the job (open the file wdskills1.doc to view a sample letter if you need some guidance in composing and organizing your letter):

   a. Launch Word using the Start menu.

   b. Following the model of wdskills1.doc, write your letter, beginning with the salutation and continuing with three or four short paragraphs, one each for your educational background, prior job experience, any other relative experience, and the reasons for your interest in this particular position.

   c. Include a closing, a few blank lines for a signature, and, finally, your name.

3. Format the text of the letter:

   a. Change the font size of the text to 11 pt.

   b. Change the font used in the letter to Garamond.

   c. Align the date with the right margin.

4. Print, save, and close the letter, and then exit Word:

   a. Use Print Preview to examine your letter and make any content or formatting changes you think are necessary.

   b. Close Print Preview and print one copy of your letter.

   c. Save the letter in your Word Files folder as Job Seek.doc.

   d. Close the document.

5. Open, edit, and save an existing document:

   a. Open Job Seek.doc from your Word Files folder.

   b. Align the date with the left margin so that it follows proper letter format.

   c. Save the changed document as a new file in your Word Files folder named Job Seek2.doc.

   d. Close the document and exit Word by clicking the application Close button on the right end of the Title bar.

interactivity (continued)

Problem Solving Exercises

1. Open a new document in Word and type your name, address, and today's date on consecutive lines. Then, skip a line and type a few sentences about an extracurricular activity or hobby that you enjoy. Format the document so that it matches the example shown in Figure 1-17. Finally, save the document in your Word Files folder as wdsolved1.doc and print it.

Figure 1-17 Problem solving exercise

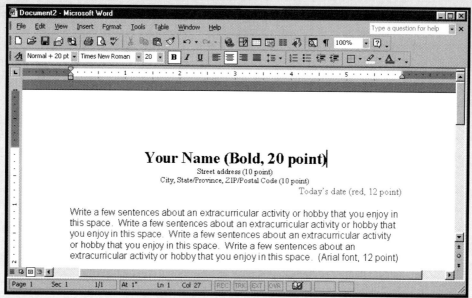

2. As the Assistant Technical Director at VER Recovery Corp., a collection agency, you have been asked to research various word processing programs to determine which is the best for your company's needs. After testing several products and considering prices, you have decided that the company would benefit most from adopting Microsoft Word 2002. Use a new blank Word document to write a memo to your boss that details this decision. Be sure to include your name as part of the document. When you are done, save the file in your Word Files folder as VER Recovery memo.doc.

3. Due to the quality of your work as Assistant Technical Director at VER, you have been promoted to Associate Technical Director. As your first act in your new capacity, you have proposed an expansion of the Information Technology department. Your proposal has been approved. Using Word, write a notice for the company bulletin board to announce the good news. Include a text in the document that calls for employees who are interested in transferring into the department to contact you (include your name). Take advantage of Word's formatting features such as bolding, underlining, font sizing, and text alignment to make your document lively. Save the document in your Word Files folder as VER IT notice.doc.

4. Your favorite entertainment-oriented Web site is looking for regular viewers who are interested in contributing movie reviews to the site on a weekly or monthly basis. If you are chosen based on your sample review, you will have your opinions published on the site on a regular basis and receive coupons for the site's online store. Use Word to write a review of the last movie you watched, either in a theater or at home. Use formatting techniques to call attention to the parts of your review that you feel are the most important, and therefore deserve emphasis. Save the document in your Word Files folder using the name Review by [Your Name].doc.

Editing Documents

Once you have entered text into a Word document, you may manipulate and edit the text to suit your needs. You can select text in a number of different ways so that you can modify portions of a document without affecting those parts of the document that do not require revision or updating. Word enables you to copy or move text, or delete it altogether.

In addition to the general blank document on which Word bases its standard new document, the program offers a multitude of other document types that can fulfill various needs. These templates serve as starting points for creating well-organized and effective documents such as letters, résumés, reports, Web pages, and so on. For even greater control over the appearance and functionality of a document template, Word provides features known as wizards. Wizards guide you through a series of steps in which you provide feedback as to what style of document you want to create and how the information in the document is presented.

You will find that the benefits of using Word are not limited to productivity features. Word places a great deal of importance on providing support for the user. For example, the program contains a powerful file search function that allows you to find documents you have saved based on a wide variety of search criteria. Word also includes a Help facility that is designed to help you access information about specific features and troubleshoot your work when you encounter problems. The Office Assistant is an animated character who acts as a liaison between you and the help files.

Lesson Goal:

Use various editing techniques to revise an existing cover letter, then create a résumé with a little assistance from Word.

- ≸ **Searching for Files**
- ≸ **Selecting Text and Undoing Actions**
- ≸ **Cutting, Copying, and Moving Text**
- ≸ **Copying and Moving Text with the Mouse**
- ≸ **Creating a Document with a Wizard**
- ≸ **Creating a Document with a Template**
- ≸ **Using the Office Assistant**
- ≸ **Other Word Help Features**

skill | Searching for Files

concept

As you may have discovered, a single computer may contain a large number of locations in which you can store documents. It is not uncommon for users to need a document but not remember exactly where they saved it. Word's Open dialog box contains powerful search tools that you can use in this situation. The Search command is particularly helpful when you remember certain characteristics of a file such as a portion of its name, text it contains, or the date you last modified it. ◖◗ If your Student Files for this book are stored on a floppy disk, make sure you have inserted the disk before beginning this Skill.

do it !

Use the Open dialog box to search for a file whose name you do not remember.

1. With Word running, click the Open button 📂 on the Standard toolbar. The Open dialog box appears.

2. Click the Tools button [Tools ▾] and then click Search on the menu that appears. The Search dialog box opens to the Basic tab. If it opens to the Advanced tab, click the Basic tab.

3. In the Search text box, type rice recipe.

4. Click the arrow on the right end of the Search in box in the Other Search Options section of tab. A list of locations will appear. If the check box next to My Computer does not contain a check mark, click the box to check it. Then click the drop-down arrow again to close the list.

5. Click the drop-down list box labeled Results should be to open a list of file types. Click the necessary check boxes so that only the one labeled Word Files contains a check mark. Then click the drop-down arrow to close the list.

6. Click the Search button [Search]. Word will begin searching all the drives on your computer for a Word file that contains the text "rice recipe." When the search is complete, you should see the file wddoit2-1.doc listed in the Results section (see Figure 2-1).

7. Double-click wddoit2-1.doc. The Search dialog box closes and the file is selected in the Open dialog box's File name box.

8. Click [Open ▾] to open wddoit2-1.doc.

9. Close the file.

more

To be more specific about where you want to search for a file, click the "plus" sign next to My Computer on the Search in drop-down list. You then can select specific drives or folders to search in rather than all of your computer. Many of the top level locations can be expanded further for an even more precise search (see Figure 2-2). Narrowing down your search locations is especially helpful if the file you are seeking does not have any unique characteristics.

The Advanced tab in the Search dialog box contains a set of controls that permit you to set very specific criteria for a file search. If you open the Text or property drop-down list, as shown in Figure 2-3, you can select from a generous list of document details and file properties that are relevant to the desired file. You then select the condition under which that property occurs in the Condition drop-down list box. Finally, you enter the actual value of the search criteria in the Value text box. For example, you could instruct Word to search for files whose file names contain the word "report." Or you could search for files whose date of creation is between May 11, 2000 and October 21, 2001.

Figure 2-1 Search dialog box

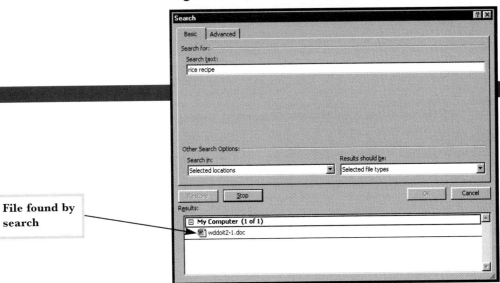

File found by
search

Figure 2-2 Selecting other search locations

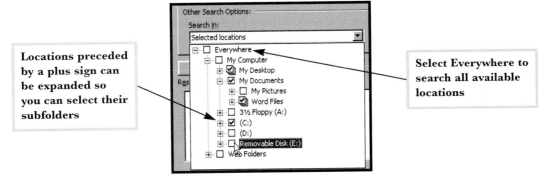

Locations preceded
by a plus sign can
be expanded so
you can select their
subfolders

Select Everywhere to
search all available
locations

Figure 2-3 Advanced tab

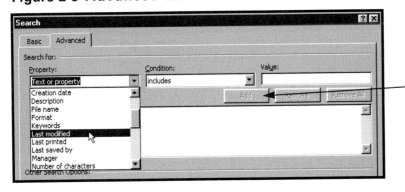

Click Add after setting
search criteria; you may
then add more sets of
criteria to the same search
and select whether one or
all of them must be true
to satisfy the search

Practice

Search your computer for a Word file that contains the word sleuth. Open the file when you find it.
Then save the file in your Word Files folder using the name mywdprac2-1.doc and close it.
Remember, if your Student Files are stored on a floppy disk, the disk must be inserted in your floppy
drive in order for you to complete this exercise.

skill | Selecting Text and Undoing Actions

concept

Sections of existing text must be selected before you can modify them. Once you have select-ed a word, phrase, paragraph, or more, the selection acts a single unit that you can move, modify, or format. When you select text, it appears highlighted on the screen. That is, text that normally appears black on a white screen will be white on a black background. It is important to be careful when working with selected text as it is possible to erase an entire document by pressing a single key. You can use the Undo command, which reverses previous commands or actions, to correct such errors.

do it !

Practice methods of selecting text and undoing actions in a document.

1. Open the file wddoit2-2.doc.

2. Scroll down to the paragraph that begins My training experience …

3. Select the paragraph by clicking just before the first letter, dragging the mouse pointer to the end of the paragraph, and then releasing the mouse button.

4. Type the letter X. The selected text will be replaced by the text you typed.

5. Click the Undo button ⟲ on the Standard toolbar to reverse your previous action (typing X) and bring back the original paragraph.

6. Cancel the selection of the paragraph by clicking a blank area of the document.

7. Click at the beginning of the paragraph to place the insertion point in front of the first letter. Then hold down the [Shift] key and click at the end of the paragraph to select it.

8. Cancel the selection of the paragraph again.

9. Triple-click any portion of the same paragraph to select the whole thing again.

10. Close the file. You do not need to save any changes.

more

When clicking and dragging to select text, the selection will follow the mouse pointer letter by letter in the first word; subsequent words will be added to the selection one by one. If you drag down to the next line before reaching the end of the current line, the remainder of the current line and the portion of the next line up to the mouse pointer will be selected. To select a single line or multiple lines quickly, use the Selection bar, a col-umn of space on the left edge of the document (see Figure 2-4). When the mouse pointer enters this area, it will appear reversed ⟩ . Clicking in the Selection bar selects the entire line to the right of the pointer. Dragging up or down in the Selection bar selects the adjacent lines in the direction you are dragging. More ways to select text are shown in Tables 2-1 and 2-2. Keep in mind that [Num Lock] must be disabled in order to use the [Home], [End], and arrow keys on the numeric keypad.

The Undo command is an essential tool that easily corrects many of the worst mistakes you may make while using Word. The Undo and Redo buttons are grouped together on the Standard toolbar. Clicking the Undo drop-down list arrow ⟲▾ opens a menu that allows you to undo multiple actions at once. The most recent action is listed first. If you want to undo an action that was not the most recent, you will have to undo all actions that followed it as well. The Redo command and its drop-down list work in a similar fashion, but instead reverse past Undo commands. ◀ After you perform many actions in Word, the Repeat command will become available on the Edit menu. You can use this command, or its keyboard shortcut [Ctrl]+[Y], to perform your last action again.

Figure 2-4 Using the Selection bar

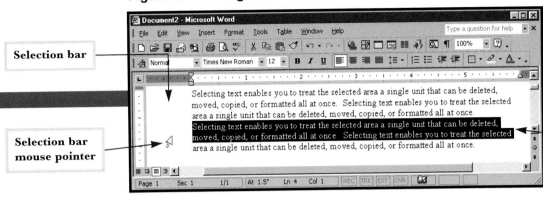

Selection bar

Selection bar mouse pointer

Selected text

Table 2-1 Selecting text with the mouse

Desired Selection	Action to take
A single word	Double-click the word
A sentence	Click the sentence while pressing [Ctrl]
A paragraph	Triple-click the paragraph or double-click next to it in the Selection bar
A line of text	Click next to it in the Selection bar
A vertical block of text	Click and drag while pressing [Alt]
The entire document	Triple-click in the Selection bar

Table 2-2 Selecting text with the keyboard

Desired Selection	Action to take
A single character	[Shift]+[◄—] or [Shift]+[—►]
Word or portion of word to the left or right of insertion point	[Ctrl]+[Shift]+[◄—] or [Ctrl]+[Shift]+[—►]
Paragraph or portion of paragraph above or below insertion point	[Ctrl]+[Shift]+[▲] or [Ctrl]+[Shift]+[▼]
To the beginning or end of a line	[Shift]+[Home] or [Shift]+[End]
To the beginning or end of a document	[Ctrl]+[Shift]+[Home] or [Ctrl]+[Shift]+[End]
A vertical block of text	[Ctrl]+[Shift]+[F8] (toggle on/off) and arrow keys
The entire document (Select All)	[Ctrl]+[A]

Practice

To practice selecting text and undoing actions, open the file wdprac2-2.doc and follow the instructions in the document. Close the file when you have completed the exercise. You do not need to save the document when you are done.

skill

Cutting, Copying, and Moving Text

concept

One of the greatest benefits of using a word processor like Word is that you can relocate existing text instead of having to type the entire document again. This saves you enormous amounts of time when you are revising your work. Within a matter of seconds, you can relocate entire paragraphs to a new place in the same document, or even in another document. Cutting and pasting text is one method of moving text. Copying and pasting text allows you to create a second instance of existing text while leaving the original text intact.

do it !

Move a paragraph in a letter using the cut-and-paste method.

1. Open wddoit2-3.doc and save it in your Word Files folder as Cutting and Copying.doc.

2. Select the paragraph that begins with This position … and the blank line below it, as shown in Figure 2-5.

3. Click the Cut button ✂ on the Standard toolbar. The selected text disappears.

4. Click after the period at the end of the first paragraph (the one that begins I am writing …) to place the insertion point there.

5. Click the Paste button 📋 on the Standard toolbar. The text you cut earlier, including the blank line, appears at the insertion point. The icon 📋 that appears when you paste is a Paste Options button. If you click the button, you can choose formatting options for the text you just pasted. These options include maintaining the formatting the text had at its previous location (the default option), acquiring the formatting in use at the new location, removing all formatting, and adding new formatting.

6. Press [Backspace] twice to delete the blank lines that have been added (as in Figure 2-6).

7. Click the Save button 💾 to save the changes you have made to Cutting and Copying.doc, and then close the document.

more

If you want to add existing text to another part of your document without moving the original text, click the Copy button 📋, press [Ctrl]+[C], or select the Copy command from the Edit menu after you select the text, and then paste. Material that you cut or copy in Word is stored in a temporary storage area known as the Office Clipboard. The Cut command (and its keyboard shortcut [Ctrl]+[X]) removes material from the document and sends it to the Clipboard, while the Copy command simply sends a copy of what you selected there.

The Office Clipboard is capable of storing up to 24 unique pieces of data at once. When you execute the Paste command (its keyboard shortcut is [Ctrl]+[V]), Word pastes the data that arrived on the Clipboard most recently. If you want to paste a selection that was copied or cut earlier, open the Edit menu and click the Office Clipboard command. The Clipboard Task Pane will appear. Each item currently on the Clipboard, whether text, picture, or other, will be displayed in the pane. When you point to a particular item, a drop-down arrow will appear. Click this arrow to access commands that will let you either paste the item or delete it from the Clipboard (see Figure 2-7). No matter what method you use to paste, the data always appear wherever the insertion point is currently positioned in the document.

The Office Clipboard is common to all Office applications, so you may use it to share data among the different Office programs. In addition, the Windows operating system has its own Clipboard that can hold one item at a time. The last item you sent to the Office Clipboard also will be available on the Windows Clipboard, so you can share data from Office with non-Office programs. Clearing the Office Clipboard removes the contents of the Windows Clipboard as well. Both Clipboards are erased when you shut down your computer.

Figure 2-5 Selected paragraph to be moved

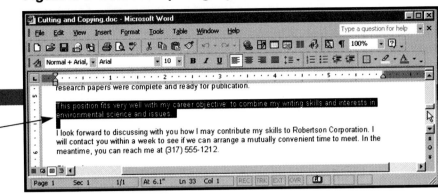

Selected text can
be cut or copied

Figure 2-6 Letter after cutting and pasting paragraph

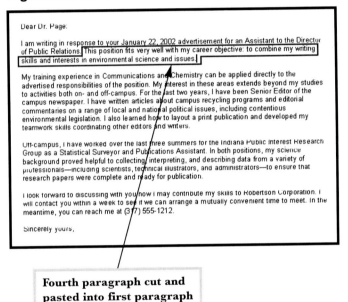

Fourth paragraph cut and
pasted into first paragraph

Figure 2-7 Office Clipboard

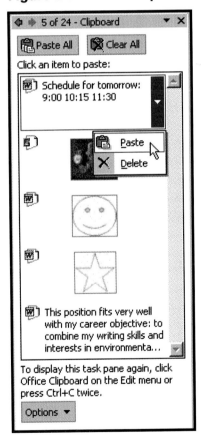

Practice

To practice cutting, copying, and pasting text, open the Student File wdprac2-3.doc and follow the instructions given in the document. Save the document as mywdprac2-3.doc when you are done and close the file.

skill Copying and Moving Text with the Mouse

MOUS Skill

concept

The drag-and-drop method of copying and moving text is quick and convenient for moving text a short distance within a Word document. In many instances, it is preferable to using the Cut, Copy, and Paste commands along with the Clipboard. Once highlighted, you can drag and drop any unit of text from a single character to multiple paragraphs.

do it !

Use the drag and drop method to move a paragraph in a letter.

1. Open the file wddoit2-4.doc.

2. Drag to select the second sentence in the first paragraph of the letter (This position … science and issues.).

3. Point to any portion of the selected text and press down the left mouse button. The mouse pointer will change to the drag-and-drop pointer, indicating that data—in this case text—are loaded and ready to be inserted. A dotted insertion point will also appear in the text. The dotted insertion point marks the point at which the text will be dropped when you release the mouse button.

4. Drag the mouse down and to the left until the dotted insertion point ⁞ is to the left of the first letter in the second paragraph of the letter, as shown in Figure 2-8.

5. Release the mouse button. The selected text disappears from its previous location and reappears at the dotted insertion point.

6. Click a blank area of the document to cancel the selection of the text. The first two paragraphs of your letter should now look like Figure 2-9.

7. Save the document in your Word Files folder as Drag-and-Drop.doc and then close the file.

more

Dragging and dropping text moves it from its previous location, much like the Cut command. To copy text to another area by dragging while leaving the original text in its place, press and hold [Ctrl] on the keyboard before dropping the text. The drag-and-drop pointer will appear with a plus sign attached to it to signify that it will make a copy of the selected text. When you release the mouse button, the selected text will appear in its original location as well as at the insertion point (make sure you release the mouse button before you release the [Ctrl] key). The ability to drag and drop text is an editing option that you can turn on and off by going to the Edit tab of the Options dialog box, which you can access by clicking the Options command on the Tools menu.

If you are copying or moving text over a long distance in a document, it might be easier to use the Clipboard instead of the drag-and-drop method. It can be difficult to stop the scrolling of the screen accurately when you drag beyond the current screen.

Figure 2-8 Dragging and dropping text

Selected text being moved

Selected text will be inserted here

Drag-and-drop pointer indicates that text is being moved

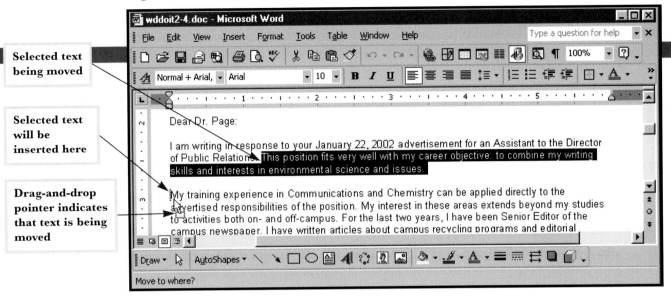

Figure 2-9 Letter after dragging and dropping

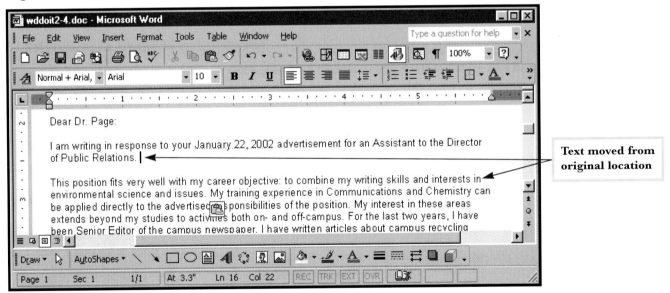

Text moved from original location

Practice

To practice moving and copying text with the mouse, open the Student File wdprac2-4.doc and follow the instructions given in the document. When you have completed the exercise, save the document as mywdprac2-4.doc and close the file.

skill

Creating a Document with a Wizard

concept

As you can probably imagine, Word is capable of producing very complex and stylized documents such as résumés, calendars, brochures, and Web pages. However, as a new user, you may not have enough confidence in your skills to begin designing one of these documents on your own. Or, you may be an experienced user who simply does not have the time it would require to design a professional-quality document from scratch. In both these cases, Word's document wizards can help you overcome your obstacles. A wizard is a series of dialog boxes that automates the document-creation process. The wizard guides you through the components of a document and asks you for the content that it needs to fill them.

do it !

Use a wizard to create a résumé for a student who is applying for a job.

1. If the Task Pane is not showing, click the New command on the File menu to display it. Click General Templates… in the New from template section of the New Document Task Pane. The Templates dialog box appears.

2. Click the Other Documents tab in the Templates dialog box to display the document templates and wizards it contains.

3. Click the Résumé Wizard icon to select it. A preview of the Résumé Wizard's typical output will appear on the right side of the dialog box (see Figure 2-10). Make sure the Document radio button is selected in the Create New section of the dialog box.

4. Click the OK button ▭ OK ▭ to launch the Résumé Wizard. The wizard begins at the Start step, which introduces the task at hand and provides an outline of all the steps to follow. The outline will be displayed throughout the wizard, with your current step marked by a green square, completed steps marked by dark gray squares, and incomplete steps marked by light gray squares. You can click these squares to jump to any step at any time.

5. Click the Next button ▭ Next > ▭ to advance to the Style step.

6. Click the Elegant radio button to select this style of résumé, then click ▭ Next > ▭.

7. For the Type step, click ▭ Next > ▭ to accept the default type, Entry-level résumé, and advance to the next step, Address. This step allows you to enter your name, address, phone and fax numbers, and e-mail address. Word automatically enters the name of the registered user in the Name text box and any other information that was provided during the software install procedure in the other boxes.

8. Type Sabrina Lee in the Name text box, 32 Oakleigh Ave. [Enter] Indianapolis, IN 46202 in the Address text box, and (317) 555-1212 in the Phone text box. Your text boxes should resemble those shown in Figure 2-11. Press [Tab] to move from one text box to another and select the extraneous information if there is any.

9. Click ▭ Next > ▭ to advance to the Standard Headings step. Once there, click the Interests and activities check box to add the heading to the résumé with the three default headings, Objective, Education, and Work Experience (see Figure 2-12). If any of those headings are not checked, click their check boxes. If any of the other headings are checked, click their boxes to remove the check marks.

10. Click ▭ Next > ▭ to advance to the Additional Headings step. No additional headings will be used in this résumé, so click ▭ Next > ▭ to advance again.

(continued on WD 2.12)

Figure 2-10 Templates dialog box

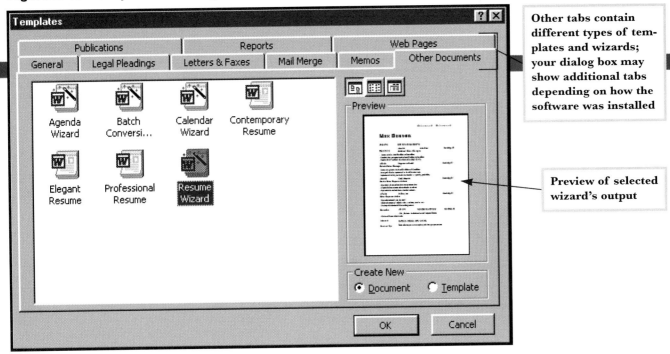

Other tabs contain different types of templates and wizards; your dialog box may show additional tabs depending on how the software was installed

Preview of selected wizard's output

Figure 2-11 Résumé address

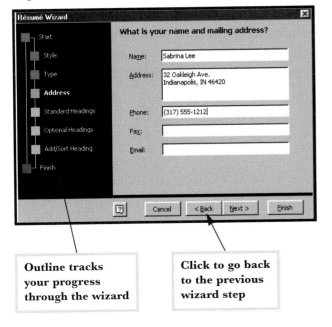

Outline tracks your progress through the wizard

Click to go back to the previous wizard step

Figure 2-12 Résumé headings

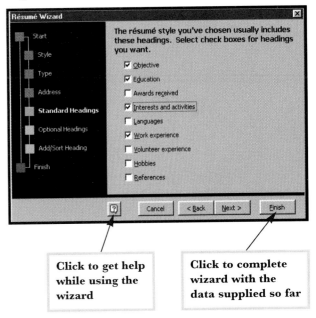

Click to get help while using the wizard

Click to complete wizard with the data supplied so far

skill

Creating a Document with a Wizard (continued)

do it !

11. The Add/Sort Heading step allows you to insert a heading that was not included in the wizard, delete a heading that you had added previously, or change the order in which your selected headings will appear. Click Work Experience to select it, and then click the Move Up button `Move Up` to place Work Experience before Interests and activities. Click `Next >`.

12. Click the Finish button `Finish`. Word constructs the résumé and displays it in Print Layout View. If the Office Assistant appears asking if you want to do more with the résumé, click the Cancel button `Cancel`.

13. Under the Objective heading in the résumé, you will see a placeholder for the Objective text: [Type Objective Here]. Click this placeholder to select it, as shown in Figure 2-13.

14. Type To secure a position in communications or research in the field of environmental sciences as the objective.

15. Select the [Dates Attended] placeholder under the Education heading and type 1998-2002.

16. Select the [Company/Institution Name] placeholder on the same line and type Indianapolis University.

17. Select the [City, State] placeholder on the same line and type Indianapolis, IN.

18. Select the [Degree/Major] placeholder and type Bachelor of Science, Chemistry.

19. Select the placeholder preceded by a bullet at the bottom of the Education section and press [Backspace] three times to delete the placeholder, the bullet, and the blank line.

20. Use Figure 2-14 as a guide to completing the rest of the résumé. Replace Sabrina's name with your own name before continuing.

21. View the résumé in Print Preview and then print a copy of the document.

22. Save the document in your Word Files folder using the suggested file name Resume Wizard.doc, and then close the file.

more

The résumé you just created was left somewhat brief due to the constraints of this particular medium and method of instruction. In comparison, a résumé you might actually submit to a potential employer probably would be fleshed out more. For an entry-level résumé such as this one, you could include academic honors and awards that you have received. You also might add a section for course work you have completed that is related to the particular position for which you are applying. A heading under which you list the particular skills you possess, such as knowledge of specific software programs, computer languages, or foreign languages, can help illustrate the quality of your candidacy for a position. If you have any published works, you might want to list those as well.

The Résumé Wizard adds the information you supply to an existing document template. You may have noticed that the Other Documents tab in the Templates dialog box contains an Elegant Résumé template. You could use this template to produce the same document you created above without working through the steps of the wizard. You will learn how to create a document precisely in this manner in the next Skill. Some wizards and templates shown in the Templates dialog box are not included in the Typical install of Word or Office. Their icons serve as shortcuts that will prompt you to install the files from your CD-ROM before you can use them.

Figure 2-13 Selecting placeholder text

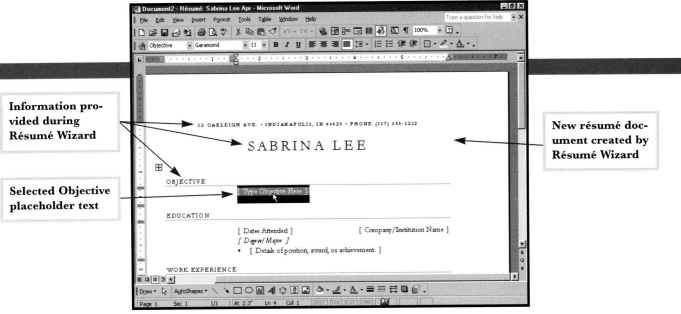

Information provided during Résumé Wizard

Selected Objective placeholder text

New résumé document created by Résumé Wizard

Figure 2-14 Completed résumé

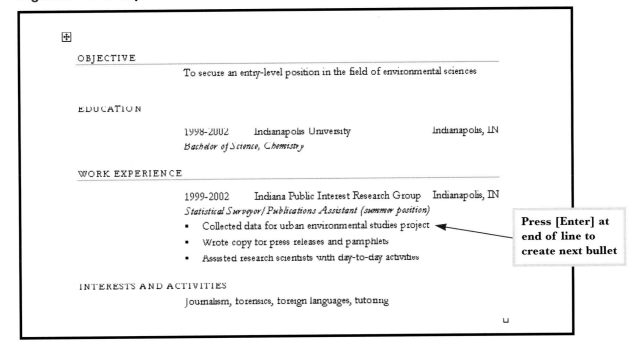

Press [Enter] at end of line to create next bullet

Practice

Use the Résumé Wizard to create a résumé for yourself. Select the Contemporary style résumé and the Entry-level type. The résumé should contain at least five Standard Headings and one Additional Heading. Once the document is set up, replace the placeholder text with the appropriate information about yourself. If you need to add more than one entry below a heading, you can do so by copying and pasting a previous entry and then editing it accordingly. When you are done, print the résumé. Then save it as mywdprac2-5.doc and close it.

skill

Creating a Document with a Template

concept

When you open a new document, its existing formatting and layout are based on a collection of stored settings. Together, these settings are known as a template. Word provides templates in many categories, including letters, faxes, memos, and Web pages; and styles, such as contemporary, professional, and elegant. When you open Word, the new document that appears is based on the Blank Document template, also known as the Normal template. Some of the settings associated with the Normal template are a blank page, the Times New Roman font, and a 12-point font size. Other templates already include text and graphics that you can customize to fit your needs. Templates serve as a great launching pad for creating documents that seem too complicated to begin from scratch. They can also help ensure consistency in documents.

do it !

Use a template to create an interoffice memo.

1. Click General Templates… in the New from template section of the New Document Task Pane. The Templates dialog box appears. If the Task Pane is not showing, click the New command on the File menu to display it.

2. Click the Memos tab in the Templates dialog box to display the document templates and wizards it contains, as shown in Figure 2-15.

3. Double-click the Professional Memo icon on the Memos tab. The dialog box closes and Word opens a memo immediately. If you would prefer to see a preview of the template before you create it, click the icon once to select it, and then open it.

4. The insertion point should already be in the first text placeholder, so you can begin entering your own information. Type 31 Smith Street [Enter] Indianapolis, IN 46202 [Enter] (317) 555-1313, as shown in Figure 2-16.

5. Drag over the placeholder text that says Company Name Here to select it, and then type Robertson Corp. to replace it.

6. Moving down the page, click the placeholder text [Click **here** and type name] in the To: field, and then type All Employees.

7. Click the placeholder text in the From: field and type Eduardo Alfonso, HR Director.

8. Click the placeholder text in the CC: (Courtesy Copy) field and type Anna Hayes, President.

9. The Date: field already should be filled in with today's date. Click the placeholder text in the Re: field and type Payroll Dates. The upper portion of the memo should now look like Figure 2-17.

(continued on WD 2.16)

Figure 2-15 Memos tab

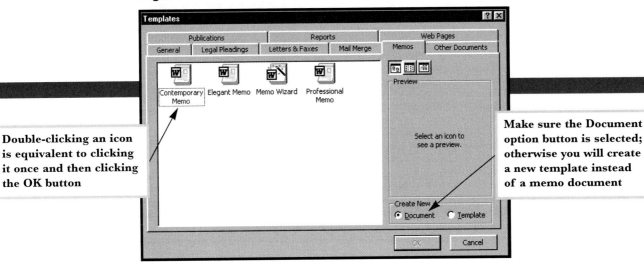

Double-clicking an icon is equivalent to clicking it once and then clicking the OK button

Make sure the Document option button is selected; otherwise you will create a new template instead of a memo document

Figure 2-16 Adding text to a template document

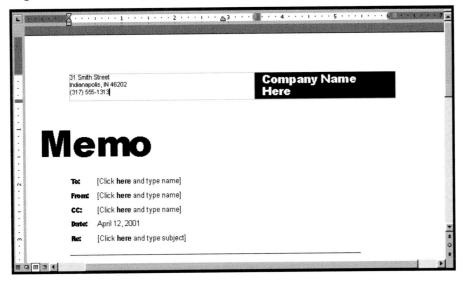

Figure 2-17 Completed upper portion of memo

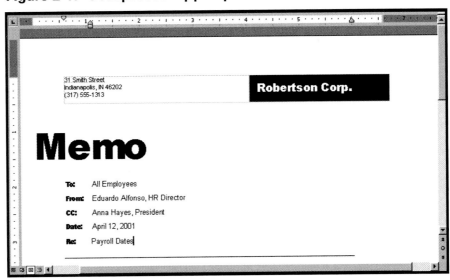

skill Creating a Document with a Template (continued)

do it !

10. Scroll down until you can see the portion of the memo below the horizontal line that divides the top of the memo from the bottom. The text you see is a brief guide to using the template.

11. Select the first line of the instructional text, How to Use This Memo Template, down to the end of the paragraph below it. All of the instructional text should now be selected (see Figure 2-18) and will be deleted as soon as you start typing your own text.

12. Type the following text:

As many of you know, our budget for the next fiscal year was recently approved. The new budget has necessitated a change in the way we run our payroll. From now on, the payroll will be run strictly on the 1st and 15th of every month instead of every two weeks regardless of date, as was done previously. We hope that this change does not present too many inconveniences for you. If you have concerns about the new policy, please feel free to see me in person. [Enter]

Your memo should now look like Figure 2-19. Add your name below the memo text.

13. View your memo in Print Preview and then print a copy of it.

14. Save the memo in your Word Files folder as Payroll Memo.doc, and then close the file.

more

Templates vary in the type and amount of information they contain. Some look like finished documents because they contain placeholders that tell you where to insert specific kinds of information. Others merely provide instructions on how to use the template in order to create the various elements needed in the document. And wizards, as you have already learned, automate part of the document-creation process by asking you to provide information that is then incorporated into the template.

Realize that the elements of a template are just a guide. You can accept them or reject them as you see fit. For example, suppose you are writing a memo like the one above, but you have no need for the courtesy copy line. You simply could select that line of text and delete it from the document. On the other hand, suppose you are using a résumé template and want to add more than one job under the Work Experience heading. All you have to do is copy and paste the existing placeholders in that section to make a duplicate set of them.

It is also important to understand how a template works from a file perspective. When you open a template, it immediately produces a fresh document file based on the template's settings. Therefore, you are not actually working in the template file. It has simply generated the document in which you are working. If you make useful changes to the elements of a document that originated from a template, you do have the ability to save that document as a template itself. That way, you can produce new documents from it in the future. To do this, select Document Template (*.dot) as the file type in the Save As dialog box.

Figure 2-18 Replacing the template's instructional text

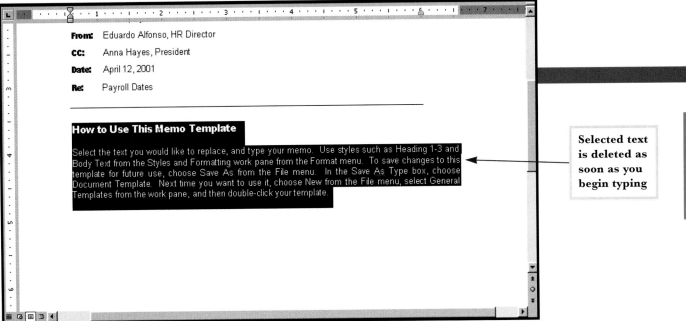

Selected text is deleted as soon as you begin typing

Figure 2-19 Completed memo

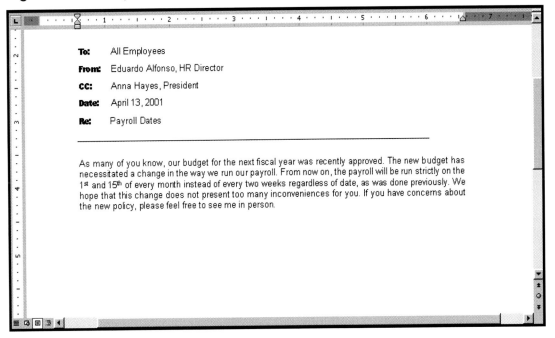

Practice

Use the Elegant Memo template to write a memo from yourself to Eduardo Alfonso, Human Resources Director, commending him and thanking him for his good work. Print a copy of the finished memo and save it as mywdprac2-6.doc. Then close the file.

skill | Using the Office Assistant

concept

Word offers a number of built-in help features that you can use when you encounter problems or just have a question about a particular aspect of the program. One of these features is the Office Assistant, an animated character who provides several methods for getting help in Word. When activated, the Assistant will provide tips related to your current activity. The Assistant also will sense when you are trying to complete a particular task and offer to guide you through it, or you can ask the Assistant a question.

do it !

Ask the Office Assistant about Smart Tags.

1. Click Help on the Menu bar, then click Show the Office Assistant. The Office Assistant will appear on your screen.

2. Click the Office Assistant to open its dialog balloon, and then type How do I use Smart Tags? as shown in Figure 2-20.

3. Click the Search button Search . The Assistant searches Word's Help files for answers to your question and presents a list of topics.

4. Click the topic named Use smart tags, as shown in Figure 2-21. A Help window containing the topic you selected appears alongside the Word window (see Figure 2-22).

5. Read the Help file, and then click its Close button ☒ to remove it from the screen. Notice that the Ask a Question drop-down list box How do I use smart tags? ▼ on the Menu bar now contains the question you asked the Office Assistant. This gives you quick access to the Help topic in case you want to consult it again.

6. Click Help on the Menu bar, then click Hide the Office Assistant. The Assistant disappears from the screen.

more

Each question you ask the Office Assistant during a Word session is added to the Ask a Question drop-down list. To access the questions you have asked previously, click the arrow at the right end of the Ask a Question drop-down list box. When you click a question on this list, the list of Help topics found earlier by the Office Assistant will appear. You then can click the topic of your choice. If you want to ask a new question without using the Office Assistant, click inside the Ask a Question box itself, type your new question, and press [Enter] on the keyboard. The Ask a Question drop-down list is erased when you exit Word.

When the Office Assistant is showing and has a tip for you, a lightbulb icon 💡 will appear above the Assistant. Click the lightbulb to receive the tip.

Once you have hidden the Assistant several times, you will be asked if you would prefer to turn off the feature instead of just hiding it. The option of turning off the Assistant is also available in the Options dialog box, which you can access by clicking the Options button Options in the Assistant's dialog balloon. The Options tab in the Office Assistant dialog box, shown in Figure 2-23, also allows you to control how the Assistant behaves and what kinds of help it provides. The Gallery tab contains animated characters that you may use as your Office Assistant in place of the default paper clip character. While previews of the other Office Assistant characters are available on the Gallery tab, you must install the characters from your Word 2002 or Office XP CD-ROM in order to use them.

Figure 2-20 Querying the Office Assistant

Figure 2-21 Selecting a Help topic

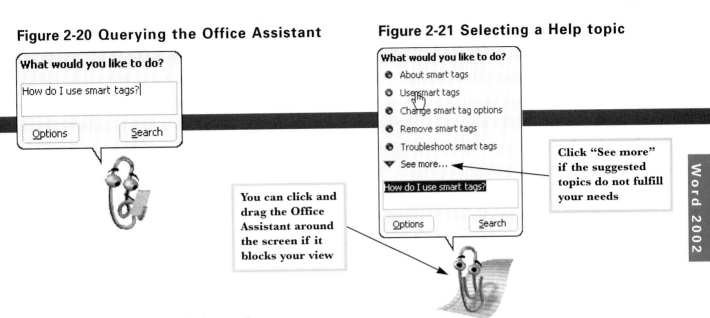

Click "See more" if the suggested topics do not fulfill your needs

You can click and drag the Office Assistant around the screen if it blocks your view

Figure 2-22 Reading a Help topic

Click to print the Help topic

Figure 2-23 Office Assistant dialog box

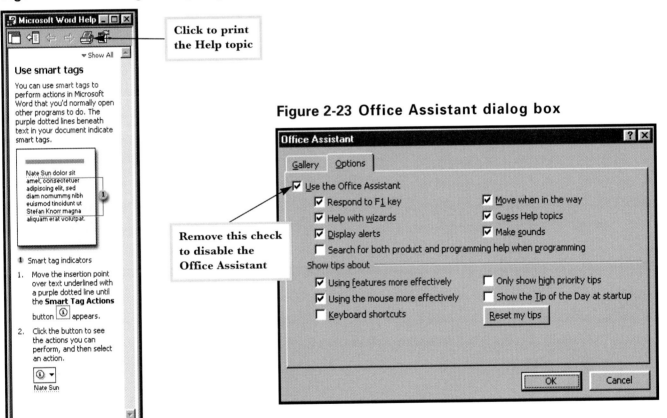

Remove this check to disable the Office Assistant

Practice

Use the Office Assistant to read Help files on the following topics: new features in Word, ScreenTips, and checking spelling in a document. If you have a printer available, print any one of the Help files that you find. Close the Help window, and then turn off the Office Assistant as described in the More section and as depicted in Figure 2-23 above.

skill | Other Word Help Features

concept

For those that would prefer to obtain help without making use of the Office Assistant, Word offers a number of alternatives. As you have seen, ScreenTips help you identify elements of the Word window such as toolbar buttons. The What's This? command extends the power of ScreenTips to include feature names and descriptions of their functions. Perhaps most importantly, all of Word's Help files are available to you in an extensive Microsoft Word Help facility that does not require the participation of the Office Assistant. If you have not turned off the Office Assistant as instructed on the previous page, do so now.

do it !

Use the What's This? command and the Help feature to improve your knowledge of Word.

1. With a blank document open, click Help on the Menu bar, and then click What's This? on the Help menu. The mouse pointer now appears with a question mark attached to it.

2. Click the Show/Hide button ¶ on the Standard toolbar with the What's This? pointer. A ScreenTip appears explaining the function of the button you just clicked (see Figure 2-24). If you click document text with the What's This? pointer, the Reveal Formatting Task Pane will appear. This Task Pane summarizes the formatting in use on the selected text.

3. Click the mouse again to erase the ScreenTip.

4. Click the Microsoft Word Help button ② on the Standard toolbar. The Microsoft Word Help window opens alongside the application window with links to particular areas of help and a list of commonly requested Help topics.

5. If necessary, click the Show button at the top of the Help window. The window expands so that you can see the Help tabs. The Answer Wizard tab functions just like the Office Assistant, allowing you to ask a question and receive a list of suggested topics.

6. Click the Index tab, which allows you to search an alphabetical list of keywords.

7. Begin to type Web page in the text box labeled 1. Type keywords. Before you finish typing, the scrolling list box below will have scrolled to match what you have typed.

8. Click the Search button Search to find Help topics related to the selected keyword. The found topics will be listed in the box labeled 3. Choose a topic (see Figure 2-25). The first topic will be selected and the text of its related Help file will be displayed on the right side of the window.

9. Click the Help topic titled Create a Web page. Its Help file now appears to the right. In this case, it is a list of subtopics. Click the subtopic titled Create a Web page based on a template for detailed instructions on how to complete the task (see Figure 2-26).

10. Click the Close button ☒ in the Help window to close the Microsoft Word Help facility.

more

The Help facility's Contents tab is organized like an outline or the table of contents you might find in a book. It begins with a main level of broad topics symbolized by book icons, each of which can be expanded to reveal more specific subtopics. You can click these subtopics on the Contents tab to display their related Help files on the right side of the window, just as on the Index tab. When the window is expanded, the Show button changes to a Hide button in case you want to collapse the window into single panel again.

Figure 2-24 What's This? ScreenTip

Show All

Displays formatting marks such as tab characters, paragraph marks, and hidden text.

Click Hide button to hide Help tabs

Figure 2-25 Help topics found by keyword

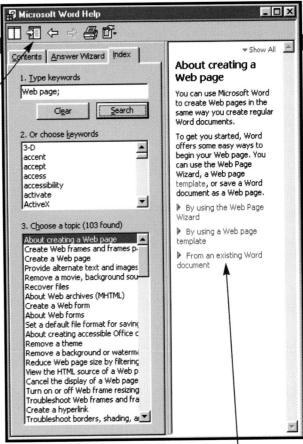

Figure 2-26 Viewing a subtopic

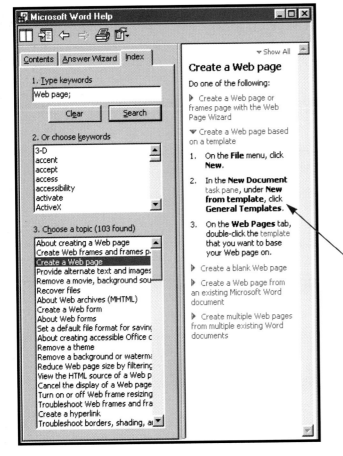

Text of selected subtopic

Subtopics of selected topic

Practice

Open the Microsoft Word Help facility and use the Index tab to find Help topics related to the keyword format. Then read the Help files for the topics named Reveal formatting and Remove formatting from text. Close the Help window when you are done. Finally, use the What's This? command to get help on the Paste button.

shortcuts

Function	Button/Mouse	Menu	Keyboard
Search for a file from Open dialog box	Tools ▾ , then click Search		
Search for a file from Task Pane	🔍	Click File, then click Search	
Undo last action	↶	Click Edit, then click Undo [action]	[Ctrl]+[Z]
Redo last undone action	↷	Click Edit, then click Redo [action]	[Ctrl]+[Y]
Repeat last action		Click Edit, then click Repeat [action]	[Ctrl]+[Y]
Cut selection to the Clipboard	✂	Click Edit, then click Cut	[Ctrl]+[X]
Copy selection to the Clipboard	📋	Click Edit, then click Copy	[Ctrl]+[C]
Paste newest item on Clipboard	📋	Click Edit, then click Paste	[Ctrl]+[V]
Get help	❓	Click Help, then click Show the Office Assistant or Microsoft Word Help	[F1]
Get a detailed ScreenTip for a screen item		Click Help, then click What's This?	[Shift]+[F1], then click the item
Show/hide nonprinting characters	¶		[Ctrl]+[*]

A. Identify Key Features

Name the items indicated by callouts in Figures 2-27 and 2-28.

Figure 2-27 Editing tools

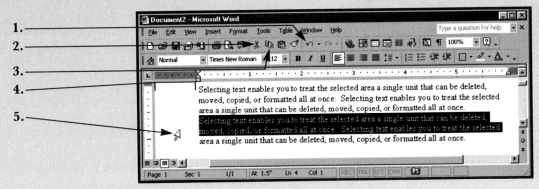

Figure 2-28 More editing tools

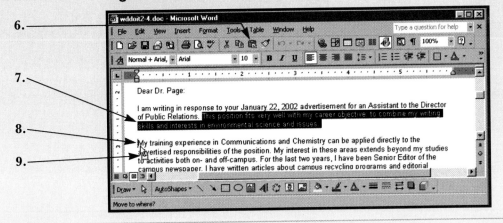

B. Select the Best Answer

10. Allows you to reverse several recent actions at once

11. Offers suggestions about using Word effectively and answers your questions

12. A series of dialog boxes that automates the creation of a document

13. Action that enables you to select an entire paragraph

14. A temporary storage area for cut and copied data

15. One of Word's Help tabs

16. A preformatted document with instructions and/or placeholder text

17. Button that appears when you insert data from the Clipboard

a. Index

b. Triple-click

c. Undo drop-down list

d. Paste Options

e. Template

f. Wizard

g. Clipboard

h. Office Assistant

quiz (continued)

C. Complete the Statement

18. When you start Word, the program opens with a document whose formatting and layout are based on the:

a. Last document used

b. Active buttons on the Formatting toolbar

c. Blank Document template

d. Résumé template

19. To copy selected text to another location with the mouse:

a. Drag and drop the selected text

b. Double-click the desired location

c. Erase the Clipboard

d. Drag and drop the selected text while pressing [Ctrl]

20. A wizard differs from a template in that:

a. A wizard contains no graphic items

b. A wizard uses information provided by you

c. Documents created with templates cannot be edited

d. A wizard can be used only once

21. To select the text from the insertion point to the end of the line:

a. Click the paragraph mark

b. Press [Ctrl]+[Home]

c. Click next to the line in the Selection bar

d. Press [Shift]+[End]

22. Double-clicking in the Selection bar:

a. Opens the Templates dialog box

b. Selects the entire document

c. Selects the adjacent paragraph

d. Minimizes the document window

23. You can revisit the Help topics produced by previous questions to the Office Assistant by using the:

a. Ask a Question drop-down list box

b. Search dialog box

c. Contents tab

d. What's This? command

24. You know the What's This? command is active when:

a. The mouse pointer includes a plus sign

b. The mouse pointer points to the right

c. The mouse pointer includes a question mark

d. The Help tabs are visible

25. Clicking the Paste button:

a. Inserts the last item sent to the Clipboard

b. Copies the selected text to the Clipboard

c. Clears the Clipboard

d. Opens the Clipboard Task Pane

26. You can use the Search dialog box to locate a file if you know:

a. Part of the file name

b. The date the document was created

c. Text that appears in the document

d. All of the above

interactivity

Build Your Skills

1. Search for a file and open it:

   a. Open the Search dialog box (from the Open dialog box) or the Basic Search Task Pane (click 🖳).

   b. Search for a Word file on your computer that contains the text Diana Voorhies.

   c. Open the file and save it in your Word Files folder as Monahan.doc.

2. Select and delete portions of the document:

   a. Select the last sentence of the second paragraph (He was really great …) by clicking it while pressing [Ctrl].

   b. Delete the selected sentence.

   c. Select the postscript near the end of the document by triple-clicking it.

   d. Add the text that follows the postscript to the end of the document to the selection by pressing [Ctrl]+[Shift]+[End].

   e. Delete the selected text.

3. Select and move paragraphs in the document:

   a. Select the third paragraph (the one that begins On a slightly …) by double-clicking next to it in the Selection bar.

   b. Drag the selected paragraph to the blank line following the next paragraph and drop it there.

   c. Select the first paragraph (Thank you very much …) by triple-clicking it.

   d. Cut the selected paragraph to the Clipboard.

   e. Paste the paragraph you just cut after the final paragraph of the document, before the name of the writer.

   d. Save the changes you have made to the document and close it.

4. Create a document using a wizard:

   a. Open the Templates dialog box and run the Memo Wizard.

   b. Create a Contemporary style memo with the title Word 2002 Memo.

   c. Address the memo to your instructor or administrator. Do not include a CC: field.

   d. Select the other options as you wish.

   e. When you finish the wizard, add text to the memo informing the addressee how you have created the document.

   f. View the document in Print Preview and then print a copy of the memo.

   g. Save the file in your Word Files folder as Word 2002 Memo.doc.

   h. Close the file.

interactivity (continued)

Build Your Skills (continued)

5. Create a document using a template:

   a. Use the Templates dialog box to open a document with the Contemporary Fax template.

   b. Fill out the fax cover sheet with the following information:
   Address: 12345 Laloma Blvd., Coral Bay, FL 01000
   To: Sir or Madam   Fax: (860) 555-6412
   From: [Your Name]   Date: [Today's Date]
   Re: Reservation   Pages: 1
   CC: Happy Travels, Inc.
   For Review

   c. Type a sentence or two in the lower half of the document explaining that you are confirming a hotel reservation.

   d. Save the document as Fax Cover Sheet.doc and close it.

6. Use Word's Help facilities:

   a. Ask the Office Assistant What are some useful keyboard shortcuts?

   b. Choose the Help topic called Keyboard shortcuts and read one of the subtopics under it.

   c. Show the Help tabs if they are not already visible in the Microsoft Word Help window.

   d. Search for topics related to the keyword view.

   e. Read each of the subtopics found under the topic About ways to view a Word document.

   f. Close the Help window and turn off the Office Assistant.

Problem Solving Exercises

1. You are about to graduate from college with a Fine Arts degree in Photojournalism. Your ambition is to find a job that will one day allow you to travel around the world taking evocative photos for a major magazine or newspaper. Since you are just starting out, you know that you may have to settle for a position with slightly less freedom for now. Use the Professional Résumé template to construct an Entry-level résumé that you can send to local newspapers and less-established magazines in search of a photojournalist position. However, do not sell yourself short. Emphasize your talents and experience as an amateur photojournalist and do not lose sight of your long-term goals. Customize the document as necessary—moving, adding, and deleting headings as necessary. When the résumé is done, print it and save it in your Word Files folder as Photo Résumé.doc.

2. As the owner and CEO of a rapidly expanding financial consulting firm, you are very proud to have had your best recruiting season ever. You have hired six outstanding recent college graduates from this year's recruiting class. Use the Letter Wizard to write a letter of congratulations to the head of your recruiting department. Select the Contemporary Letter design and the Full Block style. Preview and print the letter, then save it as Congrats Letter.doc.

interactivity (continued)

Problem Solving Exercises (continued)

3. While at a talent showcase for local bands in Ithaca, NY, you have seen an act that looks more promising than any other that you have seen in your career as a talent scout. Since you brought along your laptop, you have decided to fax your boss at National Talent right away to tell her about the band you have seen. Use the Elegant Fax template to create a fax cover sheet. Since the template includes a section in which you can add the message you want to send, the fax may consist of only this one sheet. Complete the cover sheet, including your discovery at the showcase. Preview the finished document with Print Preview, and save it as New Talent Fax.doc.

4. The résumé depicted below was originally created with the Résumé Wizard using the Contemporary style and the Functional type. The document has since been edited and formatted to some degree. Use the skills you have learned so far in Word to recreate the document to the best of your ability, substituting your own name and address. Print the document and save it as Liaison Résumé.doc.

Figure 2-29 Résumé example

22 Winger St.
Nassau, NY 10210
Phone (516) 555-1212

Tracy Alexander

Objective   To obtain a position abroad as an embassy liaison.

Employment   1/01/1999-present   United Nations   New York, NY
Translator
- Worked out of the Office of the General Secretary receiving diplomats and accompanying them to events during their stay
- Provided in-house translations of documents and speeches as required

1/01/1997-12/31/1999 Helping Hands   New York, NY
Case Worker
- Worked with immigrant families with language and economic limitations to ease their transition into life in a new country
- Met regularly with city officials to discuss the issues encountered by such families upon their arrivals and in subsequent years

Education   1992-1996   Georgetown University   Washington, D.C.
School of International Affairs
- Combined four-year Bachelors/Masters degree

Languages   English, French, Spanish, Portuguese

References   Available upon request

Advanced Editing

Word allows you to add many different types of formatting to a document. There are three types of formatting: text-level formatting, paragraph-level formatting, and document-level formatting.

Text-level formatting, which was covered in Lesson 1, refers to all formatting that applies to individual characters in a document—such as font style, font size, and options such as bold and italics. No matter where text appears, these characteristics can be applied to single letters or entire sections of text.

Paragraph-level formatting covers the characteristics that can be applied to a paragraph or group of paragraphs. These features include alignment, indents, line spacing, line numbering, and other aspects that cannot be applied to a single character.

Document-level formatting includes options such as page margins or options called headers or footers. Headers, which appear at the top—or head—of a page, often contain document titles. Footers, which appear at the bottom—or foot—of the page, often contain page numbers.

Once a document has been typed and formatted to meet your needs, Word offers several proofreading aids to assure the quality of the finished document. For example, Word has a spelling checker that spots misspelled words throughout the document. Word also has a feature called AutoCorrect that can actually fix common typing and spelling mistakes automatically, as they are made. Additionally, Word contains a built-in thesaurus—or synonym finder—that makes it easier for you to find a word with the precise meaning needed for a particular context. Finally, if you decide to change a word or phrase that occurs in several places, especially in longer documents, Word can search your document for all instances of the item and replace it with a different word or phrase that you prefer.

Lesson Goal:

Add advanced formats to individual documents and learn how to use time-saving formatting commands. Learn how to proofread documents and make changes using correction tools.

skill   Setting Up a Page

concept

Word gives you control over many aspects of formatting at the document level. These include margins, gutters (the space between two columns of text or the space formed by the inner margins of two facing pages), page orientation, paper sizes, section divisions, headers and footers, and vertical alignment of text on a page. Changing document-level formatting enables you to control how a document appears on both your screen and on a printout.

do it !

Reduce the left and right margins of a research paper.

1. Open Student File wddoit3-1.doc and save it in your Word Files folder as Report1.doc.

2. Click File, then Page Setup. The Page Setup dialog box appears.

3. If necessary, click the Margins tab to bring it to the front of the dialog box for viewing (see Figure 3-1).

4. Click the downward-pointing arrow at the right end of the Left box three times to reduce Word's default margin setting from 1.25 inches to 1 inch. The Preview area on the right side of the dialog box reflects your change to the left margin.

5. Triple-click the Right box to select it. Type the number 1 to replace the selected value of 1.25. Since inches is the default setting for measurements in Word, you do not need to add the quotations marks that represent that measurement.

6. Click ⬛ OK ⬛ to apply the changes to the document and to close the dialog box. The text of your document now may extend beyond the edges of your screen. If so, solve this viewing problem by reducing the Zoom percentage on the Standard toolbar so you can see to the edges of the page (see Figure 3-2).

7. After changing the left and right margins, save and close the document.

more

The Page Setup dialog box for Word 2002 differs somewhat from the corresponding box in previous versions of Word. Word 2002's dialog box now has three tabs—Margins, Paper, and Layout—instead of four. A few command options have been added, and some previously existing options have moved to different tabs to accommodate the simpler tab arrangement. The Margins tab enables you to adjust top and bottom document margins, as well as the left and right margins you altered in the Skill above. This tab also enables you to adjust the width and location of a gutter (the extra space at the edge of a page reserved for binding documents) and to change page orientation. The Page tab allows you to adjust page size to the type of paper in your printer, to pull paper from a different paper source in the printer, and to alter other print options as your printer's features permit. The Layout tab contains options to adjust document sections, header and footer options, the vertical alignment of text and/or graphics on a page, and line numbering and border options.

Figure 3-1 Page Setup dialog box

Click a tab to bring it to the front

Click arrows to raise or lower the values in the text boxes, or select the contents of the boxes and replace them with other desired values

Adjusts the distance added to the margin to allow extra room for binding, and for its location on the page

Formatting changes show up here for you to preview

The orientation, or direction, of the printed page

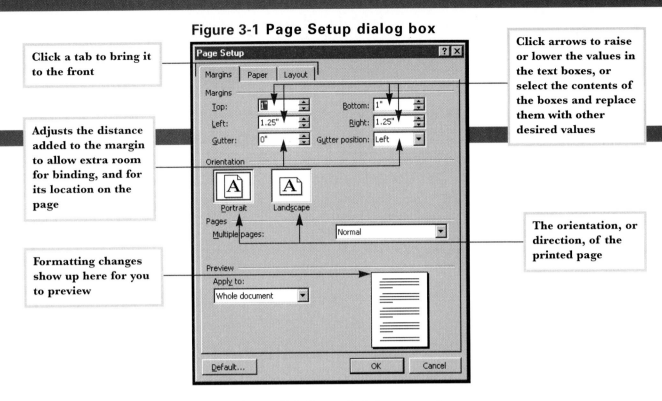

Figure 3-2 Report1.doc after setting 1″ left and right margins

Document close button

Zoom box percentage adjusted to view whole lines of text

Save button

8.5″ page width – 1″ left & right margins = 6.5″ line width

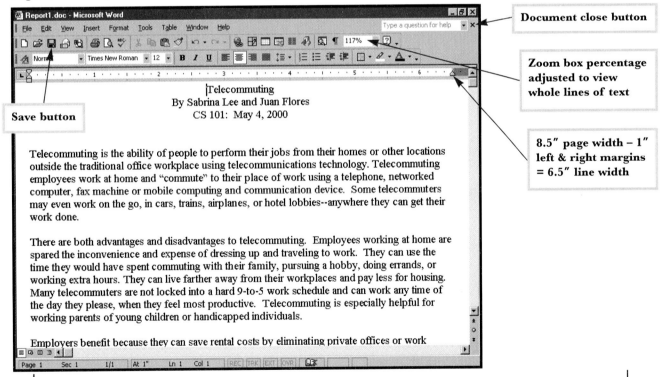

Practice

Open the Student File wdprac3-1.doc and save it in your Word Files folder as mywdprac3-1.doc. Practice adjusting page margins using the Page Setup dialog box under the File menu. When you have completed the practice exercise, resave and close mywdprac3-1.doc with your changes.

skill | Inserting Page Numbers

concept

Word can insert page numbers into documents at different locations and in various styles. Word inserts numbers automatically so you do not have to add a page number to each page individually. Additionally, you can add a prefix to each page number to identify chapters or sections, or choose to leave off the number of the first page of a document if that first page serves as a title page.

do it !

Add centered page numbers to the report and view them.

1. Open Student File wddoit3-2.doc and save it in your Word Files folder as Report2.doc.

2. Click Insert, then click Page Numbers to open the Page Number dialog box (see Figure 3-3).

3. Click the Alignment box, then click Center to change the horizontal position of each page number from the default right setting to center.

4. Click Format... to open the Page Number Format dialog box (see Figure 3-4).

5. Make sure the Page Number Format dialog box displays Arabic numerals (1, 2, 3...) instead of letters or Roman numerals. If it does not, click the box, then click 1,2,3... to select Arabic numerals.

6. Click OK to close the Page Number Format dialog box and return to the Page Numbers dialog box.

7. Click OK to confirm and apply the Arabic numeral formatting. Word automatically shifts to Print Layout View so you can see the page numbers. ⬮ If you add pages to a document that already is formatted with page numbers, the numbers will update automatically.

8. Scroll to the bottom of the page to see the inserted page number (see Figure 3-5). Click 🖫 to save the changes you have made to Report2.doc, and then close the document.

more

The numbers you've added to the document do not appear in Normal View. Recall, however, that Word allows three other major ways to view documents. You can access these three views in two ways. First, you can click the View menu and then select Web Layout View, Print Layout View, or Outline View. Second, you can move among these same three views, and in the same order, by using the View buttons at the left end of the horizontal scroll bar at the bottom of the Word window. The current view is indicated by a square white background (or, on some monitors, a soft blue background) around the selected view button. Web Layout View displays your document as it would appear if viewed with a Web browser. Print Layout View displays your document as it will appear when printed, including page numbers. This view retains the Ruler and the Standard and Formatting toolbars. Outline view enables you to use Word's outlining features to structure text with headings and subheadings. Additionally, Print Preview displays how your document will look when printed, without non-printing characters but with items not seen in the default Normal View—such as headers, footers, and page numbers. Unlike Print Layout view, Print Preview lacks the Standard and Formatting toolbars, but has a Print Preview toolbar and magnifying tool. Other view options include Header and Footer, which displays headers and footers in an editable text box, and Full Screen, which shows only the document window.

Figure 3-3 Page Numbers dialog box

These boxes determine the position of the page number on the page

Shows position of page number

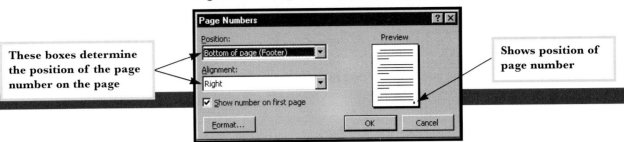

Figure 3-4 Page Numbers Format dialog box

Click to select a number style

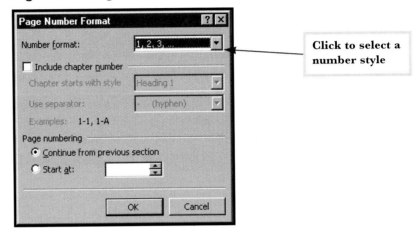

Word 2002

Figure 3-5 Report2.doc with page number

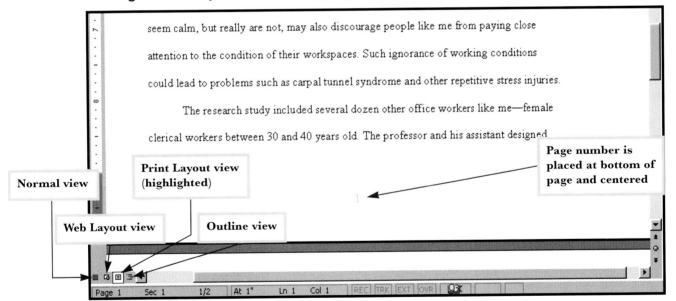

Normal view

Print Layout view (highlighted)

Web Layout view

Outline view

Page number is placed at bottom of page and centered

Practice

Open the Student File wdprac3-2.doc and save it in your Word Files folder as mywdprac3-2.doc. Follow the instructions at the beginning of the practice file to practice inserting page numbers using the Page Numbers dialog box under the Insert menu. When you have completed the practice exercise, resave and close mywdprac3-2.doc with your changes.

skill Inserting Footnotes and Endnotes

concept

Footnotes and endnotes often appear in academic or longer business documents. Footnotes—which appear at the bottom, or "foot," of a page—often comment or expand upon the main text. Endnotes—which appear at the end of a document—usually provide references for further study. Both kinds of notes contain two parts—a note reference mark (usually a number elevated slightly—or superscripted—above the main line of text) and the note text. Word has a convenient feature that helps you automatically create, format, and number such notes.

do it !

Add a footnote at the end of a research paper and then view the new note.

1. Open Student File wddoit3-3.doc and save it in your Word Files folder as Report3.doc. Make sure that you are seeing the document in Normal view.

2. Position the insertion point at the end of the first paragraph, after the words can do work. This is where the note reference mark will appear.

3. Click Insert, click Reference, and then click Footnote. The Footnote and Endnote dialog box will appear with Footnote (the Word default setting) selected (see Figure 3-6).

4. Click [Insert] to insert the footnote using the current settings. Word inserts the note reference mark at the insertion point and opens a note pane at the bottom of the Normal view window (see Figure 3-7).

5. At the insertion point, type the following text: These "anytime, anywhere" work environments are sometimes called "virtual offices" because work can be performed outside of the traditional physical office setting and work schedule. Then click [Close] to leave the note pane and return to the document window.

6. Click View, then click Print Layout. Scroll to the bottom of the page and view the footnote in its proper place (see Figure 3-8). Alternately, position the mouse pointer over the note reference mark in the text so the footnote text will appear on your screen as a ScreenTip.

7. Save and close your document, Report3.doc, with the changes you have made.

more

In the Footnote and Endnote dialog box, the Continuous option in the Numbering area and Whole Document option in the Apply changes to box are more default settings not discussed above. With these options selected, Word automatically renumbers note reference marks throughout the whole document as you add or remove footnotes and/or endnotes, so there will be no break in their continuity. By clicking the Endnotes option in the Location area, you can place notes at the end of a document. By clicking the Number Format box in the Format area, you can change the numbering system from Arabic numerals to letters or Roman numbers. The Numbering box allows you to restart your chosen numbering system on a new page or new document section. And if you've divided your document into sections, the Apply changes to box enables you to make even more adjustments.

As Figure 3-7 shows, the note pane is a separate part of the Normal view screen for entering footnote (or endnote) text. You can access all footnotes (or endnotes) through the note pane. The default formatting for footnote text is 10-point Times New Roman, left aligned. You can change this formatting while in the note pane as you can with text in any other part of a document. In Normal view, double-clicking the note reference mark opens the note pane. In Print Layout view, double-clicking the note reference mark moves the insertion point to the related footnote.

Word 2002

Figure 3-6 Footnote and Endnote dialog box

Footnotes is default setting; click *Endnotes* to place notes at end of document

Adjusts placement of footnotes and endnotes on a page

Click here to change numbering system from Arabic numerals to letters, Roman numerals, etc.

Opens Symbol dialog box to insert custom marks such as asterisk, dagger, etc. instead of numbers, letters, etc.

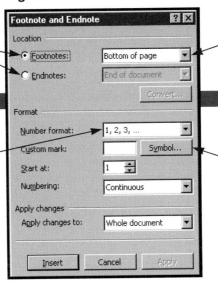

Figure 3-7 Note Pane with footnote text

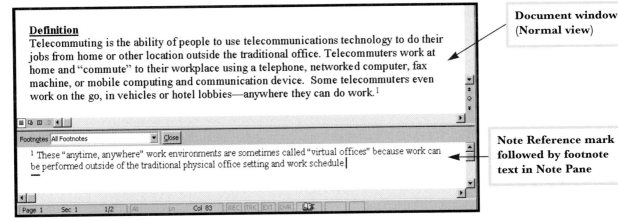

Document window (Normal view)

Note Reference mark followed by footnote text in Note Pane

Figure 3-8 Viewing a footnote at the bottom of a page

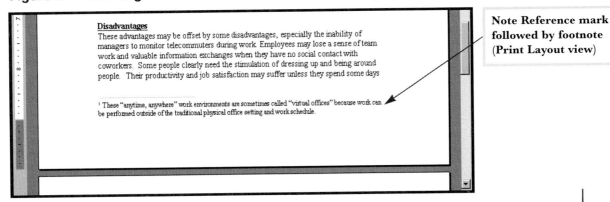

Note Reference mark followed by footnote (Print Layout view)

Practice

Open the Student File wdprac3-3.doc and save it in your Word Files folder as mywdprac3-3.doc. Practice inserting footnotes at the ends of sentences by using the Footnote and Endnote dialog box under the Reference command of the Insert menu. When you have completed the practice exercise, resave and close mywdprac3-3.doc with your changes.

skill Applying Paragraph Indents

concept

Indenting paragraphs helps to format documents so readers can follow your line of thought more easily. To indent paragraphs in Word, you can use the Tab key on the keyboard, the Paragraph command on the Format menu, the Increase Indent button on the Formatting tool-bar, or three Indent Markers on the Horizontal Ruler. The Tab key and Increase Indent button provide less indenting flexibility, while the Paragraph command and Indent Markers provide more.

do it !

Use the four indenting tools to structure a document for easier reading.

1. Open Student File wddoit3-4.doc and save it in your Word Files folder as Report4.doc.

2. Place the insertion point immediately to the left of the first word in the second paragraph, Estimate. Press the Tab key on your keyboard once to indent the first line by half an inch to the right. Word's default new blank document has Tab Stops every half inch. In this case, however, each time you press the Tab key, you are setting the First Line indent of the paragraph another half inch to the right. You could click the Smart Tag button that has appeared to change this indent to a tab.

3. Place the insertion point just to the left of the first word in the third paragraph, Choose. Click Format, then click Paragraph to open the Paragraph dialog box (see Figure 3-9). Under Indentation, click the Special arrow and then click First line. Click ⬚ OK ⬚ to close the dialog box and indent the first line of the paragraph by half an inch.

4. Place the insertion point immediately to the left of the first word in the fourth paragraph, As. Click the Increase Indent button ⬚ once on the Formatting toolbar to indent all lines of the paragraph one-half inch.

5. Click immediately to the left of the first word in the fifth paragraph, Stick. Click ⬚ at the left end of the Horizontal Ruler (see Figure 3-10). While pressing the mouse button, drag the First Line indent marker to the right until it reaches the half inch mark on the ruler. Release the mouse button to indent the first line of the paragraph one half inch.

6. Click immediately to the left of the first word in the sixth paragraph, Remember. Click Format, and click Paragraph to open the Paragraph dialog box. In the Indentation area, click the Special box, and click the Hanging option. Click ⬚ OK ⬚ to close the dialog box and indent the second and following lines one half inch.

7. Look at the variously indented paragraphs of the document in Print Layout view (see Figure 3-11). Save and close Report4.doc with your changes.

more

You can set your own tab stops by clicking the bottom half of the ruler where desired. After you set the tabs, you can drag and position them along the ruler with the mouse pointer. To remove a tab stop, click and drag it below the ruler. It will vanish when you release the mouse button. Clicking the tab alignment selector at the left end of the ruler selects various tab alignments that you can apply. As seen in the steps above, the First Line indent marker controls indentation of just the first line of selected paragraphs, while the Hanging indent marker controls all lines in selected paragraphs except for the first line. Like the Increase and Decrease Indent buttons, the rectangle below the Hanging indent marker (i.e., the Left indent marker) controls all lines of selected paragraphs. Because you can move indent markers anywhere on the ruler, the Left indent marker has more flexibility than the buttons, which you can set only to predeter-mined tab settings. When you open a blank document, the default settings for the indent markers are even with the margins.

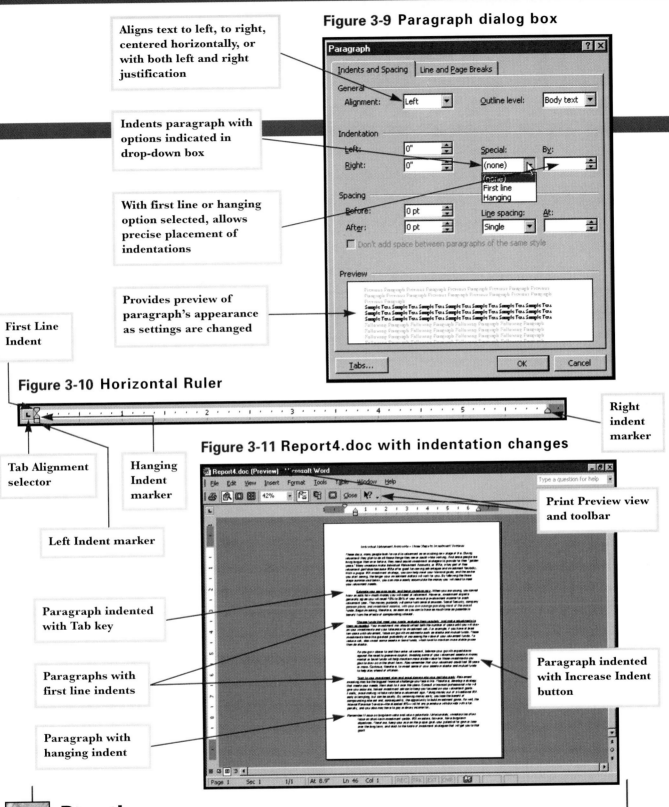

Figure 3-9 Paragraph dialog box

Aligns text to left, to right, centered horizontally, or with both left and right justification

Indents paragraph with options indicated in drop-down box

With first line or hanging option selected, allows precise placement of indentations

Provides preview of paragraph's appearance as settings are changed

First Line Indent

Figure 3-10 Horizontal Ruler

Right indent marker

Tab Alignment selector

Hanging Indent marker

Left Indent marker

Figure 3-11 Report4.doc with indentation changes

Print Preview view and toolbar

Paragraph indented with Tab key

Paragraphs with first line indents

Paragraph indented with Increase Indent button

Paragraph with hanging indent

Practice

Open the Student File wdprac3-4.doc and save it in your Word Files folder as mywdprac3-4.doc. Follow the instructions of the paragraphs that appear in the file to practice indenting paragraphs using the Paragraph dialog box under the Format menu and using the Horizontal Ruler just below the Formatting toolbar. When you have completed the practice exercise, resave and close mywdprac3-4.doc with your changes.

skill   Changing Line Spacing

concept

The line spacing—or distance between adjacent lines of text—can be modified from the Paragraph dialog box. Word also allows users to change the spacing between paragraphs, without changing line spacing within those paragraphs. Many universities and businesses require written documents to conform to certain formatting standards, which often include spacing considerations. For example, professors generally require that research papers be double-spaced, while business supervisors require that all memos and letters be single-spaced.

do it !

Remove the spaces between paragraphs and double-space a report.

1. Open Student File wddoit3-5 and save it in your Word Files folder as Report5.doc. Be sure the document displays in Normal view. Delete each of the three blank lines between the four paragraphs of the main text by selecting the blank lines and pressing [Delete].

2. Click Edit, then click Select All to select the entire document. Click Format, then click Paragraph to open the Paragraph dialog box.

3. In the Spacing area of the dialog box, click the Line Spacing list box, then click Double (see Figure 3-12). Click [OK] to accept the changes you have made. Click anywhere in the document to remove the highlighting.

4. Click View, then click Print Layout. Scroll down in the document until you can see from the title to the first line of the second paragraph, and compare your results with Figure 3-13. When satisfied with your formatting results, return to Normal view.

5. Save and close the document, Report5.doc, with the changes you have made.

more

The Paragraph dialog box has a Preview box that shows you how the changes you are making will affect your text. The Word default setting is single spacing. If the spacing interval you want does not appear in the Line Spacing list box, the At box allows you to set spacing at any interval desired, such as 1.25 spacing or 0.9 spacing. The Before and After boxes control spacing before and after a selected paragraph. These boxes allow you to space individual paragraphs automatically at any interval without adding blank lines within any paragraphs in the document.

Table 3-1 Line Spacing

Option	Description
Single	Accommodates the largest font in that line, plus a small amount of extra space. The amount of extra space varies with the font being used.
1.5 lines	One-and-one-half times that of single spacing.
Double	Twice that of single spacing.
At least	The minimum amount of line spacing needed to fit the largest font or graphic on the line.
Exactly	A fixed amount of line spacing that Word does not adjust.
Multiple	Line spacing that increases or decreases by a percentage you specify. E.g., setting line spacing to 1.3 will increase the spacing by 30 percent over single spacing.

Figure 3-12 Paragraph dialog box with double spacing

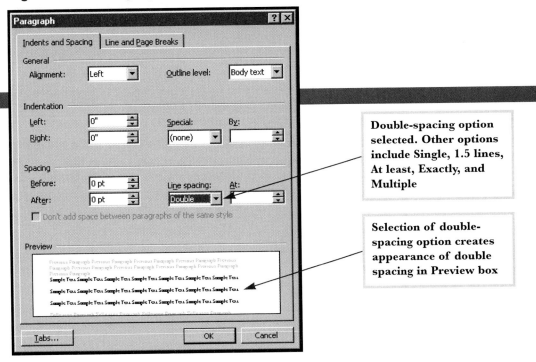

Double-spacing option selected. Other options include Single, 1.5 lines, At least, Exactly, and Multiple

Selection of double-spacing option creates appearance of double spacing in Preview box

Figure 3-13 Report5.doc, double-spaced

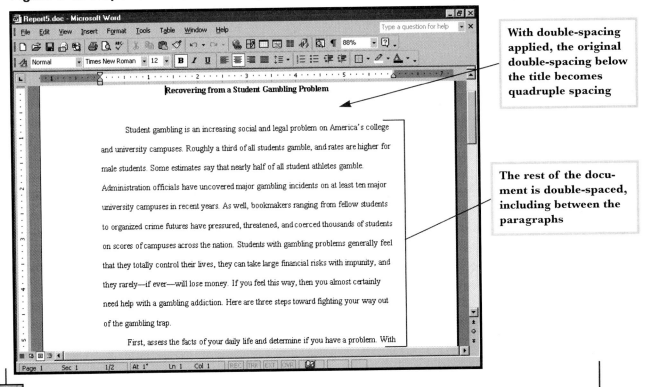

With double-spacing applied, the original double-spacing below the title becomes quadruple spacing

The rest of the document is double-spaced, including between the paragraphs

Practice

Open the Student File wdprac3-5.doc and save it in your Word Files folder as mywdprac3-5.doc. Follow the instructions of the paragraphs that appear in the file to practice line and paragraph spacing using the Paragraph dialog box under the Format menu. When you have completed the practice exercise, resave and close mywdprac3-5.doc with your changes.

skill   Inserting Page Breaks

concept

When you fill a page in Word with text and/or graphics, the program inserts an automatic (or soft) page break and starts a new page with any additional typing or images you may have. To create a page break at a specific place in a document, you can insert a manual (or hard) page break. A manual break might be proper for a Works Cited page in a report, a new novel chapter, or a table or graphic that should stand out in a business document. Word also offers various section break options for dividing longer documents into subparts.

do it !

Place the References section of a report on a separate page.

1. Open Student File wddoit3-6 and save it in your Word Files folder as Report6.doc. Be sure you are viewing it in Normal view.

2. Place the insertion point before the word References at the head of the References section of the report. This word will become the first line of the new References page.

3. Click Insert, then click Break to open the Break dialog box. In the dialog box the Page Break option already is selected (see Figure 3-14).

4. Click [OK] to insert a page break at the insertion point. The References section will now appear at the top of a new page (see Figure 3-15). Word will automatically renumber the pages of the document to account for the new page. To remove a Hard page break, you would click next to it in the Selection bar to select it, and then delete it by pressing [Delete].

5. Save and close your document, Report6.doc, with the changes you have made.

more

In Normal view an automatic or soft page break looks like a dotted horizontal line. In Print Layout view it looks like a gap between two pages over a gray background. Earlier versions of Word could not eliminate the gray gap between the pages nor reduce the top and bottom margins to view more page area. Word 2002, however, has a new feature that performs those tasks. When in Print Layout, you simply place your insertion point over the gap. When you see the Hide White Space button, 🔛, simply click it. The gap and margins will disappear, making it possible to view more page area. In the Section break types area, the Break dialog box also allows you to add Section breaks. A section is just a distinct part of your document that is separated from the rest. For example, as noted above, you could separate chapters in a book by using section breaks. Inserting a section break ends one section and dictates where the next will begin.

Consult Table 3-2 below for examples of types of section breaks that you can insert.

Table 3-2 Section Breaks

Option	Description
Next page	Inserts a section break and starts a new section on the next page.
Continuous	Inserts a section break and starts a new section on the same page.
Odd page	Inserts a section break and starts a new section on the next odd-numbered page.
Even page	Inserts a section break and starts a new section on the next even-numbered page.

Figure 3-14 Break dialog box

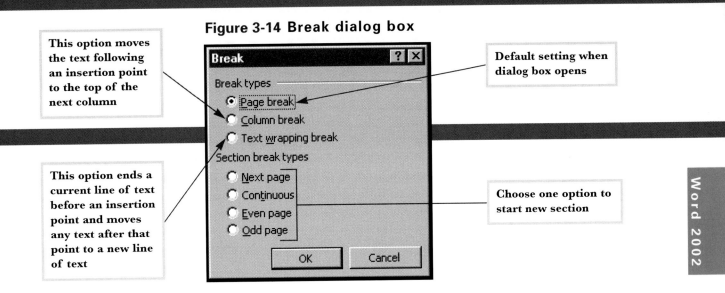

This option moves the text following an insertion point to the top of the next column

Default setting when dialog box opens

This option ends a current line of text before an insertion point and moves any text after that point to a new line of text

Choose one option to start new section

Figure 3-15 Report6.doc, after inserting manual (hard) page break

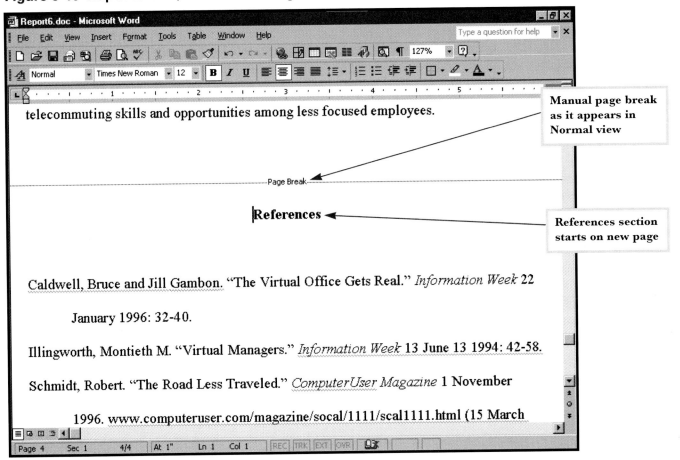

telecommuting skills and opportunities among less focused employees.

Manual page break as it appears in Normal view

References section starts on new page

References

Caldwell, Bruce and Jill Gambon. "The Virtual Office Gets Real." *Information Week* 22

January 1996: 32-40.

Illingworth, Montieth M. "Virtual Managers." *Information Week* 13 June 13 1994: 42-58.

Schmidt, Robert. "The Road Less Traveled." *ComputerUser Magazine* 1 November

1996. www.computeruser.com/magazine/socal/1111/scal1111.html (15 March

Practice

Open the Student File wdprac3-6.doc and save it in your Word Files folder as mywdprac3-6.doc. Following the highlighted instructions that appear in the file, practice inserting various page and section breaks using the Break dialog box under the Insert command. When you have completed the practice exercise, resave and close mywdprac3-6.doc with your changes.

skill Working with Multiple Documents _MOUS Skill_

concept

Word, like many other programs, lets users work with more than one document at a time. You can create a new document or open an existing one without jeopardizing the active document. You can arrange document windows so you can see one, two, or more open documents simultaneously. You also can copy and move text between open documents using the Office Clipboard. This feature can save you from the time-consuming task of having to retype text that you want to use in another document.

do it !

Copy text created in one document and paste it into another document.

1. Open Student File wddoit3-7.doc and save it in your Word Files folder as Report7.doc. Keep the file open. Then open Student File wddoit3-7a.doc and save it in your Word Files folder as Report7a.doc. Report7.doc has a 6-inch text line, so its left and right margins are set at 1.25 inches. Report7a.doc has a 6.5-inch text line, so its left and right margins are set at 1 inch. (Ignore this difference, as the next few steps will adjust for it.)

2. Select all of the one paragraph in Report7a.doc, either by dragging over the paragraph or by triple-clicking anywhere inside it. While the paragraph is selected, click 🗐 on the Standard toolbar or press the Copy command's keyboard shortcut, [Ctrl]+[C].

3. Click Window on the Menu bar, and then click Report7.doc to switch to that document. To switch to Report7.doc, you also could click its program button on the Windows taskbar at the bottom of your computer screen. If the taskbar is hidden, it is set in AutoHide mode. To make it appear, move your mouse pointer to the bottom of the screen.

4. With Report7.doc still open, click immediately after the period after the word tone at the end of the first paragraph. Press [Enter] twice to move the insertion point down two lines.

5. Click 🗐 on the Standard toolbar to paste the copy of the paragraph from Report7a.doc. Scroll to the end of the inserted paragraph. Ignore the Smart Tag that appears near the last word of the inserted paragraph, king. If needed, adjust the blank spacing between the inserted paragraph and the one that begins with the word When so there is only one blank line between the paragraphs. Notice that the inserted paragraph from Report7a.doc now conforms to the 6-inch line of Report7.doc (see Figure 3-16).

6. Save and close Report7.doc with the inserted paragraph. Close Report7a.doc without saving any changes.

more

Word provides alternate ways to open documents (or other types of Word files) that you recently worked on. First, you can click the File menu and see the directory path and filenames of the four to nine documents opened most recently in Word on the computer. (To adjust the number of displayed filenames, you would click the Tools menu, click the Options command, click the General tab to bring it forward, enter the desired number of entries in the Recently used file list box, and then close the dialog box by clicking the [OK] button.) Second, you can click the [Start] button on the Windows taskbar and move your mouse pointer over the Document command. These two steps will display a list of just the filenames from any program opened most recently on the computer. Clicking one of these filenames will open the relevant file or make it the active document if it is already open. Remember that the active file is always the one in front, highlighted by a blue title bar. Inactive files will have a medium gray title bar (see Figure 3-17).

Figure 3-16 Report7.doc with pasted paragraph

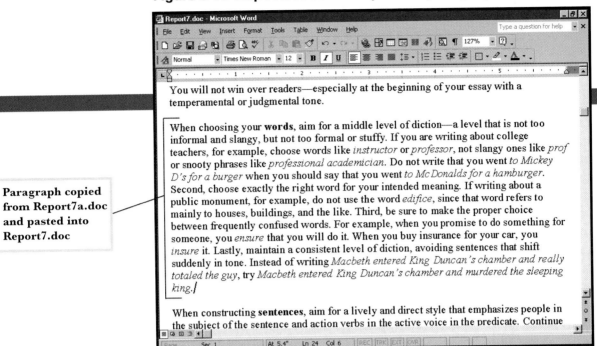

Paragraph copied
from Report7a.doc
and pasted into
Report7.doc

Figure 3-17 Active document "cascaded" on top of inactive ones

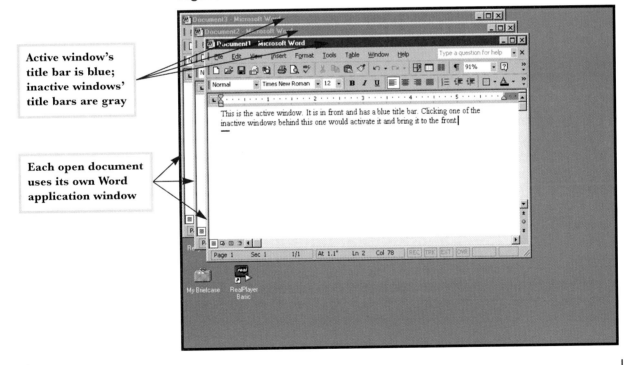

Active window's
title bar is blue;
inactive windows'
title bars are gray

Each open document
uses its own Word
application window

Practice

Open Student File wdprac3-7.doc and save it in your Word Files folder as mywdprac3-7.doc. Then open Student File, wdprac3-7a.doc. Following the instructions in the two files, practice copying and pasting paragraphs from one document into another in the proper order. When you have completed the practice exercise, resave and close mywdprac3-7.doc with your changes. Close wdprac3-7a.doc with no changes.

skill   Using the Format Painter

concept

The Format Painter enables you to copy many formatting settings from selected text to another section of text. Whether you are working with just a word or a paragraph, Format Painter unifies document formatting without having to apply each formatting change separately. By reducing the need to format new text with repeated keystrokes or mouse clicks, this feature also saves you time. Format Painter is especially useful in documents like flyers and newsletters where distinctive formatting is common, even essential, to the document's appearance.

do it !

Use Format Painter to copy the formatting from one section of text to others.

1. Open Student File wddoit3-8.doc and save it as Report8.doc. Notice that the title is formatted as 12-point Arial Black, while the rest of the text is 11-point Arial Narrow.

2. Select the first question, Question—What is the Internet? Click the Font arrow and select Arial. Click the Font Size arrow and select 12. Click **B** ; click ▤ . Click the arrow on the ▦▾ button, and click ▢ in the box that appears (see Figure 3-18). This action will apply a border around the line, margin to margin . With the first question still highlighted, click 🖋 . (The mouse pointer will change to a 🖌 when dragged onto the white document area.)

3. Move the insertion point to the left edge of your screen into the Selection bar so it changes to ↗ . Place the mouse pointer at the same level as the second question, which begins Question—How does the Internet.... Click the mouse button. Notice that the formatting of the first question applies itself to the second.

4. With the second question still highlighted, click 🖋 . Move the insertion point into the Selection Bar so it again changes to a mouse pointer. Place the mouse pointer at the same level as the third question, and click the mouse. The formatting of the first and second questions applies itself to the third. Repeat this formatting process for the fourth question so all the questions are formatted alike.

5. Double-click the word Answer at the beginning of the first answer. Click **B** , and then click **U** . This time, double-click 🖋 .

6. With the Format Painter button highlighted, double-click the word Answer at the beginning of the second, third, and fourth answers. Notice that the formatting of the first word applies itself to the other three words. Click 🖋 , or press [Esc], to deactivate Format Painter. Verify that your document now looks like Figure 3-19.

7. Save and close your document, Report8.doc, with the formatting changes.

more

As shown above, you click once on the Format Painter tool to copy a format to one other area but double-click to copy a format to multiple areas. After formatting those areas, remember to turn off Format Painter or you may format unintended spots. When formatting paragraphs, remember that the paragraph mark, ¶ , shows where you pressed [Enter] to go to a new line. Thus, to copy both text and paragraph formatting to another area, be sure to highlight the whole paragraph and its paragraph mark before activating Format Painter. To copy only text formatting, highlight the paragraph text and final period but stop short of the paragraph mark. (Display or hide the mark by clicking the Show/Hide button ¶ on the Standard toolbar.) Format Painter does have some limitations. It does copy formats such as font style, indents, line spacing, borders, etc. But it cannot convert, for example, plain text to WordArt or vice versa.

Figure 3-18 Outside border selected within Borders button

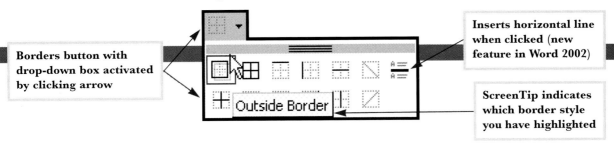

Borders button with drop-down box activated by clicking arrow

Inserts horizontal line when clicked (new feature in Word 2002)

ScreenTip indicates which border style you have highlighted

Figure 3-19 Report8.doc, formatted with Format Painter

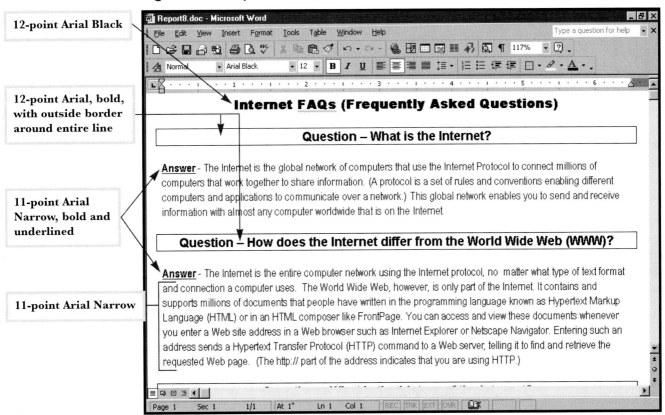

12-point Arial Black

12-point Arial, bold, with outside border around entire line

11-point Arial Narrow, bold and underlined

11-point Arial Narrow

Practice

Open Student File wdprac3-8.doc and save it in your Word Files folder as mywdprac3-8.doc. Following the instructions in the file, practice using Format Painter to copy formatting from one area of a document to another area. When you have completed the practice exercise the second time, resave and close mywdprac3-8.doc with the changes.

skill | Checking Spelling and Grammar

concept

In default mode Word automatically checks a document's spelling and grammar. Basing decisions on a built-in dictionary and grammar checking program, Word then marks with wavy colored lines any words and phrases that Word does not recognize as correct. Using pop-up menus or the Spelling and Grammar feature on the Tools menu, you then can identify possible corrections to suspected errors and, if you desire, make appropriate changes. To complete this Skill, be sure the Check spelling as you type, Check grammar as you type, and Check grammar with spelling features are active in Word. To access these features, click the Tools menu, then the Options command, and then click the Spelling & Grammar tab to bring it to the front of the dialog box.

do it !

Check a document for spelling and grammar errors, and then correct them.

1. Open Student File wddoit3-9.doc and save it in your Word Files folder as Report9.doc. This is a sample paragraph with several spelling and grammar errors in it. ⬭ Spelling errors (and correct spellings that Word's dictionary does not recognize) appear with a wavy red line under them. Grammatical errors appear with a wavy green line under them. So will grammatical constructions (such as passive verb forms) that are correct but that the grammar checker does not prefer.

2. Right-click the first word in the paragraph that is underlined with a wavy red line, processer. A pop-up menu appears with several suggested correct spellings. Move the mouse pointer over the first choice, processor (see Figure 3-20). To accept the correct spelling, click the mouse button. Word replaces the misspelled word with the selected correction.

3. Click Tools, then click Spelling and Grammar to open the Spelling and Grammar dialog box (see Figure 3-21). The next error will be highlighted in the upper area of the dialog box, and several suggestions for replacing it will appear in the Suggestions box in the lower area.

4. Select the correct word in the Suggestions box, grammar, and click [Change All] to correct all occurrences of this spelling mistake throughout the document. Word then highlights the accidentally repeated word in the phrase you you.

5. Click [Delete] that appears in place of the Change button. The second you disappears. Word now highlights the possessive form Word's. ⬭ Since inanimate (non-living) items such as computer software usually do not use the possessive form, the grammar checker highlights this construction.

6. Click [Ignore Once] to ignore this unusual construction. Word now detects a grammatical error, noting that the plural verb provide does not agree in number with the singular subject it.

7. Click [Change] to change the highlighted word to provides, thereby creating grammatical agreement between the subject and verb and clarifying the meaning of the sentence. Next, the Spelling and Grammar checker highlights a proper name that it does not recognize.

(continued on WD 3.20)

Word 2002

Figure 3-20 Automatic spell checking in a pop-up window

Click to open Spelling and Grammar dialog box from the Standard toolbar

Right-click a flagged word to open a shortcut menu of correction choices

Spell checking shortcut window with preferred correction highlighted with mouse pointer

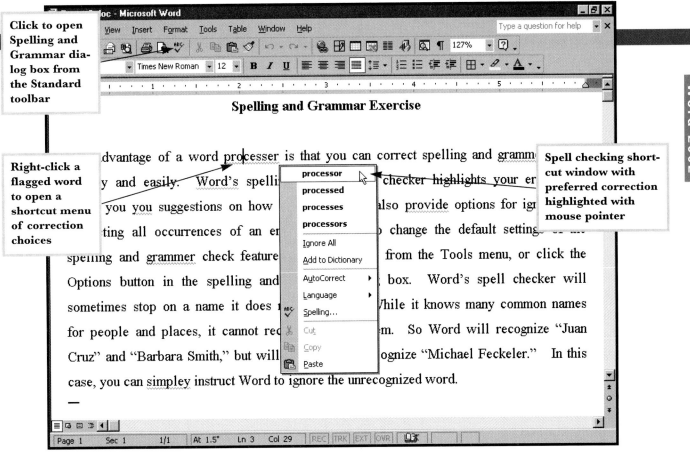

Figure 3-21 Spelling and Grammar dialog box

Spelling error highlighted in red

Suggested spellings for incorrect word

Turns grammar checking on or off

Go to Spelling & Grammar tab of Options dialog box

Click to ignore an entry only once

Click to ignore all entries throughout document

Add highlighted word to the selected dictionary

Replace the highlighted word with the selected suggestion

Replace all instances of the highlighted word with the selected suggestion

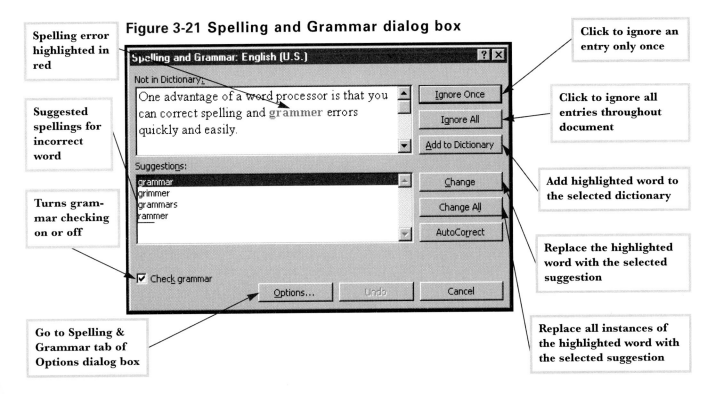

skill Checking Spelling and Grammar (continued)

do it !

8. Click [Ignore Once] to ignore the selected name, which is spelled correctly even though Word does not recognize it. Word now highlights the misspelled word, simpley.

9. Click [Change]. Word replaces simpley with the correct spelling, simply, and the Spelling and Grammar dialog box disappears. It is replaced with a small Microsoft Word message box notifying you that the spelling and grammar check is complete. To close the message box, click [OK].

10. Compare your corrected document with Figure 3-22. Correct any spelling or grammar errors that you may have missed.

11. Save and close your document, Report9.doc, with the corrections you have made.

more

As noted above, when the spelling checker comes across a word it does not recognize, it compares that word with similarly spelled words in its dictionary and marks it with a wavy red underline. These words are not based on an analysis of the sentence's meaning. Some words, even though spelled like the unrecognized word, will make no sense in the context of a corrected sentence. In the end, therefore, you must choose corrections carefully so they have not only the right spelling but also the correct meaning for your document.

The first section of the shortcut menu allowed you to select one word from a longer list of correctly spelled words resembling the word you clicked on. The second section allows you to ignore all instances of correctly spelled words (or to add correctly spelled words that you often use) that do not appear in Word's dictionary. The third section provides access to three features (a) AutoCorrect, which you will study in the next skill, (b) the Language dialog box, which permits use of dictionaries in over 200 languages or dialects other than American English (providing you have installed the required language pack) and (c) the Spelling dialog box. The fourth section allows you to cut, copy, and paste the right-clicked word.

Just as the Change All button in the Spelling and Grammar dialog box corrects all further instances of a selected word, so also the Ignore All button tells Word to skip all further instances. Word also takes capitalization into account when checking spelling. So if you told the program to ignore Interpenetrability, for example, it would still stop on interpenetrability if the lowercase form appeared in the document. Moreover, different copies of Word may recognize different words because users can add words permanently to Word's custom dictionary, a document that is unique to each copy of the program. Suppose, lastly, that the spell checker highlights a word it does not recognize but that you know is spelled correctly. By clicking [Add] in the Spelling and Grammar dialog box, you will add the word to the custom dictionary, which will not question the word again.

The grammar checker is a "natural language" tool and has the advantage that it identifies possible errors in the overall context of your document. But even a powerful word processing program such as Word has only so much computer code and operates on computers with finite amounts of power and memory. Therefore, the grammar checker cannot find all possible grammatical errors, only the most common ones.

To make Word more flexible, however, you can adjust some ways in which the program checks for errors. On the Spelling and Grammar tab of the Options command in Tools, for example, you can set preferences for which dictionaries to use, for checking words in all capital letters or words containing numbers, for checking Internet addresses, and for how formal a writing style you wish to enforce (see Figure 3-22).

Figure 3-22 Report9.doc, corrected version

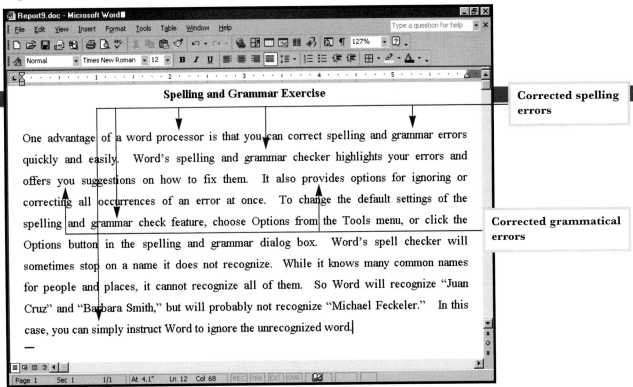

Corrected spelling errors

Corrected grammatical errors

Figure 3-23 Spelling and Grammar tab of Options dialog box

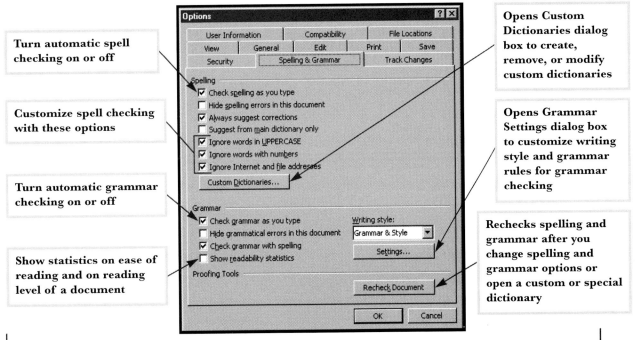

Turn automatic spell checking on or off

Customize spell checking with these options

Turn automatic grammar checking on or off

Show statistics on ease of reading and on reading level of a document

Opens Custom Dictionaries dialog box to create, remove, or modify custom dictionaries

Opens Grammar Settings dialog box to customize writing style and grammar rules for grammar checking

Rechecks spelling and grammar after you change spelling and grammar options or open a custom or special dictionary

Practice

Open Student File wdprac3-9.doc and save it in your Word Files folder as mywdprac3-9.doc. Follow the instructions at the top of the first page to practice spell checking the report. Remember—Word sometimes marks words as errors because the Spell Check dictionary does not recognize them. Examine each marked item carefully before making a change. Resave and close the document, mywdprac3-9.doc, after the changes.

skill   Using AutoCorrect

concept

Word's AutoCorrect feature automatically detects and corrects frequently misspelled words, incorrect capitalizations, and other common typographic errors. For example, if you type abbout and then a space, the feature converts the misspelling to about. AutoCorrect converts certain characters and character combinations into symbols that represent them better (for example, (c) becomes ©). A new feature in Word 2002 even detects a misplaced letter, as in I like thi sfood. When you type a space after the second misspelled word, this feature will shift the incorrectly placed letter to its proper place to create the correct phrase, I like this food. AutoCorrect's default list of corrections includes many other fixes and enables you to add entries easily. The combined features of AutoCorrect help save users lots of retyping and, therefore, lots of time.

do it !

Set AutoCorrect to fix a common typing mistake and explore AutoCorrect's other features.

1. Open a new blank document by clicking ⬜ on the Standard toolbar.

2. Click Tools, and then click AutoCorrect Options. The AutoCorrect dialog box opens to the AutoCorrect tab. An insertion point appears in the Replace box.

3. In the Replace box, type the word corect, misspelling it intentionally. Press [Tab] to move the insertion point to the With box, and type the word correct (see Figure 3-24). To accept the change and close the dialog box, click [OK]. The blank document that you opened in Step 1 now should be in the active window. ◣ Word now will replace corect with correct in any document. However, if you cannot enter the misspelled and properly spelled words, determine if you are running Word 2002 from a network. If you are, the networked program may have security precautions preventing you from adding entries. If so, skip to Step 5.

4. Type the following sentence exactly as it appears: Word will now corect mistakes that i make. Notice that as you typed the sentence, Word fixed the misspelled word corect and automatically capitalized the personal pronoun i.

5. Press [Space] after the previous sentence, and then type the word many (lowercase, as shown) followed by a space. Word recognizes many as the first word of a new sentence because the word is preceded by a period and a space and, therefore, capitalizes it.

6. After the capitalized Many, type misc. mistakes are fixed automatically. Notice that although you typed a period and a space after misc., the word mistakes did not capitalize. This is because misc. is on AutoCorrect's Exceptions list along with most other common abbreviations. ◣ To see the list of exceptions, click Tools, click AutoCorrect Options, be sure the AutoCorrect tab is showing, and click [Exceptions...] to open the AutoCorrect Exceptions dialog box (see Figure 3-25).

(continued on WD 3.24)

Figure 3-24 AutoCorrect dialog box, with added correction

Turns AutoCorrect option buttons ("Smart Tags") on or off (new feature in Word 2002)

Corrects capitalization of words and turns off Caps Lock key if left on accidentally

Turns automatic correction and replacement of type on or off

Type common mis-spelling here

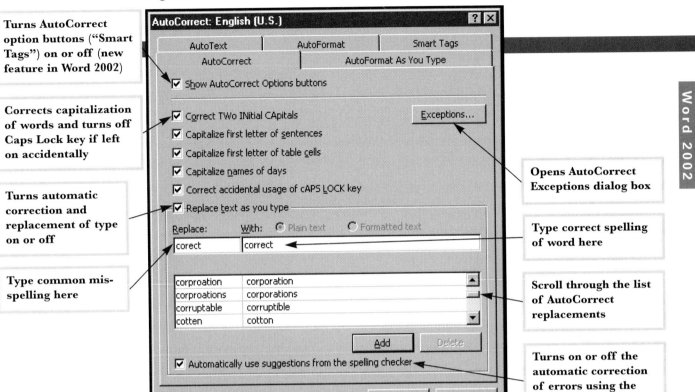

Opens AutoCorrect Exceptions dialog box

Type correct spelling of word here

Scroll through the list of AutoCorrect replacements

Turns on or off the automatic correction of errors using the spell check dictionary

Figure 3-25 AutoCorrect Exceptions dialog box

Add abbreviations here after which Word will not automatically capitalize the next word

Turn on or off the ability to add words automatically to list of AutoCorrect exceptions

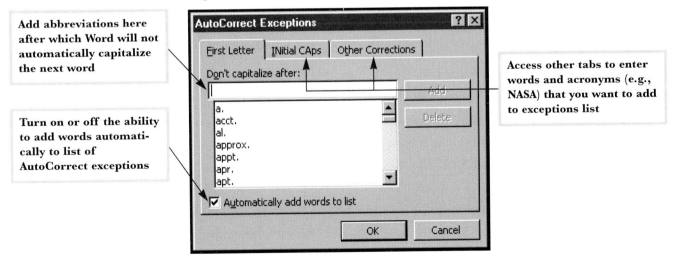

Access other tabs to enter words and acronyms (e.g., NASA) that you want to add to exceptions list

skill | Using AutoCorrect (continued)

do it !

7. Press [Space] after the previous sentence. Then type the following sentence exactly as it appears: Somem istakes are more obvious than others. Notice that as you typed the space after the letters istakes, Word shifted the misplaced letter m from the end of the word Some to the beginning of the group of letters. Press [Space] again.

8. Type the following sentence exactly as it appears: This is *bold* text, and this is _italic_ text. (In other words, type an asterisk [*] immediately before and after the word bold, and type an underscore [_] immediately before and after the word italic.) Notice that the word bold and the word italic change styles as you type. ◀▬▬▶ If these changes do not occur, click Tools, click AutoCorrect Options, and click the AutoFormat As You Type tab to bring it forward, if necessary. On this tab use a mouse click to place a check mark in the box for the option Bold and Italic with real formatting (see Figure 3-26). Close the dialog box by clicking [OK], and then retype the sentence.

9. Compare your corrected document with Figure 3-27, and then close the document. Unless directed otherwise by your instructor, do not save any changes.

more

The nine steps above expose you to several key tools in AutoCorrect, but this powerful and flexible feature can make many more types of corrections. For example, if you accidentally start a word with two capital letters, AutoCorrect will convert the second letter to lowercase. As part of its AutoFormat feature, AutoCorrect will convert the straight-styled quotation marks that were common on typewriters and early word processors (and which still can appear in Word 2002 to slightly curled marks (e.g., "La Tour Eiffel").

You can increase AutoCorrect's power and flexibility in at least three different ways. First, as you already know from Step 3 above, you can add your own common misspellings and related corrections on the AutoCorrect tab of the AutoCorrect dialog box. Second, as Figures 3-24 and 3-25 show, you can use the AutoCorrect Exceptions dialog box to add entries to its abbreviations list. Once you close the dialog box, Word will recognize the period and space after any new entries, and not capitalize the next word. (If you work in a field that uses many abbreviations, the Exceptions list will come in handy.) Third, on either AutoFormat tab in the AutoCorrect dialog box, you can turn on more correction features as your typing needs require.

If, on the other hand, you do not need all of the power that AutoCorrect provides, you can turn off some or all of its features. For example, to get rid of an entry that you do not want, select the entry on the proper list in the AutoCorrect dialog box and click [Delete]. If you are working in a computer lab or similar place where you share computers, do not delete any AutoCorrect entries that you did not add.

Smart Tags deserve special mention here because the Smart Tags tab appears in the AutoCorrect dialog box and these tags are a new feature in Word 2002 and other Office XP programs. Smart Tags are associated with various kinds of data but are not data themselves. Instead, these tags are a set of markers that appear with data you can manipulate. With Smart Tags enabled in your copy of Word, they will identify data with Smart Tag Indicators. A purple dotted line will appear under names, addresses, dates, and similar items. A small blue rectangle will appear under the beginning of Internet or e-mail addresses.

To use a Smart Tag, slide your insertion point over the indicator so a Smart Tag Actions button appears. As you click the button, a menu will appear with a list of tasks, or actions, you can perform with the data. Clicking on a name will enable you to use Microsoft Outlook to send mail, schedule meetings, and perform similar tasks. Clicking on an address will enable you to add it to your Outlook contacts, find the address on a map at www.expedia.com, and so on. The whole idea behind Smart Tags is to provide seamless, barrier-free interaction between the Office XP program you are using and many other programs, while reducing the need to move your mouse all over the screen. (For more information on Smart Tags, click [?], click the Contents tab, expand the purple Microsoft Word Help booklet, expand the Smart Tags booklet, and click on the desired topic.)

Figure 3-26 AutoFormat As You Type tab in AutoCorrect dialog box

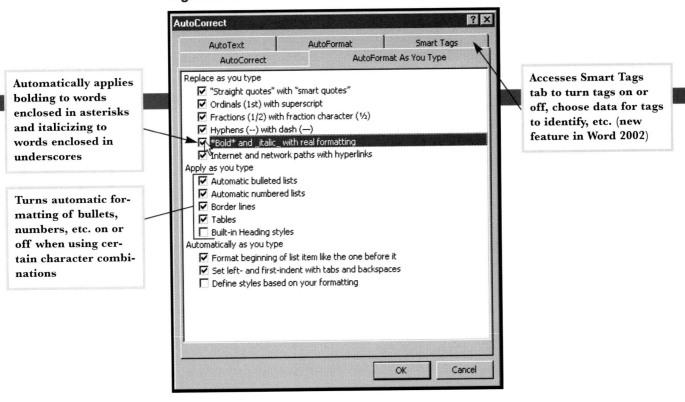

Automatically applies bolding to words enclosed in asterisks and italicizing to words enclosed in underscores

Accesses Smart Tags tab to turn tags on or off, choose data for tags to identify, etc. (new feature in Word 2002)

Turns automatic formatting of bullets, numbers, etc. on or off when using certain character combinations

Word 2002

Figure 3-27 Opened document with AutoCorrections

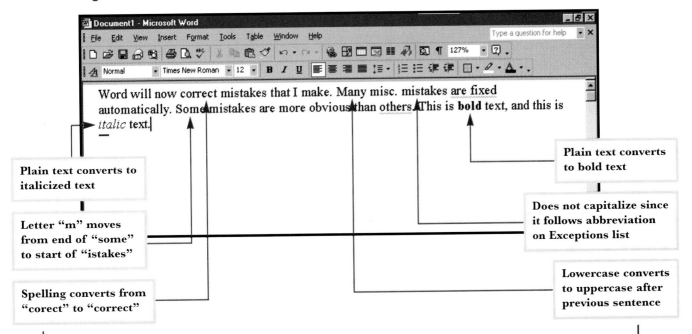

Plain text converts to italicized text

Letter "m" moves from end of "some" to start of "istakes"

Spelling converts from "corect" to "correct"

Plain text converts to bold text

Does not capitalize since it follows abbreviation on Exceptions list

Lowercase converts to uppercase after previous sentence

Practice

Open Student File wdprac3-10.doc and save it in your Word Files folder as mywdprac3-10.doc. Following the instructions at the beginning of the file, practice using Word's AutoCorrect feature. When finished typing, resave the file, mywdprac3-10.doc, and then close it.

skill

Inserting Frequently Used Text

concept

If you are like most people, you probably type a wide variety of documents for various subjects. However, you sometimes may have to type unusual, long, or complicated words or phrases over and over or use words that regularly appear in standard documents. When inserting frequently-used text in these latter situations, use Word's AutoCorrect feature to save time and effort. Also use the AutoText feature, which recognizes many words and phrases as you start typing them, predicts their outcomes in a ScreenTip, and then offers to complete them for you. For example, if you type Dear M, Word will suggest the AutoText Dear Mom and Dad. To accept the tip, press [Enter], and Word will insert the remaining text for you. If you do not want to accept the tip, or if the suggestion is incorrect, simply continue typing and the ScreenTip will disappear.

do it !

Use AutoCorrect and the AutoText features to insert frequently used text in a business letter.

1. Click ⬜ to open a new blank document, and save it as Membership.doc.

2. Start typing today's date, starting with the day of the week, not the month. When you have typed the fourth letter of the day, a ScreenTip will appears that spells out the rest of the day. Press [Enter] to accept the completed spelling, and then type a comma. When the second ScreenTip appears to add the month, day, and year, press [Enter] to insert them. Press [Enter] twice again.

3. Type the inside address of the letter as follows:

   Mr. Joseph Kucharsky
   Walton Supermarkets
   7844 Industry Park Drive
   Middletown, NY 11007

4. Press [Enter] twice. Start typing the word certified. The ScreenTip for CERTIFIED MAIL will appear upon typing the letter t. When the ScreenTip appears, press [Enter] again to accept the completed text with its uppercase formatting. Press [Enter] twice.

5. Start typing the salutation of the letter, Dear Mr. Kucharsky and a colon. When you have typed Dear M, a ScreenTip will appear for Dear Mom and Dad. Do not stop typing, and do not backspace. Instead, finish typing Kucharsky's name and the colon. Press [Enter] twice again. So far, your letter should look like Figure 3-28.

6. Click Tools, then click AutoCorrect Options to open the AutoCorrect dialog box with the AutoCorrect tab displayed. In the Replace box, type the letters sm (lowercase letters). In the With box, type SMCSL-NRD (uppercase letters). Click ▭ Add ▭ to add the entry to the scrollable list of AutoCorrect entries. To accept the new entry and close the dialog box, click ▭ OK ▭. Whenever you type the letters sm and a space, Word automatically will convert the letters to SMCSL-NRD. ◣ See Figure 3-24 for a screen shot of the AutoCorrect dialog box.

(continued on WD 3.28)

Figure 3-28 Date, inside address, and salutation of letter

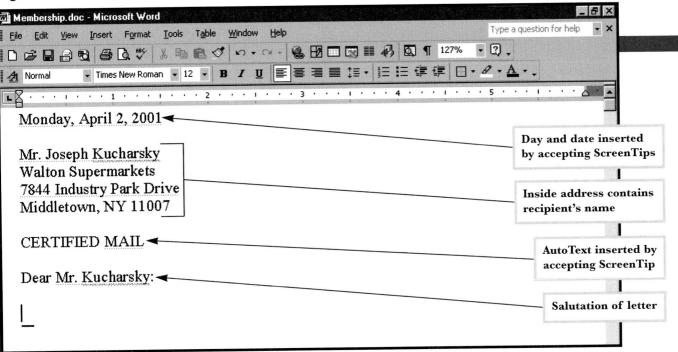

Figure 3-29 Body of letter, membership.doc

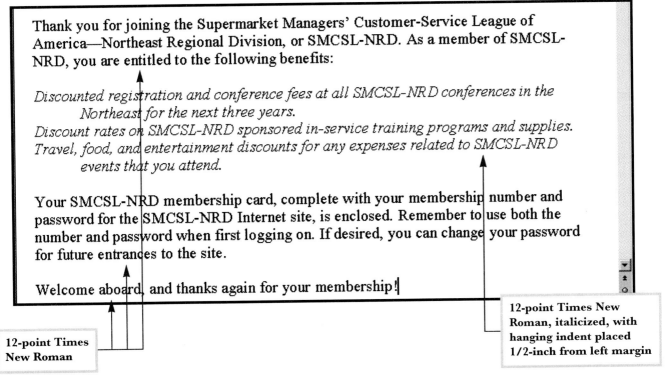

skill Inserting Frequently Used Text (continued)

do it !

7. Type and format the body of the letter as shown in Figure 3-29 (on the previous page). However, instead of typing the capital letters SMCSL-NRD, be sure to type the two lowercase letters sm and a space. Word automatically will change the lowercase letters to the eight capitalized ones. When finished typing all of the text in Figure 3-29, press [Enter] twice.

8. Click the View menu, click the Toolbars command and click AutoText to turn on the Autotext toolbar. Click the All Entries arrow, click the Closing category, and click Sincerely yours, to insert the two words and a comma as a closing (see Figure 3-30). Press [Enter] four times.

9. Type your first and last names as a signature line, and press [Enter]. Type the following text to complete the closing address, remembering to type just the lowercase letters sm and a space in place of the eight capitalized letters:

   SMCSL-NRD Director
   687 Marlboro Blvd.
   Marlboro, MA 02345

10. The closing of your document should look like Figure 3-31. Proofread, re-save, and close the document, Membership.doc.

more

In the Skill above you used the AutoText tab of the AutoCorrect dialog box to insert two pre-existing AutoText entries that might appear often in standard documents such as memos, letters, and the like. Some AutoText entries automatically include data that relates to the document. For example, if the insertion point is on the fourth page of a ten-page document and you insert the AutoText entry Page X of Y, Word will insert Page 4 of 10. You also used the AutoCorrect tab to create a new entry for frequently used text, using the shortened version of the entry to enter its longer version in a document. Just as you used the AutoCorrect tab to create a new entry, so also can you use the AutoText tab to do so (see Figure 3-32). To create an entry, you would type it in the box labeled Enter AutoText entries here. Once you created the entry, it would appear alphabetized in the scrollable box immediately below the labeled box. Additionally, when you clicked on the entry in the scrollable box, the first few lines (if any) of the entry would appear in the Preview box immediately below the scrollable box.

You also can create a new AutoText entry so that it includes graphics as well as text. To do so, begin by typing the entry in a document. Then highlight precisely that part of the entry, including any graphics you created, that you want to store as AutoText. (If you created a paragraph and wanted to include its formatting, be sure to highlight the paragraph mark too.) Next, click Insert, click AutoText, and then click New to open the Create AutoText dialog box. In this dialog box either accept the entry name that appears in the box labeled Please name your AutoText entry or type a new name. To accept the new entry and close the dialog box, press [Enter] or click OK .

Once you close the dialog box, you can access the new entry through either the AutoText toolbar or the AutoText tab in the AutoCorrect dialog box. The name of the new entry appearing on the toolbar or in the dialog box will match the name you gave it in the Create AutoText dialog box. As suggested above, the Preview box of the AutoText tab will display how the AutoText will look in a document, including formatting features such as font style, line spacing, underlining, and so on. However, you can preview only the first few lines, or about 30 to 40 words, of text.

Figure 3-30 AutoText toolbar, "Sincerely yours," option selected

Click and drag here to make toolbar "float" in other areas of screen

All Entries button on AutoText toolbar

Place mouse pointer over desired text and click to place in document

Pre-set categories of AutoText toolbar

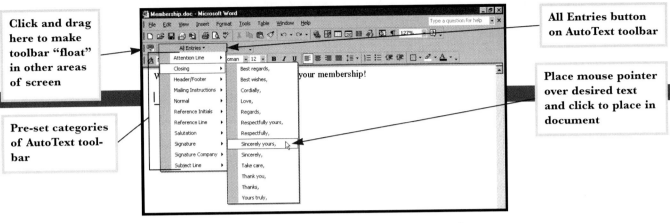

Figure 3-31 Closing of letter, Membership.doc

Type your name on signature line (without brackets)

Closing address of letter

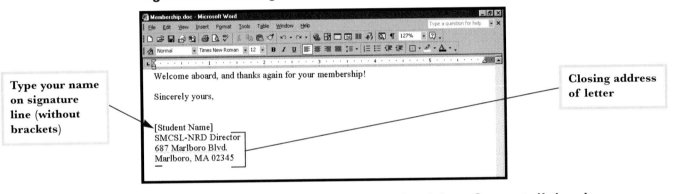

Figure 3-32 AutoText tab of AutoCorrect dialog box

Turns AutoComplete feature on or off

Enter names for AutoText entries here

Scrollable list of default and added AutoText entries

Displays AutoText toolbar and closes this dialog box

Displays the currently selected entry with its current formatting features

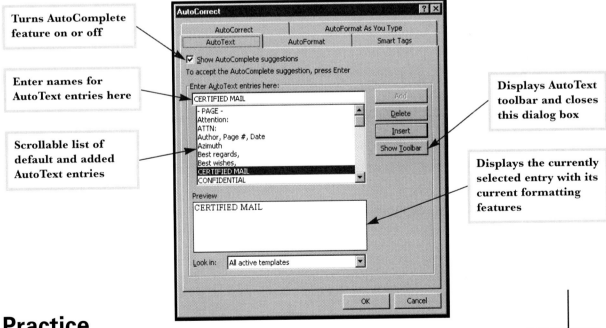

Practice

Open Student File wdprac3-11.doc and save it in your Word Files folder as mywdprac3-11.doc. Following the instructions that appear at the beginning of the file, practice inserting frequently used text based on an entry that you have created in the AutoCorrect dialog box. When you finish typing the paragraph in the file, save it again as mywdprac3-11.doc, and then delete the new entry you created in the dialog box.

skill   Using the Word Thesaurus

concept

Word has a Thesaurus feature, which is a reference tool that supplies you with synonyms (words with similar meanings) and antonyms (words with opposite meanings) for a word that you select in a document. In the Thesaurus dialog box, Word highlights a word that most closely matches the meaning of the word you selected. You then can replace the selected word with the other word, search for even a more precise word to match your desired meaning, or explore the meanings of the antonyms.

do it !

Use the Thesaurus feature to choose a more precise word for a word selected in a document.

1. Open the Student File wddoit3-12.doc and save it in your Word Files folder as Report12.doc.

2. Select or just click on the word hard in the third paragraph, fifth sentence, of the report—the sentence that begins Many telecommuters are not....

3. Click Tools, click Language, and then click Thesaurus to open the Thesaurus dialog box (or press the keyboard shortcut [Shift]+[F7]). The word that you selected will display in the Looked Up box in the upper left area of the dialog box (see Figure 3-33).

4. In the scrollable box immediately below the Replace with Synonym box, click the word inflexible.

5. Click **Look Up** to search for synonyms of inflexible, and click the word rigid that displays in the scrollable list box immediately below the Replace with Synonym box.

6. Click **Replace** to insert the word rigid in place of hard in the report. Save and close your document, Report12.doc, with your change.

more

When the Thesaurus dialog box opens, the Looked up box displays the word or phrase you just selected in a document. If you open the dialog box but have not selected a word, the Looked up box displays the word you most recently looked up. (If your selected word does not match any word in the Thesaurus, the Looked up box changes to a Not found box.) The Meanings box displays synonyms matching the word in the Looked up box. (If Word cannot find any words that seem like proper synonyms, the Meanings box will display, in alphabetic order, just a list of words spelled similarly to the selected word.) The Replace with Synonym box displays either the selected word from the Meanings box or from the scrollable list box immediately below the Replace with Synonym box, whichever you clicked last. The scrollable list box supplies synonyms (and a few antonyms) for the word selected in the Meanings box, just as the Meanings box displays synonyms for the word in the Looked up box. For quick access to synonyms for a word, right-click the word. The shortcut menu that appears will include a Synonyms command that offers suggested synonyms for the word you right-clicked and access to the Thesauraus dialog box.

As you choose the best words to put in your document, or after you have finished all your typing, you may want to know how many words you have typed overall. To do so, you can use the Word Count dialog box (see Figure 3-34) or the Word Count toolbar. (This toolbar, shown in Figure 3-35, is a new feature in Word 2002.). To open the Word Count dialog box, click Tools, and then click Word Count. The Word Count dialog box also displays the number of pages, characters, paragraphs, and lines in your document. To display the Word Count toolbar, you can click **Show Toolbar** in the lower left corner of the Word Count dialog box. Otherwise, you can click View, click Toolbars, and then click Word Count and view the same statistics there. The advantage of the toolbar is that you periodically can click **Recount** as you type to update yourself on the statistics of the active document.

Figure 3-33 Thesaurus dialog box

Displays word or phrase selected in document

Highlight word that best matches meaning of word in Looked Up box; more synonyms will appear in scrollable box to right

Replaces Looked Up word with word highlighted in scrollable box

This word will replace word in Looked Up box

Scroll through choices and click one to place it in Replace with Synonym box

Retrieves list of synonyms for highlighted word in scrollable box

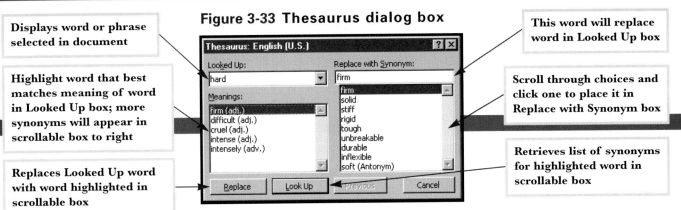

Figure 3-34 Report12.doc, after replacing text

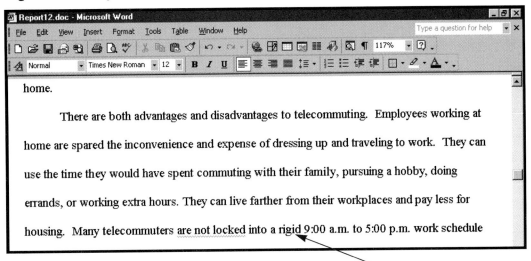

home.

    There are both advantages and disadvantages to telecommuting. Employees working at home are spared the inconvenience and expense of dressing up and traveling to work. They can use the time they would have spent commuting with their family, pursuing a hobby, doing errands, or working extra hours. They can live farther from their workplaces and pay less for housing. Many telecommuters are not locked into a rigid 9:00 a.m. to 5:00 p.m. work schedule

Word from Replace with Synonym box replaces originally selected word

Figure 3-35 Word Count dialog box

Statistics for the active document

Adds footnote and endnote statistics to totals

Displays Word Count toolbar

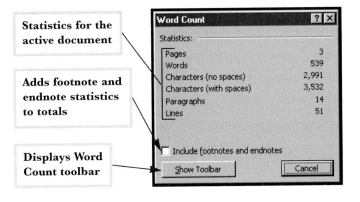

Figure 3-36 Word Count toolbar

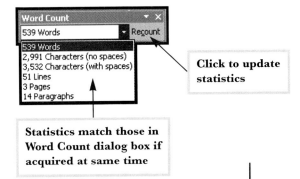

Click to update statistics

Statistics match those in Word Count dialog box if acquired at same time

Practice

Open Student File wdprac3-12.doc and save it in your Word Files folder as mywdprac3-12.doc. Following the instructions at the beginning of the file, practice using the Thesaurus dialog box to find more precise words for the ones that are identified in the practice file. When you have completed the practice exercise, resave and close mywdprac3-12.doc.

skill  Finding and Replacing Text

concept

The Find command enables you to search a document for individual occurrences of any word, phrase, or other unit of text. The Replace command enables you to replace one or all occurrences of a word that you have found. Together, the Find and Replace commands form powerful editing tools for making many extensive changes in just seconds.

do it !

Use Find and Replace to spell a word consistently throughout a document.

1. Open Student File wddoit3-13.doc and save it in your Word Files folder as Report13.doc.

2. If necessary, place the insertion point at the beginning of the document. Word will search the document from the insertion point forward.

3. Click Edit, and then click Replace. The Find and Replace dialog box appears with the Replace tab in front and the insertion point in the Find What text box.

4. In the Find What box, type the two words per cent. Click in the Replace With box, and type the one word percent (see Figure 3-37).

5. Click Replace All to search the document for all instances of per cent and to replace them with percent. A message box appears to display the results. In this case, one replacement was made (see Figure 3-38).   In short documents the Find and Replace procedure takes so little time that you usually cannot cancel it before it ends. However, in longer documents you can cancel a search in progress by pressing [Esc].

6. Click OK to close the message box. Click Close to close the Find and Replace dialog box.

7. Save and close the document, Report13.doc, with your change.

more

Clicking the Replace All button in the Find and Replace dialog box replaces every instance of the text you have placed in the Find What box. To examine and replace a word or phrase manually instead of automatically, start by clicking the Find Next button. If you desire to replace that instance, click the Replace button. Continue checking the document like this, clicking the Find Next button and then, if desired, the Replace button. Keep clicking the pairs of buttons until you have run through the entire document. Unless you absolutely must do otherwise, use this method for shorter documents only.

The first button under the Replace With box usually displays the word More. Click this button when you want to display the Search Options area of the dialog box. With the area displayed, the More button converts to a Less button. Clicking on the Less button will hide the Search Options area. The Search drop-down list under Search Options determines the direction of the search relative to the insertion point. You can search upward or downward through the document or keep the Word default setting of All to check the whole document, including headers, footers, and footnotes. The Format drop-down list enables you to include search criteria for fonts, paragraphs, tabs, and similar items. The Special drop-down list enables you to search for paragraph marks, tab characters, column breaks and related special characters. The No Formatting button removes all formatting criteria from searches. For information on the Search Option activated by the check boxes, consult Table 3-3.

The Find tab of the Find and Replace dialog box matches the Replace tab except it lacks the replace function and only searches documents for items that you specify.

Figure 3-37 Find and Replace dialog box

Enter the word or phrase to search for and replace here

Enter the replacement word here

Use check boxes to activate search options

Click to determine direction of search

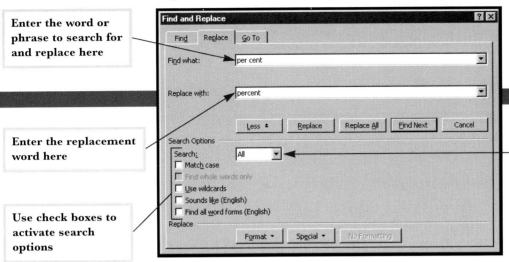

Figure 3-38 Report13.doc, after Find and Replace activity

Find and Replace makes one change in document

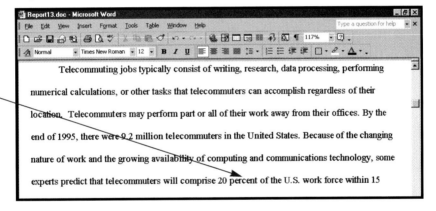

Telecommuting jobs typically consist of writing, research, data processing, performing numerical calculations, or other tasks that telecommuters can accomplish regardless of their location. Telecommuters may perform part or all of their work away from their offices. By the end of 1995, there were 9.2 million telecommuters in the United States. Because of the changing nature of work and the growing availability of computing and communications technology, some experts predict that telecommuters will comprise 20 percent of the U.S. work force within 15

Table 3-3 Search Options

Option	Description
Match case	Finds those items in capitals and/or lowercase that exactly match contents of Find What box
Find whole words only	Finds only those items that are whole words, not parts of a larger word
Use wildcards	Searches for wildcards, special characters, or special search operators found in Find What box
Sounds like	Finds words that sound the same as in Find What box but are spelled differently
Find all word forms	Replaces all forms of the text in Find What box with proper forms of the word in the Replace with box; words in both boxes should be the same part of speech

Practice

Open Student File wdprac3-13.doc and save it in your Word Files folder as mywdprac3-13.doc. Following the instructions that appear at the beginning of the file, practice using the Find and Replace dialog box to search for and replace text. When you have completed the practice exercise, resave and close mywdprac3-13.doc.

shortcuts

Function	Button/Mouse	Menu	Keyboard	
Adjust margins		Click File, then click Page Setup		
Indent selected paragraph[s]	Click and drag indent markers on the Horizontal toolbar	Click Format, then click Paragraph, then click the Indents and Spacing tab, then click Special box	[Ctrl]+[M] [Ctrl]+[T]	(Entire) (Hanging)
Adjust Line Spacing of selected paragraph[s]		Click Format, then click Paragraph, then click the Indents and Spacing tab, then click Line spacing box	[Ctrl]+[1] [Ctrl]+[2] [Ctrl]+[5]	(Single) (Double) (1.5)
Go to the next window (when working with multiple documents)	Click on the part of the next window that is showing, if the active window is not maximized	Click Window, then click the name of the next document	[Ctrl]+[F6]	
Go to the previous window (when working with multiple documents)	Click on the part of the previous window that is showing, if the active window is not maximized	Click Window, then click the name of the previous document	[Ctrl]+[Shift]+[F6]	
Use Format Painter	🖌		[Ctrl]+[Shift]+[C]	
Check for spelling and grammar errors	✓	Click Tools, then click Spelling and Grammar	[F7]	
Find next misspelling (with Automatic Spell Checking active)	Scroll down in the document to the next word with a wavy red underline		[Alt]+[F7]	
Find next grammatical error (with Automatic Grammar Checking active)	Scroll down in the document to the next word with a wavy green underline		[Alt]+[F7]	
Insert new AutoText		Click Insert, then click AutoText, then click New	[Alt]+[F3]	
Open the Word Thesaurus	Right-click a word, then point to Synonyms on the pop-up menu	Click Tools, then click Language, then click Thesaurus	[Shift]+[F7]	

A. Identify Key Features

Name the items indicated by callouts in Figure 3-39.

Figure 3-39 Identifying formatting and editing concepts

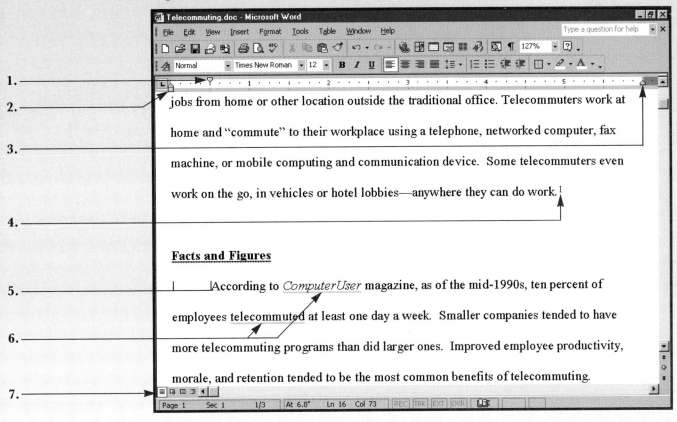

1.
2.
3.
4.
5.
6.
7.

B. Select the Best Answer

8. Objects that slide along the horizontal ruler and determine text placement

9. A Word feature that fixes common typographic mistakes as they are made

10. Markers that recognize and label data that the markers can manipulate

11. Displays the number of words, characters, paragraphs, etc. in your document

12. The invisible line marking the boundary between text and the edge of a page

13. A feature that finds synonyms and antonyms for a selected word or phrase

14. The window where footnotes and endnotes appear while in Normal view

a. Thesaurus

b. Indent markers

c. Notes pane

d. Margin

e. Word Count dialog box

f. Smart Tags

g. AutoCorrect

quiz (continued)

C. Complete the Statement

15. Document-level formatting includes:

   a. Indents

   b. Fonts

   c. Margins

   d. Footnotes

16. When a page has no more room for text and you then enter more text, Word automatically creates a:

   a. New document based on the Normal template

   b. Manual page break

   c. Drop-down list

   d. Soft page break

17. A note reference mark is:

   a. A mark in the text referring to a footnote or endnote

   b. Another name for a tab stop

   c. Text that has been highlighted

   d. An encyclopedia on floppy disk or CD-ROM

18. AutoCorrect fixes spelling mistakes when you press [Enter], enter a punctuation mark, or

   a. Press the space bar

   b. Save the document

   c. Turn on Automatic Spell Checking

   d. Access the Spelling/Thesaurus toolbar

19. Paragraph-level formatting includes:

   a. Page numbers

   b. Headers and footers

   c. Italics

   d. Line spacing

20. To view page numbers, switch to:

   a. Normal view

   b. Print Layout view

   c. Full Screen view

   d. Mirror margins

21. One way to copy text from one document to another is to:

   a. Set up File Sharing on the Control Panel

   b. Click while pressing [F11]

   c. Use the Clipboard

   d. Use the Style Gallery

22. The ⬚ button:

   a. Adds color to all black text

   b. Copies formatting from one area to another

   c. Pastes Clipboard contents into a document

   d. Displays or hides the Drawing toolbar

23. To leave the first line of a paragraph against the left margin while indenting all of its other lines, apply a:

   a. Dangling indent

   b. First-line indent

   c. Tabbing indent

   d. Hanging indent

24. The AutoCorrect dialog box does **not** contain:

   a. The AutoCorrect tab

   b. The AutoRepair tab

   c. The AutoFormat tab

   d. The Smart Tags tab

interactivity

Build Your Skills

1. Open a document and format it.

   a. Open the student file, wdskills3.doc, and save it to your student disk as Huntly1.doc.

   b. Open the Page Setup dialog box on the File menu.

   c. Set the left and right margins at 1 inch. Insert page numbers at the bottom center of the page.

2. Apply indents to the document, change the line spacing, and insert a footnote:

   a. Select all of the text in the document below the title.

   b. From the Paragraph dialog box on the Format menu, apply a first line indent of .5 inches and change the line spacing to double.

   c. Insert a footnote after (43) in paragraph 2, line 5 of the document. The footnote should read All quotes refer to the revised 1862 edition of the book.

3. Adjust the alignment and text formatting of the document:

   a. Select all of the text in the document below the title and justify it. Select the title and center it.

   b. Add bold formatting to the student author's name and to the title of the paper.

   c. Re-save the document, but do not close it.

4. Open another document and copy text from it into the original document:

   a. Open the student file wdskills3a.doc and select the paragraph it contains. It is the conclusion to the paper used above.

   b. Copy the selected paragraph to the Clipboard.

   c. Close student file, wdskills3a.doc, bringing back Huntly1.doc as the active window.

   d. Place the insertion point at the very end of the document.

   e. Paste the copied paragraph onto the end of the paper, being sure it begins on a new line as a new paragraph.

5. Use the Format Painter to change the formatting of the inserted paragraph to match the rest of the document:

   a. Select the next-to-last paragraph in the document by triple-clicking it.

   b. Click the Format Painter button to copy the formatting of the selected paragraph.

   c. Drag the I-beam (which now has a paintbrush icon next to it) across the last paragraph in the document to select it and match its formatting with that of the previous paragraph.

   d. Click once in the paragraph to deselect it.

interactivity (continued)

Build Your Skills

6. Check for spelling errors and replace all instances of one word with another.

   a. Click the Tools menu, then click Spelling and Grammar to open the Spelling and Grammar dialog box. Clear the Check grammar check box so you will check for only spelling errors.

   b. Correct the three misspelled words in the document, ignoring names and unusual words.

   c. Click Edit, then click Replace to open the Find and Replace dialog box.

   d. Use the Replace all command to replace all instances of Browne with the correct name, Brown.

   e. Close the dialog box, and save the document as Huntly2.doc, and close it.

7. Add a spelling correction and an entry for frequently used text using the AutoCorrect tab of the AutoCorrect dialog box.

   a. Open a new, blank document, and open the AutoCorrect dialog box.

   b. Use the Replace and With boxes on the AutoCorrect tab to instruct Word to replace instances of clcik with click. On the same tab, instruct Word to replace the shortened text rd with the longer entry Rough Draft.

   d. Close the dialog box, and type the following sentence exactly as it appears: Use a mouse clcik to open rd files, and use the same mouse clcik to close the rd files. Verify that your two new AutoCorrect entries converted to correctly spelled text.

   e. Return to the AutoCorrect tab, delete the two entries you created, and close the dialog box.

   f. Save the one-sentence file to your student disk as autocorrect.doc. Close the file.

Problem Solving Exercises

1. Using the skills you learned in Lesson 3, open the student file, wdproblem3-1.doc, and save it as custom.doc. Change the left and right margins to 1.25 inches. For all text below the title, apply a first-line indent of .5 inches, and change the line spacing to 1.5. Add page numbers to the top, center area of the pages, starting on page 1. Center and boldface the title, and justify the main body text of the document. Insert three footnotes into the paper. (The text of the footnotes appears in the student file wdproblem3-1a.doc.) Insert the first footnote at the end of the third paragraph, following the period after the word products. Insert the second footnote at the end of the fourth paragraph, following the period after the word inventory. Insert the third footnote at the end of the sixth paragraph, after the period after the word line. Open Spell Checking and correct all misspellings in the document. Add your name, your instructor's name, and the due date at the top, left side of page 1, observing the same revised line spacing as in the body of the document. Re-save the document, custom.doc, and close the file.

2. You are applying for a position as either a movie reviewer or restaurant critic, and you want to practice your reviewing skills before your interview. Review either your three favorite movies or three favorite fast-food restaurants in a three-paragraph, one-page document, and save the document as reviews.doc. Set up the document with 1 inch margins on all sides. After you enter all of your text, insert a Continuous Section break between the first and second, and between the second and third paragraphs. Format the first paragraph with 12-point, italicized Times New Roman text and a .5-inch, hanging indent. Format the second paragraph with 11-point Arial text and a .5-inch, first-line indent. Format the third paragraph exactly as the first. At the top, left side of page 1, add your name, instructor's name, and due date. Also add a centered title. Double-space after the due date and after the title, but keep all other line spacing at single spacing. Re-save the document, reviews.doc, and close the file.

interactivity (continued)

Problem Solving Exercises (continued)

3. Open the file wdproblem3-3.doc and save it as Westerner.doc. On the first line of the document, replace the words [Student Name] with your own name. Replace the default date of the document with the due date of this assignment. Eliminate the double-spacing between paragraphs and indent each paragraph instead with a first-line indent. Change the whole document to double-spacing. Add a page number to the bottom center of only page 2. Find and replace all instances of Lindberg with Lindbergh. Correct the spelling of the four remaining misspelled words. Save the changes you have made to the document, print it, and close the file.

4. Open the file wdproblem3-4.doc and save it as Handout.doc. Reformat the document so it resembles the one that appears below in Figure 3-40. This reformatting will involve changing the margins, centering some text, justifying other text, changing the font sizes of the sections, and adding a footnote. The footnote should say For information, contact Beatrice Jones, Head Librarian of the Slattery Public Library at 515-555-5445 during normal library hours. In the footnote, replace the Head Librarian's name with your own first and last names. After reformatting the document, use Find and Replace to change all occurrences of Slatery to Slattery and all occurrences of Libary to Library. Save the changes you have made to the document, verify that it looks like the document below, and then print and close and the file.

Figure 3-40 Identifying formatting and editing concepts

Monday, January 1, 2002
Tuesday, January 2, 2002

Slattery Public Library
125 Division Street, Slattery, TX

Come one, come all to the
FIFTH ANNUAL
Slattery Public Library Book Sale

The Library sale will include over 10,000 (count 'em, 10,000) used hardback and paperback books, starting as low as 50 cents for paperbacks and one dollar for hardbacks. A specialized mix of antiquarian, rare, and first-edition books will be sold under a written bid system, with ties on pricing going to the earliest bidder. The Library's rare book consultant will be on site on Friday evening only to verify the authenticity and condition of these special books.

All proceeds from the sale will go to the Library's Redding Fund for Literacy Training and the Slattery Memorial Development Fund for the new children's wing, to start construction early next year. Persons wishing to make tax-deductible donations to either fund may do so at any time during the book sale. Cash and check will be accepted. (Persons donating cash will receive a written receipt from the Library treasurer on the spot.)

Persons wishing to make book donations for this sale also will receive a tax deduction for a portion of the purchase price of the book, depending on condition and estimated popularity of the item.

---

[1] For more information, contact Beatrice Jones, Head Librarian of the Slattery Public Library at 515-555-5445 during normal business hours.

Tables and Charts

To present information in a document in an organized and easily understood fashion, you often can structure your data in the form of a table or chart. Word makes it easy to create, modify, and format tables in its documents. Word enables you to perform many of the more complex tasks associated with tables, such as calculating and sorting, that computer users often find only in dedicated worksheet programs.

Word can create blank tables into which you enter data, or you can transform existing data directly into table form. Once you have created a table, you quickly can insert or delete data as needed or reorganize it to communicate your point more efficiently and effectively.

Sometimes, your tables may contain so much data or textual information that readers may have trouble gleaning important facts or trends from them. In these cases you would do well to present the data in graphic form via a chart so readers will be able to grasp more readily the significance of your data. Fortunately, just as Word has the features you need to create helpful tables, the program has the features it takes to create, modify, and format charts with relative ease and efficiency.

Lesson Goal:

You will open a file that will benefit from the presence of a table, create and modify that table, and learn various ways to format the table. You will learn how to create a chart based on a table, modify and format it, and insert it in a report. You also will learn an alternate way to create tables and format them for ease of reading and attractiveness.

skills

* **Inserting and Modifying a Table**
* **Editing Tables**
* **Inserting and Deleting Rows, Columns, and Cells**
* **Sorting Data in a Table**
* **Calculating Data in a Table**
* **Formatting a Table**
* **Creating a Chart**
* **Editing a Chart**
* **Drawing a Table**
* **Adding Borders and Shading**

skill
Creating and Modifying Tables

concept

A table consists of information organized into horizontal rows and vertical columns. The box created by an intersecting row and column is a cell. You can create a table from scratch or assemble it from existing text. Tables often have row and column headers, which are labels to identify the adjacent data. Data in a table can consist of words (also called labels) or numbers (also called values).

do it !

Insert a table into a pre-existing report to organize information difficult to describe in words.

1. Open Student File wddoit4-1.doc and save it in your Word Files folder as Matthews.doc.

2. Scroll down to the third paragraph, which begins Regarding handicapped people with.... Place the insertion point at the end of the paragraph, after the colon that comes after the word disabilities.

3. Click the Insert Table button 🔲 on the Standard toolbar. A table grid appears, enabling you to select the number of rows and columns that will appear in your table.

4. Gradually move the mouse pointer from the upper left toward the lower right of the grid until you have selected an area of boxes that is two rows deep and four columns wide. The text 2 x 4 Table appears in the rectangular area below the grid to confirm that you have selected the properly sized table (see Figure 4-1).

5. Click the mouse button to insert a table into the report. The table appears on the next line of the document. Black gridlines delineate where the rows and columns are located, end-of-cell marks delineate the end of text in each cell, and end-of-row marks delineate where the last column in a row resides (see Figure 4-2). 🔷 If the cell marks do not appear, turn on the Show/Hide button ¶ on the Standard toolbar.

6. The final table for the report will be single-spaced and have four rows and five columns, but you now have only two double-spaced rows and four columns. The rows are double-spaced because the text into which the table was inserted uses this spacing. Click Table on the Menu bar, highlight the Select command, and then click Table on the Select submenu to select the entire table. Press [Ctrl]+[1] to change the table from double to single spacing.

7. With the entire table still selected, click Table, and then click Split Cells to display the Split Cells dialog box. Since the Number of columns box already is highlighted, just type 5. Press [Tab] to move to the Number of rows box, and press 4 (see Figure 4-3). Be sure that a check mark appears in Merge cells before split check box. Click 🔲 OK 🔲 to close the dialog box and to reformat the table at four rows high by five columns across.

8. The final version of Row 1 will need only three columns, so you must merge some cells. Select the second and third cells in the first row. Click Table, then click Merge Cells. Select the last two cells in the first row, click Table, then click Merge Cells. Row 1 now has three columns, while the remaining three rows have five. Do not worry about the irregular column widths, as you will reformat the columns shortly.

(continued on WD 4.4)

Figure 4-1 Using the Insert Table button

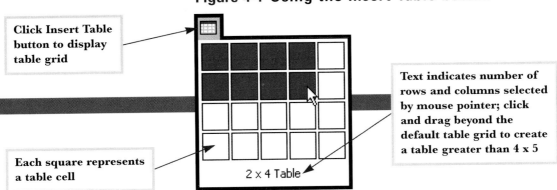

Click Insert Table button to display table grid

Text indicates number of rows and columns selected by mouse pointer; click and drag beyond the default table grid to create a table greater than 4 x 5

Each square represents a table cell

2 x 4 Table

Figure 4-2 Table inserted in Word document, matthews.doc

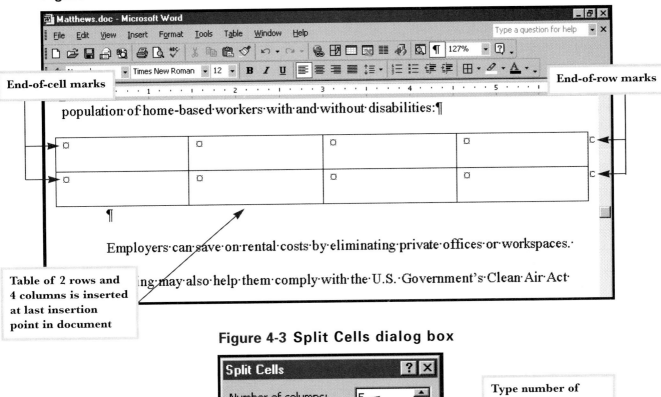

End-of-cell marks

End-of-row marks

population·of·home-based·workers·with·and·without·disabilities:¶

Employers·can·save·on·rental·costs·by·eliminating·private·offices·or·workspaces.·

ng·may·also·help·them·comply·with·the·U.S.·Government's·Clean·Air·Act·

Table of 2 rows and 4 columns is inserted at last insertion point in document

Figure 4-3 Split Cells dialog box

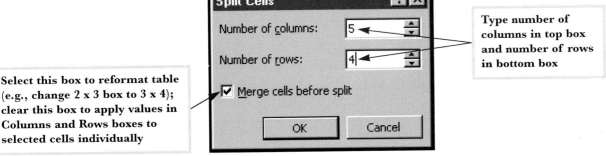

Type number of columns in top box and number of rows in bottom box

Select this box to reformat table (e.g., change 2 x 3 box to 3 x 4); clear this box to apply values in Columns and Rows boxes to selected cells individually

skill Creating and Modifying Tables (continued)

do it !

9. Since the table now has the required columns in each row, you can start entering text. Click in Row 1, Column 1, and type Percent Doing Any Paid Telecommuting If In. Click in Row 1, Column 2 (the first area of merged cells), and type Disabilities. Click in Row 1, Column 3 (the second area of merged cells), and type No Disabilities. Again, do not worry about formatting.

10. With your insertion point at the end of the text in the last column of Row 1, look at Figure 4-4. Fill in the rest of the table with the text that appears in the figure. Begin by pressing [Tab] to move to Row 2, Column 1. Type the words Private Sector, and press [Tab] to move to Row 2, Column 2. Repeat this typing and tabbing process until you enter all needed text in the table. Once again, do not worry about formatting.

11. Next, arrange the table so it looks attractive and does not use up excess white space. Begin by clicking anywhere in the table. Click Table, click AutoFit, and then click AutoFit to Contents. Also click Table, click Select, click Table, and click the Center button [≡]. The first column has widened to place its text on one line, the rest of the columns have narrowed to eliminate unneeded white space, and the overall table is centered on the page.

12. Percentages, dollar amounts, and a lot of other numerical data often contain decimal points, which generally should be vertically aligned. Select the 12 lower right cells in the table, starting with Row 2, Column 2 (with the text 2.1%) and ending with the lower right cell of the table (with the text 52.6%).

13. Click the Align Right button [≡]. Since only one decimal place and the percent symbol appear to the right of all the decimals, all of them align vertically. Click the Show/Hide button to turn it off, and click outside the table (see Figure 4-5). You also can align decimals as follows: highlight the cells that need aligning, click the tab alignment marker at the left end of the Horizontal Ruler until it changes to a decimal tab [⊥], and then click on the ruler above the related column where you want the decimals to align.

14. Save and close your document with the changes you have made.

more

Besides creating tables with the Insert Table button, you can click Table, click Insert, and click Table to open the Insert Table dialog box. Like the Insert Table button, the dialog box enables you to select the number of columns and rows for new tables. However, this dialog box also enables you to set specific column widths, autofit tables to their contents or within Web browser windows, access the Table AutoFormat dialog box (explained later in this lesson), and so on. If you have pre-existing text in a document, you can convert it to a table by highlighting the text and clicking the Insert Table button. Table cells are determined by tabs and paragraphs in the highlighted text. Another way to create a table from text is to highlight the text, click Table, click Convert, and click Text to Table to open the Convert Text to Table dialog box, which resembles the Insert Table dialog box. Whichever way you create tables, you can modify their text and formatting through the Tables and Borders toolbar (see Figure 4-6).

As part of Microsoft Office, Word enables you to insert tables from other programs. For example, you can create linked objects and embedded objects. Linked objects are created in source files from programs like Excel or Access and then inserted into destination files like Word. Linked objects maintain a connection, or link, between the source and destination files. Because of this link objects in destination files will update whenever you update them in source files. Embedded objects resemble linked objects because both are created in source files and then inserted into destination files. However, once inserted in a destination file, the embedded object becomes part of that file. Changes made to the embedded object are, therefore, part of the destination file only and not part of the source file. Such sharing of files increases the power and flexibility of all of the Office programs.

Figure 4-4 Table with text, before formatting

Click inside first cell and type needed text

After completing one cell, click in next cell or press [Tab] key to move to next cell

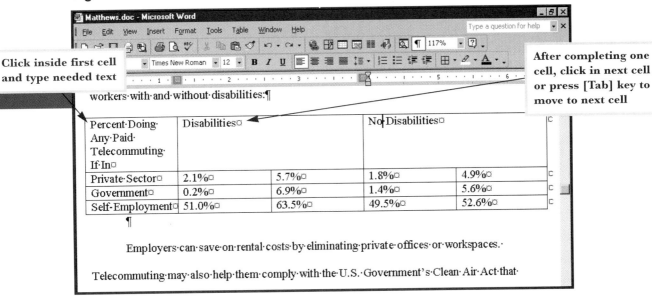

workers with and without disabilities:¶

Percent Doing Any Paid Telecommuting If In□	Disabilities□		No Disabilities□	
Private Sector□	2.1%□	5.7%□	1.8%□	4.9%□
Government□	0.2%□	6.9%□	1.4%□	5.6%□
Self-Employment□	51.0%□	63.5%□	49.5%□	52.6%□

¶

Employers can save on rental costs by eliminating private offices or workspaces.

Telecommuting may also help them comply with the U.S. Government's Clean Air Act that

Figure 4-5 Table with text, after formatting

Table is single-spaced, autofit to contents, and centered horizontally in document

Decimal points are vertically aligned

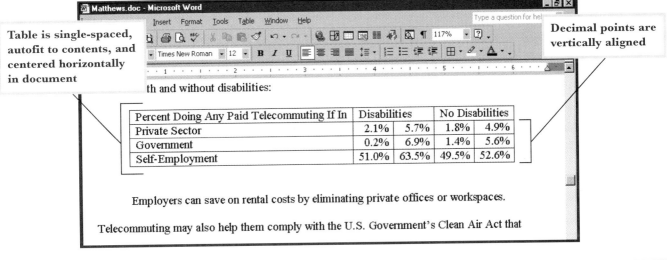

th and without disabilities:

Percent Doing Any Paid Telecommuting If In	Disabilities		No Disabilities	
Private Sector	2.1%	5.7%	1.8%	4.9%
Government	0.2%	6.9%	1.4%	5.6%
Self-Employment	51.0%	63.5%	49.5%	52.6%

Employers can save on rental costs by eliminating private offices or workspaces.

Telecommuting may also help them comply with the U.S. Government's Clean Air Act that

Figure 4-6 Tables and Borders toolbar

Merge cells and split cells buttons

Click here to set borders

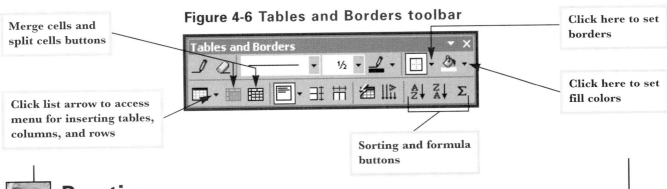

Click here to set fill colors

Click list arrow to access menu for inserting tables, columns, and rows

Sorting and formula buttons

Practice

To practice creating tables, open Student File wdprac4-1.doc. Save and close any changes you make in your Word Files folder as mywdprac4-1.doc.

skill   Editing Tables

concept

Once you have entered text and modified the format of a table, often the table still does not have all the text or formatting features that you need or want. Therefore, Word makes it as easy to edit text in cells as in regular areas of a document. Likewise, the program also offers many features for modifying formatting even further. The next few Skills focus on these text editing and table formatting features.

do it !

Change headings in a table and modify their format.

1. Open Student File wddoit4-2.doc and save it in your Word Files folder as lee.doc. Scroll down to the table that appears between the second and third paragraphs.

2. Position the insertion point just after the word Total in the table. Type a space, then type (in Millions) to complete the heading.

3. Press [Tab] to move to the next cell to the right. All the information in the cell is selected. Click immediately to the left of the word at to deselect the cell and to position the insertion point there. Type Working and press [Spacebar] to complete the cell heading.

4. Select all the headings in the table. Click the Center button ▤ to align the text horizontally in the header cells. ◕ Alternately, you can align text by using the Table and Borders toolbar. Display the toolbar by clicking View, clicking Toolbars, and then clicking Tables and Borders. (Or right-click in a gray area of the toolbars and click Tables and Borders.) After the toolbar displays, click the Align button arrow ▥▾ to display the Cell Alignment palette. Without clicking the mouse button, move the mouse pointer over the nine buttons to see where each one would place text. When finished, click the Align Top Center icon to center the text horizontally at the top of the cell (see Figure 4-7).

5. Close the Tables and Buttons toolbar to get an unobstructed view of the document (see Figure 4-8). Save and close the document with your changes.

more

As the Steps above demonstrate, you can edit text in tables just as you do in regular areas of a document. You can center or align text to either side of a cell by selecting it and clicking the appropriate formatting button: Align Left, Center, or Align Right. In a table the Selection bar (the vertical area between the left edge of the screen and left margin of a page) works in much the same way as it does with text. Therefore, clicking in the Selection bar to the left of a row selects the entire row. Dragging down or up in the Selection bar adds or deletes more rows to or from the selection, depending on whether you started dragging from the top or bottom row of a table. To move a table, drag the Table Move handle ⊞, which is available at the upper-left in Print Layout View when the mouse pointer is over the table.

In tables themselves, there is a miniature Selection bar at the left edge of each cell, so clicking there will select the whole cell and not just its text. You also can select a whole cell by triple-clicking in it, whereas double-clicking in the cell will highlight just words. To select a column, place the mouse pointer over the column's top border until the mouse pointer changes to a downward arrow ↓, then click to select the column. Dragging to the right from the leftmost column will highlight more columns, and dragging back toward the left will highlight fewer ones. To change the width of a column, place the mouse pointer over the edge of the column to display a column width pointer ◂‖▸, click and hold the mouse button to display a vertical dotted line, and then drag the edge as needed. To automatically adjust a column to match the width of the text in that column, double-click on the right edge of the desired column. This action will adjust the column to match the width of the text, plus a bit of white space at each end of the text to make for easier reading.

Figure 4-7 Align cell text button on Tables and Borders toolbar

Click View, Toolbars, and then Tables and Borders to display toolbar

Right-click in gray area to display Toolbars menu, then click Tables and Borders

Align Cell Text button

Highlight heading cells before clicking Align Cell Text button

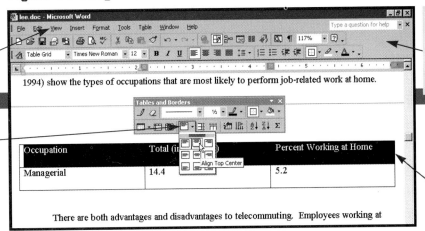

Figure 4-8 Edited cell headings in lee.doc

Second and third cell headings are edited, and all headings are horizontally centered

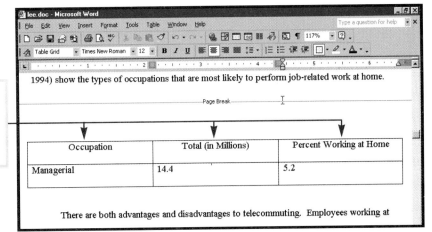

Table 4-1 Keyboard Movement and Selection Shortcuts

Desired Action	Press This
Move to next or previous cell in a table and select its contents	[Tab] or [Shift]+[Tab]
Move up or down one row	[↑] or [↓]
Move to the first or last cell in a row	[Alt]+[Home] or [Alt]+[End]
Move to the top or bottom cell in a column	[Alt]+[Pg Up] or [Alt]+[Pg Dn]
Select an entire column	[Alt]+[Click]
Select an entire table	[Alt]+[5] on the numeric keypad (with Num Lock off)

Practice

To practice editing a table, open the Student File wdprac4-2.doc. Save and close any changes you make in your Word Files folder as mywdprac4-2.doc.

skill
Inserting and Deleting Rows, Columns, and Cells

MOUS Skill

concept

Students change their course schedules, businesses modify financial projections, people come and go in organizations, and many other changes recordable in tables occur daily in life. To handle such frequent changes to data and information, Word provides a variety of ways to facilitate adding or deleting rows, columns, and cells in tables.

do it !

Add four rows and two columns, enter data, and then delete one row and one column.

1. Open Student File wddoit4-3.doc and save it in your Word Files folder as lee-1.doc. Scroll to the table that appears between the second and third paragraphs. You eventually will expand this table to six rows and five columns. Therefore, to see the whole table during this process and improve its appearance somewhat, select the entire table now and convert it to single spacing.

2. Place the insertion point at the end of the text in the rightmost cell of the second row. Press [Tab] to create a third row below the one that just contained the insertion point.

3. Select all three rows of the table. Click Table, click Insert, and click Rows Below to add three more rows to the table, for a total of six rows.

4. Select the second and third columns of the table, either by clicking and dragging through the columns or by using the downward arrow described in the previous More section. Click Table, click Insert, and click Columns to the Right (see Figure 4-9).

5. With your insertion point in the first cell of the third row, look at Figure 4-10. Fill in the rest of the table with the text that appears in the figure.

6. At this point you decide that the data in the bottom row and the rightmost column are repetitive, so you will delete that row and column. Select all of the bottom row, click Table, click Delete, and click Rows to change the table to five rows.

7. Select all of the rightmost column, click Table, click Delete, and click Columns to change the table to four columns. Compare your table with Figure 4-11. Add or delete rows, columns, and any data as needed to conform with that figure. To delete a row or column more quickly, highlight the desired area, right-click to display a pop-up menu, and then click Delete Rows or Delete Columns. Alternately, you can select the desired area and then press [Shift]+[Delete] or [Ctrl]+[X].

8. Save and close the document with your changes.

more

Inserting or deleting cells is similar to inserting or deleting rows or columns. To insert a cell, click Table, click Insert, and then click Cells to open the Insert Cells dialog box. In this dialog box select one of four radio buttons to add a cell to the right, add a cell below the selected cell, or add an entire row or column of cells. To delete cells, click Table, click Delete, and then click Cells to open the Delete Cells dialog box. In this dialog box select one of four radio buttons to shift cells to the left, shift cells up, or delete an entire row or column of cells. Do not confuse how to delete rows, columns, and cells with how to delete text. To remove text, simply use the [Backspace] or [Delete] key to remove individual letters, or select a whole cell and press only [Delete], not [Shift]+[Delete], to remove all text in the cell.

Figure 4-9 lee-1.doc with added rows and columns

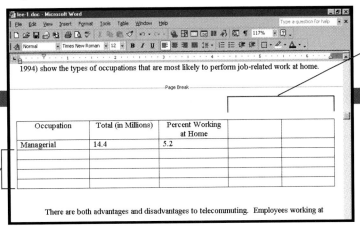

Two columns added, using the Table menu

Four rows added to table, one by tabbing and three by using Table menu

Figure 4-10 lee-1.doc with data added to new rows and columns

Click Table, click Insert, and then click desired command to add rows or columns

Bottom row repeats data of row above, just in slightly different form

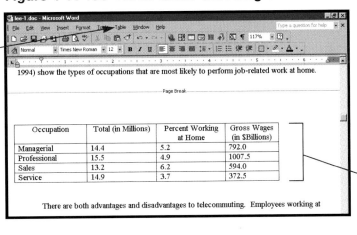

Rightmost column repeats data in fourth column, just in slightly different form

Figure 4-11 lee-1.doc after deleting unneeded row and column

Click Table, click Delete, and click Rows or Columns to delete unneeded areas

After deleting unneeded row and column, table has 5 rows and 4 columns

Practice

To practice inserting and deleting rows and columns, open Student File wdprac4-3.doc. Save and close any changes you make in your Word Files folder as mywdprac4-3.doc.

skill | Sorting Data in a Table

concept

Word's Sort feature arranges text and data according to a pattern you can dictate. For example, when you arrange text alphabetically or arrange numbers by increasing value, you have sorted in ascending order. If you arrange text in reverse alphabetical order or arrange numbers by decreasing value, you have sorted in descending order. When you sort text and data, be sure you do so in a way that makes sense for the type of information you are sorting while making sense to your readers too. For example, you probably should sort an address list by last name then first name, but sort a mail delivery guide by street address, then house number.

do it !

List occupations in a table by their decreasing order of Working-at-Home percentage.

1. Open Student File wddoit4-4.doc and save it in your Word Files folder as lee-2.doc. Make sure the insertion point is situated somewhere in the table between the second and third paragraphs.

2. Click Table, then click Sort to open the Sort dialog box. The heading Occupation appears by default in the Sort by list box because that heading appears in the first column of the table you are working with.

3. Click the Sort by drop-down list arrow, then click Percent Working at Home. Word automatically reads all of your columns headings and includes them in the list, with the first heading as the default choice. When you chose Percent Working at Home, Word analyzed the kind of data in that column and changed the Type list box from text to number.

4. In the Sort by section, click the Descending option button so Word will sort the table with the largest numerical value in the top row of data and the lowest value in the bottom row once you close the dialog box.

5. In the My list has section, click the Header row option button if it is not already selected (see Figure 4-12). Click [OK] to sort the table and to close the dialog box. Click anywhere outside the table to deselect it. The data in the Percent Working at Home column now appears in descending order, the data in all other columns move to stay with their related data in the sorted column, and the heading remains at the top of the table (see Figure 4-13).

6. Save and close your document with the sorting change you have made.

more

Word allows you to sort by up to three main criteria in a table. In a table having columns for last names, first names, street addresses, cities, states, and Zip Codes, you could sort by last name, then by first name, and then by city—or you could sort by city, then by state, and then by Zip Code. Earlier versions of Word did not allow you to sort by, for example, first and last name if both types of names resided in one column. However, a new feature in Word 2002 enables you to sort by more than one word or field inside a column. If one column contained last names and first names, you could then sort by one type of name and then by the other type as well. This ability to sort by multiple fields inside a column increases the number of criteria by which you can sort.

To sort by multiple criteria, begin by clicking anywhere in your table and opening the Sort dialog box from the Table menu. Second, in the My list has section, click an option to indicate whether your table has headings across the top. Third, in the Sort by section, choose your primary sorting criterion and whether to sort in ascending or descending order. Fourth, in the upper Then by section, choose your secondary criterion, then ascending or descending order. Fifth, in the lower Then by section, choose your tertiary (or third-level) criterion, choose ascending or descending order, and then click [OK].

Figure 4-12 Sort dialog box with desired sort criteria

Click desired column as primary basis for sorting rows of a table

Specify more columns as second-level and third-level bases for sorting

Opens Sort Options dialog box to set more sorting criteria

Sorts from start or end of alphabet, lowest or highest number, or earliest or latest date

Exclude or include first row of table when sorting

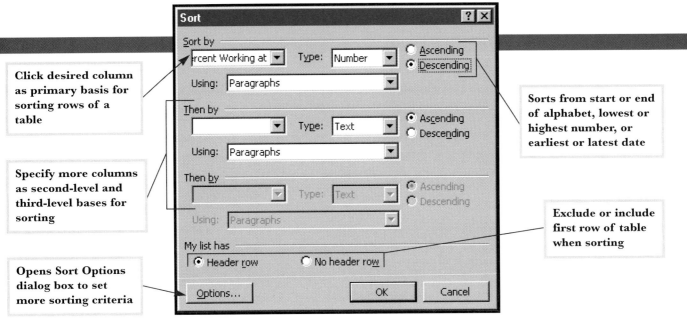

Figure 4-13 Table in lee-2.doc after sorting

Click Table, then click Sort to open Sort dialog box

Data appears in descending order; heading remains at top of table

1994) show the types of occupations that are most likely to perform job-related work at home.

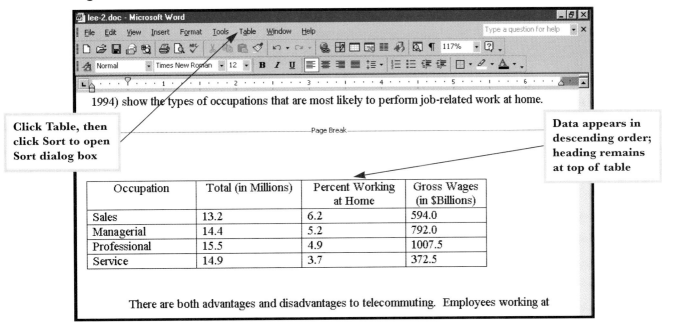

Occupation	Total (in Millions)	Percent Working at Home	Gross Wages (in $Billions)
Sales	13.2	6.2	594.0
Managerial	14.4	5.2	792.0
Professional	15.5	4.9	1007.5
Service	14.9	3.7	372.5

There are both advantages and disadvantages to telecommuting. Employees working at

Practice

To practice sorting data in a table, open the Student File wdprac4-4.doc. Save and close any changes you make in your Word Files folder as mywdprac4-4.doc.

skill | Calculating Data in a Table

concept

The Formula command makes it easy to perform calculations in tables and comes with pre-programmed formulas such as Sum, Product, and Average. You can add formulas to the default list to meet the calculation needs of tables you create. You can design simple tables to add weekly expenses or more complex ones to calculate mortgage closing costs, thereby transforming tables from simple display objects into highly functional tools. Best of all, perhaps, mastering formulas can eliminate the worry of committing costly mathematical errors.

do it !

Automatically average the values in the Percent Working at Home column and insert the average in new cells.

1. Open Student File wddoit4-5.doc and save it in your Word Files folder as lee-3.doc.

2. Position the insertion point immediately after the number 372.5 in the rightmost cell of the bottom row of the table. Press [Tab] to create a new row.

3. In the leftmost cell of the new row, type the word Average. Press [Tab] twice. The insertion point will move two cells to the right into the empty cell at the bottom of the Percent Working at Home column (see Figure 4-14).

4. Click Table, then click Formula. The Formula dialog box will appear, with the formula =SUM(ABOVE) suggested in the Formula text box (see Figure 4-15).

5. Delete the suggested formula by selecting it and pressing [Delete]. Press [=] to place an equal sign in the empty Formula box. ⬛➤ The equal sign at the beginning of the box tells Word that any text to follow should be treated as a formula, not as a label or value.

6. With the insertion point immediately to the right of the equal sign, click the Paste function list arrow, then click AVERAGE. The AVERAGE formula appears in the Formula text box with the insertion point between parentheses. Inside the parentheses, type C2:C5, which is the range of the cells that you want to average.

7. Look at Figure 4-16 to ensure that the formula reads =AVERAGE(C2:C5). If it does not, you can delete whatever text is in the box and simply type the formula into the Formula box, without getting the AVERAGE formula from the Paste Function box.

(continued on WD 4.14)

Figure 4-14 lee-3.doc with added row

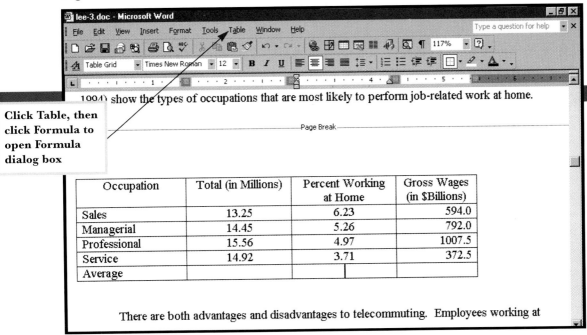

Click Table, then click Formula to open Formula dialog box

Occupation	Total (in Millions)	Percent Working at Home	Gross Wages (in $Billions)
Sales	13.25	6.23	594.0
Managerial	14.45	5.26	792.0
Professional	15.56	4.97	1007.5
Service	14.92	3.71	372.5
Average			

Figure 4-15 Formula dialog box with Paste function displayed

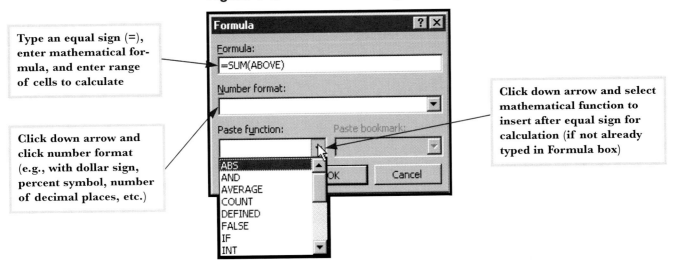

Type an equal sign (=), enter mathematical formula, and enter range of cells to calculate

Click down arrow and click number format (e.g., with dollar sign, percent symbol, number of decimal places, etc.)

Click down arrow and select mathematical function to insert after equal sign for calculation (if not already typed in Formula box)

Figure 4-16 Formula dialog box with desired formula

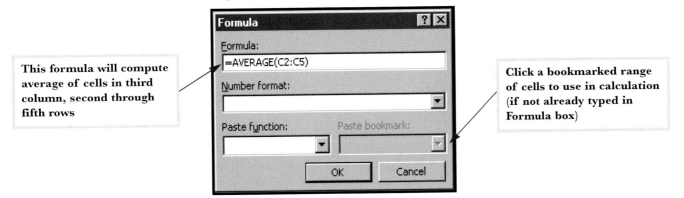

This formula will compute average of cells in third column, second through fifth rows

Click a bookmarked range of cells to use in calculation (if not already typed in Formula box)

skill   Calculating Data in a Table (continued)

do it !

8. Click [OK] to apply the formula to the column and to close the dialog box. Click outside of the table to cancel the selection. The average of the values in the column, 5.04, now appears in the last cell of the table (see Figure 4-17).

9. Save and close the file with your changes.

more

Changing data in one of the cells that the calculation is based on does not immediately affect the result seen on the screen. To account for the new data and to update the calculation, select the column that has to be recalculated and press [F9], which is the Update Fields command.

When entering your own formulas into the Formula dialog box, you will reference other cells in the table using cell references. Cell references identify a cell's position by using a column letter and row number. For example, the cell reference for the third column, second row is C2 (see Figure 4-18). You can use the Word Formula feature in many ways. In Figure 4-19, formulas are used to calculate the total monthly spending for three people as well as the resulting 12-month projected total cost. The formulas shown are the ones that you would enter into the Formula text box when you called up the Formula dialog box with the insertion point in the appropriate cells. Each formula in the Monthly Total column (Column E) adds the numbers to the left in their respective rows to arrive at the total. Likewise, the formulas in the Annual Total column (Column F) multiply the monthly total from Column E by the 12 months in the year to arrive at a projected Annual Total.

Notice in Column F that the multiplication symbol is the asterisk (*), which is the uppercase symbol on the [8] key on the top row of your keyboard. The division symbol is a forward slash (/), the lowercase symbol near the lower right of your keyboard on the same key as the question mark. After you have entered data and formulas and have achieved a mathematical result, you can format the results by using the Number Format box in the Formula dialog box. In Figure 4-19, for example, we would recommend that you choose the $#,##0.00;($#,##0.00) format from the drop-down list. This format would place a dollar sign at the left edge of a result, place any needed commas in the thousands separator, provide a decimal place and two places to the right of the decimal, and place any negative results in parentheses.

Figure 4-17 lee-3.doc after calculating formula with dialog box

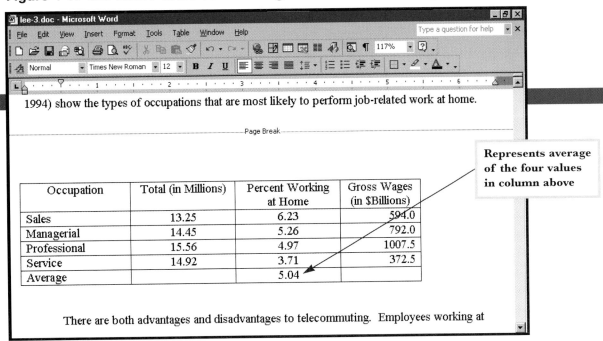

Figure 4-18 Cell References

<table>
<tr><td></td><td>A</td><td>B</td><td>C</td></tr>
<tr><td>1</td><td>A1</td><td>B1</td><td>C1</td></tr>
<tr><td>2</td><td>A2</td><td>B2</td><td>C2</td></tr>
<tr><td>3</td><td>A3</td><td>B3</td><td>C3</td></tr>
</table>

Cell C2 results from intersection of Column C and Row 2

Figure 4-19 Sample table with formulas

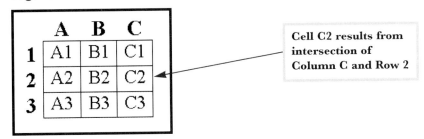

	Rent/Month	Food/Month	Other/Month	Monthly Total	Annual Total
Diane	$950	$250	$500	=SUM(LEFT)	=E2*12
Larry	$1050	$350	$400	=SUM(LEFT)	=E3*12
Margot	$1150	$300	$600	=SUM(LEFT)	=E4*12

Monthly Total represents sum of all values to the left in its row

Annual Total represents product (multiplication) of cells in Column E by 12 months

Practice

To practice calculating data in a table, open the Student File wdprac4-5.doc. Save and close any changes you make in your Word Files folder as mywdprac4-5.doc.

skill   Formatting a Table    MOUS Skill

concept

You can change a table's appearance in many ways. Word's table formatting options include, among others, shading, borders, and 3-D effects. You can format individual table elements or apply an entire set of formatting changes to a table. Both techniques can improve the organization, clarity, and appearance of tables while saving you time when trying to create attractive and readable documents.

do it !

Format a table manually and with the Table AutoFormat command to improve its appearance.

1. Open Student File wddoit4-6.doc and save it in your Word Files folder as lee-4.doc. Scroll down to make the table visible. If necessary, turn on the Show/ Hide Paragraph button ¶. Notice that none of the headings contain hard returns (which would be indicated by a paragraph mark ¶), even though the headings in Columns C and D appear on two lines.

2. In Column A place the insertion point immediately to the left of the heading Occupation and press [Enter]. This action moves the word onto the second line of the cell.

3. In Column B place the insertion point immediately to the left of the opening parenthesis at the left of the word in, press [Backspace], and press [Enter]. This action eliminates the space, inserts a hard return, and moves the last two words with their parentheses to the second line of the heading.

4. In Column C click immediately to the left of the word at, press [Backspace], and press [Enter]. This action eliminates the space, inserts a hard return, and moves the last two words to the second line of the heading.

5. In Column D click immediately to the left of the opening parenthesis at the left of the word in, press [Backspace], and press [Enter]. This action eliminates the space inserts a hard return, and moves the last two words onto the second line of the heading. Turn off the Show/Hide Paragraph button.

6. With the insertion point still in the table, click Table, then click Table AutoFormat to open the Table AutoFormat dialog box. In the Table styles section, scroll down in the listings and click Table Grid 8. Be sure that check marks appear in all of the check boxes in the Apply special formats to section. The Preview section of the dialog box shows you what the formatted table will look like, depending on which table style you have clicked and which special formats have check marks.

7. Verify that your Table style and special formats conform to those in Figure 4-20. Then click Apply to apply the Grid 8 formatting and to close the dialog box.

8. Click Table, then click Table Properties to open the Table Properties dialog box. If necessary, click the Table tab to display it at the front of the dialog box. In the Alignment section, click Center, and then click OK to center the table horizontally on the page and to close the dialog box. Click anywhere outside of the table. Verify that the table format resembles that in Figure 4-21. If the format does not, make formatting adjustments as necessary to conform with the figure.

9. Save and close your document with the formatting changes you have made.

more   If the top row of your table contains a heading and the table spans more than one page, you generally should display that heading at the top of each page where the table appears. To do so, place the insertion point anywhere in the top row, click Table, and then click Heading Rows Repeat. (Or access this command from the Row tab in the Table Properties dialog box.) You also should ensure that all lines of text and/or data in any given table row stay together in that row if the table spans more than one page. To prevent text and data from breaking across two pages, click Table, click Table Properties to open the Table Properties dialog box, click the Row tab to display it at the front of the dialog box, remove the check mark from the Allow row to break across pages check box, and click ▐ OK ▌.

Figure 4-20 Table AutoFormat dialog box

Click here to select which category of styles to display in Table styles box

Opens New Style dialog box to create new table style

Scroll through list of table styles and click desired style

Displays what selected table style will look like

Applies and saves any changes you made and closes dialog box

Turns formatting of selected parts of table on or off

Figure 4-21 lee-4.doc after applying manual and automatic formats

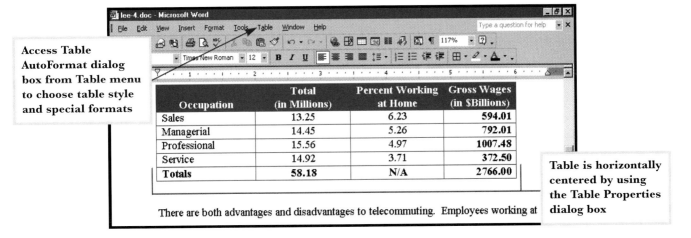

Access Table AutoFormat dialog box from Table menu to choose table style and special formats

Occupation	Total (in Millions)	Percent Working at Home	Gross Wages (in $Billions)
Sales	13.25	6.23	594.01
Managerial	14.45	5.26	792.01
Professional	15.56	4.97	1007.48
Service	14.92	3.71	372.50
Totals	58.18	N/A	2766.00

There are both advantages and disadvantages to telecommuting. Employees working at

Table is horizontally centered by using the Table Properties dialog box

Practice

To practice formatting a table, open the Student File wdprac4-6.doc. Save and close any changes you make in your Word Files folder as mywdprac4-6.doc.

skill | Creating a Chart

concept

Sometimes, readers will more readily understand a table if you present it as a chart. A chart not only represents data graphically instead of textually but also can provide an effective way to break up the monotony of line after line of text. Depending on your preference and the needs of the document that you are preparing, you can accompany the table with a chart or use the chart to completely replace the table. Word enables you to create a chart from scratch or, as you will do in this Skill, generate the chart from a pre-existing table.

do it !

Display a pre-existing table as a chart.

1. Open Student File wddoit4-7.doc and save it in your Word Files folder as lee-5.doc. Scroll to the table between the second and third paragraphs and click anywhere within it. In the bottom cell of the Percent Working at Home column, delete the letters N/A, which stand for Not Applicable, and which would frustrate your efforts to use the table-to-chart conversion subprogram.

2. Click Table, click Select, and click Table to select the entire table. Click Insert, and click Object. After a brief delay the Object dialog box opens with the Create New tab displayed.

3. Scroll down through the Object type box and double-click Microsoft Graph Chart. When this feature opens, it turns your table into a Microsoft Graph Datasheet (see Figure 4-22). A preliminary chart appears, based on the data in the table that you selected in Step 2.

4. Click Chart, then click Chart Options. The Chart Options dialog box opens with the Titles tab on top. In the Chart title text box, type Home-Based Workers. After a brief delay the title will appear at the top of the preview chart.

5. Press [Tab] to move the insertion point to the Category (X) text box, then type Occupation. After a brief delay the word will appear at the bottom of the preview chart (see Figure 4-23). Click [OK] to create the chart.

6. Click the Close Window button [X] to close the Datasheet window. The chart you have created will appear below the table in a hashmarked frame (see Figure 4-24). Some parts of the chart, especially the labels beneath it, will appear cramped and cut off. Notice that when the chart is selected, positioning the mouse pointer over a chart elements displays a ScreenTip displaying what part of the chart the element represents. Do not worry about the format, as you will learn how to modify a chart in the next Skill.

7. Click outside the chart. Save and close your document with the changes you have made.

more

The Chart Type dialog box, accessed from the Chart menu, offers 14 Standard chart types for representing data. Some of the more common chart types are the column chart, line chart, pie chart, and stock chart. Each Standard chart type offers two or more subtypes to choose from to increase your chart formatting options. On the Standard Types tab of the dialog box, you can click on the Press and Hold to View Sample button to see what your selected chart type will look like when you close the dialog box. The Custom Types tab of the dialog box offers 20 additional chart types and a preview area that displays what your selected custom chart type will look like.

Microsoft Graph automatically suggests the type of graph or chart that seems to match most closely the format of your data, since not all formats properly represent all types of data. For example, you could not represent properly the table in this Skill with a pie-chart or radar graph. Therefore, when choosing a chart type, first determine which type will best represent your data.

Figure 4-22 Chart datasheet created from table

Shows the color used for each data series in chart

Headings and data in chart come from selected table

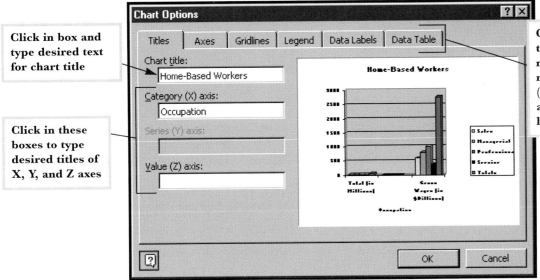

Figure 4-23 Chart Options dialog box

Click in box and type desired text for chart title

Click in these boxes to type desired titles of X, Y, and Z axes

Click to bring forward tabs for displaying, modifying, or hiding more chart elements (e.g., 3-D effects, additional gridlines, legend placement)

Figure 4-24 Chart created from table

Chart title created in Chart Options dialog box

Current chart is too small to permit proper formatting of chart labels and titles

Legend identifies categories that appear in chart and shows colors that correspond with those in the datasheet

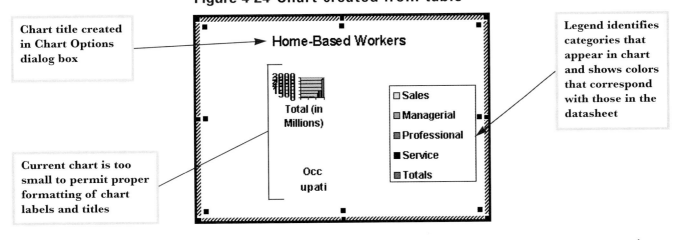

Practice

To practice creating a chart, open the Student File wdprac4-7.doc. Save and close any changes you make in your Word Files folder as mywdprac4-7.doc.

skill   Editing a Chart

concept

Word treats charts as graphic objects instead of as text, but you still can modify charts by accessing the program that created them. You can edit virtually all aspects of a chart, including its size, position, and the characteristics of each element. Proper editing not only fixes formatting problems that exist when you first create a chart, but also offers the chance to add or delete data as needed and represent data in the most graphically pleasing and informative way.

do it !

Modify the appearance of a chart, especially its size, number of columns, and column labels.

1. Open Student File wddoit4-8.doc and save it as lee-6.doc. To see a more accurate image of how the finished chart eventually will look in your document, switch to Print Layout view.

2. Scroll down to the chart in the document, and double-click the chart to open Microsoft Graph. The Microsoft Graph toolbar will replace the Standard and Formatting toolbars at the top of the screen, and a hashmarked frame will appear around the chart with sizing handles at its corners and at the midpoint of each side. If necessary, drag the Datasheet window out of the way of the column chart (see Figure 4-25).

3. Click the midpoint sizing handle on the bottom of the chart's frame, drag it downward, and release it just below the 4½-inch mark on the Vertical Ruler. The chart expands vertically, making it possible for more increments to appear along the vertical axis of the chart.

4. Click the midpoint sizing handle on the right side of the frame, drag it to the right, and release it when it is even with the 5½-inch mark on the Horizontal Ruler. The chart expands horizontally until it is almost the width of the body text and has room to display the column labels along the bottom axis of the chart without breaking them awkwardly.

5. In the Datasheet window click the gray header for column C (Gross Wages in $Billions), and press [Delete] to remove the heading and data for that column. Also in the Datasheet window, click the gray header for row 5 (Totals) and press [Delete] to remove the heading and data for that row. The chart columns associated with column C and for row 5 disappear from the chart, and the remaining columns (Total in Millions and Percent Working at Home) widen to fill the chart background. The Totals reference in the chart Legend also disappears.

6. Click outside the chart frame to return to the regular Word document window with the Standard and Formatting toolbars. Because you deleted column C and row 5, the edited chart now displays only the columns for the remaining categories Total in Millions and the Percent Working at Home (see Figure 4-26). Save your changes and close the document.

more

When working with a chart in Word, remember that the chart is a foreign element created by another application. To edit the chart itself, you first must double-click it to open its parent application. To edit a chart based on changed table data, you either must alter the datasheet for the table—available on the View menu of the Graph program—or recreate the chart. To act upon the chart as an element of your Word document (e.g., move or copy it), click it only once to select it. A box indicated by sizing handles—not the hashmarked frame indicating the parent application—will appear around it. You then may cut and paste the chart or drag and drop it to another place in the document. You also can change text added during chart creation, such as title and category, by selecting the specific element and entering new text. When you select a chart element like the title, a frame will appear around it, letting you know you may edit it.

Figure 4-25 Unedited chart displayed in MS Graph application

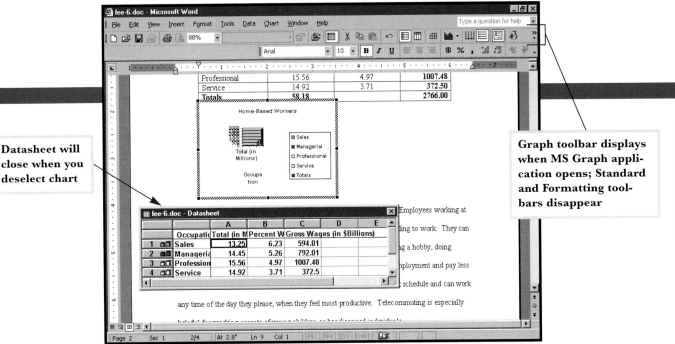

Datasheet will close when you deselect chart

Graph toolbar displays when MS Graph application opens; Standard and Formatting toolbars disappear

Figure 4-26 Edited chart displayed in Print Layout view

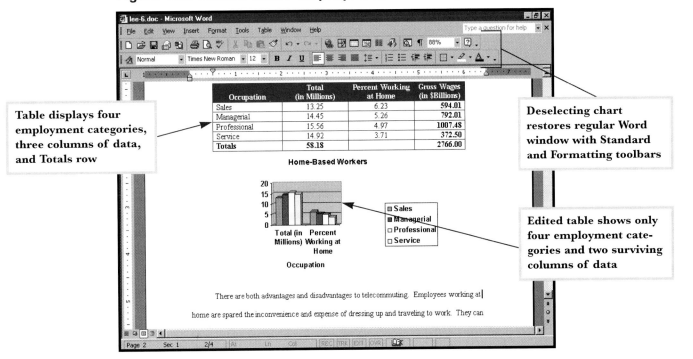

Table displays four employment categories, three columns of data, and Totals row

Deselecting chart restores regular Word window with Standard and Formatting toolbars

Edited table shows only four employment categories and two surviving columns of data

Practice

To practice editing a chart, open Student File wdprac4-8.doc. Save and close any changes you make in your Word Files folder as mywdprac4-8.doc.

skill   Drawing a Table

concept

As earlier Skills show, Word enables you to create tables with predefined borders using the Insert Table button. However, you sometimes may want to have more control over the construction of a table. Work makes this possible by letting you draw a table gridline by gridline with the Draw Table tool. With this tool you can create a table customized precisely for your needs as easily as you can create a standard table. Drawn tables still allow you to merge or split cells, change column widths, and make other edits common to standard tables.

do it !

Draw a table, merge the top row, and enter text in all of the cells.

1. Click 🗋 to open a new blank document, and save it in your Word Files folder as progress.doc.

2. Click the Tables and Borders button 🖽. The Tables and Borders toolbar will appear, floating on the screen. If the toolbar obscures your document window, drag it by its title bar to a better location—such as directly underneath the Formatting toolbar where it will be docked out of the way. The document now should be in Print Layout view.

3. Type Progress Table on the first line of the document, and press [Enter].

4. On the Tables and Borders toolbar, click the Draw Table button 🖉. The mouse pointer now should look like a pencil when it is over the document. ⬤ The Draw Table button is the first button on the Tables and Borders toolbar. Be careful not to confuse it with the Border Color button, which looks similar but has a thick line below the pencil icon.

5. Position the mouse pointer just below the word Progress. Hold down the mouse button and drag from that point down and to the right. As you drag, a dashed outline of a table will appear. Release the mouse button when the outline reaches 4 inches on the Horizontal Ruler and 3 inches on the Vertical Ruler (see Figure 4-27).

6. Place the mouse pointer on the top border of the table at the 2-inch mark on the Horizontal Ruler. Click and drag straight down to the bottom border, drawing a vertical line in the middle of the table.

7. Place the mouse pointer on the left border of the table at the ½-inch mark on the Vertical Ruler. Click and drag straight across to the right border, drawing a horizontal line.

8. Repeat the previous step to create four more horizontal lines every ½-inch down the Vertical Ruler. Verify that your table now resembles Figure 4-28. If it does not, click the Undo button ↻ until you reach an earlier stage of the table that matches the Steps listed above.

9. Click 🖉 to turn off the Draw Table tool. Resave the document with the changes you have made thus far, but do **not** close the file.

(continued on WD 4.24)

Figure 4-27 Table border drawn by hand

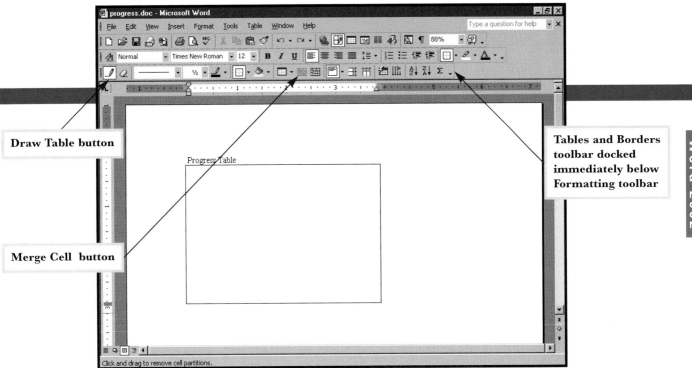

Draw Table button

Merge Cell button

Tables and Borders toolbar docked immediately below Formatting toolbar

Figure 4-28 Table with drawn gridlines

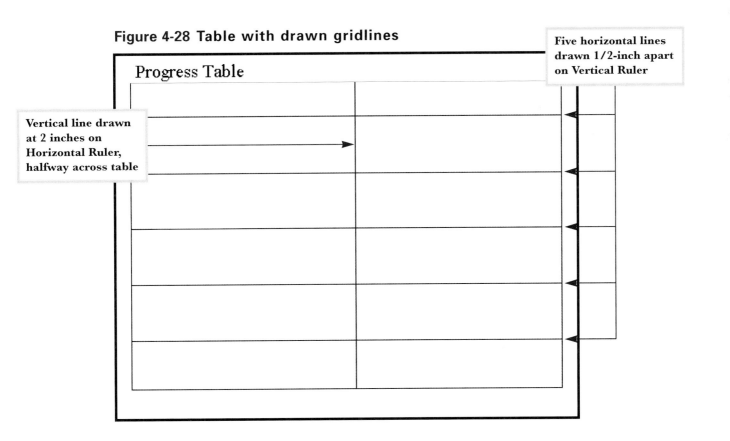

Progress Table

Five horizontal lines drawn 1/2-inch apart on Vertical Ruler

Vertical line drawn at 2 inches on Horizontal Ruler, halfway across table

skill Drawing a Table (continued)

do it !

10. Highlight the entire line of text above the table, cut it, and paste it into cell A1.

11. Click in the Selection bar to the left of Row A to select cells A1 and B1. On the Tables and Borders toolbar, click the Merge Cells button ⊞ . Cells A1 and B1 are combined into one cell.

12. With the merged cell still selected, click the Bold button **B** on the Formatting toolbar. The text in the selected cell is bolded.

13. Click in cell A2 to place the insertion point there and to deselect cell A1 (see Figure 4-29). In cell A2, type the word Task.

14. Press [Tab] to move the insertion point to cell B2. In cell B2 type the words Deadline. Use the Selection bar to highlight row 2 of the table, and then click the Underline button **U** . A line is placed beneath all text in the row.

15. Consult Figure 4-30, and type the text that appears there into the corresponding cells in your table.

16. Save and close your document with the changes you have made.

more

You can activate the Draw Table tool at any time to add more gridlines to a table. You also can remove gridlines, thereby eliminating rows and/or columns, by clicking the Eraser button ✐ on the Tables and Borders toolbar. Simply click on a gridline with the eraser to remove the line.

As you have seen, you can apply font formats to text in a table just as you would in a normal document. Most formatting options that you have applied to text in other Skills are available in tables too, including alignment, font style, font size, and font color. You even can rotate text in a cell by clicking the Text Direction button ▥ on the Tables and Borders toolbar.

Figure 4-29 Merged cell with bold font applied

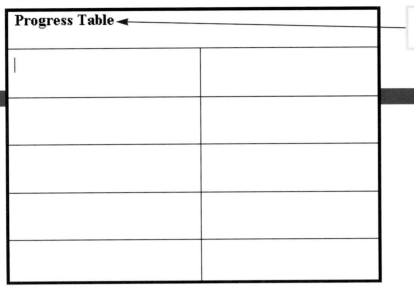

Progress Table ◀—————————————————— Merged cell with bold text

Figure 4-30 Drawn table with entered text

Progress Table	
Task	Deadline
Write text	November 1
Add text and screenshots	November 15
Proofread and edit	December 1
Deliver to printing plant	December 15

Copy text in this table to your own table, observing text formatting in second as well as first row

All text is Times New Roman, 12-point, aligned left

Practice

Use the Draw Table tool to create a table that will enable you to plot statistics from a survey in which people were asked to name their favorite season. Save and close this table in your Word Files folder as mywdprac4-9.doc.

skill   Adding Borders and Shading

concept

An earlier Skill in this Lesson teaches how to enhance the appearance of a table using the AutoFormat command from the Table menu. This command enables you to apply a predetermined set of formats to a table. Although AutoFormat does offer some options, it does not permit as many formatting changes as some people might like. Just as the Draw Table command gives you greater control over structuring a table, so also the Table Properties command provides many options for enhancing the appearance of a table.

do it !

Add a customized border and shading to a table.

1. Open Student File wddoit4-9.doc and save it in your Word Files folder as progress1.doc.

2. Click Table, click Select, and then click Table on the submenu. The entire table will be selected.

3. Click Table again, then click Table Properties. The Table Properties dialog box will open to the Table tab.

4. At the bottom center of the tab, click the Borders and Shading button <kbd>Borders and Shading...</kbd>. The Borders and Shading dialog box opens to the Borders tab.

5. In the Setting section of the tab, click the All option. In the Style box, click the third option, which looks like tightly spaced dashes.

6. At the right edge of the Color box, click the drop-down arrow to open a color palette. Then click the Blue square, which is the sixth square in the second row.

7. At the right edge of the Width box, click the drop-down arrow to open a list of line weights, or thicknesses. Then select the 2 1/4 pt option.

8. Look at the Preview diagram near the upper right area of the Borders tab. Verify that the border formats that you have selected match those that appear in Figure 4-31. If your Preview diagram does not match the figure, review the Steps above and make the needed changes.

9. Click <kbd>OK</kbd> to accept the formatting choices and to close the Borders and Shading dialog box. Click <kbd>OK</kbd> again to close the Table Properties dialog box.

10. Click outside of the modified table to deselect it. Verify that it now looks like Figure 4-32. Save your document with the changes you have made thus far, but do **not** close the file.

(continued on WD 4.28)

Figure 4-31 Border tab of Borders and Shading dialog box

Click to apply no border

Click to apply selected border style to cell, table, or paragraph

Creates custom border using options chosen in Preview diagram

Click here to return to Tables and Borders dialog box

Click sides of diagram or click surrounding border buttons to add or remove individual borders

Tells Word whether to apply borders to cell, paragraph, or table

Opens Borders and Shading Options dialog box to position paragraph text relative to borders

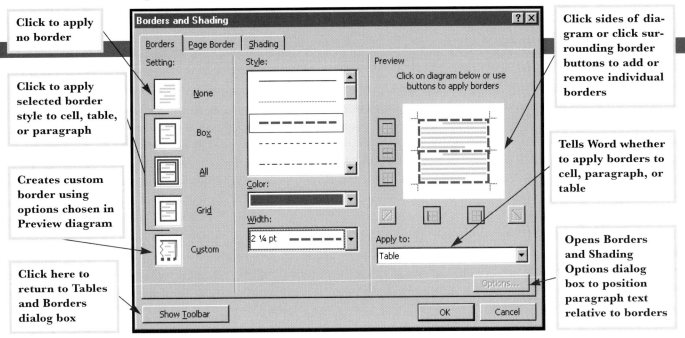

Figure 4-32 Drawn table with applied border

2 1/4-point, blue, tightly dotted border

"All" selection on Borders tab applies same border style on all internal and external borders

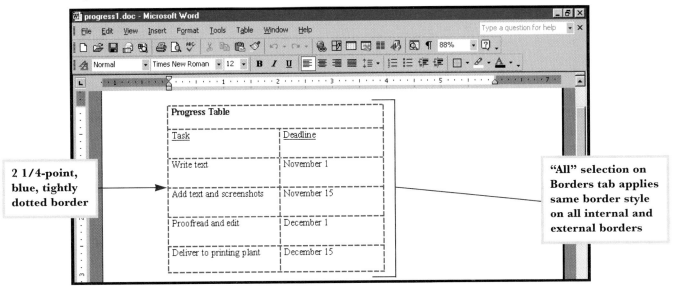

skill | Adding Borders and Shading (continued)

do it !

11. Click inside of cell A1 to activate it. If necessary, click the Tables and Borders button on the Standard toolbar to display the Tables and Borders toolbar.

12. On the Tables and Borders toolbar, click the arrow on the right edge of the Shading Color button ⬛️⏷. The Shading Color palette will appear. Click the Gray-25% option, which is the seventh square in the first row of the palette (see Figure 4-33). Word shades the active cell with the color you have selected.

13. Click in the Selection bar immediately to the left of row 2 of the table to select the entire row. Hold down the [Ctrl] key and, using the Selection bar again, highlight rows 4 and 6 as well. Release the [Ctrl] key. ◗ As a new feature in Word 2002, you can select non-adjacent areas of a document—for example, the first and fourth paragraphs of a text document or (as in this Step) the second, fourth, and sixth rows of the table. After selecting these areas, you then can format them alike.

14. Click the arrow on the right edge of the Shading Color button to display the Shading Color palette again. Click the Pale Blue option, which is the sixth square in the bottom row (see Figure 4-34). Word shades the second, fourth, and sixth rows with the color you have selected. ◗ You may apply the current Shading Color multiple times by clicking the Shading Color button itself rather than clicking the arrow next to it.

15. Click outside of the table to cancel the selection. Verify that the format of your table now matches that of Figure 4-35. If your table does not, click the Undo button as many times as needed to clear the mistaken formats, review the Steps you missed, and redo them.

16. Save and close your document with the changes you have made.

more

Figure 4-31 shows that the Borders and Shading dialog box contains not only a Borders tab but also a Page Borders and Shading tab. The Box, Shadow, 3-D, and Custom options apply formats around a whole page just as the same boxes on the Borders tab do so for tables. These four options on the Page Borders tab also resemble their counterparts on the Borders tab in that they apply formats according to the current settings in the Style, Color, and Width boxes. However, the Page Borders tab also has an Art box that offers small graphics to use in place of lined, dotted, and other borders in the Style box. The Preview diagram on the Page Borders tab works like the corresponding diagram on the Borders tab. You can apply borders by clicking the border areas on the diagram itself or the border buttons surrounding the diagram. The Page Borders tab also contains a Show Toolbar and an Options button for further formatting effects.

The Shading tab of the Borders and Shading dialog box offers fewer formatting options than do the other two tabs but it still helps you produce attractive formatting effects. Like the Shading Color button on the Tables and Borders toolbar, the Shading tab offers a color palette of over fifty colors and shades of gray to provide fill colors for rows and columns. A More Colors button opens the same Colors dialog box that the More Fill Colors area of the Shading Color button does. The Patterns section of the Shading tab contains a Style box that enables you to apply shaded or patterned colors over the top of the fill colors and a Colors box to dictate which colors will appear in those shaded or patterned areas. Lastly, the Shading tab also has a Preview area that shows what your formatting results will be and an Apply to box that dictates what precise area the Shading selection will affect.

Figure 4-33 Shading Color palette with Gray-25% option

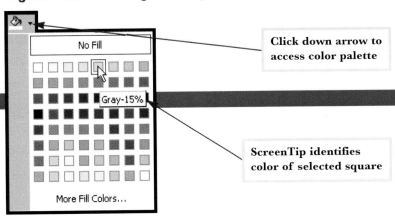

Click down arrow to access color palette

ScreenTip identifies color of selected square

No Fill

Gray-15%

More Fill Colors...

Figure 4-34 Shading Color palette with Pale Blue option

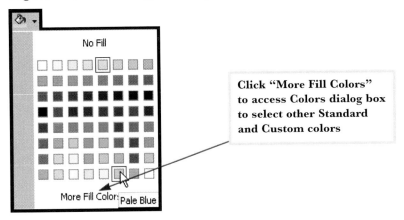

Click "More Fill Colors" to access Colors dialog box to select other Standard and Custom colors

No Fill

More Fill Colors   Pale Blue

Figure 4-35 Table formatted with all desired borders and shading

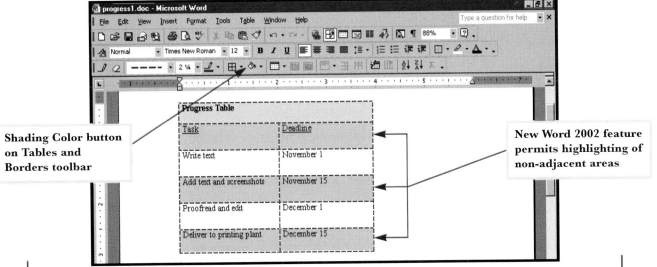

Shading Color button on Tables and Borders toolbar

New Word 2002 feature permits highlighting of non-adjacent areas

Progress Table	
Task	Deadline
Write text	November 1
Add text and screenshots	November 15
Proofread and edit	December 1
Deliver to printing plant	December 15

Practice

To practice formatting a table with borders and shading, reopen Student File mywdprac4-6.doc. Change the alternating shaded rows to light green, and the borders around the first and last rows to dashed lines. Save and close any changes in your Word Files folder as mywdprac4-10.doc.

shortcuts

Function	Button/Mouse	Menu	Keyboard
Insert a table	▢	Click Table, click Insert, click Table	
Insert a row above the selected row	Right-click to the left of selected row, then click Insert Rows	Click Table, click Insert, click Rows Above	
Insert a row below the selected row		Click Table, click Insert, click Rows Below	
Insert a column to the left of the selected column	Right-click above selected column, then click Insert Columns	Click Table, click Insert, click Columns to the Left	
Insert a column to the right of the selected column		Click Table, click Insert, click Columns to the Right	
Select entire table	Click Table Move handle ✛ (Print Layout View)	Click Table, highlight Select, then click Table	
Delete the selected table		Click Table, click Delete, click Table	
Delete the selected row	Right-click to the left of the selected row, then click Delete Rows	Click Table, click Delete, click Rows	[Shift]+[Delete]
Delete the selected column	Right-click above the selected column, then click Delete Columns	Click Table, click Delete, click Columns	[Shift]+[Delete]
Align to the left selected text in a cell or a paragraph	▤		[Ctrl]+[L]
Align to the right selected text in a cell or a paragraph	▤		[Ctrl]+[R]
Center selected text in a cell or paragraph	▤		[Ctrl]+[E]
Justify selected text in a cell or paragraph	▤		[Ctrl]+[J]
Repeat last action		Click Edit, then click Repeat [action name]	[Ctrl]+[Y]

A. Identify Key Features

Name the items indicated by callouts in Figure 2-24.

Figure 4-36 Identifying components of a toolbar and a table

1.

2.

3.

4.

5.

6.

7.

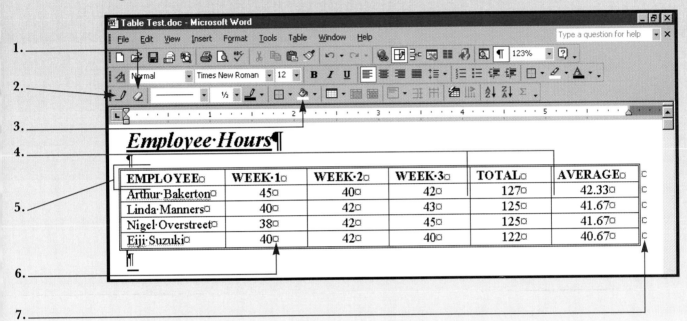

B. Select the Best Answer

8. An order in which you can sort data

9. Explains the symbols and colors being used in a chart

10. The visible boundary between cells in a basic table

11. The intersection of a row and a column

12. An existing worksheet that becomes part of a Word document

13. A command list that appears when you right-click a table

14. A graphic representation of a table

15. A visual element indicating a selected chart

16. What Word uses to calculate data in a table

a. Chart

b. Table shortcut menu

c. Embedded object

d. Legend

e. Ascending

f. Formula

g. Gridline

h. Hatchmark

i. Cell

quiz (continued)

C. Complete the Statement

17. The Insert Table button:

a. Creates a table based on the Normal template

b. Creates a table based on dimensions you choose

c. Pastes data from the Clipboard into a table

d. Inserts a default table of 4 rows and 4 columns

18. To move the insertion point to the next cell of a table in the current row:

a. Press [End]

b. Press [Tab]

c. Double-click the table

d. Press [Shift]+[Enter]

19. D14 refers to:

a. The fourteenth row in the fourth column

b. The fourteenth column in the fourth row

c. A formula with at least fourteen values

d. A document designation for a Word table

20. The first step in creating a chart from a selected table is to:

a. Click the chart button

b. Press [Ctrl]+[F8]

c. Click Insert, then click Chart

d. Click Insert, then click Object

21. Paragraphs and table columns both have:

a. Page numbers

b. Selection bars

c. Gridlines

d. Cell markers

22. The Chart Legend:

a. Summarizes a Chart Wizard's instructions

b. Must be created in Excel and linked to Word

c. Displays the Tables and Borders toolbar

d. Explains the meaning of colors used in the chart

23. You may delete columns by accessing the:

a. Table menu

b. Tools menu

c. Edit menu

d. Format menu

24. You must use an equal sign before a formula or Word will:

a. Use the wrong data to calculate the formula

b. Use the correct data, but calculate incorrectly

c. Calculate the last row of data by default

d. Read the data as a label and not calculate anything

25. To sort data in a table you should:

a. Open the Sort dialog box, and use it to sort the data

b. Open the Sort data program in Excel or Access

c. Open the Sort tool on the Edit menu

d. Open the Sort menu and choose the Ascending or Descending command

26. The Borders and Shading dialog box contains all **but** the following:

a. Border Design, Color, and Shading tabs

b. A Setting section on the Borders tab

c. A Style section on the Page Border tab

d. A Preview area on the Shading tab

interactivity

Build Your Skills

1. Open a new document, create a table, and add data to it:

   a. Open a new Word document and immediately save it as Employees.doc.

   b. Click Table, then click Insert Table to open the Insert Table dialog box. Create a table that is 5 columns by 4 rows and close the dialog box.

   c. Label the cells across the top row as follows: Name, March, April, May, and Average.

   d. Enter a first and a last name into each of the lower three cells in the leftmost column.

   e. Insert a number between 18 and 22 into each of the three cells to the right of each name, for a total of nine cells.

2. Average the columns and sort the table:

   a. Position the insertion point in the second cell down in the Average column, which is cell E2.

   b. Click Table, then click Formula to open the Formula dialog box. Enter the formula =AVERAGE(B2:D2) into the Formula text box, choose the Number format 0.00, and press [Enter].

   c. Repeat Steps a and b for the other two cells in the Average column, making sure that you use the correct cell references for the related calculation. Sort the table in the order of ascending average.

3. Format and resave the table:

   a. Place the insertion point anywhere inside the table, click Table, and then click Table AutoFormat. Select a simple Table Style that does not include any cell shading. In the Apply special formats to section, be sure that only the Heading rows and First column check boxes are checked, and press [Enter].

   b. Alter the existing formatting by shading the first row of the table with Gray-20% and bolding the heading text if needed. Also apply an All border with a Solid line, Dark Blue color, and 1-1/2 point width.

   c. Be sure the text in the Names column is aligned left and that the text in the other four columns is centered. Using the Table tab on the Table Properties dialog box, center the table horizontally on the page. Resave the table with the changes you have made thus far.

4. Create a chart from the existing table.

   a. Highlight only the first four columns of the table you created above. Click Insert, click Object, click the Create New tab if needed, click Microsoft Graph Chart, and then press [Enter] to create a chart and to close the dialog box.

   b. On the Titles tab of the Chart Options dialog box, type Monthly Workdays in the Chart title box. Type Month in the Category (X) axis box. Press [Enter] to confirm the titles and to close the dialog box.

   c. Close the Datasheet. Drag the right edge of the chart so it lines up with the decimal places in the last column of the table above it. Click outside the chart to verify that it is centered horizontally on the page. If you need to adjust the size and position of the chart, click on it only once, use the sizing handles to adjust it, and then deselect the chart.

   d. Resave and close the document with the changes you have made.

interactivity (continued)

Problem Solving Exercises

1. Create a table to display the high and low temperatures for each of the last five days (use fictional numbers if you do not have available data). Add two columns to the table to include the high and the low temperatures for the five-day period, and use the Formula dialog box to calculate the five-day averages. Then convert the table into a chart. Finally, add a row to the bottom of the table, merge the cells, and type your name. Save the file as Temperatures.doc.

2. Create a table to help calculate the grade-point averages of the students you have been tutoring for the last two years.

   a. Using the data below, calculate the Grade Point Average (GPA) for every student over the two-year period.

   b. Calculate the combined GPA of all the students for each semester that you tutored the students.

   c. Calculate the overall GPA, including every student, over the two-year period.

   d. Sort the table by the highest individual GPA, as found in question 2a, over the last two years.

   e. AutoFormat the table with a Colorful style, applying special formats to the heading row, the last row, and the first column. Make sure your name is included in the document, and save it as GPA.doc.

Student	Semester 1	Semester 2	Semester 3	Semester 4
Rosa	3.6	3.1	4.0	2.7
Zi	3.3	3.9	3.5	3.0
Donny	2.8	2.3	2.4	3.7
Melanie	3.1	1.4	2.9	2.5
Tsuyoshi	1.7	2.6	2.0	2.9

3. As the leader of a public relations team, you are responsible for your employees' business expenses. Create a table to calculate information about their expenses over the first half of the year. Format all dollar amounts with dollar signs and two decimal places. Use the Formula dialog box to calculate all totals and averages. (Hint: the table probably will fit best in Landscape page orientation).

   a. Using the data below, figure out the total each employee spent.

   b. Calculate the total that the entire team spent over the six-month period.

   c. Calculate the average amount per month spent by each employee over the six-month period.

   d. Calculate the average amount spent by the team every month.

   e. Use the default Chart type to create a chart representing the table you have created. Make any modifications to the chart that you feel are necessary to make it as informative, attractive, and readable as possible.

   f. Add your name to the document and save it as Expenses.doc.

Employees	Jan	Feb	Mar	Apr	May	Jun
Isa	113	158	306	400	322	150
Gao	150	150	258	350	300	125
Jill	200	320	354	410	300	100

Introduction to Spreadsheet Software

Excel 2002

Microsoft Excel 2002 is a computer application that facilitates your ability to organize and record data, and then extract results from the data. With Excel, you can enter text labels and numerical values into an electronic spreadsheet, which is a grid made up of columns and rows. Just like a handwritten ledger that might be used for bookkeeping or accounting, an electronic spreadsheet consists of individual worksheets that enable you to record distinct, but related, data in a common location.

Being able to use spreadsheet software can help you both professionally and personally. By providing an organized structure in which to work, Excel can increase the efficiency with which you conduct business and manage your own affairs. Excel's ability to perform and automate calculations saves you time and decreases the possibility of human error compromising the integrity of your work.

An Excel spreadsheet is nearly as versatile as a blank canvas. Businesses use spreadsheets to plan budgets, track expenses and profits, and project future values of prices and transactions. A worksheet could also be used to lay out a schedule or a record of customers. As you work with Excel, you will find that any task that involves organizing information may be well served by the spreadsheet format.

Using Excel, you will learn how to create a spreadsheet employing proper design techniques. You then will explore the fundamentals of the application and become familiar with its basic elements and operations. Later on, some of Excel's more advanced features, such as formulas, What-If analysis, and charts will broaden your ability to manipulate data in a spreadsheet. If you need assistance while using Excel, the program includes an extensive Help facility, as well as direct links to online support via the World Wide Web.

Lesson Goal:

Learn the basics of Excel as you begin to construct a worksheet that will track the income, expenses, and profits of a business.

- ⚡ **Introducing Excel and Worksheet Design**
- ⚡ **Starting Excel**
- ⚡ **Exploring the Excel Window**
- ⚡ **Moving Around the Worksheet**
- ⚡ **Entering Labels**
- ⚡ **Saving and Closing a Workbook**
- ⚡ **Opening a Workbook**
- ⚡ **Editing a Cell's Information**
- ⚡ **Using the Office Assistant**
- ⚡ **Other Excel Help Features**
- ⚡ **Exiting Excel**

skill Introducing Excel and Worksheet Design

concept

Microsoft Excel is an electronic spreadsheet application designed to make the creation and use of professional-quality spreadsheets fast and easy. A spreadsheet is a table composed of rows and columns that stores text and numbers for easy viewing and tabulation. The intersection of a row and column creates a unit called a cell, in which you can enter data. Electronic spreadsheets are very useful for performing rapid and accurate calculations on groups of inter-related numbers. Using Excel, you can:

- Organize information rapidly and accurately. With the proper data and formulas, Excel calculates your results automatically.

- Recalculate automatically. Fixing errors in Excel is easy. When you find a mistake and correct the entry, Excel recalculates all related data automatically.

- Keep track of the effect that changing one piece of data has on related numbers. You can guess changes that may occur in the future and see how they could change the results of your calculations—a feature called What-If analysis.

- Display data as graphs or charts. Excel enables you to display numeric data graphically in the form of charts that are updated automatically as the data on which they are based change. For example, Figure 1-1 shows the data in a spreadsheet also displayed in the form of a pie chart. Charts are often easier to read than raw data and make the relationships among data easier to understand. If your copy of Excel has been used previously, the appearance of the application window may differ from the one shown in the figure because another user may have resized the window or customized the screen.

A spreadsheet's organization is shaped by the goal or purpose of the data. A well-designed spreadsheet should be accurate and easily understood. Toward that end, you may choose to design your spreadsheets using the four distinct sections visible in Figure 1-2: documentation, assumptions, input, and results.

- The documentation section consists of a complete description of the name of the author, the purpose of the spreadsheet, the date it was created, and the name of the spreadsheet file. Documentation also should detail the use of named cell ranges and macros. Ranges are blocks of cells that contain similar or related data, or are acted upon as a single unit. Macros are sets of programming instructions that automate spreadsheet tasks.

- The assumptions section displays variable factors that may change in a worksheet. For example, a profit projection might assume that sales will increase by 10 percent each quarter. If the assumption is changed, or turns out to be an inaccurate projection, the amount of profit changes accordingly. If you document an assumption, it is much easier to change it later. Assumptions are useful when conducting a What-If analysis, which calculates the effects of changes in a spreadsheet. For instance, what if sales only grow by 5 percent instead of 10 percent?

- The input section of a spreadsheet stores the data that you enter and manipulate. In Figure 1-2, the input section contains data for income and expenditures. Input data are generally arranged in blocks of numbers organized in columns and rows.

- The results, or output section displays the outcome of the calculations performed on the input data. Output data are generally placed below or to the right of input data.

more

An Excel file is also known as a workbook. Excel stores each workbook you create as an individual file in your computer's memory. A workbook file can be a single worksheet or may contain many pages of data and charts. Each file should have a unique name so that you can differentiate it from other files. Excel files use the file extension .xls. A file extension is (generally) a three-character code separated from the file name with a period, pronounced "dot," that tells the computer what application is associated with a particular file and what type of data the file contains. When saving workbook files, you should avoid using additional periods in file names and changing the .xls extension. If you change the extension, Excel may no longer recognize your workbook files and may not be able to open them.

Figure 1-1 Worksheet made with Microsoft Excel

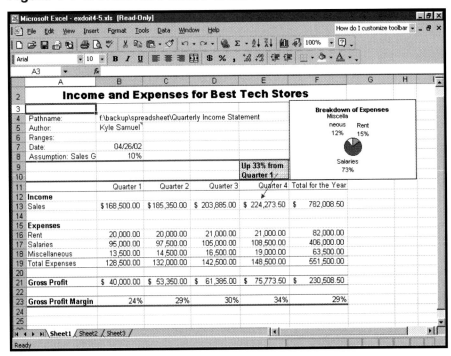

Figure 1-2 Organization of a spreadsheet

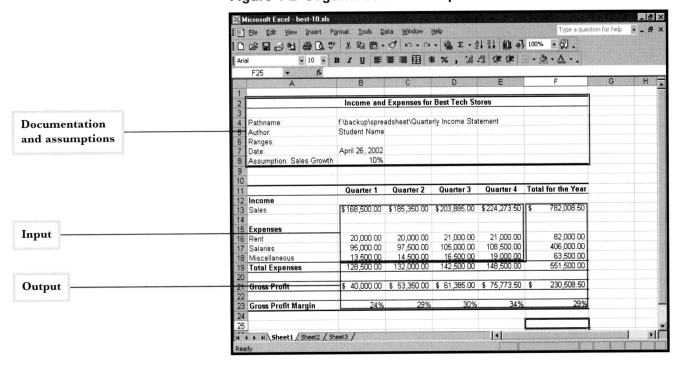

skill | Starting Excel

concept

The first step in using the Microsoft Excel program, or application, is launching it. The Windows operating system provides a number of ways to launch programs. When you install Excel (or Microsoft Office, the suite of programs of which Excel is a part), a shortcut to the program is placed on the Windows Start menu automatically. You can also open Excel by locating and running its executable file, named Excel.exe, through My Computer or Windows Explorer.

do it !

Use the Start menu to launch the Microsoft Excel application.

1. Turn on your computer and monitor and make sure that any peripheral devices such as your mouse are connected properly. When your edition of the Windows operating system finishes loading, the Windows desktop should appear on your screen (you may be asked to provide a user name and password before Windows finishes loading).

2. Click the Start button **Start** on the Windows taskbar, which generally is located at the bottom of the screen. The Windows Start menu will appear.

3. Move the mouse pointer ᛋ up the Start menu to the Programs folder. The Programs sub-menu will open beside the Start menu.

4. Move the mouse pointer over to the Programs submenu from the Start menu, and rest the pointer over Microsoft Excel. The program name will be highlighted, as shown in Figure 1-3. Newer editions of the Windows operating system such as Windows Me utilize personalized menus, which means that only the items you use most frequently are displayed on a menu when it first opens. If personalized menus are active on your comput-er and you do not see Microsoft Excel listed on the Programs menu, click the double arrow at the bottom of the menu to display the rest of the program listings. It is also possible that the program will be listed on another submenu of the Start menu.

5. Click the left mouse button once. Excel will open with a blank workbook in the window (see Figure 1-4). If your copy of Excel has been used previously, the appearance of the application window may differ from the one shown in the figure.

more

Do not be alarmed if your desktop or Start menu do not match the descriptions above or the figures on the next page exactly. With several different versions of Windows and countless software applications avail-able, variances in system configuration are more than likely. Windows itself is highly customizable, so the location or appearance of items such as the taskbar and the desktop are also subject to change. Furthermore, you can customize the way in which you interact with the operating system. For example, you can alter the functionality of the mouse so that tasks that normally require a double-click only require a single click. For the purposes of this book, the term click means to press and release the left mouse button quickly. When instructed to double-click, you should press and release the left mouse button twice in rapid succession. A right-click instruction requires you to press and release the right mouse button once. Finally, drag means to press and hold the left mouse button down, move the mouse as instructed, and then release the mouse button at the appropriate point to complete the action.

Figure 1-3 Opening Excel from the Start menu

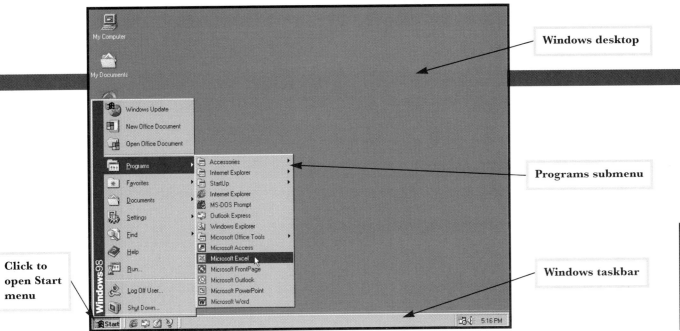

Windows desktop

Programs submenu

Click to open Start menu

Windows taskbar

Figure 1-4 Excel application window

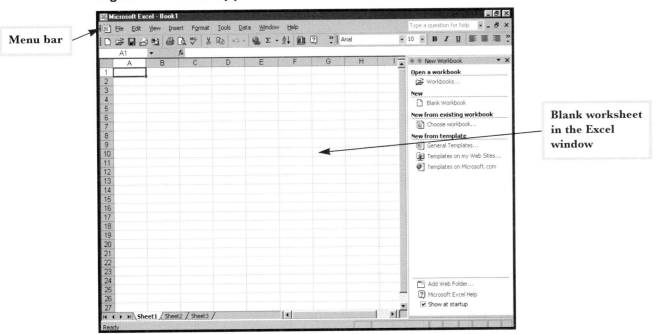

Menu bar

Blank worksheet in the Excel window

Practice

Click the File menu title on the Menu bar. The File menu will drop down below its menu title. Move the mouse pointer down the File menu and click the Exit command to close the Excel application. If you do not see the Exit command, click the double arrow at the bottom of the menu to expand the menu. When you have successfully exited Excel, use the Start menu to open the application again.

skill

Exploring the Excel Window

concept

In order to begin building a spreadsheet, it is necessary to become familiar with the Excel window and worksheet elements. The Excel application window consists of many features that are common to most applications running under the Windows operating system. These include a Title bar, Menu bar, document (worksheet) window and window control buttons, and toolbars. In addition to these items, Excel has many unique features that are designed to make worksheet production fast, flexible, and convenient.

do it !

Familiarize yourself with the Excel screen by examining various features.

1. Start Excel if the application is not already running. If the Excel window does not fill the screen, click the Maximize button ▢ on the right edge of the Title bar. The Title bar at the top of the window displays the name of the program and the name of the file that is active. When Excel opens, it automatically creates a new workbook containing three blank worksheets that is called Book1 (subsequent new files opened during the same work session are called Book2, Book3, and so on). The Title bar also houses the Minimize ▬, Maximize ▢ or Restore ▣, and Close buttons ☒, which are used to control the window. The Minimize button reduces the window to a program button on the taskbar. The Maximize button appears when the Excel window does not fill the entire screen. When the window is maximized, the Restore button, which returns the window to its previous size and location, appears in place of the Maximize button. ◣ Notice that a second set of control buttons appears just below the set on the Title bar. This second set of buttons applies to the active workbook file, not the entire application window, making it easier to work with multiple open Excel files at once. If you minimize the active file, it is reduced to a small Title bar at the bottom of the application window.

2. The Menu bar displays the titles of the menus containing Excel commands. Click File on the Menu bar to open the File menu. Excel 2002 uses personalized menus by default, so only a few commands may appear when you first open a menu. If you do not click one of the available commands, the menu will expand after a few seconds to reveal more commands. You can expedite this expansion by clicking the double arrow at the bottom of the menu or by clicking the menu title again. Alternatively, double-click the menu title to open the full menu right away. As you use Excel more and more, the program learns which commands you use most often. These commands will then be the first to appear when you open a menu. Click File again to close the File menu.

3. The Standard toolbar contains buttons that serve as shortcuts to commonly used commands. Move the mouse pointer over the New button ▢ on the Standard toolbar. A brief description of the button's function, called a ScreenTip, will appear. Guide the mouse pointer over the toolbars, pausing on each button to read its description, as shown in Figure 1-5. Next to the Standard toolbar in the same row in the default Excel setup is the Formatting toolbar, which contains buttons for formatting text, inserted objects, and the structure of the worksheet. ◣ The Standard and Formatting toolbars are just two of the many toolbars available in Excel. To activate additional toolbars, open the View menu from the Menu bar and point to the Toolbars command. A submenu of toolbar names will appear. Click a toolbar name to activate it, as shown in Figure 1-6.

(continued on EX 1.8)

Figure 1-5 Elements of the application window

Title bar

Menu bar

Standard toolbar

ScreenTip

Active worksheet in workbook window

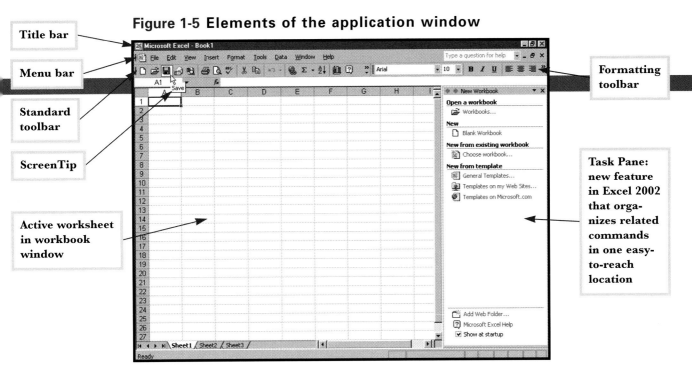

Formatting toolbar

Task Pane: new feature in Excel 2002 that orga- nizes related commands in one easy- to-reach location

Figure 1-6 Activating toolbars

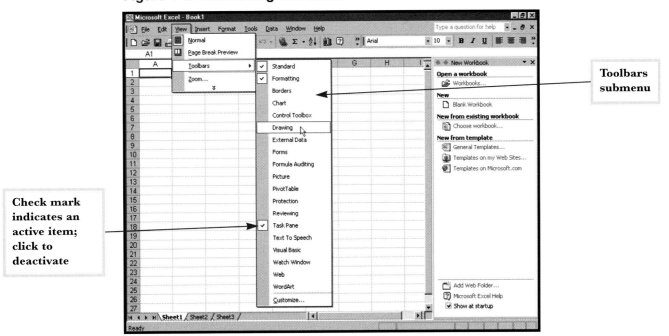

Toolbars submenu

Check mark indicates an active item; click to deactivate

skill Exploring the Excel Window (continued)

do it !

4. Click the letter A that heads the first column of the worksheet. Column A becomes highlighted indicating that it is selected, as shown in Figure 1-7. Columns in a worksheet are designated by letters, from A to Z, then AA to AZ, and so on up to IV for a total of 256 columns.

5. Click the number 1 at the left end of the first row. Row 1 becomes highlighted indicating that it is selected. Rows are labeled numerically down the left side of the worksheet from 1 to 65,536.

6. Click the space at the intersection of column D and row 7. The intersection of a row and a column is called a cell. A cell name, or address, consists of its column letter and row number. Cell D7 is now active. Excel indicates the active cell by surrounding it with a dark rectangle called the cell pointer. When a cell is active, you can enter new data into it or edit any data that are already there. You can make another cell active by clicking it, or by moving the cell pointer with the arrow keys on the keyboard.

7. Click cell F12. The Name box displays the address of the active cell.

8. Double-click cell F12. An insertion point appears in the cell and the pointer changes to an I-beam (see Figure 1-8). At the bottom of the Excel window, the text in the Status bar changes from Ready to Enter, indicating that you can enter or edit labels, values, or formulas. The Status bar provides feedback on your current activity in Excel and displays the status of particular keys such as the Caps Lock key. You can enter data in an active cell without double-clicking it, but any data already there will be erased immediately.

9. Click the down arrow on the vertical scroll bar on the right side of the worksheet to move the sheet down one row, hiding row 1. The vertical scroll bar and the horizontal scroll bar on the lower edge of the worksheet help you move quickly around the worksheet.

10. Below the active worksheet, Excel provides Sheet tabs that you can click to switch to other worksheets in the active workbook. Click the Sheet2 tab. Notice that the cell pointer moves from cell F12, the active cell on Sheet1, to cell A1, the active cell on Sheet2. The Sheet tabs enable you to organize related worksheets in a single workbook. Workbooks may contain up to 255 worksheets. Sheet tab scrolling buttons (in the lower-left corner of the window) allow you to view Sheet tabs that are hidden. Click the Sheet1 tab.

more

Standard scroll bars offer four basic ways of navigating. Clicking the arrows on either end of a scroll bar moves the worksheet view in small increments. The position of the scroll bar box relative to the ends of the scroll bar gives you an indication of where you are in the worksheet. To move in larger increments, click the scroll bar itself on either side of the scroll bar box. To move in even larger increments, drag the scroll bar box in the direction you want to move. Since Excel worksheets can grow quite lengthy, you also can hold down the [Shift] key on the keyboard while dragging the scroll bar box to advance rapidly through large portions of a worksheet. Be careful when using these last two methods, however, because scrolling by dragging is much less precise than scrolling by clicking.

As noted on the previous page, the Task Pane is a feature in Excel 2002 that brings together common, related commands in a convenient location. The Task Pane is context-sensitive, meaning that it changes according to the actions you perform. The Task Pane may be activated and deactivated just like a toolbar. The application and document control icons (see Figure 1-8) at the left end of the Title bar and Menu bar, respectively, offer menus containing the Close, Minimize, Maximize, and Restore commands.

Figure 1-7 Selecting a column

Column A heading button

Name box

Row 1 heading button

Cell D7

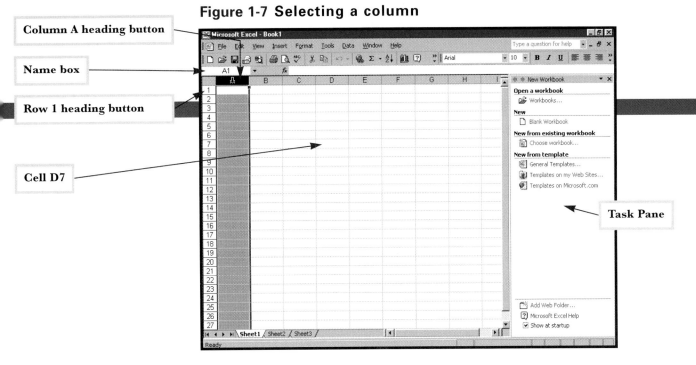

Task Pane

Figure 1-8 Working in an active cell

Control menu icons

Cell pointer

Sheet tabs

Sheet tab scrolling buttons

Insertion point: indicates where text will be entered

I-beam: allows you to place insertion point accurately

Vertical scroll bar

Horizontal scroll bar

Status bar

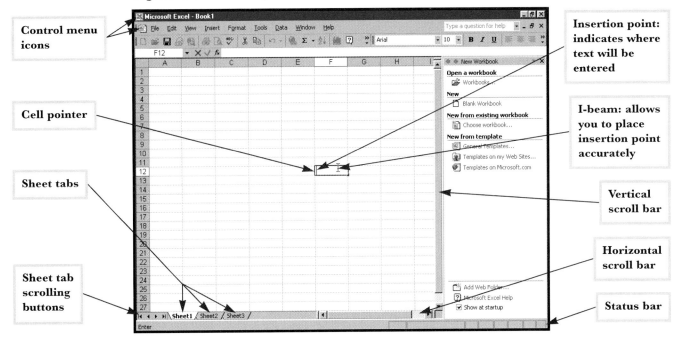

Practice

As shown in the preceding figures, the Standard and Formatting toolbars are arranged in a single row. This setting gives you more screen space, but limits the number of buttons you can see on each of the toolbars. The double arrow pointing to the right at the end of a toolbar indicates that more buttons are available. The downward-pointing arrow indicates that a menu will appear if you click the arrows. Click a set of arrows and then click Show Buttons on Two Rows. The Formatting toolbar will move below the Standard toolbar so you have better access to the buttons on both toolbars. When the buttons are shown on two rows, the command you clicked will appear as Show Buttons on One Row.

skill

Moving Around the Worksheet

concept

To use Excel effectively, you must be able to maneuver between cells in the workspace. To do this, you may use either the mouse or the keyboard depending on your personal preference or the task you are trying to accomplish. For example, if you are entering a large quantity of data quickly into cells that are close together, it may be easier and more efficient to use the keyboard. If you need to select a cell that is far from the active cell, using the mouse probably would be more effective.

do it !

Move to various points on a worksheet to familiarize yourself with Excel's navigation.

1. If Excel is not already running, start the application so you are working with a blank worksheet (if Excel is running, you should be on Sheet1).

2. Using the mouse, move the mouse pointer ✛ to cell B4 and click the left mouse button. The cell becomes surrounded by a heavy border, as shown in Figure 1-9, marking it as the active cell.

3. Press [◄—] on the keyboard. The cell pointer moves over one cell to the left to A4.

4. Press [↑] on the keyboard. The cell pointer moves up one cell to A3.

5. Press [—►] and then [↓] to return the cell pointer to cell B4.

6. Click once on the arrow at the right end of the horizontal scroll bar. The worksheet scrolls to the left so that a column further to the right is visible.

7. Scroll down one row by clicking once on the arrow at the bottom of the vertical scroll bar.

8. Click the arrow on the right end of the horizontal scroll button until column Z is visible. Notice that the scroll bar box shrinks to allow you a larger movement area, as seen in Figure 1-10.

9. Click and hold the mouse button on the horizontal scroll bar box. Drag the box to the left until you can see column A, and then release the mouse button.

(continued on EX 1.12)

Figure 1-9 Cell B4 active

Standard and Formatting toolbars now occupy two rows (see Practice on page EX 1.9)

Mouse pointer appears as a thick cross when over the worksheet

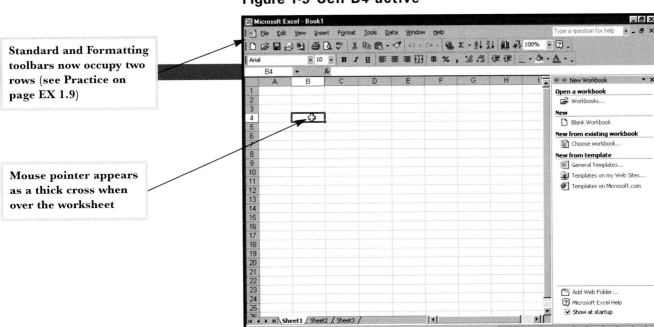

Figure 1-10 Scrolling through a worksheet

Name box still displays active cell, B4, even though it is no longer visible

Row 4 button highlighted, indicating that a cell in that row is selected

Column names extend past Z and begin again with AA, AB, and so on

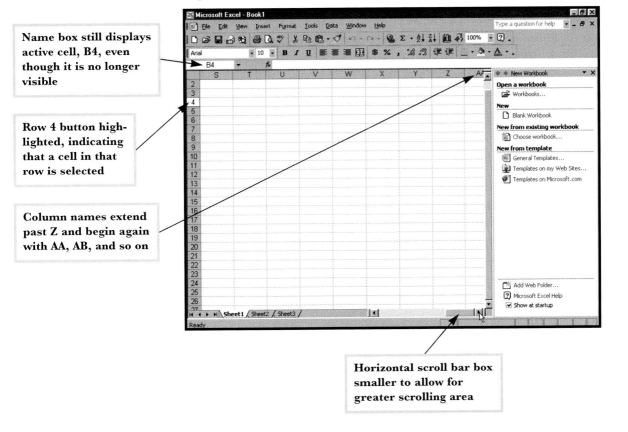

Horizontal scroll bar box smaller to allow for greater scrolling area

skill | Moving Around the Worksheet (continued)

do it !

10. Click Edit on the Menu bar, then click the Go To command. The Go To dialog box appears. The Go To dialog box enables you to go to a part of the worksheet to which it would not be convenient to scroll. ◁▷ If you do not see the Go To command on the Edit menu, click the double arrow at the bottom of the menu to reveal more commands. You also can open the Go To dialog box by pressing the keyboard shortcut [Ctrl]+[G].

11. Type E2002 in the text box labeled Reference at the bottom of the dialog box, as shown in Figure 1-11 (it is not necessary to click in the box first—the blinking insertion point indicates that the text box is ready to receive text). You may type the cell reference using lowercase or uppercase letters. Excel will convert the letters to uppercase automatically.

12. Click the OK button [OK]. Excel immediately moves the cell pointer to the cell you referenced in the Go To dialog box, E2002.

13. Press [Ctrl]+[Home] (while holding down the [Ctrl] key, press the [Home] key). This keyboard shortcut moves the cell pointer to the beginning of the worksheet, cell A1. Some of the more common methods of moving around a worksheet are summarized in Table 1-1. ◁▷ To move across a large area of blank cells, press [End] on the keyboard. The word END will appear in the Status bar. Then press an arrow key. The cell pointer will jump to the next filled cell in the direction of the arrow key you pressed.

more

As you have learned, a workbook can be made up of many worksheets. The Sheet tabs at the bottom of the worksheet, labeled Sheet1, Sheet2, and Sheet3 by default, enable you to view the different worksheets within a workbook. You can keep interrelated data across multiple worksheets in the same workbook for viewing, cross referencing, and calculation. To add a blank worksheet to a workbook, select the Worksheet command from the Insert menu. The tab for the new worksheet will appear in front of the tab for the active worksheet.

You can change the order in which a Sheet tab appears in the row of tabs by dragging it to a new position. The mouse pointer will appear with a blank sheet icon attached to it ▯ while you are dragging a tab, and a small arrow will indicate where the tab will be placed when you release the mouse button. The tab scrolling buttons |◀ ◀ ▶ ▶|, located to the left of the Sheet tabs, allow you to view tabs that do not fit in the window. Clicking one of the outer buttons moves you to the first or last tab, while clicking one of the inner buttons moves you through the tabs one at a time. The tab scrolling buttons only function when enough worksheets have been added to the workbook to cause some of the tabs to be hidden.

If you right-click the tab scrolling buttons, a shortcut menu listing all of the worksheets in your workbook will appear. Simply click the name of the worksheet you want to view to display it. You can rename a worksheet by double-clicking its tab and then editing the name like normal text. Right-clicking a tab opens a shortcut menu with commands that enable you to rename, delete, insert, and copy or move a worksheet, or change the color of the tab.

Figure 1-11 Go To dialog box

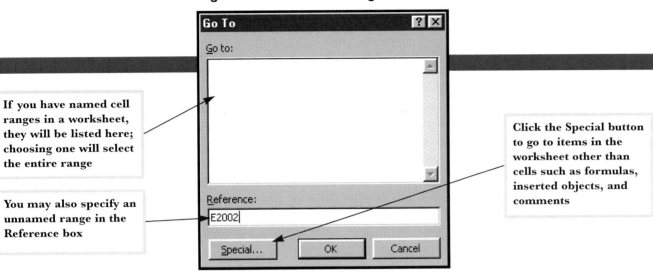

If you have named cell ranges in a worksheet, they will be listed here; choosing one will select the entire range

You may also specify an unnamed range in the Reference box

Click the Special button to go to items in the worksheet other than cells such as formulas, inserted objects, and comments

Table 1-1 Moving in a worksheet

Movement	Action
Left one cell	Press [◄—] or [Shift]+[Tab]
Right one cell	Press [—►] or [Tab]
Up one cell	Press [↑] or [Shift]+[Enter]
Down one cell	Press [↓] or [Enter] (in default setup)
Left one column or right one column	Click the left arrow or right arrow on the horizontal scroll bar
Up one row or down one row	Click the up arrow or down arrow on the vertical scroll bar
Up one screen or down one screen	Press [Page Up] or [Page Down]
Left one screen or right one screen	Press [Alt]+[Page Up] or [Alt]+[Page Down]
Go to cell A1	[Ctrl]+[Home]
Go to column A in current row	[Home]

Practice

Click cell E12 to make it active, then use the arrow keys to move the cell pointer to G7. Open the Go To dialog box and navigate to cell CH10514. Finally move the cell pointer to cell A1.

skill | Entering Labels

concept

Labels are used to annotate and describe the data you place into rows and columns on a worksheet. Properly labeled data make your spreadsheet easy to understand and interpret. Labels can consist of text or numbers and are aligned to the left of the cell to differentiate them from data used in calculations. Excel left-aligns labels for you automatically. You should enter labels into your spreadsheet first so that your rows and columns are defined before you begin to enter calculable data.

do it !

Enter the documentation and row labels for a spreadsheet.

1. On Sheet1 of a blank workbook, click cell A2 to make it the active cell.

2. Type Income and Expenses for Best Tech Stores, and then click the Enter button ☑ to the right of the Name box to confirm the entry. The label will appear in the Formula bar as you type. Even though the label is longer than the the cell's width, it will be displayed in its entirety because the cell to the right of it is empty. Your screen should look like Figure 1-12.

3. Click cell A4 and type the label Pathname:. Then press [Tab] and type f:\backup\spreadsheet\Quarterly Income Report.xls in cell B4. This is a fictional file path meant to represent that which might be used for a workbook stored on a network server. The path will not change throughout this book even though the file names you use will.

4. Click cell A5 and type Author:. Then press [Tab] and type: Kyle Samuel in cell B5.

5. Click cell A6 and type Ranges:. Press [Enter] on the keyboard to confirm the entry and move the cell pointer to cell A7.

6. Enter Date: in cell A7 and April 26, 2002 in cell B7. Then click cell A8. Notice that Excel changes the date you entered to a short format. Enter Assumption: Sales Growth in cell A8, press [Tab], and then enter .1 in cell B8. Press [Enter]. Notice that the label in cell A8 is cut off because cell B8 is not empty.

7. Press [Enter] two times to make cell A11 the active cell. Then type Income, press [Enter], and type Sales in cell A12.

8. Press [Enter] twice and make the following entries: A14—Expenditures, A15—Rent, A16—Salaries, A17—Miscellaneous, A18—Total Expenses, A20—Gross Profit. Press [Enter] after the last entry. Your worksheet should look like Figure 1-13. If your screen resolution is not set to at least 800 by 600 pixels, you likely will have to scroll down in order to complete the above entries.

9. Leave this worksheet on your screen as you will need it in the next Skill.

more

The Enter button on the Formula bar confirms cell entries just like pressing the [Enter] key on the keyboard does, except using the Enter button leaves the cell pointer in the current cell instead of moving it to the cell below. The Enter button disappears after you use it, but you can bring it back by clicking the text box in the Formula bar. The Cancel button ☒ next to the Enter button removes the contents from the active cell and restores the cell's previous contents, if there were any.

Excel automatically assumes that a number is a value and aligns it to the right by default. If you wish to use a number as a label, simply type an apostrophe ['] before the number. Excel will then align the data to the left as a label. The apostrophe will be hidden in the cell, but will appear in the Formula bar.

If you start to enter a label whose first few letters match those of an adjacent cell in the column, Excel's AutoComplete feature will complete the label to match the other one. If you do not wish to accept the suggestion, simply continue typing to overwrite the suggestion.

Figure 1-12 Entering a label

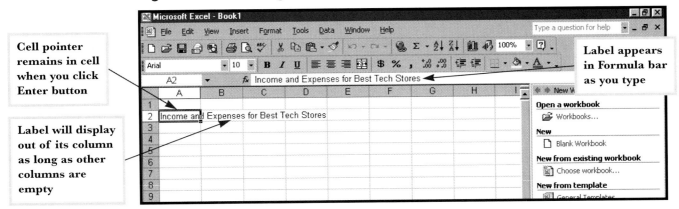

Cell pointer remains in cell when you click Enter button

Label appears in Formula bar as you type

Label will display out of its column as long as other columns are empty

Figure 1-13 Worksheet with labels added

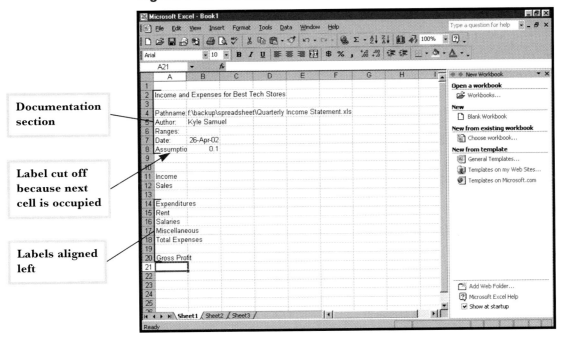

Documentation section

Label cut off because next cell is occupied

Labels aligned left

Practice

Click the New button ☐ on the Standard toolbar to open a new workbook (the Task Pane may disappear). Beginning in cell A2, enter the following cell labels, pressing [Enter] after each: your name, today's date, your instructor's name, the title of the course you are taking, and Practice1-5. Leave this file open and go on to the next Skill.

skill Saving and Closing a Workbook

concept

Saving your work is essential to being an effective computer user. By saving your files with unique names on storage devices such as hard drives, floppy disks, network drives, or Web servers, you can return to your workbooks after you have exited Excel. You also should save changes made to files frequently while you are still working on them. Saving frequently minimizes the amount of data you would lose in the event of a system crash or power failure. Closing a document removes it from the screen and puts it away for later use. You can close a file while leaving the application open in order to work with other Excel files. Or, if you are finished using Excel, you can exit the application.

do it !

Save a workbook in a folder you create specifically for your Excel files.

1. You should have two Excel files open from the previous Skill—one from the do it! section and one from the Practice section. Click Window on the Menu bar, and then click the name of the file from the do it! section—most likely named Book1. Book1 will now be the active file.

2. Click File, then click Save As to open the Save As dialog box, shown in Figure 1-14. (If you had chosen the Save command instead of Save As, the Save As dialog box would have appeared anyway, as this is the first time you are saving this file.) The file name Book1.xls automatically appears selected in the File name text box, ready to be changed. A menu command that is followed by an ellipsis (three dots) indicates that a dialog box accompanies the command. Dialog boxes permit you to set options before executing a command.

3. To give the workbook file a more distinctive name, type Quarterly Income Statement.xls. The default name, Book1.xls, will be overwritten. Windows 95 and newer versions of Windows support file names of up to 255 characters. The file name may contain uppercase or lowercase letters, numbers, and many, but not all, symbols.

4. Excel's default storage location is your computer's My Documents folder, so that folder name appears selected near the top of the dialog box in the Save in drop-down list box. To select a different location, click the Save in box to open its drop-down list, or click one of the buttons on the Places bar on the left side of the dialog box. If you have been instructed to save your Student Files on a floppy disk, open the Save in drop-down list now and click 3½ Floppy (A:) to select your floppy disk drive. Otherwise, leave the Save in box set to My Documents (or follow the specific directions of your instructor).

5. Click the Create New Folder button to the right of the Save in box. The New Folder dialog box, shown in Figure 1-15, will appear.

(continued on EX 1.18)

Figure 1-14 Save As dialog box

Click to open Web browser to a search page

Places bar: click a button to select a common storage location quickly

Click to change view of items in Contents window

Your Contents window may show different files and folders

Click to move up one level in your file hierarchy

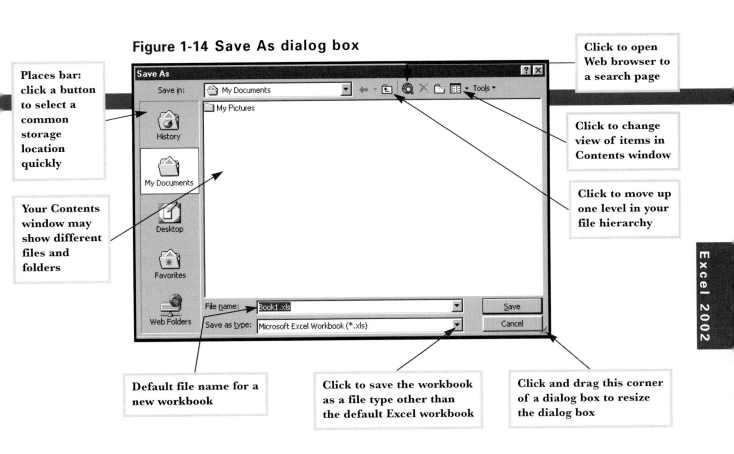

Default file name for a new workbook

Click to save the workbook as a file type other than the default Excel workbook

Click and drag this corner of a dialog box to resize the dialog box

Figure 1-15 New Folder dialog box

Type name of new folder here

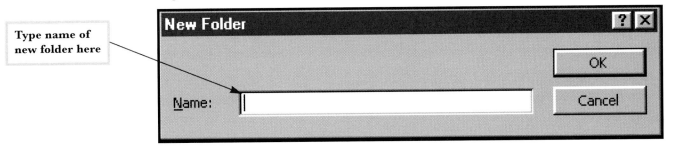

skill Saving and Closing a Workbook (continued)

do it !

6. Since an insertion point already appears in the Name text box, you can begin entering a name for the new folder. Type Excel Files as the name of the new folder.

7. Click the OK button [OK] in the New Folder dialog box to create the new folder. The New Folder dialog box closes returning you to the Save As dialog box. The new folder you just created for your Excel files is selected in the Save in box (see Figure 1-16). The folder you just created is a subfolder of the My Documents folder (or the location you selected in step 4) because that folder was selected in the Save in box when you clicked the Create New Folder button.

8. Click the Save button [Save] in the bottom-right corner of the Save As dialog box to save the Quarterly Income statement workbook in your newly created Excel Files folder. Notice that when the dialog box closes, the new file name appears in the application window's Title bar.

9. Click File, then click Close. Excel removes Quarterly Income Statement.xls from the worksheet window. The workbook you created for the Practice exercise in the previous Skill should remain open.

more

Understanding the difference between the Save command and the Save As command is an important part of working with productivity software like Excel. When you save a new file for the first time, the two commands function identically: they both open the Save As dialog box, allowing you to choose a name, storage location, and file type for the file. Once you have saved a file, the commands serve different purposes. Choosing the Save command, or clicking the Save button 🖫 on the Standard toolbar, will update the original file with any changes you have made, maintaining the same file name, storage location, and file type. The previous version of the file will no longer exist. Choosing the Save As command will permit you to save a different version of the same file, with a new name, location, type, or any combination of the three.

Another safeguard against losing data is Excel's AutoRecover feature. AutoRecover creates a "recovery" file that stores your most recent changes every time the feature activates. If your system crashes or you lose power before you have a chance to save your work, the recovery file will open the next time you start Excel. The recovery file will contain all changes you made through the last AutoRecover before the interruption. To control the AutoRecover settings, click Tools on the Menu bar, and then click the Options command. In the Options dialog box, click the Save tab, which is shown in Figure 1-17. From the Save tab, you can control whether AutoRecover is used at all, how frequently the feature runs, and where the recovery file is stored on your computer. You also may disable AutoRecover in the active workbook while leaving it available to all other workbooks. Keep in mind that using AutoRecover is not a replacement for saving your files—it is merely a backup plan. Running Auto-Recover every ten minutes is an effective amount of time because it is frequent without interfering. If you run AutoRecover too often, you could save unwanted changes. In addition, older computers may experience a slow-down for a few seconds while AutoRecover runs.

Figure 1-16 Saving a file in a new folder

New folder selected in Save in box

New file name

Click to return to previously selected save location

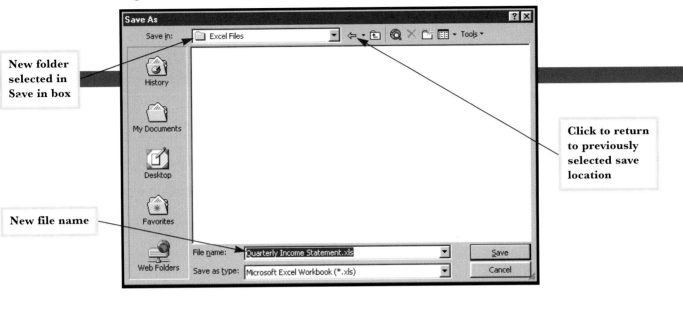

Figure 1-17 Save tab of Options dialog box

Remove check to disable AutoRecover feature

Check to disable AutoRecover in active workbook only

Click arrows to increase or decrease AutoRecover frequency

Location of recovery file

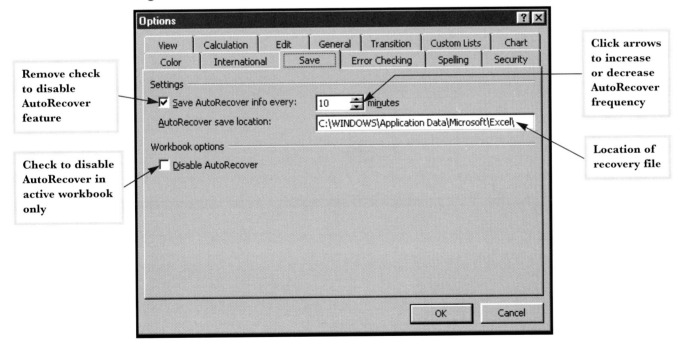

Practice

Save the workbook you created in the Practice exercise for the previous Skill in your Excel Files folder using the file name myexprac1-6.xls. Then close the file.

skill   Opening a Workbook

concept

To view or edit a worksheet that has been saved and closed previously, you must open the workbook file from the location in which it was stored. Since Excel spreadsheets are associated with the Excel application by the .xls file extension in their file names, you can double-click an Excel file in My Computer or Windows Explorer and Excel will launch automatically. However, if you are already working in Excel, you can open Excel files from directly within the application. If the Student Files for this book have been distributed to you on a floppy disk or CD-ROM, make sure you have inserted the disk in the proper drive for this Skill.

do it !

Open an existing Excel workbook that was saved previously.

1. With the Excel application running, click the Open button 📂 on the Standard toolbar. The Open dialog box will appear. You will recognize many features of the Open dialog box from the Save As dialog box. ⬤ You also can access the Open dialog box by clicking File on the Menu bar and then clicking the Open command on the File menu.

2. Click the box labeled Look in near the top of the dialog box to open a list of the locations available to your computer (see Figure 1-18).

3. Click 3½ Floppy (A:) on the list if your Student Files are stored on a floppy disk. If your Student Files are stored on a local or network drive, ask your instructor for the name of the drive you should select.

4. If your Student Files are stored in a folder on your floppy disk or hard disk, you will need to double-click that folder in the Contents window of the dialog box. Otherwise, you already should see a list of files in the Contents window. Click the file named exdoit1-7.xls to select it. ⬤ It is possible that your computer is set to hide file extensions of known file types, in which case you should click exdoit1-7.

5. Click the Open button ⬚ Open ▾ in the bottom-right corner of the dialog box. The workbook file you selected appears in the Excel window.

6. Click the Close button ☒ on the right end of the Menu bar to close the file.

more

If you cannot remember the name or location of the file you wish to open, Excel provides a search tool to help you. To access this help, click the Tools button Tools ▾ in the Open dialog box, and then click the Search command on the Tools menu (see Figure 1-19). The Search dialog box, shown in Figure 1-20, will open. On the Basic tab of the Search dialog box, you can search for files that contain specific text that you know to be in the file you need to find. You can also choose which locations the search will cover, such as all of My Computer or just the (C:) drive, and what file types the search will include. The Advanced tab allows you to search using numerous other criteria including the date when a file was last modified, the name of the person who created it, or a portion of the file name.

Excel can open a variety of file types. If you know you have selected the correct drive or folder but you still do not see your file listed in the Contents window, make sure that the Files of type box displays a setting that includes Excel files.

If you click the arrow on the right edge of the Open button, you can open the selected document in a specific manner. If you select Open Read-Only, Excel will not allow any changes to be saved unless you use Save As to create a new file. Open as Copy creates a new copy of the file so you can keep the old version and edit the new one. Open in Browser becomes active when you have selected an HTML document. The selected file will open in your default Web browser instead of Excel. Open and Repair assists you in opening and recovering a document that has been damaged by a program, system, or power failure.

Figure 1-18 Selecting a Look in location in the Open dialog box

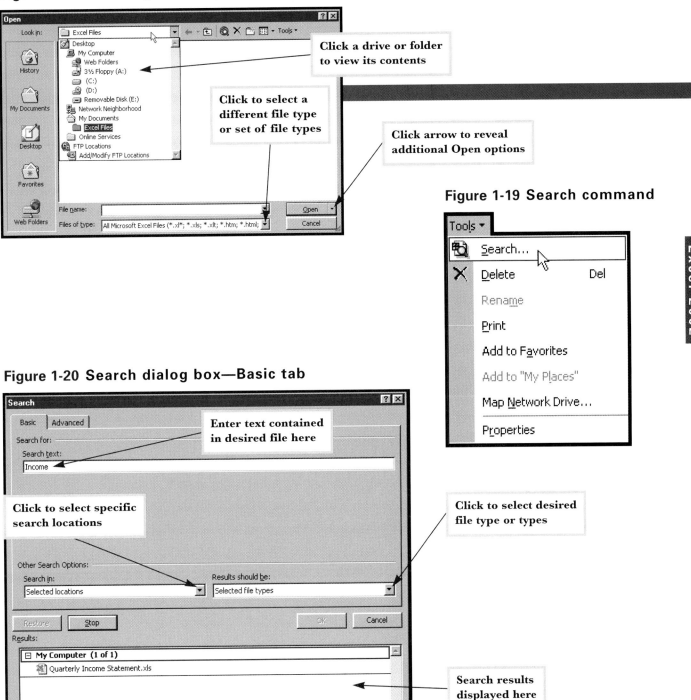

Figure 1-19 Search command

Figure 1-20 Search dialog box—Basic tab

Practice

To practice opening a workbook, open the Student File named exprac1-7.xls. Use the Save As command to save this file in your Excel Files folder with the file name myexprac1-7.xls. Close the file and leave Excel running when you are done.

skill

Editing a Cell's Information

MOUS Skill

concept

Many spreadsheets are used over a long period of time and receive constant updates. For example, suppose you work in the billing department of a company that supplies oil to homes for heating purposes. You might use a spreadsheet that tracks how much oil each customer takes upon each delivery. In order to calculate how much to bill the customers, you would also need to enter the price of oil, which changes frequently. Instead of starting a new worksheet each time the price changes, you simply can update the figure on the same worksheet. Editing the contents of a cell is very similar to editing text in a word processing document.

do it !

Edit the contents of one cell in the Formula bar and another in the cell itself.

1. Open the Student File exdoit1-8.xls.

2. Click cell A14. The cell pointer moves to cell A14 and Expenditures is displayed in the Formula bar.

3. Move the mouse pointer over the Formula bar, position it between the n and the d in the word Expenditures (the mouse pointer should appear as I-beam I when over the Formula bar), and click. A blinking insertion point will appear, the Formula bar buttons will display, and the mode indicator on the Status bar will read Edit, as shown in Figure 1-21.

4. Press and hold the left mouse button, and then drag the I-beam to the right over the last seven letters of the word Expenditures. That portion of the cell entry is now selected.

5. Type ses to replace the selected text. The cell entry now reads Expenses instead of Expenditures (see Figure 1-22).

6. Click cell B5 to make it the active cell.

7. Type your own name. As soon as you begin typing, Excel deletes the current contents of the cell, the name Kyle Samuel.

8. Click the Cancel button $\boxed{\times}$ on the Formula bar. Excel deletes your name from cell B5 and restores the cell's previous entry.

9. Save this file in your Excel Files folder using the file name QIS-Editing.xls, and then close the file.

more

As you saw in the exercise above, when you click a cell and immediately begin typing, Excel deletes the existing cell contents immediately. To edit the contents of a cell within the cell, instead of in the Formula bar, without deleting the cell's existing contents, double-click the cell. A blinking insertion point will appear in the cell where you double-clicked, allowing you to edit the cell contents in the same way as you would in the Formula bar. You can press the [Backspace] key on the keyboard to remove characters to the left of the insertion point, or press the [Delete] key to remove characters to the right of the insertion point. You also can press the left and right arrow keys on the keyboard to move the insertion point in the cell without deleting any characters. Once you are in Edit mode in a cell, double-clicking in the cell a second time will select all of the cell's contents. If you make a mistake while working in Excel, you can reverse your last action by clicking the Undo button on the Standard toolbar. Click the arrow next to the Undo button to open a list of all your previous actions in the current work session, permitting you to undo multiple actions at once. Your most recent action will be at the top of the list. If you undo an action other than the most recent, all actions that followed the one you select will be undone as well. The Redo button enables you to reverse the effect of the Undo button.

Figure 1-21 Editing a cell in the Formula bar

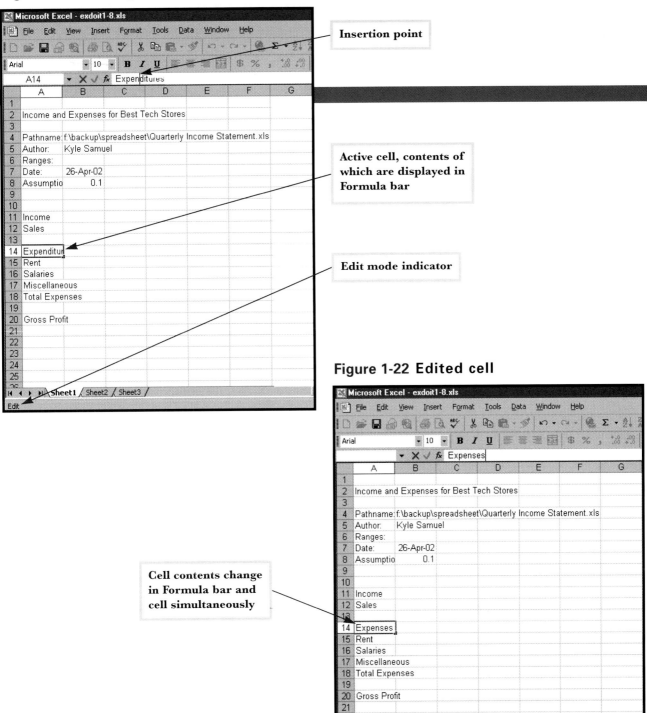

Insertion point

Active cell, contents of which are displayed in Formula bar

Edit mode indicator

Figure 1-22 Edited cell

Cell contents change in Formula bar and cell simultaneously

Practice

To practice editing information in a cell, open the Student File exprac1-8.xls and save it in your Excel Files folder as myexprac1-8.xls. Then change the first initial and last name (R. Patel) in cell A1 to your own first initial and last name using the Formula bar. Change the name (Raj Patel) in cell B4 to your name working within the cell itself. When you are done, click the Save button 🖫 on the Standard toolbar to save the changes you have made to the worksheet, and then close the file.

skill | Using the Office Assistant

concept

Even experienced computer users occasionally need help using software correctly. Excel offers a number of built-in help features that you can use when you encounter problems or when you simply have a question about a particular aspect of the program. One of these features is the Office Assistant, an animated character who provides several kinds of help. When turned on, the Assistant will provide tips related to your current activity. The Assistant also will sense when you are trying to complete a specific task and offer to guide you through it. Or you can ask the Assistant a question.

do it !

Ask the Office Assistant about Task Panes.

1. Click Help on the Menu bar, then click Show the Office Assistant. The Office Assistant will appear on your screen.

2. Click the Office Assistant to open its dialog balloon, and then type What's the difference between a workbook and a worksheet? as shown in Figure 1-23.

3. Click the Search button [Search]. The Assistant searches Excel's Help files for answers to your question and then presents a list of suggested topics.

4. Click the topic named About viewing workbooks and worksheets, as shown in Figure 1-24. A Help window containing the topic you selected appears alongside the Excel window (see Figure 1-25).

5. Read the Help file, and then click its Close button [X] to remove it from the screen. Notice that the Ask a Question drop-down list box [What's the difference betw ▼] on the right end of the Menu bar now contains the question you asked the Office Assistant. This gives you quick access to the Help topic in case you want to consult it again.

6. Click Help on the Menu bar, then click Hide the Office Assistant. The Assistant removes itself from the screen.

more

Each question you ask the Office Assistant during an Excel session is added to the Ask a Question drop-down list. To access the questions you have asked previously, click the arrow at the right end of the Ask a Question drop-down list box. When you click a question on this list, the list of suggested Help topics found earlier by the Office Assistant will appear. You then can click the topic of your choice. If you want to ask a new question without using the Office Assistant, click inside the Ask a Question box itself, type your new question, and press [Enter] on the keyboard. The Ask a Question drop-down list is erased when you exit Excel.

When the Office Assistant is showing and has a tip for you, a lightbulb icon 💡 will appear above the Assistant. Click the lightbulb to receive the tip.

Once you have hidden the Assistant several times, you will be asked if you would prefer to turn off the feature instead of just hiding it. The option of turning off the Assistant is also available in the Options dialog box, which you can access by clicking the Options button [Options] in the Assistant's dialog balloon. The Options tab in the Office Assistant dialog box, shown in Figure 1-26, also allows you to control how the Assistant behaves and what kinds of help it provides. The Gallery tab contains animated characters that you may use as your Office Assistant in place of the default paper clip character. While previews of the other Office Assistant characters are available on the Gallery tab, you must install the characters from your Excel 2002 or Office XP CD-ROM in order to use them.

Figure 1-23 Querying the Office Assistant

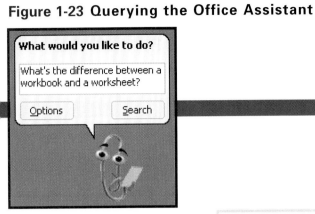

Figure 1-24 Selecting a Help topic

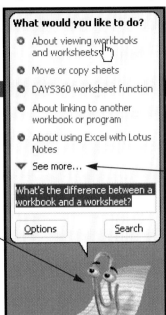

Click "See more" if the suggested topics do not fulfill your needs

Drag the Assistant to another part of the screen if it blocks your view

Figure 1-25 Reading a Help topic

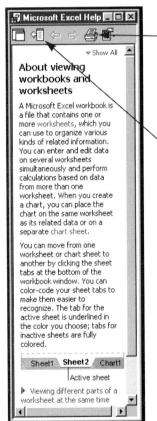

Click to print the Help topic

Help window may have one or two panes depending on the status of the Show/Hide tabs button

Figure 1-26 Office Assistant dialog box

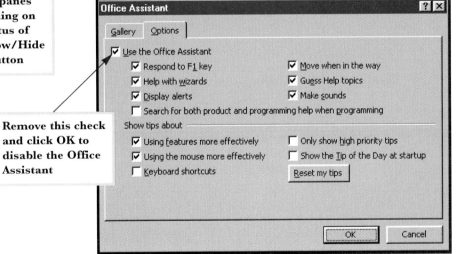

Remove this check and click OK to disable the Office Assistant

Practice

Use the Office Assistant to read Help files on the following topics: new features in Excel, ScreenTips, and Smart Tags. If you have a printer available, print any one of the Help files that you view. Close the Help window, and then turn off the Office Assistant as described in the More section and as depicted in Figure 1-26 above.

skill | Other Excel Help Features

concept

For those that would prefer to obtain help without making use of the Office Assistant, Excel offers a number of alternatives. As you have seen, ScreenTips help you identify elements of the Excel window such as toolbar buttons. The What's This? command expands the power of ScreenTips to include feature names and descriptions of their functions. Perhaps most important of all, all of Excel's Help files are available to you in an extensive Microsoft Excel Help facility that operates independently of the Office Assistant. If you have not turned off the Office Assistant as instructed on the previous page, do so now.

do it !

Use the What's This? command and the Help facility to improve your knowledge of Excel.

1. Click ▢ to open a blank workbook. Then open the Help menu from the Menu bar and click the What's This? command. The mouse pointer now appears with a question mark attached to it.

2. Click ▧ on the Standard toolbar with the What's This? pointer. A ScreenTip appears with an explanation of the item you clicked (see Figure 1-27).

3. Click the mouse again to erase the ScreenTip.

4. Click the Microsoft Excel Help ▢ button on the Standard toolbar. The Microsoft Excel Help window opens alongside the application window with links to particular areas of help and a list of commonly requested help topics.

5. Click the Show button ◀▤ at the top of the Help window. The window expands so that you can see the Help tabs. The Answer Wizard tab functions just like the Office Assistant, allowing you to ask a question and receive a list of suggested Help topics. ◆ If you see the Hide button ▤ instead of the Show button, you do not need to complete this step.

6. Click the Index tab, which allows you to search an alphabetical list of keywords.

7. Begin to type filetype in the text box labeled 1. Type keywords. Before you finish typing, the scrolling list box below will have scrolled to match what you typed.

8. Click the Search button ▭Search▭ to find Help topics related to the selected keyword. The found topics will be listed in the box labeled 3. Choose a topic (see Figure 1-28). The first topic will be selected and the text of its related Help file will appear in the right pane of the Help window. Read the text of this Help file, scrolling down as necessary.

9. Click the Help topic titled Change the program that starts when you open a file. Read the text of this Help file and then click one of the subtopic links below the text to read more (see Figure 1-29).

10. Click the Close button ☒ in the Help window to close Microsoft Excel Help.

more

The Contents tab in the Microsoft Excel Help window is organized like an outline or the table of contents you might find in a book. It begins with a main level of broad topics symbolized by book icons, each of which can be expanded to reveal more specific subtopics. You can click these subtopics on the Contents tab to display their related Help files on the right side of the window, just as on the Index tab. In addition to the Show/Hide toggle button, the Help toolbar has buttons for organizing the application and Help window (Auto Tile), browsing through the Help topics you have viewed (Back and Forward), printing a topic, and opening a menu of Options.

Figure 1-27 What's This? ScreenTip

Spelling (Tools menu)

Checks spelling in the active document, file, workbook, or item.

Click to begin new keyword search

Figure 1-29 Viewing a subtopic

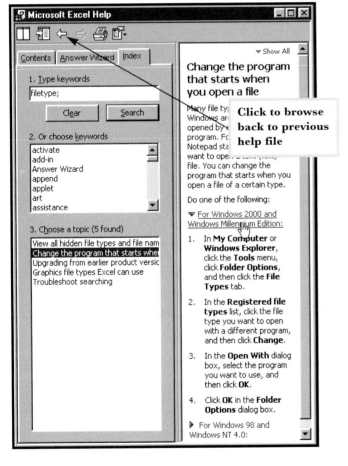

Figure 1-28 Help topics found by keyword

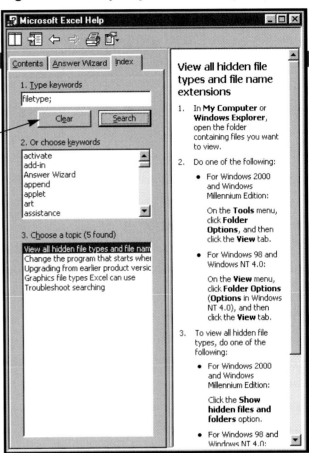

Practice

Open the Microsoft Excel Help facility and use the Index tab to find Help topics related to the keyword keyboard. Then read the Help file for the topic titled Keyboard shortcuts. Also read the subtopic in that file titled Display and use the Help window. Close the Help window when you are done. Finally, use the What's This? command to get help on the Standard toolbar's Search button. When you have completed this Practice exercise, close all open workbooks.

shortcuts

Function	Button/Mouse	Menu	Keyboard
Create a new workbook	☐	Click File, then click New	[Ctrl]+[N]
Open a workbook	☐	Click File, then click Open	[Ctrl]+[O]
Confirm a cell entry	✓		[Enter], [Tab], or arrow keys
Cancel a cell entry	✗	Click Edit, then click Undo Typing	[Ctrl]+[Z]
Save a workbook for the first time	☐	Click File, then click Save or Save As	[Ctrl]+[S]
Save changes to existing workbook	☐	Click File, then click Save	[Ctrl]+[S]
Save workbook with new name, location, file type		Click File, then click Save As	[Alt]+[F], [A]
Close the active workbook	✗	Click File, then click Close	[Ctrl]+[W]
Close the application	✗	Click File, then click Exit	[Alt]+[F4]
Undo last action	↶	Click Edit, then click Undo [action]	[Ctrl]+[Z]
Redo last undone action	↷	Click Edit, then click Redo [action]	[Ctrl]+[Y]
Get Help	②	Click Help, then click Show the Office Assistant or Microsoft Excel Help	[F1]
Search for a file from Open dialog box	Tools ▾ Then click Search		
Search for a file from Task Pane in application window	▣	Click File, then click Search	[Alt]+[F], [H]

A. Identify Key Features

Name the items indicated by callouts in Figure 1-30.

Figure 1-30 Elements of an Excel spreadsheet

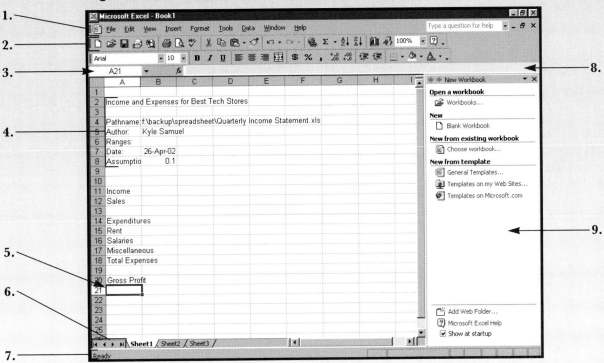

B. Select the Best Answer

10. Click this to make the Excel window fill the screen

11. Displays the active cell address

12. Gives you feedback on your current activity in Excel

13. Enables you to choose a name and location for storing a file

14. Saves the changes you have made to your file keeping its name and location

15. Unit created by the intersection of a row and a column

16. A location where you can edit the contents of a cell

17. Text in a cell that describes data displayed on the worksheet

a. Name box

b. Save command

c. Cell

d. Maximize button

e. Label

f. Status bar

g. Save As command

h. Formula bar

22

22

quiz (continued)

C. Complete the Statement

18. To select an entire column, click:

a. The first cell in the column

b. Any cell in the column

c. Its letter column heading button

d. The corresponding row number

19. Pressing [Ctrl]+[Home] will:

a. Move your view up one screen

b. Move your view down one screen

c. Move the cell pointer to cell A1

d. Move the cell pointer to column A in the current row

20. All of the following actions will move the cell pointer to another cell except:

a. Clicking the Enter button

b. Pressing the Enter key

c. Pressing the Tab key

d. Pressing an arrow key

21. A well-designed spreadsheet does not necessarily require:

a. Documentation

b. Multiple worksheets

c. Input

d. Output

22. All of these are Excel help features except:

a. The Index tab

b. The Office Assistant

c. What's This?

d. The Help Wizard

23. A file extension:

a. Allows you to see a hidden file

b. Lets you edit the information in a cell

c. Associates a file with a specific application

d. Is a component of Excel's Help facility

24. A workbook can contain up to:

a. 16 worksheets

b. 255 worksheets

c. 3 worksheets

d. 65,536 worksheets

25. Excel assumes that numbers entered on a worksheet are:

a. Values

b. Labels

c. Formulas

d. Apostrophes

26. The cell whose address is B5 is located in:

a. Row B, column 5

b. Row B, cell 5

c. Column B, row 5

d. The Name box

27. To view Sheet tabs that are not visible in the window:

a. Go to another worksheet

b. Open a new workbook

c. Use the horizontal scroll bar

d. Use the Sheet tab scrolling buttons

interactivity

Build Your Skills

1. Open the Excel application and document a new spreadsheet:

   a. Use the Start button to start Microsoft Excel.

   b. Add a documentation section to the blank worksheet using the title Class Schedule, your name, and the date.

   c. When you document the file name, use the name extest1.xls.

   d. Include labels for Ranges and Macros. Your documentation section should occupy rows 1–6 of the worksheet.

2. Design a worksheet that displays your daily class schedule:

   a. Add labels in row 8 for the days of the week, not including Saturday and Sunday. Start in cell B8 and skip a column between each day. Friday should be in cell J8.

   b. Add labels in column A for your class periods. Enter the time of your earliest class period in cell A10, and then add a label for each subsequent class period through your last class of the day. Skip a row between each time label.

   c. Enter the names of your classes in the appropriate cells where the day of the week and the time intersect.

3. Get help using the Office Assistant and the Help tabs:

   a. Use the Help menu to show the Office Assistant.

   b. Open the Office Assistant's dialog balloon.

   c. Ask the Assistant for information on how to customize toolbars.

   d. Select the Help topic titled About toolbars and read its associated Help file.

   e. Use the Index tab in the Microsoft Excel Help window to search for Help topics related to the keyword install.

   f. Select and read the Help topic titled What's installed with Excel.

   g. Close the Help window and turn off the Office Assistant from the Options tab of the Office Assistant dialog box.

4. Save a workbook file and exit Excel:

   a. Save the workbook you were constructing in steps 1 and 2 in your Excel Files folder using the file name extest1.xls.

   b. Use the File menu to exit Microsoft Excel.

interactivity (continued)

Problem Solving Exercises

1. Create a new spreadsheet following the design principles you learned in Lesson 1. Design this spreadsheet to log your daily activities. Enter labels for the days of the week just as you did in the previous exercise, but this time add Saturday and Sunday after Friday and do not leave a blank column between each day. Instead of class periods, add labels down column A for Class, Activities, Meals, Studying/Homework, Leisure, and Sleep. Do not skip rows between labels. Save the file in your Excel Files folder as 7-Day Daily.xls.

2. Due to a recent merger, your accounting firm can now increase the budgets of several departments. You are pleased to learn that you will have an additional $10,000 available for your expense account. As a member of the Human Resources department, you know how much this money will help you in your efforts to attract the top candidates for your company's job openings. Use Excel to design a spreadsheet that will detail your strategy for utilizing the new funds over the next year. You do not have to enter any monetary values yet. Simpy set up the structure of the worksheet with documentation and labels. One set of labels should divide the year in periods, such as months or quarters, and the other set should specify specific uses of the new funds, such as recruiting trips, additional job postings, or presentation materials. Save the spreadsheet in your Excel Files folder as New HR Funds.xls.

3. The restaurant you manage has been using an old computer running primitive software for its day-to-day operations. You have finally convinced the owner of the restaurant to invest in a new computer and the Office XP software suite. Now you have to prove that the purchase was a wise investment. Using Excel, design a spreadsheet that will allow you to keep track of the waitstaff's schedule over one week. Your worksheet should include columns for Time in and Time out each day of the week. Save the file in your Excel Files folder as Staff Schedule.xls.

4. Create the worksheet shown in Figure 1-31 to the best of your ability.

Figure 1-31 Lab Inventory.xls

	A	B	C	D	E	F	G	H	I	J	K	L
1	Lab Inventory											
2	Pathname:	C:\Department\Reports\Lab Inventory.xls										
3	Author:	Montgomery Moncrief										
4	Ranges:	Equipment										
5	Date:	2/3/02										
6												
7	Equipment		# Remaining		# Needed		Cost per unit		Cost to department			
8	250ml beaker											
9	400ml beaker											
10	250ml Erlenmeyer flask											
11	200ml Florence flask											
12	10ml graduated cylinder											
13	100ml graduated cylinder											
14												
15												
16												
17												
18												
19												
20												
21												
22												
23												
24												
25												

Sheet1 / Sheet2 / Sheet3 /

When you are done, replace the name in cell B2 with your own name and save the file in your Excel files folder as Lab Inventory.xls.

Manipulating Data in a Worksheet

One of the greatest advantages of using spreadsheet software is that it automates many of the processes that take up so much time when done by hand. In Excel you can enter data quickly and easily, then move or copy data from one location to another just as quickly and easily.

Excel also automates your calculations by using mathematical formulas. If you instruct Excel what operation to perform, and where to get the data, the program will execute the calculations for you. The Paste Function feature prevents you from having to enter complicated formulas that Excel already knows. Once you have entered a formula or a function, you can even paste it to a new location.

Often, businesses like to use the data they have gathered to make projections about their business. In Excel you can use assumed values, or assumptions, to perform calculations under different conditions, altering the results of the worksheet each time. This technique is called What-If Analysis, and takes full advantage of Excel's versatility.

Lesson Goal:

Fill out a worksheet with values, then use Excel's Cut, Copy, and Paste features to manipulate the labels and values in the worksheet. Use the newly located values to perform calculations with the help of formulas and functions. Change the output of the worksheet by performing a What-If Analysis. Finally, print a copy of the worksheet.

skills

- ⚡ **Cutting, Copying, and Pasting Labels**
- ⚡ **Entering Values**
- ⚡ **Entering Formulas**
- ⚡ **Using Functions**
- ⚡ **Using the Insert Function Feature**
- ⚡ **Copying and Pasting Formulas**
- ⚡ **Using What-If Analysis**
- ⚡ **Previewing and Printing a Worksheet**

skill

Cutting, Copying, and Pasting Labels

concept

Excel makes it easy to transfer text from cell to cell. Cutting or copying information places it on the Office Clipboard. The Office Clipboard enables you to temporarily store text, data, and/or graphics from any Office XP program (and many other programs) and then paste them into any other Office XP program. In Office XP, the Clipboard can hold up to 24 items. (If you copy a 25th item, the Clipboard deletes the first one.) If you exit all Office programs, or click Clear All on the Office Clipboard, all Clipboard items are deleted. Clicking the Paste command inserts at the insertion point the last item that you sent to the Clipboard. You also can move cell contents by clicking the border of a cell or group of cells, then dragging and dropping them at a new location.

do it !

Enter sales and expense values in an income statement worksheet.

1. Open Student File exdoit2-1.xls and save it as QIS-Cutting.xls.

2. Click cell C6, click Edit, and click Cut. A moving border will appear around cell C6, indicating that you now can remove its contents (see Figure 2-1). Click cell A7, click Edit, and click Paste. The contents of cell C6 will move to cell A7.

3. Right-click cell E6 to display a shortcut menu, click Cut, right-click cell A8 to open another shortcut menu, and click Paste. The contents of cell E6 will move to cell A8. Excel (and the other Office programs) often allow you to right-click an area to display a shortcut menu with commands related to that area. For many Office commands, using a shortcut menu avoids having to move the mouse pointer to a toolbar to find a command.

4. Click cell B10, and type the text Q1, standing for Quarter 1 of what will be an income statement for four quarters of a year. Click the Enter button ☑ between the Name box and Formula bar to confirm the entry (see Figure 2-2). The insertion point will disappear.

5. With cell B10 still selected, click Edit, then click Copy. (As with the Cut command, the Copy command will produce a moving border around the selected cell.) Select cells C10 through E10 (see Figure 2-3). Press [Enter]. The contents of cell B10 now appear in the three additional cells, and the moving border around cell B10 disappears.

6. Click cell C10. Click in the Formula bar right after the numeral 1, press [Backspace], press [2], and press [Tab] to move to cell D10. Click in the Formula bar right after the numeral 1, press [Backspace], press [3], and press [Tab] to move to cell E10. Click in the Formula bar right after the numeral 1, press [Backspace], press [4], and click cell B12. Cells B10 to E10 now read Q1, Q2, Q3, and Q4 to represent the four financial quarters of the calendar year.

7. Save the changes you have made to the worksheet and close the file.

more

To move the contents of a cell or cell group to another location, you also can click the left mouse button on the gray border of the area you wish to move to display the mouse pointer with a four-way arrow [↖]. Drag the border of the selected area to the new location. As you drag, a lighter gray border matching the size of the area being dragged will move with the mouse pointer. When the lighter gray border rests over the desired location, release the mouse button. The cell contents then will appear in the destination cell with the darker border around it.

To copy the contents of a cell or cell group rather than just move them, hold down [Ctrl] while clicking the left mouse button, drag the cell border, and then release it at the new location. When you copy cell contents, a mouse pointer and small cross ( ) will tell you that you are copying rather than moving the contents.

Steps 5 and 6 show you how to copy cell contents and then increase a numbered sequence with the Formula bar. However, you can create a numbered sequence more quickly by using Excel's AutoFill feature. To use AutoFill, click the lower-right corner—or fill handle—of the first cell in your sequence. While holding down the mouse button, drag the fill handle to the right or down, depending on the desired direction, and release the mouse pointer when you reach the last cell in the row or column to which you want to copy the source cell's contents. For a detailed explanation of using AutoFill, see the Skill entitled "Filling a Cell Range with Labels" in Lesson 3.

The Concept section of this Skill states that clicking the Paste command inserts at the insertion point the last item that you sent to the Clipboard. However, to paste a different item, click the destination cell, click Edit, click Office Clipboard to display the Clipboard task pane, and click the item on the task pane that you want to paste. To paste all items at once, display the Clipboard, then click the Paste All button at the top left of the task pane.

Figure 2-1 Copying a cell

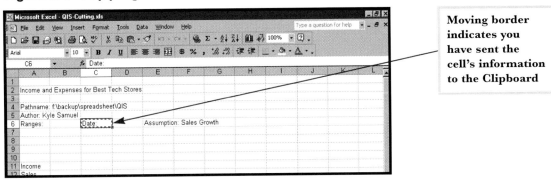

Moving border indicates you have sent the cell's information to the Clipboard

Figure 2-2 Enter button

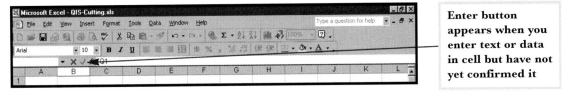

Enter button appears when you enter text or data in cell but have not yet confirmed it

Figure 2-3 Selected destination cells

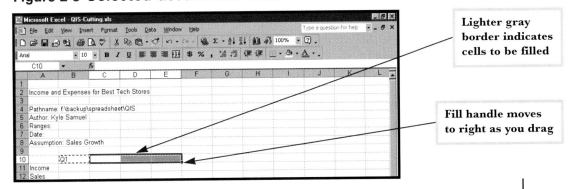

Lighter gray border indicates cells to be filled

Fill handle moves to right as you drag

Practice

To practice cutting, copying, and pasting labels, follow the instructions on the Practice2-1 Sheet tab of the practice file exprac2.xls. Save changes as myexprac2-1.xls and close the file. Make sure you have the More section of this Skill before starting the Practice exercise. Also, please see the note on Smart Tags toward the bottom of the Practice2-1 worksheet.

skill   Entering Values

concept

Values are numbers, dates, or times that Excel uses in calculations. They are the main reason that Excel exists—so that you can easily and quickly enter, manipulate, and permanently record numerical data. When entering and confirming the data, you do so in the same way as you do with labels.

do it !

Enter Sales and Expenses values in a worksheet.

1. Open Student File exdoit2-2.xls and save it as QIS-Entering.xls.

2. Click cell B12 to make it the active cell. Type 168500, then press [Tab]. The first quarter sales now appears in the cell, and the cell pointer moves to the right to cell C12. Enter the rest of the Sales values in the same row, pressing [Tab] after each: 179000, 190000, and 210000. Some Excel users will want to add commas to separate the thousands place from the hundreds, but should avoid doing so. Information on using comma separators appears in Lesson 3. Also, when typing numbers, make sure you use only digits and not letters such as O instead of 0 (zero). One way to avoid making this mistake is to use the numeric keypad on the right side of the keyboard when entering numbers. If your numeric keypad does not seem to be working, press the Num Lock key.

3. Click cell B15 to activate it. Type 20000 as the first quarter's rent expense and click ☑. Using the Edit command, copy this value to cell C15 (see Figure 2-4). Click in cell D15, and type an increased rent expense of 21000. Click ☑. Right-click in the cell and, using the shortcut menu, copy this value to cell E15 (see Figure 2-5).

4. Click cell B16 to activate it. Enter the following four values into the Salaries row, pressing [Tab] after entering each value except the last: 95000, 97500, 105000, and 108500.

5. Click cell B17 to activate it. Enter the following four values into the Miscellaneous row, pressing [Tab] after entering each value including the last: 13500, 14500, 16500, and 19000. In Step 4, you did not need to press [Tab] after the last value because clicking in cell B17 confirmed the entry in cell E16. However, you did need to press [Tab] after cell E17 because there are no more entries to be made in this Skill. You also could have pressed [Enter] or clicked ☑ to confirm the last entry.

6. Verify that your values match those in Figure 2-6. Re-enter any numbers that do not match the figure, save the changes you have made to the worksheet, and close the file.

more

You may have noticed that when you entered the values they aligned to the right when confirmed, not to the left like the text labels. Excel aligns values to the right by default and recognizes an entry as a value when it is a number or is preceded by +, −, =, @, #, or $. Excel recognizes ordinals (1st, 2nd, 3rd, etc.) and other combinations of numbers and letters as labels rather than values.

Sometimes you may want to use a number, such as a year, as a label. In such cases, you must type an apostrophe (') before the number so Excel will recognize that number as a label and will disregard it when performing calculations. The apostrophe will not appear in the cell, but will appear in the Formula bar above the worksheet window when you select the appropriate cell.

Figure 2-4 Edit command

Editing commands appear on left, with matching Shortcut key combinations on right

Icons in gray area corresponds with buttons on tool-bars

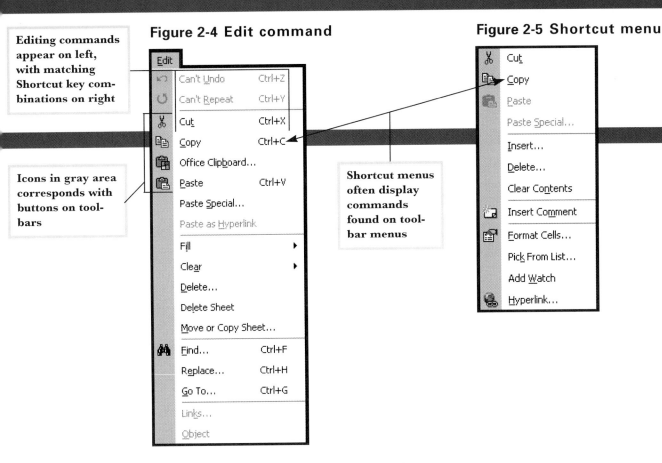

Edit
- Can't Undo   Ctrl+Z
- Can't Repeat   Ctrl+Y
- Cut   Ctrl+X
- Copy   Ctrl+C
- Office Clipboard...
- Paste   Ctrl+V
- Paste Special...
- Paste as Hyperlink
- Fill ▶
- Clear ▶
- Delete...
- Delete Sheet
- Move or Copy Sheet...
- Find...   Ctrl+F
- Replace...   Ctrl+H
- Go To...   Ctrl+G
- Links...
- Object

Figure 2-5 Shortcut menu

Shortcut menus often display commands found on tool-bar menus

- Cut
- Copy
- Paste
- Paste Special...
- Insert...
- Delete...
- Clear Contents
- Insert Comment
- Format Cells...
- Pick From List...
- Add Watch
- Hyperlink...

Figure 2-6 Worksheet's appearance after entering values

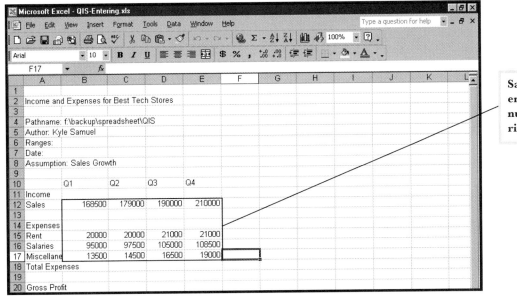

Sales and Expenses values entered into worksheet; numerals are aligned right by default

Practice

To practice entering values, follow the instructions on the Practice2-2 Sheet tab of practice file exprac2.xls. Save changes as myexprac2-2.xls and close the file.

skill   Entering Formulas

concept

Formulas are mathematical equations that perform calculations such as averages, sums, or products on worksheet data. An Excel formula always starts with an equal sign (=) to distinguish the formula from text or data. Typical Excel formulas contain cell references, mathematical operators (the symbols dictating the kind of calculation to perform), and—quite often—numerical values. For example, in the formula =B5+2, the combination B5 is a cell reference, the plus sign (+) is an operator, and the number 2 is a value. By using formulas instead of filling in averages, totals, and so on by hand, your worksheet saves you the trouble of inputting new results each time a value changes. Also, as long as your formulas are correct and relevant to the values you calculate, any changes in values automatically will produce correct results.

do it !

Calculate the Total Expenses and Gross Profit for each quarter of the income statement.

1. Open Student File exdoit2-3.xls and save it as QIS-Formulas.xls.

2. Click cell B18 to activate it. Enter the formula =B15+B16+B17 to add the three types of expenses (you can type a lowercase b). As you type the cell references, colored rectangles will appear around them, matching the references in the formula. (see Figure 2-7).

3. Click the Enter button ✓. The calculated result 128500 will appear in cell B18 as the total of the three cells referenced in the formula. The formula itself will appear in the Formula bar. ◆ Notice that the part of the words Total Expenses in cell A18 that ran into cell B18 is covered when you type the formula. Information on widening columns to display all text in a cell appears in Lesson 3.

4. Click cell C18, and enter the formula =C15+C16+C17 to add the three types of expenses in column C. In cells D18 and E18, repeat Steps 2 and 3, substituting the letters D and E respectively in each of the three cell references, and pressing [Tab] after each formula.

5. Click cell B20, enter the formula =B12-B18, and press [Tab]. Excel will subtract the first quarter's Total Expenses from the first quarter's Sales to arrive at the result 40000 for the first quarter's Gross Profit.

6. Repeat Step 4 to enter similar formulas into cells C20, D20, and E20, However, substitute the letters C, D, and E respectively where you used the letter B for the two cell references, and press [Tab] after each formula.

7. Verify that your worksheet matches Figure 2-8. If necessary, correct any incorrect formulas to ensure the same calculated results. If you are absolutely sure that all of your formulas are correct, double-check the values that you are referencing.

8. Save the changes you have made to the worksheet and close the file.

more

As this Skill demonstrates, Excel formulas use cell addresses and the arithmetic operators + for addition and – for subtraction. However, the standard computer keyboard does not contain the traditional multiplication and division symbols. Therefore, computer keyboards use the asterisk (*) for multiplication and the forward slash (/) for division. The carat mark (^) expresses exponentiation (raising a number to another power). If you select two or more cells containing values, their sum will appear in the Status bar below the horizontal scroll bar. If you right-click the sum in the status bar, a shortcut menu will display so you can select other forms of calculation.

Figure 2-7 Entering a formula

Formula from selected cell displays in Formula bar

Color of referenced cell matches color in formula

Formula in cell B18 partially covers text in cell A18

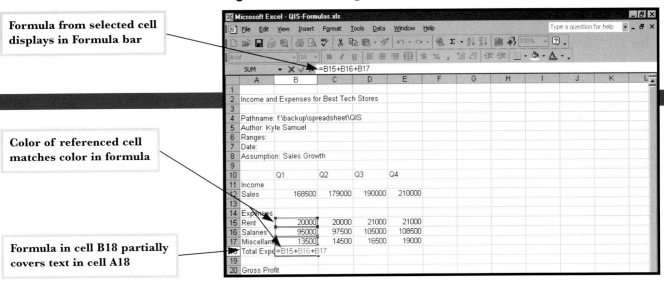

Figure 2-8 Calculating Total Expenses and Gross Profit

Calculated results appear in cells containing formulas

Calculated results in cell B20 also partially obscure text in cell A20

Formula does not display in Formula bar when cell pointer sits over empty cell

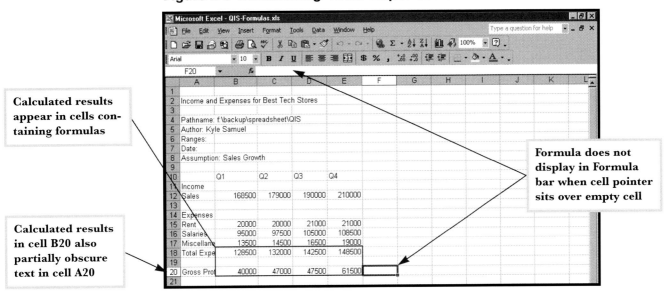

Practice

To practice entering formulas, follow the instructions on the Practice2-3 Sheet tab of the practice file exprac2.xls. Save changes as myexprac2-3.xls and close the file.

skill

Using Functions

concept

You can, of course, type a new formula each time that you want to perform a calculation in a worksheet. However, using predefined formulas, called functions, can reduce the time and trouble of typing out formulas. Excel has hundreds of these built-in formulas, and they cover the most common types of calculations you might use in a worksheet, such as AVERAGE, SUM, RATE, and so on.

do it !

Use the SUM function instead of typing in a formula to calculate Total Expenses.

1. Open Student File exdoit2-4.xls and save it as QIS-Functions.xls.

2. Click cell B18 to activate it. Click the AutoSum button Σ · (not on down-arrow to its right). The AutoSum function automatically enters the formula to add the values of the cells directly above the active cell. The SUM formula =SUM(B15:B17) appears in cell B18 and the Formula bar. The cells being added (called the function argument) are surrounded by a moving border. Below the active cell a ScreenTip appears showing the syntax (or structure) of the formula, including the form of the argument (see Figure 2-9). The argument contains the notation B15:B17, or a cell range, referring to all cells between and including B15 and B17. More information on cell ranges appears in Lesson 3.

3. Press the AutoSum button again to confirm Excel's calculation and to apply the formula to the active cell. The value 128500, matching the value that appeared before using AutoSum, appears in the cell, verifying that the AutoSum function has included the proper cells in the total. Instead of clicking the AutoSum button again, you could press [Enter] or [Tab].

4. Click cell F10 to activate it, and type a new label, Yearly Total. Click cell F12, then click the AutoSum button Σ ·. This time, a moving border appears around the cells directly to the left of cell F12. In F12 itself, the SUM function appears, followed by the correct cell range, B12:E12. The formula also appears in the Formula bar, and a ScreenTip appears, displaying a generic example of the formula (see Figure 2-10).

5. Click AutoSum again to confirm Excel's calculation and to apply the formula. The value 747500 will appear in the cell (see Figure 2-11).

6. Save the changes you have made to the worksheet and close the file.

more

In this Skill you used the AutoSum button to enter the SUM function into cell B18 in place of the formula =B15+B16+B17. However, unlike AutoSum, most Excel functions require users to enter additional information manually after the function name. This information, enclosed, or "nested," in parentheses and called the argument, can be cell references or other data that the function needs to calculate a result. The function acts upon the argument, as the SUM function acted upon the range of cells enclosed in the parentheses that followed the function.

Sometimes the cells you want to reference in an AutoSum do not appear directly above the active cell. In such cases, click the cell where you want the calculated result to appear, click the AutoSum button, click and drag through the cells desired for the argument, and press [Enter] or [Tab].

Figure 2-9 Using AutoSum to add cells in a column

Moving border indicates argument of formula

ScreenTip displays syntax, or structure, and arguments of selected function

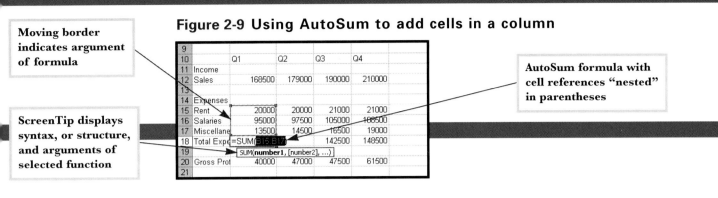

AutoSum formula with cell references "nested" in parentheses

Figure 2-10 Using AutoSum to add cells in a row

Moving border

ScreenTip

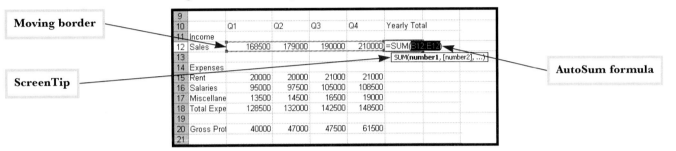

AutoSum formula

Figure 2-11 Worksheet's appearance after using AutoSum twice

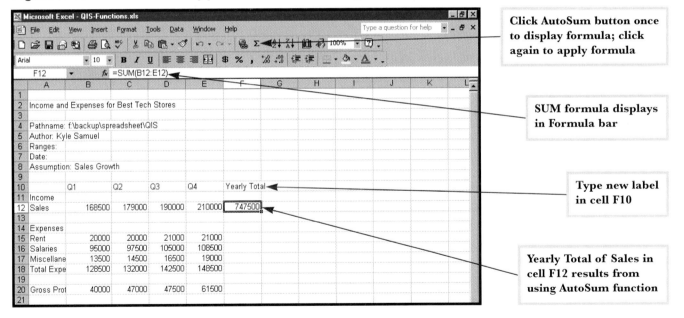

Click AutoSum button once to display formula; click again to apply formula

SUM formula displays in Formula bar

Type new label in cell F10

Yearly Total of Sales in cell F12 results from using AutoSum function

Practice

To practice entering functions, follow the instructions on the Practice2-4 Sheet tab of practice file exprac2.xls. Save changes as myexprac2-4.xls and close the file.

skill | Using the Insert Function Feature

concept

To enter a function other than SUM, you can either enter it yourself or use the Paste Function command. This command enables you to insert built-in formulas into your worksheet, saving you the trouble of remembering mathematical expressions and the time it takes to type them. And to help you find just the right function for a desired calculation, Excel 2002 has a sophisticated Insert Function dialog box that provides even more help than did earlier versions of the dialog box.

do it !

Use the Paste Function command and the Insert Function dialog box to calculate the average Total Expenses for the year.

1. Open Student File exdoit2-5.xls and save it as QIS-Insert Function.xls. Click cell A22, enter the abbreviation Avg. Exp. (Average Expenses), and press [Tab] to move to cell B22.

2. With cell B22 selected, click Insert, then click Function. The Insert Function dialog box will open, with the Search for a function text box highlighted by default. Type the description Calculate average of quarterly expenses, then click the Go button. In the Or select a category list box, the word Recommended will appear. In the Select a function list box, a list of functions will appear that Excel estimates will satisfy your calculation needs.

3. In the Select a function list box, click the AVERAGE function. The function name, the form of the related argument, and a description of what the function does will appear in the gray area directly below the list box (see Figure 2-12).

4. Click [OK]. The Insert Function dialog box will close, and the Function Arguments dialog box will open with the cell range B20:B21 appearing by default in the Number1 text box. However, this is not the cell range you want to average. If necessary, drag the dialog box out of the way so it does not block your view of row 18.

5. With the Number1 text box still highlighted, click cell B18, drag into cell E18, and release the mouse button. As you drag, a moving border will appear around the selected cells, and the Function Arguments dialog box will collapse to a smaller size. When you release the mouse button, the dialog box will re-expand, and the formula =AVERAGE (B18:E18) will appear in cell B22 and in the Formula bar (see Figure 2-13).

6. Click [OK] to apply the formula and to close the dialog box. The calculated result 137875 will display in cell B22, representing the quarterly average of Total Expenses (see Figure 2-14). Save the changes you have made to the worksheet and close the file.

more

When you open the Insert Function dialog box, the default setting for the Or select a category list box is Most Recently Used. At the same time, the Select a function list box lists the functions you have used most often in the recent past. If you have not used the Insert Function command before, the Most Recently Used category will contain a default list of commonly used functions. Each most recently used function also appears under the other general categories listed in the Or select a category list box. To find functions other than most recent ones, click the desired general category in the Or select a category list box. A list of specific functions within the general category will appear in the Select a function list box. Scroll up and down in that list box to find and click on the desired function.

Notice that the Number1 option in the Function Arguments dialog box is bold. This indicates that you must enter data into that text box in order for the function to work. Plain text in the dialog box indicates that entering cell ranges there is optional.

Figure 2-12 Insert Function dialog box

Type brief description of desired calculation, then click [Go] to display list of functions that might perform that calculation

Select function category from drop-down list of related functions; select "All" category if desired function does not appear in specific category

Click specific function to display function name, form of related argument, and brief description of what function does

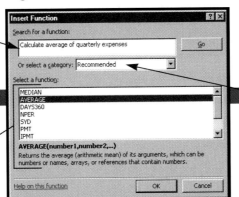

Figure 2-13 Selecting an argument for a function

Cell range of selected argument

Animated border indicates selected range

Formula appears in active cell with function and selected cell range

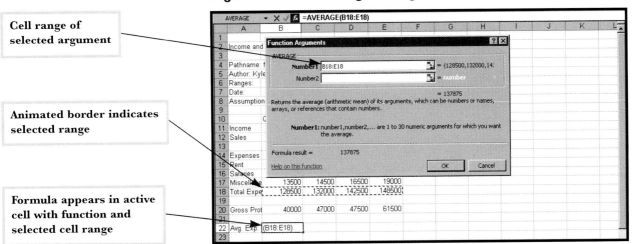

Figure 2-14 Inserted AVERAGE function

You also may open the Insert Function dialog box by clicking the Insert Function button

Calculated result of inserted function

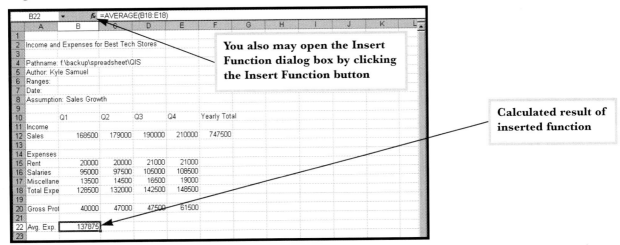

Practice

To practice inserting functions, follow the instructions on the Practice2-5 Sheet tab of the practice file exprac2.xls. Save changes as myexprac2-5.xls and close the file.

skill | Copying and Pasting Formulas

concept

You can copy and paste formulas into other cells just as you can with labels and values. By default, Excel considers the cell referred to in an argument as a relative cell reference. A relative cell reference (such as A1, B5, H16, and so on) is based on the relative position of the cell with the formula and the cell referred to by the reference. If the position of the cell with the formula changes, the cell reference changes too. With relative cell references, in other words, formulas in new locations automatically adjust to reference new cells.

do it !

Copy the SUM function from cell F12 into cells F13 through F20 to calculate Yearly Totals for Expenses and Gross Profit. Delete unneeded formulas in cells referring to empty cells to the left.

1. Open Student File exdoit2-6.xls and save it as QIS-Copying.xls.

2. Click cell F12 to activate it. Although the Yearly Total for Sales appears in the cell, the SUM function appears in the Formula bar with the argument B12:E12 inside parentheses.

3. Click the Copy button 📋 to copy the formula to the Office Clipboard. An animated border will appear around cell F12.

4. Click cell F15 to activate it. Click the Paste button 📋▾, not the down-arrow to its right, to paste the copied function into cell F15. The result 82000 will appear in cell F15. Notice that Excel has changed the argument in the Formula bar from B12:E12 to B15:E15, which is the cell range relative to the copied function's new position in the worksheet (see Figure 2-15). With this new argument the function will be applied to the row in which it appears rather than the one it was copied from.

5. A Paste Options Smart Tag appears at the lower right of cell F15. Move the mouse pointer over the Smart Tag, and click the down-pointing arrow to display a shortcut menu with the default option Keep Source Formatting (see Figure 2-16). Since this is the desired option, leave the Tag as is.

6. Move the mouse pointer over the lower-right corner of cell F15 (the cell's fill handle). The pointer will change to a black cross (✚). Holding down the mouse button, drag into cell F20 to copy the function from cell F15 into the newly selected cells as well. A gray border will appear around the cell range as you drag, and an Auto Fill Options Smart Tag will appear at the lower right of cell F20 . Release the mouse button at the lower-right corner of cell F20 (see Figure 2-17).

(continued on EX 2.14)

Figure 2-15 Copying and pasting a function

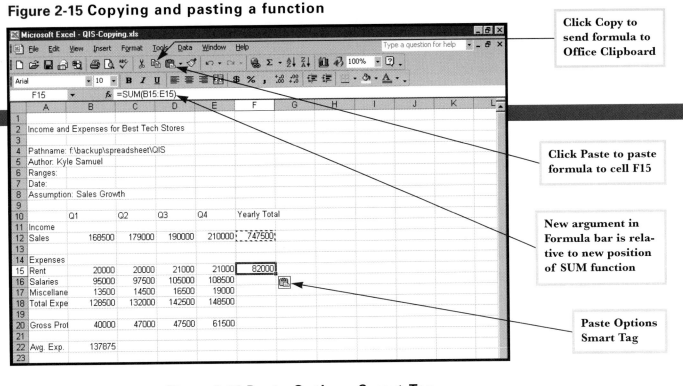

Click Copy to send formula to Office Clipboard

Click Paste to paste formula to cell F15

New argument in Formula bar is relative to new position of SUM function

Paste Options Smart Tag

Figure 2-16 Paste Options Smart Tag

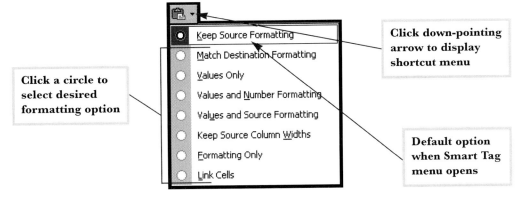

Click down-pointing arrow to display shortcut menu

Click a circle to select desired formatting option

Default option when Smart Tag menu opens

Figure 2-17 Using the fill handle to copy a function

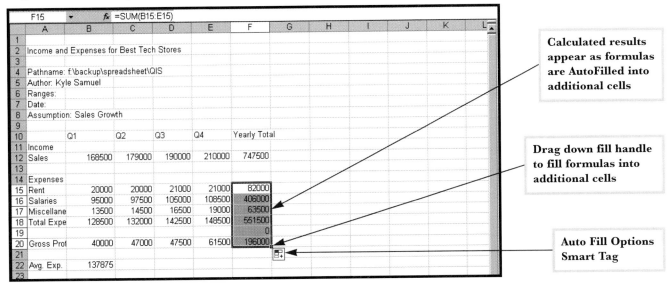

Calculated results appear as formulas are AutoFilled into additional cells

Drag down fill handle to fill formulas into additional cells

Auto Fill Options Smart Tag

skill | Copying and Pasting Formulas (continued)

do it !

7. Move the mouse pointer over the Smart Tag at the lower right of cell F20. Click the down-pointing arrow to display a shortcut menu with the default option Copy Cells (see Figure 2-18). Since this is the desired option, leave the Tag as is.

8. Cell F19 contains a zero because the function copied into that cell adds up the empty cells directly to the left of the cell. Since you do not need a function in cell F19, click in that cell and press [Delete]. Click cell F22.

9. Verify that the cell values in your worksheet match those in Figure 2-19. If any cells do not match, double-check the formulas in the mismatched cells and correct them. If you are absolutely sure that all your formulas are correct, double-check the values of the cells that are referenced by the newly pasted formulas.

10. Save the changes you have made to the worksheet and close the file.

more

As the Concept section of this Skill mentions, a relative cell reference is based on the relative position of the cell with the formula and the cell referred to by the reference. Relative cell references appear quite often in formulas. Relative cell references contrast with absolute cell references, which you can identify by the dollar signs that precede their column letters and row numbers (such as $A$1, $B$5, $H$16, and so on). In a formula an absolute cell reference always refers to one cell in a specific, unchanging location. Therefore, if the position of the cell with a formula changes, the absolute cell reference in that formula will not change, but stay the same. With absolute cell references, in other words, formulas in new locations do not adjust to reference new cells. While this Skill took advantage of the flexibility of relative cell references, the next Skill will take advantage of the benefits of absolute cell references.

Figure 2-18 Auto Fill Options Smart Tag

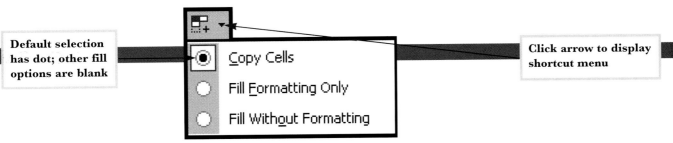

Default selection has dot; other fill options are blank

Click arrow to display shortcut menu

Figure 2-19 Worksheet's appearance after deleting unneeded function

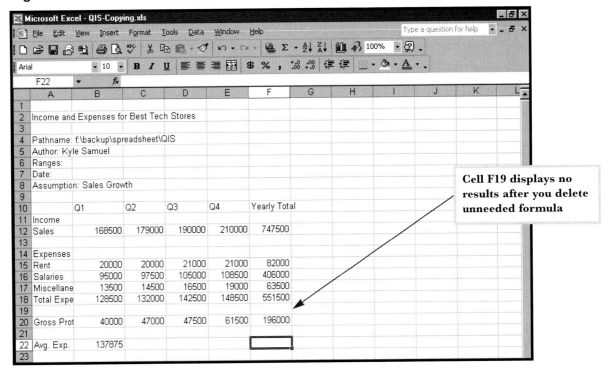

Cell F19 displays no results after you delete unneeded formula

Practice

To practice copying and pasting formulas, follow the instructions on the Practice2-6 Sheet tab of practice file exprac2.xls. Save changes as myexprac2-6.xls and close the file.

skill   Using What-If Analysis

concept

Excel facilitates changing the conditions in one area of a worksheet to see how such changes will affect calculations in another area. This altering of conditions is called What-If Analysis, and is one of Excel's most useful and time-saving features in personal and in business worksheets. Imagine, for example, that you wanted to buy a new car but could not figure out by how much a larger down payment would reduce monthly payments. A properly designed worksheet would be able to calculate such a figure. Likewise, an income statement like Best Tech's could use What-If analysis to estimate increasing Sales and how they would affect Gross Profits.

do it !

Determine how Sales would grow and how Gross Profits would be affected, assuming a Sales Growth assumption of 10% per quarter.

1. Open Student File exdoit2-7.xls and save it as QIS-Analysis.xls.

2. Select cells C12, D12, and E12—that is, the sales figures for the second, third, and fourth quarters of the year. Press [Delete] to remove the values from the selected cells. The values in cells C12:E12 now are considered to be zero. Notice that the values in cells F12 and C20:F20 change. This change results from the fact that Excel automatically recalculates formulas when values in their referenced cells have been changed.

3. Click cell C8 to activate it. Enter .1 (10% expressed as a decimal) into the active cell. This is the cell that will be referenced in the formula that calculates projected earnings. Press [Enter]. Notice that Excel inserts a zero before the .1 in cell C8 as a place holder (see Figure 2-20).

4. Click cell C12 to activate it. Here, you must create a formula to multiply the first quarter's sales by 110%, which will show the result in the second quarter of a 10% increase over the first quarter's sales figure. Enter the formula =B12*(1+$C$8) into the active cell (see Figure 2-21). The dollar signs preceding the column letter C and the row number 8 tell Excel not to change the cell address, even if you move the formula to a new location. This unchanging cell address is an absolute cell reference. ⬤ To create an absolute cell reference, be sure to place a $ before both the column letter and row number. If you place a $ before only the column letter or the row number, only the part of the formula with the symbol will remain absolute, while the other part will remain relative.

5. Press [Enter]. The result of the calculation, 185350, appears in place of the formula in cell C12. Cells F12 and C20 change to reflect Excel's recalculation of their formulas, which include cell C12 in their arguments.

6. Click cell C12 again, and move the mouse pointer over the cell's fill handle. While holding down the mouse button, drag into cell E12 to copy the formula in cell C12 to the two additional cells. As you drag, a gray border appears around cells C12:E12, and shading appears in cells D12 and E12 to indicate that you have used the fill handle to copy the formula in C12 into the shaded cells.

(continued on EX 2.18)

Figure 2-20 Cell values deleted and sales growth assumption added

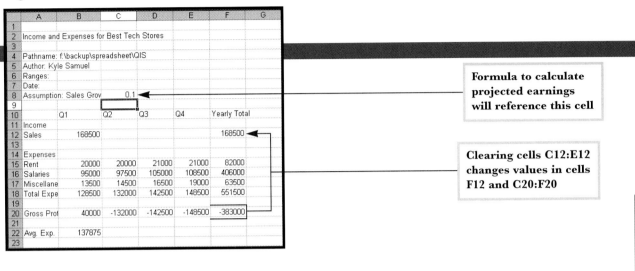

Formula to calculate projected earnings will reference this cell

Clearing cells C12:E12 changes values in cells F12 and C20:F20

Figure 2-21 Growth assumption formula using absolute cell reference

SUM   X ✓ fx =B12*(1+$C$8)

	A	B	C	D	E	F	G	H	I	J	K	L
1												
2	Income and Expenses for Best Tech Stores											
3												
4	Pathname: f:\backup\spreadsheet\QIS											
5	Author: Kyle Samuel											
6	Ranges:											
7	Date:											
8	Assumption: Sales Grow		0.1									
9												
10		Q1	Q2	Q3	Q4	Yearly Total						
11	Income											
12	Sales	168500	=B12*(1+$C$8)			337001.1						
13												
14	Expenses											
15	Rent	20000	20000	21000	21000	82000						
16	Salaries	95000	97500	105000	108500	406000						
17	Miscellane	13500	14500	16500	19000	63500						
18	Total Expe	128500	132000	142500	148500	551500						
19												
20	Gross Prof	40000	36501.1	-142500	-148500	-214499						
21												
22	Avg. Exp.	137875										
23												

Cell B12 is relative cell address, while cell C8 is absolute cell address

skill   Using What-If Analysis (continued)

do it !

7. Notice that the Auto Fill Options Smart Tag appears to the lower right of cell E12. Since the default option in the Smart Tag is the desired one, click cell F13 and press [Delete] to hide the Smart Tag.

8. Click cell D12. Notice that the cell's reference to cell B12 has changed to C12, but that the reference to cell C8 remains the same (see Figure 2-22). If you had not included the dollar signs before the column letter and row number, the copied formula would have replaced the cell reference C8 with D8, an empty cell, and the result in D12 would have been wrong. Click cell A1 (see Figure 2-23).

9. Save the changes you have made to the worksheet and close the file.

more

Formulas can contain several operations. An operation is a single mathematical step in solving an equation, such as adding two numbers, multiplying a cell by a percentage, or calculating an exponent—that is, raising a number to another power. When working with formulas containing multiple operators, Excel performs the calculations in the order displayed in Table 2-1 below. For example, in the formula =6+3*4, Excel would multiply 3 by 4 to get 12, then add 6 to get 18. However, if you want to change the order of calculations, you must add parentheses around the part of the formula that you want to calculate first. For example, in the formula =(6+3)*4, Excel would add 6 and 3 to get 9, then multiply 9 by 4 to get 36.

In a more complicated formula, such as =(B5+10)/SUM(C5:E5), Excel first would add the value in cell B5 and the quantity of 10, then divide the result by the total of the values in the cell range C5:E5. Because Excel allows you to use many operators and worksheets can have many cells, you must know how to reference cells correctly and construct formulas properly. You then must be willing to double-check the effectiveness of your formulas before saving them in a finalized worksheet and, especially, handing them off to another person to use with reliability.

Table 2-1   Order of Operations

Operator	Description
–	Negation, as in –10
%	Percentage
^	Exponentiation
* and /	Multiplication and division, from left to right
+ and –	Addition and subtraction, from left to right
&	Connection of two strings of text (concatenation)
=, <, >, <=, >=, and <>	Comparisons

Figure 2-22 Formula containing relative and absolute cell references

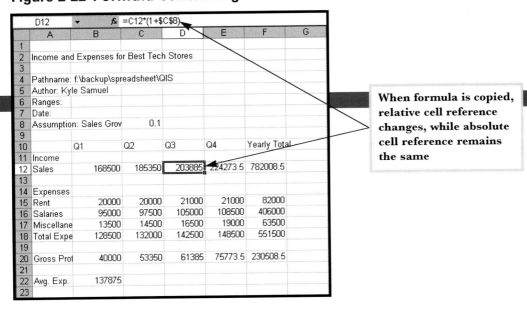

When formula is copied, relative cell reference changes, while absolute cell reference remains the same

Figure 2-23 Sales growth assumptions added to Quarters 2 through 4

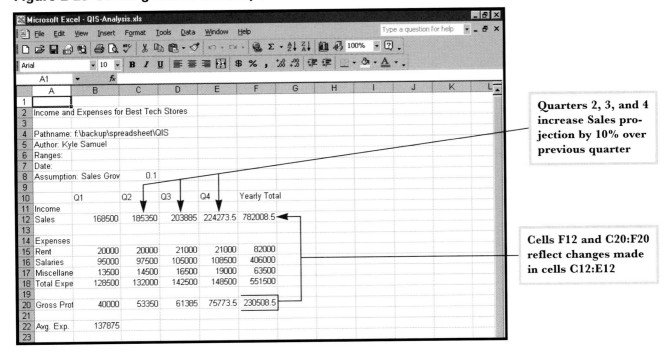

Quarters 2, 3, and 4 increase Sales projection by 10% over previous quarter

Cells F12 and C20:F20 reflect changes made in cells C12:E12

Practice

To practice performing a What-If Analysis, follow the instructions on the Practice2-7 Sheet tab of practice file exprac2.xls. Save changes as myexprac2-7.xls and close the file.

skill

Previewing and Printing a Worksheet

concept

Printing a worksheet is useful if you need a paper copy to refer to, to distribute to others, or to file. While offices are becoming more and more electronic, many people still prefer working with paper documents over viewing them on a screen. Excel allows you to view a worksheet as it will appear on a printed page before it is printed so you can spot errors or items you would like to change before going through the printing process.

do it !

Display a worksheet in Print Preview mode, then print it.

1. Open Student File exdoit2-8.xls and save it as QIS-Previewing.xls. Replace the author's name in cell A5 with your own name.

2. Make sure your computer is properly connected to a working printer, that the printer is turned on and loaded with paper, and so on (if necessary, ask your instructor for help).

3. Click the Print Preview button 🔍 on the Standard toolbar. The worksheet will display in Print Preview mode, and the mouse pointer will appear as a magnifying glass (see Figure 2-24).

4. Click near the top of the preview page. The worksheet will be magnified so you can examine it more closely, and the pointer will change to an arrow. By default, worksheet gridlines are non-printing items, so they will not appear in the preview.

5. On the Print Preview toolbar, click the Print button Print... . The view will revert to regular mode and the Print dialog box will open (see Figure 2-25). ◯ If you do not need to conduct a print preview or adjust the settings in the Print dialog box, you can print the active worksheet by clicking the Print button 🖨 on the Standard toolbar.

6. Click OK . The Print dialog box will close, a box will appear notifying you of the print job's progress, and the document will be sent to the printer.

7. Verify that the printer has printed your document. If it has not, do **not** reprint. Instead, check the connection between your computer and the printer, the condition of the printer itself, and so on. Reprint the document only after you have found the printing problem. Again, if needed, ask your instructor for help.

8. Close your worksheet without saving any changes to the file.

more

You can adjust many printing options by selecting the Page Setup command on the File menu. The Page Setup dialog box will open with four tabs: Page, Margins, Header/Footer, and Sheet. The Page tab controls the way the printed selection will appear on a page, such as its vertical (Portrait) or horizontal (Landscape) orientation, or by how large or small you can scale it on one or more pages. The Margins tab controls how you adjust the amount of space between a worksheet's print area and the edges of a page. The Header/Footer tab controls what information will appear at the top and/or bottom of each page of a printout, such as page numbers, titles, file names, author's name, and so on. The Sheet tab controls how you present your data on the printed page, such as whether to print gridlines, which parts of the worksheet to print, and whether to repeat column headings across each new page.

Figure 2-24 Previewing your worksheet

Click here to open
Print dialog box

Click with magni-
fier to zoom in on
document

Click "Close"
button to return
to Normal view

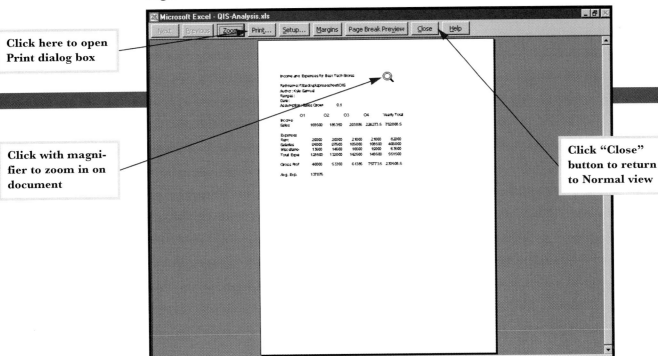

Figure 2-25 Print dialog box

Click "All" to print
all pages of a multi-
page document, or
enter page numbers
to print a partial
range of pages

Specifies that all of
the current work-
sheet will print

Alternate way to
access Print
Preview mode

Name of
selected
printer

Opens printer-
specific dialog
box to adjust
settings for
paper, graph-
ics, and other
printer features

Click arrows or
enter a number to
change quantity
of copies to print

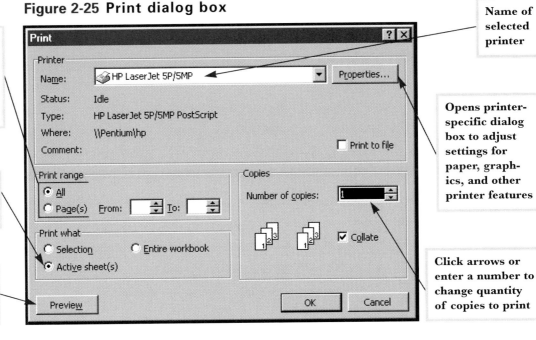

Practice

To practice previewing and printing a worksheet, follow the instructions on the Practice2-8 Sheet tab
of practice file exprac2.xls. Save changes as myexprac2-8.xls and close the file.

shortcuts

Function	Button/Mouse	Menu	Keyboard
Cut data to the Clipboard	✂	Click Edit, click Cut	[Ctrl]+[X]
Copy data to the Clipboard	📋	Click Edit, click Copy	[Ctrl]+[C]
Paste data from the Clipboard	📋 ▾	Click Edit, click Paste	[Ctrl]+[V]
AutoSum	Σ ▾		
Insert Function	fx	Click Insert, click Function	
Print Preview	🔍	Click File, click Print Preview	
Print	🖨 (to skip Print dialog box)	Click File, click Print (for Print dialog box)	[Ctrl]+[P] (for Print dialog box)

quiz

A. Identify Key Features

Name the items indicated by callouts in Figure 2-26.

Figure 2-26 Manipulating data in a worksheet

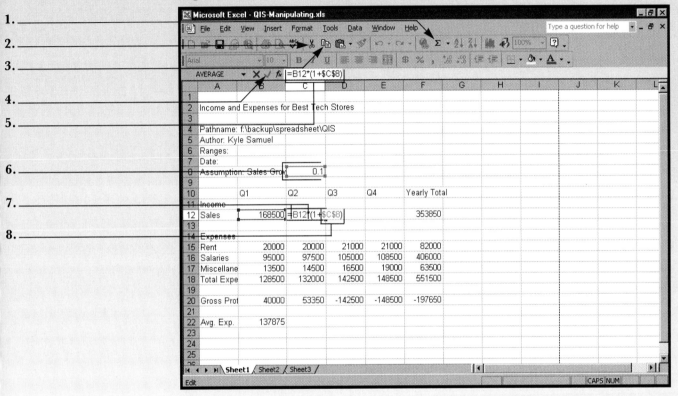

1. _____

2. _____

3. _____

4. _____

5. _____

6. _____

7. _____

8. _____

B. Select the Best Answer

9. Small square in the lower-right corner of an active cell

10. Temporary storage space for cut or copied information

11. Type this symbol to represent multiplication in a calculation

12. Allows you to see a worksheet as it will appear on a sheet of paper

13. Enables you to switch page orientation or adjust margins

14. Offers AVERAGE as one of its choices

15. Aligned to the right by default in Excel

16. Type this symbol to indicate absolute cell references

a. Values

b. Asterisk

c. Office Clipboard

d. Fill handle

e. Dollar sign

f. Insert Function dialog box

g. Print Preview mode

h. Page Setup dialog box

quiz (continued)

C. Complete the Statement

17. When you use the fill handle, cells to be filled are marked by a:

a. Gray border

b. Check mark

c. Plus sign

d. ScreenTip

18. Typing an apostrophe before a number instructs Excel to recognize it as a:

a. Formula

b. Function

c. Label

d. Value

19. None of the following actions will erase the Clipboard except:

a. Pasting an item

b. Cutting a new item

c. Copying a new item

d. Turning off the computer

20. By default, Excel considers formula cell references to be:

a. Absolute

b. AutoSums

c. Relative

d. Redundant

21. Changing conditions in one area of a worksheet to see how they affect calculations in another area is called:

a. Absolute analysis

b. Assumption analysis

c. What's-What Analysis

d. What-If Analysis

22. To copy cell contents to a new location, drag and drop the cell pointer while pressing:

a. [Ctrl]

b. [Enter]

c. [Shift]

d. [Tab]

23. An animated border indicates that the cell contents:

a. Are the result of a function or formula

b. Have been permanently deleted

c. Have been sent to the Office Clipboard

d. Have been pasted

24. Information enclosed in parentheses in a formula is called the:

a. Argument

b. Cell reference

c. Definition

d. Quantifier

25. Which of the following **could be** a correct order of operations in a formula?

a. Negation, Comparison, Multiplication, Addition

b. Negation, Percentage, Exponentiation, Multiplication

c. Comparison, Exponentiation, Addition, Multiplication

d. Addition, Subtraction, Multiplication, Division

26. The Print Preview toolbar has all of the following **except**:

a. A Zoom button

b. A Print button

c. A Setup button

d. A Page Orientation button

interactivity

Build Your Skills

1. Open a worksheet, cut and paste cell labels, and enter cell values:

   a. Open exskills2.xls and save it as ClassSked.xls.

   b. Cut and paste cells B2:B7 into cells A2:A7. Then cut and paste cells C3:C4 into cells B3:B4.

   c. Delete the contents of cell A7.

   d. Enter a number of hours, to the nearest half hour, for each activity in the cells matching the weekdays on which you do them. Do not fill in the totals.

   e. Resave the worksheet with the changes you have made.

2. Use AutoSum, the Insert Function, and the Fill Handle:

   a. Using AutoSum, calculate the total number of hours for Monday that you engage in all activities. Be sure you have accounted for all your time on Monday, so the total adds up to 24 hours.

   b. Using the fill handle, copy the AutoSum function for Monday into cells C17:F17.

   c. In cell G8, type the word Average. In cell G9 use the Insert Function command to calculate average hours spent per day on classes.

   d. Using the fill handle, copy the AVERAGE formula into cells G10:G16.

   e. Enter your name in cell A19, and enter the assignment date of this Skill in A20.

   f. Resave the worksheet with the changes you have made.

3. Preview and print the worksheet:

   a. Switch to Print Preview mode.

   b. Click the magnifying glass icon in the middle of the worksheet to enlarge the text size for easier viewing.

   c. Click the magnifying glass icon again to zoom back to the original view.

   d. Using the Print button on the Print Preview toolbar, print the worksheet.

   e. Click the Close button on the Print Preview toolbar to return to Normal view.

   f. Resave the worksheet with the changes you have made and close the file.

interactivity (continued)

Problem Solving Exercises

1. Open the file exproblem2-1.xls and save it as Revised HR Funds.xls. This worksheet will help you track a $16,000 annual human resources expense account to improve hiring rates. Cut and paste the documentation area into column A. Enter dollar amounts into the existing worksheet, staying under $4,000 per quarter. Add a Totals label at the bottom of the existing labels in column A. Use the new label to demonstrate that your monetary allotments do not exceed $4,000 per quarter. Use a formula to calculate the Quarter 1 Total. Use AutoFill to copy the formula into the remaining quarters. Use a function to calculate the Annual Total for Advertising. Use AutoFill to copy the formula into the remaining categories and the new Totals row. Enter your name and a due date in the proper documentation cells, resave, preview, and print the worksheet. Close the file.

2. Open the file exproblem2-2.xls, which is a blank schedule for keeping track of employee work hours. Save the file as Employee Schedule.xls. Using fictional names and hours for five to ten employees, complete the weekly employee schedule. Add a label to record the Total Weekly Hours for each employee. Add a label to record the Daily Totals for each employee and for all employees combined. Using the formula and function commands explained in this lesson, calculate the totals for the weekly hours and the daily hours. In the documentation area add your name and a due date to the appropriate cells. Resave, preview, print, and close the file.

3. Using the skills you have learned so far, create a new worksheet that will allow you to track your individual monthly expenses for the months of September through May. Save the file as Monthly Expenses.xls. In the top area of the worksheet, create a documentation area like the ones you have seen in the Lessons and end-of-chapter activities. In the bottom area of the worksheet, enter category labels such as Rent, Phone, Books/Supplies, Food, Recreation, and so on. Calculate your total expenses for each month, as well as your average monthly expenses over the nine months. Also include an assumption value of 5 percent to account for going over your allotted budget. Then conduct a What-If Analysis to recalculate your total and average expenses based on a 5 percent increase in one or two categories. Enter your name and an assignment due date in the proper cells of the documentation area. Resave, preview, print, and close the file.

4. Create the worksheet below; save it as Population.xls. Add a Totals row below the existing labels in column A. Use AutoSum to calculate the first decade of the Totals row, and use AutoFill to copy the formula to the appropriate cells. Insert a What-If percentage between 4% and 7% in cell B7, using it to recalculate each area's population growth for each decade, based on 1980 data. Add a name and due date in the proper cells. Resave, preview, print, and close the file.

Figure 2-27 Population.xls

	A	B	C	D	E	F	G
1							
2	Caribbean Population Trends						
3	Path name: f/backup/Stats/Population.xls						
4	Author: [Student Name]						
5	Ranges:						
6	Date: [Due Date]						
7	Population Growth:						
8							
9		1980	1990	2000	2010		
10	Antigua/Barbuda	60152	63555	66422			
11	The Bahamas	285012	290159	294982			
12	Barbados	264789	269874	274540			
13	Bermuda	60875	61200	62997			
14	Grenada	80569	82654	89018			
15	Jamaica	2158960	2254566	2652689			
16	Trinidad & Tobago	1053698	1105887	1175523			
17							

Formatting Worksheet Elements

Excel 2002 allows you to format the cells of your worksheets individually, format them as parts of rows and columns, format them automatically using the AutoFormat feature, and format them in ranges, or groups, of cells. Formatting refers to changing the appearance of information in a worksheet without changing the actual content of that information. You can use Excel's many formatting tools to improve the appearance and the readability of your worksheet. Text formatting includes font, font size, style, color, and alignment. You can format labels in a variety of styles, some of which help to express the kind of data that they represent. You also can format individual cells or ranges of cells. The AutoFormat command enables you to apply a set of pre-designed formats to an entire range of cells at once.

Although the structure of an Excel worksheet is highly organized, it also is very flexible. You can restructure cells by merging them, or splitting previously merged cells. You can change the larger structure by increasing or decreasing column widths and row heights, or by adding or deleting rows and columns as needed. You even can maintain the overall structure of a worksheet, but hide (and then unhide) rows or columns when confidentiality or display needs dictate. When making changes to the structure of a worksheet, you first should decide what data needs to appear in the final worksheet and what formatting changes will enhance rather than muddle the worksheet's appearance.

You often will find that you are using a row or column of cells, or even a larger grouping of cells, that contains closely related data. Excel allows you to define these groups of related cells as ranges and then name them as you see fit. After naming the cell grouping, you then can locate that grouping immediately in the future and manage it or manipulate it as your needs and desires dictate.

Lesson Goal:

Format cells, cell values, and rows and columns. Manipulate rows and columns, and define and format cell ranges. Learn the advantages of AutoFormat.

skills

≶ **Merging and Splitting Cells**

≶ **Formatting Cell Labels**

≶ **Formatting Cell Values**

≶ **Formatting Rows and Columns**

≶ **Inserting and Deleting Rows and Columns**

≶ **Hiding, Unhiding, and Protecting Cells**

≶ **Defining and Naming Cell Ranges**

≶ **Filling a Cell Range with Labels**

≶ **Applying Shading, Patterns, and Borders to Cells & Ranges**

≶ **Applying AutoFormat to a Worksheet**

skill | Merging and Splitting Cells

concept

Excel 2002 allows you to format your cells by merging two or more cells into one cell or by splitting a merged cell back into the component cells of the worksheet. You may want to merge cells to ensure that a large amount of text fits in only one cell, to call attention to a part of the worksheet, or to consolidate data. You may want to split cells back into their component parts if you remove a large amount of text, eliminate something on the worksheet that previously required emphasis, need more cells for additional data, and so on.

do it !

Merge cells in order to enter longer text, and then split the merged cells to separate text from data.

1. Open Student File exdoit3-1.xls and save it as best-1.xls.

2. Click in cell A21 and drag through cell B21. Click Format, click Cells to open the Format Cells dialog box, and click the Alignment tab if needed to bring it forward. In the Text control section, add a check mark to the Merge cells check box (see Figure 3-1). Click the OK button [OK] to activate the merge and to close the dialog box.

3. With cells A21 and B21 now merged into cell A21 and still selected, click the Format Painter button on the Standard toolbar. Click in cell A22 and drag through cell B22. The two selected cells in row 22 merge to match the format of merged cell A21. Press [Enter]. Format Painter is handy tool for copying the formatting of one cell or cell range to another cell or cell range. Clicking the Format Painter button once enables you to copy a format of set of formats once. Clicking the button twice enables you to copy the format or formats repeatedly until you click the button again to turn the feature off.

4. In cell A21 type Average Sales/Qrtr. In cell A22 type Average Expenses/Qrtr. You now could calculate the Average Sales and the Average Expenses by hand and type them into the relevant merged cells after adding a colon and a space to the abbreviation Qrtr in each row. However, doing so would contradict and defeat the formatting and formula capabilities of the worksheet. Therefore, you will split the merged cells and enter formulas in the restored column B cells for each category.

5. Click cell A21. Click Format, click Cells to open the Format Cells dialog box, and click the Alignment tab if needed to bring it forward. Click the Merge cells check box to remove the check mark that you placed there earlier, and click [OK]. Repeat the same process in cell A22 by using either the Alignment tab or the Format Painter button. Rows 21 and 22 now have separate cells in columns A and B.

6. In cell B21 type the formula =average(B12:E12), then press [Enter]. In cell B22, use the AVERAGE function to calculate the average of cells B18:E18, then press [Enter]. Cells B21 and B22 now contain averages for, respectively, the quarterly sales and quarterly expenses that appear in the current worksheet (see Figure 3-2). Instead of typing B12:E12 in the first formula, you could click in cell B12 and drag across into cell E12. This action identifies the selected cells as the desired range between the opening and closing parentheses of the formula.

7. Resave the worksheet with the changes you have made and close the file.

more   When you merge two or more cells, the cell reference for the merged area is the column letter and row number of the upper-left cell that was merged. Excel puts only the text and/or data from the upper-left cell into the merged area. If you had text and/or data in the other cells, Excel deletes that data from the merged cell. To change horizontal text alignment in the merged cell, click the Align Left 📄, Center 📄, or Align Right 📄 button on the Formatting toolbar. These buttons allow you to change the default alignment of labels and values. To change other features of text alignment (including vertical alignment) click Format, click Cells to open the Format Cells dialog box, click the Alignment tab to bring it forward, and use the options you need from the four sections of the tab. When you split a merged cell into its components, the Name box will display the cell reference of the upper-left cell from the latest merge, but the cell pointer border will surround all previously merged cells. To select a cell to type in, either click in the desired cell or press [Enter] until you see the desired cell reference in the Name box.

Figure 3-1 Alignment tab of Format Cells dialog box

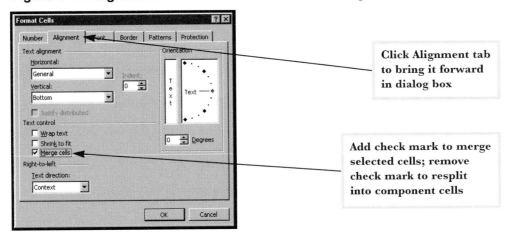

Click Alignment tab to bring it forward in dialog box

Add check mark to merge selected cells; remove check mark to resplit into component cells

Figure 3-2 Worksheet's appearance after merges, splits, and edits

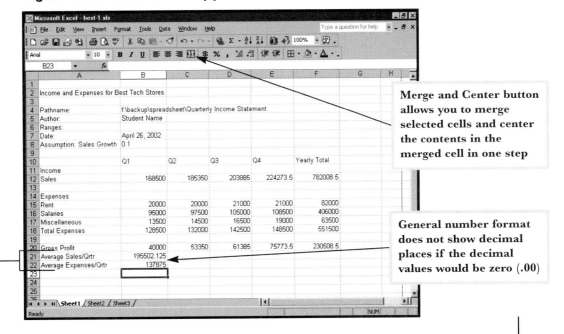

Merge and Center button allows you to merge selected cells and center the contents in the merged cell in one step

General number format does not show decimal places if the decimal values would be zero (.00)

Merged and resplit cells

Excel 2002

Practice

To practice merging and splitting cells, follow the instructions on the Practice3-1 Sheet tab of the practice file exprac3.xls. Save changes as myexprac3-1.xls, and close the file.

skill | Formatting Cell Labels

concept

Formatting cells enhances the appearance of your worksheet and makes the formatted cells stand out from the worksheet's default font so the formatted cells will be easier to read. Formatting options include changing the font style, font size, font color, text alignment, and similar cell characteristics. Before you can change the formatting of a cell or a group of cells (also called a range), you must select those cells.

do it !

Add formatting to cells to emphasize their importance to the worksheet.

1. Open Student File exdoit3-2.xls and save it as best-2.xls.

2. Click in cell A2 and drag into cell F2 to select cell range A2:F2. Click the Merge and Center button ▦ on the Formatting toolbar. The six selected cells in row 2 merge into one cell. The worksheet title centers itself across all six columns, not just cell A2.

3. With cell A2 still highlighted, click Format, click Cells to open the Format Cells dialog box, and click the Font tab to bring it forward. In the scrollable box in the Font section, click Arial Black. In the scrollable box in the Size section, click 14 (see Figure 3-3). Click ⬚OK⬚ to apply the Font formats and to close the dialog box.

4. Click in cell A4 and drag into cell A8 to select the cell range A4:A8. With the cells selected, click the Bold button ⬚B⬚. Position the mouse pointer over the right edge of the gray heading for column A so the pointer changes to ↔. Double-click to autofit the column to the width of the text in cell A8, which is slightly greater now that you have bolded it.

5. Click in cell B10 and drag into cell F10, then click the Center button ⬚≡⬚. With cells B10:F10 still highlighted, hold down [Ctrl] and click cells A11, A14, A18, and A20:A22. Release the [Ctrl] key without deselecting the nonadjacent cells. Click the Bold button ⬚B⬚.

6. Click cell A11, hold down [Ctrl], and click cells A14, A18, and the cell range A20:A22. Click the Italic button ⬚I⬚.

7. Click cell A2, hold down [Ctrl], select the cell range B10:F10 and the cell range A11:A22. Release [Ctrl] without deselecting the cells. Click the Font Color list button ⬚A⬚·⬚ to display the 40 colored squares of the color palette below the button. Click the Dark Blue square in the first row, sixth column (see Figure 3-4). Click outside the selected cells to see that the font color has changed for the text of the worksheet title, the column headings for the four quarters and the Yearly Total, and the row headings in column A.

8. Click cell A12, hold down [Ctrl], and select the cell range A15:A17. Release [Ctrl] without deselecting the cells. Click the Increase Indent button ⬚≣⬚ to indent the text in the four selected cells slightly to the right (see Figure 3-5).

9. Resave the worksheet with the changes you have made and close the file.

more

The Font tab in the Format Cells dialog box allows you to change most text attributes. The options Font, Font style, and Size each have two boxes attached to them. The lower box is a list box that indexes available fonts, font styles, and font sizes, respectively. The upper box is a text box wherein you can enter any of these choices without having to scroll through a list in a lower box. However, the point size of your font selection is not limited to only those numbers listed, and can range anywhere between 1 and 409. The Underline option contains a drop-down list with five styles of underlines that you can use. The Color option contains a drop-down palette with 56 color choices. Clicking one of these boxes will change your text to that color. Checking the Normal font box reverts any changed font formats to the default settings. You also can select the following effects: Strikethrough draws a line through text, making it appear as crossed out; Superscript shrinks the text and raises it above the baseline; Subscript shrinks and drops the text below the baseline. Any time that you alter the format of a font using the dialog box, its altered look appears in the Preview window on the Font tab, and none of the alterations take effect on the worksheet until you close the dialog box.

Figure 3-3 Font tab of Format Cells dialog box

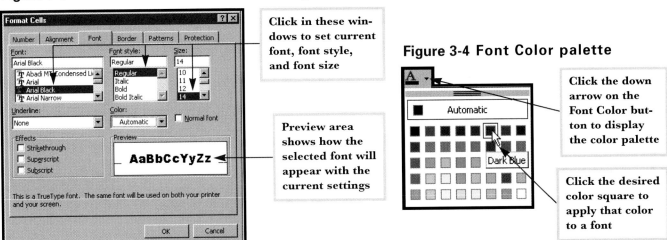

Click in these windows to set current font, font style, and font size

Preview area shows how the selected font will appear with the current settings

Figure 3-4 Font Color palette

Click the down arrow on the Font Color button to display the color palette

Click the desired color square to apply that color to a font

Figure 3-5 Worksheet's appearance after cell formats

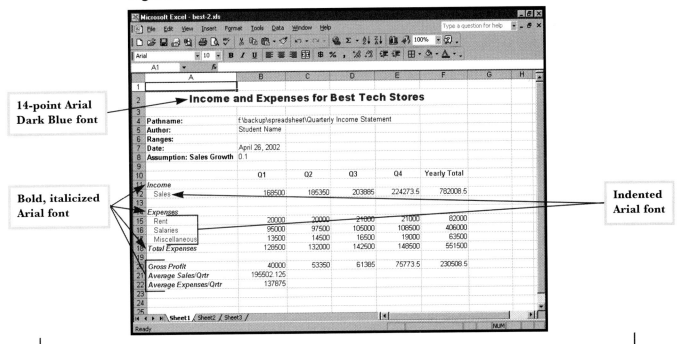

14-point Arial Dark Blue font

Bold, italicized Arial font

Indented Arial font

Practice

To practice formatting cell contents, follow the instructions on the Practice3-2 Sheet tab of the practice file exprac3.xls. Save changes as myexprac3-2.xls, and close the file.

skill Formatting Cell Values

concept Labels can help identify what kind of data a number represents. However, you still may want to format cell values themselves so that readers more readily understand what those values represent. Common formats include Currency, Percentage, Fraction, and Comma, all of which you can apply using toolbar buttons. Choose formats according to how you are using the values and how you wish them to look. You can apply cell or range formatting before or after you enter data, but you can choose formats more easily and intelligently if the values to which you apply those formats already appear in the worksheet.

do it ! Format all values with commas for easier reading, format the first and last lines of dollar amounts in Currency style, format the assumption in Percentage style, and remove the decimal places in selected cells.

1. Open Student File exdoit3-3.xls and save it as best-3.xls. Review the Formatting toolbar in Figure 3-6.

2. Select the cell range B12:F22. Click the Comma Style button ⬚. All of the cells contained within the selected range will be formatted in the Comma Style, which includes two decimal places.

3. Select the cell range B12:F12. While holding down [Ctrl], also select the cell range B20:F20. Release [Ctrl] without deselecting the cells. Click the Currency Style button ⬚. The values in the selected cells will appear with dollar signs at the left margin of the cells and two decimal places now will represent cents.

4. Select cell B8, which contains the value 0.1. Click the Percent Style button ⬚. The value will now appear as 10%. The result of the formula whose argument references this cell will remain the same.

5. Select the cell range B21:B22. Click the Currency Style button ⬚ , then click Decrease Decimal button ⬚ twice. The two decimal places in the selected cells will disappear (see Figure 3-7).

6. Resave the worksheet with the changes you have made and close the file.

more When you applied the Currency, Comma, and Percentage styles to the worksheet, you used the default style for each of these buttons. However, you can apply many more styles for 12 different categories of values by using the Numbers tab of the Format Cells dialog box. To access this tab, click Format, click Cells to open the dialog box, and click the Number tab if needed to bring it forward. In the Category section on the left side of the tab, click the name of the value that you need to format—for example, Currency, Date, Time, Fraction, and so on. After choosing a Category, click in the Type section on the right side of the dialog box for a specific style. Some values have just one box in the type section for formatting options. Other values, like Currency, allow you to choose how many decimals to display, to display a symbol such as a dollar sign, and to select a format for negative numbers.

When choosing a Category, be sure it relates to the type of data you are formatting. Don't select just the Number category, for example, to format Date or Time. When choosing a format in the Type section, be sure it is specific enough to represent the selected values adequately. For example, a worksheet for calculating weekly personal expenses probably should include two decimals to display cents. However, a worksheet for displaying annual corporate earnings can be rounded off to whole dollars.

Figure 3-6 Formatting toolbar

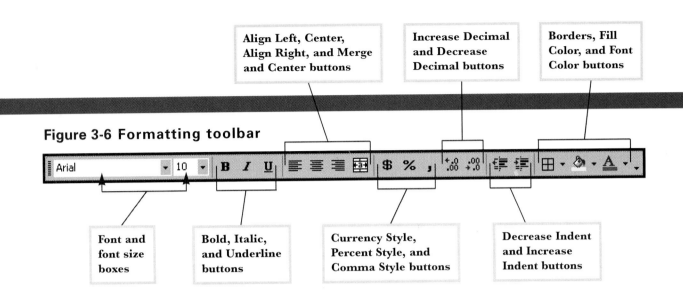

Align Left, Center, Align Right, and Merge and Center buttons

Increase Decimal and Decrease Decimal buttons

Borders, Fill Color, and Font Color buttons

Font and font size boxes

Bold, Italic, and Underline buttons

Currency Style, Percent Style, and Comma Style buttons

Decrease Indent and Increase Indent buttons

Figure 3-7 Worksheet's appearance after formatting cell values

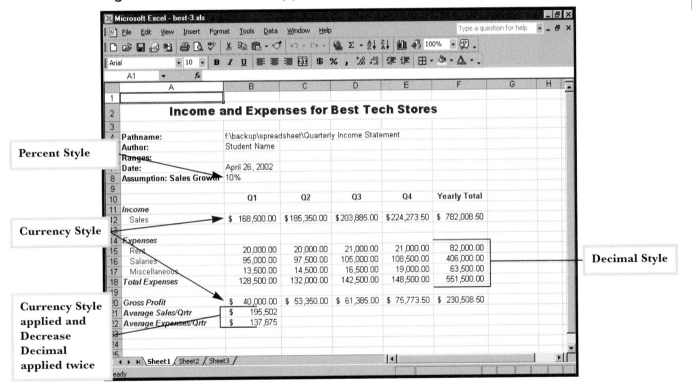

Percent Style

Currency Style

Currency Style applied and Decrease Decimal applied twice

Decimal Style

Practice

To practice formatting cell values, follow the instructions on the Practice3-3 Sheet tab of the practice file exprac3.xls. Save changes as myexprac3-3.xls, and close the file.

skill Formatting Rows and Columns

concept

Sometimes the information you enter in a worksheet will not fit neatly into a cell that is set with the default height and width. Other times, you may encounter a worksheet prepared by someone else who did not format it very well, and you may have to reformat it somewhat before working with it further. In these cases, you may need to adjust the height of a row or, more commonly, the width of a column. Standard column width is 8.43 characters, but can be set anywhere between 0 and 255.

do it !

Widen some columns to accommodate long labels and values and restore default row heights.

1. Open Student File exdoit3-4.xls and save it as best-4.xls. Notice that column A is too narrow to display all the text in cells A8, A21, and A22, and that the text in cell F10 is cut off at the beginning and runs into column G. Notice that rows 11, 14, 18, and 20 are twice the height of the other rows in the worksheet, forcing part of the worksheet below the bottom of the worksheet window (depending on your screen resolution settings).

2. Click the gray heading for column A to select the entire column. A down-pointing black arrow [↓] will appear when the mouse pointer is over the column heading. Click Format, click Column, and click Width to display the Column Width dialog box with the Column width text box already highlighted. Type 25 (see Figure 3-8). Click [OK] to change the width of column A and to close the dialog box. To display the Column Width dialog box, you also could right-click the heading of row A to display a shortcut menu, and then click the Column Width command.

3. Position the mouse pointer on the right edge of the gray heading for column F so that the pointer changes to ↔. Double-click to autofit column F, expanding the column to a width that will accommodate the contents of cell F10.

4. Click the heading for row 11, hold down [Ctrl], and click the headings for rows 14, 18, and 20. All four row headings and all the cells in the rows will highlight, just as they did when you selected column headings. Without deselecting the four rows, click the bottom edge of the heading for row 20 and hold down the mouse button to display a ScreenTip showing the current row height. While holding down the mouse button, carefully drag the bottom edge of row 20 upward until the ScreenTip reads Height: 12.75 (17 pixels), as shown in Figure 3-9, then release the mouse button. All four selected rows return to their default height.

5. Click the heading of row 12, hold down [Ctrl], and click the headings for rows 15 through 17. Click the Italic button [I]. All labels and data in the four rows will appear italicized (see Figure 3-10). Because you highlighted the row headings, not just some row cells, anything typed in any column of the four selected rows would appear italicized.

6. Resave the worksheet with the changes you have made and close the file.

more

The Steps above demonstrate that you have three ways to adjust row height or column width: (1) click and drag the right edge of the column heading or bottom edge of the row heading until you see in the ScreenTip the desired size of the row or column, (2) click the row or column heading, click Format, and click Row or Column to display the dialog box in which to enter a number, or (3) right-click on the row or column heading, click Row Height or Column Width to display the dialog box in which to enter a number. To widen several rows or columns at once, select the rows or columns to be changed, then drag any selected row or column edge as desired. To widen all rows or columns at once, click the Select All button ⬜ (to the left of the column A header, click Format, click Row or Column, and then click Height or Width to open the dialog box in which to enter a number. Remember, however, that you usually do not need to change row height manually, as Excel adjusts row height to fit the largest point size of a cell's label or data.

ScreenTips that display when you drag a column indicate the number of characters that will fit in the column, with the size of a character being equal to the average size of the digits 0-9. On a standard worksheet the default column width is 8.43 digits (64 pixels). Row height is measured in points. For a standard worksheet, which uses 10-point Arial font, the default row height is 12.75 points (17 pixels). Since there are 72 points in an inch, the font is slightly smaller than 1/7 of an inch and the row height is slightly larger, providing some white space above and below the text.

Figure 3-8 Column Width dialog box

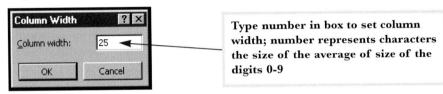

Type number in box to set column width; number represents characters the size of the average of size of the digits 0-9

Figure 3-9 Row 20 with ScreenTip

Click and drag bottom edge of row to change row height, measured in points

17	Miscellaneous	13,500.00	14,500.00	16,500.00	19,000.00	63,500.00	
18	Total Expenses	128,500.00	132,000.00	142,500.00	148,500.00	551,500.00	
19	Height: 12.75 (17 pixels)						
20	Gross Profit	$ 40,000.00	$ 53,350.00	$ 61,385.00	$ 75,773.50	$ 230,508.50	
21	Average Sales/Qrtr	$ 195,502					
22	Average Expenses/Qrtr	$ 137,875					
23							

Figure 3-10 Worksheet's appearance after row and column formatting

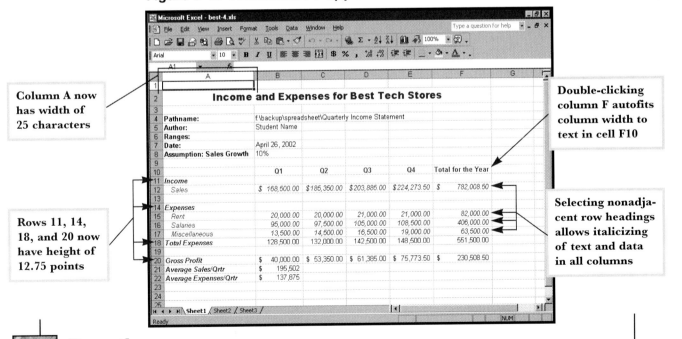

Column A now has width of 25 characters

Rows 11, 14, 18, and 20 now have height of 12.75 points

Double-clicking column F autofits column width to text in cell F10

Selecting nonadjacent row headings allows italicizing of text and data in all columns

Practice

To practice formatting rows and columns, follow the instructions on the Practice3-4 Sheet tab of the practice file exprac3.xls. Save changes as myexprac3-4.xls, and close the file.

skill

Inserting and Deleting Rows and Columns

concept

In Excel you can add and delete rows and columns to customize worksheets to meet specific needs. In a personal expenses worksheet, you might add a row to display expenses for a newly acquired car. In a business worksheet you might add more rows when you hire additional employees. You might add six monthly columns to convert from a half-year to full-year worksheet, or delete unneeded columns just to create a more tightly formatted worksheet.

do it !

Insert one row between the documentation section and the main body of the worksheet, insert rows near the bottom, and delete a blank column near the right side of the worksheet,

1. Open Student File exdoit3-5.xls and save it as best-5.xls. Notice the blank column F near the right side of the worksheet.

2. Click on cell A9. Click Insert, then click the Cells command. The Insert dialog box will open with the Shift cells down option button selected.

3. Click the Entire row option button. This button tells Excel to add a row and shift down all of the rows from row 9 and below (see Figure 3-11). Click [OK]. A new row will be inserted, the main body of the worksheet will shift down by one row, and your formulas will update to reflect the row shift. Ignore the Insert Options Smart Tag, if it appears.

4. Select the gray headings of rows 22 through 24. Click Insert, then click Rows (see Figure 3-12). Excel inserts three blank rows immediately above the three rows with text and data that you selected and renumbers the rows that moved down.

5. In cell A23 type Gross Profit Margin. In cell B23, type the formula =B21/B13 and press [Enter]. Position the mouse pointer over the fill handle in the lower-right corner of cell B23. When the mouse pointer converts to a black cross ✚, drag into cell G23 to copy the formula into the cells you selected. With cell range B23:G23 still selected, click the Percent Style button %. Ignore the formula error in cell F23, since you will delete column F shortly. Since there was no data in cell F23, Excel automatically displayed the #DIV/0! error, which appears when a cell tries to divide any number by zero.

6. Right-click on the gray heading of column F to display a shortcut menu. Click the Delete command (see Figure 3-13), removing column F and moving the text and data of column G into column F (see Figure 3-14).

7. Resave the worksheet with the changes you have made and close the file.

more

Step 4 shows you how to insert several adjacent rows at once into a worksheet. To insert several adjacent columns at once, you must select the same number of columns immediately to the right of where you want to insert the columns. After selecting the rows or columns, click Insert, then click Rows or Columns accordingly as needed. When you insert or delete rows, Excel updates formulas by adjusting references to shifted cells to account for their new location. However, new rows or columns sometimes can create problems for formulas that reference data that is adjacent to those new areas. Suppose you add a row or column at the end of a cell range—a group of related cells—that appears in a formula. In that case, you must change the formula to account for the new row or column. To avoid having to edit such a formula, include a dummy row or column at the end of, but still inside, the range that is referenced by the formula. If you then insert another row or column of data into the range, the formula automatically will change to include the new data.

Deleting a row or column can create problems for formulas that used to reference data in the deleted row or column. Suppose that you delete a row or column and then a formula in the worksheet displays the #REF error value. In this case, you have deleted one or more cells that contained data referenced by the formula. When inserting or deleting rows or columns, therefore, review the location and contents of formulas before and after a change to see if the formulas calculate data correctly.

Figure 3-11 Insert dialog box

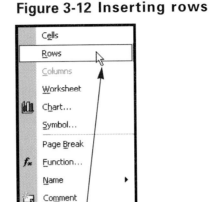

Clicking the **Entire row** option inserts a row and shifts down all rows below the new row

Figure 3-12 Inserting rows

Figure 3-13 Deleting a column

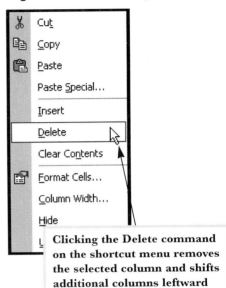

Clicking the **Rows** command on the menu inserts the same number of rows immediately above the number of selected rows.

Clicking the **Delete** command on the shortcut menu removes the selected column and shifts additional columns leftward

Figure 3-14 Worksheet's appearance after insertions and deletions

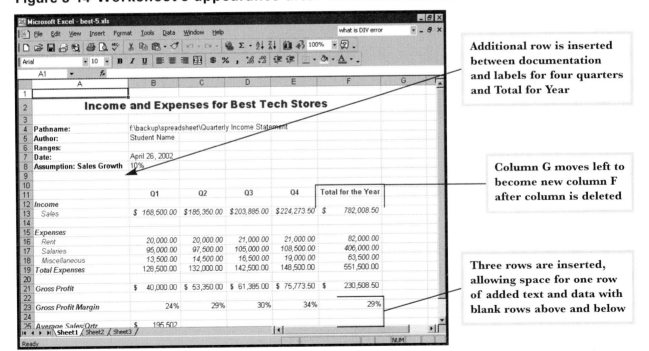

Additional row is inserted between documentation and labels for four quarters and Total for Year

Column G moves left to become new column F after column is deleted

Three rows are inserted, allowing space for one row of added text and data with blank rows above and below

Practice

To practice inserting and deleting rows and columns, follow the instructions on the Practice3-5 Sheet tab of the practice file exprac3.xls. Save changes as myexprac3-5.xls, and close the file.

skill

Hiding, Unhiding, and Protecting Cells

concept

Excel allows you to hide and unhide rows and columns and to protect many elements of a worksheet or workbook. You may want to hide worksheet elements that include confidential data or hide them simply to create a smaller worksheet, perhaps, for printing purposes. You can unhide those elements later for everyone or for just those with access rights to the data. For similar security reasons you protect worksheets and lock sensitive cells and then unprotect them and unlock them later as needed.

do it !

Hide two rows and one column and print the worksheet, then unhide the rows and column. Protect the worksheet so it cannot be changed, and then unprotect it to regain editing access.

1. Open Student File exdoit3-6.xls and save it as best-6.xls.

2. In order to create a smaller worksheet for printing purposes, you decide to hide two rows and one column of the worksheet. If necessary, scroll down slightly to display rows 25 and 26 of the worksheet. Click the gray heading for row 25 to select the entire row and drag into row 26 to select it too. Click Format, click Row, and click Hide (see Figure 3-15). The two selected rows now are hidden. Notice that the heading numbers for rows 25 and 26 are missing in the sequence of row numbers at the left edge of the worksheet window.

3. Right-click the gray heading for column F. On the shortcut menu that appears, click Hide (see Figure 3-16). Column F now is hidden. Notice that the heading letter for column F is missing in the sequence of column letters at the top edge of the worksheet window.

4. Verify that your worksheet resembles Figure 3-17. Resave the worksheet, and click the Print button 🖶. All of the unhidden rows and columns should display on a printout whether you print in Portrait or Landscape orientation. If you need help printing the worksheet, consult the Skill "Previewing and Printing a Worksheet" in Lesson 2 or "Using Advanced Printing Features" in Lesson 4.

5. Click in the heading of row 24 and drag into the heading of row 27 to select the rows immediately above and below the rows that you hid in Step 2. Click Format, click Row, and click Unhide on the submenu to unhide rows 25 and 26.

6. Click the heading of column E and drag into the heading of column G to select the columns immediately to the left and right of the column that you hid in Step 3. Right-click to display a shortcut menu and click Unhide to unhide column F.

(continued on EX 3.14)

Figure 3-15 Hide Row command

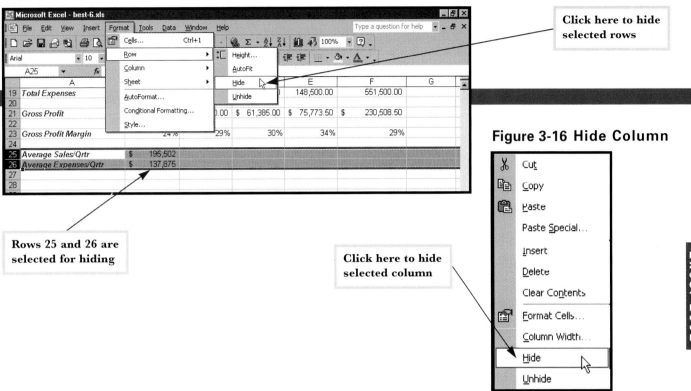

Click here to hide
selected rows

Rows 25 and 26 are
selected for hiding

Figure 3-16 Hide Column

Click here to hide
selected column

Figure 3-17 Worksheet with hidden rows and column

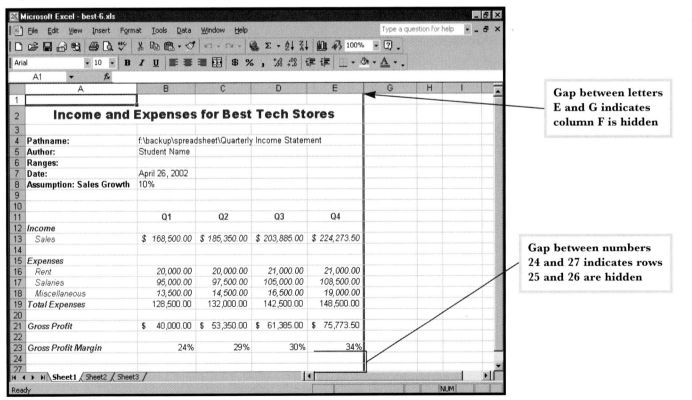

Gap between letters
E and G indicates
column F is hidden

Gap between numbers
24 and 27 indicates rows
25 and 26 are hidden

skill Hiding, Unhiding, and Protecting Cells (continued)

do it !

7. Click in cell A1 or press [Ctrl]+[Home] to place the cell pointer in the upper left cell of the worksheet. Click Tools, click Protection, and click Protect Sheet on the submenu to display the Protect Sheet dialog box (see Figure 3-18). Be sure a check mark appears in the Protect worksheet and contents of locked cells check box. Do **not** type a password in the Password to unprotect sheet text box. Click [OK] to protect the worksheet and to close the dialog box.

8. Click in any cell that contains text or a value on the worksheet. Try to type anything into the selected cell. A Microsoft Excel warning box will appear to advise you that your worksheet is protected and to explain how to unprotect it. When you have finished reading the box, click [OK]. Then, click Tools, click Protection, and click Unprotect Sheet on the submenu to regain editing access to the worksheet (see Figure 3-19).

9. Resave the worksheet and close the file.

more

In this Skill you hid and unhid rows that had an accessible row above them, and you hid and unhid columns that had an accessible column to their left. But what do you do when you need to unhide row 1 or Column A? To unhide these areas, click Edit, click Go To to display the Go To dialog box, type A1 in the Reference text box, and click [OK]. Then click Format, click Row or Column, and then click Unhide. Alternately, you can unhide row 1 just by clicking and dragging down the top edge of row 2, and you can unhide column A by clicking and dragging the left edge of column B to the right. When unhiding these areas in these simpler ways, be sure that you know what height or width the row or column should be restored to.

The purposes of this Skill do not require you to create a password in the Protect Sheet dialog box. If using a password, however, make it hard for others to guess at, but easy for you to remember. For example, avoid passwords like Excel-123 in favor of ones like eXce123-, in which the second letter is the only capital, the number "1" replaces the letter "l" from the name of the program, and the hyphen has been moved to the unlikely end position. Passwords in this dialog box are case sensitive, requiring you to remember what combination of capital and lowercase letters you used when you most recently created them. Excel passwords can use any letters, numbers, and symbols and—although not usually needed—can run up to 255 characters. To password-protect all worksheets in a workbook, click File, click Save As, click Tools, click General Options to open the Save Options dialog box, enter your desired passwords, and click [OK]. Alternatively, click Tools, click Protection, click Protect Workbook to open the Protect Workbook dialog box, complete the desired options, and click [OK].

Besides protecting worksheets or whole workbooks to prohibit altering their text and data, you also can lock selected cells. When you do so, others can see your text or data but cannot change it. To lock or unlock cells, click Format, click Cells to open the Format Cells dialog box, click the Protection tab to bring it forward, and add or remove a check mark in the Locked check box. By default Excel locks the cells in a standard worksheet, but the locking mode does not work unless you also protect the worksheet, as the Skill above demonstrates. To lock parts of a worksheet (e.g., its formulas) while leaving other areas unlocked (e.g., data-entry cells), unlock only those cells to which others need access while leaving all other cells locked, then protect the sheet as described in the Skill above.

Figure 3-18 Protect Sheet dialog box

Turns protection of work-sheet cells on and changes to locked cells on or off

Entering a password prevents unauthorized users from unprotecting a worksheet

Select options you want to activate for all worksheet users

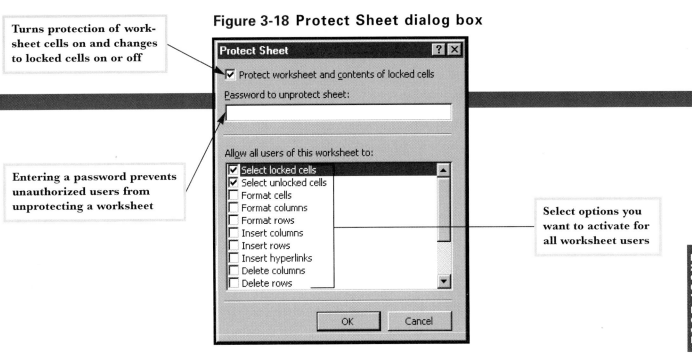

Figure 3-19 Unprotect Sheet command

Column F is unhidden after Step 6

Click to regain editing access to worksheet

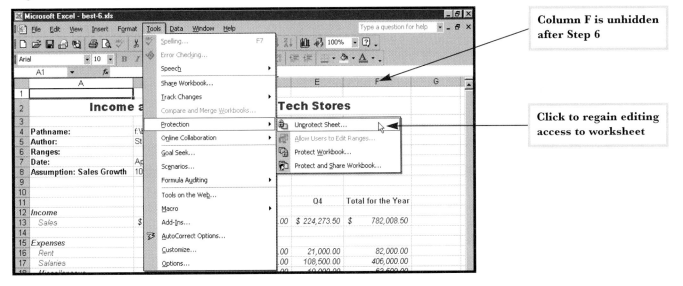

Practice

To practice hiding, unhiding, and protecting cells, follow the instructions on the Practice3-6 Sheet tab of the practice file exprac3.xls. Save changes as myexprac3-6.xls, and close the file.

skill Defining and Naming Cell Ranges

concept

Excel allows you to define and name a range of cells. A name is a string of characters, usually a word, representing a cell, a cell range, a formula, or a constant. A range is a group of cells, usually adjacent and usually referring to a related type of information or data such as book titles or employee names or inventory items. By naming a range, you can access that range just by clicking its name in the Name box and then format, edit, or otherwise modify or manipulate the range. You also can use range names in formulas instead of typing complicated cell references. Naming ranges, therefore, saves time and simplifies working with data.

do it !

Define and name cell ranges in a worksheet that contain data.

1. Open Student File exdoit3-7.xls and save it as best-7.xls.

2. Select cells B13 through E13 to define and highlight the range for Sales as B13:E13. Click inside the Name box [B13] to the left of the Formula bar. Type Sales, and press [Enter]. You now have named the range B13:E13 as Sales (see Figure 3-20). Whenever you click on the word Sales in the name box, cells B13:E13 will highlight on the worksheet. Whenever you select cells B13:E13 on the worksheet, the name Sales will appear in the Name box.

3. Repeat Step 2 to name the remaining cell ranges. Be sure to press [Enter] after you type in each name. Type Rent for the range B16:E16. Type Salaries for B17:E17. Type Miscellaneous for B18:E18. Type Total_Expenses for B19:E19. Type Gross_Profit for B21:E21. Type Gross_Profit_Margin for B23:E23. Range names cannot contain spaces, so be sure to use an underscore ([Shift]+[-]) between the words Total and Expenses, between Gross and Profit, and among the words Gross, Profit, and Margin.

4. Select cells B12 through B23 to define and highlight the range for Q1 (or Quarter 1) as B13:B23. Click Insert, click Name, and click Define, as shown in Figure 3-21, to open the Define Name dialog box. Replace Q1 with Quarter_1 (including the underscore), and press [Enter] to name the range and to close the dialog box. Excel automatically picks up a column or row label as the default range name if it adjoins or appears in the selected range, so Q1 appears by default in the Names in workbook text box. However, this combination also represents column Q, row 1, and cannot be accepted.

5. Repeat Step 4, using the Define Name dialog box, to name the cell ranges for the three remaining Quarters. For C12:C23, name the cell range as Quarter_2. For D12:D23, name the cell range as Quarter_3. For E12:E23, name the cell range as Quarter_4 (see Figure 3-22). After closing the dialog box, click outside of all of the Quarter columns to cancel the selection of the last range named in the Step above.

6. Resave the worksheet with the changes you have made and close the file.

more

Ranges do not have to be made up of cells that touch. They can contain nonadjacent blocks of cells, or many nonadjoining individual cells. To name a nonadjacent range, (1) select the first cell or group of cells you wish to include, (2) hold down [Ctrl] while selecting the second and any additional cells or cell clusters to include in the range, and (3) name the range in the Name box to the left of the Formula bar. You can select as many nonadjacent cells or ranges as needed. Clicking outside of the selected cells cancels the selection.

Figure 3-20 B13:E13 as cell range named Sales

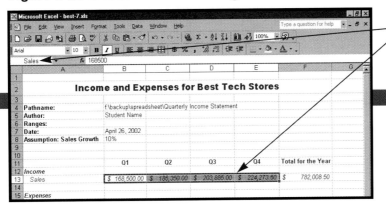

Selecting cell range name in Name box highlights related cell range; selecting cell range displays range name in Name box

Figure 3-21 Define command on submenu

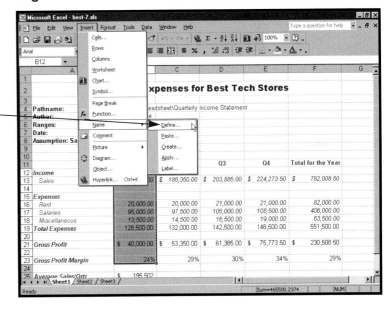

Clicking the Define command on the submenu opens the Define Name dialog box

Type here to give a name to a selected cell range

Click a name here to appear in Names in workbook text box

Displays worksheet number and cell range for the name appearing in Names in workbook text box

Figure 3-22 Define Name dialog box

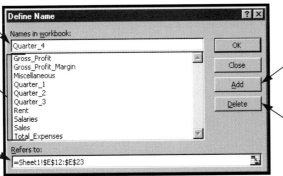

Click to add a selected range name to the list of names defined for the workbook

Click to delete a selected range name

Practice

To practice defining and naming cell ranges, follow the instructions on the Practice3-7 Sheet tab of the practice file exprac3.xls. Save changes as myexprac3-7.xls, and close the file.

skill | Filling a Cell Range with Labels

concept

Excel can automatically fill a cell range with several types of series information. Series information includes numbers, text and numbers (e.g., Quarter 1), dates, and times. Excel can step, or increase, a series by a constant set value or multiply by a constant factor. For example, you can add all of the months of the year to a worksheet by typing only the word January and then extending the series. Before you fill a cell range, be sure you know what values should appear in that range and how large an increase should occur cell by cell.

do it !

Delete the Q1, Q2, Q3, Q4 series and use the AutoFill feature to insert a new series.

1. Open Student File exdoit3-8.xls and save it as best-8.xls.

2. Select cells B11:E11, and then press [Delete] to remove the text from all of the cells.

3. Click cell B11, and type Quarter 1.

4. Position the mouse pointer ⌖ over the fill handle (small black box) in the lower-right corner of cell B11 until the pointer changes to a small black cross **✚**.

5. While holding down the mouse button, drag the fill handle to the right into cell E11. As you drag the fill handle, a border will appear, indicating the cells that you have selected. ScreenTips will appear to show what text will go in the cell where the fill handle currently resides (see Figure 3-23).

6. When you have finished filling cells B11:E11, release the mouse button. An AutoFill Options button also will appear at the right end of cell E11.The range that previously read Q1, Q2, Q3, Q4 now reads Quarter 1, Quarter 2, Quarter 3, and Quarter 4. If needed, click a blank cell and press [Delete] to close the AutoFill Options button.

7. Resave the worksheet with the changes you have made and close the file.

more

In Steps 4 and 5 above, you used AutoFill to enter a series of labels into a range of cells. Along with AutoFill, there are three other series fill types that you can use: Linear, Growth, and Date. These are advanced options and appear in the Series dialog box (see Figure 3-24). To access this dialog box, click Edit, click Fill, and click Series on the submenu. A Linear series fill, with the Trend box unchecked, adds the Step value to the value in the selected cell. With the Trend box checked, Excel disregards the Step value and calculates the trend based on the average of the difference between the values in the selected cells. Excel then uses this average to fill the range by increasing or decreasing the value by a constant amount. If necessary, the original selected cell information is replaced to fit the trend. A Growth series fill resembles a Linear series fill, except that Excel multiplies numbers to create a geometric growth trend instead of adding values. A Date series fill is based upon dates using the options in the Date unit list. You can extend selected dates by day, weekday, month, or year. You can set the Stop value to fix a value at which the series will end. If Excel fills a selected range before it reaches the Stop value, the values increase no further and do not try to reach the Stop value.

Right-clicking a selected cell displays the normal worksheet shortcut menu to cut, copy, paste, and otherwise manipulate cells. If you select a value, right-click the fill handle, drag it, and release it in a new cell, a shortcut menu appears that allows you to choose a series type to insert into the destination cells. These Excel features have been available for some time. However, as Step 6 indicates, the normal use of the fill handle now displays an AutoFill Options button, which is new to Excel in this version of the program. The AutoFill Options button enables you to copy cell values instead of autofilling the series, use the normal autofill, autofill with the formatting of the original cells, and autofill without that formatting.

Figure 3-23 Filling a cell range with labels

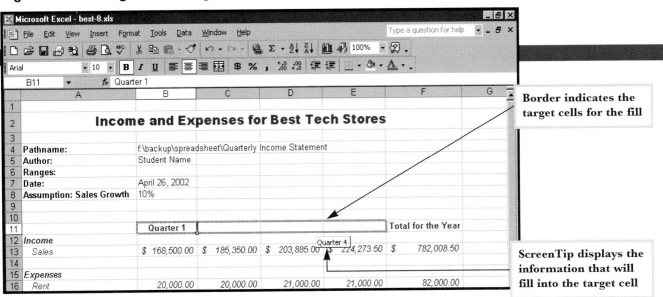

Border indicates the target cells for the fill

ScreenTip displays the information that will fill into the target cell

Click to select whether series fills across selected rows or down selected columns

Click the type of series that you want to fill

Figure 3-24 Series dialog box

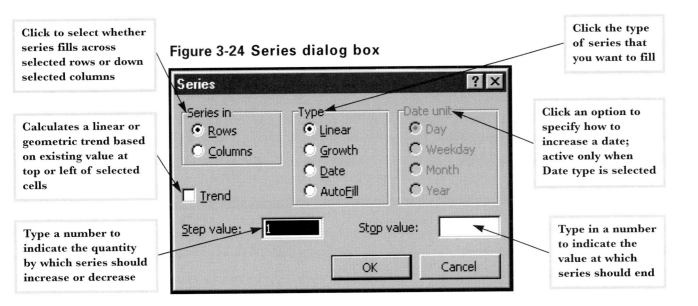

Calculates a linear or geometric trend based on existing value at top or left of selected cells

Click an option to specify how to increase a date; active only when Date type is selected

Type a number to indicate the quantity by which series should increase or decrease

Type in a number to indicate the value at which series should end

Practice

To practice filling a cell range with labels, follow the instructions on the Practice3-8 Sheet tab of the practice file exprac3.xls. Save changes as myexprac3-8.xls, and close the file.

skill | Applying Shading, Patterns, and Borders to Cells & Ranges

concept

As previous Skills have shown, you can format the look of and data in worksheet cells to make the worksheet more attractive and understandable. The AutoFormat command, which appears in the next Skill, enables you to apply a predefined set of formatting characteristics to a worksheet and then to modify that set slightly. Sometimes, however, you may want to have more precise control over the appearance of a cell or cell range. Excel therefore enables you to fill cells and ranges with colors and patterns and to outline them with special borders.

do it !

Add a color pattern and a border to the title and heading labels of a worksheet.

1. Open Student File exdoit3-9.xls and save it as best-9.xls.

2. Click cell A2 to select the merged and centered cell containing the worksheet's title. Hold down [Ctrl], select cells B11:F11 as well, and release [Ctrl]. Click the list arrow on the right edge of the Fill Color button ![fill color button] to display a color palette. Click the Light Green color square in the fifth row, fourth column of the palette. The palette will close and the selected cells will be filled with Light Green.

3. With the title cell and cells B11:F11 still selected, click Format, then click Cells to open the Format Cells dialog box. Click the Border tab to bring it to the front of the dialog box.

4. In the Line Style section, click the dashed line, which is the fourth line down in the second column. Click the Color selection arrow to display a color palette, and click the Dark Teal square from the first row, fifth column. In the Presets section click the Outline button (see Figure 3-25).

5. Click the Patterns tab to bring it forward. Notice that the Light Green color is selected in the color palette and appears in the Sample box because you already applied that color to the selected cell.

6. Click the Pattern selection arrow to display a color palette that includes patterns at the top. Click the Thin Diagonal Stripe pattern in the third row, fourth column. Click ![OK] to apply the color and border (see Figure 3-26). View the formatted worksheet (see Figure 3-27). Click outside the selected cells to cancel the selection. Although some people might have a slight difficulty viewing this pattern, the diagonal stripes look less intrusive when printed on paper. Make it a habit, therefore, to test print a page before submitting a final copy at school or work.

7. Resave the worksheet with the changes you have made and close the file.

more

The Font Color, Fill Color, and Borders buttons are all "loaded" with the most recent color or border type that you have applied, which is displayed as part of the button's icon. To apply the same color or border more than once, you do not need to click the button's arrow and open a palette. Simply click on the button itself and Excel will apply the most recent color or border that you chose. Also remember to use colors, patterns, and borders carefully. Some color shades may look light on a color screen but will print darkly on a black-and-white printer. The hue, or tint, of colors also may look different on paper than they did on the screen. Overusing colors or combining colors in a garish or cartoonish way will make your worksheets less attractive and harder to read. In these situations, therefore, aim for simplicity and consistency of appearance.

Figure 3-25 Border tab

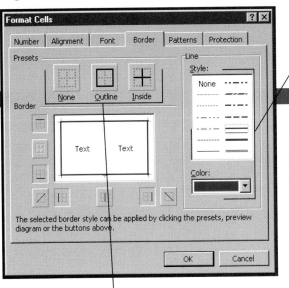

Click to select line weight and style, then click list arrow and select color for border to be applied

Click in Color area to select background color, then in Pattern area for background pattern and pattern color

Figure 3-26 Patterns tab

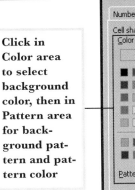

Click Presets area to apply or remove internal or external borders, or click options surrounding Preview area to choose individual borders

Sample area shows how selected cells will look with chosen color and/or pattern

Figure 3-27 Worksheet formatted with border, shading, and pattern

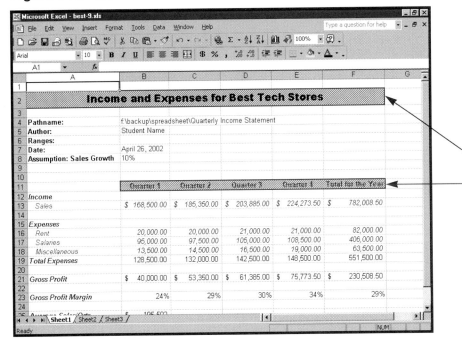

Light Green background, Dark Teal border, and Thin Diagonal Stripe pattern applied to selected cells

Practice

To practice applying shading, patterns, and borders, follow the instructions on the Practice3-9 Sheet tab of the practice file exprac3.xls. Save two files as directed in the Practice tab instructions, and close the files.

skill
Applying AutoFormat to a Worksheet

concept

Although Excel has many formatting options, sometimes you may want to format a worksheet all at once with Excel's AutoFormat command—a preset collection of format characteristics like font, font size, shadings, borders, and alignments that you can apply to a few cells or to an entire worksheet. When you choose an AutoFormat option, Excel identifies the worksheet's categories and data details and makes an assumption as to where to apply formats. Even after using AutoFormat, therefore, you may want to slightly adjust the formats that display.

do it !

Use the AutoFormat command to improve the appearance of a worksheet and to set the main body of data off from the documentation.

1. Open exdoit3-10.xls and save it as best-10.xls. The data previously in rows 25 and 26 is gone since such data, although informative, usually does not appear in income statements.

2. Click in cell A2 and drag into row 8. Because cell A2 is merged all the way to column F, the dragging action selects all the way to that column in the lower rows as well. Since no text or data in the lower rows extends beyond column F, all of the information will be included in the selection.

3. Click Format, then click AutoFormat to open the AutoFormat dialog box. Click the Simple worksheet style in row 1, column 1 (see Figure 3-28). Click [OK] to apply the worksheet style and to close the dialog box. This worksheet style (1) changes the font of the title, (2) widens column B to hold all of the text in cell B4, (3) aligns the date and Sales Growth percent to the right in cells B7 and B8, respectively, and (4) adds three horizontal borders.

4. Select cells A11:F23. Click Format, click AutoFormat, and click the Simple worksheet style again. Click [OK] to apply the style and close the dialog box. This style (1) removes the italics from column A but bolds the text in cells A12, A13, A15, A19, A21, and A23, (2) narrows column B to match the width of the data in cell B13, which is the widest cell in the lower area of the whole worksheet, and (3) adds eleven horizontal borders. The AutoFormat command offers some distinctive and colorful worksheet styles. However, as the previous Skill suggests, you generally should choose simpler styles, especially for work assignments or for situations in which you have only a black-and-white printer.

5. Notice that cell A8 is too narrow to display all of its text. Double-click the right edge of column A to autofit the column to the width of that cell. Also, the subcategory Sales under the category Income is bold while the three subcategories under the category Expenses are not. Click cell A13, and click the Bold button **B** to remove the bold style in that cell (see Figure 3-29).

6. Resave the worksheet with the changes you have made and close the file.

more

As Steps 2 and 4 indicate, you must select a range of cells before you can specify and apply an AutoFormat in the AutoFormat dialog box. The dialog box offers 16 AutoFormat options and a None option at the bottom of the scrollable worksheet window. Clicking the None option removes all formatting from the selected range. You also can click the Options button near the upper-right of the dialog box to display a Formats to apply section at the bottom of the dialog box. In this section you can clear check boxes for formatting elements that you did not want to appear in the AutoFormat option chosen in the scrollable window. For example, clearing the Font check box removes bold and/or italic formatting and returns the font to its default style.

Figure 3-28 AutoFormat dialog box, Simple style selected

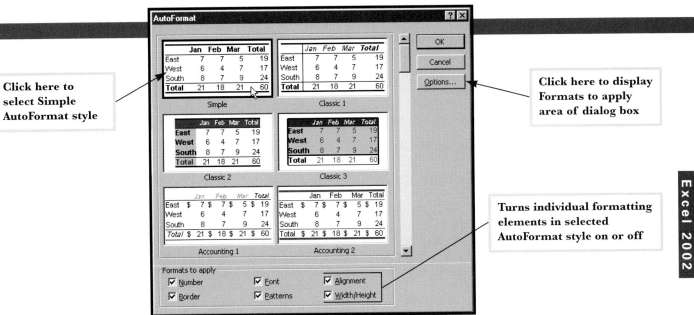

Click here to select Simple AutoFormat style

Click here to display Formats to apply area of dialog box

Turns individual formatting elements in selected AutoFormat style on or off

Figure 3-29 Simple style applied to worksheet documentation and data

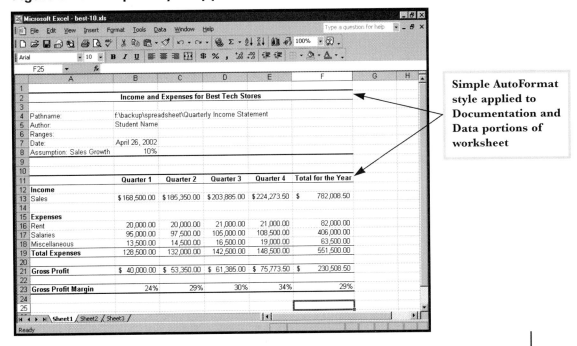

Simple AutoFormat style applied to Documentation and Data portions of worksheet

Practice

To practice AutoFormatting a worksheet, follow the instructions on the Practice3-10 Sheet tab of the practice file exprac3.xls. Save three files as directed in the Practice tab instructions, and close the files.

shortcuts

Function	Button/Mouse	Menu	Keyboard
Merge cells		Click Format, click Cells, click Alignment, then turn on Merge cells check box	
Split cells		Click Format, click Cells, click Alignment, then turn off Merge cells check box	
Copy format from selected cells to destination cells	🖌		
Merge cells and center contents of merged cells	▦	Click Format, click Cells, click Alignment, click Horizontal text box, click Center, turn on Merge cells check box	
Align cell contents to left	≣	Click Format, click Cells, click Alignment, click Horizontal text box, click Left	
Center cell contents	≣	Click Format, click Cells, click Alignment, click Horizontal text box, click Center	
Align cell contents to right	≣	Click Format, click Cells, click Alignment, click click Horizontal text box, click Right	
Bold cell contents	**B**	Click Format, click Cells, click Font, click Bold	[Ctrl]+[B]
Italicize cell contents	*I*	Click Format, click Cells, click Font, click Italic	[Ctrl]+[I]
Underline cell contents	U	Click Format, click Cells, click Font, click Underline	[Ctrl]+[U]
Select font color of selected text or data	**A** ▾	Click Format, click Cells, click Font, click Color	
Decrease or increase indent	⇥ ⇤	Click Format, click Cells, click Alignment tab, click Horizontal	
Apply Comma Style	,	Click Format, click Style, click Style name, click Comma	[Ctrl]+[Shift]+[!]
Apply Currency Style	$	Click Format, click Style, click Style name, click Currency	[Ctrl]+[Shift]+[$]
Apply Percent Style	%	Click Format, click Style, click Style name, click Percent	[Ctrl]+[Shift]+[%]
Increase or decrease decimal places	.00 .00	Click Format, click Cells, click Number tab	
Select fill color of selected cell	🎨 ▾	Click Format, click Cells, click Patterns, click Color	
Select all	▭	Click Edit, click Select All	[Ctrl]+[A]

quiz

A. Identify Key Features

Name the items indicated by callouts in Figure 3-30.

1. _____
2. _____
3. _____
4. _____
5. _____
6. _____
7. _____
8. _____
9. _____

Figure 3-30 Formatting features

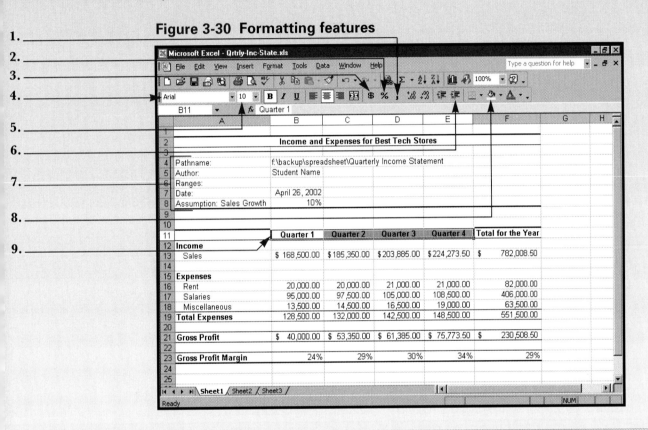

B. Select the Best Answer

10. Adds a dollar sign and two decimal places signifying cents

11. Combines multiple cells into one cell

12. Contains a tab with options for changing font, font style, and font size

13. Enables you to add a predetermined set of formatting options to a worksheet

14. Contains the Bold, Italic, and Underline buttons

15. A group of two or more cells, usually adjacent and containing related data

16. A blank cell at the bottom, but within, a defined cell range

17. A word representing a cell, cell range, formula, or constant

a. Merged cells check box

b. AutoFormat

c. Range name

d. Currency style

e. Formatting toolbar

f. Cell range

g. Format cells dialog box

h. Dummy row

quiz (continued)

C. Complete the Statement

18. All of the following are effects available on the Font tab of the Format Cells dialog box **except**:

    a. Strikethrough

    b. Strikescript

    c. Superscript

    d. Subscript

19. Excel expresses a range address as follows:

    a. B9/E9

    b. B9:E9

    c. B9;E9

    d. B9-E9

20. The Formatting toolbar offers all of the following formatting buttons except:

    a. Currency Style

    b. Comma Style

    c. Fraction Style

    d. Percent Style

21. A range name must not contain:

    a. Letters

    b. Numbers

    c. Uppercase letters

    d. Spaces

22. The standard width of an Excel worksheet column is:

    a. 8.43 characters

    b. 10.00 characters

    c. 4.83 characters

    d. 72 characters

23. Row height is measured in:

    a. Points

    b. Inches

    c. Pixels

    d. Characters

24. You can do all of the following from the Insert menu **except**:

    a. Define and name a cell range

    b. Insert a blank column

    c. Insert a blank row

    d. Access the AutoFormat command

25. Classic 2 and Colorful 2 are:

    a. Formula functions

    b. AutoFormat Styles

    c. Acceptable cell range name formats

    d. Cell values

26. When you merge two or more cells, the cell reference becomes:

    a. The last cell you typed in among the merged cells

    b. The upper-left cell of the component cells

    c. The lower-right cell of the component cells

    d. The cell you specified in the Merged cells text box

27. All of the following are examples of series data that you can enter on a worksheet **except**:

    a. Linear

    b. Currency

    c. Growth

    d. AutoFill

interactivity

Build Your Skills

1. Modify rows and columns in a worksheet:

   a. Open Student File exskills3.xls and save it as NDS Income Statement.xls. Insert one blank row above row 3. Insert two blank rows above the new row 8.

   b. In cell A8, type Current Date:. In cell B8, type today's date. Using the Format Cells dialog box, format the date using the 3/14/2001 format.

   c. In cell F10, type the label Total for the Year. Drag the right edge of the gray heading for column F until the ScreenTip reads Width: 17:00 (124 pixels). Hide rows 25 and 26, and resave the worksheet.

2. Format cell labels:

   a. Merge and center cells A2:F2 into one cell. Format the title with 14-point Tahoma font, bold and italicized. Bold the text in cells A4:A23.

   b. Double-click the right edge of column A to autofit it to the width of cell A7. Indent the text once in cell A12 and in cells A16:A20.

   c. Bold, underline, and center the text in cells B10:F10. (Do **not** merge and center the text.) Resave the worksheet.

3. Format cell values and name cell ranges:

   a. Select cells B6:B7, and format them with the Percent Style button. Select cells B11:F23, and format them with the Currency Style button.

   b. Select cells B12:F21, and use the Format Cells dialog box to delete the dollar sign symbol.

   c. Using either the Name box to the left of the Formula bar or the Define Name dialog box, name cell range B13:E13 as Gross_Profit. Name cell range B21:E21 as Total_Expenses. Name cell range B23:E23 as PreTax_Income. Resave the worksheet.

4. Apply advanced formatting to the worksheet:

   a. Click cell B10, and type Quarter 1. Using the Autofill technique, drag into cell E10 to change the remaining labels to Quarter 2, Quarter 3, and Quarter 4. (If a Smart Tag appears above cell F11, ignore it, as the next Step will clear it.)

   b. Select cell A2, cells B10:F10, and cells B23:F23. Using the Format Cells dialog box, apply a solid Indigo border around the selected cells. Also apply a Light Blue background fill and a 12.5% Gray pattern.

   c. Click the Select All button (the gray square to the left of the column A heading), click Edit, click Clear, and click Formats.

   d. Select the cells A2:F8. Using AutoFormat, select the Accounting 2 style, click Options, clear the Number check box, and press [Enter]. Remerge and center cells A2:F2.

   e. Reapply the Percent format to cells B6:B7, and reapply a Date format of your own choosing to cell B8.

   f. Select cells A10:F23. Using AutoFormat, select the Accounting 2 style, and press [Enter]. Unbold cell A15. Resave your worksheet.

interactivity (continued)

Problem Solving Exercises

1. Use the skills you have learned about spreadsheet design to help track your progress toward your diploma. Create an Excel worksheet with three parts: (1) List the general graduation requirements for your major (e.g., minimum credits for graduation, minimum credits in your major, credits required for minors, and so on). (2) List your courses already taken, current courses, and remaining courses needed for graduation. Group all of the courses by semester or quarter, depending on your school's calendar. Enter grades for only your completed courses. Calculate your semester-by-semester Grade Point Average and your cumulative GPA. Save the file as GPA Requirements.xls.

2. Design a worksheet to track stocks that you might invest in. Use a newspaper or the Internet (www.nasdaq.com, for example) to find names and stock data on nine companies (e.g., car companies, chain stores, and so on). In a Company Name column, enter their names alphabetically. In an Initials column, enter their stock initials. In a Week 1 column, enter their closing prices as of the week before last. In a Week 2 column, enter closing prices for last week. In a Price Change column, use a formula to calculate their change in price from Week 1 to Week 2. In a Percent Change column, use a formula to calculate the percent of change between the weeks, formatting it with Percent Style. In a Totals row, use the SUM formula to calculate totals for all nine stocks. Format the Week 1, Week 2, and Price Change columns with Currency Style. Merge and center the main title. Bold and center the heading labels. Format appropriate titles and headings with a solid line border and a light background color. Save the worksheet as Personal Stocks-1.xls.

3. Open Student File exproblem3-1.xls, which resembles the file, Personal Stocks-1.xls. Save exproblem3-1.xls as Personal Stocks-2.xls. Add a tenth company to the chart, filling in all its columns with appropriate data and formatting. Between the Initials and Week 1 columns, insert a column entitled No. of Shares; enter a quantity of shares between 5 and 10. After the rightmost column, add a column entitled Profit/(Loss); use a formula and AutoFill to calculate profit or loss based on No. of Shares times Price Change. Format the two new columns with appropriate formatting. Apply Names to the cell ranges in each column except the first. When applying names, include just the ten rows that correspond with the companies. After inserting the tenth company, inserting and formatting the two columns, calculating formulas, and naming cell ranges, use AutoFormat to reformat the worksheet to look organized, readable, and attractive.

4. Reproduce the worksheet in Figure 3-31 as closely as possible. Delete column C, add two additional columns to the right, use AutoFill to retitle the appropriate columns as January through June, and add additional data to the May and the June columns. Format the heading labels to be readable and attractive. Format the data below the headings properly so the data represents dollars and cents. Save the worksheet as Format Practice.xls. Print the worksheet on one page.

Figure 3-31 Formatting.xls

	A	B	C	D	E	F	G
1				Quarter 1	Quarter 2	Quarter 3	Quarter 4
2	1	Charles Bailey		850.3	900.55	910.45	950.74
3	2	Wilma Davidson		874.55	850.23	860.78	880.45
4	3	Alfred Lum		982.88	950.55	960.89	980.56
5	4	Roberto Martines		974.12	971.24	981.35	1000.23
6	5	Andrew Opperman		850.66	840.75	855.56	890.15
7	6	Libby Seasons		789.23	781.44	799.23	851.59
8	7	Samuel Tanaka		987.32	977.3	988.77	1005.26

Inserting Objects and Charts

The labels and values that you enter into a worksheet provide the main information that people need in such a document. However, objects may be more informative than pure data or illustrate your data further. Inserting these objects can break up the monotony of row after row of numbers and enable you to highlight or explain aspects of your worksheet that might otherwise go unnoticed.

You can insert a number of objects into your worksheet for the purpose of annotating specific information. These objects include text boxes, shapes such as arrows and connectors, and comments. Text boxes can be any size, but will obscure the portions of the worksheet behind them. Comments resemble text boxes, but you can hide them from view. Additionally, you can format and manipulate all graphics in many ways.

One effective way to enhance a worksheet visually is to add a chart. Excel's Chart Wizard guides you through the process of creating a graphical representation of a data series that you select from your worksheet. After creating a chart, you can move, resize, and format it. You can change the type of chart and its characteristics after creating it. You also can customize individual elements of the chart to provide emphasis or greater clarity. And once you have created, formatted, and customized the chart, you can print it along with its related data.

Lesson Goal:

Strengthen a worksheet by inserting graphics and creating a chart using the Chart Wizard. Use some of Excel's advanced printing features to print a new copy of the worksheet.

skills

- ⚡ **Inserting Text Objects**
- ⚡ **Enhancing Graphics**
- ⚡ **Adding and Editing Comments**
- ⚡ **Understanding Excel Charts**
- ⚡ **Creating a Chart**
- ⚡ **Moving and Resizing a Chart**
- ⚡ **Formatting a Chart**
- ⚡ **Changing a Chart's Type**
- ⚡ **Using Advanced Printing Features**

Excel 2002

skill | Inserting Text Objects *MOUS Skill*

concept

Lessons 1 to 3 show how to insert text into worksheet cells by clicking cells and typing. But you also can insert text into a worksheet within a text box. Such boxes enable you to add words and sentences of any size and appearance outside the constraints of a worksheet cell. A text box is an independent object, like a sticky note, that you can place anywhere on the worksheet. You also can move, resize, and reformat text boxes. And since text boxes are independent of cells, such boxes can reference worksheet data without affecting that data.

do it !

Insert a text box into a worksheet to emphasize the growth in Quarter 4 sales.

1. Open Student File exdoit4-1.xls and save it as Text Boxes.xls.

2. Click View, click Toolbars, then click Drawing to display the Drawing toolbar. If necessary, dock the toolbar at the bottom of the program window.

3. Click the Text Box button 📄 on the Drawing toolbar. When you move your mouse pointer onto the worksheet, the pointer will change to the text cursor [↓] to indicate that you can create a text box.

4. Scroll as needed to make cell E9 appear in the worksheet window. Position the pointer just below the purple line where you want the top-left corner of the text box to appear. While holding down the mouse button, drag to the lower-right corner of cell E10 so the text box will be one cell wide and two cells tall (see Figure 4-1). When you release the mouse button, the box borders will become dotted and eight small circles—called sizing handles—will appear at the corners and at the midpoints of the four box sides. A blinking insertion point will appear in the text box.

5. With the insertion point in the upper-left corner of the text box, type Up 33% from Quarter 1. When text reaches the right edge of the text box, it automatically will wrap to the second line. Click outside the text box to cancel the selection. Your worksheet should look like Figure 4-2.

6. Save and close your worksheet with the changes you have made.

more

The primary advantage of using text boxes is their flexibility. You easily can move, resize, or reformat text boxes without affecting the appearance or content of any other part of the worksheet. When text is being entered, a text box acts as a small word processing window. If the text box is not large enough to fit a word or phrase on one line, the text will wrap and continue onto the next line. If the text box is too small to accommodate all the text as you enter it, then the text will scroll upward, without changing the size or location of the box, to allow you to enter more text. You then must enlarge a text box manually to view all of the text it contains. You can do this by dragging a handle in the desired direction to expand the box. If you remove text from a text box, you can drag the proper sizing handle inward to shrink the box.

Once you create a text box, it is not fixed in place. You can move it anywhere on the worksheet. To move a text box to another part of the worksheet, click the frame of a selected text box—not a sizing handle—to select its frame, then drag the text box to the desired location. To learn how to reformat a text box, consult the next Skill.

Figure 4-1 Set Title in Black

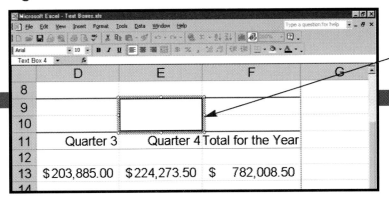

> New text box is one cell wide and two cells tall; border is dotted and displays eight sizing handles

Figure 4-2 Worksheet's appearance after adding text to text box

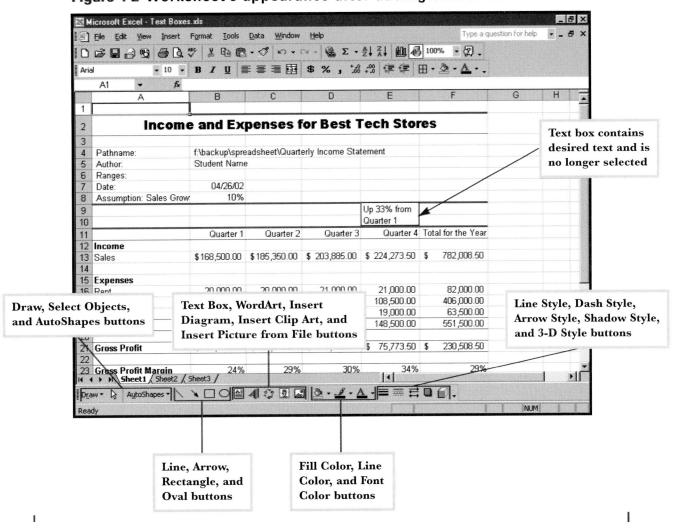

> Text box contains desired text and is no longer selected

Draw, Select Objects, and AutoShapes buttons

Text Box, WordArt, Insert Diagram, Insert Clip Art, and Insert Picture from File buttons

Line Style, Dash Style, Arrow Style, Shadow Style, and 3-D Style buttons

Line, Arrow, Rectangle, and Oval buttons

Fill Color, Line Color, and Font Color buttons

Excel 2002

Practice

To practice inserting text boxes, follow the instructions on the Practice4-1 Sheet tab of the practice file exprac4.xls. Save changes as myexprac4-1.xls and close the file.

skill Enhancing Graphics

concept

After you insert graphics such as text boxes, pictures, arrows, and the like, you can edit their appearance to make them more emphatic or attractive. Excel users might emphasize a text box or other graphic to call attention to an important part of a worksheet. By making your graphics more attractive, people are more likely to pay attention to them, especially if they are part of a color presentation, Internet site, and so on.

do it !

Add a callout arrow, add color to a text box, and bold the font so it stands out in the box.

1. Open Student File exdoit4-2.xls and save it as Enhancing Graphics.xls.

2. Click the Arrow button ⬉ on the Drawing toolbar. The mouse pointer will appear as a thin cross [+] when it is over the worksheet.

3. In the text box that covers cells E9:E10, position the pointer halfway between the number 1 and the right edge of the text box. While holding down the mouse button, drag to the top center edge of cell E13, which contains the Sales value for Quarter 4. Release the mouse button. The line that you have drawn will be fixed, and an arrowhead will appear at the lower end of the line.

4. Click the text box to select it. Its frame will become a thick, hatched line. Click the frame of the text box, but not a sizing handle. The frame will change from the thick hatched line to a dotted border.

5. On the Drawing toolbar, click the arrow on the Fill Color button 🎨⃗ to open the Fill Color palette. Click the Pale Blue square in the bottom row, sixth column, to select it. The background of the text box will change to match the selected square (see Figure 4-3).

6. Click the arrow that you drew in Step 3 to select it. A sizing handle will appear at each end of the arrow to indicate its selection. Click the arrow on the Line Color button ✏⃗ to open the Line Color palette. Click the Dark Blue square in the first row, sixth column, to select it. The arrow will change color to match the selected square (see Figure 4-4).

7. Click once in the text box, then select all of the text inside it. Click the Bold button **B** to bold the text. Click outside of the text box.

8. Compare the text box arrow, the text box shading, and the bold font with Figure 4-5. If necessary, redo the Steps above to correct any errors.

9. Save and close the worksheet with the changes you have made.

more

Excel's Format menu is context sensitive; that is, its content changes based on what worksheet item is selected. When a cell is active, the Format menu contains commands for altering a cell. When an AutoShape is active, the menu contains commands related to AutoShapes. Objects inserted into an Excel document—such as lines and Clip Art—all have their own formatting dialog boxes with tabs relating to the selected object.

The Format Text Box command, available on the Format menu when a text box is active, opens the Format Text Box dialog box (see Figure 4-6). This dialog box contains eight tabs with options for altering many aspects of a text box. While many controls in the dialog box have corresponding toolbar buttons, the dialog box permits more precise and comprehensive control over item aspects such as text box size, internal margins of a text box, and text orientation within a text box.

Figure 4-3 Fill Color palette

Click here to add Pale Blue shading to text box

Click here to add Dark Blue color to text box arrow

Figure 4-4 Line Color palette

Figure 4-5 Worksheet with enhanced graphic

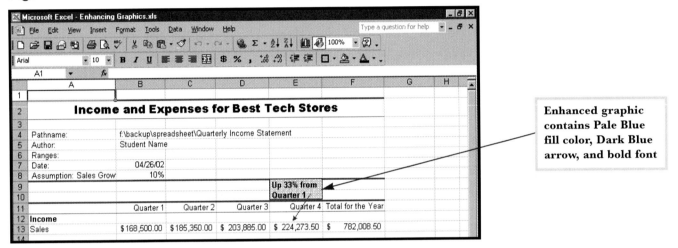

Enhanced graphic contains Pale Blue fill color, Dark Blue arrow, and bold font

Figure 4-6 Font tab of Format Text Box dialog box

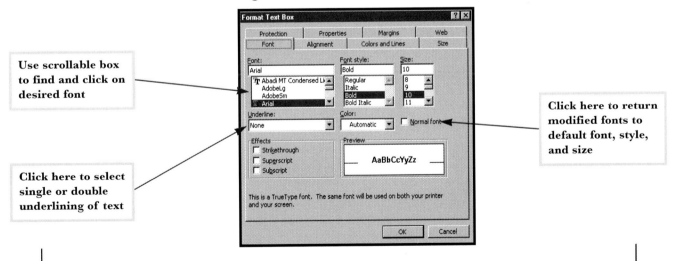

Use scrollable box to find and click on desired font

Click here to select single or double underlining of text

Click here to return modified fonts to default font, style, and size

Practice

To practice enhancing graphics, follow the instructions on the Practice4-2 Sheet tab of the practice file exprac4.xls. Save changes as myexprac4-2.xls and close the file.

skill

Adding and Editing Comments

MOUS Skill

concept

A comment is an electronic note that you can attach to a cell. A comment does not display unless the mouse pointer hovers over a cell containing that comment. Comments help to document information or provide clarifying or explanatory notes. If several people access a worksheet at school, at work, or on the Internet, comments can be used to share information without cluttering the worksheet with extra text. If the worksheet users place their mouse pointers over the proper cell, however, the comment then will appear to provide more information.

do it !

Insert a comment to list the names of cell ranges on a worksheet.

1. Open Student File exdoit4-3.xls and save it as Comments.xls. Click cell B5 to make it active. Type the name Kyle Samuel in the cell and press [Enter]. Click the cell again.

2. Click Insert, then click Comment. An active text box with the name of the program's designated user and an insertion point will appear next to the selected cell. The text box will have an arrow pointing to the cell that it references, and a small red triangle will appear in the upper-right corner of the cell to indicate that it contains a comment.

3. Select the contents of the cell by dragging the I-beam over the text in the box. Type Kyle Samuel: and press [Enter] (see Figure 4-7). Notice that the name that first appeared in the comment box appears in the Status bar at the bottom of the program window.

4. Type the following range names, exactly as listed, pressing [Enter] after each one: Gross Profit, Gross Profit Margin, Miscellaneous, Quarter 1, Quarter 2, Quarter 3, Rent, Salaries, Sales, and Total Expenses.

5. Drag down the midpoint sizing handle at the bottom edge of the comment box until you can see the words Total Expenses at the bottom of the box. Release the mouse button (see Figure 4-8).

6. Click elsewhere on the worksheet to cancel the selection of cell B5 and to hide the comment. Position the mouse pointer over cell B5 to display the comment. Notice that the words Quarter 4 are missing from the list of cell range names.

7. Click cell B5 to select it. Remember that, under this condition, the comment will display only as long as the mouse pointer is over the cell. Click Insert, then click Edit Comment. Because you have clicked the editing command, the comment will display and stay visible even if you move the mouse pointer elsewhere without clicking in a cell.

8. Click at the end of the words Quarter 3 and press [Enter]. Type the words Quarter 4 to add them to the comment box (see Figure 4-9). Click in a cell other than B5 to move the mouse pointer out of the comment box and to close it.

9. Save and close the worksheet with the changes you have made.

more

Like cells and text boxes, comment boxes and the text they contain can be formatted. To format a comment box, right-click the cell with the comment to display a shortcut menu containing the Edit Comment command used in Step 7 and a Delete Comment and a Show Comment command. If you click Edit Comment, the insertion point appears in the comment box, and you can start typing where needed as in Step 9. The comment box also will have hatch marks around it, indicating you can resize or move the box. (Wherever you move the comment box, an arrow will run from the comment to its parent cell). If you click Show Comment, you need to click the comment box before formatting. Double-clicking the comment box border opens the Format Comment dialog box with eight tabs containing options for formatting fonts, alignment, text direction, margins, and so on. Click View, click Toolbars, then click Reviewing to open the Reviewing toolbar containing commands for displaying and navigating among comments (see Figure 4-10).

Figure 4-7 Comment box with Kyle Samuel's name

Click Insert to access Comment commands

Small red triangle indicates cell containing comment

Hatchmarks indicate text within box is available for typing or editing

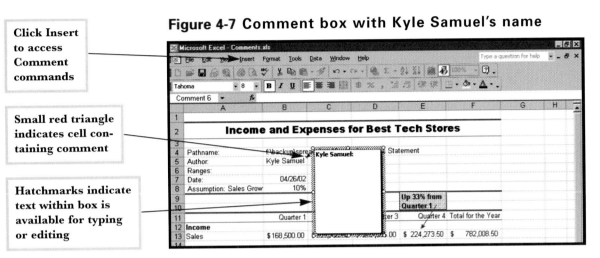

Figure 4-8 Comment box with list of cell range names

Figure 4-9 Comment box with revised list of cell range names

Kyle Samuel:
Gross Profit
Gross Profit Margin
Miscellaneous
Quarter 1
Quarter 2
Quarter 3
Rent
Salaries
Sales
Total Expenses

Kyle Samuel:
Gross Profit
Gross Profit Margin
Miscellaneous
Quarter 1
Quarter 2
Quarter 3
Quarter 4
Rent
Salaries
Sales
Total Expenses

Figure 4-10 Reviewing toolbar

Edit Comment, Previous Comment, and Next Comment buttons

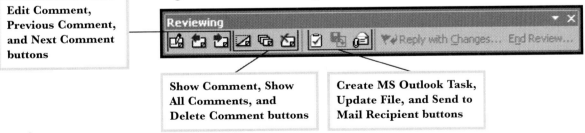

Show Comment, Show All Comments, and Delete Comment buttons

Create MS Outlook Task, Update File, and Send to Mail Recipient buttons

Practice

To practice adding and editing comments, follow the instructions on the Practice4-3 Sheet tab of the practice file exprac4.xls. Save changes as myexprac4-3.xls and close the file.

skill | Understanding Excel Charts

concept

In Excel you can create charts in worksheets to provide greater visual appeal and to help you quickly understand complicated data. For example, a chart based on an income statement such as Best Tech's can portray several rows and columns of worksheet numbers in just one graphic. This graphic can help you determine if your income is rising or falling, decide whether you are controlling expenses quarter by quarter, or display the relation between overall sales and gross profits. Whatever a chart represents, be sure it helps you understand your data more readily while portraying the data simply and attractively.

do it !

Creating Charts

Before creating a chart, you must enter data for it on a worksheet. You then must select that data and use the Chart Wizard, a series of dialog boxes that take you through four steps: (1) choosing a chart type, (2) deciding on source data, (3) selecting chart options, and (4) choosing a chart location. Alternately, you can use the Chart toolbar to create a chart and then format it. Whether you use the Chart Wizard or Chart toolbar, you can embed a chart on its related worksheets or put it on another sheet. You also can publish charts to the Web.

How Charts Represent Worksheet Data

As already noted, worksheet data provide the basis for a chart's data segments, whether they are columns, pie wedges, dots on a line, or so on. Because worksheet data and their related charts are linked, the chart automatically updates whenever you change the worksheet data on which the chart is based. A finished chart (see examples on the next page) should have all of the following elements, unless they are not appropriate to the type of chart you have chosen:

◉ **Data markers** – are columns, lines, pie wedges, or so on representing a data point, or single value, from a related worksheet; markers with the same color represent a data series.

◉ **Major gridlines** – are horizontal and/or vertical backdrops for chart values; for example, in a chart with vertical columns, horizontal gridlines will mark major value levels; larger charts also can have minor gridlines.

◉ **Category axis names** – are labels on the horizontal (X) or vertical (Y) axes identifying the individual items you are charting; these names come from row or column headings in a related worksheet.

◉ **Chart data series names** – are titles identifying the larger class or group that the individual chart items fall into; these names can come from columns or rows on a related worksheet, or you can add them in the Chart Wizard; data series names appear in the Legend.

If you rest your mouse pointer over a chart element, a ScreenTip will appear that contains the name of that element.

Embedded Charts and Chart Sheets

Embedded charts—are graphic objects saved as part of the worksheet from which you created the charts. Use these charts whenever you want to display or print one or more charts beside its related worksheet.

Chart sheets—are separate sheets in a workbook with their own sheets and, usually, sheet names. Use these sheets when you need to reserve the related worksheet for data itself and/or when the chart itself is too large or complicated for its related worksheet. With the chart on its own chart sheet, you also can view or edit it separately from the related worksheet.

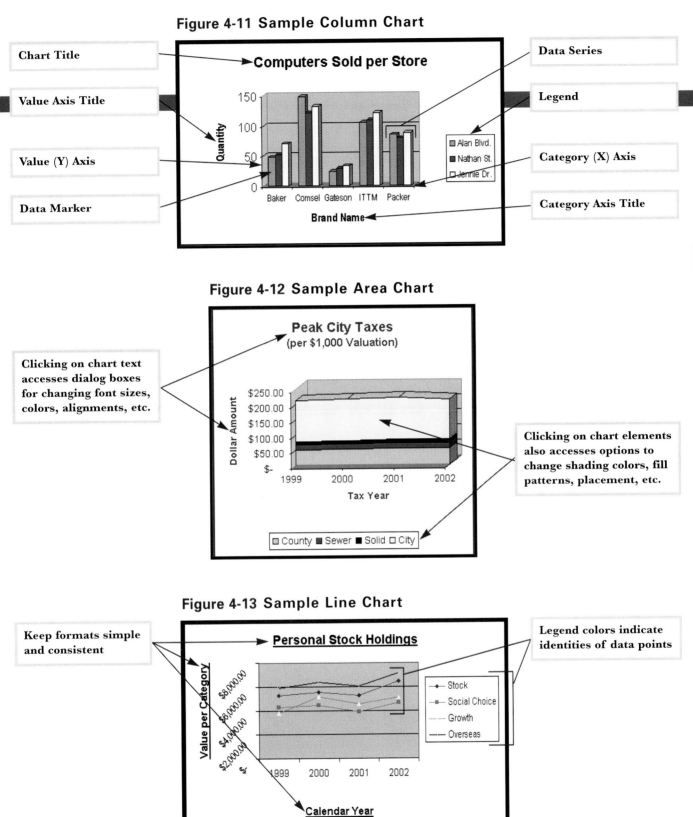

Figure 4-11 Sample Column Chart

Chart Title

Value Axis Title

Value (Y) Axis

Data Marker

Data Series

Legend

Category (X) Axis

Category Axis Title

Figure 4-12 Sample Area Chart

Clicking on chart text accesses dialog boxes for changing font sizes, colors, alignments, etc.

Clicking on chart elements also accesses options to change shading colors, fill patterns, placement, etc.

Figure 4-13 Sample Line Chart

Keep formats simple and consistent

Legend colors indicate identities of data points

skill Creating a Chart

concept

Charts are graphics that represent values and their relationships. Using charts, you quickly can identify trends in data and see contrasts among values. Excel enables you to portray data easily using a variety of two- and three-dimensional chart styles. These styles give data immediate meaning, unlike data in its raw form, which generally requires studying.

do it !

Use a pie chart to show values for Rent, Salaries, and Miscellaneous Expenses as a percentage of total yearly expenses.

1. Open Student File exdoit4-5.xls and save it as Create Chart.xls. Select cell range F16:F18 to choose the values desired for a new chart.

2. Click the Chart Wizard button 📊 on the Standard toolbar. The Chart Wizard dialog box opens with the Column chart type selected. If the Office Assistant appears, close it by clicking the No, I do not want help now option, as you do not need the Assistant for this Skill.

3. In the Chart type list box, click Pie. The Chart subtypes will change to show different types of pie charts (see Figure 4-14). The basic pie chart sub-type is selected by default.

4. Click ⬚ Next > . The Wizard will advance to Step 2 with a two-dimensional pie chart representing the selected data displayed. If you had not already selected cells, you could enter which cells to include in your chart by entering that data in the Data range text box.

5. Click the Series tab to bring it forward in the dialog box. Be sure that the Values text box reads =Sheet1!$F$16:$F$18 (see Figure 4-15).

6. Click the Category Labels text box to activate it. A flashing insertion point will appear in the text box so you can name the categories for your chart.

7. Click the Collapse Dialog button 📑 at the right end of the Category Labels text box. The dialog box will shrink so only the Category Labels text box is shown. Collapsing the dialog box allows you to view more of the worksheet so you easily can select the cells to be inserted as the labels for your chart's categories. If necessary, drag the text box to the right of Column B and scroll up slightly so rows 16–18 appear near the top of the worksheet.

8. Select cell range A16:A18. A moving border will surround the selected range, a ScreenTip will display the size of the selection, and the range will appear in the collapsed dialog box (see Figure 4-16).

9. Click the Expand Dialog button 📇 at the right end of the collapsed dialog box to bring the full dialog box back into view. Be sure that the Category Labels text box reads =Sheet1!$A$16:$A$18 (see Figure 4-17).

(continued on EX 4.12)

Figure 4-14 Chart Wizard—Step 1

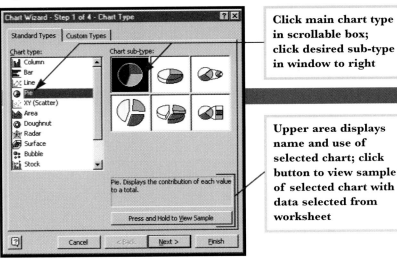

Click main chart type in scrollable box; click desired sub-type in window to right

Upper area displays name and use of selected chart; click button to view sample of selected chart with data selected from worksheet

Figure 4-15 Series tab of Step 2

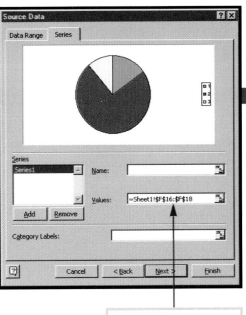

Displays cell range of series you selected in related worksheet

Figure 4-16 Collapsed dialog box

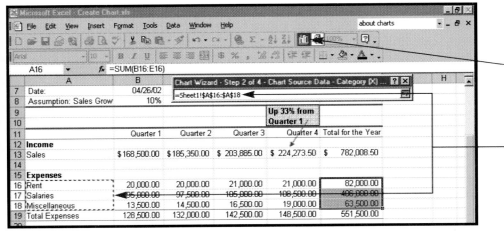

Chart Wizard button

Collapsed dialog box displays cell range selected in animated area at left

Figure 4-17 Re-enlarged Chart Wizard

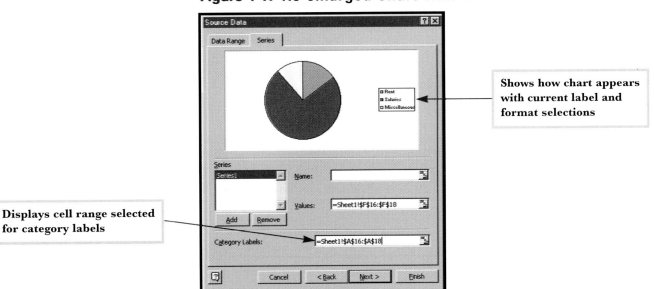

Shows how chart appears with current label and format selections

Displays cell range selected for category labels

skill Creating a Chart (continued)

do it !

10. Click the Next button [Next >]. Step 3 of the Chart Wizard will appear. Click the Chart title text box, then type Breakdown of Expenses. The title you have entered will appear in the preview area in the right side of the dialog box. The other text boxes are grayed out since they do not apply to the selected chart type.

11. Click the Legend tab to bring it forward in the dialog box. A check mark appears by default in the Show legend check box. Click the Show legend check box to deselect this option, as you will label the chart later.

12. Click the Data Labels tab to bring it forward. In the Label Contains section, put check marks in the Category Name check box and the Percentages check box. Labels and percentages will appear in the preview area at the right side of the dialog box (see Figure 4-18).

13. Click the Next button [Next >]. Step 4 of the Chart Wizard will appear. The As object in option button is selected by default, indicating that the chart would appear in the current worksheet as opposed to a new one if you closed the dialog box now (see Figure 4-19).

14. Click the Finish button [Finish]. The Chart Wizard dialog box will close, your chart will display in the center of your worksheet, and the Chart toolbar will appear in the Excel window (see Figure 4-20).

15. Save and close your workbook with the changes you have made.

more

When you select a chart, the Chart menu replaces the Data menu. The first four commands on the Chart menu open dialog boxes that resemble the steps of the Chart Wizard. These commands enable you to alter any of the characteristics of the chart without having to recreate it in the Chart Wizard. The Add Data command lets you append the ranges that are displayed.

Table 4-1 describes some common chart types and gives examples of how to you might use them.

Table 4-1

Chart Type		Description	Example
Area		Emphasizes magnitude of change over time	Increases from tax sources
Bar		Similar to column chart, but emphasizes X value	Individual sales performance
Column		Shows how data changes over time	Quarterly income projections
Line		Shows trends in data at equal intervals	Monthly gross and net sales
Pie		Shows relation of individual parts to sum of parts	Budgets, country exports
Stock		Indicates various values of stocks	Low, high, and closing prices

Figure 4-18 Data Labels tab of Step 3

Turns labels of selected chart elements on or off; options selected here replace Legend deleted on previous tab of dialog box

Turns relevant color boxes and leader lines from labels to pie wedges on or off

Click Titles tab to apply chart title and other titles appropriate for selected chart; click Legend tab to display, format, or hide Legend

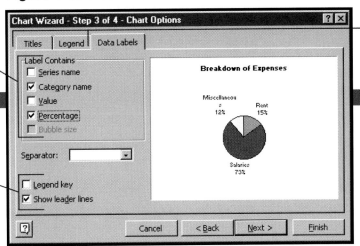

Figure 4-19 Chart Wizard—Step 4

Click option button and type name of new worksheet for chart to appear on

Accept this selection and click [Finish] button to place chart on its related worksheet

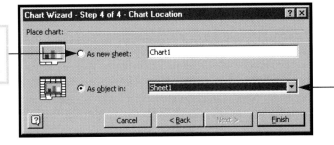

Figure 4-20 Chart displayed as object in worksheet

After closing Chart Wizard, chart appears in center of selected worksheet

With chart selected, Chart toolbar appears in worksheet window

Chart Values chosen in Step 1; Type in Step 4, Category Labels in Step 8, and Worksheet in Step 13

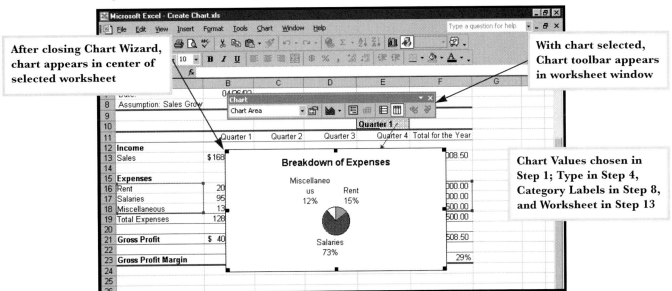

Excel 2002

Practice

To practice creating a chart, follow the instructions on the Practice4-5 Sheet tab of the practice file exprac4.xls. Save changes as myexprac4-5.xls and close the file.

skill | Moving and Resizing a Chart

concept

Once you have created a chart, you can change its location and size on the worksheet so the chart has an attractive shape and does not obstruct your view of the data in the worksheet itself. Depending on the size and orientation of your page, you generally would place the chart to the right or below the worksheet. With either of these locations, the data remains dominant, but the chart still adds important information to the overall presentation.

do it !

Move the chart below the main data of the worksheet and then resize it so its boundaries match those of existing rows and columns.

1. Open Student File exdoit4-6.xls and save it as Move Chart.xls.

2. Click once on the chart. Eight small black sizing handles appear at the corners and at the midpoints of the edges of the chart. Hold down the [Alt] key, and drag the chart down until the upper-left corner of the chart is even with the upper-left corner of cell B25 (see Figure 4-21). Release [Alt]. As you move the mouse, the mouse pointer will change to the movement pointer [↔↕], and a dotted border will indicate where the chart will appear when the mouse button is released. The worksheet will scroll upward whenever the mouse pointer is dragged below the document window.

3. If necessary, scroll down until the entire chart appears in the document window. Hold down the [Alt] key and drag the midpoint sizing handle of the right edge of the chart so the right edge of the chart is on the border between columns E and F. Release [Alt] (see Figure 4-22).

4. Hold down the [Alt] key and drag the midpoint sizing handle of the bottom edge of the chart to the boundary between rows 39 and 40 (see Figure 4-23). Release [Alt].

5. Save and close your workbook with the changes you have made.

more

Table 4-2 below summarizes different techniques you can use to move and resize charts and other objects:

Table 4-2

Action	To
Press [Shift] while dragging chart	Restrict a chart's movement to only the horizontal or vertical
Press [Ctrl] while dragging chart	Copy the chart to another place in the worksheet
Press [Ctrl] while dragging sizing handle	Maintain a chart's center point when resizing it
Press [Shift] while dragging corner sizing handle	Restrict a chart's aspect ratio when resizing it
Press [Ctrl]+[Shift] while dragging corner sizing handle	Maintain a chart's center point and aspect ratio when resizing it
Press [Alt] while dragging chart or sizing handle	Positions chart along cell borders as you drag

Figure 4-21 Chart's location after moving below worksheet

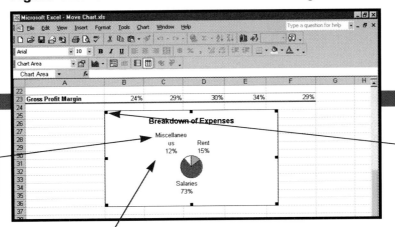

Formatting of Miscellaneous will be corrected later

Upper-left corner of chart matches upper-left corner of cell B25

Figure 4-22 Chart's appearance after moving right edge

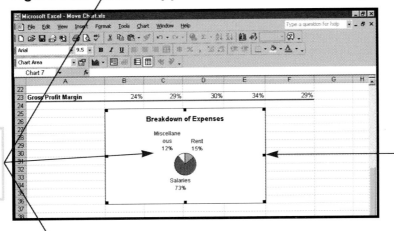

Chart elements adjust to fit redefined chart area

Right edge of chart matches boundary of columns E and F

Figure 4-23 Chart's appearance after moving bottom edge

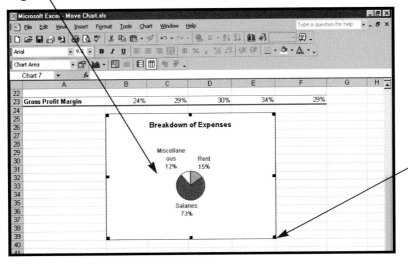

Bottom edge of chart matches boundary of rows 39 and 40

Excel 2002

Practice

To practice moving and resizing a chart, follow the instructions on the Practice4-6 Sheet tab of the practice file exprac4.xls. Save changes as myexprac4-6.xls and close the file.

skill Formatting a Chart

concept

After you create, relocate, and resize a chart, you still can alter many more of its features to make it more colorful and attractive, to highlight certain areas of the chart, to call attention to an unusual or distinctive element among several elements, and so on. Among chart features that you can change are colors, patterns, fill effects, fonts, font styles and sizes, font alignments, line widths, border effects, and so on. Before formatting an area, however, you must remember to click directly on the desired area, not a larger or smaller area of the overall chart.

do it !

Isolate the corresponding pie wedge to emphasize that a company met its goal of keeping miscellaneous expenses under 15% of total expenses. Also, change the wedge's color, format the title, and correct the formatting of a data label.

1. Open Student File exdoit4-7.xls, and save it as Format Chart.xls.

2. Click the pie in your chart to make it active. Three sizing handles will appear to indicate its selection.

3. Click the Miscellaneous pie wedge to select it. Drag the pie wedge away from the pie so the point of the wedge is even with the former border of the pie. Notice that the wedge's label moves to accommodate the wedge's new position.

4. Double-click the Miscellaneous pie wedge to open the Format Data Point dialog box. Click the Patterns tab to bring it forward. In the Area section of the tab, click the Yellow square in the third column of the bottom row. The Sample area in the lower-left region of the tab will display the newly selected color (see Figure 4-24). Click [OK] to apply the selected color and to close the dialog box.

5. Double-click the chart's title, Breakdown of Expenses, to open the Format Chart Title dialog box. On the Patterns tab, click the Shadow check box to activate it (see Figure 4-25). Click [OK] to apply the shadow and to close the dialog box.

6. Notice that the label Miscellaneous is spread over two lines. Double-click the word Miscellaneous to open the Format Data Labels dialog box. Click the Font tab to bring it forward. In the Font area, click Arial Narrow. In the Font style area, click Bold. In the Size area click 9. Click [OK] to apply the new font and to close the dialog box. Click outside the chart to cancel the selection (see Figure 4-26).

7. Save and close the workbook with the changes you have made.

more

Double-clicking any selected chart element will open a dialog box that enables you to format and alter that element. The available tabs of the dialog box that appears will provide formatting options that are relevant to the selected item. You also may select elements and their formatting dialog boxes using the Chart toolbar (see Figure 4-27).

On the Patterns tab of the chart element formatting dialog boxes, there is a Fill Effects button that lets you apply advanced formatting options such as gradients, textures, patterns, or pictures to the selected element.

Figure 4-24 Patterns tab of Format Data Point dialog box

Figure 4-25 Patterns tab of Format Chart Point dialog box

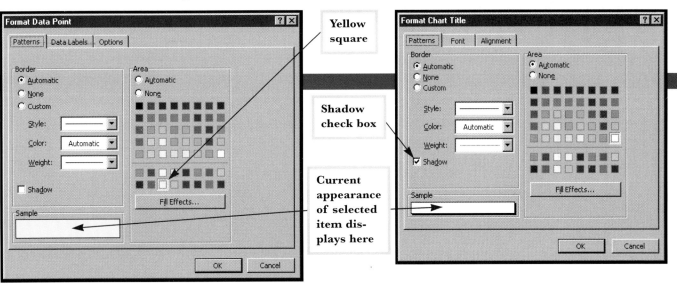

Yellow square

Shadow check box

Current appearance of selected item displays here

Figure 4-26 Formatted chart elements

All three labels have 9-point Arial, bold, format

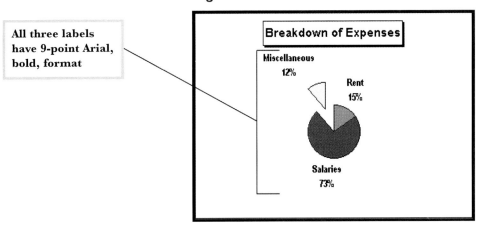

Figure 4-27 Chart toolbar

Chart Objects box: click here to select chart object desired for editing

Angle Clockwise and Angle Counterclockwise buttons

Format Chart Area and Chart Type buttons

Legend and Data Table buttons

By Row and By Column buttons

Practice

To practice formatting a chart, follow the instructions on the Practice4-7 tab of the practice file exprac4.xls. Save changes as myexprac4-7.xls and close the file.

skill | Changing a Chart's Type

concept

Excel allows you to change the type of chart you already have, while referencing the same data series. For example, you could convert a column chart to a bar chart, a line chart, and so on. You also can switch between variants of the same chart type, called sub-types, to provide variety in chart style or to enhance a chart element that needs extra emphasis. Be aware that you should not change chart types if the second type would improperly represent the selected data.

do it !

Display the pie chart with a 3-D effect and increased elevation, or tilt, to the chart's bottom.

1. Open Student File exdoit4-8.xls and save it as Change Chart.xls.

2. Select the chart, click Chart on the Menu bar, then click the Chart Type command to open the Chart Type dialog box. The Standard Types tab should be in front. If it is not, click it to bring it forward, where you will see the selected chart type and available sub-types.

3. In the Chart sub-type area, click the image in the first row, second column. It will highlight, and its name—Pie with a 3-D visual effect—will appear below the Chart sub-type area (see Figure 4-28). Click [OK] to apply the 3-D effect and close the dialog box.

4. Click Chart, then click 3-D View to open the 3-D View dialog box. In the Elevation text box, the current elevation of 15 degrees will appear. Click the Increase Elevation arrow [⇧] three times to increase the pie's elevation to 30 degrees, as shown in Figure 4-29. The preview area of the dialog box will display the changing elevation of as you click the arrow. Click [OK] to apply the new elevation and to close the dialog box. Instead of clicking the Increase Elevation arrow, you could highlight the Elevation text box, then type 30. Pressing [Enter] would apply the new elevation and close the dialog box. Alternatively, you could click the Apply button [Apply] to see how the new elevation would look, then click [OK] to accept it and to close the dialog box.

5. Click in cell G25, outside the chart area. Verify that your chart looks like the one in Figure 4-30. If necessary, redo the Steps above to match the appearance of the figure. Save and close the workbook with the changes you have made.

more

For most two-dimensional charts, you can change the type of chart for either a data series or for the entire chart. (Remember that a data series is a set of related data points that appear in a chart.) For most three-dimensional charts, you will change the entire chart when changing the type of chart. However, for three-dimensional bar charts and column charts, you can change a data series to either a cone, cylinder, or pyramid type of chart. For bubble charts you can change only the entire chart type.

To change a type of chart in which you can change either the entire chart or just a data series, you must remember to click directly on the desired area, not a larger or smaller area than you wish to change. Therefore, to change the entire chart, you must click on the overall chart. But to change just a data series, you must click on only the desired data series. After clicking on only the desired data series, you also must put a check mark in the Apply to selection check box in the Options area on the Standard Types tab of the Chart Type dialog box.

Suppose that you want to change a three-dimensional bar data series or column data series to the cone, cylinder, or pyramid type of chart. In this case, click Chart, click Chart Type to open the Chart Type dialog box, and click the Standard Types tab to bring it to the front of the dialog box. Then click either the Cone, Cylinder, or Pyramid option in the Chart type box and add a check box to the Apply to selection check box.

Figure 4-28 Chart Type dialog box with 3-D pie effect selected

Option becomes unavailable when using only one data series

Chart sub-type appears above while its name and description appear below

Add check mark to return reformatted charts to their default appearance

Sets selected chart type as default type for subsequent charts

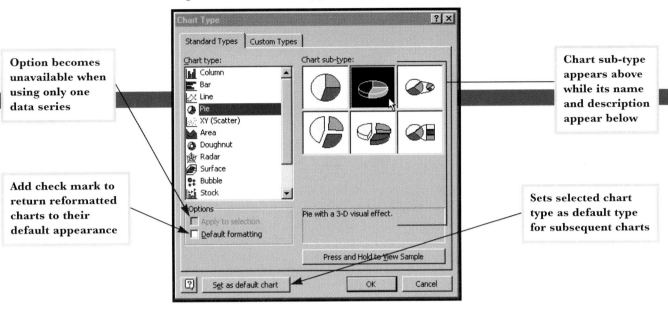

Figure 4-29 3-D View dialog box

Click respective arrow to increase or decrease chart elevation by 5-degree increments

Enter value or click buttons to rotate chart around vertical axis

Type value to increase or decrease elevation by 1-degree intervals

Returns dialog box to default format settings

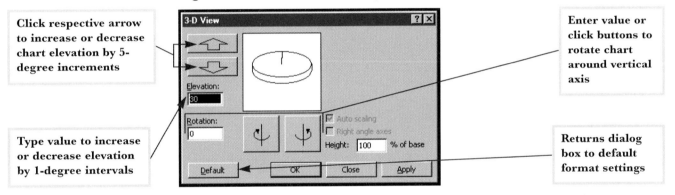

Figure 4-30 Chart with 3-D effect and increased elevation

Font, font style, font size, and data percentages remain the same

3-D pie chart elevated to 30 degrees above horizontal

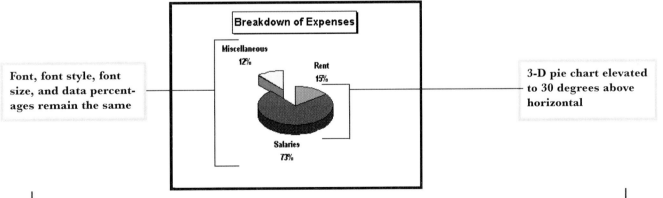

Practice

To practice changing a chart's type, follow the instructions on the Practice4-8 Sheet tab of the practice file exprac4.xls. Save changes as myexprac4-8.xls and close the file.

skill Using Advanced Printing Features

concept

A worksheet, especially one with an embedded object like a chart, may not always fit on a standard printed page using the default print settings. Excel therefore enables you to preview and change page orientation to accommodate different arrangements of data. You can choose to print specific parts of a worksheet such as a chart, a page, the active worksheet, or the entire workbook. You access these options through the Page Setup dialog box and the Print dialog box. Using these dialog boxes along with Print Preview will enable you to produce the kinds of printouts you need.

do it !

Change page orientation from Portrait to Landscape to fit an entire worksheet onto one page.

1. Open Student File exdoit4-9.xls and save it as Advanced Printing.xls. Replace the author's name in call B5 with your own name. Click the Print Preview button 🔍 to open the Print Preview mode. Notice that the worksheet and chart fit on one page in Portrait orientation. Click the Close button ⬚Close⬚ to return to Normal view.

2. Click once on the Chart Area. Hold down the [Alt] key and drag the chart up and to the right so the upper-left corner of the chart lines up with the upper-left corner of cell H2. Release [Alt], and click in cell G1. The chart now appears to the right of its related worksheet with one blank column between it and the worksheet's right column.

3. Click the Print Preview button 🔍 again. The documentation and data areas of the worksheet will appear on the page, but the chart will not, making it apparent that not all of the worksheet fits on one page. Notice that the Next button on the Print Preview toolbar is active, that the words Preview: Page 1 of 2 appear in the Status bar, and that the raised area of the Vertical scroll bar goes only halfway down the bar. These are additional indicators that your worksheet spreads over two pages (see Figure 4-31).

4. Click the Setup button ⬚Setup...⬚ to open the Page Setup dialog box. Click the Page tab to move it to the front of the dialog box. In the Orientation section of the dialog box, click the Landscape option button. In the Scaling section click the Fit to 1 page(s) wide by 1 tall option button (see Figure 4-32).

5. Click the Margins tab to bring it to the front of the dialog box. In the Center on page section, apply a check mark to the Horizontally check box. This action will center the worksheet and chart equally distant from the left and right margins (see Figure 4-33). Press [Enter] to apply the page setups and to close the dialog box. The entire worksheet with the chart now appear on one page (see Figure 4-34).

6. On the Print Preview toolbar, click the Print button ⬚Print...⬚ to open the Print dialog box. Then click ⬚ OK ⬚ to print the worksheet and chart.

7. Click on the chart to select just it for printing. Click the Print button 🖨. The chart will print on one page. Save and close the workbook with the changes you have made.

more

The Header/Footer tab of the Page Setup dialog box contains default headers and footers to apply to your pages and options for setting up customized headers and footers. The Sheet tab contains options for selecting print areas, adding sheet titles, printing worksheet gridlines, and selecting other related features.

Figure 4-31 Worksheet's layout before applying page setups

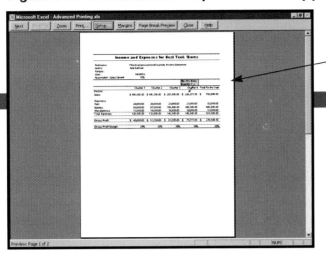

Portrait page orientation; worksheet documentation and data areas appear; chart does not display

Figure 4-32 Page tab

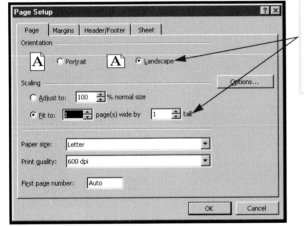

Selected settings will put all print areas on one page in Landscape orientation

Figure 4-33 Margins tab

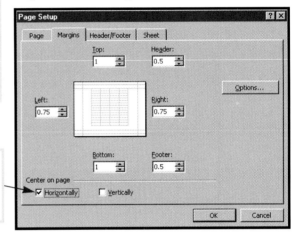

Click here to center all print areas on a page

Figure 4-34 Worksheet's layout after applying page setups

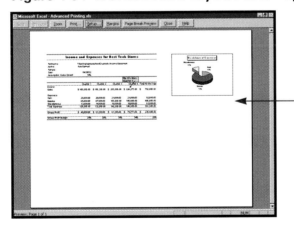

Print layout changes to landscape orientation; chart displays to right of worksheet; areas to print are centered between left and right margins on page

Practice

To practice using advanced printing features, follow the instructions on the Practice4-9 Sheet tab of the practice file exprac4.xls. Save changes as myexprac4-9.xls and close the file.

shortcuts

Function	Button/Mouse	Menu	Keyboard
Drawing Toolbar		Click View, click Toolbars, click Drawing	[Alt]+[V], [T], then select Drawing
Text Box			
Arrow			
Fill Color			
Line Color			
Chart Wizard		Click Insert, click Chart	

A. Identify Key Features

Name the items indicated by callouts in Figure 4-35.

Figure 4-35 Identify features of the Excel screen

1.

2.

3.

4.

5.

6.

7.

8.

9.

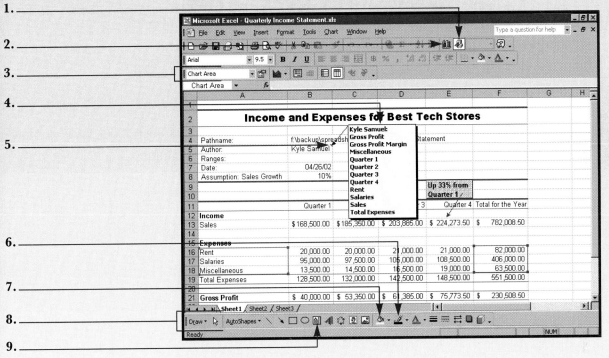

B. Select the Best Answer

10. Allows you to add text to a worksheet without being restricted to a specific cell

11. Reduces the size of a dialog box so you can easily view a worksheet

12. Displays with your chart when you complete and close the Chart Wizard

13. An electronic note attached to a cell

14. A graphic that represents values and their relationships from a worksheet

15. Alternate term for horizontal page orientation of a worksheet

16. Enables you to add text boxes, arrows, lines, and so on to a worksheet

17. Applies shading to a text box

18. Contains Show Comment, Edit Comment, Delete Comment, and similar buttons

a. Collapse dialog button

b. Comment

c. Drawing toolbar

d. Text box

e. Reviewing toolbar

f. Landscape

g. Chart toolbar

h. Fill Color button

i. Chart

quiz (continued)

C. Complete the Statement

19. To change the user name that appears on Comments, go to the:

   a. Replace dialog box

   b. Define Name dialog box

   c. General tab of the Options dialog box

   d. User tab of the Comments dialog box

20. The Arrow tool appears on the:

   a. Formatting toolbar

   b. Define Diagrams toolbar

   c. Drawing toolbar

   d. Shapes toolbar

21. To navigate from one Comment to another, use the:

   a. Comments toolbar

   b. Reviewing toolbar

   c. Formatting toolbar

   d. Standard toolbar

22. Excel contains all of the following chart types **except**:

   a. Doughnut

   b. Line

   c. Pie

   d. Volume

23. You can add a title to a chart by using the:

   a. Chart Options dialog box

   b. Chart type dialog box

   c. Format Chart Area dialog box

   d. Source Data dialog box

24. To maintain a chart's center point when resizing it:

   a. Press [Ctrl] while dragging the chart

   b. Press [Ctrl] while dragging a sizing handle

   c. Press [Shift] while dragging a sizing handle

   d. Press [Tab] while dragging a sizing handle

25. The 3-D View dialog box contains all options **except**:

   a. Elevation

   b. Height

   c. Location

   d. Rotation

26. If text in a text box exceeds the size of the box:

   a. The beginning of the text will be deleted

   b. The excess text will be deleted

   c. The text box automatically will resize itself

   d. The text will scroll up

27. The small circles at the corners and the middle of each side of a selected object are called:

   a. Fill handles

   b. Frame handles

   c. Sizing handles

   d. Format handles

28. Text boxes can contain:

   a. Text in words, phrases, or sentences

   b. Individual numbers or a series of numbers

   c. Currency and mathematical symbols

   d. All of the above

interactivity

Build Your Skills

1. Add objects and graphics to a worksheet:

   a. Open the file exskills4.xls and save it as QIS with Chart.xls.

   b. Using the Drawing toolbar, add a text box in cells E9:E10 that reads Up 37% from Quarter 1. Use the Fill Color button to add a Light Turquoise color to the text box.

   c. Draw an arrow from the lower-right area of the text box to the top center of the Quarter 4 Gross Sales cell (E13). Use the Line Color button to change the color of the arrow to Dark Teal.

   d. In cell B6, enter the name Kyle Samuel in an alphabetized Comment that displays the names of all 12 cell ranges in the worksheet. (Hint: you can view the names of the cell ranges by clicking Insert, Name, and then Define.)

2. Create a chart based on the expenses data of the worksheet:

   a. Select the four values of expenses that appear in the worksheet (cells F16:F19). Use the Chart Wizard to create a basic pie chart showing the percentage of each expense as a part of the total expenses.

   b. In Step 2 of the wizard, use the Series tab to select the appropriate Category Labels (cells A16:A19).

   c. In Step 3 add the chart title Expenses by Category; leave the Legend displayed at the right side of the chart, and show Percentage data labels.

   d. In Step 4 insert the chart into the current worksheet.

3. Move, resize, and format the chart:

   a. Move the chart so that it is centered below the data portion of the worksheet. Using the [Alt] key, position the top border of the chart at the boundary of rows 25 and 26. Position the left border at the boundary of columns A and B. Position the right border at the boundary of columns E and F. Position the bottom border at the boundary of rows 40 and 41.

   b. Change the chart's sub-type to a 3-D Exploded Pie. Increase the Elevation of the pie to 60 degrees. Rotate it 20 degrees counterclockwise so the Rotation text box reads 340.

   c. Change the color of the Phone/Utilities pie wedge to Dark Green. Add a double underline to the chart title.

4. Save and print the worksheet:

   a. Type your name in an appropriate cell and resave the file. Print the worksheet and chart in Portrait orientation.

   b. Move the chart on the worksheet to position the top border of the chart at the boundary rows 1 and 2, the left border at the boundary of columns G and H, the right border at the boundary of columns L and M, and the bottom border at the boundary of rows 15 and 16.

   c. Using Print Preview and the Setup button, select the Landscape orientation and Fit to 1 page options on the Page tab. Select the Center on page horizontally option on the Margins tab. Close the dialog box and reprint the worksheet and chart on one page.

   d. Click on the chart to select just it. Add your name to the chart title and then print the chart on one page. Resave and close the worksheet with the changes you have made.

interactivity (continued)

Problem Solving Exercises

1. Use Excel to create the worksheet and chart below. You will need to use the Drawing toolbar and the Chart command or Chart toolbar to reformat the chart once it is created. When you finish formatting the chart, add categories and data for the months of July through December. Reformat the chart as needed to make all areas of it readable, organized, and attractive. Add your name to a text box in the upper-left corner of the chart. Save the chart as Web Hits.xls, and print the worksheet and chart on one page for your instructor.

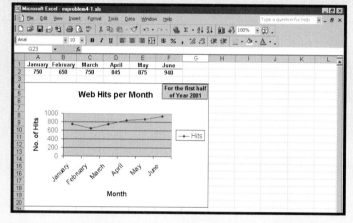

2. A friend of yours is considering learning Microsoft Excel. You want to convince your friend that the goal is worthwhile. To do this, you plan to show him or her a worksheet you have created with Excel. First, however, you decide to incorporate the Skills you have learned in this lesson to demonstrate the charting features of the program. Open the file exproblem4-2.xls and save it as Chart Features.xls. Add at least one text box, one comment, and a 3-D clustered column chart to the worksheet, using these new features to call attention to and further illustrate important data in the worksheet. Add your name to an appropriate cell, then resave and print the worksheet and chart on one page for your instructor.

3. You are training a new payroll clerk to use your school or company payroll worksheet, but you first want to modify the worksheet to make it more informative for the clerk. Open file exproblem4-3.xls and save it as Payroll with Chart.xls. Insert a text box to indicate that the clerk should type in new employee names with the last name first, then a comma, and then the first name. Add a comment to list your name and the cell range names for every column of the worksheet. Create a 3-D, exploded pie chart to show what percentage of the gross pay total is represented by the totals of the deductions and the net pay. Add your name to an appropriate cell, then resave and print the worksheet and chart on one page for your instructor.

4. Using the data in the table below, create and save a worksheet and 3-D stacked area chart with the file name Federal Taxes.xls. (If you add a Totals row at the bottom of the worksheet, do not select it when creating the chart.) Label the chart Internal Revenue Collections. Label the Y axis as Dollar Amount (in thousands). Label the X axis as Tax Year. The Legend categories should read Corporate, Individual, Employment, and Miscellaneous. Make additional formatting changes as needed so the chart looks organized, attractive, and readable. Add your name to an appropriate cell, then resave and print the worksheet and chart on one page for your instructor.

Internal Revenue Collections, Fiscal Years 1998-2001 (in thousands of dollars)				
Type of Tax	1998	1999	2000	2001
Corporation income tax	213,270,012	217,582,369	216,231,412	222,434,643
Individual income tax	928,065,857	1,003,185,952	1,000,587,123	1,150,425,581
Employment taxes	557,799,193	567,456,321	639,540,537	680,411,209
Miscellaneous	92,564,665	86,971,505	95,863,963	120,569,788

Introduction to Databases

A database is a collection of related information that is used to store, organize and extract data. Most, if not all, businesses today maintain one or more databases. For example, banks must have systems for keeping track of customers and their accounts, retail stores use point of sales systems to process the purchase of goods, and airlines use a database system for booking flights. Databases can be computerized as well as non-computerized. Some examples of non-computerized databases are telephone books, address books, and card catalogs in libraries. The advantage of a computerized database is the almost limitless capacity to store data, and the speed, accuracy, and efficiency with which you can retrieve information.

A computerized database built in Access is also flexible. Data can be reorganized and accessed in many different ways. In a computerized database, information is organized into tables. An Access database is a repository for these tables and the queries, forms, reports, and other database objects, which you will learn about in this book.

Relational databases enable you to link records from two or more tables based upon the data in a common field. The benefit is that you can save disk space and time because all of the fields in the database need not be filled in for each new entry. For example, a retail outlet would need an ordering system. For each order you would have to obtain the customer billing information, list each item the customer is purchasing and its cost, and subtract the items ordered from inventory. Instead of entering all of this information for each order, you would set up a Customer table to hold the customer billing information. Each customer will be assigned a unique customer number. An Inventory table will store details about the products the establishment stocks including the price/unit and the quantities in stock and on back order. Each product will be assigned a unique product number. Finally an Order table will store the information for each order placed with the company. The fields in the Order table will only have to include the Customer number, the Product number, and the quantity being ordered. The idea is that any piece of information is entered and stored only once, eliminating duplications of effort and the possibility of inconsistency between different records. Data entry errors are dramatically reduced because information only has to be entered once. As you continue through this book, these concepts will become clear to you. You will learn how to build a relational database with shared fields that link tables so that data redundancy is controlled and data inconsistency is avoided.

skills

※ Opening an Existing Database

※ Navigating in Datasheet View

※ Working in Table Design View

※ Formatting a Datasheet

※ Creating a Drop-Down List

※ Entering Records in a Datasheet

※ Editing Records in a Datasheet

※ Understanding Shared Fields

※ Getting Help and Exiting Access

Lesson Goal:

Become familiar with the structure of databases, the structure of tables, and the different data types that are used for the fields in a table. Learn how to navigate in a datasheet, add and edit records in a table, format a datasheet, and add a field to a table. Learn about the benefits of shared fields and how to get help while you work.

skill | Opening an Existing Database

concept

There are several ways to start the Access program. You can use the Office Shortcut Bar if you have installed it, you can right-click the desktop, highlight New, and choose Microsoft Access on the shortcut menu, or you can use the Start menu. Using the Start menu will work on any computer no matter what settings or installation methods have been employed. After you start Access, you can choose to either start a new blank database or open an existing one.

do it !

Open an existing database and examine the application window.

1. Insert the disk containing your Access Student Files in the appropriate drive (if applicable). Click the Start button [🏁 Start] on the Windows taskbar. Use the mouse to point to Programs. Click Microsoft Access on the Programs submenu to open Access.

2. Click the Open button 🗁 on the Database toolbar, or click [🗁 More files...] on the New Task Pane on the right side of the application window to open the Open dialog box.

3. Click the list arrow on the Look in list box. Locate the disk drive where your Access Student Files are located. A list of the files and folders on the disk appears in the Contents window. If necessary, double-click the folder containing your Access Student Files.

4. Click Office Furniture Inc in the Contents window and click [🗁 Open ▾]. The Office Furniture Inc database window opens.

5. Look at each of the Access window elements identified in Figure 1-1. The Objects bar on the left side of the Database window lists the seven types of database objects. Table 1-1 describes the objects.

6. Click Edit on the Menu bar. Point to the double arrows at the bottom of the menu to display all of the commands on the menu. Point to View on the Menu bar, then Insert, then Tools. Each menu opens in turn. Click the application title bar or anywhere in the application window to close the menu.

7. Place the mouse pointer over the buttons on the Database toolbar. Read the ScreenTips to begin to familiarize yourself with the program.

8. On the Database window toolbar, click the Large Icons button [▪▪]. The buttons on the Objects bar and the icons in the Database window change size.

9. Click the Queries button on the Objects bar. The commands for creating a query and the queries in the database are now displayed in the Database window.

10. Click Tables on the Objects bar. Click the List View button [▦] on the Database window toolbar to return to the default view.

more

The application Title bar contains the application Control menu icon, the name of the application and the sizing buttons. The sizing buttons located in the upper-right corner of the Access title bar control how you view the application window. The Maximize button expands the window so that it fills the entire screen. The Minimize button reduces the application window to a program button on the Windows Taskbar. When the window is maximized, the Restore button replaces the Maximize button. Clicking the Restore button will revert the window to its previous size and location.

The Database window has its own title bar, Control menu icon, and sizing buttons. The Close button on the Database window Title bar will close the database but leave the Access program running. Both the task pane (under Open a file) and the bottom of the File menu list the last four databases you have opened. You can use these shortcuts to bypass the Open dialog box and quickly open a database on which you have recently worked.

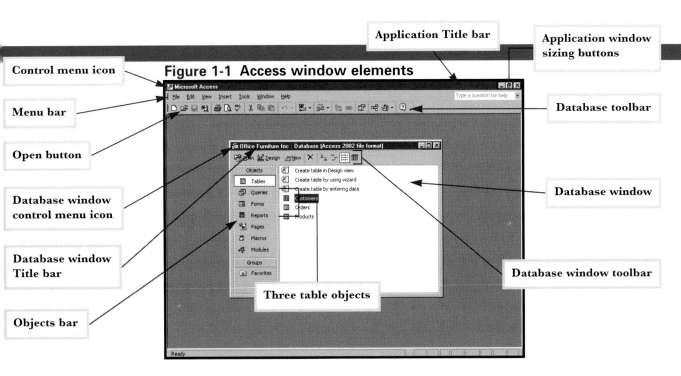

Figure 1-1 Access window elements

Application Title bar

Application window sizing buttons

Control menu icon

Database toolbar

Menu bar

Open button

Database window control menu icon

Database window

Database window Title bar

Database window toolbar

Objects bar

Three table objects

Table 1-1 Database Objects

Tables	The basis for the database. Tables are collections of records with similar data. You can link related tables to cut down on redundant or duplicated data and to make your data more manageable.
Queries	Allow you to select specific data from one or more tables. Queries enable you to create subsets of data by weeding out data you don't need at present. You use a query to clearly see and work with specific information
Forms	Data entry sheets that commonly contain the fields comprising a single record. The popular one record per screen format facilitates data entry and editing.
Reports	Used to present processed data in an organized format specifically designed for printing.
Pages	Data Access Pages (DAP). They are Web pages that allow you to view and work with data that is stored in an Access database on the Internet or a company intranet.
Macros	A series of keystrokes and commands that automate repetitive or complicated database tasks. You choose from a list of available actions and set them in a specific order to turn a multistep task into a one-click operation.
Modules	Functions and procedures written in the Visual Basic for Applications (VBA) programming language. In Access 2002 you use VBA to automate database tasks. VBA procedures can perform operations that exceed the capabilities of standard macros.

Practice

Use the Start menu to open a second Access application window. Locate and open the Home Video Collection database among your Access Student Files. Leave this application window open to complete the remaining Practice sections in this lesson. Minimize the window to return to the application window for the Office Furniture database.

skill Navigating in Datasheet View

concept

All tables are structured in a specific way. Each piece of information is called a field. A set of related fields is called a record. Each record is entered across a row. You create column headings for each field. A record contains one field for each column heading. A column contains the fields for one particular kind of data. For example, phone numbers can be listed down in one of the columns. You view the fields in a table in Datasheet View.

do it !

Open the Customers table and learn to navigate in a table.

1. With the Office Furniture Inc database open and Tables selected on the Objects bar, click the Customers table icon in the Database window. Click 🔓 Open on the Database window toolbar to open the table in Datasheet View. The Open button opens the selected object in its default view.

2. If necessary, click the Close button ☒ on the Task Pane so that you can clearly see the Customers table.

3. There are 20 customer records organized into seven fields. The field names are listed at the top of each column. Each column heading is a field selector, which you can use to select the column. Click the Company Name field selector.

4. You can also select more than one column by dragging across the fields you wish to select. Click the Billing Address field selector and drag to the right to select the City and State columns.

5. Click the first field in the Customer ID column. The Specific Record box at the bottom of the datasheet window identifies the currently selected record. To the left of the first field column is a column of gray boxes called Record selectors. The Current record symbol ▶ in the Record selector box also indicates the active record.

6. Press [Tab] on the keyboard to move to the next field in the first record. Albert's Retail should be highlighted as shown in Figure 1-2. Press [Enter]. The third field is now selected. You can press either [Tab] or [Enter] to move the focus to the next field.

7. Double-click in the Specific Record box. Type: 13. Press [Enter]. The focus moves to record 13. Click the Next Record button ▶ (to the right of the Specific Record box). The focus moves to the next record on the datasheet.

8. Click the Last Record button ▶❙. Press [Ctrl]+[Home] on the keyboard to return the focus to the first record on the datasheet.

9. The Record selector box in the row after the last record in the table contains the New record symbol ✱ (see Table 1-2). If you click the New record navigation button ▶✱ the focus will shift to this row and you can begin entering a new record.

10. Close the Customers table by clicking the Close button ☒ on the table's Title bar.

more You can also use the arrow keys on the keyboard to move between the fields in a datasheet. However, if you click a field with the mouse to select it, the program will shift to Edit mode. In Edit mode the left and right arrow keys will not switch the focus to the next field in a record. Instead, pressing the left and right arrow keys will move the insertion point within the text in the field. When you press [Tab] or [Enter] to move to the next field, the program will return to Navigation mode. You can also press the up (or down) arrow key to move to the same field in the next record (or previous record). This also returns the program to Navigation mode.

You can also use the keyboard combination [Ctrl] + [+] to move the focus to a new record. Open the Edit menu and highlight Go To to find another way to navigate within a datasheet. Commands corresponding to the navigation buttons at the bottom of the datasheet are located on the Go To submenu.

Figure 1-2 Navigating in a table

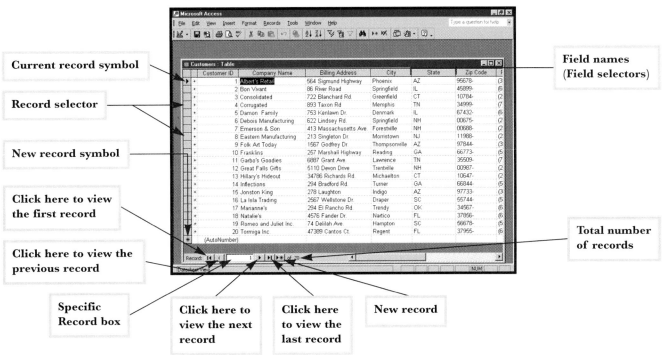

Table 1-2 Record Selectors

Button	Indicates
▶	Current record; the record has been saved as it appears
✳	A new record to which you can add data
🖉	A record that is being edited and whose changes have not yet been saved
🗊▶	A record that is set as the primary key (in a table's Design View)

Practice

Click the second Microsoft® Access database button on the taskbar to maximize the window. Open the Home Video Collection table in Datasheet View. Select the Genre column. Drag to select the Title and Genre ID columns. Use the Specific record box to navigate to record 23. Use the [Tab] key to tab through the fields in record 23. Use the Next Record button to navigate to the last field in record 24. Close the Home Video Collection table and minimize the application window.

skill

Working in Table Design View

MOUS Skill

concept

The smallest element of data is a field. When you are designing a table you should break your data down into as many fields as possible. This will give you the greatest flexibility in retrieving data later. For each field you create in a table you must specify a data type. The data type designates what kind of data the field can accept, for example, text, numbers, currency, or date and time data.

do it !

Open the Orders table and examine the data types assigned to the fields. Learn to work in the Design View window.

1. With the Office Furniture Inc database open and Tables selected on the Objects bar, click the Orders table in the Database window. Click [Design] on the Database window toolbar to open the table in Design View.

2. The Design View window is divided into two sections. In the top section you enter the field names, choose a data type for the field and enter a description of the field if necessary. The bottom half of the window is the Field Properties pane, in which you set other properties such as the field size, the number format, and the number of decimal places you want the field to include.

3. The fields in the Orders table include four different data types. Read Table 1-3 to learn about the main data types available in Access. The Order ID field is an AutoNumber field. This means that Access will automatically assign a unique number for each record in the order it is entered into the table.

4. Click in the Order Date field. Press [Tab]. Click the list arrow in the Data Type cell. Notice the different data types you can choose. Click the list arrow again to close the drop-down list. Make sure Date/Time is still the data type.

5. In the Field Properties pane in the lower portion of the window, click in the Format cell. Click the list arrow. The drop-down list displays the various Date/Time formats available in Access. Click Short Date to confirm the current choice and close the drop-down list.

6. To the left of the column of field names is a column of gray boxes called Row selectors. Click the Row selector next to the Product ID field to select the row.

7. Click the Product ID row selector again and drag upward until a black bold line appears underneath the Order ID row. Release the mouse to reposition the Product ID field directly under the Order ID field.

8. Click the Row selector for the Units Ordered field. Click the Insert Rows button [icon] on the Table Design toolbar. Click in the Field Name cell of the new row.

9. Type: Ship Via, in the Field Name cell for the new row. Press [Tab]. Text is the default data type for a new field.

10. Double-click in the Field Size cell in the Field Properties pane. Type: 25 to set the field size property for the new field to 25 characters. The Design View window should now look like Figure 1-3.

11. Click the View button [icon] on the Table Design toolbar to return to Datasheet View. Click Yes to save the changes to the design of the table when prompted. Close the table.

more

Field properties are the attributes that describe and define a field. Only two properties are required, the field name and the data type. The data type determines the kind of data that can be entered into the field. You set other field properties in the Field Properties pane to further restrict the type of data that can be entered into the field. Setting field properties can also help you to reduce data entry errors. For example, you can reduce the field size for the State field in the Customers table to 2, so that only the two-character state abbreviation can be entered. If you accidentally begin a third character, the familiar Windows Ding will remind you that this operation is not allowed. You can also use a field selector in Datasheet View to change the position of a column in the table. First click the field selector to select the column. Then drag until a bold black line indicates the correct position for the column.

Table 1-3 Data types

Text	A text field can accept almost any characters you enter: letters, numbers, symbols, and most punctuation marks. You can assign a field size to limit the number of characters. The default size is 50 characters.
AutoNumber	An AutoNumber field automatically enters a sequential number as records are added to the table.
Number	Number fields can contain only positive or negative numbers. Usually you will assign this data type for fields that will be included in calculations in the database.
Currency	A currency field contains dollar amounts that will be displayed with dollar signs, commas, decimal points, and two digits following the decimal point. Currency fields can also be used in calculations.
Memo	Memo fields are used to hold large documents. You use a memo field when you want to store descriptive or narrative information. A memo field can hold up to 65,536 characters of text.
Date/Time	A date/time field holds date and time information in various formats. You must set a field in the date/time format in order to perform date calculations such as determining the number of days between two dates.
Logical Fields	A logical field accepts only Y/N (Yes/No) data. It displays in a table as a check box, a text box, or a combo box.
OLE object	Object Linking and Embedding object. Includes bitmapped graphics, drawings, waveform audio files, and any document prepared in another program.

Access 2002

Figure 1-3 Table Design View window

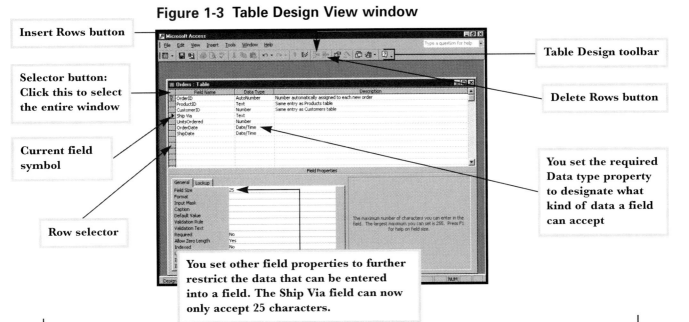

Insert Rows button

Selector button: Click this to select the entire window

Current field symbol

Row selector

Table Design toolbar

Delete Rows button

You set the required Data type property to designate what kind of data a field can accept

You set other field properties to further restrict the data that can be entered into a field. The Ship Via field can now only accept 25 characters.

Practice

Maximize the Access application window containing the Home Video Collection database. Open the Home Video Collection table in Design View. Use the Row selector to select the Comment field. Use the Insert Rows button on the Table Design toolbar to insert a new row. Name the new field Rating. Press the [Tab] key to automatically select the Text data type. Change the field size to 5. Save the changes to the design of the table and close the table. Minimize the application window.

skill | Formatting a Datasheet

concept

Reports are the database objects that are specifically designed for printing, but you may want to print a table from time to time. You can enhance the appearance of a datasheet before you print it. Although you cannot change the appearance of individual cells, you can change the font, font style, and font color for the entire table. You can also change the background color, gridline color, and border or line styles for the table.

do it !

Format the Orders table.

1. Open the Orders table in the Office Furniture Inc database in Datasheet View. On the Formatting toolbar, click the list arrow on the Font box `Arial ▾`. Use the scroll bar on the drop-down list to locate the Times New Roman font and click to select it. ⬭ If you do not see the Formatting toolbar, click View, point to the Toolbars command, and click Formatting on the Toolbars submenu to activate the toolbar.

2. Click the list arrow on the Font Size box `10 ▾` and change the font size to 12 pt.

3. Open the Format menu and click the Datasheet command to open the Datasheet Formatting dialog box. Click the list arrow on the first list box in the Border and Line Styles section at the bottom of the dialog box. Select Column Header Underline on the drop-down list.

4. Click the list arrow on the Gridline Color list box. Choose Maroon on the drop-down list. The settings in the dialog box are shown in Figure 1-4. Click `OK` to close the dialog box and apply the effects.

5. Click the list arrow on the Fill/Back Color button `🎨▾`. Select the light green color (the fourth square) in the last row of the color palette.

6. Click the list arrow on the Font/Fore Color button `A▾`. Select the brown square in the first row of the color palette.

7. Position the mouse pointer over the right boundary of the Order ID field selector until it becomes a horizontal resizing pointer ✛. Double-click the right boundary to decrease the size of the column. Double-clicking the right boundary of the field selector will size a field to its "best fit." The best fit is the size that will accommodate the longest field entry in the column. In this case the column width will decrease to fit the field heading.

8. Click the Save button 🖫 on the Table Datasheet toolbar to save the formatting changes. The formatted table is shown in Figure 1-5. Close the table.

more

You can also change the height of the rows in a table to provide more space for text or just to make the table look less packed with data. When you change the height of one row in a table, all of the rows in the table are affected. Position the mouse pointer on the border between two row selectors until the pointer becomes a vertical resizing pointer ✚. Drag up or down to increase or decrease the height of all of the rows in the table.

If you make formatting changes and forget to save them, Access will prompt you to save the changes to the layout of the table when you attempt to close it. ⬭ You can also apply a Raised or Sunken special effect to the cells in a table. Use either the Special Effect button on the Formatting toolbar or choose the appropriate option button in the Cell Effect section in the Datasheet Formatting dialog box.

Figure 1-4 Datasheet Formatting dialog box

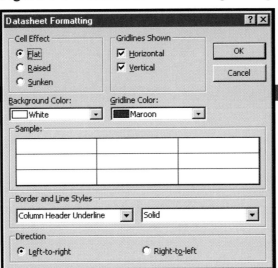

Figure 1-5 Formatted datasheet

Double-click the right boundary of a field selector to size the column to its "best fit," or drag the boundary to the left or right to custom size an individual column

Use the vertical resizing pointer to drag the border between any two row selectors to change the row height for the table

Table Datasheet toolbar

Formatting (Datasheet) toolbar

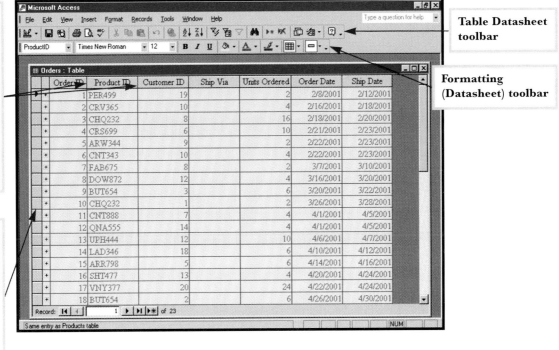

Access 2002

Practice

In the Home Video Collection database, open the Home Video Collection table in Datasheet View. Apply any design changes to the table that you wish including a new font, font size or style, font color, back color, and cell special effect. Change any column widths to their best fit as necessary. Change the height of the rows in the table. Save the changes, close the table, and minimize the window.

skill | Creating a Drop-Down List *MOUS Skill*

concept

You can use the Lookup Wizard to create a field with a drop-down list for a table. There are two kinds of Lookup fields you can create. A Lookup list displays values from an existing table or query. A Value list displays a fixed set of values that you determine when you create the field. Either way, data entry is made easier and data entry errors are reduced.

do it !

Make the Ship Via field in the Orders table a Value list.

1. Open the Orders table in the Office Furniture Inc database in Design View.

2. Click the Data Type field in the Ship Via row. Click the list arrow. Click Lookup Wizard in the drop-down list. The first Lookup Wizard dialog box opens.

3. Click the option button next to I will type in the values that I want. Click Next > .

4. Make sure the number of columns is set to 1. Position the insertion point in the field next to the current record symbol.

5. Type Federal Express. Press [Tab]. Type United Parcel Service. Press [Tab]. Type Airborne Express.

6. Double-click the right boundary of the column selector to resize the column to its best fit. The Lookup Wizard dialog box should look like Figure 1-6. Click Next > .

7. Make sure the label for the lookup column is Ship Via. Click Finish . The Ship Via field still has Text listed as its data type. Lookup fields are text fields.

8. Click to save the change to the design of the table. Click to switch to Datasheet View.

9. Click in the Ship Via field. A list arrow appears. Click the list arrow to view the new drop-down list.

10. Click the View button on the Table Datasheet toolbar to return to Design View.

11. Click the Lookup tab on the Field Properties pane. The properties for the lookup field are listed. You can see, as shown in Figure 1-7, that you have created a combo box with a Value list; the Row Source property lists the values you entered, and the Limit to List property is set to NO. This means that you can type in an alternative value that is not included in the Value list. That is the definition for a combo box; a text entry box in which the user has the option of entering text or selecting from a list.

12. Close the Design View window.

more

As you saw when you ran the Lookup Wizard, lists can contain more than one column. Additional columns can include descriptions of the list items. However, only one of the columns will contain the values for the drop-down list. The column that contains the data for the pick list is called a bound column. You will learn about bound and unbound columns as you continue through the lesson. You can change the Limit To list property on the Lookup tab to Yes to limit the user to only the values on the list.

Figure 1-6 Creating a Value List

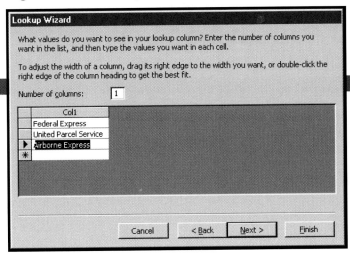

Figure 1-7 Lookup Field properties

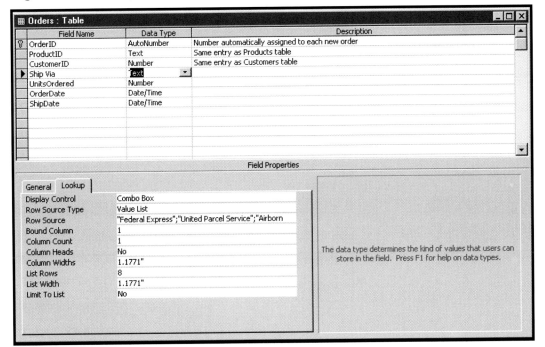

Practice

In the Home Video Collection database, open the Home Video Collection table in Design View. Click in the Data Type cell for the Rating field. Click the list arrow and choose Lookup Wizard on the drop-down list. Click the I will type in the values that I want option button. Click Next. Enter G, PG, PG-13, and R as the values for the drop-down list and complete the wizard. Click the Lookup tab to view the Lookup field properties for the Rating field. Save the changes to the design of the table, and switch to Datasheet View. View the drop-down list, close the table, and minimize the application window.

skill Entering Records in a Datasheet

concept

As you will learn, data is usually entered into a database using a form. While forms are specifically designed to facilitate data entry, you can enter data directly into a table. A new record can only be entered at the end of a datasheet. When you enter data you do not have to worry about saving. Each time you begin a new record or switch to a different window the changes you have made to the records in the datasheet are saved.

do it !

Enter a new record in the Orders table.

1. With the Office Furniture Inc database open, double-click the Orders table in the Database window to open it in Datasheet View.

2. Click the New Record button ▶* on the Table Datasheet toolbar or the New Record navigation button ▶*.

3. Press [Enter] to shift the focus to the second field in the record. The AutoNumber field will be automatically assigned. Type PER499. Press [Enter]. Type 5. Press [Enter]. Click the list arrow and select Federal Express. Press [Enter]. Type 8. Press [Enter]. Type 050801. Press [Enter]. Type 051001. Press [Enter].

4. Click the Maximize button on the Database window Title bar. Press the right arrow key on the keyboard [⟶] and enter the following record:

Product ID	DOW872
Customer ID	18
Ship Via	United Parcel Service
Units Ordered	12
Order Date	5/10/01
Ship Date	5/12/01

5. Increase the size of the Ship Via column so that entire entry can be viewed. Compare your updated Orders table with Figure 1-8.

6. Close the datasheet. You will be prompted to save the change to the layout of the table. The new record is automatically saved.   With the Database window maximized, the Database window fills the Access application window and the sizing buttons for the Database window are on the Menu bar directly below the application sizing buttons.

7. Click the Restore button ⊡ on the right end of the Menu bar to restore the database window to its previous size and location.

more
How you enter data into a field depends on how the field was designed. The Customer ID and Units Ordered fields will only accept numbers. If you enter incorrect data a warning will display to inform you that the value you entered is not valid. Currency fields will also accept only numbers, which will be automatically formatted as currency. The combo box you created will accept either typed text or a selection from the list. You may have noticed that the date fields have already been formatted with the slash marks. This is called an input mask. Input masks are character strings that determine how data will display. Like properties, input masks limit the values a user can enter into a field. You will learn how to create an input mask in Lesson 2.

The two Control menus also contain commands for resizing and closing the Database window and the Access application window. The Control menu icon for the Database window is located to the left of the database name on the Database window Title bar. With the Database window maximized, it is on the left end of the Menu bar. The Control menu icon for the program is the key symbol just to the left of Microsoft Access in the program Title bar. The Control menus contain the Restore, Move, Size, Minimize, Maximize and Close commands.

Figure 1-8 Datasheet View with the Database window maximized

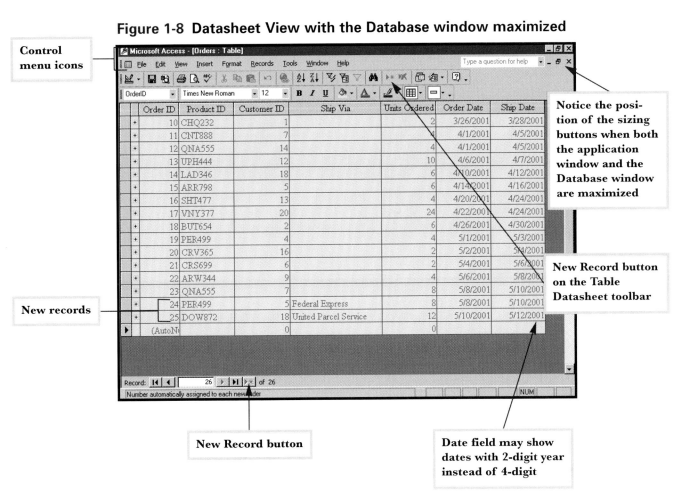

Control menu icons

Notice the position of the sizing buttons when both the application window and the Database window are maximized

New records

New Record button on the Table Datasheet toolbar

New Record button

Date field may show dates with 2-digit year instead of 4-digit

Access 2002

skill

Editing Records in a Datasheet

concept

In order to keep your database both accurate and current you will often have to edit certain records. You can change information you have entered in a field by selecting the text, positioning the insertion point, and using the Backspace and Delete keys on the keyboard. To make editing as efficient as possible you can also use a variety of other keystrokes and commands.

do it !

Edit records in the Customers table. Delete a record from the Products table for a product that the company is no longer going to carry.

1. With the Office Furniture Inc database open, double-click the Customers table icon in the Database window to open the table in Datasheet View.

2. Double-click in the Specific Record box near the bottom of the window. Type 15. Press [Enter]. Press [Tab] twice to move to the Billing Address field. Press [Delete]. Type 1667 Lansing Dr., to update the address. The Edit record symbol [✏] displays in the Record selector while you are editing a record.

3. Click to the right of River in the Billing Address field for record 2 to position the insertion point. Type side, to make the street name Riverside. Use the right arrow key [→] on the keyboard to move the insertion point to the end of Road. Press the [Backspace] key three times. Type: d. to change to the abbreviation Rd as shown in Figure 1-9.

4. Press the down arrow key [▼] 4 times to move to the Billing Address field for record 6. Position the insertion point to the right of the letter e in Lindsey. Press [Backspace] and type a. Press [Tab] to move to the next field. Press [Esc]. The editing change you just completed is reversed. When you are still editing the same record you can use the [Esc] key to undo changes.

5. Click to the left of the r in Nartico in the City field of record 18. Press [Delete]. Type: n. Press [Tab]. Change the State entry to SC. Press [→]. Click the Undo button [↺] on the Table Datasheet toolbar to reverse the changes you have made to the current record.

6. Click to the left of the n in Jonston in the Company Name field for record 15. Type h. Press [Tab] twice. Add Lake to the end of Indigo. Press [▲] twice.

7. In the City field for record 13, change Michaelton to Michaeltown. Press [Tab]. Change the state to NH. Press [▲]. Click Edit on the Menu bar. Click the Undo command. Notice that the command tells you that you are undoing the changes to the saved record. All of the changes you made to record 13 are reversed. Close the Customers table.

8. Open the Products table in Datasheet View. Select record 5. Click the Delete Record button [✖] on the Table Datasheet toolbar to delete Product ID # CNT343. You will be prompted to confirm the deletion as shown in Figure 1-10, because it cannot be reversed. Click [Yes] . Close the Products table.

more

In Edit mode you can either press [Esc] or click Undo to undo all of the changes you have made in the current record. However, after you have moved to another record and are back in Navigation mode, the changes are saved. You can no longer use the [Esc] key. You can, however, click Undo to reverse all changes to the last saved record. ◀▬▶ Press the keyboard combination [Shift]+[Tab] to return to the previous field. ◀▬▶ You can use the keyboard shortcut F2 to switch from Edit mode to Navigation mode. Use [Ctrl]+['] to insert the value in the same field in the previous record in the current field.

Figure 1-9 Editing Records

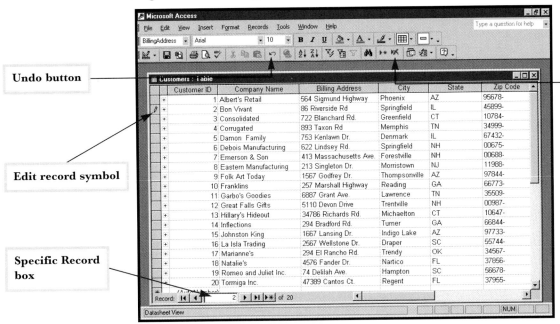

Figure 1-10 Deletion warning dialog box

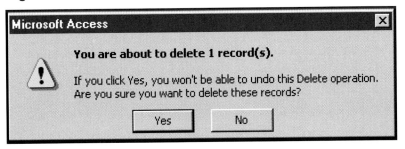

Practice

Open Microsoft Word using the Start menu. Then open the Word file acprac1-7.doc and follow the instructions it contains. When you have completed the exercise, close Word. You do not need to save any changes to the Word file.

skill   Understanding Shared Fields

concept

Each table in a database contains data about one subject. Each field, except the shared fields, should be stored in only one table. If a field in a table will cause the same piece of data to be repeated multiple times, it is in the wrong table. You want to be able to update information in only one place in the database and to avoid not only duplicate entries but entries for the same field that contain inconsistent data. Each table must also contain a unique field that identifies each record in the table. These are the shared fields that will allow you to connect data that is stored in separate tables.

do it !

Examine the relationships in the Office Furniture Inc database.

1. With the Office Furniture Inc. database open, double-click the Customers table to open it in Datasheet View. You may have noticed a column of plus signs ⊞, or expand indicators, in between the Record selectors and the first column of fields. This indicates that a sub-datasheet exists. A subdatasheet is simply a nested datasheet that contains related data. Click the expand indicator for the first record in the table. The shared Customer ID field links the record for Albert's Retail with the orders it has placed with Office Furniture Inc.

2. Click the expand indicator ⊞ to the left of the Order ID field in the Orders subdatasheet. The shared Product ID field links the Orders table with the Products table. You can now clearly see, as shown in Figure 1-11, that Albert's Retail placed an order on 3/26/01 for 2 channel quilted barstools. You can edit the data in the subdatasheets to change it in the joined table.

3. Click in the Ship Via field. Click the list arrow and choose Airborne Express on the drop-down list.

4. Click the Collapse indicators ⊟ to close the subdatasheets (or click the top indicator to close both subdatasheets at once). Close the Customers table and open the Orders table to view the updated record. Close the Orders table.

5. Click the Relationships button ⊞ on the Database toolbar to open the Relationships window as shown in Figure 1-12. Notice the line joining the Customers table and the Orders table. There is a 1 next to the Customer ID field in the Customers table and an infinity symbol ∞ next to the Customer ID field in the Orders table. This indicates that the value in the Customer ID field in the Customers table will match many records in the Orders table. The logical relationship has been established. One customer over time will place many different orders with a company. This is called a one-to-many relationship. You can see why the shared Customer ID field is so important. It allows you to build an ongoing customer purchase history with a minimum of effort. Each customer's purchasing history is automatically compiled as orders are entered in the Orders table.

6. Close the Relationships window. Open the Customers table in Datasheet View again. Understand that each customer number must be unique; that is, no two customers can be assigned the same number. Although at present the AutoNumber fields are listed in sequential order this will not always be the case. For example, if Customer ID #10, Franklins, were to go out of business, you might delete the record from the database. Customer ID #10 will never be reused.

7. Close the Customers table.

more
Access automatically creates a subdatasheet for a table on the one side of a one-to-many relationship. You will learn more about relationships and how to create the relationships between tables in the next lesson. For now, you should understand that the design of a table is the set of instructions regarding the arrangement of the data within each record. These instructions include the type of data each field can accept and the format for that data, such as the number of characters allowed in each field. The unique identifier fields are used to logically link information in the database. In a rela-tional database you will tend to create many small tables because you can use the shared fields to establish relationships that will allow you to store information only once, organize it in a logical way, and bring it back together again in meaningful ways. A well-designed database should contain organized, related data that is stored only once. It should provide efficient data entry methods and include relationships that link basic entities.

Figure 1-11 Subdatasheets for the Customers table

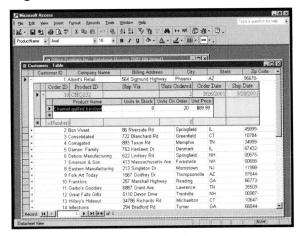

Figure 1-12 Relationships window

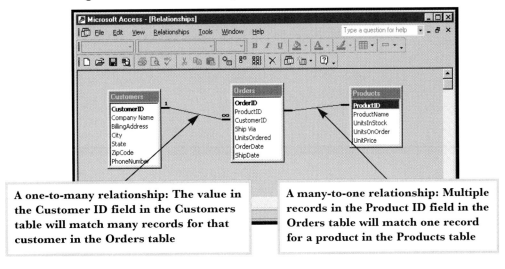

A one-to-many relationship: The value in the Customer ID field in the Customers table will match many records for that customer in the Orders table

A many-to-one relationship: Multiple records in the Product ID field in the Orders table will match one record for a product in the Products table

Practice

In the Home Video Collection database, open the Genre table in Datasheet View. Click the expand indicator for the first record in the table. The shared Genre ID field links the two tables. The movies that have been assigned the Genre ID # 1 for Sci/Fi Adventure display in the subdatasheet. Open several more subdatasheets to see the videos that have been placed in each genre category. Close the table and open the Relationships window. You can see the one-to-many relationship that has been created between the two tables. Each Genre ID # will be represented many times in the Home Video Collection table. Use the Close button on the application Title bar to close the Access application window containing the Home Video Collection database.

skill | Getting Help and Exiting Access

concept

There are a variety of ways to get help in Access. You can use the What's This command, ask the Office Assistant, or use the Ask a Question box on the right end of the Menu bar. The latter two features will generate a list of options. You click an option to open the Help window on that topic.

do it !

Learn how to use the Help facilities in Access.

1. With the Office Furniture Inc database open and Tables selected on the Objects bar, double-click the Products table icon in the Database window to open it in Datasheet View.

2. Click Help on the Menu bar. Click the What's This command. The mouse pointer changes to the What's This pointer ⌖?. Click the gray square at the top of the column of Record selectors at the intersection of the columns and rows in the table. A ScreenTip tells you that this is the Selector. You can use it to select the entire window to copy it to another program. Close the Products table.

3. Double-click in the Ask a Question box [Type a question for help ▼]. Type field properties. Press [Enter]. The list of topics shown in Figure 1-13 opens. Click the first topic to open the Help window shown in Figure 1-14.

4. Click the second topic in the Help window to display text that will remind you how to change the Field Size property for a text or number field. Close the Help window.

5. Click the Office Assistant to open a search balloon. If the Office Assistant is not on the screen, open the Help menu and click the Show the Office Assistant command.

6. Type: editing a datasheet. Click [Search]. A list of topics is added to the search balloon. Click the fourth topic, Troubleshoot editing data in a field in Datasheet or Form view, as shown in Figure 1-15.

7. Click the second topic to read why a value may not be allowed in a field. Some of the information may not be helpful at this time, but you should understand that entering a value that is not compatible with the data type for the field will cause Access to display an error message informing you that you cannot move to another field or record.

8. Click the Show button ⬚ on the Help Window toolbar to expand the window to a two-paneled format (if you see the Hide button ⬚ instead of the Show button, you are already viewing the two-paneled format). Click the Index tab at the top of the left panel. Position the insertion point in the Type keywords text box and type format. As you are typing, the list in the Or choose keywords list box scrolls to match the letters you type. ⬭ When you are using the two-paneled Help window, the Show button becomes the Hide button. Click the Hide button to collapse the Help window back to the single-panel format (do not do this now).

9. Click [Search]. All of the Help topics related to the keyword format display in the Choose a topic scrolling list box at the bottom of the window.

(continued on AC 1.20)

Figure 1-13 List of Help topics

If this list doesn't provide you with the help you need, try rephrasing your query. For example, "Print multiple copies of a file" will lead to more specific help topics than "print."

- Set or change a field's data type or size
- About expressions
- Change the record source or connection information
- Expand a field, property box or text box to make it easier to edit
- Troubleshoot tables and field properties
- ▼ See more...

Figure 1-14 Microsoft Access Help window

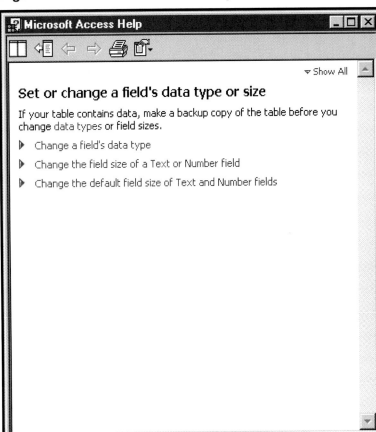

Figure 1-15 Getting help from the Office Assistant

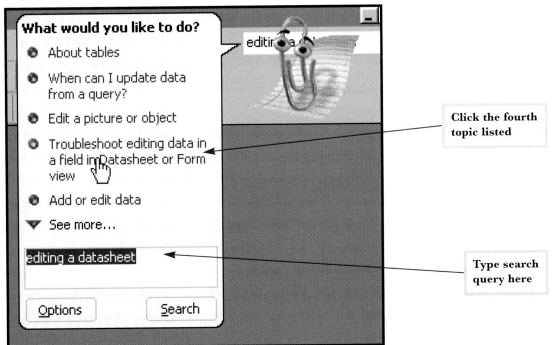

skill

Getting Help and Exiting Access (cont'd)

do it !

10. Click Format Property - Date/Time Data Type to display the Help window shown in Figure 1-16. Read about the pre-defined Format property settings for the Date/Time data type.

11. Close the Help window. Complete the Practice session.

12. Open the File menu and click the Close command to close the Office Furniture Inc. database. Open the File menu and click the Exit command to close Access. ⬳ The Close command on the File menu corresponds to the Close button on the Database window title bar and thus will close the Database window. The Exit command corresponds to the Close button on the application title bar and thus will close the Access program.

more

The Contents tab contains every Help topic in Access broken down by category. A book icon represents each main category. Click the expand indicator next to one of the book icons to open the topic and reveal the subtopics. A page icon with a question mark on it designates each individual topic document. Click a document on the left to display it in the right half of the window. To close a Help category, click the collapse indicator next to the now open-book icon. Use the Back button on the Help window toolbar to return to topics you have previously viewed.

The Answer Wizard tab functions similarly to the Office Assistant. Enter a question in the What would you like to do? text box. Click the Search button to display a list of suggested topics in the Select topic to display box.

Figure 1-16 Help on Format Property feature

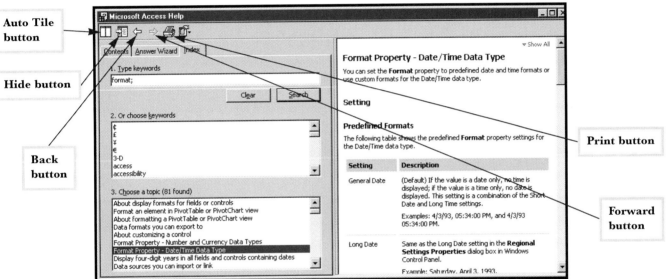

Auto Tile button

Hide button

Back button

Print button

Forward button

Practice

Type insert a field in the Office Assistant search balloon and click [Search] Open the Help window for the topic: Add a field to a table. Click Add a field to a table in Design View. Read the text to review some of the information you have learned in this lesson.

shortcuts

Function	Button/Mouse	Menu	Keyboard
Open a file		Click File, then click Open	[Ctrl]+[O]
Large Icons View in Database window		Click View, then click Large Icons	[Alt]+[G]
Small Icons View in Database window		Click View, then click Small Icons	[Alt]+[M]
List View in Database Window		Click View, then click List	[Alt]+[I]
Details View in Database window		Click View, then click Details	[Alt]+[D]
Switch to Datasheet View		In Table Design View, click View, then click Datasheet View	[Alt]+[V], [S]
Switch to Design View		In Table Datasheet View, click View, then click Design View	[Alt]+[V], [D]
Delete a row from a table		In Table Design View, click Edit, then click Delete Rows	[Alt]+[E], [R]
Insert a row in a table		In Table Design View, click Insert, then click Rows	[Alt]+[I], [R]
Begin entering a new record in a datasheet		Click Edit, point to Go To, then click New Record or click Insert, then click New Record	[Ctrl]+[+]
Delete a record from a datasheet		Click Edit, then click Delete Record	[Alt]+[E], [R]
Undo		Click Edit, then click Undo	[Esc] or [Alt]+[E], [U]
Fill/Back Color			
Font/Fore Color			
Open the Relationships window		Click Tools, then click Relationships	[Alt]+[T], [R]

A. Identify Key Features

Name the items indicated by callouts in Figure 1-17.

Figure 1-17 Microsoft Access window

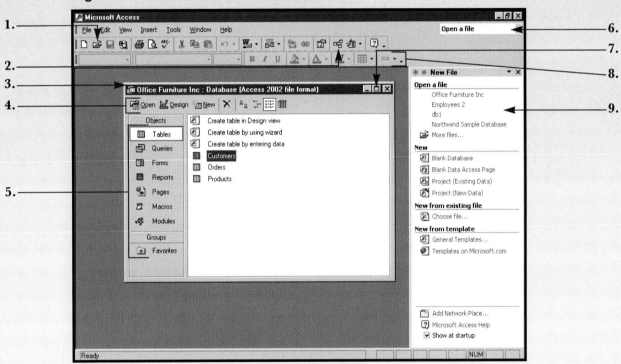

B. Select the Best Answer

10. A set of related fields is called a _____

11. To the left of the first field column is a column of gray boxes called the

12. The basis for the database—collections of records with related data

13. The Exit command on the File menu will close

14. This designates what kind of data a field can accept

15. You set these to further restrict the type of data that can be entered into a field

16. The smallest element of data is a _____

17. Data type that automatically enters a sequential number in the field as records are added to the table

18. Each column heading is a _____ that you can use to select the column

19. The Close command on the File menu will close the _____

a. Field

b. Field Properties

c. Field selector

d. Record

e. Database window

f. AutoNumber

g. Tables

h. Access

i. Record selectors

j. Data Type

quiz (continued)

C. Complete the Statement

20. A column contains:

a. Values of the same data type for different records

b. A set of related fields

c. A collection of different fields with related data

d. A collection of values in the same record

21. The set of instructions regarding the arrangement of the data within each record (the type of data each field can accept and the format for that data) is called:

a. The data type

b. The format property

c. The design of a table

d. The field properties

22. When you enter data in a table:

a. Only changes to the table design will be automatically saved, you must save new records frequently.

b. You must save frequently so that your data entry work will not be lost in the event of a power outage.

c. Each time you begin a new record or switch to a different window the changes you have made to the records in the datasheet are saved.

d. Access will remind you to save your data entry work when you close the table.

23. The two required field properties are:

a. The data type and the format

b. The field name and the data type

c. The field size and the format

d. The field name and the field size

24. The advantages of computerized databases over catalogs, index cards, and other paper methods are all of the following except:

a. The almost limitless capacity to store data

b. The speed, accuracy, and efficiency with which you can retrieve information

c. The highly organized method of storing data

d. The flexibility that enables you to reorganize and access data in many different ways

25. To navigate to the row in a table where you can begin entering the data for a new record, you can use all of the following except:

a. The keyboard combination [Ctrl]+[+]

b. The New Record navigation button

c. A field selector in Datasheet View

d. The New Record button on the Table Datasheet toolbar

26. A row contains:

a. All of the fields for one particular category of data

b. A set of related fields

c. A collection of different records with related data

d. A collection of related information

27. The advantages of a relational database are all of the following except:

a. Each piece of information must be entered and stored only once. You update data in one place and it is automatically updated throughout the database.

b. You can create links between tables to eliminate duplicate data and the possibility that the same item of data will be entered differently in two places.

c. Information is organized alphabetically for easy retrieval.

d. The number of data entry errors that can be made is dramatically reduced.

interactivity

Build Your Skills

1. Start Access and browse an existing database.

   a. Use the Start menu or any method you choose to start Access. Open the Recipes database in your Access Student Files folder.

   b. Open the Recipes table. Use the Specific Record box to navigate to record 48. Use the correct keyboard combination to return to the first record in the table.

   c. Use the correct navigation button to move the focus to the last field in the table.

   d. Press [↑] three times to move the focus to record 47. Press [Tab] three times.

   e. Press [Ctrl]+[End], the keyboard combination for moving the focus to the last field in the last record in the table.

2. Examine the Design View window, rearrange the fields, and insert a new field.

   a. Switch to Design View.

   b. Notice the Data Types used for each field. An OLE (object linking and embedding) object is simply a large object, usually a graphic but also any document prepared in another program. In the recipe database, the instructions for each recipe are (or will be when the database is complete) contained in an embedded Word document.

   c. Click in the TimetoPrepare field. Change the Field Size to 30.

   d. Use the Row selector to select the FoodCategoryID field. Move it underneath the RecipeID field.

   e. Select the TimetoPrepare field. Insert a new row. Click in the Field Name cell for the new row. Name the new field WhichMeal?

   f. Save the changes to the design of the table. Click Yes when warned about lost data. Return to Datasheet View.

3. Format a datasheet.

   a. With the Recipes table open in Datasheet View, maximize the window.

   b. Change the font for the table to Book Antiqua in a Bold style.

   c. Open the Datasheet Formatting dialog box and change the Gridline Color to Teal. Change the Cell Effect to Sunken. Close the dialog box.

   d. Change the Fill/Back Color to light yellow.

   e. Save the changes to the design of the table.

4. Create a drop-down list.

   a. Open the Recipes table in Design View. Click in the Data Type cell for the WhichMeal? field.

   b. Click the list arrow and select Lookup Wizard on the drop-down list.

interactivity (continued)

Build Your Skills (cont'd)

c. Click the I will type in the values that I want option button. Click Next.

d. Make sure 1 column is selected in the Number of columns text box. Type Breakfast in the first field. Press [Tab]. Enter Lunch, Dinner, Dessert and Appetizer as the other choices for the pick list. Size the column to the best fit. Click Next.

e. Make sure Which Meal? is selected as the label for the lookup column and click Finish.

f. Switch to Datasheet View. Save the change to the design of the table when prompted.

g. Click in the Which Meal? field of the first record, Hot Sausage Rolls. Click the list arrow and select Appetizer on the drop-down list.

5. Entering a record in a datasheet.

a. Click the New record button on the Table Datasheet toolbar.

b. Enter the following 2 records:

Recipe ID	Food Category ID	Recipe Name	Which Meal?	Time to Prepare	Number of Servings	Instructions	Vegetarian
Auto Number (Press[Tab])	1	Pepper Sirloin Steak	Dinner	25 min	6	(Skip)	No (leave unchecked)
Auto Number (Press[Tab])	10	Chocolate Turtle Cheesecake	Dessert	35 min	12	(Skip)	N/A (leave unchecked)

c. Right-click in the Instructions field for the Pepper Sirloin Steak record. Click Insert Object on the shortcut menu. Click the Create from file option button in the Microsoft Access dialog box. Click Browse to open the Browse dialog box. Use the Look in list box to locate your Access Student Files. Select the Pepper Sirloin Steak document and click OK. Click OK to close the Microsoft Access dialog box. The Instructions field now says Microsoft Word Document. Double-click in the field to view the embedded object.

d. Follow the instructions in the previous step to embed the Chocolate Turtle Cheesecake recipe in the Instructions field for the record.

6. Editing Records in a datasheet.

a. Change the Recipe Name field for Record 4 to Vegetable Chicken Pasta.

b. On record 11, change the number of servings to 6 and enter Dinner in the Which Meal? field.

c. On record 14, fix the spelling on Deviled and enter Appetizer in the Which Meal? field.

d. Change the Food Category ID on record 24 to 11. Enter Dessert in the Which Meal? field.

interactivity (continued)

Build Your Skills (cont'd)

7. Examine the relationship between the two tables.

   a. Close the Recipes table. Open the Food Category table in Datasheet View.

   b. Open the subdatasheet for the first record, Beef. The two recipes in this category display. Examine the other sub-datasheets. The shared Food Category ID field links the two tables.

   c. Close the Food Category table. Open the Relationships window.

   d. A one-to-many relationship exists between the Food Category and Recipes tables. Each Food category will apply to many entries in the Recipes table.

   e. Close the Relationships window.

8. Get Help and exit Access

   a. Type designing a database, in the Ask a question box. Click About designing a database. Read the page.

   b. Click the Show button if necessary. Open the Contents tab. Click the expand indicator next to Microsoft Access Help.

   c. Click the Expand indicator next to Tables. Click the About Tables document.

   d. Click How data is organized in tables. Read the information and close the Help window

   e. Click the Close button on the application Title bar to exit Access.

Problem Solving Exercises

1. For each example of a database given below, write down at least five fields you would expect to find and examples of two possible records. Write down the data type for each field.

   a. CD collection

   b. Address book

   c. Book store inventory

   d. Coin collection

   e. Recipe file

   f. Teacher's grade book

   g. Sporting equipment catalog

2. You have been hired by Ruloff and Dewitt, a rapidly growing advertising agency that specializes in promoting new products and services. For your first project you must compile data on the magazine preferences of a cross-section of people. This data will eventually be stored and maintained in an Access database. Your initial assignment is to plan the database on paper following database design principles. First, make a list of the fields that should be included in the database. Create fields for the following:

interactivity (continued)

Problem Solving Exercises (cont'd)

a. a unique identification number for each record

b. First Name

c. Last Name

d. Age

e. Gender

f. Occupation

g. Number of Magazines Read Regularly

h. Favorite Magazine

i. Hobbies

Either collect or fabricate data for 25 people and write it down in a table format. Next, group the fields to form three different tables. Plan all three tables keeping in mind that you are planning a relational database. Make sure you write down the fields for each table and the data type for each field. Be sure to name all three tables. The three tables must share at least one common field (one of the unique identification fields) so that they can be joined later.

Creating Tables and Queries

Now that you are familiar with the Access application window, the basic structure of a database, and the structure and design of a table, you are ready to begin building your own databases. When you plan a database, you must first decide how many and what kind of tables your database will need. You will need to determine how the data you are collecting can be organized into separate smaller groups and how the fields in the tables can be related to each other. As you have learned, each table will contain fields related to one topic and each field will be assigned an appropriate data type to designate the kind of data that can be entered into the field. By focusing each table on a particular topic you simplify the structure of each table making them easier to modify later. As you have seen, the shared fields will enable you to link related information in other tables so that you can easily view all of the orders associated with a particular customer, all of the movies in a particular genre, or all of the recipes in a particular food category.

When you create a new database, you first create and save an empty database and then create the objects the database will contain. You can use a Database Wizard to quickly create a complete database on one of ten business topics. The simplest way to create a table is to use the Table Wizard. The Wizard guides you through a series of dialog boxes that help you to choose the fields for the database or the fields for the table. However, you will eventually want to create your tables in the Design View window to have more control over the finished product. As you have seen, in the Design View window you work with the underlying structure of the table. You enter the names for your fields and the data type for each field and set field properties for fields in which you want to alter the format or otherwise restrict the data that the field can accept. You must also identify the field that will serve as the primary key for the table. Primary keys are the fields containing the value that will uniquely identify each record in the table. In other words, the primary key is the shared field that will enable you to link the records in one table to records in other tables. When you have built all of the tables for your database you will create the relationships by forming joins between the shared fields.

After you have created your tables you can use various methods to reorganize data. You will learn how to sort data so that it is displayed in either ascending or descending order and filter data so that you can work with a temporary subset of records. You will also learn how to locate a specific piece of data using the Find command.

You create queries to answer questions about the data in your tables. These questions create permanent subsets of data. For example, you might want to know what customers have placed orders with your company in the last three months or what movies in your home video collection are rated PG. Queries allow you to focus on the data that you need to work with at present by eliminating all records in a table that do not match the criteria that you set.

Lesson Goal:

Create a database from a template. Create the tables to store the employee data for a company. Set and modify field properties. Learn to find, sort, and filter data and create queries.

skills

≩ **Creating a Database with the Database Wizard**

≩ **Using the Table Wizard**

≩ **Modifying Field Properties**

≩ **Creating an Input Mask**

≩ **Setting a Validation Rule**

≩ **Creating a Table in Design View**

≩ **Establishing Table Relationships**

≩ **Sorting and Finding Records**

≩ **Filtering Records**

≩ **Using the Simple Query Wizard**

≩ **Creating a Calculated Field in a Query**

skill

Creating a Database with the Database Wizard

MOUS Skill

concept

The easiest way to create a new database is to use a Database Wizard. The Access Database Wizards provide a number of different databases that are commonly used in business. When you use a Wizard, all of the fields, tables, queries, forms, and reports that you will need in the database are created for you. You can examine one of the completed templates to give you a better idea of what all of the objects will look like and how to design your own custom database.

do it!

Create a database using a Database Wizard.

1. Start Access. Click General Templates in the New from template section on the Task Pane. The Templates dialog box opens. Click the Databases tab.

2. Select the Order Entry icon as shown in Figure 2-1. Click ⬛ OK ⬛.

3. The File New Database dialog box opens. Click the list arrow on the Save in list box and select the drive where your Access Student Files folder is located. Double-click the folder in the Contents window of the dialog box to place it in the Save in list box. Order Entry1 has been entered for you in the File name text box as shown in Figure 2-2. Click ⬛ Create ⬛. 🔘 Whenever you create a new database either with a wizard or from a blank file, you must first save it with the name you have chosen and in the location where you want to store it.

4. The Order Entry1 database is created and saved in your Access Student Files folder window and the Order Entry1 Database window opens. The first Database Wizard dialog box opens on top of it. Read the list of information the database will contain and click ⬛ Next > ⬛ to continue.

5. The next Wizard dialog box contains boxes that display the Tables in the database and the Fields in the table. You can scroll to the bottom of the fields in the Fields in the table list box to add the optional fields, E-mail address or Notes to the Customer information table.

6. Click each table name in the Tables in the database box and read the list of fields the table will contain. Click ⬛ Next > ⬛.

7. Click Sumi Painting to select it as the style for your screen displays and click ⬛ Next > ⬛.

8. Click Corporate, if necessary, to select it as the style for your reports. Click ⬛ Next > ⬛.

9. Keep the selected title for the database, Order Entry, and click ⬛ Finish ⬛.

10. The Database Wizard creates the database objects for the Order Entry database (this may take a minute or more). Then a dialog box opens telling you that you must enter your company information before you can use the database application. Click ⬛ OK ⬛.

(continued on AC 2.4)

Figure 2-1 Choosing a Database Wizard

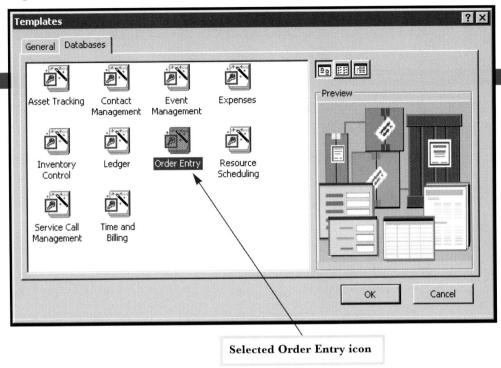

Selected Order Entry icon

Figure 2-2 File New Database dialog box

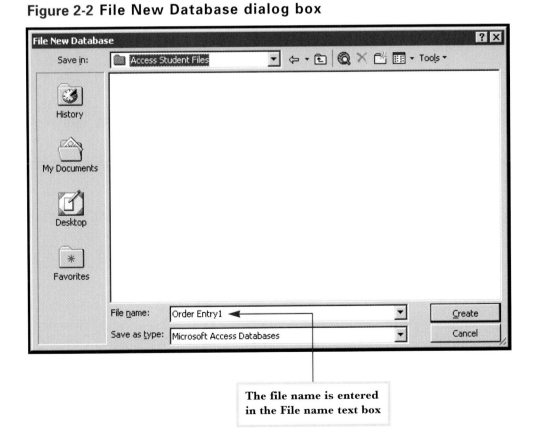

The file name is entered
in the File name text box

skill Creating a Database with the Database Wizard (cont'd)

do it!

11. The My Company Information form opens. Enter the information given below into the form pressing the [Tab] key to move to each new field. Click the Close button on the form Title bar when you are finished.

Browder's Comics, 6871 Franklin Dr., Ashlawn, MO, 84538, USA, .07, (skip the Default terms and Invoice description fields) 816-555-1766, 816-555-1767

12. The Main Switchboard opens as shown in Figure 2-3. Click Enter/View Other Information button ▦. Click Enter/View Employees button ▦. The Employees form opens as shown in Figure 2-4. You can see how a form will simplify data entry. Each employee record will be listed on a separate screen. Close the form. Close the switchboard.

A switchboard is a custom window that contains command buttons for opening the objects in the database that a user is most likely to need. It will often contain buttons for opening the forms that data entry operators will use to enter information into the database. It will also usually enable management personnel to easily access the reports they will need to make strategic decisions.

13. Click the Restore button ⊡ on the Order Entry title bar in the lower-left corner of the application window.

14. Click Tables on the Objects bar, then open the Employees table in Datasheet View, as shown in Figure 2-5. The Employees form you opened in Step 12 will be used to enter the Employee information into this table. Close the table.

15. Use the Objects bar to view the objects the Wizard has created for the database. Click Queries, then Forms, then Reports. Open several tables and their corresponding forms.

16. When you have finished close the Database window.

more

If a database contains a switchboard it usually opens first when the database is opened. All of the databases created with the Database Wizard include a switchboard. When you become more proficient with Access you can add a switchboard to the databases you create. You can use a switchboard to make it easier for new users to access the forms, reports or queries that they will need to use. You can also use a switchboard to control what objects in the database you will allow users to access.

Figure 2-3 Switchboard for an Access database

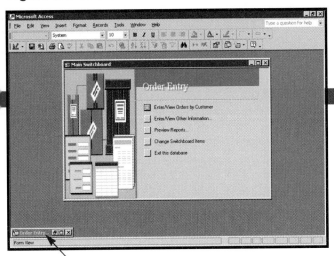

Order Entry Title bar

Figure 2-4 Employees form for the Order Entry database

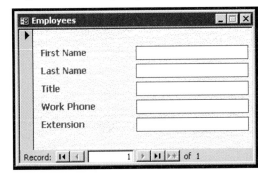

Figure 2-5 Employees table

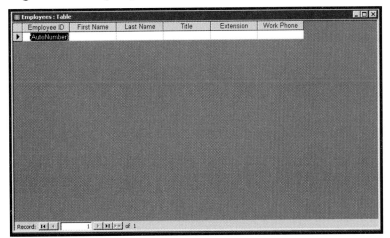

Practice

Click the New button ▯ on the Database toolbar to reopen the task pane. Use the Database wizard to create the Expenses database. Apply any screen display style and Report style you choose. When the database is complete, use the switchboard to open and view the Expense eports by Employee form. Open several tables and their corresponding forms. Open the Relationships window and view the relationships between the tables. When you have finished, close the database. If storage space is a concern for you, you may delete this database.

skill | Using the Table Wizard

concept

After you have determined what tables your database will need and what fields you will need in your tables, you can begin to build your database. You can use the Table Wizard to easily build your first table. The Table Wizard provides a variety of pre-made business and personal tables. You can choose from among the fields offered in each type of table to create a table that fits your needs. The Table Wizard will choose the correct data types and field sizes for you and organize and assemble the fields in the table.

do it!

Create a new database file and use the Table Wizard to create a table.

1. Click the New button on the Database toolbar to re-open the Task Pane. Click Blank Database under New on the Task Pane. The File New Database dialog box opens.

2. Use the Save in list box to locate your Access Student Files folder. Double-click in the File name text box and type Employees 1. Click [Create]. The Employees 1 database is created and saved in your Access Student Files folder and the Database window for the Employees 1 database opens.

3. Double-click Create table by using wizard in the Employees 1 Database window. The first Table Wizard dialog box opens as shown in Figure 2-6.

4. With the Business option button selected as shown in Figure 2-6, click Employees in the Sample Tables scrolling list box.

5. Click Employee ID in the Sample Fields scrolling list box. Click the Add Field button [>] to add the field to the Fields in my new table box.

6. Double-click Last Name in the Sample Fields scrolling list box to add it the Fields in my new table box.

7. Use one of these two methods to add the First Name, Address, City, State or Province, and Postal Code fields to the Fields in my new table box. You will have to use the down scroll arrow on the Sample Fields scrolling list box to locate the fields. Click [Next >].

8. Keep the name for the table the Wizard has selected, Employees, and leave the Yes, set a primary key for me option button selected as shown in Figure 2-7. Click [Next >].

9. Click the Modify the table design option button as shown in Figure 2-8 and click [Finish]. The table opens in Design View. Notice the primary key symbol in the Row selector next to the Employee ID field. The Wizard has chosen the Employee ID field as the field you will use to link the records in the Employees table to records in other tables.

10. Leave the table open in Design View for the next skill.

more

The Table Wizard will automatically assign the Number data type and an appropriate field size to fields that will require only numbers. Fields for costs or prices will be assigned the Currency data type and fields such as the Required by Date and Promised by Date in the list of fields for the Orders table will be correctly assigned the Date/Time data type. When you use the Table Wizard to create a table you can choose fields from different sample tables, click Rename Field button [Rename Field...] to change a field name, and open the table in Design View to further modify the structure.

Figure 2-6 First Table Wizard dialog box

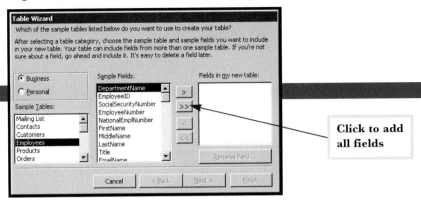

Figure 2-7 Second Table Wizard dialog box

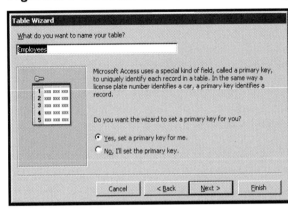

Figure 2-8 Final Table Wizard dialog box

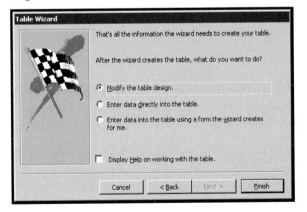

Practice

Use the Start menu to open a second Access application window. Open the Tuning Tracker database available in your Access Student Files folder. Use the Table wizard to create an Orders table. Select the Order ID, Customer ID, Order Date, RequiredbyDate, and PromisedbyDate fields. Let Access select the primary key for you and leave the name for the table, Orders. When you get to the third Wizard dialog box, simply click Next >. You will create the table relationships later in the lesson. Leave the Enter data directly into the table option button selected and click Finish. Resize the fields to display the complete column headings and save the changes. Close the table and minimize the application window.

skill

Modifying Field Properties

MOUS Skill

concept

You can use the Table Wizard to quickly create a table and then modify its properties in the Design View window to meet your needs. For example, you can modify the field names, set additional field properties, add field descriptions, or add fields that the Wizard does not offer.

do it!

Change field names, add field descriptions, add a field, and change field properties for the Employees table.

1. Click in the StateOrProvince field. Use [Backspace] and [Delete] keys to delete OrProvince. Double-click in the Field Size cell in the Field Properties pane and type 2, to restrict the field size. Press [Tab] to move to the Format cell.

2. Type >. The greater than symbol instructs Access to make all characters in the field upper-case. Each two-letter state abbreviation will be automatically capitalized. Press [Tab] twice to move to the Caption cell.

3. Change the Caption property for the field to State. Press [Tab].

4. Type NY, in the Default Value cell. For a company located in New York, this would be the most likely entry for the field. Setting a default value will save data entry personnel time when entering records.

5. Click in the Description cell for the State field. Type Default is NY; 2 characters limit; converted to uppercase. Press [Enter]. The Design View window should look like Figure 2-9. ⬛ The description will display in the Status bar in the lower-left corner of the Access application window when the field is selected in Datasheet View.

6. Click in the PostalCode field. Change the field name to ZipCode. Press [Tab] twice and enter the description 10 character limit. Click in the Caption cell in the Field Properties pane. Change the Caption property to Zip Code. ⬛ The Caption property controls the text that displays in the Field selector in Datasheet View. When a Caption property has been assigned, changing the Field Name property will not change the column heading.

7. Change the field size for the Zip Code field to 10.

8. Click the Row selector for the LastName field. Click the Insert Rows button ⬛ on the Table Design toolbar to insert a new row. Name the new field DateHired. Press [Tab].

9. Click the list arrow in the Data Type cell. Select Date/Time on the drop-down list. Press [Tab]. Type: Acceptable formats are 6/13/01, Jun 13, 01, or June 13, 2001.

10. Click in the Format cell in the Field Properties pane. Click the list arrow and select Short Date on the drop-down list. Data entry operators can enter any of the valid formats listed in the description, but all will be converted to the short date format, 6/13/01. This ensures that all data in the table will be displayed in a consistent format.

11. Enter Date Hired as the Caption property for the field. Check Figure 2-10 to make sure you have entered all of the properties correctly.

12. Click ⬛ on the Table Design toolbar to save the changes to the design of the table.

more It is considered good database programming practice not to include spaces in field names. Database programmers use an underscore to create spaces in their field names. This is because in programming languages object names cannot contain spaces. If a database programmer must write code for the field, they will have to change the field name. Tables that you create with the Table Wizard will follow this convention. The Caption property is used to create the conventional heading, with spaces, for the field. If you do not enter a Caption property, the field name will be used for the column heading.

Figure 2-9 Field Properties for the State field

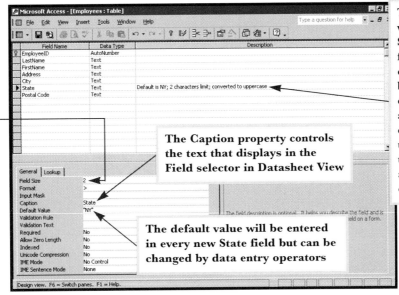

The greater than symbol instructs the program to capitalize the entries in the field

The Caption property controls the text that displays in the Field selector in Datasheet View

The field description will display in the Status bar when the field is selected. It explains that NY will be automatically entered into the field and that the field will only accept 2 characters, and the characters entered will be automatically converted to uppercase

The default value will be entered in every new State field but can be changed by data entry operators

Figure 2-10 Field Properties for the Zip Code field

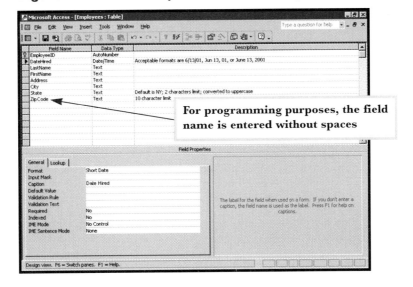

For programming purposes, the field name is entered without spaces

Practice

Open the Customers table in the Tuning Tracker database in Design View. Set the Format property for the State field so that all entries will appear as uppercase letters. Enter a description for the State field. Change the Field Size property for the City field to 25. Change the Field Size property for the Zip field to 10. Create a new field at the end of the table for PhoneNumber and enter the Caption property for the field. Save the changes. Click Yes if you receive a warning about changing a field size, no entry in the City field is over 25 characters so no data will be lost. Minimize the application window.

Access 2002

skill

Creating an Input Mask

concept

Input masks are character strings that determine how data will display in a field. You can use the Input Mask Wizard to set the Input Mask property. The Input Mask property, just like all properties, is used to restrict the data a user can enter into a field. An input mask consists of literal characters (spaces, parentheses, dots, etc.), and placeholder characters. Placeholder text consists of characters such as underscores, which indicate to the user where the values for the field should be entered.

do it!

Use the Input Mask Wizard to set the Input Mask property for the Zip Code field.

1. With the Employees table in the Employees 1 database open in Design View, click in the Zip Code field. Click in the Input Mask cell in the Field Properties pane.

2. Click the Build button ... to the right of the Input Mask cell. The Input Mask Wizard opens.

3. Click Zip Code in the Input Mask/Data Look box. Use the scroll bar to view the various pre-defined input masks available in Access. Click [Next >].

4. Click the list arrow on the Placeholder character list box and select # on the drop-down list.

5. Click in the Try It box. Navigate to the first placeholder character if necessary, and type 223076677. Each placeholder character is replaced as you type a literal character. The field is automatically formatted with the hyphen after the main 5 numbers in the zip code as shown in Figure 2-11. Click [Next >].

6. Click the With the symbols in the mask, like this option button to display the hyphen in the data in the table. Click [Next >]. Click [Finish]. Press [Enter].

7. The completed Input Mask property is shown in Figure 2-12. The 0's for the first five digits of the zip code indicate that an entry is required for each placeholder. The 9's for the last four digits of the zip code indicate that these digits are optional. The slash before the (-) indicates that the hyphen is a literal character that will display in the field.

8. Click 💾 to save the change to the design of the table. Click 📧 to switch to Datasheet View.

9. Scroll to the right and click in the first Zip Code field in front of the first character of the input mask. The input mask appears. Type 2230. Press [Enter]. A Microsoft warning dialog box opens because the first five required digits have not been entered. Click [OK]. Type 7. Press [Enter]. The zip code is entered in the field with the hyphen as the final character. The last four digits are optional. Close the table.

more The Input Mask Wizard can only be used for Text or Date/Time fields. If you want to create an input mask for a Number or Currency field you must enter the formatting symbols yourself to create a custom input mask in the Input Mask property field.

Telephone numbers and zip codes should be assigned the Text data type even though they generally contain numbers. This is because you may want to enter a phone number containing letters and because when sorting fields with the Number data type Access will interpret a telephone number or zip code as a value. If you have entered the zip code 22307 in one place and the zip code 22307-7766 in another, and you sort a table to group records with like zip codes, 22307 will be interpreted as 22,307 and 22307-7766 will be interpreted as 223,077,766. The two zip codes in the same area of the country will not be grouped together in the table. You use an input mask to control not only how data will display as the Format property does, but also how data is entered into a field and stored in the database. The input mask forces the user to enter data in the format that you have set.

Figure 2-11 Using the Input Mask Wizard

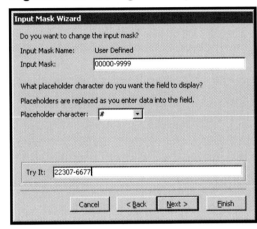

Figure 2-12 Input Mask property

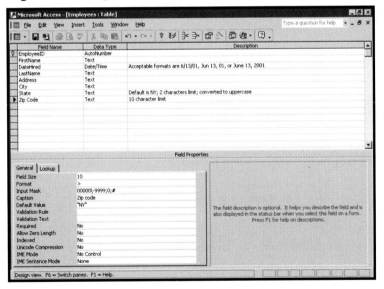

 ## Practice

In the Customers table in the Tuning Tracker database, use the Input Mask Wizard to set the Input Mask property for both the Zip Code field and the Phone Number field. Use any placeholder characters you choose and store the data with the symbols in the mask. Save the changes after you create each mask. Switch to Datasheet View and increase the size of the Zip Code field to accommodate the zip code extensions. Save the change, close the table and minimize the application window.

skill
Setting a Validation Rule

concept

One more method for restricting the values that users can enter into a field is to set the Validation Rule property for a field. A validation rule is a short expression that will test the reasonableness of an entry. If the value the user enters does not satisfy the validation rule criteria, an error message will display. You can set the Validation Text property to designate specific text for the error message. Validation rules allow you to precisely control the data that a field can accept and are yet another method of ensuring that your database contains accurate information.

do it!

Add a field for Gender to the Employees table. Set the Validation Rule property so that only the letters M or F will be accepted in the field. Set the Validation Text property to display a custom error message.

1. Open the Employees table in the Employees 1 database in Design View. Click in the first empty cell below the ZipCode field.

2. Type Gender. Press [Enter]. Leave the default, Text, as the data type.

3. Double-click in the Field Size cell in the Field Properties pane. Type 1. Press [Enter] to move to the Format property.

4. Type >, to program Access to capitalize all entries in the field. Press [Enter] four times to move to the Validation Rule property.

5. Type = M or F to set the validation rule. Access will test the data entered in the field to see if it passes the test. If the user does not enter an m or an f an error message will display. Press [Enter]. Quotation marks are inserted around the two acceptable characters.

6. Type You may only enter M or F to set the validation text. This message will display in the error dialog box if a user enters invalid data. The properties for the new field are shown in Figure 2-13.

7. Click 🖫 on the Table Design toolbar to save the change to the design of the table. The dialog box shown in Figure 2-14 opens. When you add a validation rule you must test the existing data to make sure that it conforms to the new rule. Since this is a new field and no data has yet been entered, click No .

8. Click ⊞⋅ to switch to Datasheet View. Scroll to the right and click in the Gender field for the first record. Type W. Press [Enter]. The warning dialog box shown in Figure 2-15 opens with the text you supplied in the Validation Text property.

9. Click OK . Delete the w and type m. Press [Enter]. The entry is automatically capitalized as designated by the Format property. Close the table.

more Validation rules such as the one created in the exercise, which are based on only one field, are called field-level validation rules. A more complex type of validation rule in which the value of a field depends on an entry that has already been made in another field in the current record is called a table-level validation rule. Data validation rules use expressions that result in one of two values, either True or False. If the result of the expression is True, the data is entered in the field. If the result is False, the error message you entered as the validation text will display.

Figure 2-13 Setting a Validation Rule

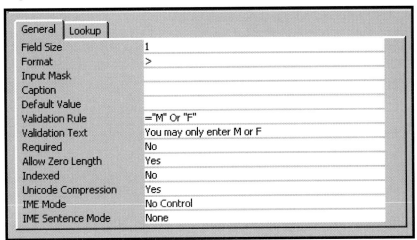

Figure 2-14 Warning dialog box that displays when a validation rule is added to a table

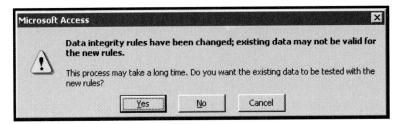

Figure 2-15 Warning dialog box containing the Validation Text

Practice

Open the Service Records table in the Tuning Tracker database in Design View. Change the Field Size property for the Use field to Byte. The Byte field size is the most efficient way to store numeric data that will not be greater than 255. Create a data validation rule to limit the entries in the field to 1–5. The expression is: >0 And <6. Save the change and click Yes to test the existing data. Enter the validation text: Only numbers between 1 and 5 are allowed. Save the change, switch to Datasheet View, and change the data in a record's Use field to test the new properties. Close the table and minimize the application window.

skill | Creating a Table in Design View

concept

Although a table created with the Table Wizard can be modified to fit your data, you will want to create tables on your own in order to have complete control over the field names, data types, and field properties. As you have learned, first you must identify the type of information your table will contain and then determine what data entities to include. Each data entity will be assigned to a field in the table.

do it!

Use all of the skills you have learned thus far to create a table in the Design View window called Positions for the Employees 1 database.

1. With Tables selected on the Objects bar on the Employees 1 Database window, double-click Create table in Design View. The Design View window for Table 1 opens.

2. Type EmployeeID in the first Field Name cell. Press [Enter]. Click the list arrow and select Number on the drop-down list. Press [Tab] two times.

3. Type Department. Press [Enter]. Set the Field Size property to 25.

4. Create a Text field for Title. Create a Currency field for HourlyRate.

5. Create a Yes/No field for StockOptionPlan. Click the Lookup tab. If Check Box is not already entered in the Display Control property, click the list arrow and select it from the drop-down list.

6. Create a field called Status. Use the Lookup Wizard to create a drop-down value list for the field. Enter Temporary, Part-Time, and Full-Time as the values for the pick list. Open the Lookup tab on the Field Properties pane as shown in Figure 2-16.

7. Create a Yes/No field for HealthPlan. Set the Default Value property for the field to Yes. (Type Yes, in the Default Value property cell.) On the Lookup tab, set the Display Control property to Check Box if necessary. The properties of the field are shown in Figure 2-17.

8. Set Caption properties for each field that you want to display in the column heading with spaces included.

9. Click the Row selector for the EmployeeID field. Click the Primary Key button ⎘ on the Table Design toolbar. The key symbol is inserted in the Row selector for the EmployeeID field as shown in Figure 2-17. ◣◢ Remember the primary key field is used to uniquely identify each record in the table. It will be used to link the employee records in the Positions table with the employee records in the Employees table.

10. Click ⊟ on the Table Design toolbar. The Save As dialog box shown in Figure 2-18 opens. Type: Positions in the Table Name text box. Click ⎐ OK ⎏. The table is saved in the Employees 1 database and the table name, Positions, displays in the Design View window title bar.

11. Click ⊞⁃ to switch to Datasheet View. Adjust the column widths to display the complete column headings. Notice that the Health Plan check box is checked because you set the default value for the field to Yes.

12. Save the changes and close the table. Notice that the new table, Positions, is listed under the Employees table in the Database window. Close the Employees 1 database.

more A Yes/No field can appear as a check box, as a text box that displays Yes or No, or as a combo box that has Yes and No on a drop-down list. As you saw in the exercise, you set the Display Control property on the Lookup tab to choose the format you want. If you use a text box, data entry operators will enter -1 and it will be converted to Yes. 0 will be converted to No.

There are three kinds of primary keys. You can create the fields you need in a table without creating a unique identifier field. When you save the table, Access will ask if you want to have the program create a primary key for you. If you click Yes, an AutoNumber primary key field will be automatically created for you. In the exercise above, you created a single-field primary key. You used the Employee ID field which will have a unique value for each employee. If you need data from more than one column in order to meet the uniqueness requirement, you can designate two or more fields as the primary key. This is called a multiple-field or composite primary key.

Figure 2-16 Properties for the Lookup Field

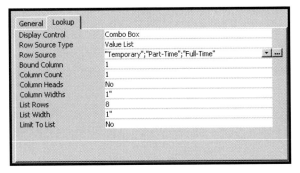

Figure 2-17 Design View Window for the Positions Table

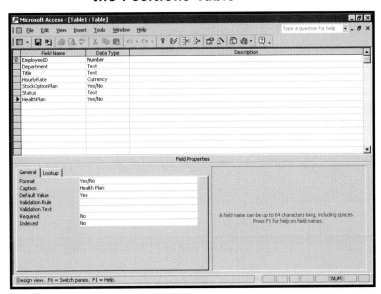

Figure 2-18 Saving a Table

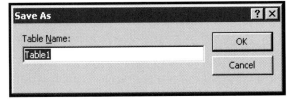

Practice

Create a new table in Design View in the Tuning Tracker database. Name the new table Service History. Create a Number field for CustomerID, a Date/Time field for the TuningDates, and a Yes/No field for TuningDue. Apply the Short Date format to the TuningDates field. Set the Display Control property for the TuningDue field to check box. Set the Caption properties as necessary. Save the table and do not set a primary key. Close the table and minimize the application window.

skill

Establishing Table Relationships

concept

After you have established a way of relating two tables with a common field, you can use the Relationships window to define the type of relationship and establish the joins. There are three types of relationships. You have already viewed a one-to-many relationship in which each record in one table is matched to one or more records in another table. In a one-to-one relationship, each record in one table is matched to only one record in the second table. In a many-to-many relationship, each record in one table is matched to many records in a second table and vice versa.

do it!

Open the Employees 2 database and establish table relationships.

1. Click ⬜ on the Database toolbar to re-open the Task Pane. Click 📂 More files... to access the Open dialog box. Use the Look in list box to locate the drive or folder where your Access Student Files are located. Double-click the folder to place it in the Look in list box. Double-click Employees 2 to open the database.

2. The Employees 2 database contains the Employees table that you built with the Table Wizard, a Position table similar to table that you built in the Design View window, and a third table in which the hours worked by each employee are recorded each week. Records for 51 employees have been added to all three tables.

3. Click the Relationships button 🔗 on the Database toolbar. The Show Table dialog box opens on top of the Relationships window. ✏️ If the Show Table dialog box does not open, click the Show Table command 🔲 Show Table... on the Relationships menu.

4. Press [Shift] and click the two un-highlighted tables in the Show Table dialog box to select all three tables as shown in Figure 2-19. Click 🔲 Add . The field lists for all three tables are added to the Relationships window.

5. Close the Show Table dialog box. Click the Employee ID field in the Employees table field list. Drag the selected field name toward the Employee ID field in the Hours table. As you drag, a small rectangle will display. Do not release the mouse button until the rectangle is over the Employee ID field in the Hours table's field list. The Edit Relationships dialog box opens as shown in Figure 2-20. Access has determined that you are creating a one-to-many relationship as shown at the bottom of the dialog box. Each employee will have one record in the Employees table and a record for the hours worked every week in the Hours table. ✏️ The primary key field for a table will be bold in the field list. To display all of the field names on a field list, Drag the bottom border to increase its size.

6. Select the Enforce Referential Integrity check box (see Figure 2-20). Referential integrity helps reduce data entry errors by ensuring that information in the two related fields matches. You cannot enter data in the field on the Many side of a relationship that does not exist in the related field on the One side.

(continued on AC 2.18)

Figure 2-19 Show Table dialog box

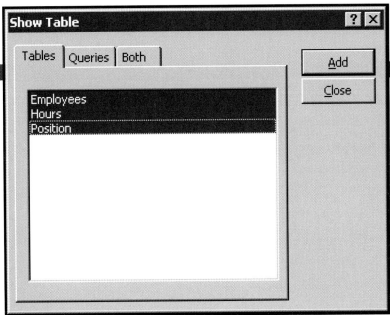

Figure 2-20 Edit Relationships dialog box

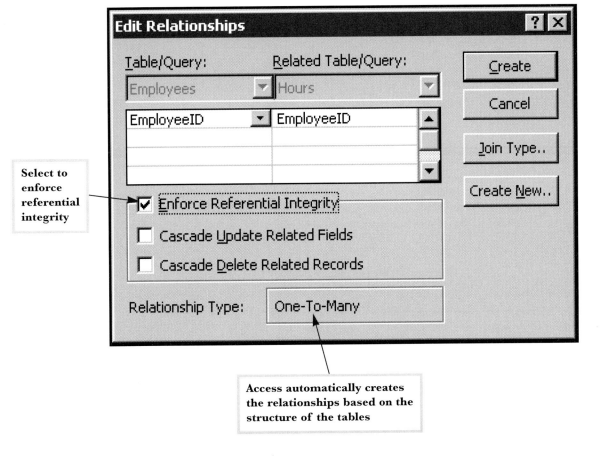

Select to enforce referential integrity

Access automatically creates the relationships based on the structure of the tables

skill Establishing Table Relationships (continued)

do it!

7. Click [Create]. The join is created and a line appears between the two fields to indicate that they are related. The infinity sign [∞] indicates the many side of the relationship.

   ◢ If you do not enforce referential integrity, the joins will be created but the 1 and the infinity symbol will not appear on the line between the joined fields.

8. Select the Employee ID field in the Employees table field list again. Click and drag the field to the Employee ID field in the Position table field list. The Edit relationships dialog box again opens. This time Access has correctly interpreted that you are creating a one-to-one relationship as shown at the bottom of the dialog box and in Figure 2-21.

9. Enforce referential integrity and click [Create].

10. Move the Position field list by clicking and dragging the title bar so that you can clearly see the relationships and your window looks like Figure 2-22.

11. Close the Relationships window. Click [Yes] to save the changes to the layout of the window.

more

When you create relationships, the related fields must have the same data type. However an AutoNumber primary key field can be linked to a Number field as long as the Field Size property for both fields is set to Long Integer. Long Integer is the default field size for a number field. Two Number fields must also have the Long Integer field size in order to establish a link. You set the Field Size property for a Number field to raise or lower the storage requirement for the field. The Byte field size has the lowest storage requirement (takes up the least space in the memory of the computer). You can use it for fields that will only need to hold entries between 0 and 255. The Integer field size is the next most efficient data type. You can use it to store entries between –32,768 and +32,768. Long Integers can be between –2,147,483,648 and +2,147,483,648.

You enforce referential integrity to protect against the accidental deletion of related records. A record in the primary table cannot be deleted if there is a matching record in the related table. Referential integrity will also disallow you from adding a record to the related table that does not have a matching record in the primary table. Furthermore, you cannot change the value of the primary key in the primary table if there is a matching record in the related table. All of this ensures that the relationships between records are valid and that the data in the related fields matches.

Figure 2-21 Defining the Employees/Position table relationship

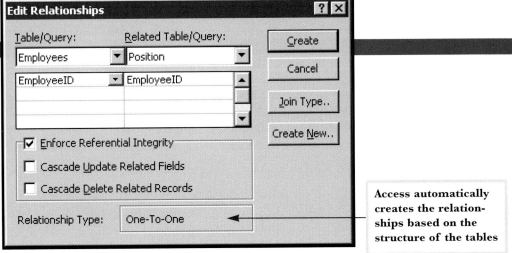

Figure 2-22 Relationship between Employees/Hours Tables and Employees/Position Tables

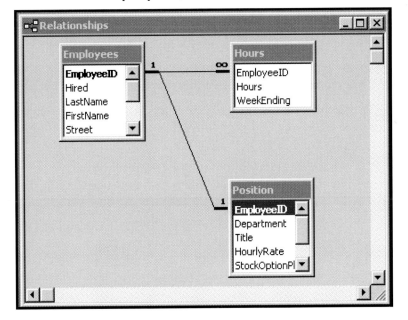

Practice

Open the Relationships window in the Tuning Tracker database. Add the field lists for the Customers, Service Records, and Service History tables to the window. Create the one-to-one relationship between the CustomerID fields in the Customers and Service Records tables. Enforce referential integrity. Create the one-to-many relationship between the CustomerID field in the Customers and Service History tables. Enforce referential integrity. Close the window, saving the changes when prompted. Minimize the application window.

skill

Sorting and Finding Records

concept

Even though you enter records into a table in some kind of logical order, at some point you may need to work with your data in a different order. You can rearrange or sort the records in your tables according to any field you choose. You sort in either Ascending (A to Z, 1 to 10) or descending (Z to A, 10 to 1) order. You also can use the Find command to locate a specific data item within a table. For example you may want to find the record for a particular employee or a particular video.

do it!

Perform a sort on the Employees table in the Employees 2 database based on the Last Name field. Use the Find command to locate and edit a record.

1. Open the Employees table in the Employees 2 database in Datasheet View.

2. Either use the field selector to select the Last Name column or position the insertion point in any of the Last Name fields. Click the Sort Ascending button 🔼 on the Table Datasheet toolbar. The records are sorted by last name alphabetically from A to Z.

3. Click the Find button 🔍 on the Table Datasheet toolbar. The Find and Replace dialog box opens as shown in Figure 2-23. Access has automatically chosen to search within the selected field.

4. Type Van Pelt to replace the current selection in the Find What text box. Click Find Next .

5. The record containing the text Van Pelt is located and highlighted in the table. Click the Replace tab. Type Geddes, in the Replace with list box as shown in Figure 2-24. Click Replace to replace Van Pelt with the employee's new married name.

6. Van Pelt should be selected in the Find What list box. Type De. Click Find Next . A dialog box informs you that the search item was not found. Click OK . A whole field search will only locate an exact match with the Find What box.

7. Click the list arrow on the Match list box. Select Any Part of Field on the drop-down list. Click Find Next . Access selects the record for Adelman, which contains the De sequence in any part of the field. Continue clicking Find Next to view the other records that will be located with this search. Click OK to close the dialog box when the search is complete.

8. Click the list arrow on the Match list box. Select Start of Field on the drop down list. Press [Enter]. This time Access locates the record for DeBois. Press [Enter] again. There are no more records with the De sequence at the start of the field. Click OK and close the Find and Replace dialog box.

9. Close the Employees table. Click Yes to leave the table sorted alphabetically by last name.

more You can use wildcard characters as placeholders for other characters when you only know part of the value you want to find or you want to find values that begin with a certain letter or match a certain pattern. For example, you can enter st* to find start, still and stitch, or w?ll to find well, wall and will. Figure 2-25 explains the various wildcard symbols you can use to help you locate specific items of data. You can also check the Match Case check box to locate entries that match the uppercase and lowercase configuration of the text in the Find What list box.

Figure 2-23 Find tab in Find and Replace dialog box

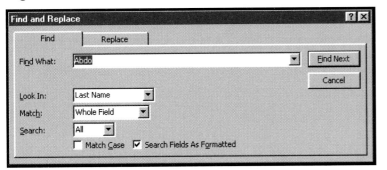

Figure 2-24 Replace tab in Find and Replace dialog box

Click to make search sensitive to uppercase and lowercase letters

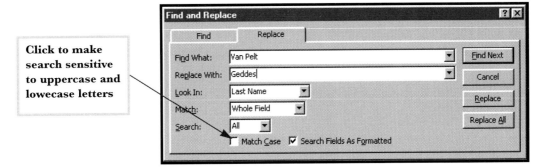

Figure 2-25 Wildcard characters used as search parameters

Wildcard	Used For	Example
*	Matching any number of characters; may be placed at the beginning, end, or in the middle of text	thr* finds throw, through, and thrush
?	Matching any single alphabetic character	t?n finds tan, ten, and tin, but not town
[ ]	Matching any single character within the brackets	t[ae]n finds tan and ten, but not tin
[!]	Matching any character not in the brackets	t[!ae]n finds tin and ton, but not tan or ten
[-]	Matching any one of a range of characters, specified in alphabetical order	ta[a-m] finds tab and tag, but not tan or tap
#	Matching any single numeric character	4#0 finds 410 and 420, but not 4110 or 415

Practice

Sort the Customers table in the Tuning Tracker database alphabetically by last name. Find the record for the person who lives on 38th St. Hint: You will have to select the apporiate field first and then use an Any Part of Field match. Save the change to the table design, close the table and minimize the application window.

skill   Filtering Records

concept

While sorting allows you to control the order in which records are displayed, filters control which records are displayed. Filtering temporarily narrows down the number of records according to criteria that you select. Records that do not meet your specifications are filtered out. A filter is a temporary subset of data that you can format and print. You can also save a filter as a permanent data subset by saving it as a query. A query is a subset of specific data that is extracted from a table or from another query.

do it!

Use Filter by Selection to isolate the records of employees who live in Elmsford. Filter by Form to create a data subset of all female employees who live in Irvington or Dobbs Ferry. Save this filter as a query.

1. Open the Employees table in the Employees 2 database. Click in any City field. Click $\boxed{\overset{A}{z}\!\downarrow}$ to sort the datasheet alphabetically by City.

2. To Filter by Selection you must locate an instance of the value you want the filtered records to contain. With the table sorted, you can easily locate and place the insertion point in one of the City fields containing the value Elmsford. Click in one of the City fields containing Elmsford.

3. Click the Filter by Selection button $\boxed{\mathbb{V}}$ on the Table Datasheet toolbar. Seven records are selected as shown in Figure 2-25. Filter by Selection is a quick and easy way to filter a datasheet based on the value in a single field.

4. Click the Remove Filter button $\boxed{\mathbb{Y}}$ to display the full datasheet. ⬭ The Remove Filter button is really the same button as the Apply Filter button. The button is depressed and changes function when a filter is in effect.

5. Click the Filter by Form button $\boxed{\mathbb{H}}$ on the Table Datasheet toolbar. Click the list arrow in the City field. Select Irvington on the drop-down list.

6. Click in the Gender field. Click the list arrow and select F on the drop-down list. ⬭ This is an AND condition, Access will filter out all employees who live in Irvington and are female.

7. Click the Or tab in the bottom left hand corner of the Filter by Form window. Select F in the Gender field again.

8. Click in the City field. Click the list arrow and select Dobbs Ferry on the drop-down list.

9. Click the Apply Filter button $\boxed{\mathbb{Y}}$ on the Filter/Sort toolbar. The four female employees from either Irvington or Dobbs Ferry are displayed as a data subset as shown in Figure 2-26.

10. Open the Records menu, point to Filter and click Advanced Filter/Sort on the Filter submenu. The details of the filter open in Design View as shown in Figure 2-27.

11. Click the Save as Query button $\boxed{\blacksquare}$ on the Filter/Sort toolbar. Type: Female, Irvington or Dobbs Ferry in the Query Name text box and click $\boxed{\text{OK}}$.

12. Close the Design View window and the data subset. Click $\boxed{\text{No}}$ when you are asked if you want to save the changes to the design of the table, so that you leave the datasheet sorted by Last Name rather than by City. Click Queries on the Objects bar to view the filter that you saved as a query in the queries list.

Figure 2-25 Filtering by Selection

	Employee ID	Hired	Last Name	First Name	Street	City	State	Zip	Gend
+	41	8/1/1998	Castle	Frank	51 Stone Ave	Elmsford	NY	10523-	M
+	31	3/27/1997	Young	Trent	77 Silver Rd	Elmsford	NY	10523-	M
+	27	5/4/1996	Rush	Francis	2122 Lincoln Rd	Elmsford	NY	10523-	M
+	23	7/2/1995	James	Arthur	89 Indian Bluff Blvd	Elmsford	NY	10523-	M
+	19	4/19/1995	Rosafort	Lyle	1 Upland Ln	Elmsford	NY	10523-	M
+	16	3/25/1994	Collins	Elmer	17 Cornell Ave	Elmsford	NY	10523-	M
+	2	6/5/1993	Young	Tracy	665 Boylston St	Elmsford	NY	10523-	F

Employees : Table — Record: 1 of 7 (Filtered)

Figure 2-26 Filtering by Form

	Employee ID	Hired	Last Name	First Name	Street	City	State	Zip	Gender
+	29	5/11/1996	Smith	Rhonda	11 Smith Ave	Dobbs Ferry	NY	10522-	F
+	48	3/28/1999	Greco	Hannah	12 Woodland Ave.	Irvington	NY	10533-	F
+	47	3/28/1999	McBride	Meghan	777 Pear Pl.	Irvington	NY	10533-	F
+	24	3/21/1995	Harris	Stephanie	1431 Lakeview Cir.	Irvington	NY	10533-	F
*	(AutoNumber)						NY		

Employees : Table — Record: 1 of 4 (Filtered)

Figure 2-27 Filter by Form in Design View

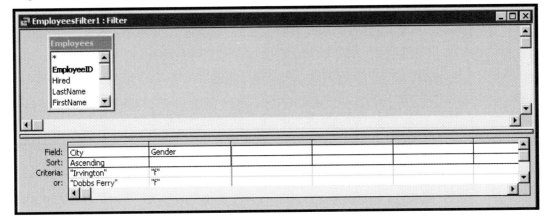

EmployeesFilter1 : Filter

Employees
*
EmployeeID
Hired
LastName
FirstName

Field:	City	Gender				
Sort:	Ascending					
Criteria:	"Irvington"	"f"				
or:	"Dobbs Ferry"	"f"				

Practice

Open the Customers table in the Tuning Tracker database in Datasheet View. Sort the records in ascending order by zip code. Highlight an instance of the 10010 zip code and use Filter by Selection to display only the records of customers who live in that zip code. Remove the filter. Use Filter by Form to isolate the records of customers who live in 10010, Or 10011, Or 10012. Save the filter as a query named 10010, 10011, and 10012. Close the Design View window and the data subset. Do not save the changes to the table design. You want the records to remain sorted by last name not by zip code. Minimize the application window.

skill

Using the Simple Query Wizard

concept

A query is a formal way to sort and filter data. You can designate which fields you want and in what order you want them to appear. You can also specify separate filter criteria for each field and the order in which you want each field to be sorted. You can use queries to analyze your data. Queries are similar to filters in that they both create data subsets, but the important difference is that queries are saved as objects in the database. While a filter is a temporary view of the data, a query is a permanent data subset.

do it!

Create a query to answer the question: Which employees are on the company health plan?

1. With Queries selected on the Objects bar in the Employees 2 database, double-click Create query by using wizard in the Database window. The Simple Query Wizard opens.

2. With Table: Employees selected in the Table/Queries list box, click EmployeeID, if necessary, in the Available Fields scrolling list box. Click > to add the field to the Selected Fields box.

3. Select Last Name in the Available Fields scrolling list box. Click > to add it to the Selected Fields box. Follow the same procedure to add the First Name field.

4. Click the list arrow on the Table/Queries list box. Select Table: Position on the drop-down list. Add the Department, Title, and Health Plan fields to the Selected Fields box. The dialog box should look like Figure 2-28. Click Next > .

5. Leave the Detail (shows every field for every record) option button selected and click Next > .

6. A suggested query title is selected for modification. Type: Health Plan Query. Click Finish .

7. The query is created and opened in Datasheet View. Click on the Query Datasheet toolbar to switch to Query Design View.

8. The top half of the Query design grid displays the field lists for the tables from which you have selected fields and the relationship between the tables. The bottom half displays each field you have selected for the query and which table it is in, and provides cells in which you can choose the sort order, choose to display or hide the field in the query, and set criteria for which records to extract.

(continued on AC 2.26)

Figure 2-28 Selecting Fields for the Query in the Simple Query Wizard dialog box

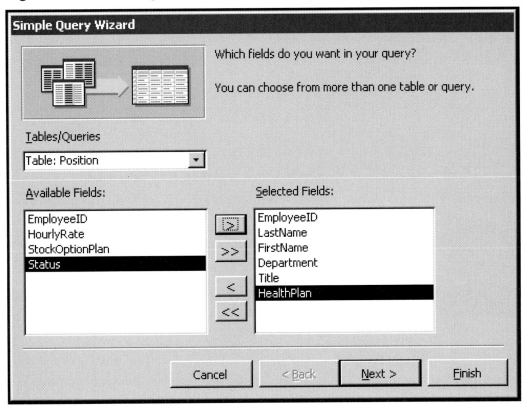

skill
Using the Simple Query Wizard (continued)

do it!

9. Click in the Sort cell for the Last Name field. Click the list arrow and select Ascending. Click in the Sort cell for the First Name cell. Click the list arrow and select Ascending. This is the secondary sort field for the datasheet. In cases where two employees have the same last name, the records will be sorted alphabetically based on the first name.

10. Click in the Criteria cell for the Health Plan field. Type: Yes. The Query design grid is shown in Figure 2-29.

11. Click the Run button [!] on the Query Design toolbar. The records for all employees on the company health plan are displayed in alphabetical order (see Figure 2-30). Notice that Collins, Elmer is listed before Collins, John.

12. Save the changes to the design of the query and close the datasheet.

more

The Simple Query Wizard creates a simple Select query. Select queries retrieve and display records in Datasheet View. Select queries are the most common type of query, but you will learn in later lessons how to create several kinds of action queries. Action queries create new tables or modify data in existing tables. There are four types of Action queries: Make-table, Append, Delete and Update. Append queries add new records to tables and Delete queries delete records from tables that correspond to the rows of the query result set. Update queries change the values of existing fields in a table corresponding to rows of the query result set. For example, you can raise the salaries for people in a certain job category by 3%. You will also learn how to create a Parameter query, which is a flexible query that is used over and over again with simple changes made to its criteria each time it is run. Each time you run a parameter query, Access displays a dialog box that prompts you for the new criterion.

Figure 2-29 Sorting and Adding Criteria to the filter

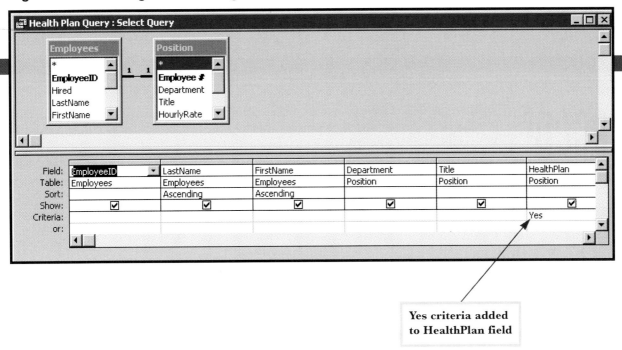

Yes criteria added
to HealthPlan field

Figure 2-30 Employees on health plan listed alphabetically

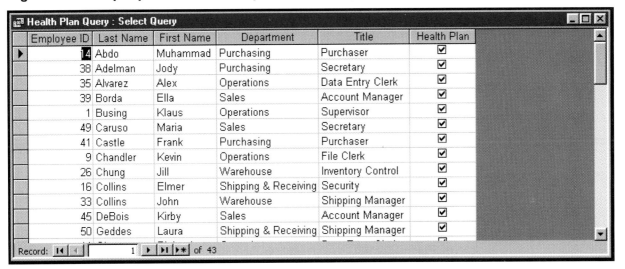

Practice

In the Tuning Tracker database, create a query to answer the question: How many customers have not had their pianos tuned in 2 years? Use the Simple Query Wizard to add the Customer ID, Last Name, and Last Tuned fields to the query. Open the query in Design View. In the Criteria cell for the Last Tuned field, enter the expression that will isolate the correct records. For example, if today's date is 9/30/01, enter < 9/30/99. Run the query, save it as 2 Years, and close the datasheet. Minimize the application window.

skill

Creating a Calculated Field in a Query

concept

A calculated field uses data in one or more fields to create a new field. Arithmetic operators and functions can be used to perform calculations on data already included in your database. When you create a new field based on existing database fields, always use a query rather than defining a new field in a table in Design View. This will ensure that the new field updates as data is added and changed in the related tables.

do it!

Create a query to answer the question: What is the gross pay each week for every employee?

1. With Queries selected on the Objects bar in the Employees 2 Database window, double-click Create query by using wizard.

2. Create a query using the Employee ID, Last Name and First Name fields from the Employees table, the Hours and Week Ending fields from the Hours table, and the Hourly Rate field from the Position table.

3. You want the query to show every field from every record. Name the query Gross Weekly Pay and open it in Design View.

4. The thin gray box at the top of each column in the bottom half of the design grid is the column selector. Hover the mouse pointer over one of the column selectors until it becomes a small black arrow. Click to select the column. Click anywhere else in the Design grid to cancel the selection.

5. Hover the mouse pointer over the gridline on the right side of the first empty column. (This will be the seventh field in the datasheet.) When the pointer becomes a horizontal resizing pointer, drag to the right to increase the width of the column and create a clear space to complete the following steps (see Figure 2-31).

6. Click in the Field cell for the column you just widened. Type: Gross Weekly Pay:. This will be the column heading for the calculated field.

7. In the same cell, continue typing CCur([Hours]*[HourlyRate]). This will multiply the Hours worked each week by the employee's hourly pay. ⬥ Make sure to include the colon following the field name, and not to use a space in the Hourly Rate field name.

   ⬥ The function CCur converts a numeric value to a Currency data type.

8. In the Show cells for the Hours and Hourly Rate fields, click the check boxes to clear the selection. This will hide the two fields in Datasheet View. Check your design grid with Figure 2-32.

9. Click the Run button [!] on the Query Design toolbar to run the query. The query with the gross weekly pay calculation opens as shown in Figure 2-32.

10. Close the datasheet, saving the changes to the design when prompted. Complete the Practice session and exit Access.

more   The * operator is used for multiplication. You use the +, –, /, and ^ operators to perform addition, subtraction, division, and exponentiation. Fields which are having calculations performed on them must be enclosed in brackets. The parentheses must surround the calculation so that the function CCur is performed on the result. The colon must be included after the field name to indicate that an expression will follow. If you do not type a field name Access will enter the default Expr1 as the calculated field name.

You can drag a selected column in the Query design grid to change the order for the fields in the query. To delete a field, select it and either press the [Delete] key or click the Delete command on the Edit menu. When you remove a field from the design grid you are only removing it from the query stipulations, the field and the data it contains are secure in the under-lying table.

Figure 2-31 Creating a Calculated Field

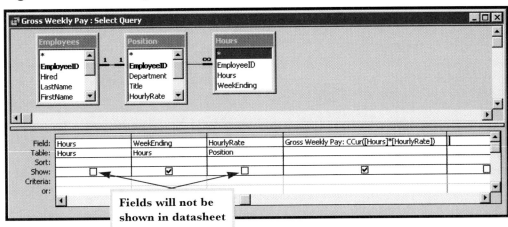

Fields will not be
shown in datasheet

Figure 2-32 Gross Weekly Pay Query

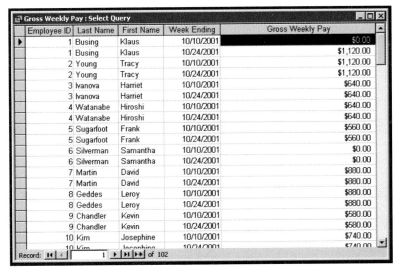

Practice

In the Tuning Tracker database, create a query to answer the question: How old are our customer's pianos. Use the Simple Query Wizard to collect the Customer ID, Piano Make, Piano Model and Year fields from the Service Records table. Save the query as Customer's Piano Age and open it in Design View. Create a calculated field named Piano Age using the expression, "Current Year"-[Year]. For example if the year is 2002, enter the expression "2002" - [Year]. Run the query. The piano with an unknown age will return an error message. Save the change to the query design and close the application window.

shortcuts

Function	Button/Mouse	Menu	Keyboard
Create a new database	📄	Click File, then click New	[Ctrl]+[N]
Set primary key	🔑	In Table Design View, click Edit, then click Primary Key	[Alt]+[E], [K]
Open the Show Table dialog box	On the Relationships toolbar 🗄	With the Relationships window open, click Relationships, then click Show Table	[Alt]+[R], [T]
Sort records in ascending order	⬇	Click Records, point to Sort, then click Sort Ascending	[Alt]+[R], [S], [A]
Find an item of data	🔍	Click Edit, then click Find	[Ctrl]+[F]
Filter By Selection	▽	Click Records, point to Filter, then click Filter by Selection	[Alt]+[R], [F], [S]
Apply Filter/Remove Filter	▽ ▼	Click Records, then click Apply Filter/Sort or Remove Filter/Sort	[Alt]+[R], [Y] or [Alt]+[R], [R]
Filter By Form	🗐	Click Records, point to Filter, then click Filter by Form	[Alt]+[R], [F], [F]
Save As Query	💾	In the Filter By Form window, click File, then click Save As Query	[Alt]+[F], [A]
Run a query	❗	In Query Design View, click Query, then click Run	[Alt]+[Q], [R]

A. Identify Key Features

Name the items indicated by callouts in Figure 2-33.

Figure 2-33 Employees table in Datasheet View

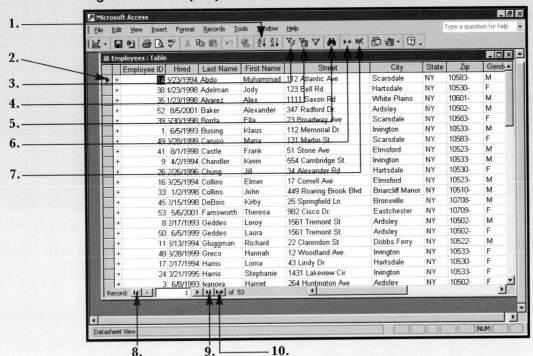

1.
2.
3.
4.
5.
6.
7.
8.
9.
10.

B. Select the Best Answer

11. This is a custom window that contains command buttons for opening the objects in the database that a user is most likely to need.

12. You set this property to choose the format for a Yes/No field

13. You set this property to automatically enter the value the user is most likely to enter in a field

14. This property controls the text that displays in the Field selector in Datasheet View

15. This is a character string that determines how data will be entered and displayed in a field and how it will be stored in the database

16. This is a short expression that will test the reasonableness of an entry

17. This is used to ensure that the relationships between records are valid and that the data in the related fields matches

18. You can use this as a placeholder for other characters when you only know part of the value you want to find in a datasheet

19. This is a temporary subset of data that you can format and print

20. This is a permanent data subset that is saved as an object in the database

a. Input mask

b. Default Value

c. Validation rule

d. Query

e. Switchboard

f. Wildcard character

g. Filter

h. Caption

i. Display Control

j. Referential Integrity

quiz (continued)

C. Complete the Statement

21. This symbol in the Format property for a Text field instructs the program to capitalize the entries in the field

a. <

b. +

c. >

d. ~

22. These temporarily narrow down the number of records that are displayed according to criteria that you select.

a. Sorts

b. Queries

c. Properties

d. Filters

23. These allow you to control the order in which records are displayed.

a. Sorts

b. Queries

c. Properties

d. Filters

24. These are used to answer questions about the data in a database and are saved as objects in the database.

a. Sorts

b. Queries

c. Properties

d. Filters

25. For programming purposes, you should enter the field names:

a. With quotation marks surrounding them

b. Without spaces or with underscores between words

c. With all capital letters

d. With slash marks to indicate literal characters

26. The field descriptions will display:

a. In the error message when a validation rule has been broken

b. In a ScreenTip when you hover the mouse pointer over the Field selector

c. In the Status bar in Datasheet View when the field is selected

d. Only in the Description cell in the Design View grid

27. The field you will use to link the records in the primary table to records in other tables is called:

a. A principal join

b. A composite key

c. An AutoNumber field

d. A primary key

28. You set the Field Size property for a Number field to:

a. Change the number of characters allowed in the field

b. Raise or lower the amount of storage space the field will require in the memory of the computer

c. Format the field as a General number, or as a Fixed decimal, Percent or Currency value

d. Designate the number of decimal places you want in the field

29. When you create a calculated field based on existing database fields you should do all of the following except always:

a. Use brackets around the field names

b. Use a query rather than defining a new field in a table in Design View

c. Create the expression in the Display Control property in Table design view.

d. Include a colon after the name for the calculated field, before you enter the expression

interactivity

Build Your Skills

1. Create a new database and use the Table Wizard to construct the first table

   a. Start Access and click Blank Database on the task pane. Name the new database Address Book.mdb.

   b. Use the Table Wizard to create the Addresses table in the Personal category. Use the AddressID, LastName, FirstName, SpouseName, Address, City, StateOrProvince and PostalCode fields. Use the Rename Field button to rename the StateOrProvince field, State, and the PostalCode field ZipCode.

   c. Let Access set the AddressID field as the primary key for you and open the table in Design View.

2. Modify the field properties for the new table.

   a. Decrease the field sizes for the Last Name and First Name fields to 25 each. Decrease the size of the Address field to 50. Decrease the ZipCode field to 10 characters.

   b. Make the State field 2 characters long and format it in uppercase letters. Enter your state as the default value for the field. Enter a description for the field.

   c. Enter Zip Code as the Caption property for the ZipCode field.

3. Create an input mask and add a data validation rule.

   a. Use the Input Mask Wizard to create a mask for the Zip Code field. Store the data with the symbols in the mask.

   b. Add a Text field for Gender. Set the field size to 1. Format the field as a capital letter.

   c. Set the data validation rule so that the field will only accept m or f.

   d. Enter validation text to display in the error dialog box.

   e. Save the changes and test the rule.

   f. Enter data for 5 people you know in the table and close the datasheet.

4. Create tables in Design View.

   a. Create a new table in Design View named Communication in the Address Book database. Create a Number field for the AddressID. Leave it in the default Long Integer format.

   b. Create a Text field for EMailAddress. Create a Text field for PhoneNumber and apply an input mask. Decrease the field size for the Phone Number field to 15. When you save the table do NOT set a primary key. You may enter several e-mail addresses or phone numbers for each Address ID. This will be the many side of the relationship.

   c. Enter the data for the 5 people you have in the Addresses table with the matching Address ID. Make sure you enter two e-mail addresses and/or two phone numbers for at least some of the entries. Close the datasheet.

   d. Create another new table named Contact Details. Create a Number primary key field for the AddressID field. Create a field called Relationship. Use the Lookup Wizard to create a value list with the choices: Acquaintance, Business Contact, Friend, and Relative. Decrease the field size to accommodate the longest entry in the list. Save the changes.

interactivity (continued)

Build Your Skills (continued)

e. Create a Yes/No field named VisitScheduled. Enter the Caption properties for each field as necessary. Add a Date/Time field named Birthday. Apply the Long Date format. Save the changes.

f. Create a field called TimesCalledperMonth. Create a value list with the choices: 1–3, 4–6, 7–9. Decrease the field size appropriately and save the changes. Switch to Datasheet View, increase the column widths and save the changes. Enter data in the table and close the datasheet.

g. Establish the One-to-Many relationship between the AddressID fields in the Addresses and Communications tables and the One-to-One relationship between the Contact Details and Addresses tables. Enforce referential integrity and save the changes.

5. Create queries.

a. Use the Simple Query Wizard to create a permanent data subset to answer the question: Which of my contacts are friends? Include the Last Name, First Name, and Relationship fields. Name the query Friends and open it in Design View.

b. In the Criteria cell for the Relationship field type: friend. Press [Enter], run the query, and save the changes. Close the Address Book database.

6. Open the Home Video Collection database. Use the Simple Query Wizard to create a query to answer the question: Which of my videos are rated PG-13? Use the Title, Genre and Rating fields, name it PG-13, and open it in Design View. Type: PG-13, in the Criteria cell for the Rating field. Press [Enter], run the query, and save the changes. Close the database.

7. Open the Recipes database. Use the Simple Query Wizard to answer the question: Which of my recipes can be created in half an hour or less? Use the Recipe Name, Which Meal? and Time to Prepare fields. Name the query Quick Recipes and open it in Design View. Type: <31 in the Criteria cell for the Time to Prepare field. Press [Enter], run the query, and save the changes. Fill in the Which Meal fields as necessary. Open the Recipes table to see that these fields have been entered in the underlying table. Close the database.

Problem Solving Exercises

1. Build the Magazine Preferences database that you outlined on paper for Lesson 1. Begin a Blank database and name it Magazine Preferences. Construct the three tables you planned in Design View. Assign appropriate data types and field sizes. Make sure not to duplicate any fields. Follow database programming principles when you name the fields and enter Caption properties as necessary. Use the most efficient Byte field size for the Age and Number of Magazines Read Regularly fields. Make sure you use the Auto Number and Number data type in the Long Integer size for the fields you will use to establish relationships. Set the primary keys. The table containing the Hobbies field will not have a primary key. It will be on the many side of the relationship. You will be able to enter several hobbies for each survey respondent.

2. Format the Gender field so that it appears as 1 uppercase letter. Create an input mask for the Social Security field. Create a data validation rule and validation text for the Gender field. Save and name each table. Switch to Datasheet View for each table and enter the data you have compiled. Adjust the column widths as necessary. Apply formatting to the datasheet for the primary table.

interactivity (continued)

Problem Solving Exercises (continued)

3. Establish the table relationships. You should have one one-to-one relationship and one one-to-many relationship. Enforce referential integrity. Sort the records in the primary table in descending order by age. Filter by Selection to display a subset of only the female survey respondents. Filter by Form to display a subset of records for survey respondents who are Female AND 22 OR Female AND 23 OR Female AND 24.

4. Create queries using the Simple Query wizard to answer the questions: How many survey respondents are between the ages of 18 and 34 (>18 And <34), between the ages of 35 and 49 (>35 And <49), between the ages of 50 and 64 (>50 And <64), and over 65 (>65). Include the ID #, Occupation, # of Magazines Read Regularly, Age, and Gender fields in each query and then set the appropriate criteria in the Age field. If these age groups are not represented in your data you can use other criteria for example under 17 (<17), 18 to 25 (>18 And <25) or 26 to 34 (>26 And <34) etc. Save each query with the age group name.

3

Creating Forms

As you have seen, tables serve as the backbone of a database, and you can enter your data directly into them. However, after you have tested your database design by adding sample data to your tables, you will want to build forms to simplify data entry. Forms will serve as the user interface for your database. Although you can use Datasheet View in either a table or a query to access, edit and add data, a form will provide a more user friendly environment. Forms are constructed from any number of objects called controls or control objects. You use text box controls for entering and editing data. Label controls are used to identify the text boxes and other control objects, and toggle button, option button, or checkbox controls are used for Yes/No fields.

Using a form you can enter data into several tables at once. More importantly, you can choose a format that displays only one record at a time to simplify data entry and reduce errors. There are three ways to create a form. The easiest way to create a form is with an AutoForm Wizard. If you simply want a form that displays all of the records from a single table or query, you can let Access create a standardized form for you. AutoForm is the least flexible but quickest way to create a form.

The Form Wizard enables you to create a form by following a series of dialog boxes and choosing which fields to include. The Form Wizard offers less control than creating a form on your own, but it is much faster. One advantage to using the Form Wizard is that you can choose fields from more than one table creating a form that will enable users to enter data into several tables simultaneously. Finally, you can create a form in Form Design View. You will have more control over where to put each field and how to format the fields, but it is the most complicated method. In the Form Design window you add the dynamic controls that you will use to enter and edit data and the static controls that will hold the identifying labels and titles.

There are three types of form controls. Bound controls are fields containing data from a table or query. There must be a bound control for each field you want to be able to enter data into. Labels and titles are unbound controls. Unbound controls are the identifiers that tell the user what data to enter where. Calculated controls display values created from expressions. You can use calculated controls to include totals, subtotals, averages, percentages, or date calculations. If you use a value in the expression that is stored in one of the other data fields, the calculated control will be bound to that field. Otherwise it will be an unbound control. In other words, the term bound indicates a link to a field in a table.

Lesson Goal:

Create an AutoForm. Create a form with the Form Wizard. Modify and format form controls. Create a calculated control and add records using a form.

- ⚡ Creating an AutoForm
- ⚡ Creating a Form with the Form Wizard
- ⚡ Modifying a Form
- ⚡ Setting Tab Order
- ⚡ Adding a Field to a Form
- ⚡ Using the Expression Builder
- ⚡ Using Property Sheets
- ⚡ Entering Records Using a Form

Access 2002

skill

Creating an AutoForm

concept

To create a simple form that only includes the fields from a single table or query you can use an AutoForm Wizard. AutoForm Columnar is the most popular format because it creates a form that aligns the fields in columns with each record displayed individually. This is the advantage of creating a columnar form. You can use the navigation buttons at the bottom of the form to scroll through the data, one record per screen, to locate, view, and edit records individually.

do it!

Create an AutoForm to enter data into the Employees table.

1. Start Access and open the Employees 2 database. Click Forms on the Objects bar to display the options for creating a form in the objects list.

2. Click ⊞ New on the Database Window toolbar. The New Form dialog box opens.

3. Click AutoForm: Columnar. Click the list arrow on the box with the instructions: Choose the table or query where the object's data comes from, as shown in Figure 3-1.

4. Click Employees on the drop-down list to select this table as the record source for the form. The record source is the table or query where you are getting the data for the form. Click OK.

5. A standard columnar form is created with all of the fields from the Employees table, as shown in Figure 3-2. The fields are created in the same order as in the datasheet.

6. Use the navigation buttons at the bottom of the form to view the records in the form. Close the form without saving it. All Form Wizards "remember" the previous styles you have applied. The last autoformat that was used to create a form will be used by the AutoForm Wizard.

more

You can choose from three basic AutoForm formats: columnar, tabular, or datasheet. In a tabular form, the fields in each record appear on one line with the labels displayed once, at the top of the form, as shown in Figure 3-3. In a datasheet form, the fields in each record appear in row and column format with one record in each row and one field in each column. The field names appear at the top of the column, just like in a table. Pivot table forms are used to create forms from Excel pivot tables.

You can also create a columnar AutoForm based on the record source that is selected in the Database window. For example, with Queries selected on the Objects bar, you can select the Health Plan query in the Database window. Then you can open the Insert menu and select the AutoForm command to automatically create a form that includes all of the fields in the query. You can also click the list arrow on the New Object button on the Database toolbar and select the AutoForm command. The New Object button displays the last object you created. For example, if the last object you created was an AutoForm, the New Object: AutoForm button 🗃 displays.

Figure 3-1 Creating an AutoForm

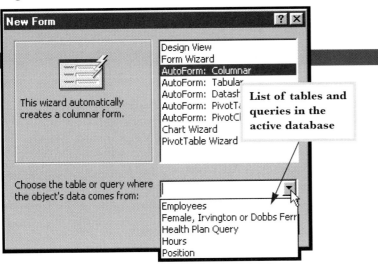

Figure 3-2 A Columnar AutoForm

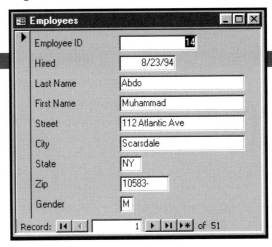

Figure 3-3 A Tabular AutoForm

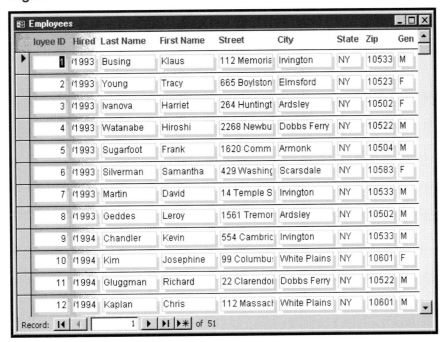

Practice

Open a second Access application window. Open the Tuning Tracker 2 database in your Access Student Files folder. The phone numbers have been entered in the Customers table and the Service History table has been completed. Create a columnar AutoForm for entering records into the Customers table. Save it as Customers AutoForm and minimize the application window.

skill | Creating a Form with the Form Wizard

concept

As you have seen, your options are limited when you create an AutoForm. If you want to change the layout, choose a background template, or choose fields from several different tables, you should use the Form Wizard to create your form. The Form Wizard provides a compromise between the ease of the AutoForm and the total control of designing a form in Design View. You can use the Form Wizard to quickly create a form and then modify its properties in the Design View window.

do it!

Create a form to enter the data into the Employees and Positions tables.

1. In the Employees 2 database window, click Forms on the Objects bar. Double-click Create form by using wizard in the database window. The first Form Wizard dialog box opens.

2. Table: Employees should be selected from the Tables/Queries list box. If it is not, click the list arrow and select it from the drop-down list.

3. Click the Select All Fields button >> to move all the Available Fields to the Selected Fields box.

4. Click the list arrow on the Tables/Queries list box. Select Table: Position from the drop-down list. Click >> .

5. Select the Position.EmployeeID field in the Selected Fields box. Click the Remove Field button < . The EmployeeID field has already been added to the form from the Employees table. The Selected Fields box is shown in Figure 3-4. Click Next > .

6. Leave the Columnar option button selected, and click Next > .

7. Click Blends to choose it as the style for your report. Click Next > .

8. Type: Employees/Position as the title for the form. Leave the Open the form to view or enter information option button selected and click Finish .

9. The Form is created and saved and opens in Form View as shown in Figure 3-5. Notice that the Yes/No fields from the tables are check box controls on the form and the drop-down value list you created with the Lookup Wizard is a combo box control. The rest of the form controls are either text boxes or labels.

more

The main advantage to using the Form Wizard is that you can choose fields from several tables. You can choose the fields you want to include from as many different tables or queries as you want. When choosing fields from several different record sources, be sure not to duplicate the shared fields. Generally you will include all of the fields from several tables so that the form can be used to easily enter data into more than one table at the same time.

Figure 3-4 Choosing the fields for the form

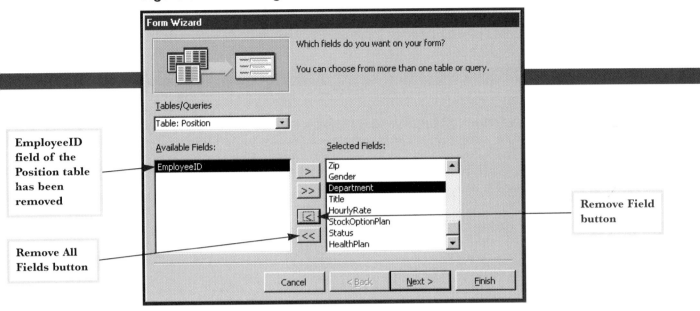

EmployeeID field of the Position table has been removed

Remove Field button

Remove All Fields button

Figure 3-5 Employees/Position form

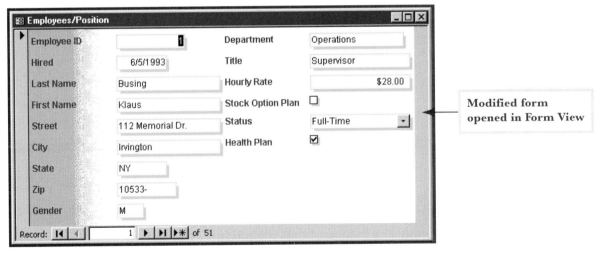

Modified form opened in Form View

Practice

In the Tuning Tracker 2 database, use the Form Wizard to create a form for entering records into the Customers and Service Records tables. Make sure you remove the duplicate CustomerID field from the Selected Fields box. Use a columnar layout and the SandStone style. Name it Customers/Service Records. Close the form and minimize the application window.

skill

Modifying a Form

concept

Even if you choose to create your forms using a Wizard, you can make changes in Design View to manually tweak your forms into exactly the format you need. You can make the form easier to work with by rearranging the layout and resizing the fields. You can also apply borders and shading, change the text color or text style for certain controls, and apply other formatting changes to make your forms visually appealing.

do it!

Modify the control properties for the Employees/Position form.

1. Open the Employees/Position form in the Employees 2 database in Design View. Since you will not be adding any new controls yet, you can close the Toolbox either by clicking its close button or by clicking the Toolbox button 🔨 on the Form Design toolbar to toggle it off.

2. Drag the lower-right corner of the Form window downward and to the right to reveal the entire form. Release the mouse button when you can see the Form Footer. ◖◗ There are two components to every field, the text box control and the corresponding static, unbound label control.

3. Click the EmployeeID text box as shown in Figure 3-6. Sizing handles surround the selected object. Hover the mouse pointer over the border of the bound text box control; it becomes an open hand. You can use this pointer to move both the bound text box control and its corresponding unbound label control together as a unit.

4. Hover the mouse pointer over the black box in the upper-left corner of the text box control. This is called the move handle. As you can see, the move handles are larger than the sizing handles. The pointer becomes a hand with an extended finger. You can use this pointer to move an individual control.

5. Hover the mouse pointer over the midpoint sizing handle on the right end of the EmployeesID text box. When the pointer becomes a horizontal resizing arrow, drag to the left to the 1¼ inch mark on the horizontal ruler to decrease the size of the text box.

6. Click the HourlyRate text box to select it. Press [Shift] on the keyboard and click the Status combo box. Drag the midpoint resizing handle on the right end of either control to the 4¾ inch mark on the horizontal ruler to decrease the size of both controls at the same time. ◖◗ The Object list box, at the left end of the Formatting (Form/Report) toolbar, lists every control on the form. You can also click the name of an object on the drop-down list to select the corresponding control on the form.

7. Click 🔲 to switch to Form View and make sure the control are sized correctly. Make sure the longest entry in the combo box will be visible in Form View. Then click 📐 to switch back to Design View.

8. Drag the midpint sizing handle on the right end of the Department text box to the 5¼ inch mark on the horizontal ruler. Drag the right midpoint sizing handle on the Title text box to the 5⅛ mark. Drag the right midpoint sizing handle on the Last Name and First Name text boxes to the 2¼ mark. Make sure that the longest entry fits in the text boxes in Form View.

9. Select and move the Gender field (both the text box and its label) so that it is positioned underneath the Health Plan field as shown in Figure 3-7.

(continued on AC 3.8)

Figure 3-6 Form Design View window

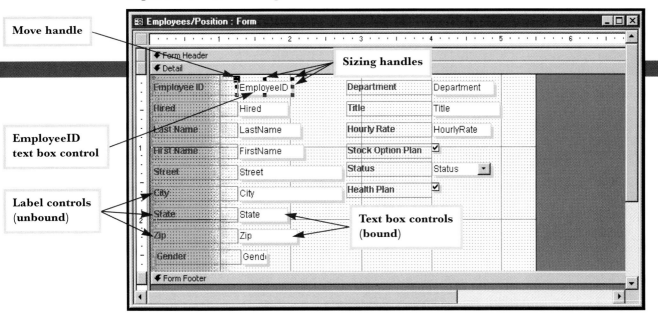

Move handle

Sizing handles

EmployeeID
text box control

Label controls
(unbound)

Text box controls
(bound)

Figure 3-7 Moving the Gender field

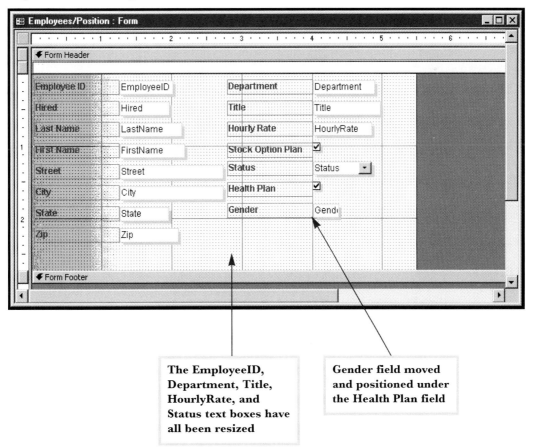

The EmployeeID,
Department, Title,
HourlyRate, and
Status text boxes have
all been resized

Gender field moved
and positioned under
the Health Plan field

skill
Modifying a Form (continued)

do it!

10. Select the EmployeeID text box. Press [Shift] and click each text box control on the form. Click the list arrow on the Line/Border Width button ⬚▾ on the Form Design toolbar. Change the border width for the controls to 2 as shown in Figure 3-8.

11. With all of the controls still selected, click the list arrow on the Font/Fore Color button ▲▾. Change the font color for the controls to dark blue (the sixth square in the first row on the color palette).

12. Click a blank area of the form to cancel of the selection of the controls. Select the Hired text box. Click the list arrow on the Font list box and change the font to Courier. Click the list arrow on the Fill/Back Color button ▨▾. Change the background color for the control to the lightest yellow.

13. Now change the back color for the control to Transparent. Switch to Form View. The background looks white. Select the Hired field. The background changes to the light yellow color when the field is selected as shown in Figure 3-9.

14. Save the changes to the design of the form and close the form.

more

The Bold, Italic, and Underline buttons modify the style of the selected text. The three alignment buttons, Align Left, Center, and Align Right, control the placement of text within a text box or label control. The last button on the Formatting toolbar is the Special Effects buttons, which controls the appearance of the outlines of a label or text box. You can choose a Raised, Sunken, Chiseled, Shadowed, or Etched effect. The Blends style uses a shadowed border effect.

Don't worry too much about resizing and moving your controls so that they are perfectly aligned. It is a very precise proce-dure, which requires excellent mouse skills. You will become better at it with practice. Just make sure that you understand which are the sizing-handles and which are the move-handles and that the open hand mouse pointer moves the text box and label control as a unit, while the extended finger mouse pointer moves the controls separately.

Figure 3-8 Changing the Border Style for selected controls

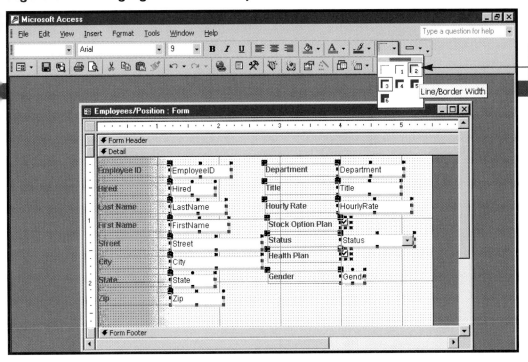

Figure 3-9 Changing the Background color for a control when it is selected

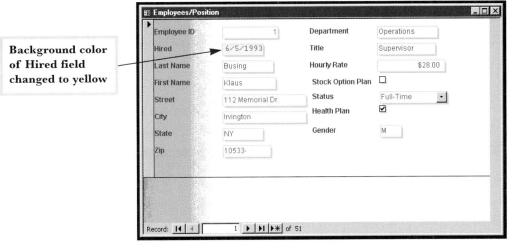

Practice

Open the Customers/Service Records form in the Tuning Tracker 2 database in Design View. Decrease the sizes of the text boxes, making sure that the longest entry fits in Form View. Decrease the size of the Piano Make and Piano Model label controls. Move the Year, Use, and Last Tuned fields downward. Move the Piano Make and Piano Model fields into the space you create so that the fields from the Service Records table are the second column in the form. Use the appropriate pointers to align the labels and text boxes. Select all of the text box controls in the Customers/Service Records form. Apply a 2 pt border with a Shadowed special effect. Change the font in the Piano Make text box to Bookman Old Style and apply a bold font style. Move the Last Tuned field so that it is directly below the Piano Model field. Save the changes and minimize the window.

skill | Setting Tab Order

concept

Tab order refers to the sequence in which controls receive the focus when a user is pressing the Tab key to move through a form. When you first create a columnar form, the Tab order runs from top to bottom according to the order in which the fields were added to the form. When you move and rearrange fields, the Tab order does not automatically change. You can adjust the Tab order for your form so that users will be able to quickly and accurately enter data in a logical order.

do it!

Change the tab order for the Employees/Position form so that the moved Gender field will be last in the tab order. Set the Tab stop property for the State field.

1. Open the Employees/Position form in the Employees 2 database in Form View. Press the [Tab] key to tab through the controls on the form. You can see that the Gender field is not in the correct order.

2. Switch to Form Design View. Open the View menu and click the Tab Order command to open the Tab Order dialog box as shown in Figure 3-10.

3. Click the Gender row selector button as shown in Figure 3-10. Drag the Gender field to the bottom of the fields in the Custom Order scrolling list box. The Tab order is now set to move the focus down the first column of fields and then down the second column. You can click the Auto Order button to instruct Access to automatically set the tab order. The focus will start in the upper-left corner of the form and move across the first line. Then it will move down and proceed from left to right again.

4. Click [OK] to close the Tab Order dialog box.

5. Since NY has been entered as the default value for the State text box and very few employees live out of state, data entry personnel will rarely need to stop at this control. To increase data entry efficiency, you can set the Tab Stop property for the control to No so that the focus will skip the State text box. Click the State text box to select it.

6. Click the Properties button 🖼 on the Form Design toolbar. A window with Text Box: State in the Title bar opens. This is the property sheet for the State text box.

7. Click the Other tab. You can now easily locate the Tab Stop property. Click in the Tab Stop property settings box. Click the list arrow and select No on the drop-down list as shown in Figure 3-11. Controls whose Tab Order property has been set to No can still be selected and edited in the form; they will simply never receive the focus as the user tabs through the form.

8. Click the Close button ☒ to close the property sheet. Save the changes to the form design.

9. Switch to Form View and press [Tab] to tab through the form controls. The Gender field is now last in the tab order and the State field is skipped. Close the form. The Enter and arrow keys also respond to the new tab order. The focus will correctly shift to the controls you have specified when the user presses these keys to move through the fields in the form.

more
Remember that moving and rearranging the order of fields in a form will not automatically change the tab order. Tab order will have to be adjusted to reflect the new form structure. You can also change the tab order to suit your particular needs. For example, if you find that one field requires more editing than the others, you might want to put it first on the tab order without changing its location on the form. Or if a large number of the records you enter skip several fields, you might want to put those fields last in the tab order instead of changing their Tab Stop properties to No so that they can still be easily skipped.

Figure 3-10 Tab Order dialog box

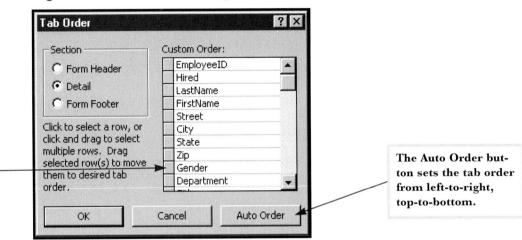

Gender row selector button

The Auto Order button sets the tab order from left-to-right, top-to-bottom.

Figure 3-11 Setting the Tab Stop property

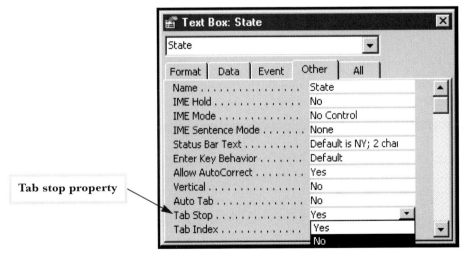

Tab stop property

Practice

Open the Customers/Service Records form in the Tuning Tracker 2 database in Design View. Open the Tab Order dialog box and move the Last Tuned field so that it is after the Piano Model field in the tab order to conform to its new position on the form. Save the change and test the tab order in Form View. Close the form and minimize the application window.

skill | Adding a Field to a Form

concept

You can use the Toolbox to add a field to your form that is not in the original record source/s. This type of text box is called an unbound control because it is not linked or bound to a field in a table or query. All of the text boxes in the form so far are bound controls. Each field in the form is linked to a field in the Employees or Position table. Unbound text boxes can be used to supply values to other fields or to display the results of calculations.

do it!

Use the Toolbox to add an unbound text box to the form.

1. Open the Employee/Position form in the Employees 2 database in Design View. Click the Toolbox button 🛠 on the Form Design toolbar.

2. Select the Last Name text box. Press [Shift] and select the First Name, Street, City, State and Zip text boxes. Move the selected block of controls down on the form to make room for a new text box.

3. Click the Text Box button 🔲 on the Toolbox. Move the mouse pointer over the form. The pointer becomes the symbol for the Text Box button combined with a crosshair. The center of the crosshair will define the position of the upper-left corner of the text box.

4. Click once directly below and aligned with the Hired text box to insert a text box with the word Unbound and a label that says Text: 30 as shown in Figure 3-12. ⬭ The label caption (Text: 30) will vary depending on how many controls are on the form. This is the thirtieth control added to the Employees/Position form.

5. Drag one of the midpoint sizing-handles on the top or bottom of the text box to increase the width to match the Hired text box. Decrease the length to match the Hired text box.

6. With the two controls, the text box and its corresponding label, still selected, move the mouse pointer over the move handle in the upper left-hand corner of the label. When the mouse pointer becomes a hand with a pointing finger, drag to move the label into position below the Hired label.

7. Click the Text: 30 label to select it, and use the sizing handles to adjust the width to match the Hired label. Double-click the label control (on top of the text) to select the text. Type Years of Service to replace the default text.

8. Select all of the labels in the first column. Open the Format menu and point to the Align command. Click Left to align the new label on the left margin with the other labels.

9. Save the changes to the design of the form and switch to Form View. The new field appears in the form as shown in Figure 3-13. ⬭ Each new field automatically becomes the last field in the Tab order. You will need to adjust the Tab order if users will be entering data into a field that you add to a form.

more

You can also add a bound field to a form in Design View. If you have forgotten a field that you need from one of your record sources you can easily add it to the form. First click the Field List button 🗐 on the Form Design toolbar to open the field list. All of the fields from the record sources for the form will be included in the field list. Drag a field name to the form. When you drag the field, the mouse pointer will turn into 🔲. Position this field symbol where you want the upper-left corner of the text box to be positioned. When you release the mouse button, a text box for the field and a numbered label control will be added to the form. You will have to move, resize and edit the label appropriately just as you did in the Skill.

Figure 3-12 Adding an unbound text box to a form

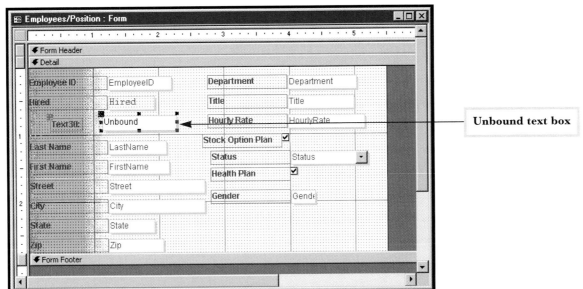

Figure 3-13 New Field in Form View

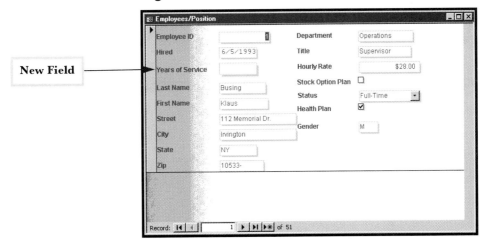

Practice

In the Tuning Tracker 2 database, open the Customers/Service Records form in Design View and add an unbound text box control directly below the Use text box. Move the new label control directly under the Use label. Use the Align Left command to line up all the labels. Drag the midpoint sizing handle on the right edge of the label control to the right until it reaches the Unbound text box. Drag the midpoint sizing handle on the bottom edge of the label downward to the 1¼ inch mark on the vertical ruler. Double-click the label control to select the text. Type Months Since Last Tuning to replace the default text. Save the changes, close the form, and minimize the application window.

skill
Using the Expression Builder

concept

You use the Expression Builder to help you create equations for calculated controls on a form or a report. Calculated text boxes are used to display the results of expressions. Expressions can use any of the Access functions you will find in the Expression builder, mathematical operators, raw values, and any field values on the form. Functions are predefined formulas that simplify the process of building equations. You can use these Access tools to display many useful calculations in a form such as the cost per unit of a particular product, or the number of years each employee has worked for a company.

do it!

Use the Expression Builder to build an equation that will calculate the number of years each employee has worked for the company and display the result in a new text box.

1. Open the Employee/Position form in Design View. Double-click the Unbound text box to open the property sheet.

2. Click the Data tab. Click in the Control Source property settings box. You use the Control Source property to specify what data appears in a control.

3. Click the Build button ⋯ that appears to the right of the Control Source property settings box after you select it. The Expression Builder opens.

4. Type: = since all Access expressions must begin with an equal sign.

5. Click the Common Expressions folder at the bottom of the left window in the lower half of the dialog box. Click Current Date in the middle window. Double-click Date() in the right window to add the current date function to the top window in the dialog box and begin the equation.

6. Click ⊡ (the minus sign operator) in the row of operator buttons just below the top window to add it to the equation.

7. Click the Employees/Position folder in the left window. Select the Hired text box in the field list that displays in the middle window. Click the Paste button [Paste] to add the value contained in the Hired field to the expression. The equation currently subtracts the date of hire from the current date to compute the number of days the employee has worked for the company. ◆ The text box is now a bound control. If you include a field value in the expression for a calculated control, the text box is bound to that field. The Years of Service field is bound to the Hired field because it must use the value in the Hired field to calculate the equation.

8. To calculate the number of years the employee has worked for the company, you must divide this equation by 365. First you must insert parenthesis around the equation so that the subtraction operation is performed first. Position the insertion point in front of Date. Click the opening parenthesis button ⟮.

9. Position the insertion point after the closing bracket on the Hired field. Click the closing parenthesis button ⟯.

10. Click the backslash button ⟋ to enter the division operator. Type: 365. The completed expression in the Expression Builder is shown in Figure 3-14.

(continued on AC 3.16)

Figure 3-14 The completed expression

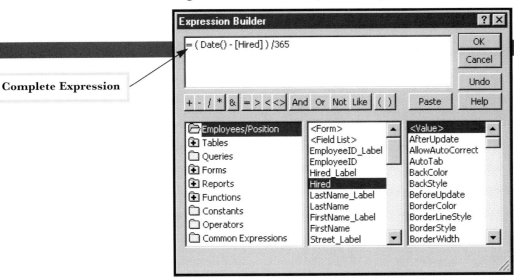

Complete Expression

Figure 3-15 The expression entered in the Control Source text box

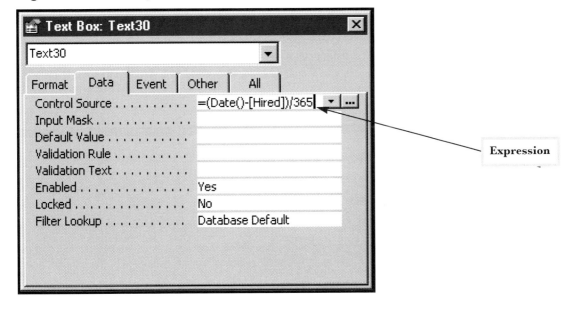

Expression

skill Using the Expression Builder (continued)

do it!

11. Click [OK] to close the Expression Builder. The equation has been entered in the Control Source property as shown in Figure 3-15 (see page AC 3.15). Click the Format tab on the property sheet.

12. Click in the Format property settings box. Click the list arrow and select Fixed on the drop-down list.

13. Click in the Decimal Places settings box. Click the list arrow and select 1 on the drop-down list. The Fixed decimal point settings on the Format tab are shown in Figure 3-16.

14. Click the Other tab. Set the Tab Stop property for the calculated control to No.

15. Close the property sheet. Close the Toolbox. Save the structural changes to the form.

16. Switch to Form View. Use the navigation buttons at the bottom of the form to view several records. The calculated control displays the number of years of service rounded to the nearest tenth. Close the form.

more

You must set the Tab Stop property for the Years of Service text box to No because users will not be entering or editing information in this field. The calculation will automatically update as the current date changes.

You can also simply type your equation in the text box control. For example, when you become comfortable with constructing equations without the help of the Expression Builder, you can simply type: =(Date()-[Hired])/365 in the text box control in Design View. Field names must be surrounded by square brackets. In Design View, you will see that the expression has replaced the word Unbound in the text box as shown in Figure 3-17.

Figure 3-16 Format tab settings

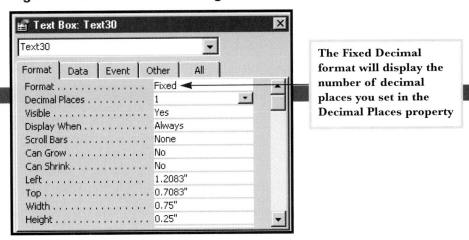

The Fixed Decimal format will display the number of decimal places you set in the Decimal Places property

Figure 3-17 Expression entered in the text box in Design View

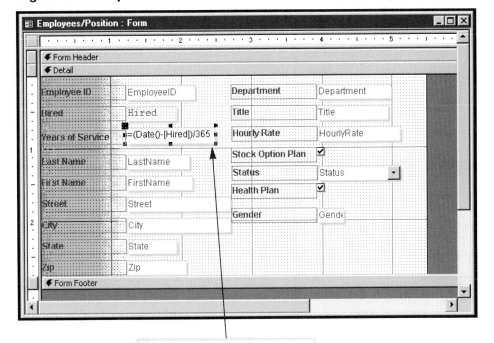

The length of the text box has been increased so that the entire equation is visible.

Practice

In the Tuning Tracker 2 database, open the Customers/Service Records form in Design View. Then, open the property sheet for the unbound text box. Click the Build button for the Control Source property. Use the Expression Builder to construct the equation that will calculate the months since the last tuning date,=(Date()-[Last Tuned])/30. Format the text box to round the answer to the nearest month (no decimal places). Save the change, view the calculations and close the form. Minimize the application window.

skill

Using Property Sheets

concept

You can also change properties for a control such as the font, font style, control size, border style, or special effects on the property sheet for that control. When you change the properties for a control using the Formatting toolbar, the new values are automatically entered on the property sheet. Generally, you use the property sheet only if a toolbar button or menu choice is not available on the Formatting toolbar.

do it!

Use the property sheets to format several controls on the form.

1. Open the Employee/Position form in the Employees 2 database in Design View.

2. Double-click the Last Name text box to open its property sheet.

3. Click the Format tab on the property sheet if necessary. Use the scroll bar to scroll down the list and locate the Font Size and Font Weight properties. Change the Font Size property to 10. Change the Font Weight property to Semi-Bold as shown in Figure 3-18.

4. Click the list arrow on the Object list box at the top of the property sheet. Select FirstName on the drop-down list. Apply the same two formatting changes.

5. Click the list arrow on the Object box and select Text 30 on the drop-down list. Locate the Fore Color property. Click in the settings box. Click the Build button [...] , as shown in Figure 3-19.

6. Select the fifth square in the fifth row of the color palette as shown in Figure 3-20, to apply the same blue color to the text in the calculated control, and click [OK] . Change the Border Width property to 2pt to match the rest of the controls on the form.

7. Close the property sheet. Select the Department label. Press [Shift] and select all of the labels in that column. Click the Properties button [icon]. A Multiple selection property sheet opens.

8. Locate the Left property. Double click .7917 to highlight it. Type: 83 to enter 2.83 as shown in Figure 3-21. This will move the column of labels slightly to the right so that there is no overlap between the Street text box and the Health Plan label. Close the Multiple selection property sheet.

9. Save the changes. Switch to Form View to view the formatting changes. Close the form.

more

Using the property sheets to format your form is most useful when you must change minute details such as the spacing between controls. You can use the Left and Top properties to move controls to exact locations on the form. The Width and Height properties can be used to resize controls to your exact specifications. You can use the Border Style property to apply borders with dots or dashes in various styles. The Back Style property can be changed to transparent to make the background color for the form show through the control. If you try to close the form without saving the formatting changes, you will be prompted to save the changes to the design of the form.

Figure 3-18 Changing the Font Weight property

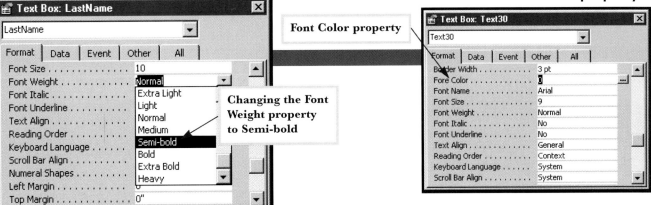

Font Color property

Changing the Font Weight property to Semi-bold

Figure 3-19 Changing the Fore Color property

Figure 3-20 Selecting the font color

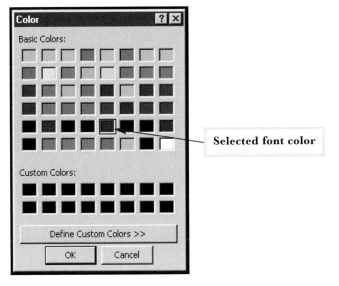

Selected font color

Figure 3-21 Changing the Left property for a multiple selection

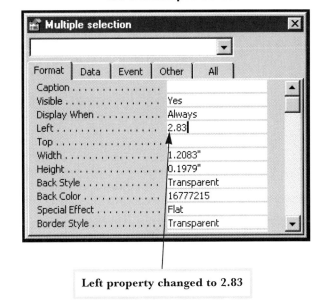

Left property changed to 2.83

Practice

Open the Customers/Service Records form in the Tuning Tracker 2 database in Design View. Format the Piano Make field so that it is Semi-bold instead of Bold. Change the Tab Stop property for the calculated control so that it is not included in the tab order and apply a 2 pt border and the Shadowed Special Effect. Close the property sheet. Select all the labels in the second column and set their Left property to 2.95. Close the multiple selection property sheet. Select the first five text boxes in the second column. Set their Left property to 3.7. Save the changes, close the form, and minimize the application window.

skill

Entering Records Using a Form

MOUS Skill

concept

The purpose of a form is to simplify data entry and editing. The one-record-per-screen format is particularly useful for locating, entering, and editing records in the underlying record source. When you add a new record using the form, it is automatically added to the table or query to which the fields are bound. When you edit a record, the record sources are automatically updated.

do it!

Several new employees have been hired and the Employees database must be updated. Use the Employee/Position form to update the two tables.

1. Open the Employees/Position form in Form View. Click the New Record button ▶* on the Form View toolbar or the New Record navigation button ▶* at the bottom of the form.

2. Enter today's date in the Hired field. Press [Tab]. The Years of Service field is skipped because its Tab Stop property is set to No.

3. Type: Baker. Press [Tab]. Type: Alexander. Press [Tab]. Type: 347 Radford Dr. Press [Tab]. Type: Ardsley. Press [Tab]. The State field is skipped because it has a Tab Stop property of No.

4. Type: 10502. Press [Tab]. Type: Operations. Press [Tab]. Type: Data Entry Clerk. Press [Tab]. Type: 11.00. Press [Tab]. The Hourly Rate field is automatically formatted as Currency.

5. Press [Tab] to tab through the Stock Option Plan field. New employees are not eligible for the stock option plan until they have passed their six month anniversary. Press [Tab]. Select Full-Time on the drop-down list. Press [Tab]. Press [spacebar] to enter a check in the Health Plan check box. Press [Tab]. Type m. Press [Tab]. The M will be automatically capitalized as shown in Figure 3-22, but you will now see a blank record form.

6. Enter the record from Table 3-1.

7. Close the form. Click the Tables button on the Objects bar. Open the Employees table in Datasheet View and sort it in ascending order by the Employee ID field. Click the Last Record ▶I button. The two records have been added to the table as shown in Figure 3-23.

8. Close the table and the database without saving changes to the design of the table.

more

When you have many records to enter, creating a form and using it to enter your records is the most efficient method. The one-record-per screen format provides a clear working space for entering data and thus reduces data entry errors. If data must be entered into several tables in a relational database, a form that includes all of the pertinent fields will enable you to enter new records in one operation rather than having to open each table individually. In a table, you often have to scroll to locate a particular field in a record. When you create a form on the other hand, you can have all of the fields in one record display at one time. You can use the Find command to locate records and the Find and Replace dialog box to quickly edit text. You can also use the Filter by Selection button to locate records that meet certain criteria. For example, you can highlight the Zip Code field for record 1 and click the Filter by Selection button to locate all records of employees who live in the 10533 zip code area.

Figure 3-22 Entering a Record

Table 3-1 Record to be entered

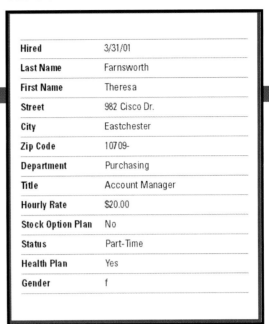

Hired	3/31/01
Last Name	Farnsworth
First Name	Theresa
Street	982 Cisco Dr.
City	Eastchester
Zip Code	10709-
Department	Purchasing
Title	Account Manager
Hourly Rate	$20.00
Stock Option Plan	No
Status	Part-Time
Health Plan	Yes
Gender	f

Figure 3-23 New records are entered in the record source

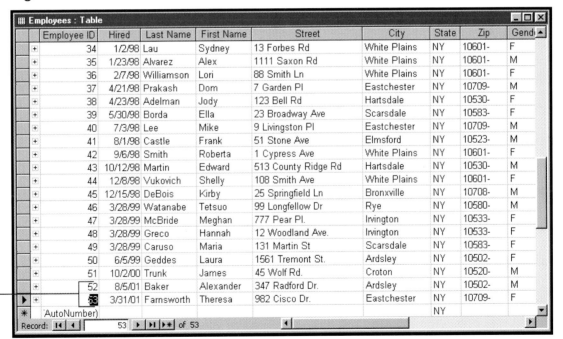

Two new records added to the table

Access 2002

Practice

Use the Start menu to open Microsoft Word. Then, open the Word file acprac3-8.doc and follow the instructions.

shortcuts

Function	Button/Mouse	Menu	Keyboard
Switch to Form View		In Form Design View, click View, then click Form View	[Alt]+[V], [F]
New Object: AutoForm		Click Insert, then click AutoForm,	[Alt]+[I], [O]
Show Toolbox/Hide Toolbox		In Form Design View, click View, then click Toolbox	[Alt]+[V], [X]
Properties (Open the property sheet)		In Form Design View, click View, then click Properties	[Alt]+[V], [P]
Show Field List/Hide Field List		In Form Design View, click View, then click Field List	[Alt]+[V], [L]

A. Identify Key Features

Identify the items indicated by callouts in Figure 3-24.

Figure 3-24 Microsoft Access window

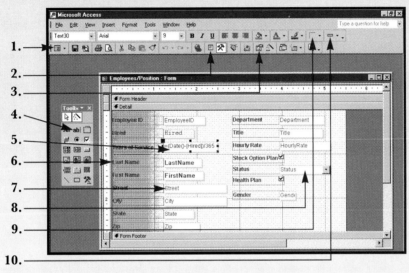

1.
2.
3.
4.
5.
6.
7.
8.
9.
10.

B. Select the Best Answer

11. This is used if you want to change the layout, choose a background template, or choose fields from several different tables when you create a form

12. This is used if you simply want to create a form that displays all the records from a, single table or query

13. This is used to change many form characteristics such as the font, placement of text, and background color for a form

14. Property used to specify what data appears in a control—you can create a calculated control in any control that has this property

15. Refers to the order in which controls receive the focus when a user is pressing the Tab key to move through a form

16. Property that is set to No so that the focus will skip the control on the form when the user is entering data

17. Control that is not linked to a record source

18. This is opened to add a bound field from a record source to a form

19. This is used to help you create equations for calculated controls on a form

20. This is used to set the size and position for a control precisely and to change characteristics such as the border style and back style

a. Formatting toolbar

b. AutoForm

c. Tab order

d. Unbound

e. Property sheet

f. Expression Builder

g. Control Source

h. Field List

i. Tab Stop

j. Form Wizard

quiz (continued)

C. Complete the Statement

21. When you use the Form Wizard you choose fields from:

    a. Only a single record source

    b. Only tables

    c. Multiple record sources

    d. A single table only

22. A bound control:

    a. Links to a field in an underlying database object

    b. Displays results of expressions that use functions and any field values on the form

    c. Is a predefined formula that simplifies the formula for building an equation

    d. Does not link to a record source

23. In Design View, you can enter an expression for a calculated control in all of the following ways except:

    a. Text box control where you want the result to display

    b. Expression Builder for the Control Source property for the control

    c. Label control for the corresponding text box

    d. Control Source property settings box for the control

24. You can create a columnar AutoForm using all of the following methods except:

    a. Select a record source in the Database window, open the Insert menu, and select the AutoForm command

    b. With Forms selected on the Objects bar, click Open on the Database window

    c. With Forms selected on the Objects bar, click New on the Database window toolbar and select AutoForm: Columnar in the New Form dialog box

    d. Click the list arrow on the New Object button on the Database toolbar and select the AutoForm command

25. The Auto Order button in the Tab Order dialog box will set the tab order so that the focus moves:

    a. According to the order of the fields in the record source

    b. Across the first line, down to the second line, and continuing left to right again

    c. According to the order in which the fields were added to the form

    d. Down the first column of fields and then down the second column

26. This type of control generally contains data from an underlying table or query.

    a. Bound control

    b. Unbound control

    c. Calculated control

    d. Text box control

27. This type of control is generally an identifier that tells the user what data to enter where.

    a. Bound control

    b. Unbound control

    c. Calculated control

    d. Text box control

28. The most common unbound control is a:

    a. text box

    b. checkbox

    c. label

    d. combo box

interactivity

Build Your Skills

1. Create and reformat an AutoForm. Enter a record using the form.

a. Open the Home Video Collection database. Click Forms on the Objects bar. Open the New Form dialog box. Create a columnar AutoForm using the Home Video Collection table.

b. Switch to Design View. Select both the VideoID text box and the GenreID text box. Open the Multiple selection property sheet and set the Width property to .3 to decrease the side of the controls Set the Width property for the Rating combo box to .7.

c. Select the Title text box. Drag the midpoint sizing handle on the right end of the text box to the 3-inch mark on the horizontal ruler. Switch to Form View. Use the navigation buttons to scroll through the records in the form. Return to Form Design View and increase the size of the text box to fit the longest title.

d. Change the font color in all of the text boxes to dark blue. Underline all of the labels. Save the changes. Name the form Home Video Collection.

e. Enter the following record using the form. Then close the form and the database.

Title	Genre ID	Genre	Rating	Comment	Star
Life Is Beautiful	3	Drama	PG-13	Excellent	Benigni, Braschi

2. Use the Form Wizard, modify a form, and set tab order.

a. Open the Office Furniture Inc database. Use the Form Wizard to create a form for entering new products into the Products table. Use the Justified layout and the Sumi Painting style. Leave the name for the form Products and open it in Design View.

b. Move the Units in Stock and Units on Order fields (both the text boxes and the labels) to the bottom row. Move the Unit Price field up to the end of the top row. Move the Units in Stock and Units on Order fields over to the left margin aligned with the Product ID field (see Figure 3-25, below).

c. Open the Tab Order dialog box and use the Auto Order button to set the tab order from left to right, top to bottom.

d. Save the changes, switch to Form View, and test the tab order.

Figure 3-25 Products form

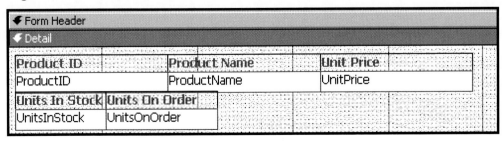

Access 2002

interactivity (continued)

Build Your Skills (continued)

3. Add a field to a form and use the Expression builder to construct a calculated control.

a. In the Office Furniture Inc database, open the Products form in Design View. Open the Toolbox. Add an unbound text box to the form to the right of the Units on Order field.

b. Use the move handles to position the text box and label in the justified layout to the right of the Units on Order field.

c. Select the new label control. Position the mouse pointer over the text until you have an I-beam pointer. Drag across the default text to select it. Type: Value in Inventory. The label size will automatically increase to fit the text that you type.

d. Double-click the Unbound text box to open the property sheet. Click the Data tab. Open the Expression Builder for the appropriate property.

e. Type: =. Remember, all expressions must begin with an equal sign. Create the expression that will calculate the inventory value of each product: =[UnitsInStock]*[UnitPrice].

f. On the Format tab, set the Format property to display the field as Currency. Format the new label with a Solid Border Style. Close the property sheet and save the changes.

g. Switch to Form View and use the navigation buttons to view the new calculated control. Is the calculated control a bound or an unbound control?

h. Return to Form Design View and resize and move any controls as necessary. Save the changes. Close the form and the database.

4. Use the Form Wizard, rearrange fields, set a new tab order, set properties using the property sheets, and create a calculated control.

a. Open the Address Book database. Use the Form Wizard to create a form using all the fields from both the Address and Contact Details tables. Be sure not to duplicate the shared field. Use the columnar layout and the Sumi Painting style. Keep the default name for the form (Addresses) and choose to modify the form's design.

b. In Design View, move the Relationship field one dot underneath the Birthday field so that it is the final field in the form. Move the Relationship field to last in the tab order to match the structural change you made to the form.

c. Move the TimesCalledPerMonth field up so that it is one dot below the Gender field. Move the TimesCalledPerMonth combo box directly underneath its label and increase the width of the label to the 1¾ inch mark on the horizontal ruler.

d. Add an unbound text box to the form underneath the Relationship combo box at the 4 inch mark on the horizontal ruler. Position the new controls one dot below the Relationship field and align the left edges of the labels in the second column of the form. Enter: Days Until B-Day in the Caption property for the new label control. Increase the width of the Days Until B-Day label to the 4 inch mark on the horizontal ruler.

e. Using the Expression Builder, construct an equation to calculate the number of days until the birthday for each Address Book entry {=[Birthday]-Date()}. Remember that you create a calculated control in the Control Source property and that all Access expressions must begin with an equal sign.

f. Change the correct property so that the Tab order will not include the calculated control. Save the changes.

g. Switch to Form View. Scroll through the records to view the new calculated control. Birthdays that have already passed in this calendar year must be entered for next year in order to calculate the number of days until the person's next birthday. Otherwise the formula will calculate the number of days since the birthday occurred, a negative value. Edit your data accordingly.

h. Return to Form Design View and resize the controls as necessary. Increase the width of the Birthday text box to the 6 inch mark on the horizontal ruler. Save the change. View the change in Form View, close the form and the database.

interactivity (continued)

Problem Solving Exercises

1. Open the Magazine Preferences database. Use the Form Wizard to create a form to enter data into the two tables with the one-to-one relationship. Be sure not to duplicate the shared field. Use the Columnar layout and any style you choose. Name the Form Magazine Subscribers.

2. View the form in Form View. Scroll through the records. Switch to Form Design View and resize the controls appropriately.

3. Change the typeface in one of the text boxes to Calisto MT in a 10 pt size. Change the Font color in the ID # text box to dark blue. Change the Font style to Bold.

4. Change the Font weight for the Last Name text box to Semi-bold. Save the structural changes to the form.

5. Since data entry personnel will not have to enter or edit data in the ID # field, set the Tab Stop property for the ID # text box to No. Save the changes.

6. Rearrange the order of the fields by moving fields on the form. Adjust the Tab Order accordingly. Save the change.

7. Use the property sheet to experiment with different border styles, border widths and border colors on one of the text box controls. When you are satisfied with the result save the change.

8. Use the form to add three more records to the tables. Close the database and Access.

Creating Reports

As you have learned, reports are the database objects that are specifically designed for printing. A report is a summary of the data contained in one or more tables or queries that can include calculations, graphics, and customized headers and footers. A report will often provide answers about the information in your database such as the yearly sales for a specific product or the payroll data for a particular week or month. When you create an Access report you can include calculations that are not included in other database objects. You can also include headers and footers to print identifying information at the top and bottom of every page. You can group and sort data to organize information efficiently and apply formatting effects to make your report both more attractive and easier to read and understand.

skills

* **Creating an AutoReport**
* **Using the Report Wizard**
* **Formatting a Report**
* **Adding a Calculated Control to a Report**
* **Using a Query to Create a Report**
* **Previewing and Printing a Report**
* **Creating Mailing Labels**

Just like forms, reports can be created using a variety of methods. The AutoReport Wizards create a simple report containing the fields from a single record source. A columnar AutoReport is organized with each field on a separate line and the label for the field on the left. A tabular AutoReport is organized with each record on a single line and each of the field labels at the top of the page.

The Report Wizard will guide you through a series of dialog boxes which will enable you to choose the kind of report you wish to create. You can choose fields from multiple record sources and apply sorting and grouping options. The Label Wizard will create a report that is automatically formatted for printing mailing labels. After you have created any report you can modify its design in the Design View window.

When you have finished customizing your report you can preview it in either Print Preview or Layout Preview. Print Preview displays the report exactly as it will look when printed. Layout Preview displays the report with only a few sample rows of data to give you an idea of how the report will look without having to view every detail in the report.

Lesson Goal:

Create a report with an AutoReport Wizard. Use the Report Wizard to create a grouped report and the Label Wizard to create mailing labels. Customize reports, add calculated controls to a report, and preview and print a report.

skill | Creating an AutoReport

concept

You can create a standard report based on a single table or query using one of the AutoReport Wizards. An AutoReport can use either a columnar or a tabular layout. Just like AutoForm, AutoReport is the easiest and quickest way to create this type of database object, but it offers the most limited options. The AutoReport Wizard will arrange and format the data in the selected record source as an appealing report, which you can customize as necessary before printing.

do it!

Create an AutoReport in the Employees 2 database.

1. Start Access and open the Employees 2 database. Click Reports on the Objects bar to display the options for creating a report in the objects list.

2. Click 📄 New on the Database window toolbar to open the New Report dialog box.

3. Click AutoReport: Tabular. Click the list arrow on the Choose the table or query where the object's data comes from list box.

4. Click Employees on the drop-down list as shown in Figure 4-1 to select the Employees table as the record source. Click ⬚ OK ⬚.

5. A standard tabular report is created using all of the fields in the Employees table. The report is opened in Print Preview. Use the navigation buttons at the bottom of the Print Preview window and the scroll bars to preview the three pages of the report. ◯ As you can see the output from an AutoReport is only slightly better than a printout from a datasheet (tabular) or a form (columnar). To create more appealing and useful reports you should use the Report Wizard.

6. Click 🗹 ▾ to switch to Design View. Click the AutoFormat button 🗐 on the Report Design toolbar to open the AutoFormat dialog box. Leave the Corporate style for the report selected and click ⬚ OK ⬚.

7. Practice resizing and moving the labels in the Page Header section of the report and the text boxes in the Detail section of the report to create more space between the columns in the report as shown in Figure 4-2.

8. Close the report without saving it.

more

You can also open the New Report dialog box by clicking the list arrow on the New Object button on the Database toolbar. Select Report on the drop-down menu. The New Object button displays the last object you created. If the last object you created was an AutoReport the New Object: AutoReport button 📄 ▾ displays.

You can also create a simple columnar AutoReport based on a record source you select in the Database window. For example, with Queries selected on the Objects bar, you can select the Gross Weekly Pay query in the Database window. Then you can either open the Insert menu and select the AutoReport command or click the list arrow on the New Object button and select AutoReport. Access creates the report using the last autoformat you used. If you have not previously created a report with a wizard or used the AutoFormat command, the Standard AutoFormat is used. Reports created using this method do not include report headers or footers or page headers or footers.

Figure 4-1 New Report dialog box

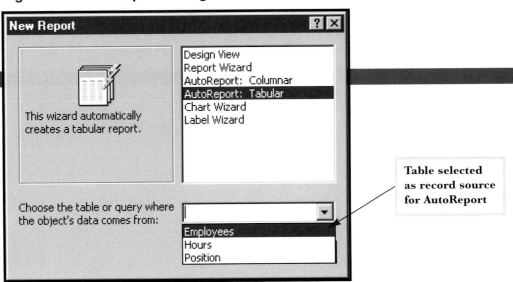

Figure 4-2 Employees AutoReport with the Corporate AutoFormat applied

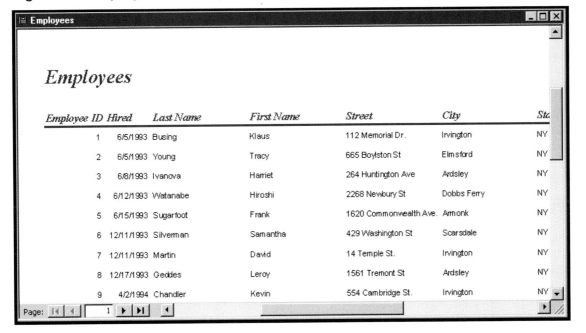

Practice

Open another Access application window and the Recipes database. Create a tabular AutoReport using the Quick Recipes query. Do not save it. Leave the application window and Recipes database open for subsequent Practice sessions. Minimize the application window.

skill

Using the Report Wizard

concept

When you create a report with the Report Wizard, you can select fields from more than one record source, determine the style for the report as it is being created, choose from among several different layout designs, and decide how you want the records in the report to be grouped and sorted. When you group a report based on a field each group is a separate section in the report. For example, you can group employees by Department so that managers will be able to easily skim a report to locate the information for their department.

do it!

Use the Report Wizard to create an Employees report.

1. Click the Reports button on the Objects bar in the Employees 2 Database window. Double-click Create report by using wizard. The first Report Wizard dialog box opens.

2. With Table: Employees selected in the Tables/Queries list box, click the Select All Fields >> button to move all of the fields from the Available Fields scrolling list box to the Selected Fields box.

3. Use the Remove Field < button to remove the Employee ID, Hired and Gender fields as shown in Figure 4-3. ◀▬▶ Another way to move a field from the Available Fields box to the Selected Fields box or vice versa is to double-click it. No matter which side the field is on, when you double-click it, it will move to the opposite side.

4. Click the list arrow on the Tables/Queries list box. Select Table: Position on the drop-down list.

5. Select the First Name field in the Selected Fields box. Access will add the new fields from the Positions table after the field you select in the Selected Fields box.

6. Use the Add Field > button to add the Department and Title fields to the Selected Fields box as shown in Figure 4-4. Click Next > .

7. Select the Department field in the box underneath the question; Do you want any grouping levels? Click > . The fields in the report will be grouped by Department as shown in Figure 4-5. Click Next > .

8. Click the list arrow on the first sort order list box. Select Last Name on the drop-down list.

9. Click the list arrow on the second sort order list box. Select First Name on the drop-down list. The records will first be sorted by last name. In cases where there are identical last names, First Name will serve as the secondary sort field. Click Next > . ◀▬▶ By default, Access will sort the fields in ascending order. To switch to a descending sort, click the Ascending button to change the button caption to Descending.

10. Leave the layout in the Stepped format and click the Landscape option button in the Orientation section. Click Next > . ◀▬▶ If you do not choose any grouping levels for a report, your layout choices will be limited to three: Columnar, Tabular, or Justified. The layouts in Step #10 are only available for grouped reports.

(continued on AC 4.6)

Figure 4-3 Removing fields from a report

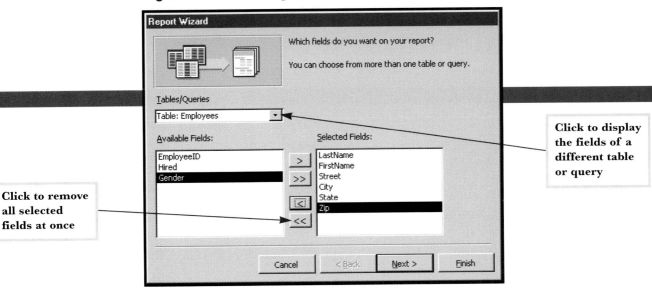

Click to display
the fields of a
different table
or query

Click to remove
all selected
fields at once

Figure 4-4 Adding fields from a second record source

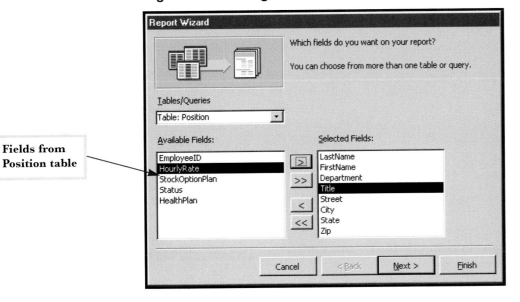

Fields from
Position table

Figure 4-5 Adding a grouping level to a report

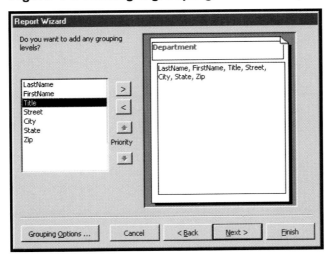

skill   Using the Report Wizard (continued)

do it!

11. Choose the Corporate style and click [Next >] .

12. Leave the name for the report Employees and click [Finish] to open the report in Print Preview as shown in Figure 4-6. Increase the size of the window as necessary.

13. Click the list arrow on the Zoom list box. Select 75% on the drop-down list. The onscreen magnification is decreased allowing you to see more of the report.

14. Click the Multiple Pages button [⊞] on the Print Preview toolbar. Drag across the top row on the drop-down palette to select the 1x3 display and click the left mouse button to display all three pages of the report.

15. Use the magnification glass pointer to click the lower left hand corner of the second page of the report. The page footer for the report displays the date in the left hand corner of each page and the page number out of how many total pages in the report in the right-hand corner of each page. Click the magnification glass pointer again to zoom out.

16. Click the One Page button [▣] on the Print Preview toolbar. Close the report.

more

The report header which prints once at the beginning of the report contains the title for the report. The page header prints at the top of every page and contains the labels or column headings. When you group records, the Report Wizard automatically creates a group header which contains the name for the like field that defines each group. You can add a group footer, as you will see in the next two skills, to include summary information about the group such as a count, sum or average.

Print Preview displays reports as they will appear when printed. As you saw in the exercise, you can change the onscreen magnification percentage in the Zoom list box either by selecting a different percentage on the drop-down list or by typing in the magnification percentage you want. Changing the magnification does not change the size at which the document is printed. The Fit setting adjusts the magnification of the page to fit the size of the window. You can switch between the magnification you selected and Fit using the magnification glass pointer or the Zoom button [🔍] on the Print Preview toolbar.

Figure 4-6 Employees report grouped by Department

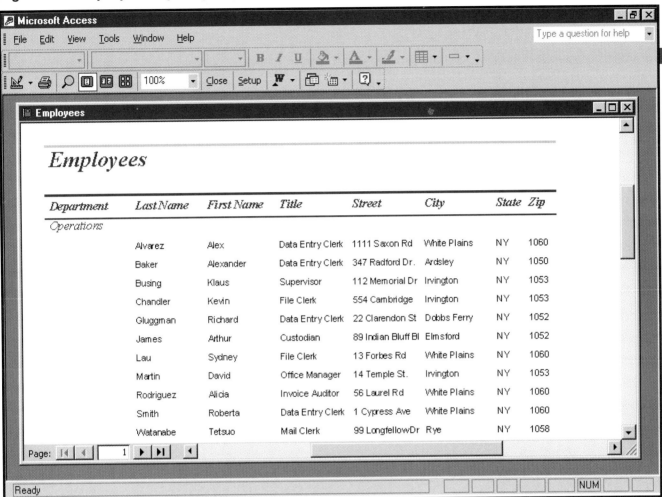

Access 2002

Practice

Fill in all of the Which Meal? fields in the Recipes table. Use the Report Wizard to create a report containing the Recipe Name, Food Category, Which Meal? Time to Prepare, and Number of Servings fields. Choose to view the data by Food Category. Add a grouping level for Which Meal? Click the Raise Priority button to make it the primary grouping field. Use the Outline 2 layout and the Corporate style. Keep the default name.

skill   Formatting a Report

concept

Just as in a form, all of the objects in a report can be modified in Design View. You can change the organization or layout of your report and apply formatting changes to the entire report or to individual sections. You can rearrange and resize fields, add special effects, align and format text, and add color. In a grouping report you can also add group footers and set group properties to improve the appearance of your report.

do it!

Apply formatting effects and add a group footer to the Employees report.

1. Select the Employees report in the Employees 2 database window. Click [Design] on the Database window toolbar to open the report in Design View.

2. Select the label control with the report title in the Report Header section of the report. Click the Underline button [U] on the Formatting (Form/Report) toolbar.

3. Click in the vertical ruler to the left of the Department label in the Page Header section of the report to select all of the label controls in the page header. Increase the font size for the controls to 12 pt.

4. Select the Department text box in the Department (group) Header section. Make the text bold and underlined.

5. Select the Last Name text box in the Detail section of the report. Make the text bold and change the font color to the medium blue color (the third row, sixth square) on the Font/Fore Color palette.

6. Select the text box containing the Now function (=Now()) in the Page Footer section of the report. Decrease the size of the text box and change the background color for the text box to light blue (the last row, fifth square on the Fill/Back Color palette).

7. Click the Sorting and Grouping button [≣] on the Report Design toolbar.

8. Click in the Group Footer settings box in the Group Properties section at the bottom of the dialog box. Click the list arrow and select Yes on the drop-down list to add a group footer to the report.

9. Click in the Keep Together property settings box. Click the list arrow and select Whole Group. Check your settings against Figure 4-7.

10. Close the Sorting and Grouping dialog box. Save the changes and click [🔍] to switch to Print Preview. Use the navigation buttons to view the formatting changes (see Figure 4-8).

more

To access the property sheet for the entire report (Figure 4-9), double-click the small gray box [ ] in the upper-left corner of the report window at the intersection of the vertical and horizontal rulers. This is called the Report Selector icon. When the form is selected, the Report Selector icon will contain a black square [■].

Each section of the report also has a property sheet. To the left of each section bar is a small gray box on the vertical ruler. These are the Section Selectors. Double-click a Section Selector to open the property sheet for the section.

If you have the appropriate data you can group a report by more than one level, creating a report that resembles an outline, with subgroups nested within the primary group. The Group On property is used to instruct Access when to begin a new group of records. The default Each Value setting tells the program to group identical values. You can use the Interval setting to organize your report based on a range of entries. For example, if you group a number data type field using an interval of 25, Access will group records with the values, 0 to 24, 25 to 49, 50 to 99, and 100 to 124 and so on.

The With First Detail setting for the Keep Together property instructs Access to print all of the data from the group header through the Detail section for the first entry in the group on the same page. It ensures that a group header will not print at the bottom of a page with no records underneath it.

Figure 4-7 Sorting and Grouping dialog box

Sorting and Grouping symbol indicates that Access uses the field or expression to group the records

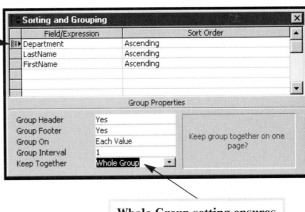

Whole Group setting ensures that the entire group will be kept together on one page of the report

Figure 4-8 Formatted Employees report

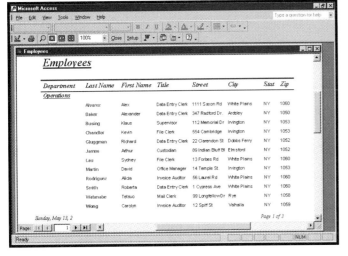

Figure 4-9 Property sheet of the Entire Report

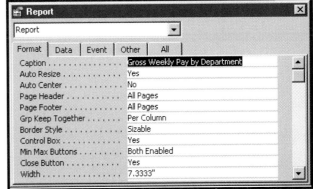

Practice

In the Recipes database, open the Recipes report in Design View. Open the Sorting and Grouping dialog box and set the Keep Together property to Whole Group. Format the Which Meal text box so that the entries display in an 11 pt Tahoma font in royal blue. Drag the right midpoint sizing handle on the Which Meal? label to the 1¼ inch mark on the horizontal ruler to decrease the label size. Move the Which Meal? text box to the left so that it is two dots to the right of the label. Save the changes and close the report.

skill

Adding a Calculated Control to a Report

concept

You can add fields to a report by adding unbound text box controls just as you did in the form. You can also use the Expression Builder to create an equation to calculate a value that you want to include in the report. Calculated controls are often quite useful in a report. You can calculate the quantity on hand of a certain product times its unit price to determine the value of your inventory, or you can use the Sum, Average or Count functions to summarize data for each group of records in a report.

do it!

Add unbound text boxes to the Group Footer and Report Footer sections of the report. Use the Count function to calculate the number of entries in each group and the total number of employees listed in the report.

1. Open the Employees report in the Employees 2 database in Design View.

2. Click the Toolbox button ⚒ on the Report Design toolbar. Click the Text Box button 🔲 to activate the Text Box pointer.

3. Click at the left edge of the Department Footer section. Use the move handles to position the new unbound text box and label control.

4. Click the label to select it. Drag to select the default numbered text in the label control. Type: Count.

5. Double-click the text box to open its property sheet. Click the Data tab. Type: =Count([Department]) in the Control Source property settings box. Close the property sheet. ◣◝ Remember, all formulas must begin with an equals sign and all field names must be enclosed in brackets. Parentheses must surround the expression on which a function is being performed.

6. Position the mouse pointer on the bottom edge of the Report Footer section bar until it turns into a vertical resizing pointer. Drag downward to create a section just large enough for a calculated control.

7. Click 🔲 in the Toolbox. Click once at the left edge of the Report Footer section to insert an unbound text box and label. Use the move handles to reposition the two controls. Close the Toolbox. Replace the default label text with: Grand Count.

8. Click the calculated control in the Group Footer section to select it. Drag to select the expression in the text box. Click the Copy button 📋 on the Report Design toolbar.

9. Click the unbound text box in the Report Footer section to select it. Click the control again to enter text. Click the Paste button 📋 to enter the formula. The Report Design window is shown in Figure 4-10.

10. Save the changes to the report and switch to Print Preview. Click the Last Page button ▶| . The last page of the report is shown in Figure 4-11. The expression using the Count function has totaled the number of records in each group and the number of records in the report.

11. Close the report, saving the changes if necessary.

more When you are entering a lengthy expression in the Control Source property for a report control, you can either right-click the settings box and click Zoom on the shortcut menu or use the keyboard combination [Shift]+[F2] to open the Zoom dialog box. The Zoom dialog box will enable you to see the entire equation as you are entering it.

The report footer is printed after the last group and appears only once, at the end of the report. The page footer is always the last section to print at the bottom of each page.

Figure 4-10 Calculated controls added to the group and report footers

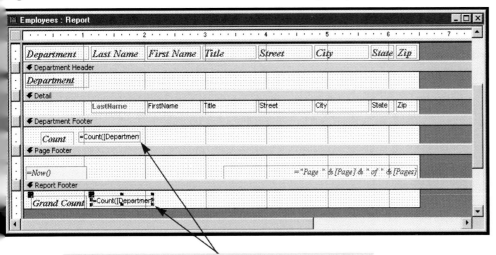

The same expression counts the numbers of records in each group in the group footers and the total number of records in the report in the report footer

Figure 4-11 Calculations in the report

Practice

Add an unbound text box to the report footer. Create a calculated control to count the total number of recipes in the database. Format the calculated text box in an 11 pt. Times New Roman font in dark blue to match the report. Enter Total Recipes as the label text. Create a light gray, sunken, 2 pt. border around both controls. Save the changes and close the report.

skill | Using a Query to Create a Report

concept

Although you can select fields from different tables and queries in the first step of the Report Wizard, you may find it easier to create a query to consolidate the fields that you want first. This will simplify the process if you decide to add fields or criteria later. You can easily add fields to the underlying query to add them to the field list for the report. You can also change criteria in the Query design grid to expand or limit the number of records displayed in the report.

do it!

Create a report based on a query including a summary of the records for each department.

1. In the Employees 2 database, click Queries on the Objects bar. Create a query with the Simple Query Wizard. From the necessary record sources, include (in order) the EmployeeID, LastName, FirstName, Department, Title, WeekEnding and Gross Weekly Pay fields as shown in Figure 4-12.

2. Make the query a detail query, and name it Gross Pay Report Query. Close the query.

3. Click Reports on the Objects bar. Double-click Create a report by using wizard to begin the Report Wizard. Add all of the fields in the Gross Pay Report Query except Week Ending to the Selected Fields box. Click [Next >].

4. Group the report based on the Department field. Click [Next >].

5. Sort the report in Ascending order based on the Last Name and First Name fields. Click [Summary Options ...].

6. Click the Sum checkbox in the Summary Options dialog box as shown in Figure 4-13 to instruct Access to calculate the sum of the gross weekly pay field for each department. Leave the Detail and Summary radio button selected and click [OK]. Click [Next >].

7. Leave the report in the Stepped layout and Portrait orientation. Apply the Corporate style if necessary. Name the report Gross Weekly Pay by Department and open it in Design View.

8. Rearrange the Employee ID, Last Name, and First Name fields (both the text boxes and the labels) so that the Employee ID field is the first field after the Department grouping. To select adjacent controls you can also click and drag to create a rectangle around the controls you want to select. The Select Objects button [ ] must be selected on the Toolbox.

9. Increase the size of the Employee ID label control. Select the report title and add 10/24/01 to the title. The changes to the report design are shown in Figure 4-14.

(continued on AC 4.14)

Figure 4-12 Creating a record source for a report

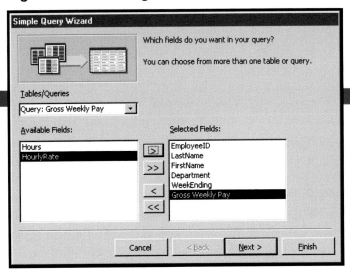

Figure 4-13 Summary Options dialog box

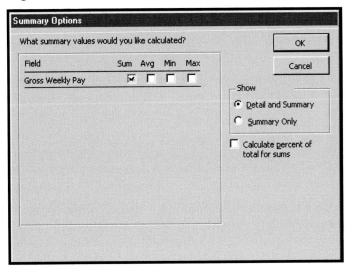

Figure 4-14 Gross Weekly Pay 10/24/01 report in Design View

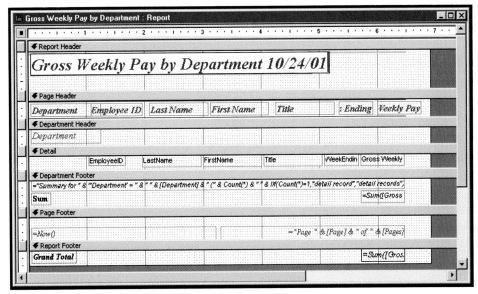

skill

Using a Query to Create a Report (continued)

do it!

10. Select the two calculated text boxes labeled Sum and Grand Total in the Department Footer and Report Footer sections and open the multiple selection property sheet. Set the Format property to Currency as shown in Figure 4-15 and close the property sheet. You can also right-click a selected control or group of controls and click Properties on the shortcut menu to open the property sheet.

11. Switch to Print Preview and use the scroll bars and the navigation buttons to view the report. A summary has been created for each group. The number of records and gross weekly pay total for each department display in the group footers. However, there are two weeks of pay displayed for each employee (see Figure 4-16). Save the changes to the report and close it.

12. Open the Gross Pay Report Query in Design View. In the Criteria cell for the Week Ending field, type =10/24/01. Press [Enter]. Save the change and close the query.

13. Open the Gross Weekly Pay by Department report in Print Preview. Changing the criteria in the underlying record source has eliminated the unwanted records in the report. Close the report.

14. Right-click the report name in the Database window. Click the Rename command. Position the insertion point at the end of the title and add: 10/24/01 to the report name. Press [Enter].

more

Creating a query to gather the fields you want for your report into one database object is a good practice. If you decide you want to add fields later, it is easier to add the fields to the underlying query. To add fields and criteria to the report itself you must either change the properties of the report or add unbound text box controls and create expressions to retrieve the desired value. It is much easier to create a query to select the fields and use it as the record source for the report.

Figure 4-15 Applying the Currency format to a multiple selection

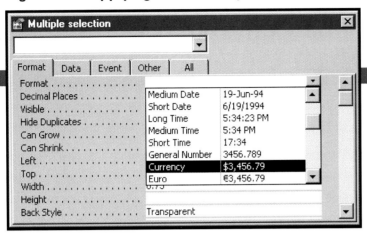

Figure 4-16 Completed report

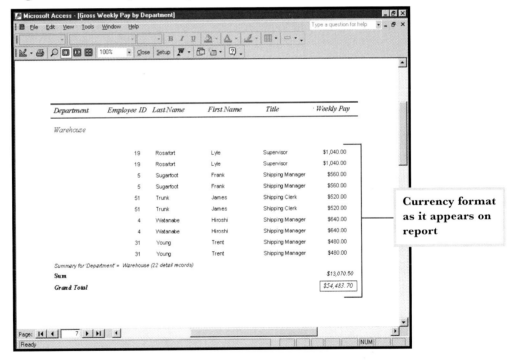

Practice

Use the Simple Query Wizard to create a query containing the Which Meal, Recipe Name, Food Category, and Vegetarian fields. Name the query Vegetarian and enter Yes in the Criteria cell for the Vegetarian field in the Query design grid. Create a report with the Recipe Name, Food Category and Which Meal fields from the query grouped by Food Category. Use the Stepped layout, Corporate style, and name it Vegetarian.

skill Previewing and Printing a Report

MOUS Skill

concept

Before you print a report you should make sure that all of the controls are correctly aligned. Misaligned controls in a report will be obvious and will detract from the effectiveness of the printed document. You can display just a few sample records in Layout view to check that the controls in every section of the report are properly displayed. Then you can adjust the margins, change the page orientation, or adjust the paper size if necessary in the Page Setup dialog box. Finally you can return to Print Preview and print the report.

do it!

Align the controls in the Gross Weekly Pay by Department 10/24/01 report, preview the report in Layout Preview, adjust the page margins, and print the report.

1. Open the Gross Weekly Pay by Department 10/24/01 report in the Employees 2 database in Design View.

2. Click in the vertical ruler to the left of the Department label in the Page Header section of the report to select all of the label controls in the section. Open the Format menu, highlight Align and click Top. The top edges of all of the controls are aligned with the uppermost selected label.

3. Click in the vertical ruler to the left of the Employee ID text box in the Detail section of the report. Open the Format menu, highlight Align, and click Bottom. There is now a straight line along the bottom edge of the five controls.

4. Click at the ¼ inch mark on the horizontal ruler to select all of the controls on the left edge of the report. Align the controls Left as shown in Figure 4-17.

5. Click at the 6 inch mark on the horizontal ruler to select the controls on the right edge of the report. Align the controls along the Right edge of the report.

6. Open the View menu and click the Layout Preview command. A sample report showing all of the controls but not all of the Detail section opens. You may still need to align some of the text boxes in the center of the report with their corresponding labels. If so, return to Design View, select the appropriate controls, and use the correct Align command to fix their placement on the report. Save the changes.

7. Open the File menu and click the Page Setup command. The Page Setup dialog box opens on the Margins tab.

8. Double-click in the Top text box to highlight the setting. Type .75 to set the margin to ¾ of an inch. Press [Tab]. Type: .75 to reset the Bottom margin, as shown in Figure 4-18.

9. Click the Page tab. If necessary you can change the page orientation or paper size on this page of the dialog box. Click   OK   .

10. Return to Design View. Click 🔍.

11. Open the File menu and click the Print command. Click the Pages radio button in the Print Range section. Enter 1 in both the From and the To text box to print only the first page of the report. Click   OK   to print the page. Close the Print Preview window.

more

Access stores the page setup settings for forms and reports so you only have to set them once. For tables and queries, you must set the page setup options every time you print. The default margin settings (1 inch Top, Bottom, Left, and Right) can be changed on the General tab in the Options dialog box. You open the Options dialog box by clicking the Options command on the Tools menu. Changing the default margins will not affect the margin settings on existing forms and reports.

The Printer section in the Print dialog box tells Access which printer it is sending data to and where that printer is located. The Properties button opens the Printer Properties dialog box where you can change the paper size and page orientation, or adjust the print quality and color intensity.

Figure 4-17 Aligning controls

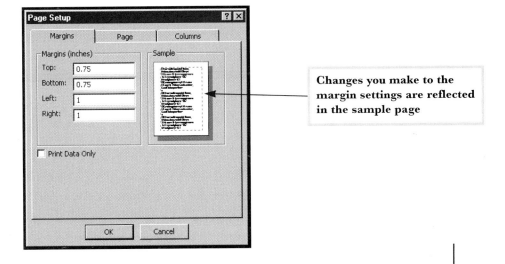

This aligns the left edge of each of the seven selected controls

Figure 4-18 Adjusting page margins in the Page Setup dialog box

Changes you make to the margin settings are reflected in the sample page

Practice

Open the Vegetarian Report in Design View. Use the Report Selector to select the report and click the AutoFormat button. Change the report style to Bold. Open the report in Layout Preview. Click the Two Pages button. Open the Page Setup dialog box and decrease the left and right margin to ½ inch. Close the report, saving the changes. Close the Recipes database.

Access 2002

skill   Creating Mailing Labels

concept

In an office many tasks involve bulk-mailings, for example, correspondence with employees, invoices to customers, and remittances to suppliers. The Label Wizard can be used to create mailing labels directly from a database. Mailing labels are a special type of multi-column report specifically designed to be printed on many different brands of adhesive labels.

do it!

Create mailing labels for the Employees 2 database.

1. With Reports selected on the Objects bar on the Employees 2 Database window click 🆕 New on the Database window toolbar to open the New Report dialog box.

2. Click Label Wizard in the New Report dialog box. Choose the Employees table as the record source. Click ⟨ OK ⟩.

3. Drag the scroll bar down the list of Product numbers in the: What label size would you like? scrolling list box to locate the Avery USA 5095 label as shown in Figure 4-19. Click to select it and click ⟨ Next > ⟩. ◗◗◗ If you cannot locate the correct label, click the English radio button in the Unit of Measure section and click the list arrow on the Filter by manufacturer list box and select Avery on the drop-down list.

4. Click the list arrow on the Font name list box and select Lucinda Handwriting on the drop-down list.

5. Click the list arrow on the Font weight list box and select Semi-bold on the drop-down list.

6. Click the list arrow on the Font size list box and select 10 on the drop-down list. Click ⟨ Next > ⟩.

7. Select First Name in the Available fields scrolling list box. Click the Add Field button ⟨ > ⟩. Press the space bar and add the Last Name field. Press [Enter].

8. Select the Street field and click ⟨ > ⟩. Press [Enter]. Double-click the City field to add it to the label. Type a comma (,), press the space bar, and double-click the State field to add it to the label.

9. Press the space bar. Double-click the Zip field to add it to the label. The prototype label is shown in Figure 4-20. Click ⟨ Next > ⟩.

10. Double-click the Last Name field in the Available fields list box. Double-click the First Name field to make it the secondary sorting criterion. Click ⟨ Next > ⟩.

11. Click ⟨ Finish ⟩ to accept the default name for the report and open it in Print Preview as shown in Figure 4-21. Close the report.

more

The Label Wizard includes the correct dimensions for numerous commercial adhesive labels made for dot-matrix or laser printers. After you select the label type, Access sets up the number of columns, rows per page and margins for the Detail section of the report. In the first wizard dialog box you can create your own custom label to accommodate labels with unusual sizes or for manufacturers that are listed in the dialog box.

Figure 4-19 Choosing the label type in the Label Wizard

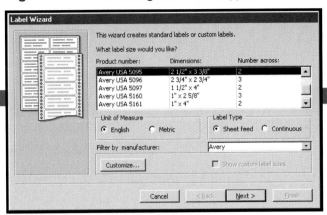

Figure 4-20 Prototype label

Select fields
for label here

Type your own fields
on the prototype here

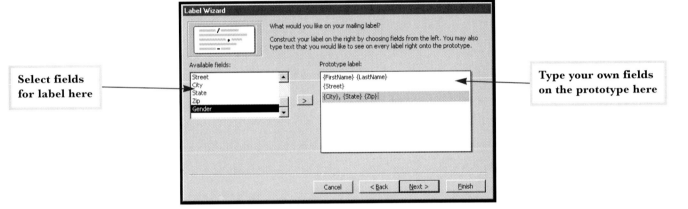

Figure 4-21 Labels in Print Preview

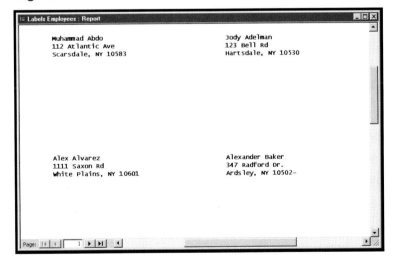

Practice

Open the Tuning Tracker 2 database. Use the Customers table to create mailing labels for the company. Use the Avery 5095 label and the Times New Roman font in an 11 pt size and a semi-bold weight. Create the prototype label with the correct punctuation and spacing. Sort the labels by last and first name. Close Access.

shortcuts

Function	Button/Mouse	Menu	Keyboard
Print Preview		In Report Design View: click View, then click Print Preview	[Alt]+[V], [V]
AutoFormat		In Form or Report Design View: Click Format, then click AutoFormat	[Alt]+[O], [F]
New Object: AutoReport		On the Database toolbar: click Insert, then click AutoReport	[Alt]+[I], [E]
Show Sorting and Grouping/Hide Sorting and Grouping		In Report Design View: click View, then click Sorting and Grouping	[Alt]+[V], [S]
One Page, Two Pages, Multiple Pages		In Print Preview: click View, point to Pages, then click One, Two, Four, Eight or Twelve	[Alt]+[V], [A], ([O], [T], [F], [E], or [W])
Print	(to bypass the Print dialog box)	Click File, then click Print	[Alt]+[F], [P]
Zoom			

A. Identify Key Features

Name the first three items indicated by callouts and match the rest with the correct answer below.

Figure 4-22 A report in Design View

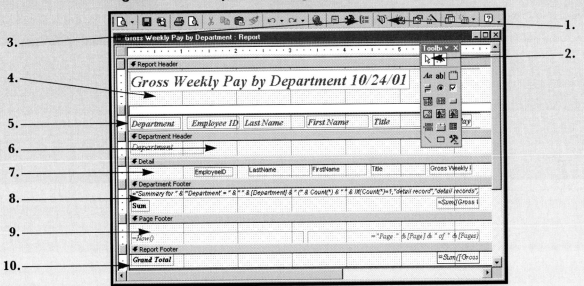

1.
2.
3.
4.
5.
6.
7.
8.
9.
10.

B. Select the Best Answer

11. Either prints an entire group from header to footer on the same page or prints all of the data from the group header through the first entry in the Detail section on the same page

12. Property you set to Currency to display calculated controls with a dollar sign and two decimal places

13. Used to create a standard report based on a single record source

14. Small gray box in the upper-left corner of the report window that is used to access the property sheet fo the entire report

15. Used to switch between a selected magnification percentage and a report sized to fit in the window

16. Used to create a special type of multicolumn report specifically designed to be printed on an adhesive label

17. Small gray box on the vertical ruler that you can use to open the property sheet of a report section

18. Dialog box found within the Report Wizard where you can set Access to calculate the sum, average, minimum value, or maximum value for each data set in a grouped report

19. Displays a report with only a few sample rows of data to give you an idea of how the report will look without having to view every detail

20. Contains commands for viewing one, two, or multiple pages of a repot

a. Summary Options

b. Section Selector

c. Label Wizard

d. Layout Preview

e. Format property

f. Keep Together property

g. Print Preview toolbar

h. Report Selector

i. Auto Report Wizard

j. Zoom

quiz (continued)

C. Complete the Statement

21. To group a report based on a selected field you must:

a. Set the Group On property to Each Value in the Sorting and Grouping dialog box

b. Set the Group Header, Group Footer or both properties to Yes on the property sheet for the field you want to group by

c. Set the Group Header, Group Footer or both properties to Yes in the Grouping and Sorting dialog box

d. Set the Grouping property to Yes on the property sheet for the field you want to group by

22. When you are entering a lengthy expression in the Control Source property for a report control, you can create a clearer working space to see the entire equation as you are entering it by: Pick two

a. Opening the View menu and clicking the Zoom command

b. Using the keyboard combination [Shift] + [F2] to open the Zoom dialog box

c. Clicking the Zoom button on the Print Preview toolbar to open the Zoom dialog box

d. Right-clicking the settings box and clicking Zoom on the shortcut menu

23. To select multiple controls on a report you can do all of the following except:

a. Press the Shift key down and click each control you want to include.

b. Click the Section selector for a section of the report in which you want to select all of the controls

c. Click in the horizontal or vertical ruler above or to the left of the row or column of controls you want to select

d. Make sure the Select Objects button is selected on the Toolbox and click and drag to create a rectangle around the controls you want to select

24. The Detail section of a report will usually contain this type of control

a. Text box controls

b. Label controls

c. Calculated controls

d. Combo box controls

25. A group footer will usually contain this type of control

a. Text box controls

b. Label controls

c. Calculated controls

d. Combo box controls

26. The page header will usually contain this type of control

a. Text box controls

b. Label controls

c. Calculated controls

d. Combo box controls

27. The correct expression for calculating the sum of the values in the Extended Price field is:

a. Sum([ExtendedPrice])

b. = Sum[ExtendedPrice]

c. =Sum({ExtendedPrice})

d. =Sum([ExtendedPrice])

28. You can use this function to insert the current system date and time in a field

a. Date()

b. Time()

c. Now()

d. Date/Time()

interactivity

Build Your Skills

1. Use the Report Wizard to create a grouped report. Add a group footer and calculated controls and customize the report.

   a. Open the Home Video Collection database. Use the Report Wizard to create an Inventory report grouped by Rating. Include the Title, Genre, Rating, Comment, and Star, fields. Sort the report in ascending order alphabetically by Title within each group. Use the Outline 1 format in portrait orientation in any style you choose. Name the Report Home Video Inventory.

   b. Open the Report in Design View. Add a group footer to the report and program Access to keep each group together on the same page.

   c. Add an unbound text box to the group footer. Enter the expression that will count the number of videos in each rating group. Also add a calculated control to the report footer to count the total number of videos in the inventory. Enter appropriate label text for each calculated control. Switch to Layout Preview.

   d. Align the calculated controls and format the text boxes so that they display with a semi-bold font style and are enclosed in a 3 pt. gray border with a shadowed effect.

   e. View the complete report in Print Preview and move and resize any fields as necessary. If the style you have chosen has any lines separating the labels in the group header from the Detail section, select the line controls and increase their lengths as necessary. Align the controls as necessary.

   f. Save the changes and close the report.

2. Create a query to serve as the record source for a report. Use the Report Wizard to create a report including group and report summaries and totals. Format the report and change the criteria in the record source to remove records from the report.

   a. Open the Office Furniture database. Use the Simple Query Wizard to generate a detail query that includes (in order) the Order ID, Order Date, Company Name, Units Ordered, Product Name, and Unit Price fields. Name the query Orders Query and open it in Design View.

   b. Create a calculated field in the Query design grid named Invoice Total. Create the expression that will calculate the result. Note: In the real world this would be a more complex calculation including the tax, shipping, and any discounts applied to the order. For now just create the simple expression.

   c. Save the changes to the query and run it to make sure you have entered the expression correctly. Close the query.

   d. Use the Report Wizard to create a report using all of the fields from the query except Order ID. Group the report by Order Date. Sort the fields in each group alphabetically by Company Name. Create a summary to display the total number of units of product ordered per month and the Invoice total for each month.

   e. Use the Stepped layout, Landscape orientation, and the Corporate style. Name the report Orders Report.

   f. View the report. Switch to Report Design View and resize and realign controls as necessary. Format the sums of the invoice totals as currency. Format all four calculated text boxes with a medium font weight, dark blue fore color (8388608), and a raised 2 pt. border.

   g. Drag the Page Footer downward slightly to increase the size of the group footer (Order Date) section and thus increase the space between the group footer and the report footer.

   h. Complete any other formatting, layout, and alignment changes you think are necessary, save them, and close the report.

interactivity (continued)

Build Your Skills (continued)

i. Open the Orders Query in Design View. Enter criteria to display only orders placed in May. Use the wildcard character (*) for the day, to instruct the program to select all order dates in May of 2001. Press Enter and run the query. Access will insert the Like operator. All entries that match the pattern 5/*/01 or 5/*/2001 (depending on which Short Date format your system is using) will be extracted. Save the change to the query design and close the query.

j. Open the Orders Report and view the change. You have created a report for only the month of May. Change the title for the report to May Orders Report. Save and close the report. Rename the report in the Database window.

3. Create Mailing Labels:

a. Use the Label wizard and fields from the Customers table in the Office Furniture database to create mailing labels for the billing department. Use the Avery 5095 label.

b. Use the Arial font with a medium weight in a 10 pt. size. Create the prototype label with the correct spacing and punctuation. Sort the labels alphabetically by the company name and keep the default name for the report.

Problem Solving Exercises

1. Open the Magazine Preferences database. Use the Report Wizard to create a report using the Age, Gender, Occupation and # of Magazines Read Regularly fields. Group the report by age. Click the Grouping Options button to open the Grouping Intervals dialog box. Click the list arrow on the Grouping Intervals list box and select 10s on the drop-down list. This will group the report into age group blocks of 10 years. Do not select a sorting field. Use the Outline 2 layout with a portrait orientation. Use the Casual style and name the report Survey Respondents.

2. View the report. Switch to Report Design View and resize, move and realign the controls appropriately. Open the Grouping and Sorting dialog box and set the Keep Together property so that no age group will be split between two pages of the report. Use the Report Selector to select the report. Use the Auto Format button on the Report Design toolbar to change the style of the report to Bold. View the report in Layout Preview. Decrease the size of the Left and Right page margins to .5 each so that the report fits on two pages.

3. Reformat the report title in any way you choose. You can change the font, font weight, font color, back color, border, special effect, etc. Use both the commands on the Formatting toolbar and the property sheet to achieve a result you are satisfied with. Reformat the Age by 10s text box. Resize the text boxes in the page footer that display the date and page numbers.

4. Add a group footer. Add a calculated control to the group footer to count the number of survey respondents in each age category. Resize and move the controls to the left side of the report aligned with the Age text box and label. Create a border around the calculated control and its label and apply a special effect.

5. Click the AutoFormat button on the Report Design toolbar. Click the Customize button. Select the Create a new AutoFormat based on the Report (report name) radio button. Click OK. The New Style Name dialog box opens. Enter a name for the new format you have just created and click OK. Access will create the new AutoFormat and return you to the AutoFormat dialog box. Your new format is listed in the Report AutoFormats list. You can reuse the design on other reports. Click the Close button. Close the report and save the changes.

1

Introduction to PowerPoint

Microsoft PowerPoint is a computer application that helps you create professional-looking presentations. With PowerPoint you can make on-screen presentations, overhead transparencies in black and white or color, paper printouts, 35mm slides, or handouts that include notes or outlines of your presentation. You even can publish a PowerPoint presentation on the World Wide Web where anyone with Internet service and a Web browser can view it. PowerPoint is an effective tool that enables you to organize and present information easily. Creating and editing text and graphics are made easier by PowerPoint's user-friendly features.

With PowerPoint you can design a presentation using a pre-made template—that is, a file with a pre-existing layout, background colors, fonts and bullets of certain sizes, and so on. If you do not use a template, you can create your own presentation from blank slides. A quick and easy way to create a presentation is to let PowerPoint aid you in designing one by using a tool called the AutoContent Wizard. PowerPoint enables you to add Clip Art, charts, photographs, video, and sound to enhance your presentation.

If you need help on how to use PowerPoint, you can ask questions of the Office Assistant or enter them in the Ask a Question box to receive tips and/or Help topics potentially related to your questions. An extensive Help facility complements the Assistant and Question box. This facility has additional tabs for displaying and printing information from either the program's built-in database of Help topics or from Microsoft's Web-based Help sites.

Lesson Goal:

Start PowerPoint and familiarize yourself with the application by creating a short presentation using the AutoContent Wizard. Also use PowerPoint's key Help features to obtain assistance.

skills

≶ **Introducing PowerPoint and Presentation Design**

≶ **Starting PowerPoint**

≶ **Using the AutoContent Wizard**

≶ **Exploring the PowerPoint Window**

≶ **Viewing Your Presentation**

≶ **Saving and Closing a File**

≶ **Using the Office Assistant**

≶ **Other PowerPoint Help Features**

skill

Introducing PowerPoint and Presentation Design

concept

A PowerPoint presentation is a file composed of slides, each slide being a single screen of the presentation. You can create overhead transparencies and other presentation materials containing main headings and subpoints. You can use simple graphics like Clip Art or photographs to complement your text or more complicated graphics like tables, charts, or diagrams to illustrate complex ideas or data. If you display a presentation on a computer, not just an overhead projector, you can exploit PowerPoint's increasingly powerful animation features to create dynamic presentations rivaling television and the movies. As mentioned on the previous page, you even can publish PowerPoint presentations to the World Wide Web.

Teachers and students alike use PowerPoint to explore every subject from art to English to math to zoology. Business professionals use PowerPoint to create simple handouts or complex presentations on acquiring other companies, marketing products to consumers, building new facilities, and so on. PowerPoint presentations are popular with non-profit organizations, social and political clubs, and the military and government as well.

Building a PowerPoint presentation involves starting with a basic design, adding new slides and content, then modifying slide design, often with different formats and color schemes. As suggested above, computer-based presentations often contain additional slide transitions, animation, sound effects, and narration. The four bullet points below explain the most common ways in which people build presentations:

- With a Blank presentation you must add all of the background elements, text, graphics, and other visual elements people normally associate with professional-looking presentations.

- With a Design Template you begin with a file containing a pre-selected background complete with a color scheme, placeholders dictating the location and size of text and/or graphics, fonts and bullets of pre-determined sizes, and other formatting elements common to finished presentations. You can apply this template to all of your slides or to just selected slides. With PowerPoint 2002, you also now have the freedom to apply more than one type of template within a presentation.

- With a Content Template you begin with a design template as described above. However, this template also contains suggested text for each slide to help you stay focused on the purpose and content of your presentation. By replacing the suggested text with your own, you stay on topic but have a presentation that is custom designed for your own situation. The AutoContent Wizard, discussed later in this Lesson, uses Content Templates.

- With a Web Template you begin with a template stored on a Web site, such as the Microsoft Office Template Gallery at http://officeupdate.microsoft.com/templategallery/. Web designers, graphic artists, and other Internet-trained users provide categorized PowerPoint templates on their sites, sometimes for free and sometimes for a fee. You can access these Web sites from within an Internet browser or directly through PowerPoint.

Figure 1-1 Sample Title slide

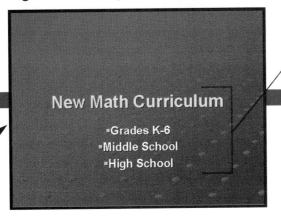

Title slides summarize presentation topic, grab viewer's attention, and list key upcoming points

Change slide designs, backgrounds, layouts, colors, fonts, bullets, etc. to create customized presentations

Figure 1-2 Sample Title, Text, and Content slide

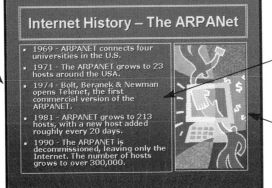

Use bulleted or numbered slides to list detailed points

Add Clip Art, photos, diagrams, or other graphics to enliven and illustrate text or data

Figure 1-3 Multiple slides created with AutoContent Wizard

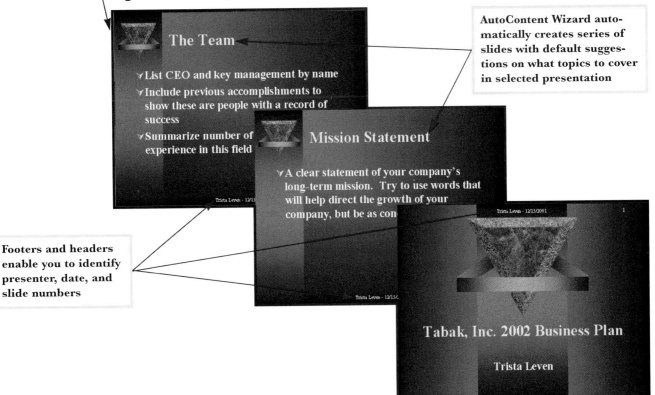

AutoContent Wizard automatically creates series of slides with default suggestions on what topics to cover in selected presentation

Footers and headers enable you to identify presenter, date, and slide numbers

skill | Starting PowerPoint

concept

To use PowerPoint, you first must start the application from your computer's desktop. The Windows operating system permits you to start an application in a variety of ways. You can start PowerPoint and other programs by using the Start menu on the Windows taskbar, a Quick Launch on the Windows taskbar, a desktop shortcut, or by finding the program's executable file through My Computer or Windows Explorer.

do it !

Begin using PowerPoint by starting the application from the Start menu.

1. Turn on your computer and monitor. After a brief delay the Windows Desktop will appear (generally with a greenish background). Shortcuts (images with program names underneath them) will appear on the Desktop for accessing the main utility and application programs in your computer's hard drive or on your organization's network. A gray Windows taskbar will appear at the bottom of the screen. Click the Start button 🔳 Start located at the left end of the taskbar. A gray Windows Start menu will appear above the button.

2. On the Start menu, move the mouse pointer over the word Programs to select it near the top of the menu. The gray Programs submenu will appear with, generally, an alphabetized list of programs that are installed on your computer.

3. After pointing to the word Programs, slide over to select the Programs submenu and then down to select the words Microsoft PowerPoint (see Figure 1-4).

4. With Microsoft PowerPoint still selected, click the left mouse button to start the program. By default, PowerPoint will display the Normal view of the application with the Outline and Slides tabs at the left side of the program window, a blank slide in the middle Slide Pane of the window, and the New Presentation task pane at the right side of the window. (see Figure 1-5).

5. Do not worry if your program window does not exactly resemble Figure 1-5. Users can install PowerPoint in more than one way, and the Microsoft Windows environment comes in more than one version. The actions of previous users also may affect the setup of your program window. 🖱️ To make a consistent view appear each time you open PowerPoint, click the Tools menu near the top of the screen, click Options to open the Options dialog box, and click the View tab if needed to bring it to the front of the dialog box. Under the Default View section of the View tab, click the down-pointing arrow, click the option Normal - thumbnails, notes and slide, then click the OK button [OK].

6. The next Skill introduces the AutoContent Wizard, which appears in the New Presentation Task Pane under the category New. Therefore, leave the file open.

more

Notice also that a Notes Pane appears below the blank slide. Clicking and typing in this pane enables you to record speaker notes for the current slide on the screen. For example, for the opening slide of a presentation, you might type welcoming remarks in the pane, and for a concluding slide you might suggest follow-up actions for your audience to undertake after leaving a meeting. After preparing a presentation, you can print regular handouts, transparencies, or similar items for your audience but print Notes pages for yourself as the presenter. Later Skills will discuss printing various versions of a presentation.

Figure 1-4 Opening PowerPoint from the Windows Start menu

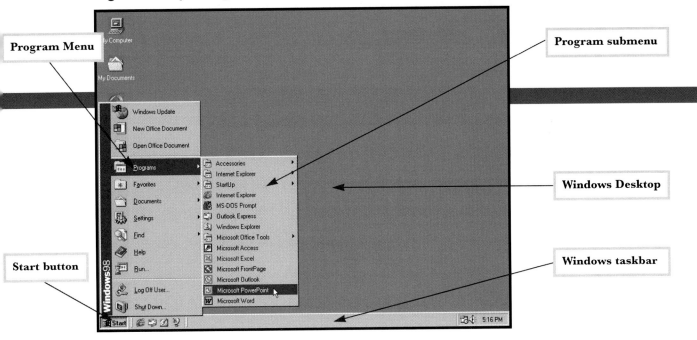

Program Menu

Program submenu

Windows Desktop

Start button

Windows taskbar

Figure 1-5 PowerPoint Normal View, default setting

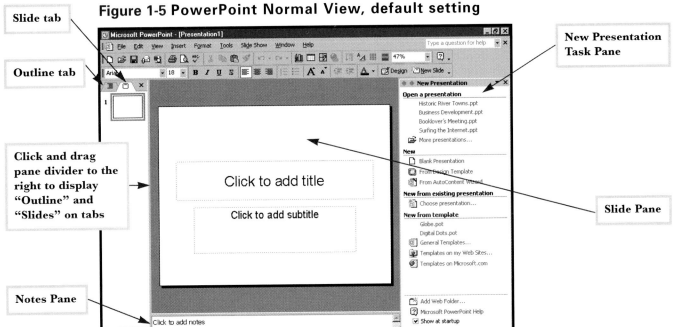

Slide tab

Outline tab

Click and drag pane divider to the right to display "Outline" and "Slides" on tabs

Notes Pane

New Presentation Task Pane

Slide Pane

Practice

Task panes are a new feature of PowerPoint 2002 and other Office XP programs. These panes are Web-styled areas containing commands that you can use to undertake operations or choose options. You can dock these panes anywhere in the program window and resize them by clicking and dragging their edges. You also can open and close them as work needs dictate. A task pane's appearance can vary according to previous usage. For example, the first four entries under the heading Open a presentation represent four previously opened PowerPoint presentations.

skill Using the AutoContent Wizard

concept

PowerPoint's AutoContent Wizard provides you with templates that include pre-selected layout designs, styles, and output types. To complete a presentation, all you have to do is add content in pre-established locations of each slide. The AutoContent Wizard therefore is the quickest, easiest way to design a presentation in PowerPoint. New PowerPoint users and users who need to create presentations quickly will find the AutoContent Wizard particularly helpful.

do it !

Use the AutoContent Wizard to design a presentation.

1. With the default PowerPoint window open on your screen, click the words From AutoContent Wizard under the New section of the New Presentations task pane. The task pane will disappear, and the blank slide that appeared in only the middle of the window will appear across the right two-thirds of the window. On top of the blank slide, the AutoContent Wizard dialog box will appear. In the left half of the box, a green box-shaped bullet will appear next to the word Start, indicating you are in the first step of the Wizard.

2. If the Office Assistant does not appear with the Wizard, click the Microsoft Office Assistant button at the bottom of the dialog box ⌗. This Assistant will offer helpful tips as you work your way through PowerPoint and will be discussed in detail later.

3. Move the mouse pointer over the blue bullet labeled Yes, please provide help in the Assistant's balloon, then click the left mouse button. The Assistant now will provide you with descriptions of the AutoContent Wizard's steps as you advance (see Figure 1-6).

4. Click the Next button   Next > . In the left half of the dialog box, the green bullet will appear next to the second step of the Wizard, Presentation type. This step asks you to select the type of presentation you're going to give. The presentation types are divided into categories. The General category button is selected in the middle of the dialog box, and its presentation types appear in the list box to the right of the category buttons.

5. Click the All button   All   to view all of the presentation types at once. The first presentation type, Generic, should be selected by default (see Figure 1-7).

6. Click Next   Next > . The green bullet will appear next to the third step of the Wizard, Presentation style. This step asks you to choose what type of output your presentation will use. Leave the On-screen presentation radio button selected (see Figure 1-8).

7. Click Next   Next > . The green bullet will appear next to the fourth step of the Wizard, Presentation options. This step enables you to add a title to the presentation and decide what information will appear in the footer, or bottom, of each presentation slide.

8. Move the mouse pointer over the Presentation title text box so the pointer changes to an I-beam, and click the mouse button. A flashing insertion point will appear in the text box. (If any unwanted information appears in the text box, click and drag over all of the information, press [Backspace] to delete that information, then type the desired text.)

(continued on PP 1.8)

Figure 1-6 AutoContent Wizard with Office Assistant

Position of green bullet shows which step of wizard is active

Office Assistant icon with Help balloon

Click here to activate Office Assistant

Click [Next] button to move to next step of wizard

Tabs, Slide Pane, and Notes Pane remain displayed in background

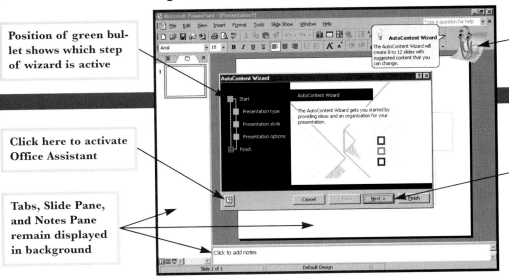

Figure 1-7 AutoContent Wizard, Step 2

Green bullet moves to second step of wizard

Instructions in Office Assistant change as you move to new wizard panel

Buttons show categories of presentations available for selection

Instructions ask you to select presentation type

Click [Back] button to return to previous step in wizard

Scrollable list displays presentation types of selected category

Figure 1-8 AutoContent Wizard, Step 3

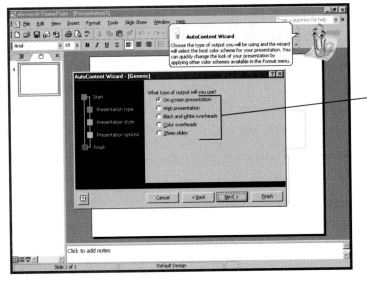

Users can select only one option from among radio buttons

skill Using the AutoContent Wizard (continued)

do it !

9. In the Presentation title text box, type Learning PowerPoint. Press [Tab] to move the insertion point to the Footer text box. In the Footer text box, type Trista Leven. Trista's name will appear at the bottom of each slide. Below the Footer text box are two check boxes that allow you to include on each slide the date that you last updated your presentation and the number of each slide. Leave these check boxes checked (see Figure 1-9).

10. Click ‎[Next >]‎. The green bullet will appear next to the last step of the Wizard, Finish. This step tells you that it has enough information to complete your presentation (see Figure 1-10). At this point you still can click the Back button ‎[< Back]‎ to return to any step of the Wizard to edit the content that you have provided.

11. Click the Finish button ‎[Finish]‎ to apply your content edits and to close the Wizard dialog box. The presentation will appear in Normal view, and the Office Assistant will close automatically (see Figure 1-11).

12. The AutoContent Wizard has created a number of slides, each with its own title and suggested discussion points. The first slide is displayed and includes Trista's name in the title. (You also may notice a wavy red line under Trista's name. When PowerPoint's Check spelling as you type option is on, the program places these lines under words it does not recognize. These lines appear on only the screen and do not appear in printed slides.)

13. The next Skill explains the different toolbars and windows of the PowerPoint program window. Therefore, leave the file open.

more

The AutoContent Wizard provides you with 24 commonly used presentations—from simple certificates for one person to sophisticated presentations for large groups. Be sure to choose a type that fits the purpose and content of the message you want to convey. For example, if you want people to commit to a goal, while explaining how to move from your current situation to that goal, you probably would use the Recommending a Strategy presentation. If you are starting a new business and need to explain its mission, introduce its leadership, describe a start-up marketing plan, and so on, you almost certainly would use the Business Plan presentation.

Once you create slides with the Wizard, you will see default text on each slide that gives advice on information to type in its place. You can follow the advice as closely or loosely as you wish. However, remember that each presentation type is designed with a particular purpose and content in mind. Wandering too far from the default text could create some rather confusing slides, especially if the new text were to contradict the default text. The idea here is not that you absolutely must follow the advice given on each slide, but that your new text should make sense in the context of the presentation type you have chosen.

The dialog box for the second step of the AutoContent Wizard, or Presentation type, contains Add and Remove buttons below the box that lists the various presentation types available in that step. Clicking the Add button opens the Select Presentation Template dialog box, from which you can choose additional presentation types. You may have to install these templates from your Office XP or PowerPoint 2002 CD-ROM. You also can create your own presentation templates and make them available to the Wizard through this dialog box. Clicking a presentation type in the list box mentioned above, then clicking the Remove button will delete the presentation type you just have highlighted. When removing presentation types, be sure to remove only those that you yourself have created or those authorized by your instructor.

As you work through the AutoContent Wizard, you can click the Finish button in any dialog box within the Wizard. However, be aware that the Wizard will complete the presentation with only the information you have provided to that point.

Figure 1-9 AutoContent Wizard, Step 4

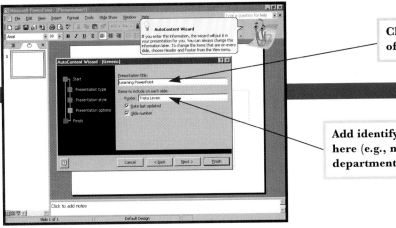

Click and type title of presentation

Add identifying information here (e.g., name of presenter, department, or company)

Figure 1-10 AutoContent Wizard, Step 5

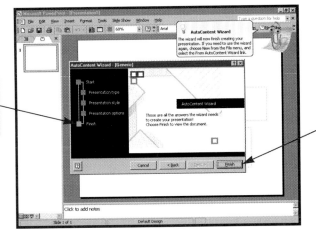

Green bullet in lowest box indicates last step of wizard

Click to close wizard and to create Generic presentation

Figure 1-11 Generic presentation created with AutoContent Wizard

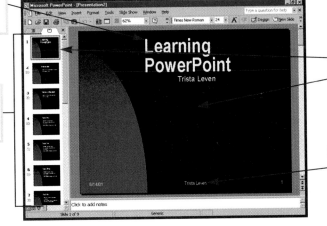

Title entered in Step 4 of wizard appears at top of Slide 1

Series of slides in Generic presentation appears on Slide tab

Slide 1 selected on Slides tab; Slide 1 appears in Slide pane

Name entered in Step 4 appears in footer of each slide

Practice

Do not worry if the name that appears immediately below the slide title does not match the name in Figure 1-11, since the user name for the computer you are using is what will appear there. To change the user's name, click Tools, click Options to open the Options dialog box, and click the General tab. In the User information section, type the desired name in the Name box, and click ☐ OK ☐.

skill Exploring the PowerPoint Window

concept

Exploring a program's application window is important in learning to use the program successfully. PowerPoint's window contains several time-tested and user-friendly features, including toolbars, icons or buttons, and window viewing controls. PowerPoint is designed so you can perform most of the program's functions from the main window. Clicking the Tools menu near the top-center of your screen also allows users access to commands for customizing or modifying options in the application window to suit individual preferences.

do it !

Familiarize yourself with the PowerPoint window to gain a better understanding of its functions and features.

1. Be sure that the presentation you created with the AutoContent Wizard appears in Normal view in the active window, as shown in Figure 1-12. If the window looks different, click the Normal View button [▣] at the lower-left of your screen to match the figure.

2. At the top of the active window is the blue Title bar. At the left end of the Title bar are the PowerPoint program Control Menu button [▣], program name, and name of the current presentation. The Control Menu button opens a menu of commands to restore, move, size, minimize, or maximize the program window and for closing the entire program. The right end of the Title bar has three sizing buttons: Minimize [▬] reduces the window to a program button on the Windows taskbar; Restore [▣] reverts the window to its original size and location; and Close [✖] terminates the entire program. ◤ If the window is not fully open, the Maximize button [☐] will appear in place of the Minimize button. Click the Maximize button to create the largest possible screen area for working in PowerPoint.

3. Below the Title bar is the gray Menu bar, containing menus of PowerPoint commands. Click once on File to display the File menu. Move your mouse pointer over a command on the menu and that command will become highlighted. You perform PowerPoint operations by clicking commands on a menu. Each menu contains a list of related commands and has two levels. The first level appears as soon as you open the menu and contains the commands you use most often. If you do not choose a command, the menu expands after several seconds to reveal all commands for that menu. (To see a full set of commands immediately, double-click the desired menu.) Near the right end of the Menu bar is the Ask a question text box. Type brief questions here and press [Enter] to display a list of Help screens that might display information about the questioned feature. At the right end is another Close button. Clicking this button closes the current presentation but leaves the program running and ready for you to open a new file.

4. The row of buttons and boxes immediately below the Menu bar contains two toolbars, the Standard toolbar and the Formatting toolbar. The Standard toolbar contains buttons for opening a new blank presentation, opening a previously created file, saving files, printing files, and so on. The Formatting toolbar contains boxes for changing the size of presentation fonts (i.e., typefaces), changing font size, bolding fonts, and so on. To see a list of all toolbars available in PowerPoint, click View on the Menu bar and highlight the Toolbars command. A submenu will appear with the names of all toolbars. A check mark will appear next to those toolbars that are active. Users can move and resize toolbars, so your screen may look slightly different than in Figure 1-12. When you rest the mouse pointer over a toolbar button, a small ScreenTip will display to identify the button's function.

(continued on PP 1.12)

Figure 1-12 PowerPoint program window

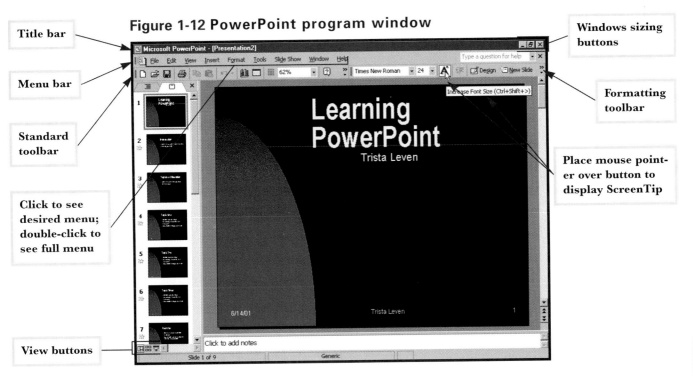

Title bar

Menu bar

Standard toolbar

Click to see desired menu; double-click to see full menu

View buttons

Windows sizing buttons

Formatting toolbar

Place mouse pointer over button to display ScreenTip

skill   Exploring the PowerPoint Window (continued)

do it !

5. Below the Standard and Formatting toolbars are the main PowerPoint work areas. The earlier Skill entitled "Starting PowerPoint" instructed you to select the default option Normal - thumbnails, notes and slide from the Tools menu. Therefore, the left-hand work area contains an Outline tab hidden behind a Slides tab. The Slides tab displays thumbnail-sized images of the presentation you created with the AutoContent Wizard. A vertical scroll bar appears at the right side of the Outline and Slides tabs, indicating that more slides exist below the bottom of the program window. A border surrounds Slide 1 on the Slides tab, so a large image of Slide 1 appears in the right-hand work area, or Slide Pane, of the program window. Below the Slide Pane is the Notes Pane discussed in the More section of the Skill entitled "Starting PowerPoint" (see Figure 1-13).

6. You may see vertical and horizontal scroll bars at the edges of the Slide Pane. If you do not see both scroll bars, click the arrow at the right edge of the Zoom box 62% ▾ near the top center of your screen. Click 100%, then press [Enter]. The vertical and horizontal scroll bars enable you to view the parts of a slide missing from the Slide Pane because the slide is too large to fit into the area all at once. You can use the scroll bars in a few ways. First, you can click on a scroll bar arrow to move the display in small increments. Second, you can click in the scroll bar slightly above or below the directional arrows so the display will move up or down one screen at a time. Third, you can drag the scroll bar box (which looks like a raised button) up or down to scroll to a specific place in the display. Clicking the Previous slide ▲ or Next slide ▼ buttons near the bottom-right corner of the program window moves the display up or down, respectively, one slide at a time (see Figure 1-14). When you have finished reviewing the scroll bars, click the Zoom box arrow again, then click Fit to make all of Slide 1 appear in the Slide Pane.

7. The next Skill explains different ways of viewing a PowerPoint presentation. Therefore, leave the file open.

more

Some menu commands have keyboard shortcuts next to them. Pressing a key combinations is equivalent to clicking the corresponding command from the menu. Clicking a command followed by an ellipsis (...) opens a dialog box with additional options related to the command. Using a keyboard shortcut makes sense when you are in the middle of typing text, while clicking commands saves time when your hand already is on the mouse.

In the left-hand work area, clicking the Outline tab will display the headings and subpoints of the active presentation. Clicking a slide icon or any text for that slide will display the selected slide in the Slide Pane. Similarly, on the Slides tab clicking a slide number or slide thumbnail will display the selected slide in the Slide Pane. The vertical scroll bar at the right edge of the Outline and Slides tabs work area works similarly to the scroll bars discussed above.

The Status bar at the bottom of the program window gives you feedback on your current activity in PowerPoint, including which slide you are viewing and the name of the design template being used (see Figure 1-14). If you double-click the current design name on the Status bar, the Slide Design task pane—a new feature in PowerPoint 2002—will appear in the right-hand area of the program window, with options for other Design Templates, Color Schemes, and Animation Schemes.

Figure 1-13 Panes in PowerPoint program window

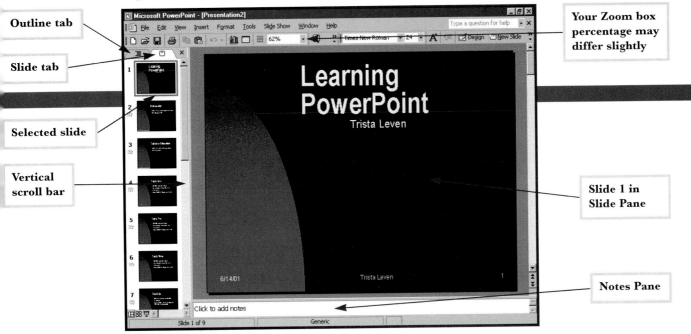

- Outline tab
- Slide tab
- Selected slide
- Vertical scroll bar
- Your Zoom box percentage may differ slightly
- Slide 1 in Slide Pane
- Notes Pane

Figure 1-14 Additional PowerPoint program window features

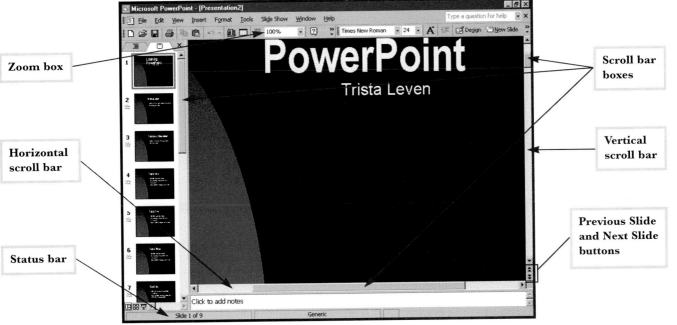

- Zoom box
- Horizontal scroll bar
- Status bar
- Scroll bar boxes
- Vertical scroll bar
- Previous Slide and Next Slide buttons

Practice

By default PowerPoint and other Office XP programs display only parts of the Standard and Formatting toolbars and only recently used menu commands. To display all of the toolbars and commands in your Office programs without sacrificing significant display area, click the Tools menu, then click the Customize command to display the Customize dialog box. Click the Options tab to bring it to the front of the dialog box. In the Personalized Menus and Toolbars section, click to add check boxes to the options Show Standard and Formatting toolbars on two rows and Always show full menus. Click the Close button [Close] to apply the toolbar formats and to close the dialog box.

skill Viewing Your Presentation

concept

PowerPoint offers a few ways to view presentations. The different views enable you to focus on specific aspects of your presentation. The view you select will depend on what you want to do with the presentation, such as adding or deleting text, adding or editing graphics, organizing your slides, or previewing your presentation.

do it !

See how the current presentation will appear in each of PowerPoint's views.

1. Be sure the presentation you created with the AutoContent Wizard appears in Normal view. If the window looks different, click the Normal View button ⊞ at the lower-left of your screen to match the figure. This view enables you to focus on one slide at a time. You can add to, edit, or delete presentation content, including text, graphics, and overall slide appearance. Clicking a numbered slide in the left-hand work area offers you a quick way to display the corresponding slide in the Slide Pane.

2. Click the Slide Sorter View button ⊞ at the lower-left of your screen to switch to Slide Sorter View. This view displays thumbnail images of all of a presentation's slides in their current order. This view makes it easy to add, delete, hide, or rearrange individual slides. It also makes it easy to add, delete, or edit notes in slides, to create or edit animation effects, and to modify slide design (see Figure 1-15). If the Slide Sorter toolbar does not display, click the View menu, click the Toolbars command, and click Slide Sorter. If you cannot see all of your slides at once, lower the percentage in the Zoom box on the Standard toolbar or use the vertical scroll bar to move up and down in the display area.

3. Click the View menu, then click Notes Page. In this view each slide appears on the upper half of a page and a large text box appears in the lower half (see Figure 1-16). In this text box you can add notes, graphics, tables, and so on for each slide, but not have them appear on the slides themselves. You then can print the slides with the notes, refer to them during a presentation, and/or hand them out to your audience. If you save a presentation as a Web page, notes will appear in the Web browser but pictures or objects will not.

4. Click the Slide Show button 🖵 in the lower-left area of the screen (see Figure 1-17). PowerPoint runs the presentation as a full-screen slide show, starting at the currently selected slide. Click the left mouse button or press [Enter] to advance through each slide. When all slides have appeared, the program will return you to the previous view. Pressing [Esc] during a slide show cancels it at that point and returns you to the previous view.

5. The next Skill explains how to save and close a PowerPoint presentation. Therefore, leave the file open.

more

PowerPoint's multiple views add depth to presentation design. Each view but Slide Show allows you to zoom in and out. Normal View and Notes Page View permit enlargements up to 400%, but Slide Sorter View permits enlargement to just 100%. Since Slide Show takes up the whole screen, there is no Zoom box in that viewing mode. When using a view with multiple panes, you can change the sizes of the panes to suit your needs. Place the mouse pointer over the border between two panes, then click and drag the border to shrink one pane while expanding the other. Clicking the Close button ☒ on the top gray bar of a side pane will close that pane and expand the Slide Pane.

Figure 1-15 Slide Sorter View

Slide Sorter toolbar

Click slide, then move it, insert slide just after it, or delete it

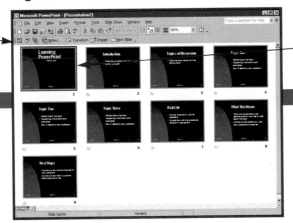

Figure 1-16 Notes Page View

Image of currently selected slide

Text box for inserting notes, graphics, tables, charts, diagrams, etc.

Standard and Formatting toolbars now fully displayed (see PP 1.13)

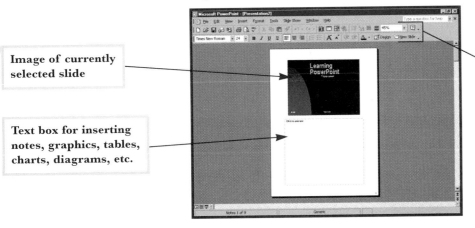

Figure 1-17 Slide Show

Slide Show starts at selected slide from previous slide view

In Slide Show, slide fills entire screen; click [Esc] to interrupt show

Practice

Most people use the Slides tab of Normal View to create and edit a presentation since PowerPoint exploits the appeal of visual images. However, click the Outline tab and type, edit, and organize your text slide by slide to prepare a word-intensive presentation. Switch to the Slides tab to add and view enhancing graphics. Remember to use Notes Page View to add information that only you should see when giving a presentation. Likewise, use the Slide Sorter View to add, delete, or move slides; and use the Slide Show to review the overall message, look, and sound of your presentation.

skill Saving and Closing a File

concept

Saving your work is crucial to learning how to use application software and preserving your efforts. Once you save a file, you can reopen it anytime for viewing or editing. Many users save presentations to either an internal hard drive or floppy disk on their computer. Many other uses, however, can save their work to network drives, CD-ROMs, and even storage areas on the Web. Even after you save a file with a unique file name, you should continue to save changes to the file often. Otherwise, you could lose hours of hard work due to hardware, software, or power failures. Only after saving a file should you close it, because closing a file removes it from the screen. You can close a file while leaving PowerPoint open for use with other files. Or, if you have finished using PowerPoint, you can exit the application.

do it !

Save the presentation created with the AutoContent Wizard in a new folder. Then close the file and exit PowerPoint.

1. Be sure the presentation you created with the AutoContent Wizard appears in Normal View.

2. Click File on the Menu bar, then click the Save As command to open the Save As dialog box.

3. Click the drop-down arrow at the right edge of the Save in box. A list of your available disk drives and folders will appear (see Figure 1-18).

4. If you will be saving your files on an internal hard drive, click the drive labeled (C:). If you will save files on a floppy disk, insert a formatted disk and click the drive labeled 3 1/2 Floppy (A:). Follow your instructor's directions if you files should be saved else-where. The drive you select will appear in the Save in box and its contents, if any, will appear in a list below in the contents window.

5. Click the Create New Folder button 🗁. The New Folder dialog box will open with an insertion point blinking in the Name text box.

6. Type PowerPoint Files as the new folder's name (see Figure 1-19). Press [Enter]. A new folder named PowerPoint Files has been created on the drive you selected in the Save in box in Step 4. The contents window is blank as this new folder contains no files yet (see Figure 1-20).

(continued on PP 1.18)

Figure 1-18 Save As dialog box, Save in box displayed

Click File, then click Save As to open dialog box

Create New Folder button

My Documents folder on (C:) drive is default location for saving files; click a different drive to change saving location

Click drop-down arrow to display list of available drives and folders for saving files

New feature in Office XP allows you to resize both Open and Save (As) dialog boxes

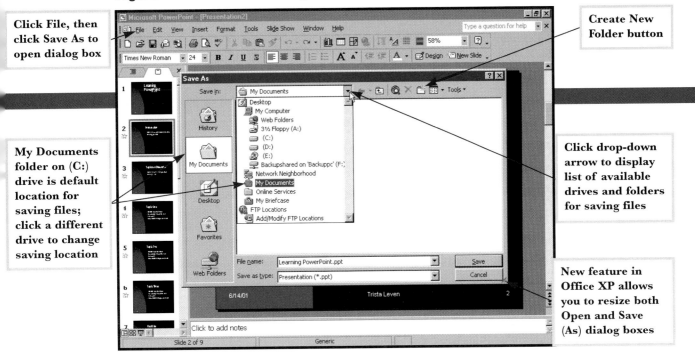

Figure 1-19 New Folder dialog box

Click and type name of new folder

Click to create newly named folder and to close dialog box

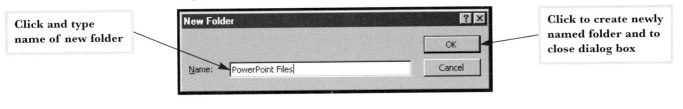

Figure 1-20 Save As dialog box with new folder name

Name of newly created folder appears here

Since new folder is empty, contents window is blank

Name given to presentation in AutoContent Wizard appears by default in File name box

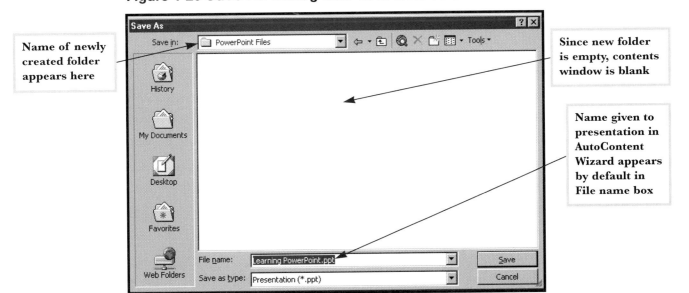

skill | Saving and Closing a File (continued)

do it !

7. Having chosen a storage location for your file, you must give it a unique file name. The default name chosen by the program, Learning PowerPoint, should be highlighted in the File name box. Depending on how your copy of Windows is configured, this name may have the file extension .ppt. File extensions help an operating system associate individual files with their corresponding programs. The extension .ppt identifies this file as a PowerPoint presentation file. In the Save as type box, you should see Presentation (*.ppt), which also tells you that you will save the file as a PowerPoint presentation.

8. In the File name box, type My First Presentation.ppt to replace the default file name (see Figure 1-21). Do not type the .ppt extension if the program automatically adds it.

9. Click the Save button [Save]. This file will be saved, and you will be returned to the presentation window. Notice that the new file name now appears in the application window's blue Title bar (see Figure 1-22).

10. To close the file, click File, then click Close. The file will disappear from the screen, leaving a blank gray application window.

11. To exit the application, click File, then click Exit. The PowerPoint application window closes. If this is the only application you had open, you will be returned to the Windows Desktop (see Figure 1-23).

more

Understanding the difference between the Save and Save As commands is essential to ensuring that you save a file in the version you actually want. When you save a new file for the first time, the two commands function identically: they both open the Save As dialog box, enabling you to choose a storage location, file name, and file type for the file. Once you have saved a file, the commands work differently. Choosing the Save command, or clicking the Save button 🖫 on the Standard toolbar, will update the original file with any changes you have made, maintaining the same location, file name, and file type. The previous version of the file no longer will exist. Choosing the Save As command will permit you to save a different version of the same file, with a new location, file name, and file type.

If you modify a file and do not save the changes before you try to close it, PowerPoint will ask you if you want to save the changes you have made. If you do not save, any changes you have made to the file since the last time it was saved will be lost. PowerPoint also will ask you if you want to save changes if you try to exit the program with unsaved changes in a file. Remember also the difference between the document Close [X] and application Close buttons [X]. The document Close button, appearing at the right end of the gray Menu bar, closes only the active file you see on your screen. The application close button, appearing at the right end of the blue Title bar, closes the entire program and any of its files that still might be open.

Another safeguard against losing data is PowerPoint's AutoRecover feature, which creates a recovery file storing your most recent changes each time the feature activates. If your program "crashes" (i.e, stops working) or you lose power before you could save your work, AutoRecover will open the next time you launch PowerPoint. The recovery file will contain all changes you made through the last AutoRecover before the interruption. Realize that you should not use AutoRecover as a substitute for saving your files, but just as a backup procedure in emergencies. To activate AutoRecover, click the Tools menu, then click the Options command to open the Options dialog box. Click the Save tab, if needed, to bring it to the front of the dialog box. In the Save options section of the tab, be sure a check mark appears in the Save AutoRecover info every check box. A save interval of 10 minutes is recommended for the list box to the right of the AutoRecover option. This is an effective interval for ensuring that the program protects your work, but is not so frequent as to frustrate the process of creating a presentation. In addition, older computers may slow down for several seconds while AutoRecover runs.

Figure 1-21 Typing new file name

Click and type desired name of new file in File name box; do not add file extension if program automatically will add it

Program to associate with new file appears in Save as type box

Click to save file, close dialog box, and return to program window

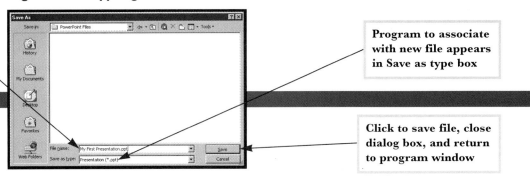

Figure 1-22 Program window after saving new file

New file name now appears in Title bar

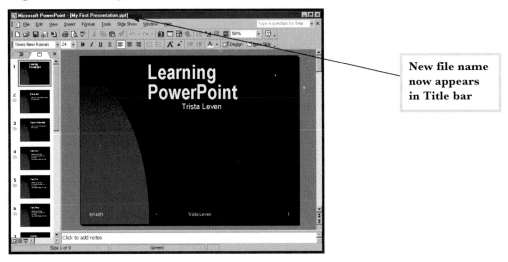

Figure 1-23 Windows Desktop after closing file and program

Windows Desktop

Windows taskbar

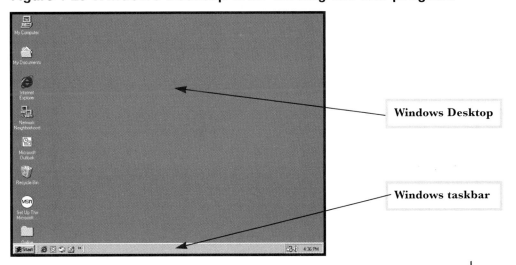

Practice

The File menu contains a Save as Web Page command that allows you to save presentation files in Hypertext Markup Language (HTML). You must save presentations this way if you want to publish them to the World Wide Web. When saving a presentation in HTML, you can give the file a descriptive name for the Web browser's Title bar that differs from the file name. To do so, click the Change Title button in the Save As dialog box, type the descriptive name, press [Enter], then save the file.

skill Using the Office Assistant

concept

Even the most experienced computer users need help from time to time. The Office Assistant is a Help feature that enables you to ask questions in plain language related to PowerPoint presentations. This assistant will reply with several options that may provide helpful information about the question. You also can configure the Office Assistant so that it senses your actions and offers relevant Help tips as you work.

do it !

Use the Office Assistant to obtain answers to questions about presentation design tools.

1. Restart PowerPoint using the first four Steps in the Skill entitled "Starting PowerPoint."

2. At the right end of the Standard toolbar, click the Microsoft PowerPoint Help button [?] to display the Office Assistant. The Assistant and its dialog balloon will appear, asking what you would like to do, and its text box will instruct you to type a question. ⬤ If the Office Assistant does not appear, click the Help menu, click the Show the Office Assistant command, then click on the Office Assistant when it appears on screen.

3. With the text box in the dialog balloon highlighted, type How do I create a presentation? (see Figure 1-24). Click the Search button ⎸ Search ⎸ or press [Enter]. The Office Assistant scans PowerPoint's Help files and returns topics that it believes relate to your question.

4. Click the Help topic called About creating presentations. A Help window will appear, displaying the topic and related information (see Figure 1-25). ⬤ To get the best view of the Help topic, (a) click the Maximize sizing button on the Menu bar and (b) click the Hide button [▣] on the Help toolbar to display only the right pane of the Help facility.

5. Read the topic, using the vertical scroll bar to any view hidden text. Some Help files contain underlined blue text, or hyperlinks, to another Help topic or to a Help file on the Internet. ⬤ In the topic About creating presentations, clicking the link Microsoft Office Template Gallery would take you to a Microsoft Web site where you can access many Office XP templates, including over 30 for PowerPoint.

6. The next Skill discusses more aspects of Microsoft Help, so leave the Help window open.

more

The Office Assistant occasionally will offer you tips on how to use PowerPoint more effectively. The appearance of a small light bulb 💡, next to the Assistant or on the Microsoft PowerPoint Help button, indicates there is a tip to be viewed. To see the tip, click the light bulb. Note that you also can customize the Assistant. In the dialog balloon that appears with the Assistant, click the Options button ⎸ Options ⎸ to display the the Office Assistant dialog box. This dialog box has two tabs: Gallery and Options. The Gallery tab enables you to change from the default Office Assistant character to another one, as long as you can access the program CD-ROM with the characters. The Options tab provides options to turn the Assistant on or off, modify how and when it supplies Help topics, and modify which tips—if any—will appear when problems arise.

Each question asked during a PowerPoint session gets added to the drop-down list in the Ask a Question box. To access previous questions, click the arrow at the right end of the Ask a Question drop-down list box. Click a question on the list that appears, and the same list of suggested Help topics found earlier by the Office Assistant will appear. Click the desired Help topic, and you will see the same information that appeared when using the Assistant. To get the best results with the Office Assistant, type phrases or questions, not just words, in the dialog balloon. Be sure to spell all of your words correctly, and use computer terms if you know them rather than vaguer words. For example, the question How do I save a file? will yield more relevant results than Storing work.

Figure 1-24 Office Assistant with typed question

Click and type question in dialog balloon

Click to access other Assistant images, change Assistant settings, and select Tip options

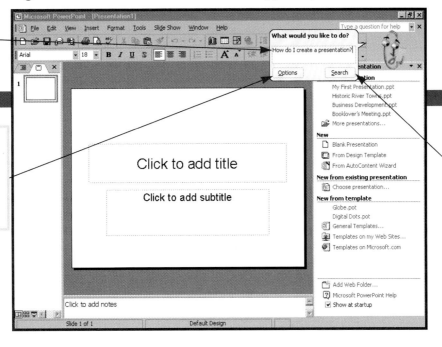

Click to open list of up to 9 potentially relevant Help topics

Figure 1-25 Help topic entitled "About creating presentations"

Help toolbar

Help topic heading and subheadings

Click to display all text, definitions, How to tasks, and Tips

Click blue text to display definitions of selected text; click underlined blue hyperlinks to access other Help topics, including those on Internet

PowerPoint 2002

Practice

If the text of a Help topic is too large or too small, click the Options button 🗗 on the Help toolbar, then click Internet Options to open the Internet Options dialog box. If necessary, click the General tab to bring it to the front of the dialog box. Click the Accessibility button [Accessibility...] to open the Accessibility dialog box. Add a check mark to the Ignore font sizes specified on Web pages check box. Click [OK] to close the Accessibility dialog box, then click [OK] to close the Internet Options dialog box.

skill
Other PowerPoint Help Features

concept

PowerPoint provides an extensive Microsoft PowerPoint Help facility that complements help features discussed already by providing more information than any of them can do. After opening the Help facility, you can search for Help topics three different ways, read Help topics on screen, print selected topics, and access more information using Web hyperlinks.

do it !

Use PowerPoint's Help tabs to find out more about PowerPoint features.

1. The Microsoft PowerPoint Help window still should be open on the screen, showing the Office Assistant and the Help topic About creating presentations. Right-click the Office Assistant to display a shortcut menu, and click Hide to turn off the Assistant. Click the Show button 🔲 near the top of the window to expand the window to a two-pane format. The left pane will consist of three tabs that organize PowerPoint's Help topics differently. The right pane will display whichever Help topic you select in the left pane.

2. Click the Contents tab to bring it to the front of the left pane. Click the Plus sign ➕ for Microsoft PowerPoint Help at the top of the Contents pane to display the main Help categories. Click the Plus sign for Creating Presentations. Notice that the first Help topic under that category is About creating presentations. More Help topics appear, including the last one, WEB: Creating a presentation for a kiosk (see Figure 1-26). Clicking a WEB entry will take you to a Help topic on the Internet. ⬥ To display the main categories or their Help topics, you also can double-click the purple book icon 📖 for each entry.

3. Click the Answer Wizard tab in the left pane to display two sub-panes. In the upper sub-pane entitled What would you like to do?, type Create a handout. Then click the Search button ⌷Search⌷ or press [Enter]. Over 15 Help topics will appear in the lower sub-pane, entitled Select topic to display. Click the Help topic About handouts to display it in the right pane (see Figure 1-27).

4. Notice that this Help topic contains a labeled graphic, headings, and text, some of which is blue. In the upper-right corner of the topic, click the words Show all. Notice that the blue terms are now defined with green text. Read the topic, then click the words Hide all in the upper-right corner of the topic to hide its definitions. ⬥ Clicking Show all also will expand blue heading sections, How? sections that explain PowerPoint tasks, and Tips sections that provide gentle warnings about program problems or limitations.

5. Click the Close button ❌ in the Help window. Click the Close button on the PowerPoint Title bar. If PowerPoint asks if you want to save the presentation, click ⌷No⌷.

more

Use the Contents tab when you are unclear on what you need to do or want to work from a broad perspective on Help topics to more specific topics. Use the Answer Wizard when you have a question that is likely to produce relevant responses for that question. If you know which task you want to perform or which feature you want to review, try the Index tab. This tab presents PowerPoint's Help topics in a large, alphabetical list of keywords, or terms used to search for information. To use this tab, type a keyword in the top text box, labeled Type keywords, then click the Search button ⌷Search⌷ just below the window. Otherwise, double-click on a keyword from the scrollable list in the middle window, labeled Or choose keywords. When you click the Search button or double-click a keyword, a list of potentially relevant Help topics will appear in the bottom list box, labeled Choose a topic. Clicking on a topic in the bottom list box will display it in the right pane of the Help window (see Figure 1-28).

Figure 1-26 Using the Contents tab

Clicking plus sign displays main Help categories and changes plus to minus sign

Help topic selected in left pane displays in right pane

Clicking a Help category displays related Help topics

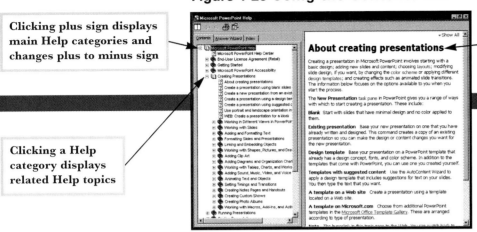

Figure 1-27 Using the Answer Wizard tab

Click and type question or desired task

Click desired Help topic

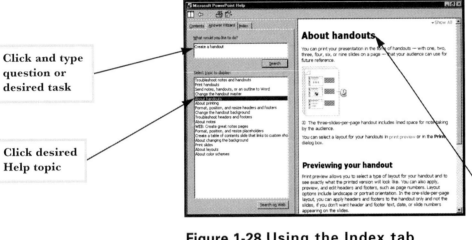

Selected Help topic from lower left pane displays in right pane

Figure 1-28 Using the Index tab

Click and type key-word(s), then click [Search] button

Otherwise, double-click keyword from middle pane

Click desired Help topic

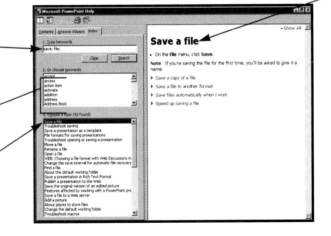

Practice

The upper-right corner of a PowerPoint wizard or dialog box contains a Help button ?. Click on this button to display a question mark attached to the mouse pointer ▶?, then click on virtually any element in the wizard or dialog box to display an information rectangle with a faint yellow background. Alternately, you can right-click on the element to display the What's This command
What's This? , then left-click on the command to see the same rectangle.

shortcuts

Function	Button/Mouse	Menu	Keyboard
Office Assistant		Click Help, click Microsoft PowerPoint Help	[F1]
Minimize		Right-click Title bar, click Minimize	
Maximize		Right-click Title bar, click Maximize	
Restore		Right-click Title bar, click Restore	
Close file		Click , click Close	[Ctrl]+[F4] or [Ctrl]+[W]
Exit PowerPoint		Click File, click Exit	[Alt]+[F4]
Normal View		Click View, click Normal	
Slide Sorter View		Click View, click Slide Sorter	
Slide Show		Click View, click Slide Show	[F5]
Save / Save As		Click File, click Save (As)	[Ctrl]+[S]
Create New Folder			[Alt]+[5]

A. Identify Key Features

Name the items indicated by the callouts in Figure 1-29.

Figure 1-29 Exploring the PowerPoint window

1. _____
2. _____
3. _____
4. _____
5. _____
6. _____
7. _____
8. _____
9. _____

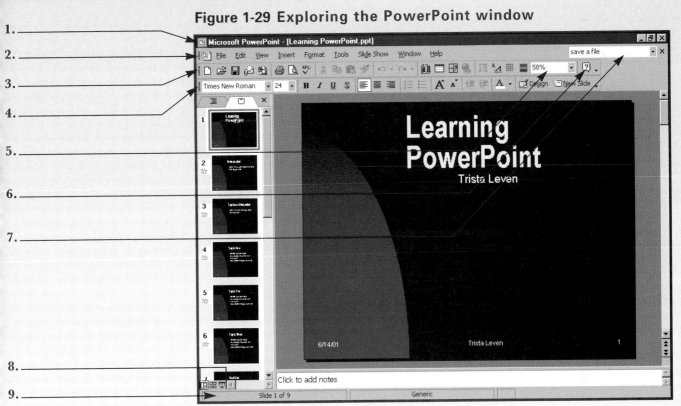

B. Select the Best Answer

10. A tool for quick and easy design in PowerPoint

11. Enables you to set options before executing a command

12. Useful for inserting, deleting, and/or reorganizing slides in a presentation

13. Increases size of the program window so it fills the computer screen

14. Organizes Help topics by main categories and specific topics

15. Enables you to focus on all aspects of a slide at one time

16. Permits you to choose a storage location, file name, and file type

17. A Help tab that functions like the Office Assistant

a. Answer Wizard tab

b. AutoContent Wizard

c. Contents tab

d. Dialog box

e. Maximize button

f. Save As dialog box

g. Normal View

h. Slide Sorter View

quiz (continued)

C. Complete the Statement

18. You can create a new presentation by choosing:

   a. Blank Presentation

   b. From Design Template

   c. General Templates

   d. All of the above

19. To save changes to a file, keeping its current name and location, click the:

   a. Save As button

   b. AutoContent Wizard

   c. Insert menu

   d. Save button

20. All of the following are PowerPoint views except:

   a. Normal View

   b. Slide Show

   c. Slide Sorter View

   d. Create Slide View

21. The AutoContent Wizard contains:

   a. 24 commonly used presentations

   b. A "Recommending a Strategy" presentation

   c. A "Business Plan" presentation

   d. All of the above

22. The best View for looking at slides all at once and rearranging them is:

   a. Normal View

   b. Slide Sorter View

   c. Notes Page View

   d. Outline View

23. The blue bar at the top of PowerPoint's window is:

   a. The Title bar

   b. The Menu bar

   c. The Standard toolbar

   d. The Status bar

24. The file extension for a PowerPoint presentation is:

   a. .pow

   b. .doc

   c. .xls

   d. .ppt

25. If your computer and/or lab allows it, you can save a presentation to:

   a. A floppy drive

   b. A hard drive

   c. A network drive

   d. All of the above

26. The AutoRecover feature of PowerPoint creates:

   a. A copied presentation each time you open PowerPoint

   b. A crash program to stop computer viruses

   c. A recovery file storing your most recent changes

   d. The best substitute for routinely backing up files

27. To get the best results with the Office Assistant:

   a. Type phrases or questions, not just single words

   b. Spell all of your words correctly when typing

   c. Use computer terms if you know them

   d. All of the above

interactivity

Build Your Skills

1. Start PowerPoint and run the AutoContent Wizard:

   a. Launch the PowerPoint program from the Start button on the Windows taskbar.

   b. Run the AutoContent Wizard from the New Presentation task pane.

   c. Turn on the Office Assistant.

2. Use the AutoContent Wizard to create a presentation:

   a. Click the Projects category of presentations. Select the presentation type called Reporting Progress or Status.

   b. Select the output type option called On-screen presentation.

   c. Give your presentation the title Reporting Progress. In the footer include your name, the slide number, and the date last updated.

   d. Click the Finish button to display the presentation. Save the modified file as Progress.ppt.

3. View your presentation:

   a. In Normal View click the Outline tab in the left pane, and click any slide in the presentation other than Slide 1.

   b. Switch to Slide Sorter View, count the total number of slides, then click Slide 1.

   c. Run a Slide Show of your presentation.

   d. Return the presentation to Normal View.

4. Use PowerPoint's Help facility, close the file, and close the program:

   a. Ask the Office Assistant about Using PowerPoint templates.

   b. Select, read, and summarize on paper a topic provided in the Office Assistant's dialog balloon related to your question.

   c. Activate the full Help facility, then hide the Office Assistant.

   d. Use the Contents tab to locate the same Help file that you selected in the dialog balloon.

   e. Use the Answer Wizard tab to ask for help on Saving new PowerPoint files. Read and summarize on paper the Help topic you believe most closely relates to this subject.

   f. Use the Index tab to list Help topics associated with the keywords rename and file. Read the Help topic entitled Rename a file, and summarize it on paper.

   g. Close the Help window, close the modified file, and close the PowerPoint program.

   h. Write your name and the due date on your Help topic summaries and hand them in, per your instructor's directions.

PowerPoint 2002

interactivity (continued)

Problem Solving Exercises

1. Tabak, Inc., a retail book distribution company, recently has expanded its operations to eight new cities across North America, and you are its Regional Personnel Director. People staffing the new offices must be made to feel welcome working for the company. More importantly, they must be properly motivated for the expansion to be successful. Using the AutoContent Wizard, choose a presentation type that relates to motivating a team, and choose the proper output type for an Internet presentation. The title of the presentation should be The Tabak Way. In the footer, type your name, a dash, and the due date of this exercise. Remove the check mark in the check box for Date last updated. Finish the wizard and save the file as Motivation.ppt. If possible, save it on a hard drive or network drive. Close the file.

2. The National Director of Personnel of Tabak, Inc. has heard about the motivational Internet presentation that you are creating for employees at the company's eight new sites. The National Director thinks the presentation would be a valuable motivational tool for new employees at the company's headquarters. First, however, she wants to examine your work so she can use it as the foundation for a revised presentation of her own. Save a new version of the file, called Duplicate Motivation.ppt. If possible, save it on a 3-1/2 inch floppy disk. Close the file.

3. Your own supervisor has had bad experiences with losing or damaging files of large and important presentations. He wants to ensure that PowerPoint has safeguards to prevent the loss of files before he decides to update the department's programs to PowerPoint 2002. Use the Office Assistant to find out about Recovering lost files. When you find Help topics related to this subject, print the one that most directly relates to it. On the top of the printout, write your name, the phrase Office Assistant, and the due date. To demonstrate PowerPoint's additional Help features, use either the Contents tab or Index tab to print a related topic. On the top of this second printout, write your name, the name of the tab used to find the topic, and the due date. Submit the Help topics to your instructor according to his/her directions.

4. You have been hired as Assistant to the Marketing Director at RedWeb, an Internet service provider. In the coming months you will be attending several trade shows in order to increase the company's profile among schools, colleges, and other non-profit organizations. Using the AutoContent Wizard, choose a presentation type that relates to selling a product and/or service, and choose the output type for either black-and-white overheads or color overheads, depending on the type of printer in your classroom and your instructor's directions. Give the presentation a simple, clear title that would attract the attention of non-profit organizations. Include your name, a dash, and the due date of this exercise in the footer. Delete the check mark for the Date last updated check box, but keep the Slide numbers. Do not worry about the remaining content of the presentation. Save the presentation as Non-Profit.ppt.

Designing Your Presentation

Presentation design is just as important as production. Choosing one style over another can make a big difference in how your presentation works as well as looks. In PowerPoint you can design a presentation from scratch by choosing templates, colors, and object placement.

PowerPoint makes designing a project from the beginning, starting with a blank presentation, easy to do. Slide AutoLayouts will help you organize the content of your presentation, and the design you select will depend on the data you wish to display. AutoLayouts are pre-formatted slides that contain placeholders for various objects, the most useful of which are text boxes. It is in the text boxes that you will enter the information to be presented to your audience.

As Lesson 1 demonstrates, PowerPoint allows you to see your presentation in a few different views. Using multiple views lets you work with your presentation most effectively. While using the Slides tab in Normal View, you can focus on and manipulate every element of a single slide. Using the Outline tab in Normal View, you can focus on a text-oriented display and refine text more easily. To work with all of your slides at once, in the order they will appear in a presentation, you would use Slide Sorter View. Notes Page View lets you enter text that will not appear in your slide show but that you can refer to while giving the presentation; this View also enables you to print slides and notes for yourself and/or the audience. Remember to choose a View depending on the main task you want to perform with a presentation at a given time.

Lesson Goal:

Design a presentation for a sod company on your own from the beginning. Start with a blank presentation, and use PowerPoint's design features to lay the groundwork for the project. Also begin to add content to the presentation.

skills

- ⚡ **Opening a New Presentation**
- ⚡ **Opening an Existing PowerPoint File**
- ⚡ **Entering Text in Normal View**
- ⚡ **Adding a New Slide to Your Presentation**
- ⚡ **Working with Text on the Outline Tab**
- ⚡ **Adding Speaker's Notes**
- ⚡ **Printing Slides and Notes Pages**

PowerPoint 2002

skill

Opening a New Presentation

MOUS Skill

concept

PowerPoint allows you to create customized presentations from beginning to end. You can choose the style and layout of all features to give your presentation a personalized touch. Starting with a blank presentation gives you complete control over every aspect of the presentation's design. PowerPoint also gives you the option of beginning with a Design Template, which can provide a starting point for determining a project's overall organization and look.

do it !

Create a presentation of your own, starting with a blank presentation.

1. Using the Start button on the Windows Taskbar, start the PowerPoint application. When the program opens, be sure it is set to Normal View, with the Outline and Slides tab in the left pane, the Slide pane in the middle above the Notes Pane, and the New Presentation task pane at the right.

2. In the New section of the New Presentation task pane, click the Blank Presentation option. The Slide Layout task pane will replace the New Presentation task pane, with a blue border around the Title Slide layout by default. The Slide Layout task pane offers four categories of AutoLayout slides—Text Layouts, Content Layouts, Text and Content Layouts, and Other Layouts. As the category titles suggest, slides are grouped according to which presentation elements appear on the slides within a category—for example, titled text, bulleted text, pictures, charts, diagrams, and so on. The layout you select should depend on how you want to present information on a particular slide.

3. Scroll to the bottom of the Slide Layout task pane and click once on the last slide layout (not on the arrow to its right), called Title and Chart (see Figure 2-1). Notice that the selected layout appears in the Slide pane. Scroll back to the top of the Slide Layout task pane and click once on the Title Slide (not Title Only) layout to return it to the Slide pane.

4. Click Format, then click Slide Design. The Slide Design task pane will replace the Slide Layout task pane at the right, with three design options listed at the top of the pane— Design Templates, Color Schemes, and Animation Schemes. Design Templates should be selected by default. The task pane offers the design categories Used in this Presentation, Recently Used, and Available for Use. Scroll down and click on the design called Capsules.pot (see Figure 2-2) to apply it to the Title slide in the Slide pane.

5. Save the file as GSU Presentation.ppt in your previously created PowerPoint Files folder. Be sure that your Title slide matches Figure 2-3. Then close the file, but leave the program running.

more

After you start the PowerPoint application, it offers you other ways to create a new presentation. Clicking the New button ☐ on the Standard toolbar or pressing [Ctrl]+[N] will display by default a blank Title slide and the Slide Layout task pane. With any PowerPoint task pane open, you can open any of the program's other task panes. To do so, click the Other Task Panes arrow ▼ near the right end of the current task pane's gray title bar to display a shortcut menu, then click on the desired task pane name (see Figure 2-4). You can display the Slide Design task pane by clicking the Design button ☑ Design near the right end of the Formatting toolbar. Finally, clicking the Back ◀ or Forward ▶ arrows at the left end of a task pane's title bar will take you to other task panes you already have used in your current PowerPoint session.

Figure 2-1 Title and Chart Layout

Figure 2-2 Capsules.pot design

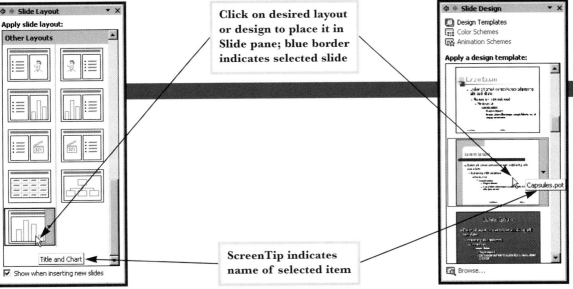

Click on desired layout or design to place it in Slide pane; blue border indicates selected slide

ScreenTip indicates name of selected item

Figure 2- 3 GSU Presentation Title slide

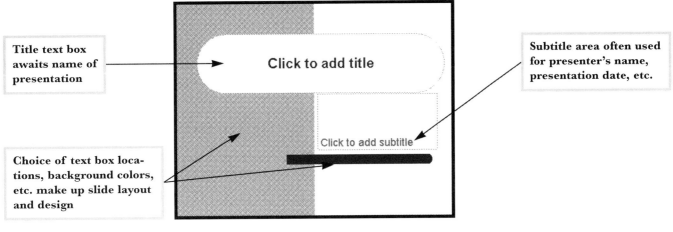

Title text box awaits name of presentation

Subtitle area often used for presenter's name, presentation date, etc.

Choice of text box locations, background colors, etc. make up slide layout and design

Figure 2-4 Choosing another task pane

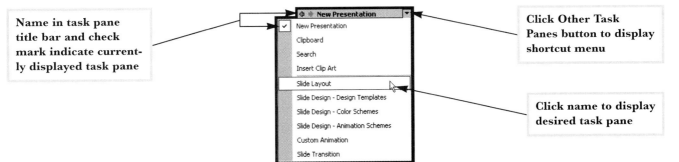

Name in task pane title bar and check mark indicate currently displayed task pane

Click Other Task Panes button to display shortcut menu

Click name to display desired task pane

Practice

Start PowerPoint. Be sure that the program opens in Normal View, displaying the Slides tab, a Title slide in the Slide pane, the Notes pane below it, and the New Presentation task pane. In the New category in the New Presentation task pane, click From Design Template. Scroll near the bottom of the task pane, and click the Profile.pot design. Save your file as myppprac2-1.ppt, and close it.

skill   Opening an Existing PowerPoint File

concept

The AutoContent Wizard used in Lesson 1 and the Blank Presentation option used in the previous Skill are tools for creating new presentations. But suppose you want to open a file that you already have created. To do so, you can use the File menu on the Menu bar, the Open File button on the Standard toolbar, or a keyboard shortcut. The method you use to open a file will depend on whether PowerPoint is already running, your familiarity with the software, and personal preferences. This Skill teaches how to use the File menu.

do it !

Open the GSU Presentation created in the previous Skill.

1. Click the File menu, then click the Open command. The Open dialog box will appear. The PowerPoint Files folder should appear in the Look in box since that is where the GSU Presentation.ppt file was saved in the previous Skill. If the folder does not appear, click the drop-down arrow at the right end of the Look in box, click the drive that contains your PowerPoint Files folder, then double-click the folder in the large contents window. The PowerPoint Files folder will appear in the Look in box.

2. If the GSU Presentation.ppt file is not already highlighted, click once on its name to select it. A preview of the first slide of the presentation should appear in the preview pane at the right side of the dialog box (see Figure 2-5). The Open dialog box, like the Save and Save As dialog boxes, permit several ways to view your files. If the first slide does not appear in a preview pane, click the drop-down arrow on the Views button to display a shortcut menu, then click the Preview command. Alternately, you can click and re-click on the Views button itself until the preview pane displays.

3. Click the Open button. With the program set to the default Normal View, the first slide of the presentation will appear in the Slide Pane (see Figure 2-6). Leave it open.

more

If you have just opened PowerPoint to work with an existing file, look in the New Presentation task pane under the category Open a presentation. If the desired file is one of the last four you opened, just click its name. If the desired file was opened five or more files ago, click the More presentations option to display the Open dialog box. Then, as in this Skill, use the Look in box to find the disk drive and folder name of your desired file. Click the desired file name when it appears in the contents window of the dialog box, then click the Open button. To open the file without having to use the Open button, you can just double-click on the desired file in the contents window. Also notice that the Open command in the File menu and the More presentations option in the New Presentations task pane have an icon that resembles a partially opened manila folder and matches the Open button on the Standard toolbar. The matching icons indicate that you can click on the Open button to open the same dialog box displayed by the Open command or the More presentations command.

The Open button in the Open dialog box includes an arrow on its right edge. Clicking this arrow opens a shortcut menu that provides commands for opening a file in different ways. The Open Read-Only command permits you to view a file, but prohibits you from saving changes to it using the same file name. The Open Copy command creates a copy of the file you want to open, then opens the copy instead of the original file. The Open in Browser command opens HTML files in your default Web browser rather than in PowerPoint.

To search for a file that is difficult to find, click the Tools button in the Open dialog box, then click the Search command on the shortcut menu to display the Search dialog box. Use this box to conduct your search, using file properties such as the author's name, words that appear in the file, the potential location of the file, the type of file you saved it as, and so on (see Figure 2-7).

Figure 2-5 Open dialog box

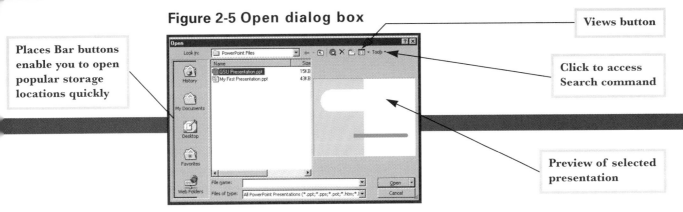

Places Bar buttons enable you to open popular storage locations quickly

Views button

Click to access Search command

Preview of selected presentation

Figure 2- 6 GSU presentation just after opening

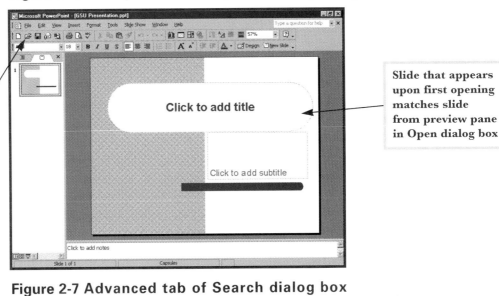

Open button matches icon on Open and More presentations commands

Slide that appears upon first opening matches slide from preview pane in Open dialog box

Figure 2-7 Advanced tab of Search dialog box

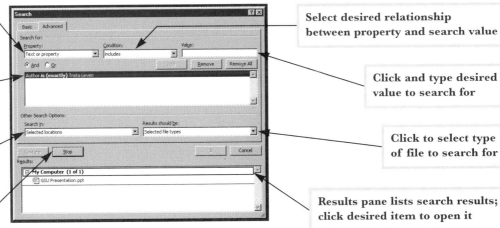

Click to select author, keywords, or other property to search for

Upper pane lists query conditions constructed for searches

Type a path or select search location from drop-down list

Starts or stops search chosen in upper pane

Select desired relationship between property and search value

Click and type desired value to search for

Click to select type of file to search for

Results pane lists search results; click desired item to open it

Practice

Click File, then Open to display the Open dialog box. Without clicking, place your mouse pointer over the icons and buttons that appear in the dialog box to review the ScreenTips. Open Student File pppprac2-2.ppt, read Slide 1, save the file as myppprac2-2.ppt, then close it. At the top of your page, write your name, Myppprac2-2.ppt, and today's date. Hand in the page if asked for it.

skill

Entering Text in Normal View

MOUS Skill

concept

Text is an essential part of a presentation. It must be informative, organized effectively, and displayed appropriately. Entering text in Normal View allows you to see in the Slide Pane how it will look on the actual slide, while still allowing you to view it clearly and edit it on the Outline tab in the left pane. Many slides come with predetermined text placeholders containing instructions for their use. These text boxes are designated by dashed borders.

do it !

Add text to your title slide using both the Outline tab in the left pane and the Slide Pane.

1. Be sure that the title slide for the GSU Presentation.ppt file appears in the Normal View of your program window.

2. Click the gray Outline tab. The Outline tab and panel will turn white and come to the front of the left pane, while the Slides tab will turn gray and recede to the background. The left pane also will widen to about twice its original size to make it easier to type text.

3. Click just to the right of the dimmed slide icon 🔲 labeled 1 on the Outline tab (this first icon represents the title slide). The icon will change to an active slide icon 🔲 and a blinking insertion point will appear next to the icon (see Figure 2-8).

4. Type the company name, Green Side Up. Notice that as you type on the Outline tab, the text also appears in the text box that contained the instruction Click to add title on the slide in the Slide pane. The text on the slide is formatted with a font, font size, and color that are included in the Title Slide AutoLayout for the Capsules Design Template.

5. In the Slide pane, not on the Outline tab, click the text box labeled Click to add subtitle to activate it. A border will appear around the text box. Type the company motto, Merrily We Roll a Lawn (see Figure 2-9). Click a blank area of the slide to cancel the selection of the text box. The subtitle you just entered now has formatting that differs slightly from that of the main title of the slide and that it has appeared below the slide title on the Outline tab.

6. Click the Save button 🔲 on the Standard toolbar to save the changes you have made.

more

When you enter text on a blank title slide, the text automatically goes into the title placeholder, not the subtitle placeholder. A placeholder is a box with a border for holding text or objects like Clip Art or photographs, charts or tables, diagrams, and so on. Text placeholders appear on all slides in the Text Layouts and Text and Contents Layouts categories and in most of the Other Layouts category in the Slide Layout task pane. When you click on a text placeholder, a hatchmarked border appears. Content placeholders appear in all slides in the Content Layouts and Text and Contents Layouts categories, and on a few of the Other Layouts category. When you click on a content placeholder, a wide dotted border appears.

Instead of clicking in the subtitle placeholder to type the subtitle, you can use the Outline tab. Using the Outline tab involves more steps, but may take less time since you do not have to shift between using the keyboard and the mouse. To enter the subtitle using the Outline tab, press [Enter] after typing the main title. Pressing [Enter] will create an active Slide 2 icon in the Outline tab and display a second slide in the Slide pane. With the second slide still activated on the Outline tab, type the subtitle, then press [Tab]. Pressing [Tab] will delete the Slide 2 icon and indent the subtitle under the title of Slide 1. It also will delete the second slide from the Slide pane and display the subtitle in its proper location on Slide 1.

Figure 2-8 Outline tab with Slide 1 activated

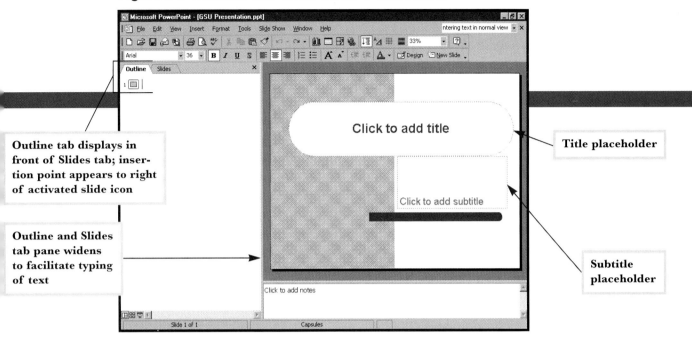

Outline tab displays in front of Slides tab; insertion point appears to right of activated slide icon

Outline and Slides tab pane widens to facilitate typing of text

Title placeholder

Subtitle placeholder

Figure 2-9 Title slide with title and subtitle added

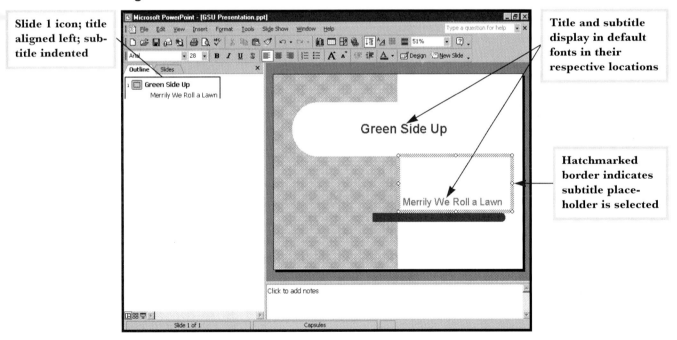

Slide 1 icon; title aligned left; subtitle indented

Title and subtitle display in default fonts in their respective locations

Hatchmarked border indicates subtitle placeholder is selected

PowerPoint 2002

Practice

Open the file mypppprac2-1.ppt. In the title placeholder, enter the name of a fictitious company. In the subtitle, enter your name. Save your changes as mypppprac2-3.ppt, then close the file.

skill   Adding a New Slide to Your Presentation

concept

If you create your presentation without the help of the AutoContent Wizard, you will need to add each slide manually. Before adding a slide, you should have a clear idea of what kind of information you want to place on it and how you want to present that information. Once you have determined these factors, you can use one of several methods for adding a new slide to a presentation.

do it !

After finishing the title slide, you will add a second slide to the GSU Presentation.

1. Be sure that the title slide for the GSU Presentation.ppt file appears in the Normal View of your program window.

2. Click the New Slide button [New Slide] on the Formatting toolbar. A second active slide icon will appear on the Outline tab with a blinking insertion point, and a new slide will appear in the Slide pane. The Slide Layout task pane will display with the Title and Text layout under the Text Layouts category selected by default. PowerPoint automatically places a new slide immediately after the slide that is active when you click the New Slide button. Notice that the Status bar now reads Slide 2 of 2 (see Figure 2-10).

3. Since you will use the default Title and Text slide in this Step, close the Slide Layout task pane. In the now enlarged Slide pane, click the text box with the instruction Click to add title to activate it. Notice the hatchmarked border discussed in the previous Skill. Then type Growing to meet your needs as the title of Slide 2.

4. Click the text box labeled Click to add text to activate it. Again, notice the hatchmarked border. Enter the following lines of text, pressing [Enter] after the first two entries:

   Thirty square miles of turf laid since company was founded in 1989
   Four varieties of grass produced on 1450 acres
   Business has grown by an average of 18% annually

5. This text now is aligned left and is displayed as a bulleted list. Click outside the slide's borders to cancel the selection of the text box. Verify that your slide matches the one displayed in Figure 2-11. If your slide does not match the figure, click the Undo button on the Standard toolbar until you revert to a correct version of the slide. Then redo the Steps listed above until you get the correct result. You also can click the arrow on the button to see a list of your most recent actions so you can undo several at once.

6. Click the document close button ☒ to close the presentation. When the program asks you to save changes to your presentation, click the Yes button [Yes].

more

There are multiple ways to create a new slide for a presentation. First, you can click the Insert menu, then click the New Slide command. Second, you can use the keyboard combination [Ctrl]+[M]. Both of these approaches will open the Slide Layout task pane, where you can accept the default slide that appears or choose a different one. Third and finally, if the Slide Layout task pane is open, you click the arrow at the right edge of a desired layout, then click Insert New Slide. If you want to prevent the Slide Layout task pane from displaying every time you insert a new slide, remove the check mark from the Show when inserting new slides check box at the bottom of the task pane.

Figure 2-10 New Title and Text slide

Active slide icon indicates addition of new slide

New slide appears in Slide pane

Click to add new slide immediately after active slide

Border around slide in Slide Layout task pane indicates which layout has been added

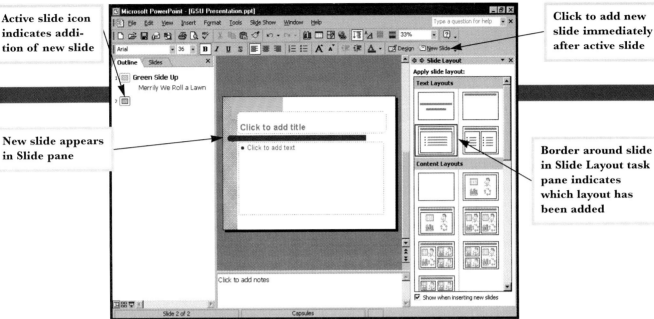

Figure 2-11 Completed Title and Text slide

Title added on Outline tab pane and to new slide

Bulleted list added on Outline pane and to new slide

Undo button

Text of each bulleted item automatically wraps to next line, if so needed

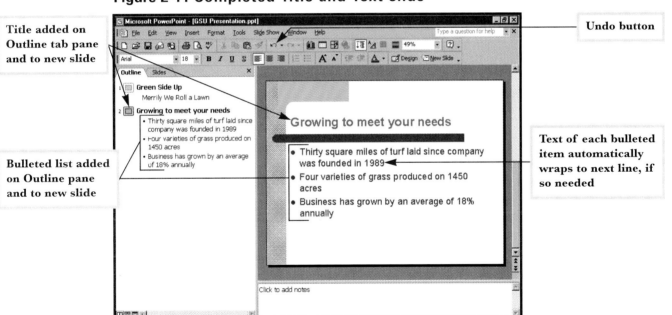

Practice

Open the file mypppprac2-3.ppt. Add a Title and 2-Column Text slide. In the title placeholder, type the word Divisions. In the left bulleted placeholder, type Sales. In the right one, type Accounting. Save your changes as mypppprac2-4.ppt, then close the file.

skill | Working with Text on the Outline Tab

 MOUS Skill

concept

As earlier skills have shown, PowerPoint enables you to view all of your text in outline form. On the Outline tab you can enter, edit, or move text freely on existing and newly created slides, and even move or copy text between different slides in the presentation. The Outline tab is useful also for promoting and demoting text, thereby increasing or decreasing its importance relative to other text in the same slide. While you can perform these tasks in other Views, the Outline tab makes it easier to focus exclusively on your text.

do it !

Use the Outline tab to check the accuracy of your text and to make any needed changes.

1. Open Student File ppdoit2-5.ppt and save it in your PowerPoint Files folder as GSU Presentation 2.ppt. Notice that the Slides tab is forward in the left pane of the program window.

2. Click the Outline tab to bring it forward in the left pane of your screen. The Outline tab will display the text of the slides in this pre-existing file, and the slides in the Slide pane on the right side of your screen will display the same text in their respective placeholders (see Figure 2-12). If a task pane appears in your program window, close it.

3. Click the Scroll Down arrow ▼ on the Vertical scroll bar for the Outline tab until you can see all of the text for Slide 4. Click just to the left of the third-to-last bullet in the slide, which reads Received the prestigious Velvet Turf award two years running. The mouse pointer will change to a four-headed arrow (✛), and the bulleted text will be selected.

4. Keeping the four-headed arrow to the left of the bullet, click and drag the selected text up to Slide 2, entitled Growing to meet your needs. Position the text below the third bullet at the bottom of the slide, then release the mouse pointer. As you drag the bulleted text, the mouse pointer will change to a vertical, two-headed arrow (↕), and a solid horizontal line will move with the pointer. The solid line shows where the text will appear whenever you release the pointer. When you release the pointer, the two-headed arrow will revert to a four-headed arrow, and the moved text will remain highlighted until you click the mouse anywhere in the text.

5. With the moved text still highlighted, verify if the size of that text in the Slide pane matches the size of the first three bullets of text. If it does not, click the Increase Font Size button 𝐀 once to increase the fourth line of text to 28-point (see Figure 2-13).

6. On the Outline tab place the insertion point after the item labeled Playing Fields, the fifth bulleted item on Slide 4, by moving the mouse pointer there and clicking. Press [Enter] to create a new bullet point, then type the word Commercial.

(continued on PP 2.12)

Figure 2-12 GSU Presentation 2 with Outline tab and Slide pane

Slide 1 high-
lighted on
Outline tab

Slide 1 also shows
in Slide pane

Deactivated
slides have
bulleted
subpoints

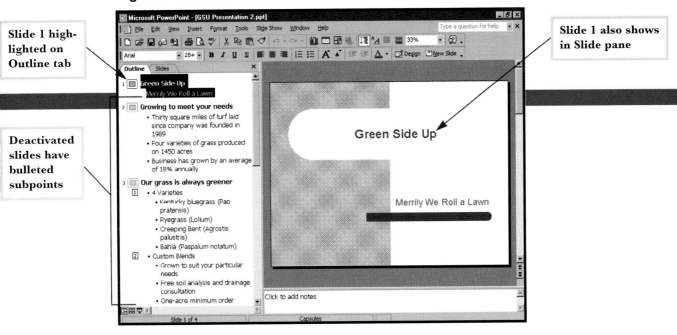

Figure 2-13 Slide 2 after moving text from Slide 4

Highlighted toolbar
buttons indicate
current formatting
for text on displayed
slide

Increase Font
Size button

Text moved
from Slide 4
appears at
bottom of
Slide 2

Three original
bulleted items
and added fourth
one now have
same font size

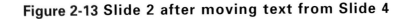
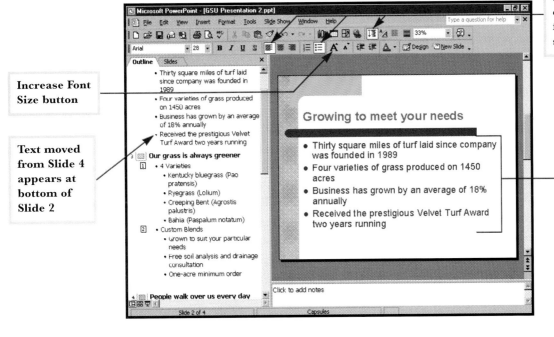

PowerPoint 2002

skill Working with Text on the Outline Tab (continued)

do it !

7. Click the View menu, select the Toolbars command, and click Outlining on the submenu that opens. The Outlining toolbar will appear along the left side of the PowerPoint window. ◥ If, for any reason, the toolbar does not appear at the left side of the screen, click and drag its Title bar to the left until the mouse pointer reaches the left edge of the screen. The toolbar will dock, or park itself, there. You can use the click-and-drag method to dock any PowerPoint 2002 toolbar at the top, bottom, left, or right of your computer screen.

8. Click the bullet next to the words Golf Courses to select it. Hold down [Shift] on the keyboard and click the bullet next to the words Playing Fields. This action will add Playing Fields and any text in between it and Golf Courses to the highlighted selection.

9. On the Outlining toolbar click the Demote button ⬛. The selected items will indent so as to be inferior in importance to the heading immediately above them, Recreation. The text on the slide in the Slide pane also will indent and reduce slightly in font size.

10. Click and drag through the last five bulleted items on Slide 4. Press [Tab] on the keyboard, which is the equivalent of clicking ⬛, to demote these five items.

11. On Slide 4 in the Slide pane, click the word Commercial. Then, on the Outlining toolbar, click the Promote button ⬛ to move the word back to the same level of importance and font size as Recreation. On the Outline tab, click at the end of the last line of Slide 4, after the word medians (see Figure 2-14). ◥ Whether you promote or demote text using the Outline tab or Slide pane, all text in the selected placeholder of the selected slide in the Slide pane automatically will adjust, or autofit, in font size, if needed, to keep the text within the placeholder. This autofit of font sizes is a new feature new in PowerPoint 2002.

12. Click the Save button ⬛ on the Standard toolbar to save the changes you have made to your presentation. Leave the file open.

more

Pressing [Enter] on the Outline tab creates a new item at the same level as the currently selected item. For example, if you are at the top of the hierarchy, slide level, pressing [Enter] will create a new slide. You then can press [Tab] or [Shift]+[Tab] where the insertion point is in order to demote or promote the currently selected item. Along with autofitting text, another new feature in PowerPoint 2002 (as well as all other Office XP programs) is the Smart Tag. A Smart Tag is a type of button that appears after selected program actions—for example, after an autocorrection, a cut and paste operation, an autofit action, or an automatic layout change. Clicking on the Smart Tag will display a shortcut menu of options to perform more tasks related to the current action. When PowerPoint first resizes text in a placeholder, it will display the AutoFit Options button ⬛. You then can click the button and accept the autofit feature, turn it off, split text between two slides, or perform other tasks related to text formatting.

Besides the Promote and Demote buttons, the default Outlining toolbar provides eight more buttons (see Table 2-1). The Collapse All button reduces all of the slides to their title text only, hiding all other text. The Expand All button displays all lines of text on currently selected slides. The Expand and Collapse buttons function just as the Expand All and Collapse All buttons, but act upon only single or adjacent slides. The Move Down and Move Up buttons relocate entire paragraphs or titles. Text that is moved up or down exchanges places with the next item in its path. The Summary Slide creates a new first slide, displaying a bulleted list of the titles of all selected slides in the presentation. The Show Formatting Slide, if activated, displays text with all its formatting, such as font size or italics; when deactivated, presentation slides appear as they normally do.

Figure 2-14 Slide 4 after demoting and promoting text

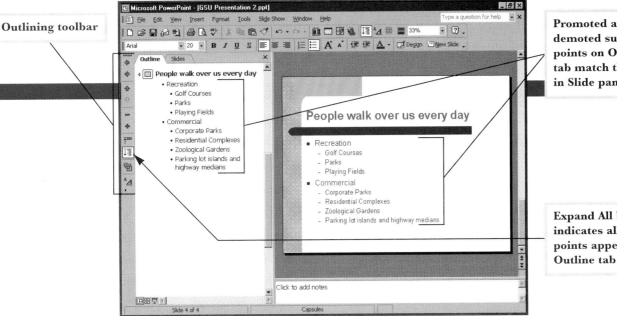

Outlining toolbar

Promoted and demoted sub-points on Outline tab match those in Slide pane

Expand All button indicates all sub-points appear on Outline tab

Table 2-1 Outlining toolbar buttons

Button	Name	Function
←	Promote (indent less)	Moves selected item to the left, or up one level
→	Demote (indent more)	Indents selected item to the right, or down one level
↑	Move Up	Moves selected item up in the outline by exchanging it with previous item
↓	Move Down	Moves selected item down in the outline by exchanging it with next item
−	Collapse	Displays only the titles of selected slides
+	Expand	Displays the titles and all of the bulleted items of selected slides
↑≡	Collapse All	Displays only the title of all slides
↓≡	Expand All	Displays the titles and all of the bulleted items of all slides
▣	Summary Slide	Creates a new slide with a bulleted list of the titles of selected slides
A̲A̲	Show Formatting	When selected, displays text with all its formatting, such as italics or font size; when deselected, all text appears as normal on screen

Practice

Open the file myppprac2-4.ppt and switch to the Outline tab in the left pane of Normal View. Insert a new slide between the two existing slides. Give it the title We Produce, then create three bullets that list three products supplied by the fictitious company. Save your changes as myppprac2-5.ppt, then close the file.

skill | Adding Speaker's Notes

concept

When giving a presentation, you may want to have notes that refer to each slide in the order it which it will appear. PowerPoint allows you to create notes pages that contain presentation notes along with small pictures of the slides being referenced. These notes do not display in a presentation, but can be viewed privately by you or printed out for rehearsal or distribution. You can enter notes in the Notes Page View or in the notes pane of any tri-pane view.

do it !

Add notes to two of your slides so you can refer to them during a presentation.

1. Be sure that GSU Presentation 2.ppt file still is open with the Outline tab displayed. Click anywhere in the slide title Our grass is always greener to activate Slide 3.

2. Click in the Notes pane, which reads Click to add notes, so these instructions are replaced by a blinking insertion point. Click the gray bar dividing the Slide pane from the Notes pane to display a double-headed resizing arrow (⇳), then drag the border up so the Notes pane can display three lines of text.

3. Type the following text to accompany Slide 3. Then scroll the text up, if needed, to see both lines of text in the Notes pane (see Figure 2-15):

   As you can see, we grow four types of grass to meet many soil and light conditions. If these sods do not meet your needs, we can create—for a slight additional charge—a customized or signature turf for you.

4. Click the Next Slide button ⬇ below the Vertical scroll bar in the Slide pane to advance to Slide 4. Click View, then click Notes Page. In Notes Page View, the active slide will appear on a page with a text box under it in which you can enter notes for that slide. Click the Zoom box drop-down list arrow 100% ▾ , then click 100%. The text box that appears beneath the slide will now be easier to read.

5. Click inside the text box. A hatchmarked border will appear around the text box, a blinking insertion point will appear in the upper left corner of the text box, and a mouse pointer with a four-headed arrow (✛) will appear. In the text box, type the following sentence (see Figure 2-16):

   We have nearly two decades experience in handling both large and small jobs, laying sod on everything from exclusive 36-hole golf courses to parking lot islands measuring only three feet across.

6. Click anywhere outside the text box to deselect it. Save the changes you have made.

more

The image of the slide that appears at the top of the page in Notes Page View helps when trying to coordinate your comments with your slides during a presentation. If you want a slide to appear larger on the page, click the slide to display small circular sizing handles at the corners and midpoints of the slide, and to a mouse pointer with a four-headed arrow. Click any resizing handle to display a two-headed arrow, then drag the handle outward to enlarge the slide. (Holding down [Shift] while you resize a corner handle will maintain the slide's proportions.) To recenter an enlarged slide, click on the slide itself, not a resizing handle, to display the mouse pointer with the four-headed arrow, then drag the slide back to the mid-point of the page. You can resize and move the text box using the same techniques that you use with the slide. Just remember that, when selected, the text box will have a hatchmarked border. Resizing a slide or text box in Notes Page View will affect only Notes Page View, not slides in an actual presentation.

Figure 2-15 Adding speaker's notes in the Notes pane

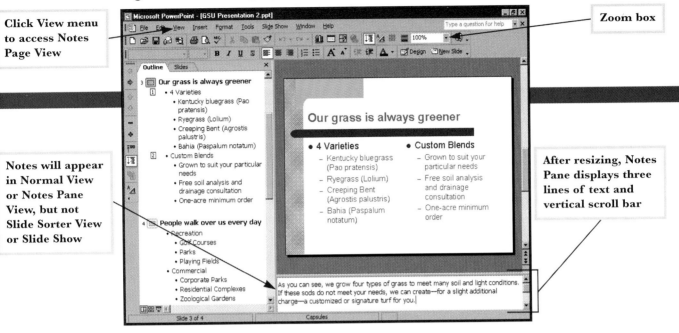

Click View menu to access Notes Page View

Zoom box

Notes will appear in Normal View or Notes Pane View, but not Slide Sorter View or Slide Show

After resizing, Notes Pane displays three lines of text and vertical scroll bar

Figure 2-16 Adding notes in Notes Page View

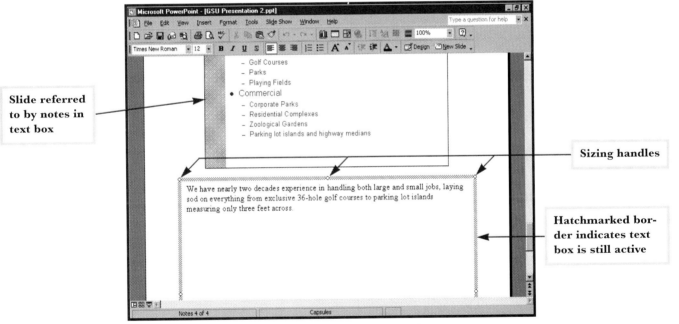

Slide referred to by notes in text box

Sizing handles

Hatchmarked border indicates text box is still active

Practice

Open myppprac2-5.ppt and add speaker notes to the first slide. These notes should provide a brief introduction to the name and the mission (i.e., the main customer-oriented goals) of your company. Save your changes as myppprac2-6.ppt, then close the file.

skill | Printing Slides and Notes Pages

 MOUS Skill

concept

You can use PowerPoint's print features to produce speaker's notes, audience handouts, or a hard copy of your presentation. Printing a presentation can involve a single click of a button or setting many options to determine what elements of a presentation are printed and how they are printed. You can use printouts to preview and evaluate your work or to share with your presentation audience.

do it !

Print hard copies of a presentation's slides and notes pages.

1. Make sure your computer is properly connected to a printer and that the printer is turned on and loaded with toner and paper. Also be sure that the GSU Presentation 2.ppt file appears on your screen in Normal View.

2. Click File, then click Print. The Print dialog box will open. Verify that the Print range is set to All, that the Copies section is set to 1, and that the Print what box is set to Slides (see Figure 2-17).

3. Click the OK button [OK] to print. Your printer will produce four pages, each displaying one slide from the presentation. If your printer does work, do **not** repeat the printing process. Double-check your printer connections, paper supply, and so on. If your pages still do not print, consult your instructor.

4. Repeat Step 2 to reopen the Print dialog box.

5. Click the drop-down arrow at the right edge of the Print what box. Click on Notes Pages to select that printing option from among the several options displayed there, as shown in Figure 2-18. In the Print Range section of the dialog box, click the Slides radio button, then type 3-4 in the text box next to it. Click [OK] to print. The notes pages that you created for Slides 3 and 4 will print.

6. Close your file and the PowerPoint program.

more

The Print dialog box offers you many print options. The Printer section of the dialog box enables you to select any printing device your computer properly connects to. Clicking the Name box opens a drop-down list of printers from which to choose. The Properties button opens a printer-specific dialog box for controlling options such as page orientation, graphics, printer features, and related options. As this Skill shows, the Print range section allows you to determine how much of your presentation will print. With the All option selected, the entire presentation will print. The Current Slide option prints only the slide that appears on screen immediately before opening the dialog box. The Selection option prints only those slides that you have highlighted. And the Slides option enables you to enter slide numbers so you can print nonconsecutive slides or limited ranges of slides, and to print slides in reverse order by stating the slide numbers in reverse (e.g., 6-1). The Copies section enables you to control how many times each selected slide will print, while checking the Collate box tells the computer to print one copy of a full set of slides before starting to print the next copy. If the box is unchecked, the printer will not arrange multiple copies of a presentation in slide order, but will print all copies of one slide, then the next, and so on. The Handouts section and bottom section of the dialog box enable you to select even more of the advanced options that the dialog box offers. The Preview button in the lower-left corner of the dialog box is a new feature in PowerPoint 2002 and opens a Print Preview screen like those in other Microsoft programs. PowerPoint's Print Preview screen enables you to navigate among slides, reopen the Print dialog box, choose which slide version to print, and so on.

Figure 2-17 Print dialog box

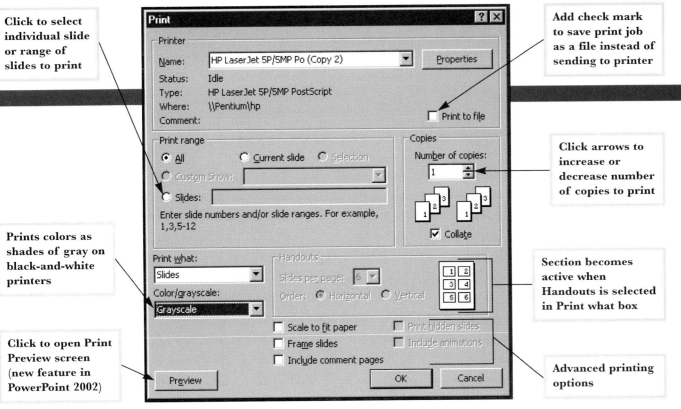

Click to select individual slide or range of slides to print

Add check mark to save print job as a file instead of sending to printer

Click arrows to increase or decrease number of copies to print

Prints colors as shades of gray on black-and-white printers

Section becomes active when Handouts is selected in Print what box

Click to open Print Preview screen (new feature in PowerPoint 2002)

Advanced printing options

Figure 2-18 Printing speaker's notes

Click to select desired option

Click to print selected item and to close dialog box

PowerPoint 2002

Practice

Open the file myppprac2-6.ppt, print speaker notes for it, then close the file. If asked to do so, write your name and today's date on the top of Slide 1, and hand in all slides.

shortcuts

Function	Button/Mouse	Menu	Keyboard
New file	🗋	Click File, click New	[Ctrl]+[N]
Slide design	📝 Design	Click Format, click Slide Design	
Open file	📂	Click File, click Open	[Ctrl]+[O]
New slide	🗐 New Slide	Click Insert, click New Slide	[Ctrl]+[M]
Increase font size	A	Click Format, click Font	[Ctrl]+[Shift]+[>]
Decrease font size	A	Click Format, click Font	[Ctrl]+[Shift]+[<]
Promote selected text	⬅		[Shift]+[Tab] or [Alt]+[Shift]+[Left]
Demote text	➡		[Tab] or [Alt]+[Shift]+[Right]
Move text up	⬆		[Alt]+[Shift]+[Up]
Move text down	⬇		[Alt]+[Shift]+[Down]
Collapse slide text	−		[Alt]+[Shift]+[−]
Expand slide text	+		[Alt]+[Shift]+[+]
Collapse all slide text	⤒		[Alt]+[Shift]+[1]
Expand all slide text	⤓		[Alt]+[Shift]+[9]
Summary slide	📑		[Alt]+[Shift]+[S]
Show formatting	ᴬ⊿		
Print file	🖨	Click File, click Print, click [OK]	[Ctrl]+[P], [Enter]

A. Identify Key Features

Name the items indicated by the callouts in Figure 2-19.

Figure 2-19 Designing your presentation

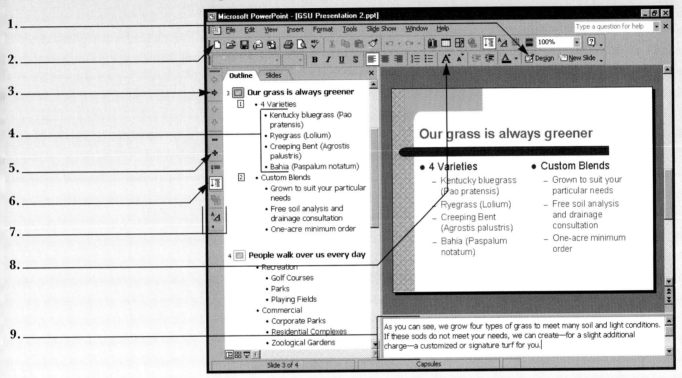

1. _____
2. _____
3. _____
4. _____
5. _____
6. _____
7. _____
8. _____
9. _____

B. Select the Best Answer

10. Area that contains a presenter's remarks about corresponding slides

11. Area that displays background, layout, placeholders, and text of a slide

12. Area that contains main titles and subpoints of a slide in text form

13. Name of a slide design

14. Name of a slide layout

15. Enables you to determine which slides will appear on hard copies

16. Includes a Views button, Tools button, and Preview area

17. A box with a border for holding text or objects on a slide

18. Type of button that appears after selected program actions (e.g., cut and paste)

a. Smart Tag

b. Placeholder

c. Slide pane

d. Title and Text

e. Outline tab

f. Print dialog box

g. Capsules.pot

h. Notes Pane

i. Open dialog box

quiz (continued)

C. Complete the Statement

19. The Outlining toolbar contains all of the following buttons **except** for:

  a. The Promote button

  b. The Move Up button

  c. The Show Placeholders button

  d. The Summary Slide button

20. The Print dialog box allows you to print which of the following?

  a. Slides

  b. Handouts

  c. Notes Pages

  d. All of the above

21. You can view notes entered in the Note pane:

  a. In a Notation View panel

  b. In Normal View

  c. In Slide Sorter View

  d. In Slide Show

22. To work more effectively on the Outline tab, activate:

  a. ScreenTips

  b. Grayscale Preview mode

  c. The Drawing toolbar

  d. The Outlining toolbar

23. Text that you type into a presentation slide is contained in:

  a. Icons

  b. Placeholders

  c. AutoLayout slides

  d. External files

24. Clicking the Back or Forward arrows at the left end of a task pane's title bar will:

  a. Take you to other task panes you already have used

  b. All task panes in other Office XP programs

  c. Previous or later slides in the current presentation

  d. None of the above

25. The Open button in the Open dialog box can access:

  a. The Open Read-Only command

  b. The Open as Copy command

  c. The Open in Browser command

  d. All of the above

26. All of the following are ways to create a new slide for a presentation **except**:

  a. Click Insert, then click New Slide

  b. Use the keyboard combination [Ctrl]+[M]

  c. Click the New Slide button on the Formatting toolbar

  d. Click Insert New Slide on the Slide Layout task pane

27. The Outline tab in Normal View enables you to:

  a. Enter, edit, or move text freely on a slide

  b. Move or copy text between different slides in a presentation

  c. Promote or demote text

  d. All of the above

28. Smart Tags may appear in PowerPoint after which of the following actions?

  a. An autocorrection

  b. An autofit action

  c. An automatic layout change

  d. All of the above

Build Your Skills

1. Design a presentation about your favorite musicians from scratch:
   a. Start PowerPoint, and verify that a blank Title Slide appears by default as Slide 1.
   b. Apply the Design Template Network.pot to your presentation.
   c. On Slide 1, enter the title My Top Five Musical Acts.
   d. Save the file in your PowerPoint Files folder as Music.ppt.

2. Develop your presentation:
   a. Add five Title and Text slides to your presentation, maintaining the Network.pot slide design.
   b. Click Slide 2 on the Slides tab in Normal View, and enter the name of your favorite musical act.
   c. Click Slide 3 on the Slides tab, and enter the name of your second favorite musical act.
   d. Click Slides 4, 5, and 6, adding the name of your third, fourth, and fifth favorite musical acts, and resave your file with the changes you have made.

3. Focus on the text of your presentation:
   a. Switch to the Outline tab of Normal View. On Slides 2–6, type Favorite Albums as the first bullet point.
   b. List your three favorite albums for each musical act on the appropriate slide as bullet points demoted one level below Favorite Albums.
   c. On Slides 2–6, add a bullet point that says Favorite Songs on the same level as the Favorite Albums bullet.
   d. List your three favorite songs for each musical act on the appropriate slide as bullet points demoted one level below the Favorite Songs bullet.
   e. Move the Favorite Albums section of text so that if follows the Favorite Songs section on Slides 2–6.
   f. Collapse Slides 1 and 2, then collapse the remaining slides. Resave your file with the changes you have made.

4. Create speakers' notes for your presentation.
   a. Select Slide 1. Using the Notes Pane in Normal View, write an introduction to your presentation.
   b. Switch to Notes Page View, and add notes to Slides 2–6 that include basic biographical information that you know about each musical act and why you enjoy its music.

5. Create output for your presentation:
   a. Switch to Normal View, with the Slides tab showing, and Slide 1 selected.
   b. Click the Color/Grayscale button on the Standard toolbar, then click the Grayscale command and preview your slides one by one.
   c. Print one copy of each slide. Print one copy of each Notes Page. Close the file and exit PowerPoint.

Note: If you prefer books or films over music, feel free to substitute them for musical acts. For example, if you choose books, substitute your five favorite authors for the musical acts. Substitute your three favorite characters of each author for favorite songs, and substitute favorite books for favorite albums. If you prefer films, substitute your five favorite movie types (drama, comedy, adventure flick, musical, etc.). Instead of songs, substitute three favorite actors for each movie type. And instead of albums, substitute three favorite movies. In Notes Page View, be sure to use biographical information about authors or actors, and use plot summaries or thematic interpretations about books or movies.

interactivity (continued)

Problem Solving Exercises

1. A Problem Solving Exercise in Lesson 1 asked you to lay the groundwork for a motivational presentation to be used by managers at the new offices of Tabak, Inc., a retail book distributor. Now that you have started to develop your PowerPoint skills, you can begin to convert the presentation you created from a framework into a functional, customized document. Open the file Motivation.ppt, from Lesson 1, which should be based on an AutoContent Wizard for motivating a team. Each slide should contain placeholder text that advises what information to place on each slide. Replace the text in these placeholders with text that relates to Tabak and the goals of its presentation. Add speaker's notes for at least half of the slides, including the first and last slides. Save the new presentation as Revised Motivation.ppt. Be sure that your name still appears on every slide, and print the presentation according to your instructor's directions.

2. In your search for a new job, you have encountered an employment agency that encourages you to present yourself as being highly skilled in Office XP software. Along those lines the agency has suggested that you use PowerPoint to create an interactive resume. Your resume should include at least seven slides, beginning with a Title Slide that provides personal information such as your name, address, telephone number, and e-mail address. Each slide that follows should provide bulleted information about standard resume topics such as job objective, education, paid and volunteer work experience, computer skills and related hobbies, and so on. Choose a Design Template that you like, but that is also appropriate for a business presentation. When you finish the presentation, preview it in grayscale, making sure that your name appears on each slide. Save the project as Resume.ppt. Print the presentation according to your instructor's directions.

3. Create a presentation that will map your progress as you learn PowerPoint. Create a Title Slide that states the name of this book in the title placeholder and your name in the subtitle placeholder. For each Lesson in this book, create a Title and Text slide. On each Lesson slide put the title of the Lesson in the title area. As you complete the Skills in each Lesson, enter the names of the Skills in the corresponding bulleted placeholder. By this point, of course, you need to complete the bulleted areas for only Slides 2 and 3, which correspond with Lessons 1 and 2. Be sure your name appears on each slide, then save your presentation as Progress.ppt. Print the presentation according to your instructor's directions.

4. The Marketing Director at Redweb has approved the presentation layout that you submitted in Lesson 1. With the first round of trade shows just a few weeks away, you must start developing a presentation that will attract schools, colleges, and other non-profit organizations to your company's Internet service. Open the Non-Profit.ppt presentation that you created with the AutoContent Wizard at the end of Lesson 1. Using the placeholder text on selling a product and/or service as a guide, add your own text to the presentation to make it a clear and persuasive marketing tool for RedWeb. Add speaker's notes that explain exactly what the presenter should say as each slide is shown. Be careful not to repeat just what is on the slide that audience members can see, but add additional information that would help them understand what RedWeb can provide and how RedWeb can help their organization. Be sure your name appears on each slide, then save the new version of the presentation as Revised Non-Profit.ppt. Print your Notes Pages so you can submit them to your boss for approval.

3

Developing Your Presentation

During the presentation-building process, you will need to add, edit, and format text. PowerPoint comes equipped with an extensive collection of tools that you can use to manipulate text and text boxes. The ability to add your own text boxes at any location on a slide adds flexibility to your presentation designs. You are not limited to the text boxes, which are those preformatted and prepositioned placeholders for text, provided by the AutoLayout slides. The placement of text on a slide can help you to accentuate the point you are making. With a simple drag of the mouse, you also can move text boxes to any position on a slide.

Editing text includes revising existing text, correcting typos, rearranging text, and checking and correcting misspellings. PowerPoint handles text much like the word processors you may have used. You can specify what font you wish your text to be in and can add formatting. Text embellishments such as bolding and italics make text stand out. With PowerPoint's advanced editing tools, you can check your spelling and quickly search for and replace specified words or phrases. Each of these editing features will aid you in creating an impressive, grammatically correct presentation.

Once you have conquered the text of your presentation, you may want to enhance the presentation visually by adding drawing objects. Drawing objects can serve a functional purpose or simply be decorative and can be saved along with the text in a presentation. You then can print audience handouts with those graphics and with places for audience members to take notes. At the same time, however, you also should know how to save files without graphics for those occasions that require graphics-free or smaller files.

Lesson Goal:

Develop a presentation by editing existing text and adding custom text boxes. Use PowerPoint's editing tools to refine the text. Enhance the appearance of the presentation by using PowerPoint's drawing toolbar. Print audience handouts, and save presentations in file versions without graphics.

skills

- Editing and Adding Text Boxes
- Formatting Text
- Moving Text Boxes and Aligning Text
- Using the Spelling Checker
- Finding and Replacing Text
- Using AutoCorrect
- Drawing and Formatting Objects
- Modifying and Enhancing Drawn Objects
- Printing Audience Handouts
- Saving Slide Presentations as RTF Files

PowerPoint 2002

skill

Editing and Adding Text Boxes

concept

Text in a PowerPoint presentation appears in text boxes, which are rectangular areas in which you add text so you may manipulate it independently of other text on a slide. You can create two types of text boxes with the Text Box tool: text label and word processing. In a text label box, words do not wrap to the next line when they reach the edge of the text box. This type of box is best used for single words and short phrases. If you have a longer passage of text and want it to wrap onto the next line, then you should create a word processing box.

do it !

Edit some of the text that exists on a previously added fifth slide of a presentation. Add another slide and create your own text boxes on it.

1. Open Student File ppdoit3-1.ppt in Normal View with the Slides tab forward in the left pane. Save the file in your PowerPoint Files folder as GSU Presentation 3. ⬤ If any task pane opens along the presentation, click the Close task pane button [X] to close the task pane and to enlarge the Slide pane.

2. Advance the presentation to Slide 5, which has a Title and 2-Column Text layout that compares the Green Side Up company to its competition, Lawns by Louis. Notice that the slide title, We Mow Down the Competition, uses initial capital letters, whereas the previous slide titles use an uppercase letter for only the first word.

3. Move the mouse pointer over the title text. The pointer will change from the standard pointing arrow to an I-beam (Ĩ). Position the I-beam just after the M in Mow, and click the left mouse button. A hatchmarked border will appear around the text, defining the box's dimensions and indicating that it is active. A blinking insertion point also will appear where you clicked to mark the place where entered text will be inserted or deleted.

4. Press [Backspace] to delete the uppercase M, then type a lowercase m.

5. Press the right arrow key [→] until the insertion point is just in front of the D in Down. Press [Delete], which will erase the character just in front of the insertion point. Then type a lowercase d.

6. Using the mouse, click and drag over the C in Competition to select it. Then type a lowercase c to replace it. Verify that the slide now matches Figure 3-1.

7. Press [Ctrl]+[M], the shortcut key combination for creating a new slide, to create a new slide. Slide 6, with the Title and Text layout, will appear by default, and the Slide Layout task pane will appear. Under the Content Layouts category on the Slide Layout task pane, click the Blank AutoLayout. Slide 6 will convert to a Blank layout in the Slide pane, and a blue border will surround the Blank layout in the task pane (see Figure 3-2). Click the Close Task Pane button [X] to close the Slide Layout task pane.

8. If necessary, click View, select Toolbars, then click Drawing to display the Drawing toolbar. If necessary, click on the toolbar's title bar and drag the toolbar to the bottom of your program window to dock it there (see Figure 3-3).

(continued on PP 3.4)

Figure 3-1 Slide title changed to lower case

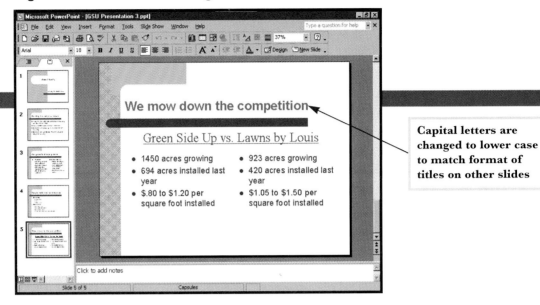

Capital letters are changed to lower case to match format of titles on other slides

Figure 3-2 New slide with Blank layout

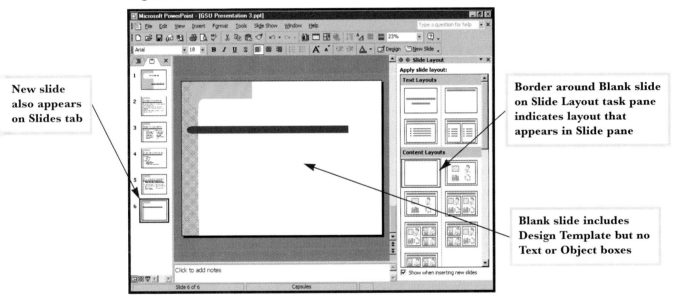

New slide also appears on Slides tab

Border around Blank slide on Slide Layout task pane indicates layout that appears in Slide pane

Blank slide includes Design Template but no Text or Object boxes

Figure 3-3 Drawing toolbar

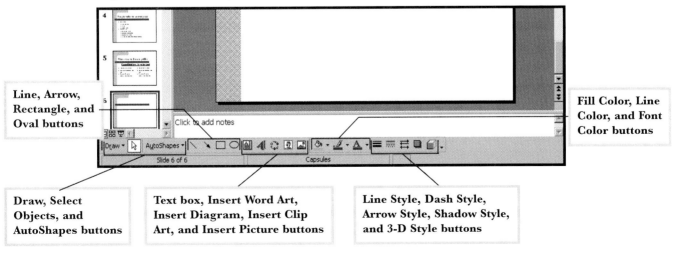

Line, Arrow, Rectangle, and Oval buttons

Fill Color, Line Color, and Font Color buttons

Draw, Select Objects, and AutoShapes buttons

Text box, Insert Word Art, Insert Diagram, Insert Clip Art, and Insert Picture buttons

Line Style, Dash Style, Arrow Style, Shadow Style, and 3-D Style buttons

PowerPoint 2002

skill | Editing and Adding Text Boxes (continued)

do it !

9. On the Drawing toolbar, click the Text Box button 🗐. The mouse pointer will change to a text box pointer (↓) when it is in the Slide pane. The position of the text cursor on the slide will determine where the text box will appear when you click the mouse button.

10. Place the text cursor in the white area between the light green background and the horizontal blue bar separating the upper and lower areas of the slide, then click once. An active text label box will appear. Type We're on a roll. The text box will extend to accommodate the text as you type (see Figure 3-4).

11. Click the Text Box button 🗐 again. Position the mouse pointer below the horizontal blue bar. Align the pointer with the left edge of the text box you already have created. Click and drag to the lower-right corner of the slide. ◖◗ As you drag, the text box pointer will change to a drag pointer (+), and a dashed border will appear, indicating where you have dragged the pointer. When you release the pointer, the box will retain its width, its height will be reduced to one line, and a blinking insertion point will appear inside the left edge of the box.

12. Type the following text, including the misspellings, which you will correct later in this lesson. Be sure to press [Enter] at the ends of the first two lines, as indicated below:

    Argyle County Municiple Stadium [Enter]
    Winter Crow Golf Course and Country Club [Enter]
    Arthur Milton Golden Cloud Seniors Place, Infirmary Care, and Recreational Facility

    The last line wrapped onto the next line when it reached the boundary of the text box because the word processing text box you created allows this feature (see Figure 3-5). The text label box created earlier would not wrap, but would continue on the same line. ◖◗ The line spacing for Figure 3-5 assumes the following settings in the Line Spacing dialog box, accessed from the Line Spacing command on the Format menu: Line Spacing: 1 Lines; Before paragraph: 0.5 Lines; After paragraph: 0 Lines.

13. Click the Text Box button 🗐, and click once near the bottom center of the slide to create a text label box. Type Recently Acquired Accounts. Click outside of the box to cancel the selection (see Figure 3-6).

14. Save the changes you have made to the presentation, but leave the file open.

more

The drag-and-drop method of copying or moving text is a convenient way to rearrange text on your slides. To move text that you already have selected, click and drag the mouse pointer. As you drag the text, the mouse pointer will appear with a small box (⧉), indicating that the text is loaded and ready to be dropped. A dotted insertion point (|) will move through the text with the drag-and-drop pointer, indicating where the loaded text will be dropped when you release the mouse button. To duplicate existing text elsewhere on a slide, first select the text you want to move. Hold down [Ctrl], then click and drag the text to the desired location. As you drag the text, the mouse pointer will appear with a small box and small plus sign (⧉), indicating that you are copying rather than moving the text to the new location. To place items on a slide more accurately, you can display horizontal and vertical rulers by right-clicking a blank area of the slide and selecting Ruler from the shortcut menu that appears. You also can display horizontal and vertical grids by clicking View, then clicking Grid and Guides to display the Grid and Guides dialog box. In the dialog box you can select Snap objects to grid, Snap objects to other objects, Display grid on screen, and Display drawing guides on screen, then click ▭OK▭.

Figure 3-4 Text label box

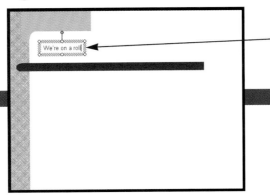

Manually placed
text box with
added text

Figure 3-5 Word processing text box

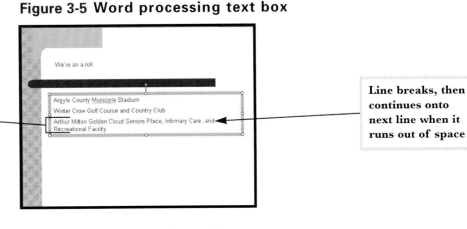

Spacing between
wrapped lines is
less than between
paragraphs

Line breaks, then
continues onto
next line when it
runs out of space

Figure 3-6 Slide 6 with added text boxes

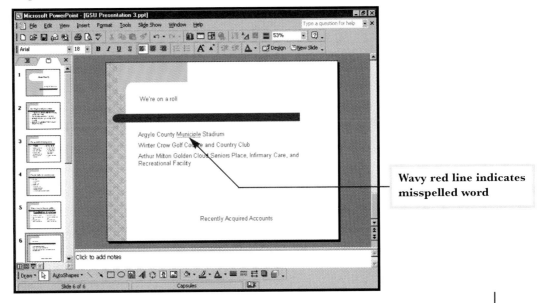

Wavy red line indicates
misspelled word

Practice

Open the file myppprac2-6.ppt, created according to instructions on PP 2.15. Add a Blank slide to the end of the presentation. Create a Text Label text box in the upper-left corner that says Board of Directors. Add a Word Processing text box in the body of the slide with three names in it. Save the changed presentation as myppprac3-1.ppt.

skill   Formatting Text

concept

Most text added to the presentation so far has appeared with preassigned characteristics known collectively as formatting. Formatting includes the overall appearance of the text, which is determined by the font that has been applied to it. Formatting also includes font size, font color, and style. PowerPoint gives you the ability to format text as you please, even if it was preformatted as part of a Design Template. You can apply formatting for informational, organizational, and stylistic purposes.

do it !

Change the formatting of text added in the previous Skill.

1. Be sure that the GSU Presentation 3.ppt file appears in your program window in Normal View, with Slide 6 selected on the Slides tab. Notice the Formatting toolbar in Figure 3-7.

2. In Slide 6 click the text We're on a roll to activate the text box. Click at one end of the text box, then drag the I-beam across the text to the opposite end to select the whole title. To quickly highlight a whole paragraph, you can triple-click anywhere within it. To quickly highlight a sentence, hold down [Ctrl] while clicking the sentence. To quickly highlight just a word, just double-click anywhere within it.

3. Click the drop-down list arrow on the right end of the Font Size box 18 ▾. The Font Size drop-down list will appear with the current size highlighted.

4. Scroll down the list and click 36. The point size of the title will increase. Points are the measurement unit used for character size. Roughly speaking, 72 points equal one inch, so the modified title will print about 1/2-inch tall (for Arial, about 3/8-inch tall).

5. On the Drawing toolbar, click the Font Color drop-down list arrow ▲ ▾. The Font Color palette will appear, with a border surrounding the box containing the current text color. The ScreenTip for this box will read Follow Text and Lines Scheme Color.

6. In the Font Color palette, click the fourth box in the row. The ScreenTip for this box will read Follow Title Text Scheme Color (see Figure 3-8).

7. Click the Bold button **B** to apply bold style to the selected text.

8. In the middle text box, click the list of new accounts, then select the three account names by dragging the I-beam from the beginning of the first line of text to the end of the last.

9. Click the number in the Font Size box 18 ▾ to highlight it, type 28, then press [Enter] to enlarge the list of accounts to that size of font. Click the Center button ≡ on the Formatting toolbar to center the list of accounts in its text box. Click outside the list of accounts to cancel the selection of the text box. Verify that the formatting of your slide so far matches the formatting in Figure 3-9. To enlarge the text for the list of accounts, you also could click the Increase Font Size button **A** on the Formatting toolbar until the Font Size box displays 28. Since your fingers were on the keyboard for increasing the font size, you then could have centered the text by pressing [Ctrl]+[E].

(continued on PP 3.8)

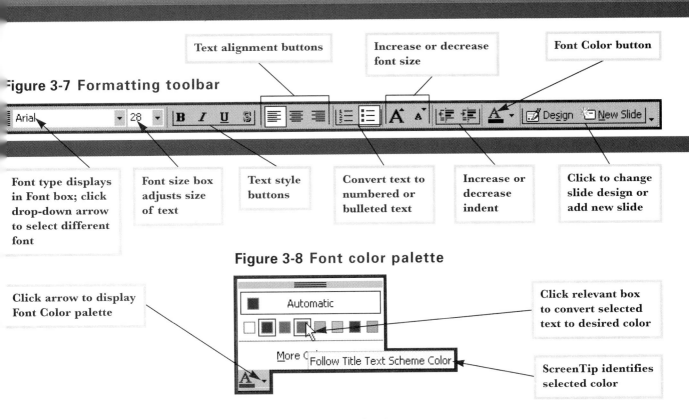

Text alignment buttons

Increase or decrease font size

Font Color button

Figure 3-7 Formatting toolbar

Font type displays in Font box; click drop-down arrow to select different font

Font size box adjusts size of text

Text style buttons

Convert text to numbered or bulleted text

Increase or decrease indent

Click to change slide design or add new slide

Figure 3-8 Font color palette

Click arrow to display Font Color palette

Automatic

More C Follow Title Text Scheme Color

Click relevant box to convert selected text to desired color

ScreenTip identifies selected color

Figure 3-9 Formatted title text on Slide 6

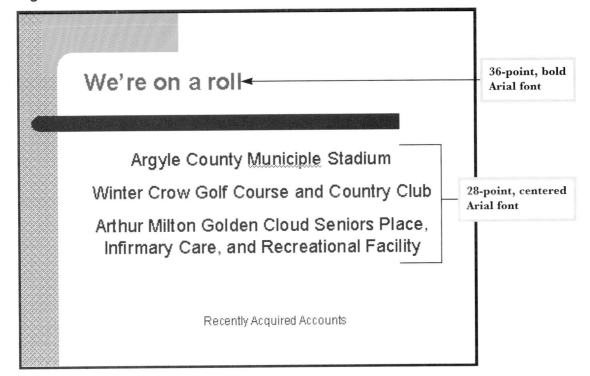

36-point, bold Arial font

28-point, centered Arial font

PowerPoint 2002

skill Formatting Text (continued)

do it !

10. Click once in the word Recently in the bottom text box. While holding down [Ctrl], click once to highlight the words Recently Acquired Accounts.

11. On the Standard toolbar click the Font drop-down list arrow [Arial ▾]. An alphabetized list of fonts installed on your computer will appear, and each font will appear in its own style. ⬭ If fonts appear in a plain typeface, you can turn on their styles. To do so, click Tools, click Customize to open the Customize dialog box, then click the Options tab to bring it to the front of the dialog box. In the Other section add a check mark to the List font names in their font check box and close the dialog box.

12. With the text in the Font box highlighted, press [T] to move to that part of the alphabet, then click the font named Times New Roman. The text in the bottom text box will change from Arial to Times New Roman font.

13. With the text Recently Acquired Accounts still highlighted, click the Increase Font Size button [A] on the Formatting toolbar five times to increase the font size to 36. Click the Underline button [U], then click the Center button [≡] on the Formatting toolbar to underline the text and to center it in its text box. Click outside of the bottom text box to cancel the selection. Verify that the formatting of Slide 6 matches that in Figure 3-10. Notice that the now-enlarged text and text box appear at the right edge of the slide. Do not worry about this placement, as a later Skill will teach you how to relocate text boxes.

14. Save the changes you have made to your presentation, but leave the presentation open.

more

If the exact point size that you want to apply to selected text is not available on the Font Size drop-down list, you can type any whole number between 1 and 4000 into the Font Size text box. The point size of the selected text will change to reflect your entry. If you need to apply several formatting changes to selected text, you may want to use the Font dialog box, which you can open from the Format menu (see Figure 3-11). This dialog box enables you to view all of the characteristics of the selected text at once. It also offers additional formatting options that do not appear on the Formatting toolbar. For example, the Effects section of the dialog box enables you to add an embossed look to the text and format text as a subscript or superscript. After changing a format, you can click the Preview button [Preview] (a new feature in PowerPoint 2002) to see on the slide what a formatting change will look like if you close the dialog box at that point. If you do not like certain formatting changes, simply undo them in the dialog box until text on the slide looks the way you want, then close the dialog box.

Figure 3-10 Slide 6 with text formatting changes

36-point, underlined Times New Roman font, centered in text box, but not on slide

Figure 3-11 Font dialog box

Click desired font, style, and size, or select from list

Add check marks to apply desired formatting effects to selected text

Describes selected font in Font box

Click to apply formats and to close dialog box

Click to display slide as it will look when printed

Click box or arrow to display palette from which to choose color

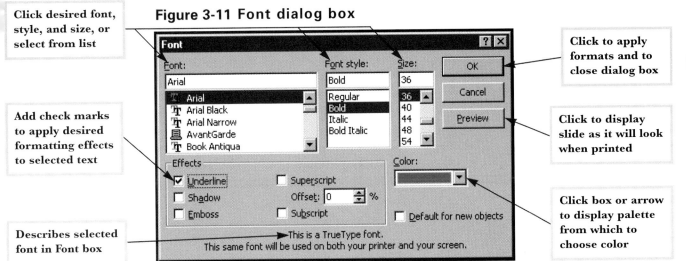

Practice

To practice formatting text, open the file ppprac3-2.ppt. Follow the instructions on the slide. Save and close the modified file as myppprac3-2.ppt.

skill Moving Text Boxes and Aligning Text

MOUS Skill

concept

To improve a slide's layout, you can move text boxes and realign their text. You can move text boxes easily by dragging them or pressing the keyboard's arrow keys. The four alignment options in a text box are left, center, right, and justify (that is, aligned at both the right and left margins). Besides aligning text according to the boundaries of its text box, you also can adjust the spacing between paragraphs within any selected text box.

do it !

Move and align the text boxes on Slide 6 and change paragraph spacing within one text box.

1. Click the title text, We're on a roll, to activate the text box. Small circles, called sizing handles, will appear at the corners and at the midpoints of each side of the border.

2. Position the pointer over the hatchmarked border to display a mouse pointer with a four-headed arrow (✥). With the pointer touching the border, not a sizing handle, drag the text box to the right, centering it between the left and right edges of the slide. Be sure that the text box also remains centered vertically between the green shading above and the horizontal blue bar below it. ◑ As you drag the text box, a dashed rectangle will move with the pointer. When you release the mouse button, the text box will relocate at the last location indicated by the rectangle.

3. Click the list of new accounts to activate its text box. Click the hatchmarked border to activate it. Press the down-arrow key (▼) several times to move the text box into the lower half of the slide. Press the left (◄) or right (►) arrow keys, if needed, to ensure that the text box remains centered between the left and right edges of the slide.

4. Click any text in the Recently Acquired Accounts text box. Use the mouse pointer with the four-headed arrow (✥) to drag this text box above the text box containing the list of new accounts. When you finish dragging the text box, be sure it also is centered between the left and right edges of the slide.

5. Click the Toolbar Options button ⬝ at the right end of the Formatting toolbar to display a menu. Point to Add or Remove Buttons to display a submenu, then point to Formatting to display another submenu. Click Increase Paragraph Spacing to add its button to the toolbar (see Figure 3-12).

6. Click to the left of the first word in the first line in the new accounts text box, which is now the lowest of the three text boxes. While holding down [Shift], click to the right of the last word in the last line to select all of the text between those two points.

7. Click the Increase Paragraph Spacing button ⬛ three times to increase the space between each account name. Click outside of the text box to cancel the selection of the text. Verify that your slide now looks like the one in Figure 3-13.

8. Save the changes you have made, but leave the presentation open.

more

You can resize text boxes by dragging one of their sizing handles. Placing the mouse pointer over a sizing handle changes the pointer to a double-headed arrow showing the direction in which you can move that handle. Dragging a corner sizing handle will adjust a text box in two relevant directions. You can maintain the proportions of a text box while resizing it by holding down [Shift] while you drag a corner sizing handle. Dragging a mid-point sizing handle will adjust a text box in only the one horizontal or vertical direction that you move it.

Figure 3-12 Adding a toolbar button

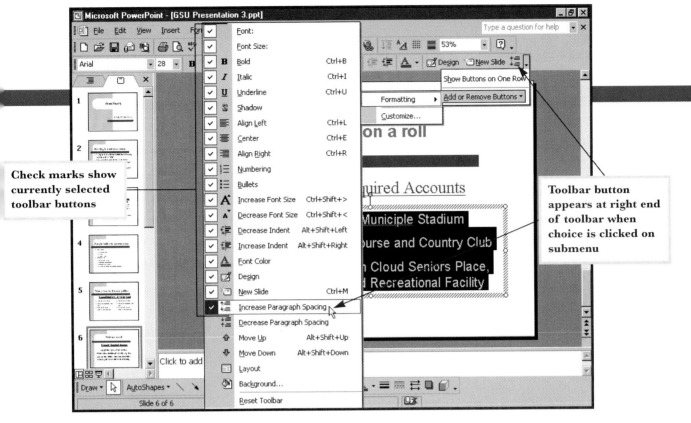

Figure 3-13 Slide 6 after moving text boxes and aligning text

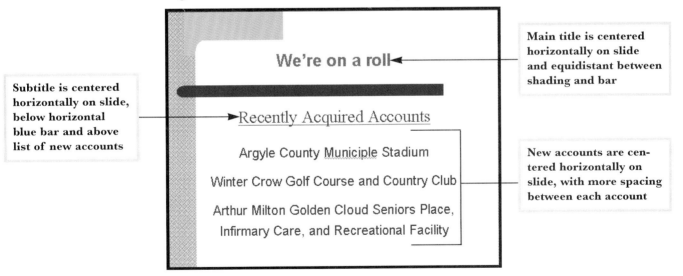

Main title is centered horizontally on slide and equidistant between shading and bar

Subtitle is centered horizontally on slide, below horizontal blue bar and above list of new accounts

New accounts are centered horizontally on slide, with more spacing between each account

Practice

To practice moving text boxes and aligning text, open the file ppprac3-3.ppt. Follow the instructions on the slide. Save and close the modified file as myppprac3-3.ppt.

skill | Using the Spelling Checker

concept

Even the most careful typists can make typing mistakes that they will not catch with their own eyes. PowerPoint has a spelling checker feature that finds spelling errors in a presentation and offers you choices for correcting them. Be aware that the spelling checker cannot determine if a word has been misused, as in using "there" when you should use "their." Also, it will tag any words it does not recognize, including most proper names and most words in languages other than the main one installed in the PowerPoint program.

do it !

Check for misspelled words in a presentation.

1. Be sure that Slide 6 of the GSU Presentation 3.ppt file still appears on screen in Normal View.

2. On the Standard toolbar click the Spelling button [ABC✓]. The Spelling dialog box will appear on screen, The first questionable word that the spelling checker has found will appear in the Not in Dictionary text box. The Change to box will contain the first of two suggested replacements for the misspelled word, which are shown in the Suggestions box. The misspelled word Municiple also will appear selected on the slide behind the dialog box (see Figure 3-14).

3. Click the Change button [Change] to change Municiple to the suggested and correct spelling, Municipal. With the correction made, the Spelling dialog box advances to the next questionable word in the presentation, which is on Slide 3. The word also is selected on the slide behind the dialog box (see Figure 3-15).

4. The questionable word, Pao, is part of the scientific name of a grass variety grown by Green Side Up. The spelling checker flags the word because PowerPoint's dictionary does not recognize it. However, since the word is spelled correctly, click the Ignore button [Ignore] to leave the word unchanged and to advance to the next questionable word.

5. Click [Ignore] seven more times to ignore the remaining scientific names that PowerPoint does not recognize. When the spelling checker stops finding questionable words, a dialog box will appear to inform you that the spelling check is complete. Notice that all of the wavy red lines, indicating questionable spellings, have disappeared.

6. Click the OK button [OK] to exit the spelling checker and to return to your presentation. Save the change you made, but leave the presentation open.

more

Clicking [Ignore] tells the spelling checker feature to leave an unrecognized word unchanged and to move to the next questioned word. The feature will stop if it finds the same word again in the file. If you click the Ignore All button [Ignore All], however, the feature will skip any more instances of that word. Likewise, the Change All button [Change All] will change every instance of the questioned word to whatever is in the Change To text box. Ordinarily, the feature places its primary suggested change directly into the Change to box. However, you may click another suggestion or type a new word to replace the preferred suggestion. In the Skill above, the feature recognized several proper names but failed to recognize the Latin terms for the grass varieties. If you wanted to use these Latin terms often, you could add them to the the feature's custom dictionary so the feature would no longer question them. To add an uncommon word to the the feature's database, select the desired word, then click the Add button [Add]. You can change the language used by the spelling checker by selecting the Language command from the Tools menu. Finally, The Custom Dictionary is a database unique to each installed copy of PowerPoint that you have added during each spelling checker process.

Figure 3-14 Spelling dialog box

Questioned word is highlighted on slide and appears in Not in Dictionary text box

Click to leave questioned spelling unchanged and to continue the spelling checker

Change to box contains word highlighted in Suggestions text box

Click to replace questioned word with word in Change to box and to continue the spelling checker

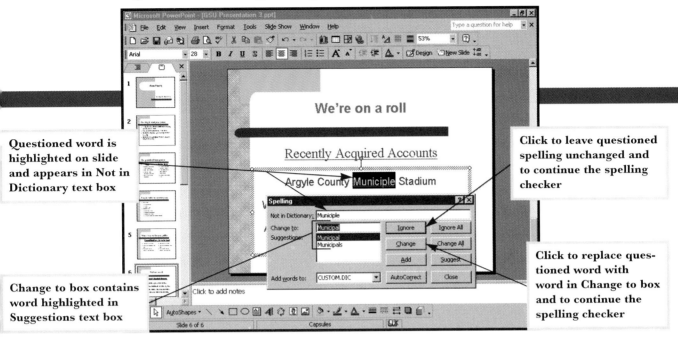

Figure 3-15 Spelling dialog box questions additional words

Adds highlighted word to selected dictionary and continues the spelling checker

Leaves all instances of the questioned word unchanged and continues the spelling checker

Replaces all instances of questioned word with word in Change to box

Adds questioned spelling and correction in Change to box to AutoCorrect list

Searches selected dictionary for possible spellings of questioned word

Selects dictionary in which to store added spellings

Stops the spelling checker and closes the dialog box

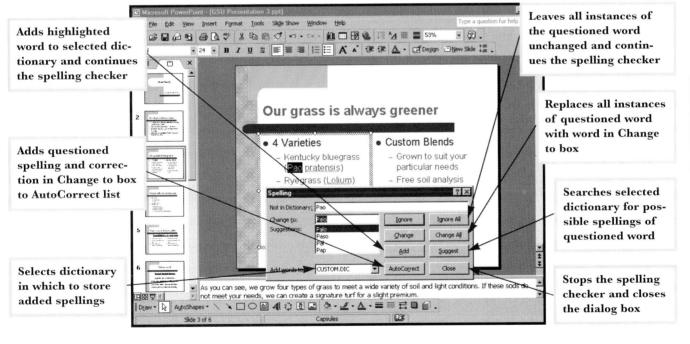

Practice

To practice using Spelling Checker, open the file ppprac3-4.ppt. Use the Spelling dialog box to find and correct the errors in the presentation. Save and close the modified file as myppprac3-4.ppt.

skill | Finding and Replacing Text

concept

If you want to change a specific word or phrase throughout your presentation, PowerPoint offers a Find and Replace function that saves you the time, effort, and potential inaccuracies of long, manual searches. You can view each instance of a desired item and change it individually or instruct PowerPoint to change all instances of the item at once. You also can set an option to search for only those items that match the capitalization of the items and an option to find only those items that match whole words, and not parts of larger words.

do it !

Find and replace a statistical error that had been made in the presentation.

1. Be sure that Slide 1 of the GSU Presentation 3.ppt file appears on your screen in Normal View.

2. Click Edit, then click Replace. The Replace dialog box will appear with a blinking insertion point appearing by default in the Find what box.

3. Type the number 1450, then press [Tab] to move the insertion point into the Replace with box. In the Replace with box, type the number 1405 (see Figure 3-16).

4. Click the Find Next button [Find Next]. PowerPoint will highlight the first instance it finds on a slide (beginning from the active slide) of the entry that you typed in the Find what box (see Figure 3-17).

5. Click the Replace All button [Replace All] to replace all instances of the number 1450 with the number 1405. An information box will appear with the results of the Find and Replace operation (see Figure 3-18).

6. Click [OK] to continue. Close the Replace dialog box.

7. Save the changes you have made to your presentation, and close the file.

more

When you are working with a presentation that contains multiple slides, you can use the Replace command to search the entire presentation at once. To replace a word on a case-by-case basis, click the Replace button [Replace] in the Replace dialog box instead of the Replace All button. Be aware that the Find What and the Replace with text boxes have drop-down lists that contain your previous Find and Replace entries so that you can conduct repeat searches quickly.

To find and replace only those words that match the capitalization of a word or phrase you are searching for, add a check mark to the Match case check box near the lower-left corner of the Replace dialog box. To find and replace only whole words, rather than parts of words, that match a word you are looking for, add a check mark to the Find whole words only check box. For example, this second feature will help you find the word fact only when it stands alone, not when it appears as part of a word such as factory or a phrase such as de facto.

The Find dialog box resembles the Replace dialog box except that it lacks the Replace function and just searches your presentation for words or phrases that you specify. This search feature is helpful when you want to find out how many times you have used certain words in your presentation, or if you need to go to a specific word or phrase but do not remember which slide that word or phrase appears on. Clicking [Replace...] in the Find dialog box transforms it into the Replace dialog box. (The additional ellipsis, or three periods, on the button indicates that clicking this kind of button will take you to a new menu or dialog box rather than just perform a replacement.)

Figure 3-16 Replace dialog box

Takes capitalization into account when searching for words

Tells PowerPoint to ignore requested word when it is part of another word

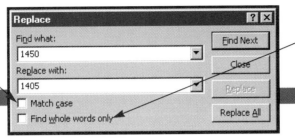

Figure 3-17 Finding the first item to replace

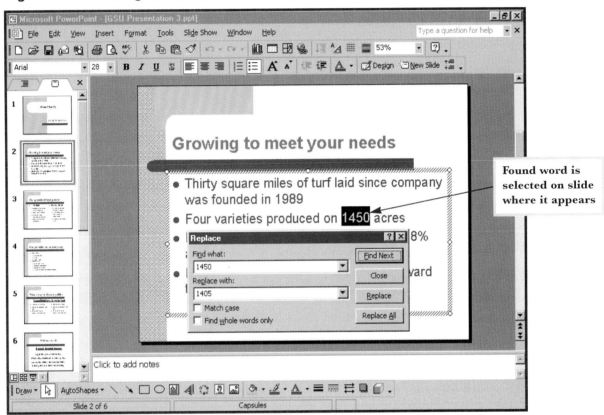

Found word is selected on slide where it appears

Figure 3-18 Results of Find and Replace operation

PowerPoint 2002

Practice

To practice finding and replacing text, open the file ppprac3-5.ppt. Follow the instructions on the slide. Save and close the modified file as myppprac3-5.ppt.

skill Using AutoCorrect

concept

PowerPoint's AutoCorrect feature takes the idea of a spelling checker feature one step further. In addition to finding your spelling errors, AutoCorrect corrects them as soon as you type them. This feature recognizes a predetermined set of common typing errors, such as teh for the. Additionally, you can customize AutoCorrect to act upon specific words that you frequently enter incorrectly.

do it !

Set AutoCorrect to correct automatically a typing mistake that is often made.

1. Click the New button ⬜ to create a new presentation. A blank Title Slide will appear in the Slide pane, and the Slide Layout task pane will appear on the right side of the screen.

2. Click Tools, then click AutoCorrect Options. The AutoCorrect dialog box will open. If necessary, click the AutoCorrect tab to bring it to the front of the dialog box, with the insertion point located by default in the Replace box. Type presentatin, misspelled without the letter o. Notice that the Title bar of this dialog box also states the name of the language operating in the current presentation.

3. Press [Tab] to move the insertion point to the With box. Type the word presentation (see Figure 3-19). Click ⬜ OK ⬜ to accept the changes you have made and to close the AutoCorrect dialog box. Whenever you type the incorrect spelling, presentatin, PowerPoint now will replace it automatically with the correct one, presentation.

4. The default slide from the new presentation will appear in the Slide pane. Click the Title text box to activate it. Type the misspelling, presentatin, then a space. When you press [Spacebar], AutoCorrect will correct the misspelling. It also will capitalize the word, as it recognizes the word as the first word of a sentence (see Figure 3-20).

5. Close the new presentation without saving it.

more

AutoCorrect automatically capitalizes any word after you have pressed [Enter] or typed a period and a space, as the program identifies that word as the first word of a new sentence. To keep AutoCorrect from automatically capitalizing words after abbreviations, AutoCorrect takes into account a list of Exceptions when deciding if a previous sentence has ended, or if just a common abbreviation has been typed. Clicking the Exceptions button ⬜ Exceptions... ⬜ on the AutoCorrect tab of the AutoCorrect dialog box opens the AutoCorrect Exceptions dialog box. The First Letter tab of the AutoCorrect Exceptions dialog box enables you to enter abbreviations after which you do not want automatic capitalization. Likewise, the INitial CAps tab enables you to enter words or abbreviations for which you do not want automatic capitalization fixes. (Remember to respect the rights of others and never add or delete Exceptions on a shared computer without an instructor's or supervisor's permission.) The AutoCorrect dialog box also enables you to turn on or off capitalizing the first letter of text in table cells, capitalizing names of days, correcting the incorrect use of [Caps Lock], and so on.

Place your mouse pointer over the word Presentation just after AutoCorrect has created it, and the pointer will convert to an I-beam. A small blue rectangle also will appear under the capital P. Place your mouse pointer on the rectangle to display the AutoCorrect Options button, one of PowerPoint 2002's new Smart Tags, then click the drop-down arrow on the smart tag to open a shortcut menu (see Figure 3-21). This menu enables you to undo the most recent spelling correction, undo the most recent capitalization correction, remove the AutoCorrect listing for the current autocorrection, and access the AutoCorrect dialog box. If you find the smart tag bothersome, you can turn it off by removing the check mark in the Show AutoCorrect Options buttons check box. This check box is on the AutoCorrect tab of the AutoCorrect dialog box.

Figure 3-19 AutoCorrect dialog box

Turns AutoCorrect Options button on or off

Accesses options to autoformat quote marks, fractions, hyphens, bullets, numbers, etc.

Turns other AutoCorrect options on or off

Type word, phrase, or abbreviation to be replaced by autocorrection

Opens dialog box to add, edit, or delete Exceptions to autocorrections

List of words, phrases, or abbreviations to be replaced and the words or graphics to replace them

Type word, phrase, or graphic to replace entry in Replace text box

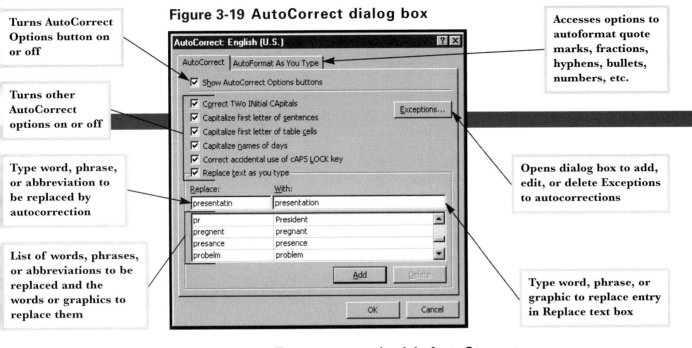

Figure 3-20 Text corrected with AutoCorrect

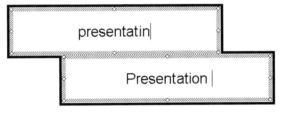

Figure 3-21 AutoCorrect Options button

Click button or arrow to display shortcut menu

Click here to open AutoCorrect dialog box

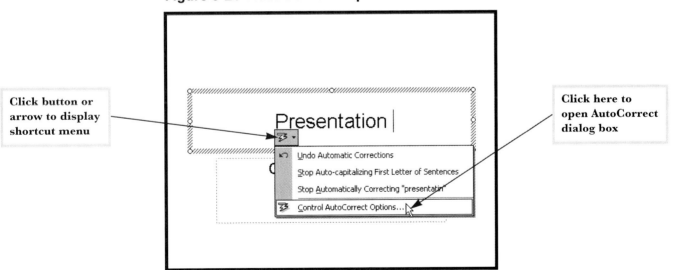

Practice

On the AutoCorrect tab of the AutoCorrect dialog box, add an entry that will replace Powerpoint with PowerPoint.

skill
Drawing and Formatting Objects

concept

Including drawn objects in your presentation helps to enliven it, to break up the routine of text-only slides, and to stir the interest of more visually oriented audience members. PowerPoint's Drawing toolbar has tools for creating lines, shapes, pictures, and other graphics. You have complete control over where to place these items and how much space they will occupy on a slide. In PowerPoint 2002 you now also can create cycle, radial, pyramid, Venn, and target diagrams, and design organizational charts more easily than before.

do it !

Create an arrow with a color gradient to enhance a presentation's Title Slide.

1. Open the GSU Presentation 3.ppt file in Normal View, with Slide 1 in the Slide pane.

2. On the Drawing toolbar, click the AutoShapes button `AutoShapes ▾`. The AutoShapes menu will appear.

3. Highlight Block Arrows, then click the Up Arrow button ⬆ on the submenu that appears (see Figure 3-22). The mouse pointer will change to a crosshairs pointer (＋) when you move it over the Slide pane.

4. With the crosshairs displayed, click near the upper-left corner of the slide, about a 1/2 inch down from the top and 1 and 1/2 inches in from the left edge. Drag down and about an inch to the right, creating an arrow that runs all the way to the bottom of the slide. When you let go of the mouse, the arrow will appear filled. The object also will appear with eight small circular sizing handles, one small green rotate handle, and one small yellow diamond-shaped adjustment handle (see Figure 3-23).

5. On the Drawing toolbar, click the Fill Color drop-down arrow ⬛▾. The Fill Color palette will appear with several color boxes and commands enabling you to access More Fill Colors or Fill Effects (see Figure 3-24).

6. Click Fill Effects. The Fill Effects dialog box will appear. If necessary, click the Gradient tab to bring it to the front of the dialog box.

7. In the Colors section of the dialog box, click the Two colors option button. A drop-down list box labeled Color 2 will appear below the Color 1 list box. These boxes are used for selecting the two colors that will make up the Fill Color gradient.

8. Click the Color 1 drop-down list arrow, then select the second box from the left on the color palette, with the ScreenTip that reads Follow Text and Lines Scheme Color. Click the Color 2 drop-down list arrow, then select the sixth box from the left, labeled Follow Accent Scheme Color. ⬭ Notice that, as you select colors in their drop-down boxes, the Sample square at the lower-right of the dialog box changes to match your selections.

(continued on PP 3.20)

Figure 3-22 Choosing an AutoShape

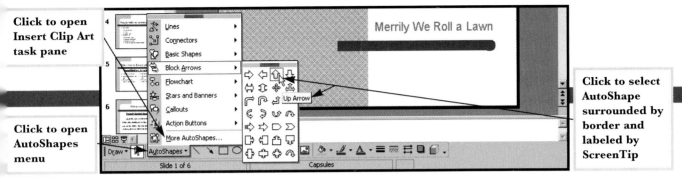

Click to open Insert Clip Art task pane

Click to open AutoShapes menu

Click to select AutoShape surrounded by border and labeled by ScreenTip

Figure 3-23 Drawing an AutoShape

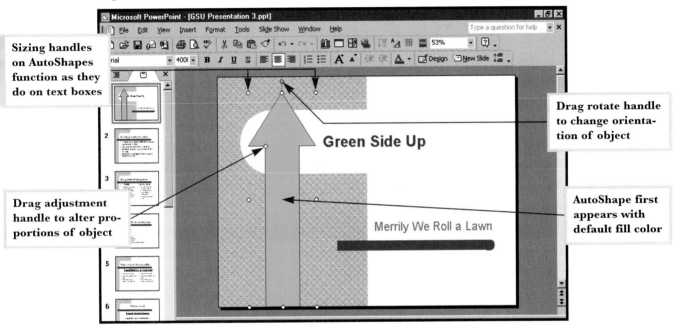

Sizing handles on AutoShapes function as they do on text boxes

Drag adjustment handle to alter proportions of object

Drag rotate handle to change orientation of object

AutoShape first appears with default fill color

Figure 3-24 Selecting the Fill Effects option

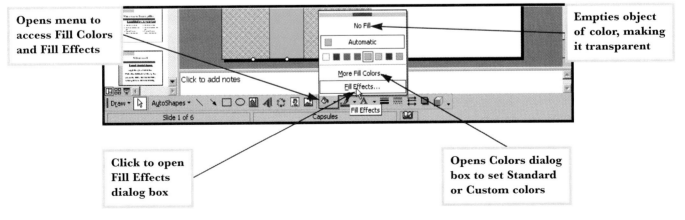

Opens menu to access Fill Colors and Fill Effects

Empties object of color, making it transparent

Click to open Fill Effects dialog box

Opens Colors dialog box to set Standard or Custom colors

skill | Drawing and Formatting Objects (continued)

do it !

9. In the Variants section of the Fill Effects dialog box, click the lower-left box, so the gradient seems to run from dark to light to dark (see Figure 3-25).

10. Click the Preview button [Preview] to see how the gradient will look when applied to the AutoShape. You can see the results on the selected slide on the Slides tab, or drag the Fill Effects box out of the way and look at the affected slide in the Slide pane.

11. Click [OK] to add the two-color gradient to AutoShape and to close the dialog box.

12. Click anywhere outside the slide to cancel selection of the AutoShape arrow. Verify that your slide now resembles Figure 3-26.

13. Save the changes you have made to your presentation, but leave the file open.

more

The Texture tab in the Fill Effects dialog box provides a palette of textures, such as marble or wood, that you can apply to objects you create. The Pattern tab resembles the Texture tab, but instead provides 48 patterns, such as dotted or wavy, from which to choose. The Picture tab enables you to fill an object with a picture or other graphic that you have in a file.

You can rotate objects you have created by dragging the small green rotate handle (⊙) that extends out from the top of an object when that object first appears on your slide. When you place the mouse pointer over the rotate handle, the pointer changes to a small circular-shaped arrow (↻). When you click the rotate handle in order to rotate the object, the circular-shaped arrow changes to four arrows forming a circle (⟳). Ordinarily, an object will rotate about its center. If you hold down [Ctrl], however, the object will rotate around the point that is opposite to where you are dragging the object. You can rotate objects freely to any degree you wish, or you can restrict the rotation to 15-degree increments by holding down [Shift] while you drag. You can rotate a selected object in 90-degree increments or flip it horizontally or vertically by using the commands on the Rotate or Flip submenu of the Draw menu, located at the left end of the Drawing toolbar.

The AutoShape arrow you created, and many other shapes in PowerPoint, have a small yellow adjustment handle (◇). You can use this adjustment handle to change, for example, the size of the arrowhead relative to its shaft. You also can use the handle to widen or narrow the shaft in relation to the base of the arrowhead. When you place your mouse pointer over the adjustment handle, the pointer will change to a small triangle indented at its base (▷). As you drag the adjustment handle, the triangle will maintain its shape.

Figure 3-25 Fill Effects dialog box

Accesses preset gradients such as Desert, Ocean, Fog, etc.

Adjusts transparency level of gradient

Shading styles determine orientation of gradient

Applies selected gradient temporarily to slide without closing dialog box

Click a square to set pattern of variation

Turns on or off the ability to rotate gradient as object rotates

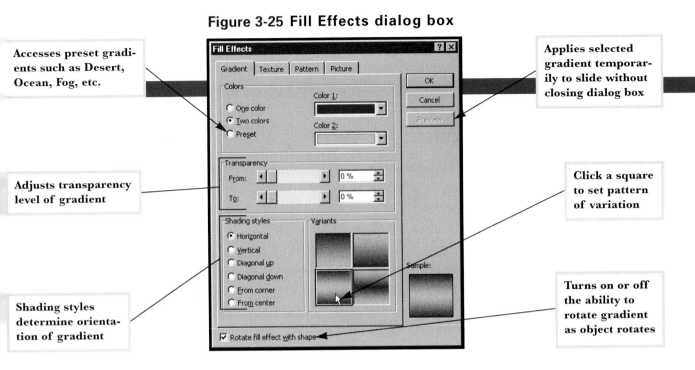

Figure 3-26 Title Slide with finished object

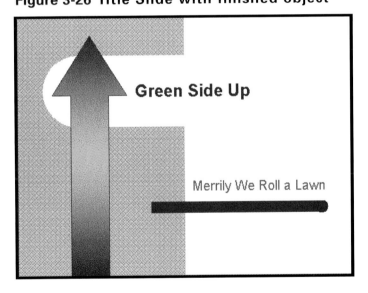

Green Side Up

Merrily We Roll a Lawn

Practice

To practice creating an AutoShape with a Fill Effect, open file pppprac3-7.ppt. Follow the instructions on the slide. Save and close the modified file as myppprac3-7.ppt.

skill Modifying and Enhancing Drawn Objects

concept

Occasionally, when you add a drawn object to a presentation, it does not appear exactly as you had imagined it would. Fortunately, you can modify objects such as AutoShapes so they look better within the scheme of a slide. This modification can include enhancing the object itself and changing how the object interacts with the other elements on the slide.

do it !

Add a shadow to the AutoShape created in the previous Skill.

1. Be sure that the GSU Presentation 3.ppt file appears in Normal View, with Slide 1 in the Slide pane.

2. Click the block arrow on Slide 1 to select it.

3. On the Drawing toolbar, click the Shadow Style button. A palette of shadow types will appear.

4. Click Shadow Style 4, the fourth shadow in the first row. A shadow will be cast from the base of the block arrow through the middle of the slide (see Figure 3-27).

5. On the Drawing toolbar, click the Draw button Draw ▾. The Draw menu will appear.

6. On the Draw menu, point to the Order command to open its submenu. The Order submenu contains four commands that enable you to layer the objects on your slides according to your needs. Since the Block Arrow was the last object that you added, it is on the top layer of the order, and its shadow is obscuring part of the subtitle, Merrily We Roll a Lawn.

7. On the Order submenu, click Send to Back. The Arrow and its shadow are sent to the back of the order, revealing the text of the subtitle that was obscured (see Figure 3-28). Notice that the shadow still passes in front of the decorative band just below the subtitle. The order of elements that are part of the Design Template cannot be changed, so they always will be behind any elements you add.

8. Click off of the slide to cancel selection of the arrow, save the changes you have made, but leave the file open.

more

Even though a shadow is a part of the object to which it is applied, you can modify some aspects of a shadow independently. With the object selected, click the Shadow Style button, then click the Shadow Settings command. The Shadow Settings toolbar, Figure 3-29, will appear. The buttons on this toolbar enable you to turn a shadow on or off, nudge it up or down, left or right, and change its color and opacity.

On the Order submenu the Send Backward command enables you to send an object down one place in the layering order rather than all the way to the bottom layer. The Send to Front and Send Forward commands mirror the Send to Back and Send Backward commands by moving objects upward in the layering order.

To add 3-D effects instead of shadow effects to an object, click the 3-D Style button on the Drawing toolbar. A palette will open, from which you can select any of twenty 3-D Styles. Clicking the 3-D Settings command at the bottom of the palette will open the 3-D Settings toolbar. This toolbar enables you to turn a 3-D Style on or off, tilt it up or down, and tilt left or right. You also can modify its depth, direction, lighting, surface, and color.

Figure 3-27 Block arrow with shadow on top layer

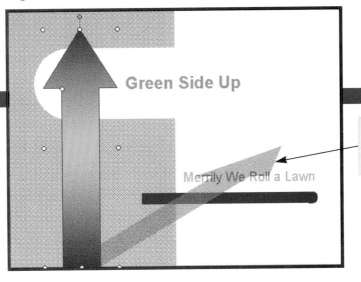

As newly added object, shadow appears at top layer of order

Figure 3-28 Shadow sent to back

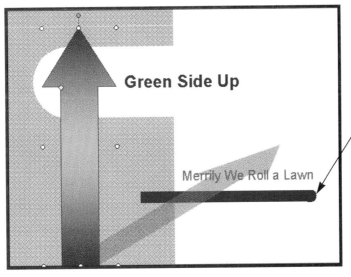

Shadow, sent to back, is behind text, but elements of Design Template remain at bottom level

Figure 3-29 Shadow Settings toolbar

Surrounding box indicates Shadow On/Off is selected button

Click to display Shadow Color palette

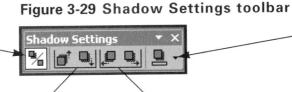

Nudge Shadow Up and Nudge Shadow Down buttons

Nudge Shadow Left and Nudge Shadow Right buttons

Practice

To practice modifying and enhancing drawn objects, open file ppprac3-8.ppt. Follow the instructions on the slide. Save and close the modified file as myppprac3-8.ppt.

skill | Printing Audience Handouts

concept

One of the most important aspects of giving a presentation is keeping the attention of your audience. Audiences often follow and retain a presentation more closely when they have material to follow during the presentation. For this purpose you may want to use PowerPoint to generate audience handouts. Your audience members can use the handouts to take notes, and then have their notes and your slides available to review on their own.

do it !

Print audience handouts of a presentation.

1. Be sure that the GSU Presentation 3.ppt file appears in Normal View, with Slide 1 in the Slide pane. Also be sure that your computer is properly connected to a printer, that the printer is turned on, and that the printer contains toner and paper.

2. Click File, then click Print to open the Print dialog box.

3. At the right end of the Print what box, click the drop-down arrow. A drop-down list of printing options will appear.

4. On the drop-down list, click Handouts to select it. The Handouts section of the dialog box will become active.

5. In the Handouts section of the dialog box, click the Slides per page drop-down list arrow and select 3 from the drop-down list (see Figure 3-30). Notice that the Horizontal and Vertical option buttons become dimmed since the slide order cannot change for one, two, or three slides per page. Notice also that the small preview of how your handouts will print out changes as you select different numbers on the Slides per page drop-down list.

6. Click the Preview button [Preview]. The Print Preview window will open, giving you a larger, more detailed image of how your handouts will appear on paper (see Figure 3-31). On the Print Preview toolbar, click the Print button [Print...] to return to the Print dialog box.

7. Click [OK]. PowerPoint will print two pages, each containing pictures of three slides per page and lines for notes next to each slide.

8. Leave the presentation open on your screen.

more

Besides printing slides on paper, you also can print slides on transparencies for use with an overhead projector, as long as you have a printer that can accept the plastic sheets. Load the transparencies into the proper printer tray, and print your presentation as you would on paper. You can print transparencies in color or in black and white, using the Portrait (vertical) or Landscape (horizontal) page orientation.

The new Print Preview window in PowerPoint 2002 offers several options for previewing and modifying printouts while leaving the presentation's contents as is. The two left buttons on the Print Preview toolbar move between the Previous Page and Next Page of an upcoming printout. The Print button opens the Print dialog box. The Print What box enables you to choose among printing Slides, various versions of the Handouts, the Notes Pages, or the Outline View. The Zoom box displays the printout at different magnification levels. The next two buttons switch the printout between Landscape (horizontal) and Portrait (vertical) orientation. The Options button access options to open the Header and Footer dialog box, change an output from Color to Grayscale or Black and White, scale a printout to fit the current paper in the printer, and so on. The Close button returns you to the previous View you were using, and the Help button opens the Office Assistant.

Figure 3-30 Printing audience handouts

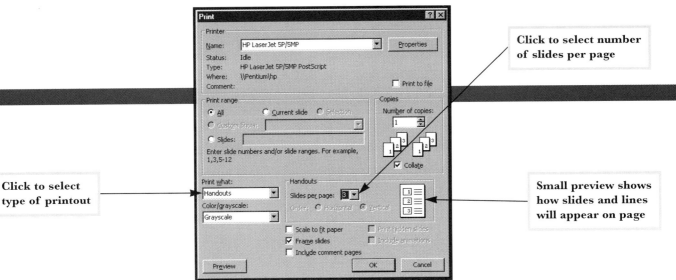

Click to select number of slides per page

Click to select type of printout

Small preview shows how slides and lines will appear on page

Figure 3-31 Print Preview window

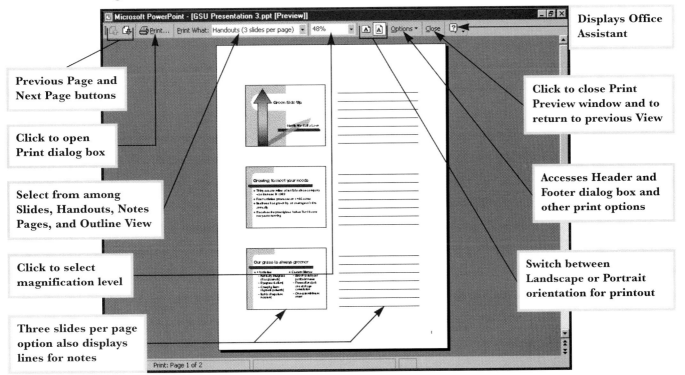

Displays Office Assistant

Previous Page and Next Page buttons

Click to open Print dialog box

Select from among Slides, Handouts, Notes Pages, and Outline View

Click to select magnification level

Three slides per page option also displays lines for notes

Click to close Print Preview window and to return to previous View

Accesses Header and Footer dialog box and other print options

Switch between Landscape or Portrait orientation for printout

Practice

To practice printing audience handouts, open file ppprac3-9.ppt. In the Print dialog box, select Handouts in the Print what box, and select 3 in the Slides per page box. Click the Preview button to preview the presentation, click the Print button to return to the Print dialog box, then print the presentation. Close the file without saving any changes.

skill | Saving Slide Presentations as RTF Files

concept

When saving a PowerPoint presentation, you normally save all of text and graphics you have created. Such presentations often consume lots of storage space on a floppy or hard disk drive. However, you may need to save only a presentation's text, not its graphics too, or may want to shrink the overall file to allow more storage space for other files. For such situations consider saving your PowerPoint files in a Rich Text Format, or RTF, file. Since you already have saved GSU Presentation 3 in a graphical version, you now can save it in RTF format.

do it !

Save your presentation as an RTF file, then close it.

1. Be sure that the GSU Presentation 3.ppt file appears in Normal View, with Slide 1 in the Slide pane.

2. Click File, then click Save As to open the Save As dialog box.

3. If necessary, click the drop-down arrow at the right end of the Save in text box, then find and click on your PowerPoint Files folder so the new file will save in that folder.

4. In the Save as type box, click the drop-down arrow, then scroll to the bottom of the drop-down list and click on Outline/RTF (*.rtf) to select the RTF format for saving the file. When you select the RTF format, the contents window will appear blank, confirming that you have not yet saved any RTF files. In the File name box, the GSU Presentation 3 file now will have an .rtf rather than .ppt file extension (see Figure 3-32).

5. Click the Save button [Save]. The GSU Presentation 3.rtf file will be saved, and the dialog box will close, returning you to the Normal view of the presentation.

6. Close the presentation. Close PowerPoint.

more

In the future, when you open the RTF file, you will see only text and not graphics in the presentation. To open the RTF file, not the PPT file, do as follows. (1) Click File, then click Open to display the Open dialog box. (2) Click the Look in drop-down box and find the PowerPoint Files folder (or whichever disk drive and folder in which you have saved the file). (3) Click the Files of type drop-down box and select the All Files (*.*) option. This option will display not only typical PowerPoint presentations in the PPT format, but also any other file in the selected drive and folder. (4) Look in the large contents window in the middle of the dialog box, click the desired RTF file, then click the Open button. (Alternately, you can double-click on the desired RTF file, and it will open without having to use the Open button).

So far you have learned that you can save PowerPoint presentations as PPT or RTF files. Table 3-1 on the next page lists and describes other file formats in which you can save a PowerPoint presentation.

Figure 3-32 Saving a presentation as an RTF file

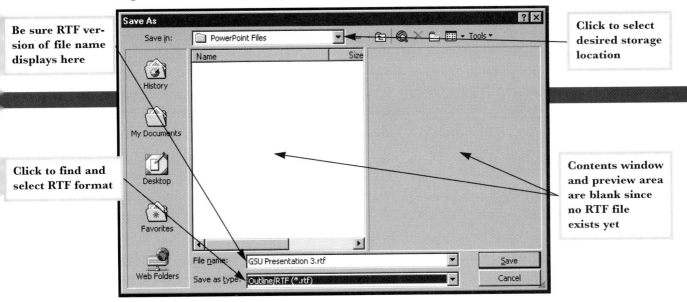

Be sure RTF version of file name displays here

Click to find and select RTF format

Click to select desired storage location

Contents window and preview area are blank since no RTF file exists yet

Table 3-1 Additional File Formats for Saving Presentations

Save as type	File Extension	Use for Saving
Design Template	.pot	A presentation as a PowerPoint template
GIF (Graphics Interchange Format)	.gif	A slide as a graphic for using on Web pages
JPEG (File Interchange Format)	.jpg	A slide as a graphic for using on Web pages
PNG (Portable Network Graphics Format)	.png	A slide as a graphic for using on Web pages
PowerPoint Show	.pps	A presentation that always will open as a Slide Show
Web Archive	.mht, .mhtml	A Web page as a file including all support files
Web Page	.htm, .html	A Web page as a folder with an .htm file & all support files
Windows Metafile	.wmf	A slide as a graphic

Practice

Open the file myppprac3-10.ppt. Save the file in RTF format as myppprac3-10.rtf. If instructed to do so, print both files, then close them. Be prepared to explain, verbally or in writing, any differences that might exist between the two printouts.

shortcuts

Function	Button/Mouse	Menu	Keyboard
Text Box		Click Insert, click Text Box	
Font Size	18	Click Format, click Font, select size	
Font Color		Click Format, click Font, select color	
Bold text	B	Click Format, click Font, click Bold	[Ctrl]+[B]
Italicize text	I	Click Format, click Font, click Italic	[Ctrl]+[I]
Underline text	U	Click Format, click Font, check Underline	[Ctrl]+[U]
Apply text shadow	S	Click Format, click Font, check Shadow	
Align text to left		Click Format, click Alignment, click Align Left	[Ctrl]+[L]
Center text		Click Format, click Alignment, click Center	[Ctrl]+[E]
Align text to right		Click Format, click Alignment, click Align Right	[Ctrl]+[R]
Check spelling		Click Tools, click Spelling	[F7]
AutoShapes	AutoShapes	Click Insert, click Picture, click AutoShapes	[Alt]+[U]
Fill Color		Click Format, click AutoShape, select fill color	
Draw	Draw		
Apply object shadow			
3-D Style			

A. Identify Key Features

Name the items indicated by callouts in Figure 3-33.

Figure 3-33 Formatting and Drawing toolbars

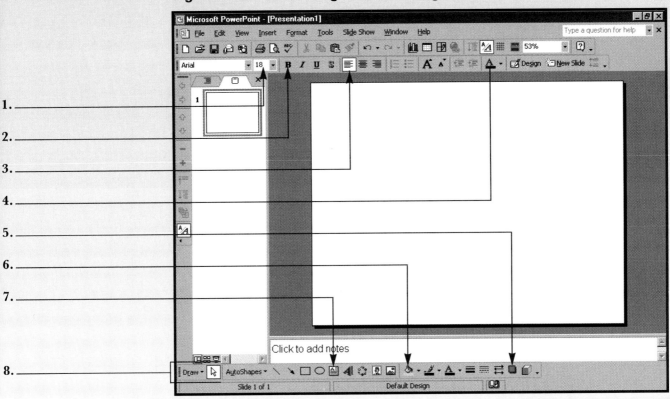

1.
2.
3.
4.
5.
6.
7.
8.

B. Select the Best Answer

9. Automatically fixes spelling errors as you type

10. Enables you to ignore or change a misspelled word

11. Leads to a list of abbreviations after which the next word will not capitalize

12. Offers a full range of text formatting options

13. Contains options for filling an object with a gradient

14. An example of an AutoShape

15. A file format that saves text but not graphics

16. Area where you can add typing and manipulate it separately from other slide text

17. Enables you to change each or all instances of a word or phrase at once

a. RTF file

b. Text box

c. AutoCorrect

d. Block Arrow

e. Exceptions button

f. Fill Effects dialog box

g. Spelling dialog box

h. Font dialog box

i. Find and Replace function

quiz (continued)

C. Complete the Statement

18. A text box that automatically wraps to the next line when the insertion point reaches its right edge is a:

a. Text label text box

b. Title text box

c. Flexible text box

d. Word processing text box

19. To move an object such as an AutoShape to the top level of a slide, choose the:

a. Send Forward command

b. Send Backward command

c. Send to Front command

d. Send to Back command

20. The Replace command appears:

a. In the Spelling dialog box

b. On the Edit menu

c. On the Standard toolbar

d. On the Editing toolbar

21. If you are adding a single word or short phrase to a slide, it is best to use a:

a. Text label text box

b. Word processing text box

c. Text shadow application

d. Bold, italicized, and/or underlined font

22. All of the following control the size of a font **except**:

a. The Font box

b. The Font dialog box

c. The Font Size box

d. The Increase/Decrease Font Size buttons

23. The small green circle on a selected object is the:

a. Master Sizing handle

b. Rotate handle

c. Adjustment handle

d. Object handle

24. The small yellow diamond on a selected object is the:

a. Master Sizing handle

b. Rotate handle

c. Adjustment handle

d. Object handle

25. Draw, Line, Insert Word Art, and Dash Style are buttons that appear on the:

a. Menu bar

b. Standard toolbar

c. Formatting toolbar

d. Drawing toolbar

26. The Font, Bold, Align Left, and Increase Font Size buttons appear on the:

a. Menu bar

b. Standard toolbar

c. Formatting toolbar

d. Drawing toolbar

27. The Next Page, Print, Options, and Close buttons appear in the:

a. Print dialog box

b. Print Preview window

c. Fill Effects dialog box

d. Draw menu

interactivity

Build Your Skills

1. Practice entering and moving text.

   a. Open a new file. The presentation should open in Normal view with a Title Slide as the default slide for Slide 1. Save the file as Family.ppt.

   b. Change the Title Slide layout of Slide 1 to a Blank slide layout. Apply the Profile.pot slide design to the presentation.

   c. Use the Text Box button to create a text label text box in the middle of Slide 1. In the text box, type My Family.

   d. Move the text box to the left side of the slide, above the upper horizontal red line.

   e. Click the Text Box button again and drag a large word processing box in the area between the upper and lower horizontal red lines. Type a brief history of your family in this text box. Resave the file.

2. Practice formatting text:

   a. Click the My Family text box to activate it. Drag the midpoint sizing handle on the right edge of the box toward the right edge of the slide so the text box is centered horizontally on the slide.

   b. Center the text in the My Family text box, bold it, and increase its size to 40 point. If necessary, click on the edge of the text box to display a mouse pointer with a four-headed arrow, then drag the text box so it is centered vertically between the top edge of the slide and the upper horizontal red line.

   c. Click the lower text box to activate it. Increase the paragraph spacing slightly and italicize the text. Resave the file.

3. Build and refine your presentation.

   a. Using the Blank slide layout, add a slide for each member of your family.

   b. Format each slide as you did the first one. On these slides replace the My Family text box with a text box containing each family member's name, and replace the family history text box with a text box of the corresponding family member's history.

   c. Format the text in each family member's name box with that family member's favorite color, if you know it, or with different colors of your own choosing.

   d. Use Find and Replace to replace all instances of My with The [insert family's last name]. When finished with all of the family members' slides, check the spelling of the presentation. Resave the file.

4. Add, format, and modify drawing objects:

   a. Select the AutoShape 5-Point Star. Draw the star near the upper-left corner of Slide 1. Adjust the size and location of the family name text box, if necessary, to make room for the star.

   b. Fill the star with a two-color gradient that uses the Vertical shading style and consists of the Fills Scheme Color and Accent Scheme Color.

   c. Apply Shadow Style 2 to the star. Draw the 32-Point Star AutoShape over the 5-Point Star, but slightly larger. Change the color of the 32-Point star to the Accent Scheme Color.

   d. Use the Order command to move the 32-Point Star behind the 5-Point Star. Resave the file.

   e. Review the look of your presentation in the Print Preview window, then print audience handouts with two slides per page.

interactivity (continued)

Problem Solving Exercises

1. After years of work at a 9 to 5 job, you finally have saved enough money to quit and realize your dream of opening a country inn. Use PowerPoint to create a six-slide presentation you can show to investors helping you start the inn. Begin the presentation with a Title Slide that names the inn, lists your name as owner, and gives a presentation date. Since the inn still is in planning, additional slides should consist of Title and Text slides that describe what the inn will look like, where it will be located, the general atmosphere you hope to provide, and other key information for investors and travelers. Add at least one AutoShape with Fill Effects to each Title and Text slide. Include a final slide, using Text Boxes, that summarizes your presentation. Make the presentation clear, organized, and interesting, then check the spelling of it. Save the presentation as Country.ppt and as Country.rtf. Print audience handouts (three slides per page) from the Country.ppt file, since the Country.rtf file will not print the added text boxes and graphics.

2. Peppercorn's, a national restaurant chain, has launched a campaign to place ads in five national magazines—*Sports Digest, Women's Quarterly, Men Today, Entertainment Extract,* and *News Now.* The company wants to use a different half-page ad in each magazine, with each ad geared toward a specific reader group. You must provide five ads in the form of a PowerPoint presentation for the director of advertising to preview. When finished with the five ad slides, create a Title Slide that states the presentation's title, your name as presenter, and the presentation's due date. Also create a final slide stating the campaign's key benefits to the company. The Title Slide and final slide must include Text Boxes, AutoShapes, and Fill Effects. Check the spelling of the presentation, and save it as Peppercorn.ppt and as Peppercorn.rtf. Print both files as audience handouts (two per page). If instructed to do so, hand in both presentations with a cover page summarizing the contrasts between the printouts of the two files.

3. Use PowerPoint to create the slide shown in Figure 3-34. Then make the appropriate changes to the slide to make it resemble Figure 3-35. Replace [Student Name] with your name, and [Date] with the presentation's due date. Save the files as Figure 3-34.ppt and Figure 3-35.ppt, respectively.

Figure 3-34

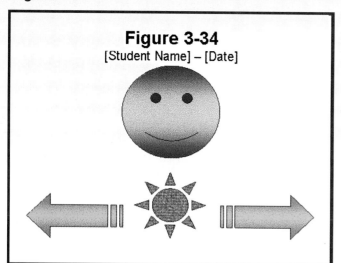

Figure 3-35

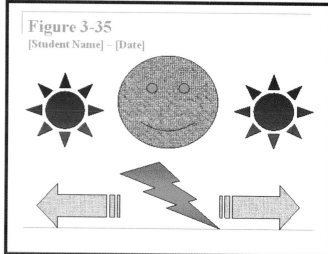

interactivity (continued)

Problem Solving Exercises (continued)

4. Use PowerPoint to create the slide shown in Figure 3-36. Then make the appropriate changes to the slide to make it resemble Figure 3-37. Replace [Student Name] with your name, and [Date] with the presentation's due date. Save the files as Figure 3-36.ppt and Figure 3-37.ppt, respectively.

Figure 3-36

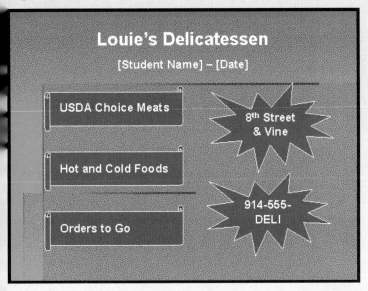

Figure 3-37

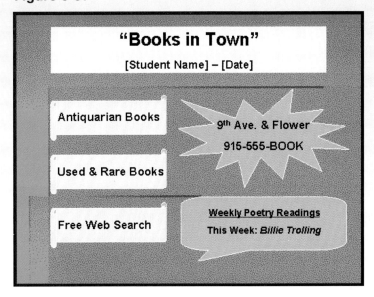

4

lesson four

Strengthening Your Presentation

skills

- ≷ **Adding Clip Art**
- ≷ **Editing Clip Art**
- ≷ **Inserting a Picture from File**
- ≷ **Inserting a Chart**
- ≷ **Customizing the Datasheet**
- ≷ **Changing a Chart's Type**
- ≷ **Setting Chart Options**
- ≷ **Formatting Chart Elements**
- ≷ **Adding Transition Effects**
- ≷ **Timing Slide Transitions**
- ≷ **Annotating Slides**
- ≷ **Navigating during a Slide Show**

A strong presentation often requires more than just text and simple shapes to make an attractive and visually interesting slide show. You can enhance your presentation with detailed pictures provided by PowerPoint called Clip Art. Once you insert a piece of Clip Art, you will find that you can edit and format it so it is compatible with the particular presentation in which it appears. You also can insert your own image files into a presentation.

Another important visual aspect of a presentation is the way in which you represent data. Raw statistics serve an important purpose in many presentations, but sometimes lack clarity and persuasiveness when presented in just a text format. PowerPoint enables you to create graphical charts to display any kind of data. Different chart types, such as line, bar, or pie, are available so you can choose the type that will best display your data. Once you have created a chart, you can control its placement on the slide, the colors and sizes of individual chart objects, its text style, and its overall size.

The end product of most PowerPoint presentations that include graphics is a slide show, wherein the slides are displayed with all of the graphics, text, and other features that were included during their creation. Though you can create a presentation solely for producing paper copies or overhead transparencies, PowerPoint's true strengths show through when the slides are animated and presented on a computer screen. Using the program's slide transition features, you can control exactly how each slide will make its appearance on the screen and how long it will remain there before the presentation advances to the next slide. You also can predetermine whether slides will advance on their own or with a prompt from the presenter.

Lesson Goal:

Add pictures to a presentation, both from Microsoft's Clip Gallery and from your own file. Transform raw data that you have accumulated into a chart, then customize the chart for your needs and preferences. Finally add transition effects to slides and set slide timings.

skill   Adding Clip Art

concept

You already have seen how you can enhance your presentation by drawing objects such as AutoShapes. To take the visual aspect of your presentation a step further, you may want to use Clip Art. Clip Art is a collection of ready-made pictures that PowerPoint provides for the user. Clip Art pictures are more numerous, varied, and generally more detailed than drawings created with AutoShapes.

do it !

Add Clip Art to the presentation.

1. Open the Student File ppdoit4-1.ppt. Save it in your PowerPoint Files folder as GSU Presentation 4.ppt in Normal view. Close the Drawing toolbar if it appears. Activate Slide 2, entitled Growing to meet your needs. Notice that the last two bullet points are in reverse order from those in GSU Presentation 3.ppt.

2. Click Insert, select Picture, then click Clip Art. The Insert Clip Art task pane will open, divided into three sections: Search For, Other Search Options, and See also (see Figure 4-1). ◖◗ If this is the first time in PowerPoint 2002 that a user has asked for Clip Art, the program will display a dialog box asking if you want to organize previously installed Clip Art images. Consult your instructor on organizing the images.

3. In the Search For section, click in the text box labeled Search text. Type the keyword business, then click the Search button ⬚Search⬚ just below the text box. PowerPoint will search the Clip Gallery for images associated with the keyword, and display its findings in a scrollable Results pane.

4. In the Results pane, scroll down until you reach the Clip Art of a stylized business growth chart on a gold background and a stylized tree on a red background. Place the mouse pointer over the image. A ScreenTip containing the picture's keyword, pixel size, file size, and file type will display (see Figure 4-2).

5. Click the Clip Art to insert it onto Slide 2. The slide converts to a Title, Text, and Content layout with the bulleted text on the left and Clip Art selected on the right side of the slide. The Automatic Layout Options button ⬚🖅⬚ appears to the lower-right of the Clip Art. The Picture toolbar appears. If necessary, drag the Picture toolbar down and dock it between the Notes pane and the Status bar. Close the Insert Clip Art task pane (see Figure 4-3).

6. Save the changes you have made to your presentation, but leave the file open with the Clip Art still selected and the Automatic Layout Options button still active.

more

Each section of the Insert Clip Art task pane serves a different function. As the above Skill shows, the Search For section lets you enter keywords associated with available Clip Art images, use the Search button to find and display them in the Results window, then scroll to and click on one to insert it into a slide. The Other Search Options section lets you select one or more collections of Clip Art to search in. The default collections are My Collections, Office Collections, and Web Collections. It also lets you search in one or all of the following categories of Clip Art: Clip Art, Photographs, Movies, and Sounds. The See Also section enables you to organize your clips, search for online clips, or find Help on searching for clips. If you know a presentation slide will include Clip Art, you can choose a slide layout for that purpose. For example, a Title, Text, and Content slide includes a placeholder for inserting Clip Art or other graphics in its layout. Double-click on the Clip Art image in the placeholder, and the Select Picture dialog box will open with all of your installed Clip Art displayed in a scrollable pane. You can scroll through the many Clip Art images to find what you want. Or you can limit your search as follows: (1) type a relevant keyword in the text box labeled Search text; (2) click the Search button. PowerPoint then will find the same Clip Art images you would have found if using the Insert Clip Art task pane.

Figure 4-1 Insert Clip Art task pane

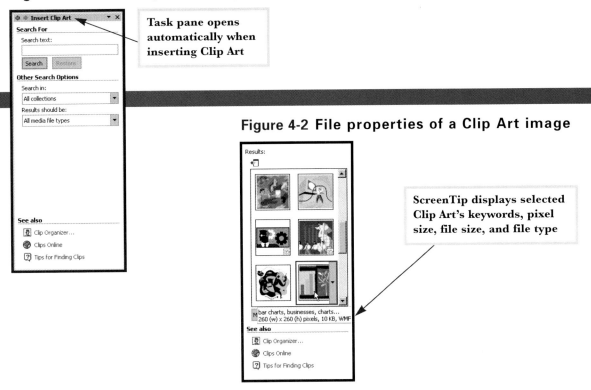

Task pane opens automatically when inserting Clip Art

Figure 4-2 File properties of a Clip Art image

ScreenTip displays selected Clip Art's keywords, pixel size, file size, and file type

Figure 4-3 Clip Art inserted onto slide

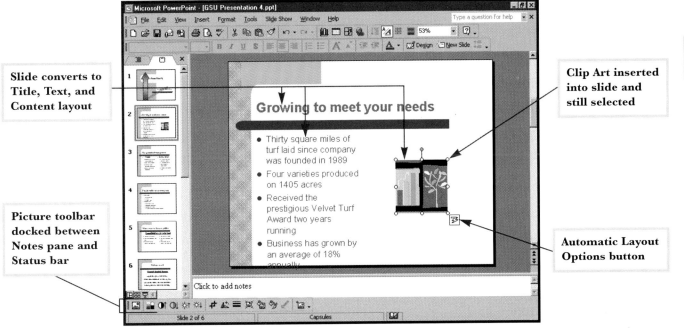

Slide converts to Title, Text, and Content layout

Clip Art inserted into slide and still selected

Picture toolbar docked between Notes pane and Status bar

Automatic Layout Options button

Practice

To practice adding Clip art, open the file ppprac4-1.ppt, and follow the instructions on the slide. Save and close the modified file as myppprac4-1.ppt.

skill   Editing Clip Art

concept

Clip Art files are quality, finished pictures. They have particular dimensions and colors that are part of the file. However, like other objects you insert into a PowerPoint slide, they can be repositioned, resized, and reformatted to fit the slide on which they appear. To alter most characteristics of a piece of Clip Art, you can use the Picture toolbar.

do it !

Resize the ribbon Clip Art previously inserted and move it to its proper place on the slide. Change the picture's color so it matches the color scheme of the presentation.

1. Be sure that GSU Presentation 4.ppt appears on the screen in Normal view, and that the Clip Art still is selected and the Automatic Layout Options button (part of Office XP's new Smart Tag feature) still appears. ⬭ When you inserted the Clip Art in the previous Skill, the slide layout changed. To accept this change, you would leave the Automatic Layout Options button alone and format the Clip Art in the new layout. However, the bulleted text reads faster in the longer lines of the original layout, so you will return the slide to that format.

2. Place your mouse pointer over the Automatic Layout Options button to display its drop-down arrow. Click the drop-down arrow to display the button's shortcut menu. Click the Undo Automatic Layout option to restore the slide to its original layout (see Figure 4-4).

3. On the Standard toolbar, click the Show/Hide Grid button ▦ to display a dotted grid over the slide. With the Clip Art still selected, click in the middle of it to display a mouse pointer with a four-headed arrow (⬌). Drag the image toward the lower-right corner of the slide. Stop and release the mouse pointer when the upper-left sizing handle sits over the intersection of the sixth horizontal grid row from the top of the slide and the seventh vertical grid row from the left of the slide. The bottom edge of the image will run off the bottom of the slide.

4. On the Picture toolbar, click the Format Picture button 🖼. The Format Picture dialog box will appear. Click the Size tab to bring it to the front of the dialog box. Notice that the dimensions of the Clip Art image are almost exactly equal in the Height and Width boxes of the Size and rotate section. Notice also that the Height and Width boxes of the Scale section read 100%. ⬭ The Size and rotate section of the tab lets you adjust the height and width of the picture using linear measurements such as inches. The Scale section of the tab lets you adjust the height and width as a percentage of the picture's original size, which appears at the bottom of the tab. If the Lock aspect ratio check box is checked, changing the height will alter the width proportionally, and vice versa. When it is unchecked, you can alter the width and height of an image separately from each other.

5. If necessary, click the Lock Aspect ratio check box to remove its check mark. In the Size and rotate section, triple-click the Height box, and type 1.4. Press [Tab] to select the measurement in the Width box of the Size and rotate section. Type 2.5 (see Figure 4-5).

6. Click ▭ OK ▭. Click the Show/Hide Grid button ▦ to turn off the grid, but leave the Clip Art selected. The Clip Art image now fits neatly on the slide (see Figure 4-6).

(continued on PP 4.6)

Figure 4-4 Automatic Layout Options button

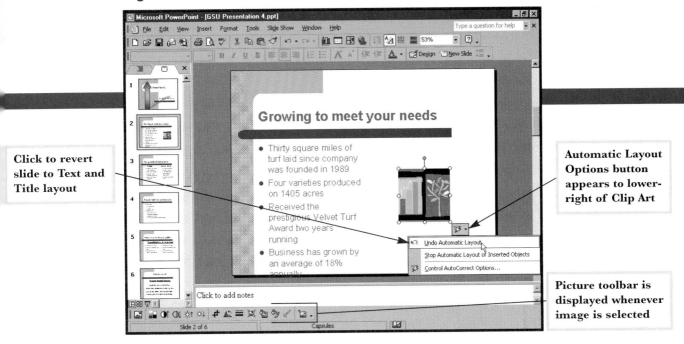

Click to revert slide to Text and Title layout

Automatic Layout Options button appears to lower-right of Clip Art

Picture toolbar is displayed whenever image is selected

Figure 4-5 Format Picture dialog box

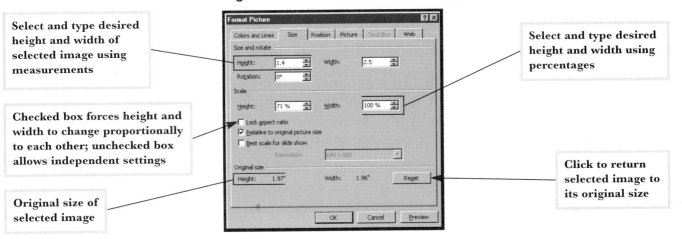

Select and type desired height and width of selected image using measurements

Select and type desired height and width using percentages

Checked box forces height and width to change proportionally to each other; unchecked box allows independent settings

Click to return selected image to its original size

Original size of selected image

Figure 4-6 Edited Clip Art on Slide 2

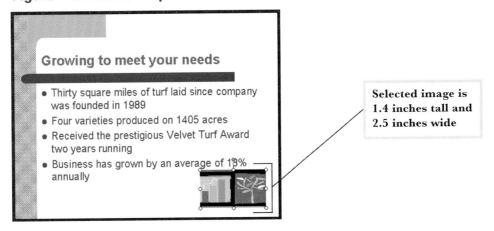

Selected image is 1.4 inches tall and 2.5 inches wide

skill　Editing Clip Art (continued)

do it !

7. On the Picture toolbar, click the Recolor Picture button 🖼. The Recolor Picture dialog box will appear. The dialog box's Original column displays every color in the picture. The New column contains related boxes that let you change a color everywhere it appears in the picture. The preview area in the middle of the dialog box lets you see how the selected picture would look if you were to close the dialog box with its current color selections.

8. In the Change section of the dialog box, click the Fills option button. This action excludes lines from the list of items you can change, leaving only the background and fill colors.

9. Under the New column, click the arrow on the topmost color box for the red background in the image. In the color palette that appears, place the mouse pointer over the sixth box from the left to display a border around the light green Fill color (see Figure 4-7).

10. Click the light green box. The background color of the image will change in the preview area but not on the slide. Click ⬚ OK ⬚ to apply the color change to the slide and to close the dialog box.

11. Click anywhere outside of the Clip Art to cancel the selection. The Picture toolbar will close. Verify that your slide resembles Figure 4-8. Save the changes you have made to the presentation, but leave the file open.

more

In the previous Skill you used the Format Picture dialog box's Size tab to resize a Clip Art picture. If you are not concerned about exact measurements, you can resize a piece of Clip Art by dragging its sizing handles, just as you can with other objects. To resize Clip Art and other objects quickly and easily, feel free to use the Show/Hide Grid button ▦ to display the grid just as you did when moving the Clip Art. Although you probably will want to use the Format Picture dialog box to make precise adjustments to an image, the Picture toolbar still is a powerful tool for adjusting a picture's features. Table 4-1 below list and describes the key buttons on the Picture toolbar.

Table 4-1 Additional Picture toolbar buttons

Button		Description
🖼	Insert Picture	Opens Insert Picture dialog box for retrieving available picture files
🔲	Color	Sets Automatic, Grayscale, Black & White, or Washout coloration
◑ ◐	More Contrast / Less Contrast	Increases or decreases degree of contrast between dark and light colors
☀ ☼	More Brightness / Less Brightness	Increases or decreases brightness of picture
🖽	Crop	Removes vertical and/or horizontal edges to trim picture size
🖾	Rotate Left	Rotates picture counterclockwise by 90-degree increments
≡	Line Style	Displays palette to select different line widths or styles
🖼	Compress Pictures	Reduces file size by reducing picture resolution or deleting cropped areas
✎	Set Transparent Color	Creates transparent areas in selected colors of picture if file type permits
🖼	Reset Picture	Undoes changes to picture's contrast, color, brightness, borders, or size

Figure 4-7 Recolor Picture dialog box

Shows original colors of selected picture; clear check boxes to restore original colors

Click box of desired color to replace original one

Allows you to change line, background, or fill colors

Allows you to change only background or fill colors

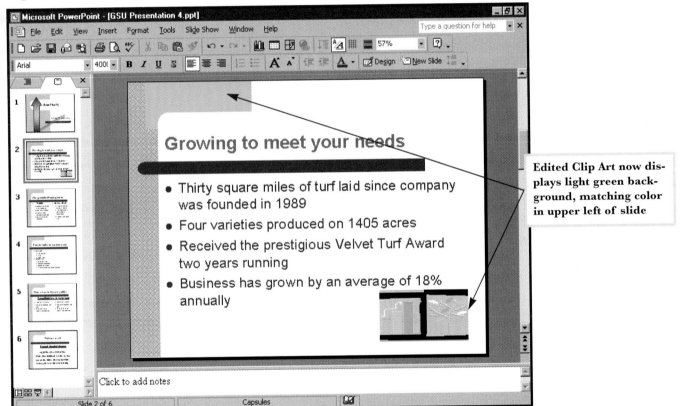

Figure 4-8 Slide 2 after recoloring Clip Art image

Edited Clip Art now displays light green background, matching color in upper left of slide

Practice

To practice editing Clip Art, open the file ppprac4-2.ppt, then follow the instructions on the slide. Save and close the modified file as myppprac4-2.ppt.

skill

Inserting a Picture from a File

concept

When adding graphics to a presentation, you do not have to limit yourself to the clips found in the Insert Clip Art dialog box. If you are handy with image or drawing software such as Microsoft Paint, or if you have other art files on disk, you can insert your own pictures into a presentation.

do it !

Insert a picture created with the Windows Paint program in one of the slides, then crop the picture.

1. Be sure that GSU Presentation 4.ppt appears on your screen in Normal view. Activate Slide 6 of the presentation.

2. Click Insert, click Picture, and click From File. The Insert Picture dialog box will appear. Use the Look in box to select the drive, folder, or other location that contains your Student Files. Double-click the location in the large contents window of the dialog box to open the location.

3. In the contents window, click once on the file named ppcheckbox.bmp to select it. A preview of the picture will appear in the right half of the dialog box (see Figure 4-9).

4. Click the Insert button [Insert ▾]. The dialog box will close and the ppcheckbox.bmp picture will appear in the middle of the slide. The Picture toolbar should display automatically. If the Picture toolbar does not appear, right-click any blank gray area of the toolbars to display the shortcut menu listing PowerPoint's toolbars. Left-click Picture to redisplay the Picture toolbar.

5. On the Picture toolbar, click the Crop button to activate the Crop tool. When the mouse pointer hovers over blank areas of the slide, the pointer will be accompanied by an icon resembling the Crop button.

6. Place the mouse pointer over the cropping handle ( ) at the upper-right corner of the picture. The pointer resembling the Crop tool will change to an icon resembling a smaller version ( ) of the cropping handle. Drag to the left until the right border of the picture completely cuts off the text Check! (be careful not to cut off the top of the check mark). Release the mouse button. The text portion of the picture will disappear.

7. Use the arrow keys on your keyboard to move the cropped picture so it is located just to the right of the words Recently Acquired Accounts. Cancel selection of the Crop tool and the picture, then save your changes. Verify that your slide now resembles the one in Figure 4-10. Leave the presentation open.

more

PowerPoint enables you to insert various image file formats into a presentation. Pictures made with the Paint program are bitmap files, using the file extension .bmp. Clip Art files that come with PowerPoint are Windows metafiles, using the extension .wmf. You generally can edit other image files just as you can Clip Art, but there are some exceptions. For example, you cannot use the Recolor Picture feature on a bitmap file. Lastly, if you click the arrow on the right edge of the Insert button in the Insert Picture dialog box, you can choose to link the picture you are inserting to its source file. Then, changes made to the source file will appear in the linked picture in the presentation.

Figure 4-9 Insert Picture dialog box

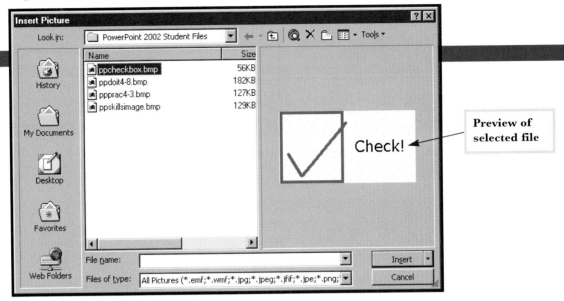

Figure 4-10 Cropped picture inserted from file

Practice

Create a one-slide presentation and insert the picture file ppprac4-3.bmp from your Student Files folder. If you cannot find the file in the contents window, be sure the Files of type text box at the bottom of the Open dialog box reads All Files (*.*). Remember to save and close the modified presentation as mypprac4-3.ppt.

skill Inserting a Chart

concept

As you become more skilled at designing presentations, you will discover that certain types of information are presented best through certain media. So far, the content of your presentation has used mostly text to express key points. Some data, such as numbers and statistics, often are more informative for a viewer when they appear graphically in charts. PowerPoint enables you to embed a chart in a slide, while still permitting you to alter its data and appearance.

do it !

Present some gathered data on a new slide that favorably compares Green Side Up with several competitors.

1. Be sure that GSU Presentation 4.ppt appears on your screen in Normal view.

2. With Slide 6 activated, click the New Slide button ⌐New Slide⌐, which will add a Title and Text slide as Slide 7 and display the Slide Layout task pane. In the Other Layouts section of the task pane, click the Title and Chart layout at the bottom of the task pane. The new slide will convert to a Title and Chart slide. In the Title placeholder, type How our sod stacks up (see Figure 4-11). Close the Slide Layout task pane.

3. Double-click the chart placeholder to start Microsoft Graph, a separate application used to create charts in Office XP files. A datasheet filled in with default data will appear over the slide, and a chart that corresponds to the default data will be embedded in the slide (see Figure 4-12). ⬛ MS Graph inserts the default data so the chart has structure until you enter data. The datasheet consists of numbered rows and lettered columns. The point where a column intersects a row is a cell. Cells are named by combining their column letter and row number. Thus, the cell that results from the intersection of the third column and fourth row is cell C4. Text entries in the cells in the left column and top row of the datasheet are data labels describing the data that follow them to the right or below. Data that occupy a column or row are a data series. Data series are represented in charts by a data series marker, or graphic object such as a bar, line, column, or pie piece.

4. When you place the mouse pointer over the datasheet, it changes to a ✚, or a pointer that you will recognize if you have used Microsoft Excel. The active cell in a data sheet has a thick border around it, known as the cell pointer. You can change the active cell by clicking on a new cell, or by moving the cell pointer with the arrow keys on the keyboard.

5. Click cell A2 to make it active (see Figure 4-13). Click outside the chart on Slide 7 to exit Microsoft Graph.

6. Save the presentation with the changes you have made, but leave the file open.

more

Inserting a chart does not require that you add a Title and Chart slide to a presentation. You can add a chart to any slide by choosing the Chart command from the Insert menu, or by clicking the Insert Chart button ⬛ on the Standard toolbar. Both operations start MS Graph as you did above by double-clicking the chart placeholder. You will notice that, whenever MS Graph is running, the Standard toolbar transforms to include buttons related to working with charts. The standard PowerPoint menu commands also will be replaced by chart-related commands when MS Graph is running.

Figure 4-11 New Title and Chart slide

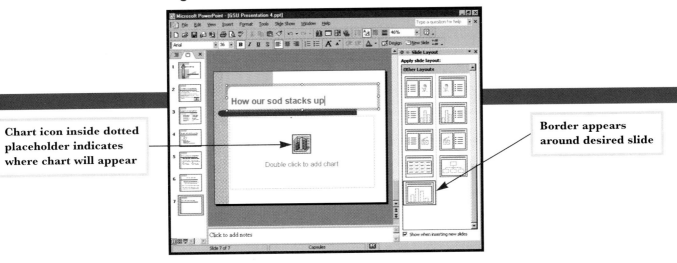

Chart icon inside dotted placeholder indicates where chart will appear

Border appears around desired slide

Figure 4-12 Inserted chart and datasheet

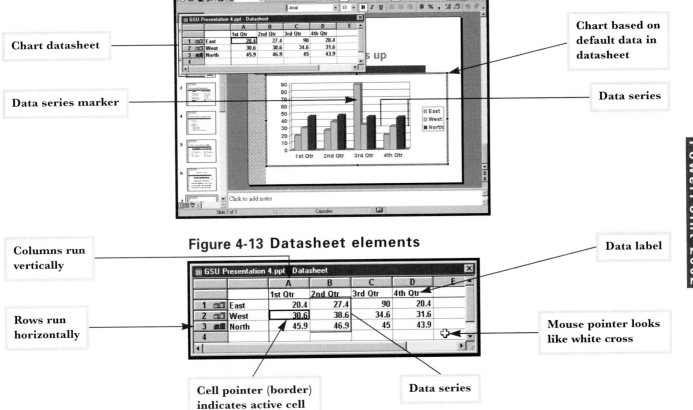

Chart datasheet

Data series marker

Chart based on default data in datasheet

Data series

Figure 4-13 Datasheet elements

Columns run vertically

Rows run horizontally

Data label

Mouse pointer looks like white cross

Cell pointer (border) indicates active cell

Data series

Practice

To practice inserting a chart, open file ppprac4-4.ppt, then follow the instructions on the slide. Save and close the modified file as mypprac4-4.ppt.

skill Customizing the Datasheet

concept

Once you have inserted a chart in a PowerPoint slide, you need to edit the datasheet so the resulting chart reflects your own data and not the default data provided by the program. Otherwise, your chart will have no significance or relevance in the presentation. The datasheet window is always available to you, so you can edit a chart as often as necessary.

do it !

Enter the comparison data in the chart's datasheet.

1. Be sure that GSU Presentation 4.ppt appears on your screen in Normal view.

2. Double-click the chart on Slide 7 to open MS Graph and the datasheet. If the datasheet does not appear when you double-click the chart, click the View Datasheet button on the Standard toolbar.

3. Click the blank cell above the East data label and to the left of the 1st Qtr label. Type Sod Farms, then press [Enter] to confirm the data label and to select the cell below it that contains the East data label.

4. Type Green Side Up to replace the East data label, then press [Enter] again. Type Lawns by Louis to replace the West data label, press [Enter], type Marquis de Sod to replace the North data label, press [Enter], then type Turfin' USA in the blank cell, and press [Tab].

5. Click the cell containing the 1st Qtr label to select it, replace the label with Acres Growing, and press [Tab]. Replace the 2nd Qtr label with Acres Installed Last Year, and press [Tab] again.

6. Right-click the gray header for column C [C], and click the Delete command on the shortcut menu that appears. Repeat the process to delete the data that moved into column C when you deleted it the first time.

7. Enter the following numbers to complete the datasheet:

Cell A1: 1405	Cell B1: 694
Cell A2: 923	Cell B2: 420
Cell A3: 896	Cell B3: 346
Cell A4: 890	Cell B4: 402

   Your completed datasheet now should resemble Figure 4-14.

8. Click a blank area of the presentation window to close the datasheet and MS Graph. Click outside of the chart to cancel the selection of it. The chart on Slide 7 will be updated with your data (see Figure 4-15).

9. Save your presentation with the changes you have made, but leave the file open.

more

When you work in MS Graph, you can point to any data series marker on an activated chart with the mouse pointer to receive a ScreenTip that summarizes the marker. For example, if you point to the first column, the ScreenTip will say Series "Green Side Up" Point "Acres Growing" Value: 1405. These ScreenTips will appear only when you select the chart, not when you select the datasheet.

Figure 4-14 Completed datasheet

This data label displays fully because the cell to its right is empty, but labels cut off by their neighbors will appear completely on charts

		A	B	C	D	E
	Sod Farms	Acres Grow	Acres Installed Last Year			
1	Green Sid	1405	694			
2	Lawns by	923	420			
3	Marquis d	896	346			
4	Turfin' US	890	402			

GSU Presentation 4.ppt - Datasheet

Figure 4-15 Updated chart

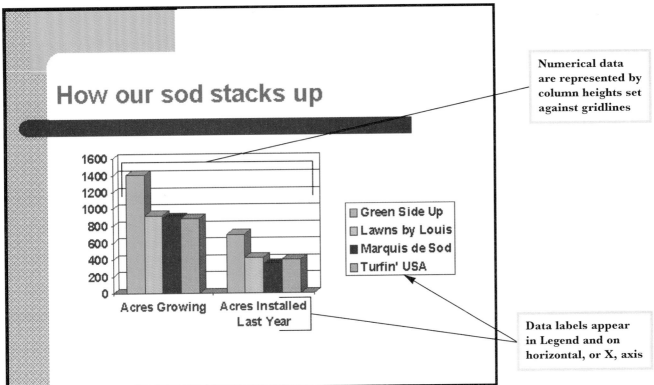

Numerical data are represented by column heights set against gridlines

Data labels appear in Legend and on horizontal, or X, axis

Practice

To practice customizing a datasheet, open the file ppprac4-5.ppt, then follow the instructions on the slide. Save and close the modified file as myppprac4-5.ppt.

skill | Changing a Chart's Type

concept

When you inserted a chart earlier in this lesson, PowerPoint's default choice for the type of chart was a Clustered Column chart with a 3-D visual effect. However, even after you have finished a chart, you still can change its type. You may want to do this because you think another chart type will better represent your data, or simply because it interacts better with other slide elements.

do it !

Change the chart from a Clustered Column to a Clustered Bar chart.

1. Be sure that GSU Presentation 4.ppt appears on your screen in Normal view. Double-click the chart on Slide 7. Click the Close button [X] on the datasheet's blue Title bar to close the datasheet, if it appears.

2. On the Menu bar, click Chart, then click Chart Type. The Chart Type dialog box will open to its Standard Types tab. The Chart type scrolling list box displays the basic chart types you can use in PowerPoint. The Chart sub-type section to the right of this list box displays the sub-types available for the chart type selected in the list box. The sub-type selected in black is the current type of chart on the slide. ◯ When you open the dialog box, the Office Assistant may appear. Close the Assistant by right-clicking on it (not on its yellow Help balloon) and clicking Hide on the shortcut menu.

3. In the list of chart types in the dialog box, click Bar to select it and to display its sub-types. The first sub-type, Clustered Bar, will be selected automatically. Click the sub-type just below Clustered Bar to select it. Its description, which will appear below the sub-types, will read Clustered bar with a 3-D visual effect (see Figure 4-16). ◯ Click and hold the Press and Hold to View Sample button in the Chart Type dialog box to preview your chart with its new type without changing the actual chart.

4. Click [OK] to change the chart type and to close the dialog box. Deselect the chart. Verify that your chart resembles the one in Figure 4-17. Save the changes you have made to your presentation, but leave the file open.

more

Consult Table 4-2 below to learn more about different chart types available in PowerPoint.

Table 4-2 Common chart types

Chart Type	Description	Example
Bar	Shows how data changes over time or compares quantities	Individual sales performances
Column	Similar to Bar chart, but emphasizes vertical value (Y axis)	Quarterly income projections
Line	Shows trends in data at equal intervals	Monthly gross and net sales
Pie	Shows relation of individual parts to sum of parts	Budgets, country exports
Stock	Indicates various values of stocks	Low, high, and closing prices

Figure 4-16 Chart Type dialog box

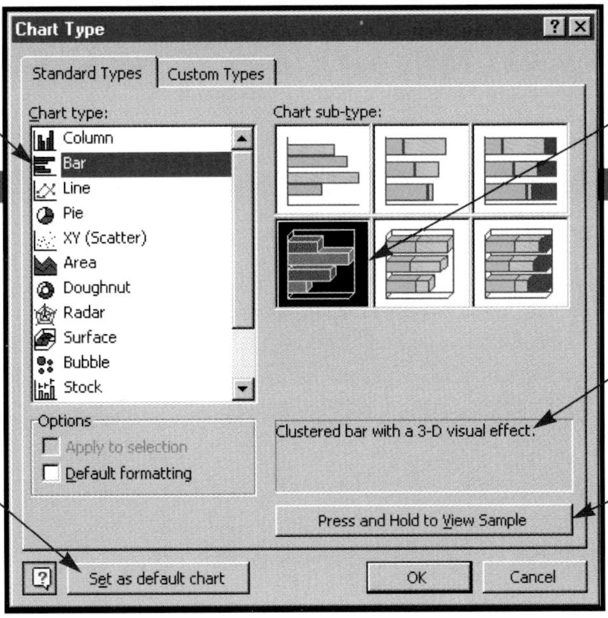

Selected chart type

Selected sub-type
of chart

Description of
selected sub-type

Click to make selected
chart type the default
type for future charts

Click to display
image of selected
chart and sub-type

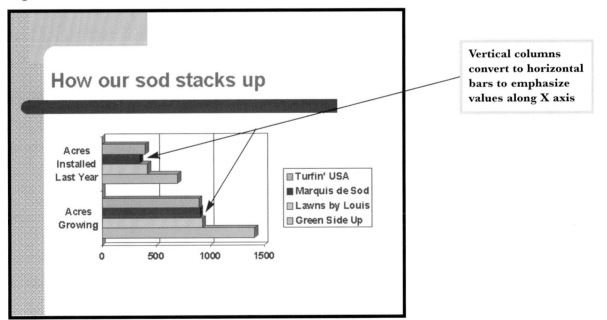

Figure 4-17 Clustered Bar Chart with 3-D visual effect

Vertical columns
convert to horizontal
bars to emphasize
values along X axis

Practice

To practice changing a chart's type, open the file ppprac4-6.ppt, and change the chart on Slide 2 to a
Line chart. Save and close the modified file as myppprac4-6.ppt.

skill | Setting Chart Options

concept

A chart can have many components, including data labels such as columns, titles for horizontal and vertical axes, horizontal and vertical gridlines, data labels, and a legend. The Chart Options dialog box enables you to determine how and where these components will appear, or if they will appear at all. When including components, choose only those elements that clarify or add understanding to a chart. Do not add components simply because you can or doing so makes the chart look fancy.

do it !

Give the chart a title and reposition the chart's legend.

1. Be sure that GSU Presentation 4.ppt appears on your screen in Normal view.

2. Double-click the chart on Slide 7. Close the datasheet and the Office Assistant if they appear.

3. On the Menu bar, click Chart, then click Chart Options. The Chart Options dialog box will open. The dialog box contains six tabs, each of which enables you to add, edit, or delete certain aspects of the chart. Each tab also includes a preview of the chart that reflects your changes as soon as you make them on the tab.

4. If necessary, click the Titles tab to bring it to the front of the dialog box. Click in the text box labeled Chart title to place the insertion point there.

5. Type Growth Comparison for Industry Leaders. The title will appear in the text box and in the preview (see Figure 4-18). Do not worry if the preview appears crowded as the actual chart will display correctly.

6. Click the Legend tab to bring it to the front of the dialog box. By default the Placement option for the legend is set to Right. Click the radio button labeled Bottom to move the legend below the chart (see Figure 4-19).

7. Click [OK] to accept the changes you have made and to close the dialog box. Verify that the new chart options appear on the deselected chart (see Figure 4-20).

8. Save the changes you have made to the presentation, but leave the file open.

more

After you alter Chart Options, you may need to adjust the size of the chart to compensate for items you have added, edited, or deleted. You can do this without working in MS Graph. If you click on a chart once, it will be selected just like a text box or other object you have inserted. You then can resize the chart by dragging one of its sizing handles. You also may reposition the entire chart on the slide by dragging it from its center.

You do not need a Legend on every chart, especially if you have added Data labels or a Data table to the chart. To remove the Legend, remove the check box from the Show legend check box on the Legend tab in the Chart Options dialog box.

Figure 4-18 Chart Options dialog box

Click and type in these boxes to entitle horizontal and vertical axes

Title appears in preview pane as you type it in Chart title text box

Approximated image of chart appears in preview pane

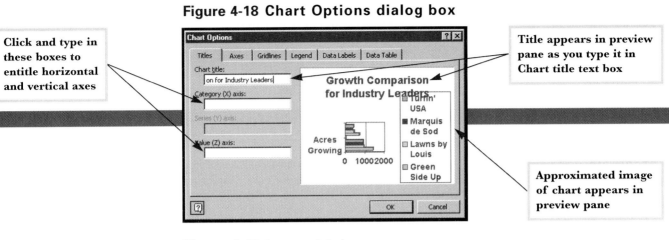

Figure 4-19 Legend tab

Legend appears, in position selected in Placement section, only when box is checked

Legend moves to bottom of preview pane when you check Bottom radio button

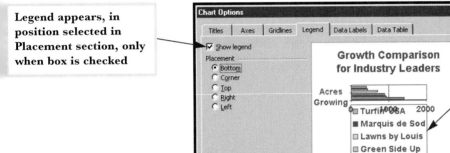

Figure 4-20 Chart with new options

Chart title appears at top of chart

Legend appears in bottom position on slide

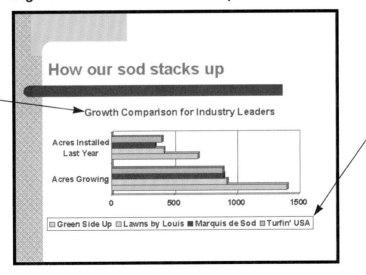

Practice

To practice setting chart options, open the file ppprac4-7.ppt. Add the title MyPractice4-7 to the chart on Slide 2. Move the chart's legend to the left of the chart. Save and close the modified file as mypppracc4-7.ppt.

skill   Formatting Chart Elements

concept

Now that you have learned how to convert a chart to a completely different chart type and to modify its general structure, you can learn how to improve your chart by working with individual elements. You can modify many aspects of a chart, including its text, colors, textures, and organization. Though you can select the chart as a single entity, you also can select and format each element individually. This flexibility enables you to enhance the chart's overall appearance and call attention to specific data.

do it !

Italicize and change the color and font of the Category Axis labels, increase the chart's depth, and add texture to one of the data series markers.

1. Be sure that GSU Presentation 4.ppt appears on the screen in Normal view.

2. Double-click the chart on Slide 7 to open MS Graph. If necessary, close the datasheet and the Office Assistant.

3. Click the Category Axis label Acres Installed Last Year on the chart to select the entire Category Axis. On the Formatting toolbar, click the Italic button *I* to italicize the two Category Axis labels.

4. With the axis still selected, click Format on the Menu bar, then click Selected Axis. The Format Axis dialog box will appear.

5. Click the Font tab to bring it to the front of the dialog box. Notice that Bold Italic is selected in the Font style list box. The Bold style formatting automatically was applied when you created the chart.

6. Click the drop-down arrow on the right end of the Color box, which currently says Automatic. A color palette will open. Click the Dark Green color square (first row, fourth column), as shown in Figure 4-21. Click   OK   to apply the color change and to close the dialog box.

7. With the axis still selected, use the Font box Arial ▾ on the Formatting toolbar to change the font from Arial to Arial Narrow. Click the border of the Legend to select it, not one of its individual elements. Use the Font box again to change the Legend's font to Arial Narrow. The Category Axis labels and Legend now should resemble those in Figure 4-22.

8. Click one of the two horizontal bars that represent Green Side Up's data in the chart. Both of the Green Side Up data series markers will be selected.

9. Click Format, then click Selected Data Series. The Format Data Series dialog box will appear. If necessary, click the Options tab to bring it to the front of the dialog box.

10. Double-click inside the Chart depth box to select its current value. Type 500 to replace the default value with the new one (see Figure 4-23). Click   OK   to confirm the change in value and to close the dialog box.

(continued on PP 4.20)

Figure 4-21 Format Axis dialog box

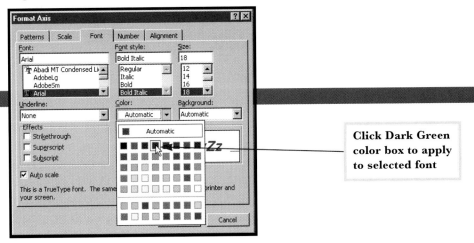

Click Dark Green color box to apply to selected font

Figure 4-22 Reformatted Category Axis labels and Legend

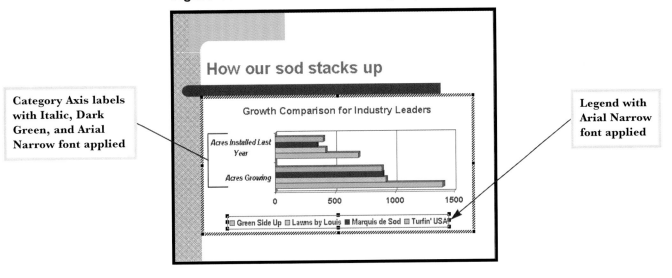

Category Axis labels with Italic, Dark Green, and Arial Narrow font applied

Legend with Arial Narrow font applied

Figure 4-23 Format Data Series dialog box

Sets distance between data markers in 3-D charts

Sets distance between data categories in chart

Sets depth of chart relative to its width

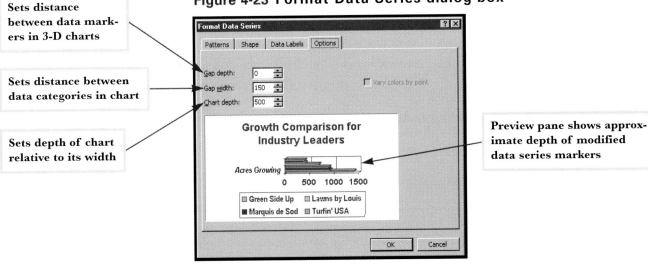

Preview pane shows approximate depth of modified data series markers

skill Formatting Chart Elements (continued)

do it !

11. Verify that your chart now resembles Figure 4-24. Notice that although you selected only one data series marker, the change to the Chart depth option affected all of them.

12. With the Green Side Up data series still selected, click the Format Data Series button [icon] on the Standard toolbar. The Format Data Series dialog box will open. If necessary, click the Pattern tab to bring it to the front of the dialog box.

13. In the Area section of the Pattern tab, click the Fill Effects button [Fill Effects...]. The Fill Effects dialog box will open. Click the Texture tab to bring it to the front of the dialog box. This tab offers several premade textures that you can apply to a chart object. When you click on a texture to select it, its name will appear below the Texture box. By accessing the Select Texture dialog box, you also can apply your own texture if you already have a file of it.

14. Click the Other Texture button [Other Texture...]. This action will open the Select Texture dialog box, which resembles PowerPoint's Open dialog box for opening files. Use the Look in box and contents window to find the file ppdoit4-8.bmp. This is a grass texture image file located where you keep your Student Files. When you locate the file, double-click it in the contents window. The Select Texture dialog box will close, and the grass texture will appear selected on the Texture tab of the Fill Effects dialog box (see Figure 4-25).

15. Click [OK] to close the Fill Effects dialog box and to return you to the Format Data Series dialog box. Click [OK] to apply the texture and to close this remaining dialog box. The grass texture will appear on the Green Side Up data series markers.

16. Deselect the chart (see Figure 4-26). Save your modified file, but leave it open.

more

You can access special formatting options for 3-D charts by clicking Chart, then 3-D View. The 3-D View dialog box enables you to change a chart's elevation so you can view it from another angle than the default one. You can rotate a chart clockwise or counterclockwise, which yields different effects depending on the selected chart type. Other more general formatting options appear on the toolbars when you are working in MS Graph. Some of the more popular of these options appear in Table 4-3 below:

Table 4-3 MS Graph formatting tools

Button	Command	Function
[icon]	Import File	Opens the Import File dialog box, enabling you to import a file, an entire sheet of data, or a selected range into a chart
[icon]	View Datasheet	Displays the datasheet window, or hides it if it is showing
[icon] [icon]	By Row or By Column	Plots chart data series from data across rows or down columns
[icon]	Data Table	Displays the values for each data series in a grid below the chart
[icon] [icon]	Category / Value Axis Gridlines...	Shows or hides category axis or value axis gridlines in charts
[icon]	Legend	Displays or hides chart Legend

Figure 4-24 Chart with depth change

Use Chart Objects drop-down list to select any desired chart object

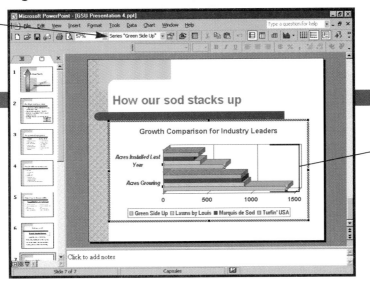

Change to Chart depth affects all data series markers

Figure 4-25 Texture tab of Fill Effects dialog box

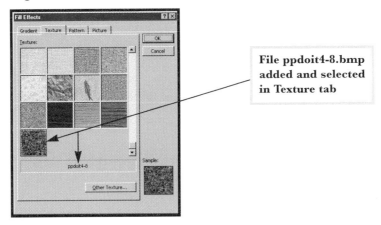

File ppdoit4-8.bmp added and selected in Texture tab

Figure 4-26 Texture applied to data series marker

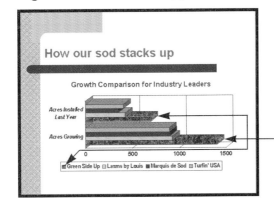

New texture appears in both selected data series markers and in chart legend

Practice

To practice formatting chart elements, open the file ppprac4-8.ppt, then follow the instructions on the slide. Save and close the modified file as mypppprac4-8.ppt.

skill   Adding Transition Effects

 MOUS Skill

concept

After you have constructed your slides, you can think about the manner in which you will present them. Adding slide transition effects adds visual interest and makes a presentation look more professional. Unlike traditional slide shows, PowerPoint's features enable you to set controls to determine how each additional slide displays on the screen after its previous one. You can set slides to move off the screen in different directions, to appear as if they are fading in or out of view, or even to dissolve into one another.

do it !

Add transition effects to presentation slides.

1. Be sure GSU Presentation 4.ppt appears on your screen in Normal view.

2. At the lower-left corner of the screen, click the Slide Sorter View button 🔳. The presentation will display in Slide Sorter view, which displays small versions, or thumbnail views, of the presentation's seven slides. The slide you were viewing when you switched to Slide Sorter View will be selected, as indicated by a heavy blue border. The Slide Sorter toolbar also will display. If necessary, click the left end of the toolbar and drag it so the toolbar docks just below the Standard toolbar (see Figure 4-27).

3. If necessary, click Slide 1 to activate it.

4. On the Menu bar, click Slide Show, then select Slide Transition from the menu. The Slide Transition task pane will open. The Apply to selected slides section of the task pane lets you to select a transition effect to apply to one presentation slide or all slides. The Modify transition section lets you set the speed at which an effect runs, to accompany the effect with a sound, and to repeat the sound until the next sound occurs. The Advance slide section lets you choose to move forward in a show via a mouse click or after a selected number of seconds or both. If you select both, the presentation will advance upon whichever choice occurs first. Additional features let you (a) apply an effect to all presentation slides, (b) play transitions and animations of selected slides, (c) run a slide show starting at the selected slide, and (d) set or cancel a preview of effects and animations if you add or modify a slide.

5. To select a transition effect, click the scrollable list in the Apply to selected slides box. Scroll down until you reach the Uncover Up option, then click it (see Figure 4-28). Clicking this effect will apply it to Slide 1, add a transition effect icon below the slide's lower-left corner (⬛), and make a preview of it run on the slide.

6. In the Modify transition section, click the arrow on the Speed list box, then click the Slow option. A second preview of the transition effect will run on Slide 1.

7. In the Advance slide section of the dialog box, click the On mouse click check box to clear it. Later in the Lesson you will set automatic transition timings. Click the Apply to All Slides button Apply to All Slides . The selected settings will be applied to every presentation slide. The transition effect icon that appeared below Slide 1 will appear below all of the other slides, indicating that the transition effect is applied where marked (see Figure 4-29).

(continued on PP 4.24)

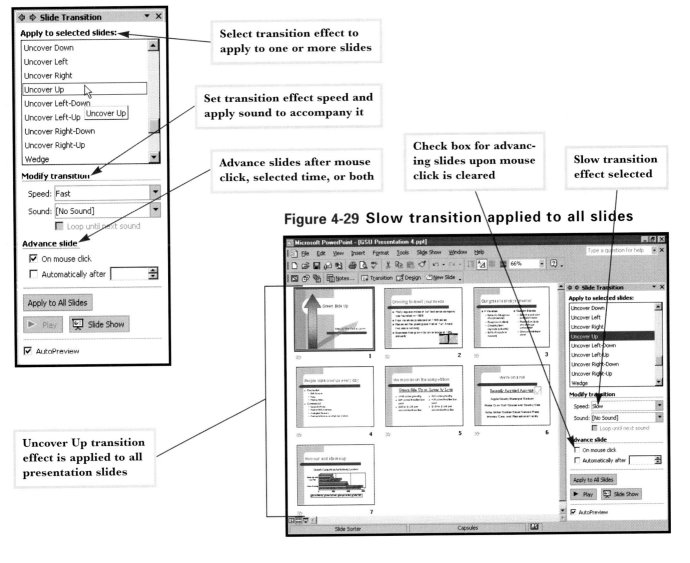

Figure 4-27 Slide Sorter view

Figure 4-28 Uncover Up option

Figure 4-29 Slow transition applied to all slides

Slide Sorter toolbar

Selected slide

Select transition effect to apply to one or more slides

Set transition effect speed and apply sound to accompany it

Advance slides after mouse click, selected time, or both

Check box for advancing slides upon mouse click is cleared

Slow transition effect selected

Uncover Up transition effect is applied to all presentation slides

skill | Adding Transition Effects (continued)

do it !

8. With Slide 1 still selected, scroll down in the Apply to selected slides list box, and click to select the Fade Through Black transition effect (see Figure 4-30). A preview of the effect will display on Slide 1. Applying transitions in this way affects only the selected slide, not the whole presentation.

9. Select Slide 3, and use the Apply to selected slides list box to apply the Wipe Down transition effect to the slide (see Figure 4-31). Select Slide 7, and use the Apply to selected slides list box again to apply the Dissolve transition effect (see Figure 4-32).

10. With Slide 7 still selected, hold down [Shift] and click Slide 1. This action will select all the slides in the presentation. Click the Play button ▶ Play at the bottom of the task pane. The entire presentation will run through its varying transition effects, starting with Slide 1. Verify that Slides 1, 3, and 7 display the new transition effects that you applied to them, while Slides 2, 4, 5, and 6 still have the Uncover Up effect.

11. Save the changes you have made to your presentation, but leave the file open.

more

The Slide Sorter toolbar, Figure 4-33, contains eight buttons that are appropriate for the Slide Sorter view. The Hide Slide button, for example, hides or displays selected slides during the running of a slide show. The Rehearse Timings button starts a slide show and displays the Rehearse toolbar, which you can use to set the amount of time each slide will display in the show. The Summary Slide button, which also appears on the Outlining toolbar, creates a summary Title and Text slide of selected slides. The Speaker Notes button opens the Speaker Notes dialog box for adding presentation notes without having to go to Normal View. The Slide Transition button opens the Slide Transition task pane. If you have not selected a slide in Slide Sorter view, the task pane displays inactive, grayed-out options. Clicking any slide will activate the options. The Slide Design button opens the Slide Design task pane. The New Slide button inserts a new slide just after the slide selected in Slide Sorter view.

Figure 4-30 Fade Through Black transition effect

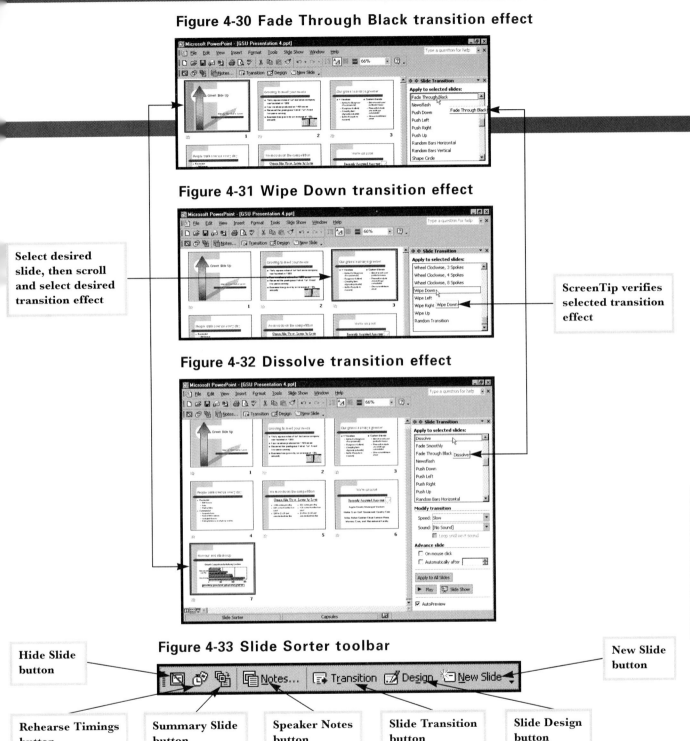

Figure 4-31 Wipe Down transition effect

Select desired slide, then scroll and select desired transition effect

ScreenTip verifies selected transition effect

Figure 4-32 Dissolve transition effect

Figure 4-33 Slide Sorter toolbar

Hide Slide button

New Slide button

Rehearse Timings button

Summary Slide button

Speaker Notes button

Slide Transition button

Slide Design button

Practice

To practice adding transition effects, open the file ppprac4-9.ppt. Apply the following transition effects: Slide 1—Wipe Left, Slow; Slide 2—Checkerboard Across, Medium; and Slide 3—Cover Right, Slow. Save and close the modified file as myppprac4-9.ppt.

skill | Timing Slide Transitions

concept

PowerPoint allows you to control the amount of time a slide spends on the screen before the next one appears during a slide show. By adjusting the display time for the content of a slide, you provide yourself with more time to explain more complex slides. You also demonstrate your courtesy and professionalism by providing more time for audience members to read and absorb the slide's content.

do it !

Based on the content of each slide, set appropriate slide transition timings.

1. Be sure that GSU Presentation 4.ppt appears on your screen in Slide Sorter view.

2. If necessary, click Slide 1 to activate it and click the Slide Transition button [Transition] on the Slide Sorter toolbar to open the Slide Transition task pane.

3. In the Advance slide section of the dialog box, click the Automatically after check box to add a check mark to it. The default value, 00:00, will appear selected in the time text box and below the lower-left area of Slide 1.

4. In the time text box on the task pane, triple-click the 00:00 default setting to select it, then type 5. Click Slide 1 to apply the new time to it. PowerPoint recognizes the number entered as seconds. Thus, the time text box and the area below Slide 1 read 00:05, indicating that the slide will advance after displaying for 5 seconds in a show (see Figure 4-34).

5. Click Slide 2 to activate it. Hold down [Ctrl] and click Slide 4, Slide 5, and Slide 6 to add them to the selection.

6. The four selected slides all have the Uncover Up transition effect. Return to the Slide Transition task pane and set these four slides to advance automatically after 15 seconds. With Slides 2, 4, 5, and 6 still selected, click any one of them to apply the new time.

7. Set Slide 3 to advance automatically after 17 seconds. Set Slide 7 to advance automatically after 10 seconds. Verify that your Slide Sorter view now resembles Figure 4-35.

8. Click Slide 1 to activate it, then click the Slide Show button near the lower-left corner of your screen. The slide show will begin at the selected slide and run until the last slide appears. At the end of the slide show, click to exit, and you will return to your previous view, Slide Sorter view.

9. Save the changes you have made to your presentation, but leave the file open.

more

When setting transition times, take into account the content of each slide. A brief slide like the Green Side Up Title slide does not need as much time as the third slide containing two columns of information, including scientific names of grasses. Sounds, movies, complex animations, and other slide elements all add to the time needed for the audience to view the slide and understand its content. Also consider the length of a presenter's explanation for a slide, including speaker's notes. If any speaker's notes are long, consider advancing a slide manually with the mouse, which provides more flexibility for controlling a presentation's timings. Also note that you can hide a slide by clicking the Hide Slide button on the Slide Sorter toolbar. A gray box with a line through it will appear over the slide number that appears below the lower-right corner of the hidden slide.

Figure 4-34 New timing added to Slide 1

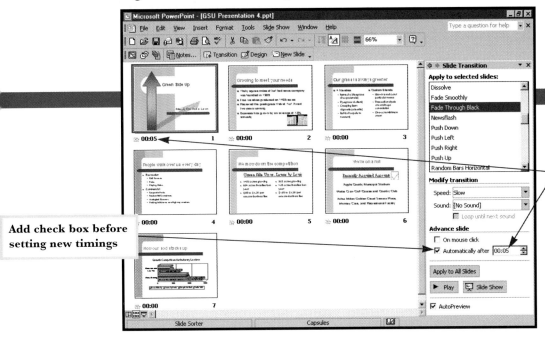

New slide timing appears in time text box and under selected slide

Add check box before setting new timings

Figure 4-35 New timings added to remaining slides

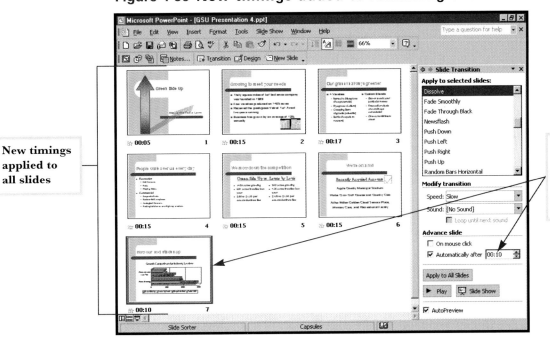

New timings applied to all slides

As only slide currently selected, Slide 7's timing appears in time text box

Practice

To practice setting slide transition timings, open file ppprac4-9.ppt. Set Slide 1 to advance automatically after 6 seconds, Slide 2 to advance when you click the mouse, and Slide 3 to advance after 12 seconds. Save and close your changes as myppprac4-10.ppt.

skill Annotating Slides

concept

Sometimes, you may want to halt the slide show to explain further an especially important or interesting point. PowerPoint has a pen feature that enables you to draw on, or annotate, your slides. You even can pause your presentation to allow more time for explaining your annotations without having to worry about being cut off by the next slide transition.

do it !

Highlight data on Slide 5 of a presentation.

1. Be sure that GSU Presentation 4.ppt appears on your screen in Slide Sorter view.

2. Click Slide Show, then click Set Up Show. The Set Up Show dialog box will open.

3. Click the Pen color drop-down list arrow. The Pen color palette will appear. Click the Teal color box, or the fourth box in the row from the left (see Figure 4-36). The Pen color palette will close, and the selected color will appear in the Pen color box.

4. Click [OK] to close the dialog box. Select Slide 5 and click the Slide Show button 🖵 to begin a slide show on Slide 5. As soon as the slide show starts, move the mouse. A transparent icon will appear in the lower-left corner of the slide.

5. Click the Slide Show pop-up menu icon 🖉◣. Select the Pointer Options command, then click the Pen command on the submenu (see Figure 4-37). The mouse pointer will change to the annotation pen pointer (🖉).

6. Click and drag the annotation pen pointer in a circle around the two numbers that represent the number of acres growing. The numbers will be circled in the color you chose in Step 5 (see Figure 4-38). ⬬ To make perfect horizontal or vertical lines while using the annotation pen pointer, press [Shift] while drawing. Release [Shift] to add curves again. Alternating between straight and curved lines in this way will make your drawings appear more precise.

7. Click 🖉◣ again. Click the Screen command on the shortcut menu, then click the Pause command on the submenu. The presentation now will pause and not advance to the next slide.

8. Use the Pointer Options command again to switch back to the Automatic mouse pointer. Use the Screen command to resume the slide show. After the slide show ends, click to exit and to return to your previous view. Leave the presentation open.

more

When the annotation pen pointer is active, your slide show will not advance, allowing you to write or draw without interruption. Selecting Automatic from the slide show Pointer Options submenu causes the mouse pointer to revert to its standard appearance, and allows the slide show to proceed if it is not set on Pause. You can move to another slide by selecting Previous or Next from the Slide Show pop-up menu, which will take you out of annotation mode and return you to the slide show at the requested point. Markings made with the annotation pen are not permanent and are erased as soon as another slide displays or the show ends. Alternately, pressing [E] erases all annotations without having to leave the current slide.

Figure 4-36 Set Up Show dialog box

Add check mark to enable slide show to run repeatedly

Click From button and enter numbers to specify which slides will appear in slide show

Click Teal color box to apply color to annotation pen pointer

Click to advance slides via mouse click

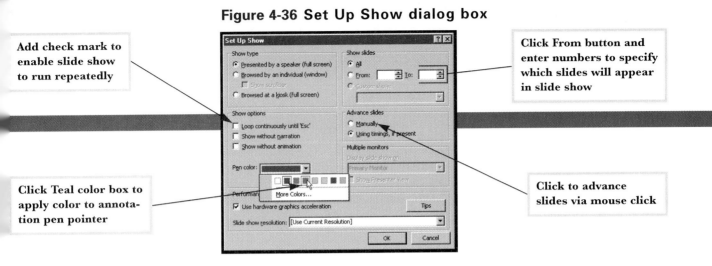

Figure 4-37 Selecting the annotation pen pointer

Click to access annotation pen pointer options

Click to display annotation pen pointer

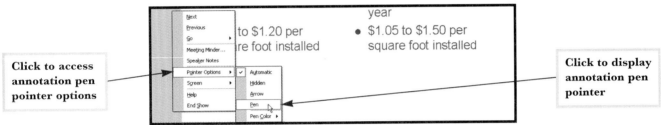

Figure 4-38 Annotating numbers on Slide 5

Annotations drawn with pen pointer

Slide Show pop-up menu icon

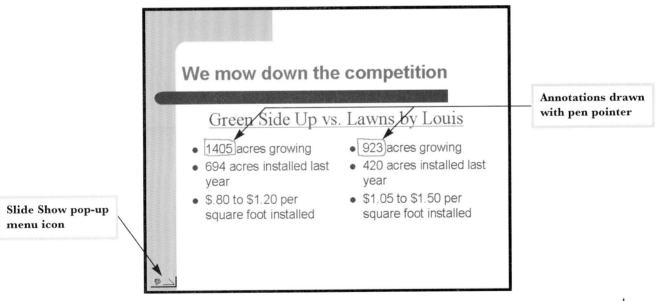

Practice

Run GSU Presentation 4 starting at Slide 1, and practice annotating each slide. After you mark the last slide, pause the presentation, switch back to the Automatic mouse pointer, then let the presentation conclude.

skill   Navigating during a Slide Show

concept

While slide presentations generally follow a sequence, times may arise when you want to display slides out of order—for example, if an audience member needs you to repeat an earlier slide or if you want to jump over a slide and show a later one. PowerPoint provides several ways to show any of your presentation's slides at any point during a slide show without having to end the show and restart it.

do it !

Explore the PowerPoint Slide Show navigation capabilities.

1. Be sure that GSU Presentation 4.ppt displays on your screen in Slide Sorter view.

2. Run a Slide Show of the presentation starting at Slide 2.

3. When the presentation starts, right-click anywhere on the slide to open the Slide Show shortcut menu. This is the same menu that opens when you click the Slide Show pop-up menu icon at the lower-left corner of the Slide Show screen.

4. Select the Go command on the shortcut menu, then click the Slide Navigator command on the Go submenu. The Slide Navigator dialog box appears.

5. Click 7. How our sod stacks up to select Slide 7 (see Figure 4-39). Click the Go To button `Go To`. The slide show will resume, but starting at Slide 7.

6. Right-click Slide 7 to open the shortcut menu again. Select the Go command, then highlight the By Title command on the Go submenu. A second submenu, consisting of all your numbered slide titles and the Slide Navigator command, will appear. A check mark precedes the current slide.

7. On the By Title submenu, click 1 Green Side Up to go to Slide 1 (see Figure 4-40). Allow the slide show to run through to the end. Click to exit the slide show.

8. Close the presentation. Close PowerPoint.

more

Pressing [F1] during a slide show or clicking the Help command on the Slide Show pop-up menu displays a comprehensive list of slide show controls. Some popular controls are described in Table 4-4 below.

Table 4-4 Slide Show keyboard commands

Key	Function
[N], [→], [Enter], or [PgDn]	Advance to next slide
[P], [←], or [PgUp]	Return to previous slide
[B] or [W]	Displays blank Black or White screen
[Slide Number]+[Enter]	Go to slide indicated by number
[H]	Go to hidden slide
[Esc], [Ctrl]+[Break], or [–]	End slide show

Figure 4-39 Slide Navigator dialog box

Click slide you want to move directly to when dialog box closes

Click to move to slide selected in Slide titles pane

Title for Slide 6 does not appear because you created it with Text Boxes from Drawing toolbar, not from Title and Text slide layout

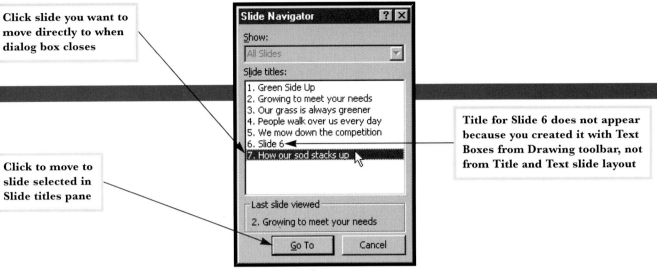

Figure 4-40 Navigating with the By Title submenu

Current slide in show displays check mark

Click to move directly to Slide 1

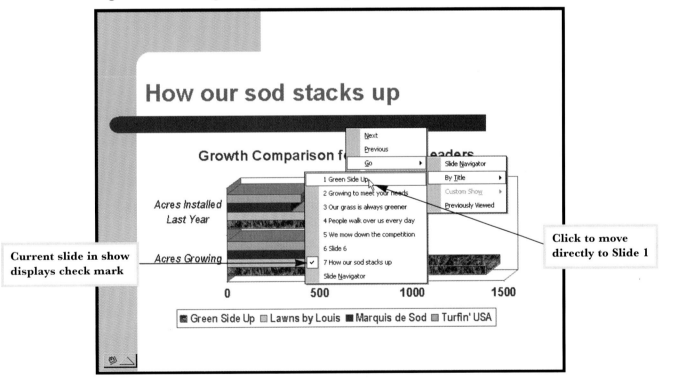

Practice

To practice navigating during a slide show, open the file ppprac4-12.ppt. Start a slide show at Slide 5. Open the Slide Navigator and go to Slide 8. Use the By Title command to go to Slide 1. Exit the slide show and close the file without saving changes.

shortcuts

Function	Button/Mouse	Menu	Keyboard
Show/Hide Grid	▦	Click View, click Grid and Guides	[Shift]+[F9]
Insert Chart	📊	Click Insert, click Chart	
View Datasheet	▦	Click View, click Datasheet	
Select Font	Arial	Click Format, click Font	[Ctrl]+[1]
Format Data Series	🖼	Click Format, click Selected Data Series	[Ctrl]+[1]

A. Identify Key Features

Name the items indicated by callouts in Figures 4-41 and 4-42.

Figure 4-41 Microsoft Graph elements

1. _____

2. _____

3. _____

4. _____

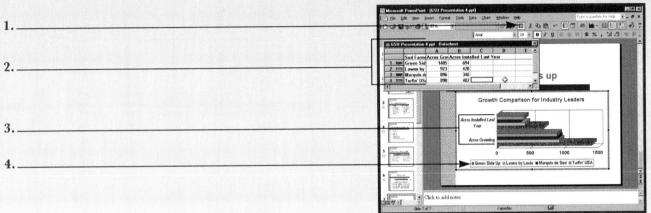

Figure 4-42 Slide Sorter view elements

5. _____

6. _____

7. _____

8. _____

9. _____

10. _____

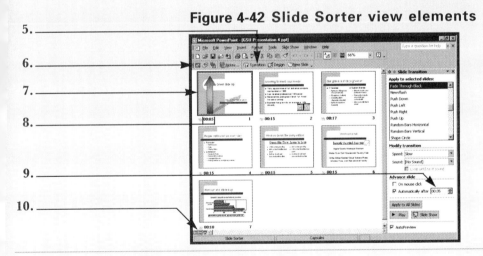

B. Select the Best Answer

11. Enables you to mark a slide temporarily during a slide show

12. Controls the manner in which slides appear on the screen

13. An example of a slide transition effect

14. Stores in tabular form the information that drives a chart

15. The intersection of a column and a row in a table

16. Enables you to jump to any slide during the delivery of a presentation

17. Provides pictures that you can add to your presentation

a. Datasheet

b. Insert Clip Art task pane

c. Annotation Pen pointer

d. Slide Navigator

e. Dissolve

f. Slide Transition task pane

g. Cell

PowerPoint 2002

quiz (continued)

C. Complete the Statement

18. You can edit and format Clip Art by using the:

a. Microsoft Clip Gallery

b. Picture toolbar

c. Slide Navigator

d. Standard toolbar

19. You can add texture to a chart object using an option on the:

a. Chart toolbar

b. Fill Effects dialog box

c. Font tab

d. Pattern tab

20. A column is an example of a:

a. Category axis

b. Data label

c. Data series marker

d. Value axis

21. When working in a datasheet, pressing [Enter] moves the cell pointer:

a. One cell to the right

b. One cell to the left

c. To the next row in the same column

d. To the next column in the same row

22. You can add chart titles and legends to a chart in the:

a. Chart Options dialog box

b. Chart Type dialog box

c. Datasheet window

d. None of the above

23. You can change the elevation of a chart in the:

a. Chart Options dialog box

b. Format Data Series dialog box

c. Presentation window

d. 3-D View dialog box

24. To change a Pie chart to a Bar chart, use the:

a. Chart Options dialog box

b. Chart Type command

c. Datasheet

d. Formatting toolbar

25. You can add transition effects and slide timings most easily in the:

a. MS Graph

b. Normal View

c. Slide Sorter View

d. Slide Show mode

26. To maintain precise control over your presentation, set your slides to advance:

a. Automatically

b. Automatically after 10 seconds

c. On mouse click

d. With sound effects

27. A datasheet:

a. Contains columns and rows

b. Can be hidden or displayed while its chart is visible

c. Contains data that will appear in its related chart

d. All of the above

interactivity

Build Your Skills

1. Open a file and insert Clip Art, insert an image from your files, and recolor the first Clip Art:

   a. Open the Student File ppskills4-1.ppt. Save it as Summer.ppt.

   b. Open the Insert Clip Art task pane, and search for Clip Art named summer. When your results appear, click the picture that looks like alternating squares of lighter blue and darker blue with yellow and white sunbursts in the squares.

   c. Resize and reposition the Clip Art so it sits below the lower row of circles and extends from the left edge of the leftmost circle to the right edge of the rightmost circle.

   d. Insert the picture file named ppskillsimage4-1.bmp from your Student Files folder. Position the image above the upper row of circles and extend it from the left edge of the leftmost circle to the right edge of the rightmost circle.

   e. Select the summer Clip Art that you added in Step 1 and activate the Picture toolbar.

   f. Open the Recolor Picture dialog box. Click the down arrow for the dotted blue color in the second row, second column. In the color palette that appears, click the darker lavender color (seventh box from left) to replace the first color. Click the [OK] button.

   g. Click View, then click Header and Footer to open the Header and Footer dialog box. Click the Update automatically option button. Type your name in the Footer text box. Click the Apply to All button. Resave the presentation.

2. Open a blank presentation and prepare the Title slide:

   a. Start a new blank presentation with a Title slide as Slide 1. Save the presentation as Accounts.ppt.

   b. In the title placeholder, type Accounts Acquired by Region. Underline the title.

   c. In the subtitle placeholder, type your name and a due date for the presentation.

3. Add a chart slide and edit its data:

   a. Add a new slide, which should be a Title and Text by default. Convert it to a Title and Chart slide layout.

   b. Entitle the slide (not the chart) East Accounts by Quarter. Underline the title.

   c. Open the chart. In the datasheet remove the rows for the West and North data, leaving only the East data

   d. Close the datasheet. Change the chart from a Column chart to a plain Pie chart.

4. Add a second and third chart slide and edit their data:

   a. Add a new slide, convert it to a Title and Chart layout, entitle it West Accounts by Quarter, and underline the title.

   b. Open the chart, delete the East and North data, leaving only the West data, and close the datasheet.

   c. Convert the West chart to an Exploded pie with a 3-D visual effect.

   d. Repeat Steps (a) through (c) to create a North region chart, adjusting the above instructions accordingly to create the proper underlined title and chart. Convert the North chart to a Doughnut chart, and apply a texture to the largest section of the doughnut.

   e. Resave the presentation.

5. Add transition effects and advance timings to a presentation:

   a. Open the file ppskills4-5.ppt. Save it as Transition.ppt.

   b. On Slide 1, apply the Box in transition effect at Slow speed. Set the slide to advance automatically after five seconds.

   c. On Slide 2, apply the Blinds Horizontal transition effect at Medium speed. Set the slide to advance after ten seconds.

   d. On Slide 3, use the Slide Transition task pane to apply the Random Bars Vertical transition effect. Set the slide to advance when you click the mouse.

(continued on PP 4.36)

interactivity (continued)

Build Your Skills (continued)

6. Practice running a slide show:

    a. Run a slide show for Transition.ppt, starting on Slide 2.

    b. When you get to Slide 3, use the annotation pen pointer to underline the word Congratulations! on the screen.

    c. Use the Slide Navigator to go to Slide 1.

    d. Use the By Title command to go back to Slide 3.

    e. End the slide show. Resave and close the file.

Problem Solving Exercises

1. Open the file Country.ppt, which is the presentation you created at the end of Lesson 3 for the country inn you are opening. Use PowerPoint's gallery of Clip Art to enliven the presentation. Add one piece of Clip Art to each slide, using illustrations that relate to the topic of each slide. Recolor the added Clip Art pictures so they match the Template Design scheme used in the presentation. Add a Title and Chart slide to the presentation. Entitle the slide Room Rates per Night. Open and create a chart that compares your projected room rates with those of competing inns in your region. You may use any chart type that properly represents contrasting prices at various locations. You do not need to add AutoShapes or Clip Art to this last slide. An example of such a chart appears to the right. Update the due date of the exercise. Save the presentation as Revised Country.ppt.

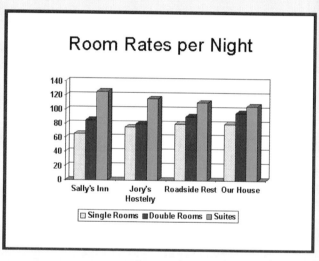

2. Create a six-slide comic strip giving practical advice on solving a relationship problem at school or work. Slide 1 should be a Title slide stating the comic strip's name in the title placeholder and your name and the exercise due date in the subtitle placeholder. Slide 2 should set up the problem, Slides 3 and 4 should give advice. Slide 5 should show a resolution to the problem. Use Clip Art pictures for the characters in your strip. Use Callouts from the AutoShapes button of the Drawing toolbar for the dialog balloons of the strip. Use appropriate Fill Effects and Textures to match the colors of your images to the colors of your selected Design Template. Program the presentation so each slide advances after 15 seconds or on a mouse click, whichever comes first. A sample version of Slide 2 appears to the right. Save the presentation as Comic Strip.ppt.

interactivity (continued)

Problem Solving Exercises (continued)

3. To help the environment and cut down on parking problems at your school or business, the organization is trying to change commuting habits. The Facilities Director has asked you to create a five-slide PowerPoint presentation promoting ways of getting to work other than by one-person car. Slide 1 should state the program name, your name, and the presentation's due date. Slide 2 should list alternate commuting options (e.g., car pool, bus, etc.). Slide 3 should list the program benefits to individuals and your organization. Slide 4 should show a chart of financial savings of various commuting methods. Slide 5 should list the names, job titles, and contact numbers of program leaders. Include one appropriate Clip Art picture on each slide, except Slide 4. Program the presentation so Slide 1 advances after 7 seconds and the other slides after 17 seconds. Save the presentation as Commuting.ppt. A sample of Slide 2 appears below.

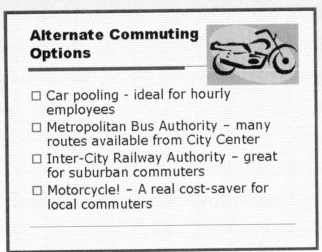

4. An all-news radio station has hired your consulting firm to do a demographic study of its listeners and present the findings in PowerPoint. Slide 1 should state the name of your firm, your name, and the presentation's due date. Slide 2 should list your data-gathering methods (e.g., phone, street interview). Slide 3 should list the demographics of the station's major listening groups (e.g., teens, at-home spouses, commuters). Slide 4 should have a chart displaying statistics about the groups of Slide 3. Slide 5 should list your suggestions on how to improve the station's appeal to each group. Make full use of a Design Template, Clip Art, AutoShapes, slide transitions, slide timings, and the major forms of text formatting. Save your presentation as Demographics.ppt. A sample of Slide 5 appears below.

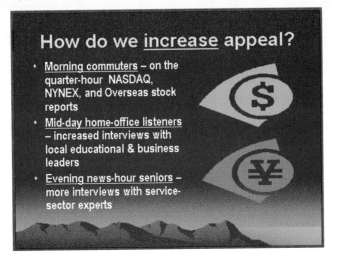

Office Integration and Web Features

Once you have mastered the individual tools that make up the Office XP suite, you may find it useful to use these tools together. Word, Excel, Access, and PowerPoint are designed to work together seamlessly. You already have seen how some features, like the Office Assistant and the Office Clipboard, are shared by all four applications. The documents and data you produce with these programs can be shared among them as well. For example, you may have produced a chart on an Excel worksheet that you want to include in a PowerPoint presentation. You may need to convert a presentation into a Word document. You may want to use an Access database to drive a mail merge that will create documents such as form letters, mailing labels, or even product catalogs in Word. You can transfer data between two Office applications with various techniques, the most common of which are pasting, linking, and embedding.

Another feature that Office XP applications share is their Web capabilities. Each Office program enables you to save a file as a Web page, which enables you to publish it on the World Wide Web without losing formatting, structure, or functionality. Once this is done, anyone with a Web browser can view your Office documents. You can, in turn, "round-trip" your Web documents back into their original Office applications for editing, and then publish them again. With these features you can publish documents easily and even save a file directly to a Web server.

Lesson Goal:

In this lesson, you will learn how to embed an Excel chart in a PowerPoint slide and how to link Excel and Word files. The lesson also includes editing the linked Excel data. Additionally, you will learn to convert a PowerPoint presentation into a Word document, merge Access data with a Word document, and create a hyperlink and Web pages.

skills

≽ **Embedding an Excel Chart in a PowerPoint Slide**

≽ **Linking Excel and Word Files**

≽ **Editing Linked Excel Data**

≽ **Converting a Presentation into a Word Document**

≽ **Adding a Word File to a Word Document**

≽ **Merging Access Data with a Word Document**

≽ **Creating Hyperlinks and Web Pages**

Office XP

skill | Embedding an Excel Chart in a PowerPoint Slide

concept

The strength of the PowerPoint application is its ability to present information in an informative and appealing manner. While you also can use PowerPoint to produce the information you present, it is sometimes easier to generate your data in another application that is better suited for a particular task. You then can insert the data from the second application into PowerPoint as an object.

do it !

Embed an Excel chart that contains the data in a PowerPoint slide.

1. Open the PowerPoint Student File ofdoit1-1a.ppt.

2. Navigate to Slide 5 of the presentation.

3. Click [New Slide] on the Formatting toolbar. The Slide Layout Task Pane opens.

4. Click the Blank layout from the Contents Layout section of the Slide Layout Task Pane. This adds a blank slide to the presentation.

5. Click Insert on the Menu bar, then click the Object command. This displays the Insert Object dialog box.

6. Click the Create from file option button, and then click [Browse...]. This displays the Browse dialog box.

7. Use the Look in drop-down list of the Browse dialog box to find and select the Excel file ofdoit1-1b.xls (see Figure 1-1). Click [OK].

8. Click [OK] in the Insert Object dialog box.

9. The Excel chart from ofdoit1-1b.xls is displayed on the PowerPoint slide (see Figure 1-2). Ignore any spelling or grammatical errors found in the files that you open, as you will correct them in later Skills.

10. Save the file as EmbeddedExcel.ppt and close the file.

more

In addition to embedding an object, you can link the object with the source file. When you embed an object, the object becomes part of the file into which you have moved it. All connections to the original file or source file are broken. Linked objects retain their connections to the source file. Any changes you make to the source file will be updated in the linked object the next time its file is opened. To link an object, activate the Link check box in the Insert Object dialog box before you insert an object.

Figure 1-1 Insert Object dialog box

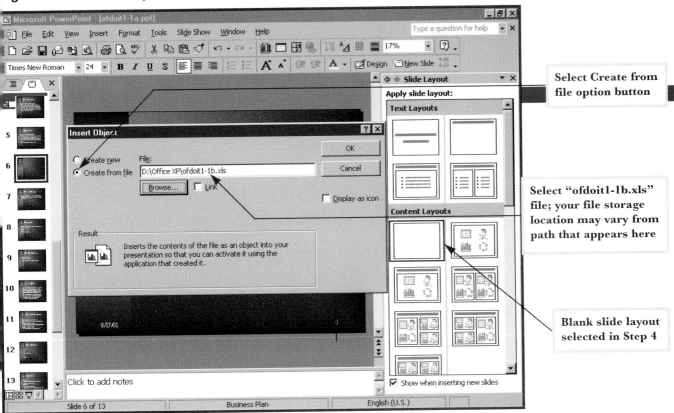

Select Create from file option button

Select "ofdoit1-1b.xls" file; your file storage location may vary from path that appears here

Blank slide layout selected in Step 4

Figure 1-2 Slide with an embedded Excel chart

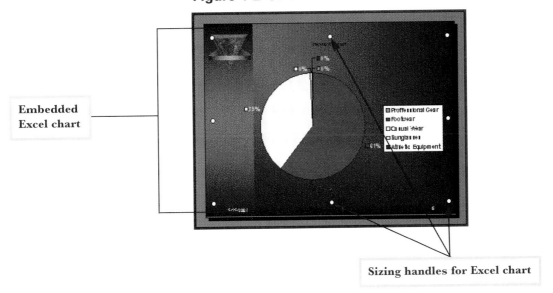

Embedded Excel chart

Sizing handles for Excel chart

Practice

Open ofprac1-1a.ppt. Create a new Blank slide just after Slide 2. On this new slide, embed the Excel 3-D column chart (not its worksheet) from ofprac1-1b.xls. Save the modified presentation as myofprac1-1.ppt and close the file.

skill | Linking Excel and Word Files

concept

Sometimes it is more appropriate and useful to link documents rather than embed them. For example, if you know that the source file for an inserted object changes frequently, and you want those changes to be reflected in the object automatically, it makes sense to link the object. Linking saves you the time it would take to edit or update two files.

do it !

Link an Excel file to a Word file.

1. Open ofdoit1-2a.xls and view Sheet 1. Leave the misspelling, Proffessional, alone, as you will correct it in a later Skill.

2. Open ofdoit1-2b.doc.

3. Right-click the taskbar and click the Tile Windows Vertically command. Both documents appear on the screen, side by side.

4. Click in the Excel window to activate it, and select the range A11 to E18.

5. Click Edit on the Menu bar, then click the Copy command. A moving border appears around the cells you copied.

6. Click inside the Word window to activate it. Then click after the secretary's initials, TY, at the bottom of the memo to place the insertion point there.

7. Press [Enter] to move the insertion point to a new line.

8. Click Edit on the Menu bar, then click the Paste Special command. The Paste Special dialog box is displayed, as shown in Figure 1-3. ◖◗ The Paste Special command is part of the advanced section of the Edit menu. If it does not appear right away, wait for a few seconds for the menu to expand or click the arrow at the bottom of the menu to expand it immediately.

9. Click the Paste link option button, and select Microsoft Excel Worksheet Object in the As list box. Click ▭ OK ▭ .

10. The selected cells you copied from the worksheet appear in the Word document. If necessary, scroll to the left edge of the Word document to display the leftmost columns of the Excel worksheet (see Figure 1-4). Once you save the memo, the data you pasted as a link will be updated in accordance with its source worksheet whenever you open the Word file.

11. Save the modified Word file as ExcelWord.doc, then close it. Save the Excel file without changing its file name.

more

The process for linking a chart to a Word document is the same, although you could also use the Object command on the Insert menu to accomplish the task. If you do not use Paste Special, but simply Paste, then you are simply embedding a copy of the object in the Word document rather than linking it. By using the Insert Object command, you also can embed or link an entire worksheet in a Word document or PowerPoint slide instead of just a chart or cell range.

Figure 1-3 Paste Special dialog box

Click here to create shortcut to source file; changes to source file will appear in destination file

Select the format for linking an object

Describes the relationship between the documents

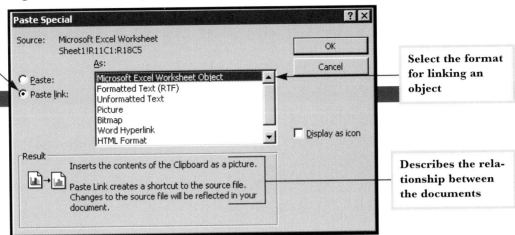

Figure 1-4 Windows vertically tiled and Word document with the pasted Excel cells

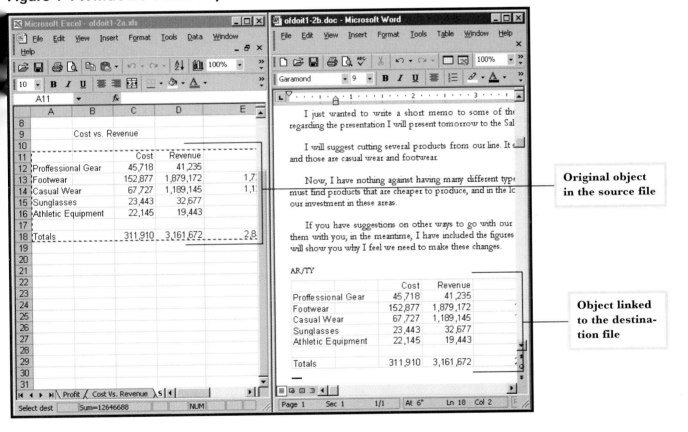

Original object in the source file

Object linked to the destination file

Practice

Open a blank Word document, open the Excel file ofprac1-2.xls, then tile the two files vertically on your computer screen. Using the Paste link command as you did in this Skill, link the Excel worksheet (not its chart) to the blank Word document. Save the Word document as myofprac1-2.doc, then close the file. Close the Excel file without making any changes.

skill

Editing Linked Excel Data

concept

The advantage of linking data rather than inserting them is that any changes you make to a source file are reflected automatically in any files that are linked to it. Editing linked data does not require any special procedures. You can use the same simple editing techniques you have already learned to update your linked files. The Edit menu also contains a command for working with the selected linked object. The name of the command changes to reflect the type of linked object that is selected. The submenu of the command allows you to open, edit, or convert the link.

do it !

Edit an Excel worksheet, which is linked to a Word document.

1. Open the Word Student File, ofdoit1-3.doc.

2. Double-click the linked Excel data that is inserted at the bottom of the memo. The source file of the linked Excel data, the Excel workbook ofdoit1-2a.xls, will open in Excel, and the Excel window will partially obscure the Word window.

3. Right-click the Windows taskbar; click the Tile Windows Vertically command. The Word and the Excel documents appear side by side. Click the Excel Title bar (see Figure 1-5).

4. Double-click in cell A12, which contains the misspelled label Proffessional Gear.

5. Place the mouse pointer after the second f in Proffessional, in the Formula Bar and click to place the insertion point there.

6. Press [Backspace] to delete the second f.

7. Click another cell in the worksheet to confirm the change to cell A12. The extra f in Proffessional will be removed from the linked worksheet in ofdoit1-3.doc, as shown in Figure 1-6.

8. Save the modified Excel file as ModifiedExcel.xls, save the modified Word file as ModifiedWord.doc, then close both files.

more

It is possible to change a linked object into an embedded object once you have already linked it from one file to another. To make this change, click the object that is linked in the destination file to select it. Then, click Edit and select the Links command on the Edit menu. In the Links dialog box there is an option, Break Link. Once you select this option, the linked object becomes an embedded object and any changes made to the object no longer reflect on the source file, and vice versa. The Links dialog box also allows you to change other aspects of a link, including its source file and whether it is updated automatically or manually. If your file contains more than one linked object, each link will be listed in the Links dialog box. Click the link you wish to work with to select it before making changes to it.

Figure 1-5 Editing a linked object

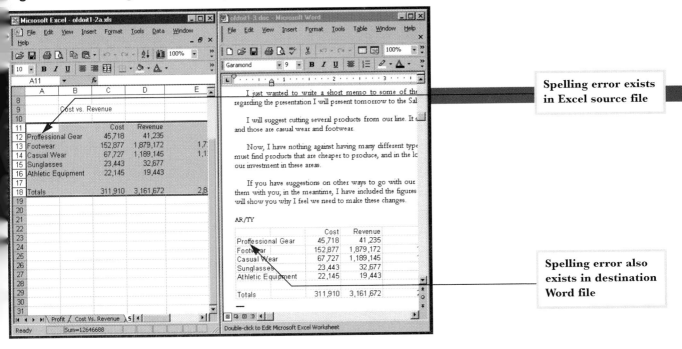

Spelling error exists in Excel source file

Spelling error also exists in destination Word file

Figure 1-6 Corrected and updated linked object

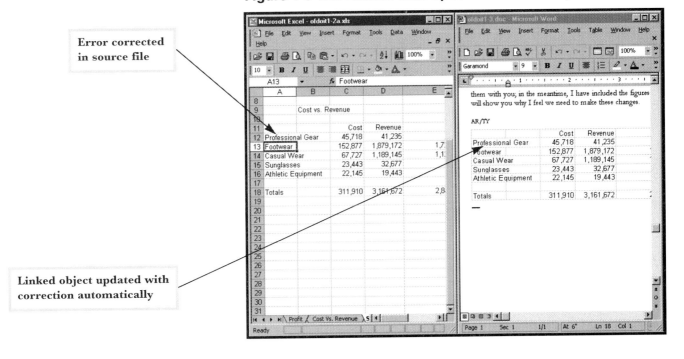

Error corrected in source file

Linked object updated with correction automatically

Practice

To practice editing a linked object, open the practice file ofprac1-3.doc. Double-click the table of expenses at the bottom of the memo to open ofprac1-3.xls. In the Excel file, decrease the Transportation expense by $100 and increase the Beverage expense by $100. After verifying that the expenses have changed in the Word memo, save it as myofprac1-3.doc. Close the Excel file without saving any changes.

skill

Converting a Presentation into a Word Document

concept

Converting an existing Office document to another type of Office file can be useful for completing certain tasks or for increasing your own comfort level. For example, you may be a novice PowerPoint user who wants printed images of slides and some speaker's notes to go with them for a presentation. Although you can create such notes in PowerPoint, you may be more proficient in Word, a program designed for working with text. You could export the PowerPoint presentation to Word, type notes to go with related slides, then print the slides and notes from Word to refer to during the presentation. ◀━━━▶ If you add Notes Pages to your slides in PowerPoint, these notes will transfer to the new Word document as well if you export the presentation to Word using a layout that includes notes.

do it !

Convert a presentation into a Word document and add notes to give at a presentation.

1. Open the PowerPoint presentation ofdoit1-4a.ppt.

2. Click File on the Menu bar, then point to Send To.

3. When the Send To submenu appears, click the Microsoft Word command. The Send To Microsoft Word dialog box is displayed, as shown in Figure 1-7. The top section of the dialog box, labeled Page layout in Microsoft Word, lets you choose how the presentation will be organized in Word.

4. Click Notes below slides, a layout that places each presentation slide on its own page and includes an area below each slide for typing notes.

5. Click [OK]. The Word application launches and, after a delay of a few seconds, creates a document with the Notes below slides layout. If necessary, click View, click Print Layout, and then scroll down slightly in the Word document to display both the first slide and the Notes area below the slide.

6. If necessary, click under Slide 1 in the Word window to place the insertion point there for typing. Type the words Welcome to the Fix Brothers presentation on Marketing goals for the year 2001. (see Figure 1-8).

7. Save the Word document as ConvertPresentation.doc, then close the file. Close the PowerPoint file without making any changes to it.

more

The bottom section of the Send To Microsoft Word dialog box determines whether the Word document you create will include your actual slides or just links to them. If you are concerned about the size of the file created when you send a presentation to Word, choose the Paste link option instead of the Paste option.

It is also possible to create PowerPoint presentation text in Word. You can create an outline of a presentation in Word by using heading styles from Word, such as Heading 1 for slide titles, Heading 2 for secondary text, and so on. When you open PowerPoint, click Insert, then click Slides from Outline. Choose the proper Word file and PowerPoint will produce a presentation based on the Word outline.

Figure 1-7 Send To Microsoft Word dialog box

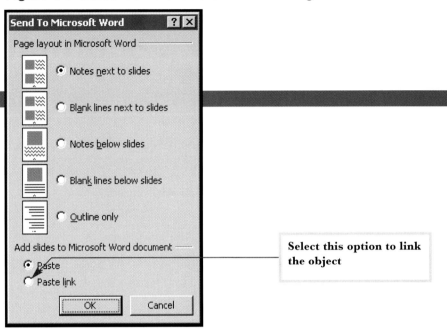

Select this option to link
the object

Figure 1-8 PowerPoint slide in Word

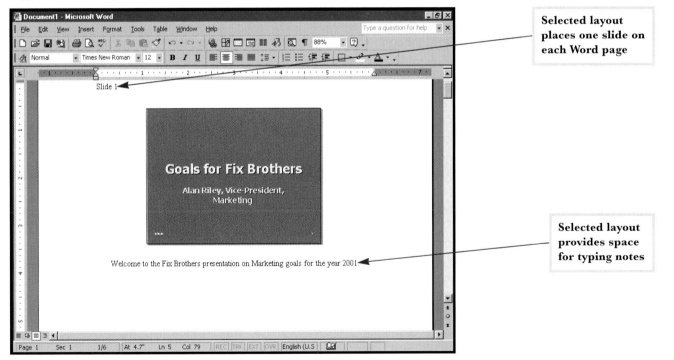

Selected layout
places one slide on
each Word page

Selected layout
provides space
for typing notes

Practice

Export the PowerPoint presentation ofprac1-4a.ppt to Microsoft Word. (Use the default setting in the
Send to Microsoft Word dialog box. The slides will appear on the left side of the Word document with
room for notes on the right side.) Save the Word document as myofprac1-4b.doc, then close the file.
Close the PowerPoint file without making any changes.

skill | Adding a Word File to a Word Document

concept

Word makes it easy to combine two files into one. You can add the text of one file to another without even having to open the file being inserted. This allows for quick collaborations while minimizing the possibility of errors. When you insert a file, it will be placed where the insertion point is currently located.

do it !

Add data from one memo to another memo.

1. Open the Word file, ofdoit1-5b.doc.

2. Click Insert on the Menu bar, then click the File command. The Insert File dialog box is displayed, as shown in Figure 1-9.

3. Use the Look in drop-down list box to select the student file Money Management.doc and then click Insert .

4. The text of the Money Management.doc file appears at the top of the active document, as shown in Figure 1-10.

5. Save the file as CombinedMemo.doc so that you have both versions of the memo on file.

6. Close the file.

more

You can import numerous types of files into Word documents. At the bottom of the Insert File dialog box there is a drop-down list box labeled Files of type. Click the drop-down arrow and you can choose the type of file you want to insert in your Word document. The possibilities range from other Office documents to sound and image files and even Web pages. By clicking the Range... button in the Insert File dialog box you can insert a particular range of cells from an Excel file into your Word document rather than an entire worksheet.

Figure 1-9 Insert File dialog box

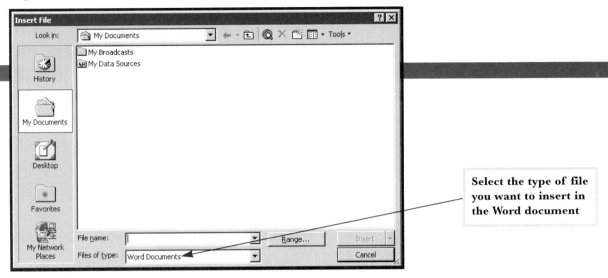

Select the type of file you want to insert in the Word document

Figure 1-10 Two Word documents combined

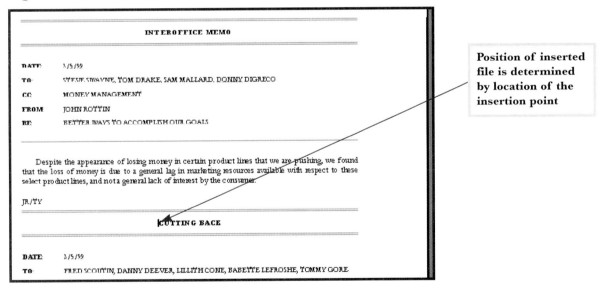

Position of inserted file is determined by location of the insertion point

Practice

Open the Word file ofprac1-5a.doc, which explains some initial steps in a document insertion process. After the existing text in ofprac1-5a.doc, press [Enter] to create a new line, and insert the Word file ofprac1-5b.doc, which provides more steps and a note. Save the combined file as myofprac1-5c.doc, then close it. Close ofprac1-5b.doc without any changes.

skill | Merging Access Data with a Word Document

concept

Databases that generate mailing lists, inventory reports, and statistical reports are a key component to many businesses. Using databases for practical purposes can be as challenging as it is imperative. Using them efficiently can be the greatest challenge of all. With Office XP, you can merge Access data fields with a Word document to create a powerful data management and output tool. ⬤ If you use mail merge commands frequently, click View, then point to Toolbars, and finally click Mail Merge to display the Mail Merge toolbar.

do it !

Merge an Access database table with a new Word document to produce a list of products and information about each product.

1. Open a new blank Word document.

2. Click Tools on the Menu bar, then point to Letters and Mailings and click the Mail Merge Wizard command. This displays the Select document type Pane of the Mail Merge Task Pane (see Figure 1-11).

3. Click the Directory option button to create a document containing a catalog.

4. Click the Next: Starting document hyperlink. This displays the Select starting document Pane. The Use the current document option button is selected by default.

5. Click the Next hyperlink. This displays the Select recipients Pane. The Use an existing list option button is selected by default.

6. Click the Browse hyperlink to select the existing list. This displays the Select Data Source dialog box.

7. Click the Files of type arrow and select Access Databases as the file type, as shown in Figure 1-12.

8. Select the Access file ofdoit1-6.mdb from the location where you have stored the student files.

9. Click ⬚ Open ⬚. This displays the Mail Merge Recipients dialog box. The Mail Merge Recipients dialog box displays the entries of the Products table in the List of Recipients list. All the check boxes of the table are checked by default (see Figure 1-13).

10. Click ⬚ OK ⬚. This action closes the Mail Merge Recipients dialog box and displays the Select recipients Pane.

11. Click the Next hyperlink. This displays the Arrange your directory Pane.

12. Click the More items hyperlink to select the fields you want to add to the document as merge fields. This displays the Insert Merge Field dialog box. The Field list box of the Insert Merge Field dialog box displays all the fields of the Products table. The ID field is selected by default (see Figure 1-14).

13. Click ⬚ Insert ⬚. This will insert the ID field in the Word document.

(continued on OF 1.14)

Figure 1-11 Word document with the Mail Merge Task Pane

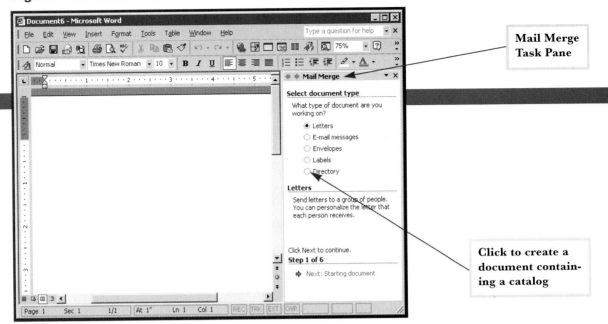

Mail Merge Task Pane

Click to create a document containing a catalog

Figure 1-12 Select Data Source dialog box

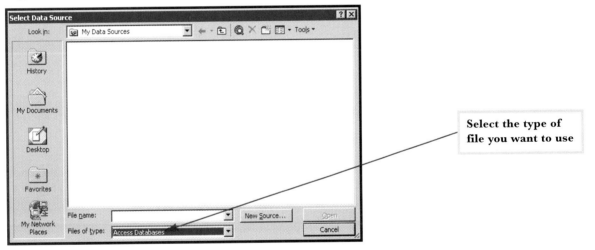

Select the type of file you want to use

Figure 1-13 Mail Merge Recipients dialog box

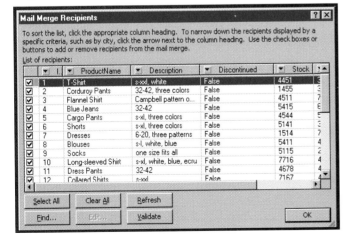

Figure 1-14 Insert Merge Field dialog box

skill | Merging Access Data with a Word Document (continued)

do it !

14. Repeat step 13 to add ProductName, Description, and Price as merge fields. Click the Close button [Close] to close the Insert Merge Field dialog box and view the Word document.

15. Just after the closing chevrons of the ID merge field and of the the ProductName merge fields, add a semicolon (;) and a space. Just after the closing chevrons of the Description merge field, add a semicolon, a space, and a dollar sign ($), as shown in Figure 1-15. Press [Enter] at the end of the line in the Word document.

16. Click the Next hyperlink in the Arrange your directory Pane. This displays the Preview your directory Pane.

17. Click the Next hyperlink. This displays the Complete the merge Pane.

18. In the Merge section of the Complete the merge Pane, click To New Document. This displays the Merge to New Document dialog box. In the Merge records section, the All option button is selected by default.

19. Click [OK]. The Mail Merge executes and creates a new document in Word that includes the data in all of the merge fields you selected for all of the records in the Products table, as shown in Figure 1-16.

20. Save the document generated by the merge as ProductsCatalog.doc, then close it. Save the document with the one line of sample merge fields as ProductsMerge.doc, then close it.

more

The Mail Merge toolbar is a useful feature for quickly performing tasks during the merging of a source document like an Access database with a form document such as the new Word document into which you placed merge fields. Some of the more commonly used toolbar buttons appear in Table 1-1 below.

Table 1-1 Mail Merge toolbar buttons

Function	Buttons	Action
Record Navigation buttons	⏮ ◀ ▶ ⏭	View specific records
View Merged Data	«» ABC	Preview the data that will be merged
Merge to New Document	📄	Create the Mail Merge document
Merge to Printer	🖨	Print the Mail Merge
Find Record	🔍	Find specified records
Mail Merge Recipients dialog box	✎	Edit data source

Figure 1-15 Merge fields chosen from Access table

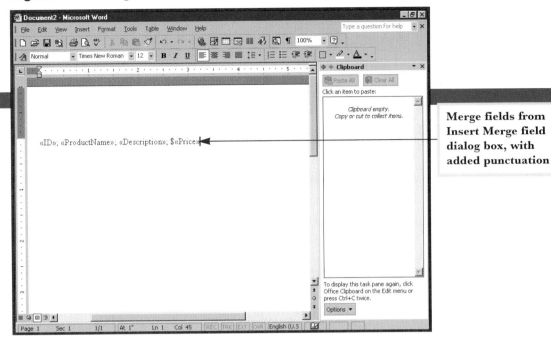

Merge fields from
Insert Merge field
dialog box, with
added punctuation

Figure 1-16 Access table merged with Word document

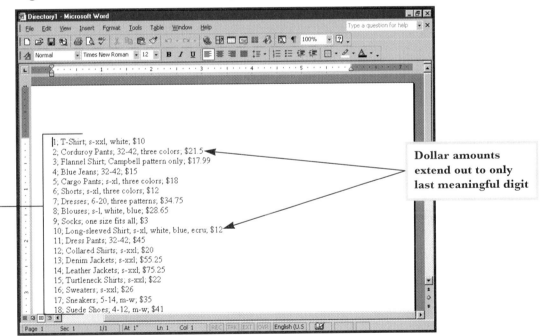

Dollar amounts
extend out to only
last meaningful digit

Data from Access
database merged
with form created
in Word document

Practice

Open, print, and close the Word document ofprac1-6.doc. Following the instructions in the document, compose a form letter in Word and merge it with the Contacts table in the Access database ofprac1-6.mdb. Be sure to save the form letter as myofprac1-6.doc, but close the Access file without any changes.

skill | Creating Hyperlinks and Web Pages

concept

The rapid growth of the Internet has increased the individual's ability to share information with others around the world. By publishing documents on the World Wide Web, posting information in newsgroups, and sending messages and files via e-mail, you can reach previously unavailable audiences with remarkable speed and ease. To assist you in taking advantage of this technology, Office XP allows you to insert hyperlinks in a document and to save your documents as Web pages. Saving a document as a Web page converts it to HTML, or HyperText Markup Language, the current standard for Web page authoring.

do it !

Insert a hyperlink in a Word document and save the document as a Web page.

1. Open the Student File ofdoit1-7.doc and save it as Directory.doc. Scroll to the second page of the document so that the last entry in the directory, Technical services, is visible.

2. Click and drag over the text Technical services to select it, and then click the Insert Hyperlink button 🔲 on the Standard toolbar. The Insert Hyperlink dialog box will be displayed with a blinking insertion point in the Address box.

3. Type http://www.domain.com/fixbros/techserv.html as shown in Figure 1-17. This is a fictional Internet address to which the text you selected will be linked.

4. Click ⌴ OK ⌴. The Insert Hyperlink dialog box closes. Notice that the text you selected has been converted to a hyperlink. Once this page is published on the Web, clicking on this link will take the user to the Technical Services page of the Fix Brothers Web site.

5. Click File on the Menu bar, then click the Web Page Preview command. Your default Web browser will be launched so that you can view your document as it will appear on the Web (see Figure 1-18).

6. Close the Web browser.

7. Click File on the Menu bar, then click the Save as Web Page command. The Save As dialog box is displayed.

8. Use the Save in drop-down list box to choose a storage location and click ⌴ Save ⌴. Your document now is saved as a Web page and can be published on the World Wide Web. 💿 While saving the Directory.htm file, Word also has created the Directory_files folder, containing other files. Word creates this kind of folder under various circumstances —for example, when a Web page includes graphics. When it comes time to publish the Directory.htm file, you also would need to move the Directory_files folder and its contents to the Web.

more

While saving a document as a Web page, you can change the page title, which is displayed in the title bar of the browser. To change the title, click ⌴ Change Title... ⌴. This displays the Set Page Title dialog box. In the Page Title text box of the Set Page Title dialog box, you can specify the desired name for the Web page. 💿 The Save as Web Page command is also available in Excel and PowerPoint.

Figure 1-17 Insert Hyperlink dialog box

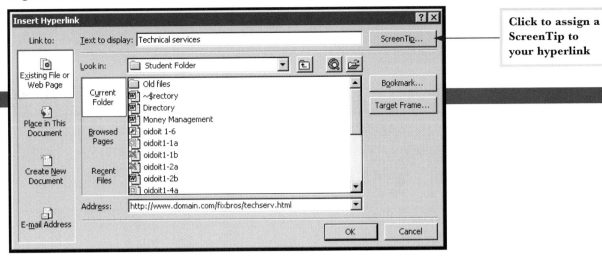

Click to assign a ScreenTip to your hyperlink

Figure 1-18 Previewing a Web Page

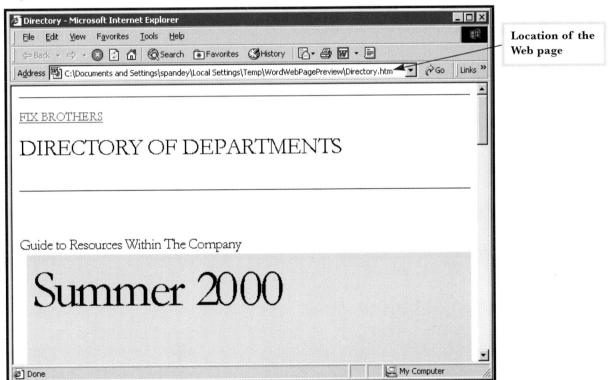

Location of the Web page

Practice

Open the Word document ofprac1-7.doc. Change the name of the university from Azimuth to Excelsior. Create hyperlinks for the names Mary Masterson, Ed.D. and for Rupert Muddrick, M.S. Save the file as a Web page called myofprac1-7.htm. Preview the Web page in your Web browser and close the file.

shortcuts

Function	Button/Mouse	Menu	Keyboard
New Slide (PowerPoint)	New Slide	Click Insert, click New Slide	[Ctrl]+[M]
Insert Hyperlink (Word)		Click Insert, click Hyperlink	[Ctrl]+[K]

quiz

. Identify Key Features

ame the items indicated by callouts in Figure 1-19.

Figure 1-19 Mail Merge toolbar

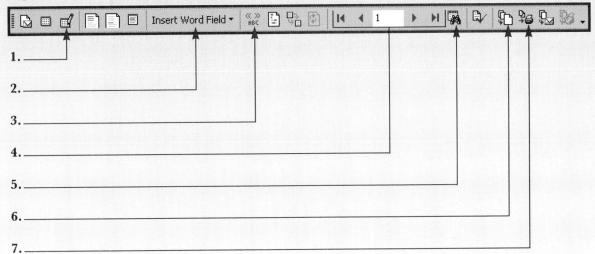

1. _____
2. _____
3. _____
4. _____
5. _____
6. _____
7. _____

B. Select the Best Answer

8. An alternate method of embedding an object from one Office program in another

9. Traditional method of inserting an object into a PowerPoint presentation

10. Where an object originates

11. Where an object is inserted

12. An object that is updated automatically whenever its source file is changed

13. An object that originates from another file, but maintains no ties to its source

14. Allows you to combine data and fields from one program in another

15. Programming language used in Web pages

16. Text that connects you to another data source when you click it

a. Copy and paste

b. Data source

c. Destination file

d. Embedded object

e. HTML

f. Hyperlink

g. Insert Object slide

h. Linked object

i. Mail Merge

quiz (continued)

C. Complete the Statement

17. To see merged records after you have completed the setup of a mail merge, click the:

a. Merge to Printer button

b. Merge to New Document option

c. Mail Merge Helper button

d. View Merged Data option

18. Office XP allows documents to be saved and viewed as Web pages by:

a. Eliminating all complicated objects

b. Changing the format of the documents

c. Saving documents as Web pages

d. Adding Web servers

19. You can change a linked to an embedded object by:

a. Using the Break Link option

b. Clicking the Unlink command on the Standard toolbar

c. Accessing the Chart Tools dialog box

d. Right-clicking it in the destination file

20. Office XP makes it easy to move a PowerPoint presentation to Word by:

a. Cutting and pasting notes and slides from the presentation

b. Accessing the Send To Microsoft Word dialog box from the File menu

c. Clicking Insert, then clicking Presentation File

d. Clicking File, then Import From, then PowerPoint presentation

21. You can create a presentation in Word and import it in PowerPoint by:

a. The exact process needed to move a PowerPoint presentation into Word

b. Writing the outline in Word, then opening the Insert menu in PowerPoint

c. Creating the presentation in Word, then clicking Save as PowerPoint presentation

d. Clicking Insert, then clicking PowerPoint Slides

22. The Paste Special dialog box is useful when you are trying to:

a. Break a link

b. Paste data as a link

c. Both a and b

d. Neither a nor b

23. To create a document containing a catalog or a printed list of addresses, click the :

a. Directory option on the Mail Merge task pane

b. Insert Directory command on the Insert toolbar

c. Directory button on the Catalog toolbar

d. Any of the above

24. HyperText Markup Language:

a. Enables the existence of hyperlinks

b. Is abbreviated HTML

c. Is a standard programming language for Web page authoring

d. All of the above

interactivity

uild Your Skills

Using PowerPoint with other Microsoft Office XP programs:

a. Open the PowerPoint presentation ofskills1-1.ppt. Add a new Blank slide at the end of the presentation.

b. Insert the chart (not the worksheet) in the Excel file ofskills1-1.xls into the PowerPoint presentation's new slide. Resize the chart as needed to fit attractively on the slide.

c. Export the modified PowerPoint presentation ofskills1-1.ppt to Word. Type your name in the upper-left corner of Page 1 of the Word document, and save the document as Integration1-1.doc. Print and close the document. Close the other files without any changes.

Using Excel with other Microsoft Office XP programs:

a. Insert the Excel worksheet (cell range A5:F9) from ofskills1-2.xls as a linked object at the bottom of the Word document ofskills1-2. If necessary, resize the linked worksheet so the Word document appears on only one page.

b. On the Excel worksheet, correct the spelling error, 1st Quatter. After making the correction in Excel, verify that the Word version of the linked object also is correct.

c. In the Word document, change the name of the letter writer to your name. Save the revised Word document as Integration1-2.doc. Print and close the Word document. Save and close the Excel file as Integration1-2.xls.

3. Using Access with other Microsoft Office 2000 programs:

a. Open the Word document ofskills1-3.doc, which contains a table with a completed column header row and a blank row for merge fields. In the page header, replace [Student Name] with your first and last names.

b. Start the Mail Merge Wizard. In the Select document type pane, select the Directory option.

c. In the Select starting document pane, select the Use the current document option.

d. In the Select recipients pane, browse for and open the Access file ofskills1-3.mdb. Close the Mail Merge Recipients dialog box. be sure that the insertion point appears in the leftmost blank cell of the Word table.

e. In the Arrange your directory pane, click the More items option to open the Insert Merge Field dialog box. Insert the merge field <<Description>> in the leftmost blank cell. Insert the merge field <<PaymentMethod>> in the middle blank cell. Insert the merge field <<TransactionDate>> in the rightmost blank cell. (Hint: To format the directory properly, insert the first merge field, close the dialog box, click in the second table cell, reopen the dialog box, insert the desired merge field, and so on.)

f. In the Preview your directory pane, verify that the proper merge fields appear in the previously blank table cells. Save the Word document as Integration1-3.doc.

g. In the Complete the merge pane, click the To New Document option. Accept the All option in the Merge to New Document dialog box. Print and close the Word document.

4. Use Word to create a Web page:

a. Reopen the Word document Integration1-3.doc created in the previous exercise.

b. Delete the entire page header. Type the title Student Name - Sample Budget at the top of the Word document, replacing the words Student Name with your first and last names. Create a fictional hyperlink to your first and last names.

c. Save the Word document as a Web page with the file name Integration1-4.htm.

d. Preview the page with your Web browser. Make sure the title in the browser's Title bar is correct.

e. Make any modifications to the Web page you think are necessary. Resave, print, and close the Web page.

interactivity (continued)

Problem Solving Exercises

1. You work for the company Randolph & Mortimer. You have the task of developing a proposal to reduce expenses, there by increasing revenue. Use Excel and PowerPoint to create a presentation to address the Board of Directors' concerns at a upcoming meeting. Slide 1 should be a title slide with the company's name in the title placeholder and your first and last names in the subtitle placeholder. Slide 2 should list two key problems facing the company. Slide 3 should list two key steps you will take to cut expenses (see Exercise 2 below for examples of steps). Slide 4, entitled Profits & Losses Worksheet, should display an Excel worksheet that represents the six departments of the company: Sales, Bonds, Investment Services, Accounts, Online Investing, and Equity, with their profits or losses for the year 2001. Slide 5, entitled Profits and Losses Chart, should display a 3-D column chart that graphically represents the profits and losses from the worksheet. For the year ending 2001, Sales lost $70,100, Accounts lost $13,500, and Equity lost $62,800. For the same year, Online Investing made $181,000, Bonds made $195,200, and Investment Services made $950,500. Save the Excel worksheet and chart in one file named Randolph.xls. Save the PowerPoint presentation, including the linked (not embedded) worksheet and chart as Randolph.ppt.

2. Create a one- or two-page Word document describing exactly what your proposal is, with the company name and your name at the top center of the first page in bold text. You are going to propose that you cut Equity and Sales from the company because they are losing too much money. Briefly list and explain no more than three reasons why it would be wise business practice to eliminate these failing departments (e.g., they always have lost money, their main offices are on the opposite coast from headquarters, they don't fit with future growth plans, etc.). Illustrate the reasons by inserting either the linked spreadsheet or chart that you created in the Excel file in Exercise 1 above. Save the Word document as Randolph.doc. Print and close the file.

3. Create an Access database from the data listed below. Name the database ServicesOffered.mdb. Using the Mail Merge Wizard, create an organized and attractive directory (i.e., catalog or list) resembling the table below in a new Word document. Be sure to include the company name, Randolph and Mortimer, and your name at the top center of the document. Save and close the Word document that has only the unmerged fields as UnmergedMortimer.doc. Save the merged Word version with the data from Access as MergedMortimer.doc. Print and close the MergedMortimer.doc file.

Departments	Services
Accounts	Checking
	Savings
	Certificates of deposit
Equity	Mortgages
	Auto loans
	School loans
Sales	Customer service
	Gift certificates
	Warranties

4. Reopen MergedMortimer.doc. Change the document title to Randolph and Mortimer Financial Services. Create a hyperlink from the word Accounts to a banking Web site (actual or fictional). Create a hyperlink from the word Equity to an investment firm's Web site. Create a hyperlink from the word Sales to a retail chain Web site. Move your name from the top to the bottom of the document, and identify yourself as Webmaster. Save the modified file as a Web page with the file name WebMortimer.htm. View the file in your Web browser, then reformat any errors in the file if needed. After making revisions, print and close the file.

glossary

 a

Absolute cell reference
In Excel, a cell reference that will remain fixed, even if the formula containing the reference is moved. To make a cell reference absolute, place a dollar sign ($), before both the column letter and row number.

Accessories
Programs built into Windows 2000 that are useful for everyday tasks.

Action query
An Access query that is used to select records and perform operations on them, such as deleting them or placing them in new tables.

Active cell
The selected cell in a table, as indicated by the insertion point, or in a worksheet, as indicated by the cell pointer.

Active Desktop
In Windows 2000, gives you the ability to integrate live Web content and animated pictures into your desktop.

Active window
The window you are currently using. When a window is active, its title bar changes color to differentiate it from other open windows and its program button is depressed.

Address Bar
Used for entering a Web address manually; also can be used to view a local folder or drive.

Address Book
Component of Outlook Express that enables you to store contact information.

Adjustment handle
A small yellow diamond that appears when certain PowerPoint objects are selected. Dragging the handle enables you to alter the shape of the object.

Alignment
The position of text or objects in relation to the margins of a document, or the location of values or labels within a cell in relation to the cell borders.

Anchor cells
In Excel, the first and last cells in a cell range; the cells used to express a range address (for example, B9:E9).

Animated border
Indicates that a cell's contents have been sent to the Clipboard.

Animation effect
Movement of items, especially objects, on a PowerPoint slide to create a dynamic presentation.

Annotation pen pointer
A tool that enables you to draw freely on PowerPoint slides during a slide show.

Answer Wizard tab
The Help tab that replicates the Office Assistant by allowing you to ask questions or enter search topics in your own words to produce Help topics most closely related to your question.

Appearance tab
In the Display Properties dialog box of Windows 2000, lets you customize the appearance of individual system items or apply an appearance scheme.

Append Query
An Access query that adds groups of records from one or more tables to the end of a specified table.

Applications program
See "Program."

Argument
Information (such as a cell address, range, or value) enclosed in parentheses, used by a function or macro to produce a result.

Arithmetic operators
Symbols used to perform formula calculations such as +, −, *, and /.

Arrow keys
The [→], [←], [↑], and [↓] keys on the keyboard. Used to move the insertion point, select from a menu or a list of options, or in combination with other keys to execute specific commands such as selecting text.

Ascending order
See Sort order.

Assumption
In Excel, a variable factor useful for conducting What-If analysis in a worksheet.

Attach button
In Windows 2000, a button that permits you to e-mail a computer file.

AutoCalculate box
In Excel, automatically displays the total of the values in a selected group of cells in the status bar.

AutoComplete

Automatically finishes entering a label when its first letter(s) match that of a label used previously in the column.

AutoContent Wizard

A feature that assists you in designing a PowerPoint presentation quickly and easily. The AutoContent Wizard guides you through the steps of choosing basic layout design, style, and output type.

AutoCorrect

A feature that corrects common typing errors automatically as you type. AutoCorrect can be customized to correct specific mistakes that you frequently make.

AutoFill

Automatically fills a range with series information such as the days of the week when the range after the first value is selected using the fill handle.

AutoFit

A feature that automatically resizes items in a program. In a table, it resizes table columns to match their contents. On a Web page, it resizes the entire table so it fits on the visible page when the window is resized. In PowerPoint, it resizes text in a slide placeholder if the current text size drives the lower lines of text below the placeholder.

AutoForm

Creates a form automatically from the Access table or query that you select. You can use AutoForm by selecting it from the New Form dialog box or by clicking the drop-down arrow on the New Object toolbar button.

AutoFormat

Adds a pre-designed set of formatting to selected ranges. AutoFormats can modify numbers, borders, fonts, patterns, alignment, symbols, and the height and width of rows and columns.

AutoFormat button

Allows you to open the AutoFormat dialog box, which helps you change the template upon which a form is based; you can choose a template that is predefined or customize your own.

AutoLayout

Any of 26 pre-designed PowerPoint slides set up to accommodate different combinations of text, pictures, charts, and other objects.

Automatic save

A feature that automatically saves document changes in a temporary file at specified intervals. If power to the computer is interrupted, the changes in effect from the last save are retained. Enabled by default, you can turn off this feature from the Save tab of the Options dialog box on the Tools menu.

AutoReport

Creates a report automatically from the Access table or query that you select. You can use AutoReport by selecting it from the New Report dialog box or by clicking the drop-down arrow on the New Object toolbar button.

AutoShape

One of numerous figures that can be drawn by simply selecting a shape from the Drawing toolbar and dragging the mouse. The user determines the dimensions and the location of an AutoShape.

AutoSum

In Excel, a function that automatically adds the values in the cells directly above or to the left of the active cell.

AutoText

Text that Word is programmed to recognize. When you begin to type a word or phrase that Word recognizes, the program offers to complete it for you.

Axis

A horizontal, vertical, or diagonal line on a chart that provides a frame of reference for measuring the chart's data; the horizontal line is the X-axis; the vertical line is the Y-axis, the diagonal line suggesting depth is the Z-axis.

Back button

Allows you to return to the Web page or system window you viewed previously.

Background tab

In the Display Properties dialog box of Windows 2000, used to apply wallpaper to your desktop.

Best Fit

An Access command that sizes the width of a column so that it can accommodate the widest entry in the column, including the field name. You can also apply Best Fit by double-clicking the right border of a column's field name.

Bitmap (.bmp)

Basic image file format used by Windows.

Black and White View

In PowerPoint, this view shows how your presentation will appear when printed in black and white in case you do not have a color printer.

Blank Document template

The collection of settings used in the blank document you see when you first launch Word or when you click the New button on the Standard toolbar.

Bound/Unbound objects

Unbound objects stay the same through every Access record in a form, while bound objects are linked to particular fields in a database.

Break

A feature that ends a current line, section, or page of text and/or graphics and starts the material on the next line, section, or page.

Browser

An application that enables you to find and view information on the World Wide Web. Major browsers include Netscape Navigator and Microsoft Internet Explorer.

Browsing

Examining Web pages in the manner of your choice.

Bullet

A small graphic element, usually a round or square dot, used to designate items in a list.

C

Cancel button

In Excel, removes the contents of a cell and restores the cell's previous contents if there were any; marked by an X on the Formula bar.

Cascade Delete Related Records

An Access command that, when active, ensures that deleting a record from the primary table will automatically delete it from the related table as well.

Case

Refers to whether or not a letter is capitalized. Some search features are case-sensitive; that is, they will differentiate between words that are spelled the same but have different capitalization.

CD Player

Windows application that lets you play audio CDs.

Cell

The box or rectangle created by the intersection of a row and a column in a table, worksheet, or database.

Cell address

A cell's identification code made up of a column letter and row number; E4 would be the cell in the fifth column and fourth row.

Cell pointer

The black rectangle that outlines the active cell in a chart's datasheet.

Cell reference

See "cell address."

Character style

A combination of character formats from the Font dialog box that is identified by a style name. Changing an element (such as the font size) of a character style changes all text that has been formatted with that style.

Chart

A graphical representation of data.

Chart elements

The objects that represent information in a chart such as bars, columns, or text labels.

Chart type

Determines the style in which a chart graphically interprets data.

Chart Wizard

A series of specialized dialog boxes that guide you through the creation or modification of a chart.

Check box

A small square box that enables you to turn a dialog box option on or off by clicking it.

Classic Style

A folder option that requires a double-click to open an icon and a single-click to select it.

Clear Layout button

Allows you to eliminate relationships between Access tables, but does not eliminate just one relationship.

Click

To press and release a mouse button in one motion; usually refers to the left mouse button.

Click and drag

To press and hold the mouse button, move the mouse along a flat surface, and then release the mouse button when an action is done.

Client–Server

A computing model in which computers known as clients request and receive data from a central computer with high storage capacity called a server.

Clip art

The pre-created artwork or photographs from the Microsoft Clip Gallery in an Office XP program, or from Microsoft's Web-based Design Gallery live; alternately, the pre-created, often copyright-free, graphic image that can be inserted into a document to illustrate a point or to add visual interest. Clip art often comes in large collections.

Clip Gallery

A Microsoft Office feature that acts as a library of Clip Art, pictures, sounds and videos. It enables you to import, store, and reuse these objects in Word and other Office applications.

Clipboard, Office XP

A temporary storage area for cut or copied text or graphics. You can paste the Clipboard contents into any area of the PowerPoint slide, such as a placeholder. If data, you can paste it to another cell in a chart's datasheet. The Clipboard holds an item until replaced by another item, or until you shut down the computer. The Clipboard holds up to 24 items and is viewable in the application window as a task pane.

Close

To quit an application and remove its window from the Desktop. The Close button appears in the upper-right corner of a window, on the Title bar.

Close button

A button at the top-right corner of every window and box that appears in Microsoft Office. It automatically closes that particular window or box.

Collapse

On the Outline tab, reduces the selected PowerPoint slide to its title only, hiding all other text.

Collapse All

On the Outline tab, reduces all PowerPoint slides to their titles only, hiding all other text.

Collate

A printing option that instructs your computer to print one complete copy of a document before beginning the first page of the next copy.

Color scheme

The default colors assigned to basic aspects of a presentation such as text, background, and fill color.

Column

A vertical grouping of cells that contains the values for a single field in a table, worksheet, or database table.

Column Selector button

The gray rectangle that appears above each column and displays its column letter.

Combo box

A lookup list that is added to a form rather than a table.

Command

Directive that carries out an application feature or provides options for carrying out a feature.

Command button

In a dialog box, a button that carries out an action. A command button usually has a label that describes its action, such as OK, Cancel, or Help. If the label is followed by an ellipsis, clicking the button displays another dialog box.

Comment

An electronic note that can be attached to a cell. Similar to a text box, but can be hidden from view.

Contents

One of the tabs as part of the Access Help features. Once clicked this tab displays the contents of the Access Help feature.

Contents tab

A comprehensive Help facility that organizes program information by main subject categories and individual Help topics.

Control menu

A list of commands available from the Title bar that contains commands for resizing, moving, or closing a window.

Control Panel

In Windows 2000 utility used for changing computer settings. You can access the various control panels through the Start menu, My Computer, or Windows Explorer.

Controls

The functions in databases that control the data that is presented. Editing these controls changes the way data functions are performed and the way data is represented.

Copy

To place a duplicate of a file, or portion thereof such as text or graphics, on the Clipboard to be pasted in another location.

Criteria

Conditions you set that instruct Access to select certain records for a query or filter.

Crop

To cut off portions of a graphic that you do not wish to display.

Crosstab query

An Access query that performs calculations and presents data in a spreadsheet format. It displays one type of data listed down the left side and other types of data across the top.

Cursor

The blinking vertical line in a document window that indicates where text will appear when you type. Also referred to as the insertion point.

Custom Animation

A text or object movement, sometimes accompanied by sound, that animates a PowerPoint slide element in order to call attention to it or simply add to the overall effectiveness of the presentation.

Custom dictionary

A document containing all the words that have been "learned" by Word's spell checker. More than one custom dictionary can be created and referenced by a single copy of Microsoft Word.

Custom Help

Allows you to provide customized advice and tips that can help someone using the form you create.

Cut

To remove a file, or a portion of a file such as text or graphics, and place it on the Clipboard.

Cut

To remove a file, or a portion of a file, and place it on the Clipboard.

Cut and paste

To remove information from one place and insert it in another using the Clipboard as the temporary storage area.

d

Data

The fields, values, records, and other information entered and stored in a database.

Data label

Text or numbers that name and/or describe the data that you enter in rows and columns.

Data series

The selected data taken from a worksheet and converted into a chart, or data taken from a row or column of a datasheet.

Data series marker

In a chart, a graphic object such as a bar, line, column, or pie piece that represents the data series in the chart's datasheet.

Data type

Allows you to specify and limit what kinds of data Access will accept in a particular field.

Database

A system for storing, organizing, and retrieving information.

Database management system (DBMS)

Permits you to create a database and then edit and manipulate its elements.

Database toolbar

Contains graphical buttons that execute specific commands when clicked.

Database window

The main control center for building and working with an Access database. Displays the database object buttons.

Datasheet

Displays the data from a table, form, or query in tabular form; alternately, a table of information serving as a data source for a chart.

Datasheet View

Displays the Access table as it was created in Design View.

Date/Time Properties dialog box

In Windows 2000, allows you to set your system clock and calendar.

Default

A predefined setting for variables such as PowerPoint slide margins, fonts and their sizes and styles within a place-holder, etc.

Default value

A field property that automatically enters an assigned value into a field for every Access record.

Defaults

Predefined settings for variable items such as page margins, tab spacing, and shortcut key assignments; these can be changed when necessary.

Delete

To remove the contents from a cell or an object such as a chart from the worksheet.

Delete

To remove text, graphics, or values from a document, worksheet, slide, or database.

Delete Query

A query that deletes a group of records from a specified Access table.

Delete Rows button

A command that enables you to delete a row from your table by clicking this button.

Deleted Items folder

Outlook Express folder that functions much like the Windows Recycle Bin.

Demote

To indent a line of text so that it is moved down a level in an outline hierarchy.

Descending order

See Sort order.

Design Gallery Live

See "Microsoft Design Gallery Live."

Design grid

The Design View grid in which you create an Access query or advanced filter.

Design Templates

Prepared designs you can apply to presentation PowerPoint slides that include organizational patterns, formatting, and color schemes.

Design View

The window in which you create and edit an Access database object.

Desktop

The on-screen area, created using the metaphor of a desk, that provides workspace for your computing tasks.

Destination file

The file to which you transfer a source file—for example, a business report in Word that uses a table from another program like Excel or Access.

Dialog box

A graphical box that offers additional command options for you to review or change before executing the command.

Disk Cleanup

Windows 2000 utility that removes unnecessary files from your computer, creating more free space.

Disk Defragmenter

Windows 2000 utility that rearranges the data on your hard disk so that it can be accessed more efficiently.

Docked toolbar

See "toolbar."

Document window

The Word window on the screen in which a document is viewed and edited. When the document window is maximized, it shares its borders and title bar with the Word application window.

Documentation

The first section of an Excel worksheet. It contains important information such as the spreadsheet's author, purpose, date of creation, file name, macros, and ranges.

Dotted border

Indicates that the selected object can be resized or repositioned.

Double-click

To press and release a mouse button twice rapidly; usually refers to the left mouse button.

Drafts folder

In Outlook Express, enables you to store messages that you have not finished composing.

Drag

To hold down the mouse button while moving the mouse.

Drag-and-drop

Method of moving selected text and objects by dragging them from one location to another with the mouse.

Draw Table tool

Allows you to create the borders and gridlines of a table freehand.

Drawing toolbar

Contains tools and buttons for creating and formatting shapes, text boxes, and WordArt.

Drive

The mechanism in a computer that reads recordable media (such as a disk or tape cartridge) to retrieve and store information. Personal computers often have one hard disk drive labeled C, a drive that reads floppy disks labeled A, and a drive that reads CDs, usually labeled D.

Dummy row/column

A blank row or column at the end of a defined range that holds a place so that Excel can recalculate formulas correctly if a new row or column is added to the range.

Dynaset

An Access table that is generated from a select query, it is dynamically linked to a source table.

Edit

To add, delete, or modify cell contents or other elements of a file.

Effects

Text formats such as small caps, all caps, hidden text, strikethrough, subscript, or superscript.

Electronic spreadsheet application

A computer program designed to organize information in columns and rows on a worksheet and facilitate performing rapid and accurate calculations on groups of interrelated numbers.

Elevation

An option that enables you to change the angle at which you view a 3-D chart.

Ellipsis (...)

Three dots after a menu command indicating that, when clicked, the command will lead to a dialog box with options for executing the command.

E-mail

A method of sending electronic messages from one computer to another over the Internet.

Embedded object

Information contained in a source file and inserted in a destination file; after embedding, the object becomes part of the destination file; changes made in the embedded object are reflected in only the destination file (see also Linked object).

Endnote

In Word, the explanatory material, usually marked by a sequential number or letter, that appears at the end of a document (see Footnote).

Enforce Referential Integrity

A command that ensures that for each Access record in the primary table, there is at least one corresponding record in the related table.

Enter button

In Excel, confirms cell entries. The Enter button is located on the Formula bar and is symbolized by a check mark.

Entire Network icon

Gives you access to the other workgroups that are a part of your network.

Expand

On the Outlining toolbar, reveals all of the selected PowerPoint slide's text if it has been collapsed previously.

Expand All

On the Outlining toolbar, reveals all text on all PowerPoint slides if any of them have been collapsed previously.

Exploded pie slice

A pie chart slice that has been dragged away from the rest of the pie to emphasize it.

Export

Allows you to save database objects into other databases to be used there.

Expression

A mathematical equation or other form of data control that makes data entry more efficient.

Expression Builder

A dialog box offering you the option of creating a pre-selected expression or put an expression together yourself using the values presented.

Extend selection

In Word, to increase the selected area. When a selection is extended, it grows progressively larger each time [F8] is pressed. To shrink the selection, press [Shift]+[F8]. The arrow keys may also be used with the [Shift] key to enlarge or shrink the selection.

Favorite

A shortcut to a local, network, or Internet address that you have saved so that you can access the location easily.

Favorites Explorer bar

In Windows 2000, it makes your Favorites menu part of the browser window so that it is always available.

Favorites menu

In Windows 2000, it allows you to store shortcuts to your favorite Web pages and other files for easy access.

Field

A column of information in a database table that contains a specific type of information; alternately, the place in a main document where a specific portion of a record, such as a postal code, will be inserted when the document is merged. Also known as a merge field.

Field list box

In Access, the small window appearing in such places as query Design View and the Relationships window that displays the fields contained in a particular table.

Field properties

Characteristics that control how a field appears, what kinds of data will be accepted in a field, and how that data will be formatted.

Field selector

In Access, the gray bar at the top of each datasheet column that contains the field name. Clicking the field selector selects the entire field.

Field size

In Access, a field property that limits the number of characters you can enter in a field.

File

A computer document, worksheet, presentation, or database that has been created and saved under a unique file name.

File hierarchy

A logical order for folders and files that resembles how you would organize files and folders in a filing cabinet. Your file hierarchy displays where your folders and files are stored on your computer.

File management

The skill of organizing files and folders.

File path

The address of a computer file's location; it contains the drive, folder, any subfolders, and file name. For example, a complete file path for a PowerPoint presentation might be C:\My Presentations\Work\Marketing.ppt.

Fill handle

The small black square at the bottom right corner of the cell pointer. Dragging the fill handle copies a cell's contents to adjacent cells or fills a range with series information.

Filter

Criteria you set that Access uses to find and display certain records.

Filter by Form

An Access command that enables you to select several different criteria from different tables to use to filter your table.

Filter Excluding Selection command

An Access filter that, when applied, searches for every record that does not include the data you have specified.

Find

Allows you to locate specific types of data or specific records in a database by searching for criteria that you specify.

Find and Replace

To search automatically for text or graphics in a document and then to substitute other text or graphics in its place.

Floating toolbar

See "toolbar."

Folders

Subdivisions of a disk that work like a filing system to help you organize files.

Folders Explorer bar

Default left panel of Windows Explorer; shows all of the drives and folders available on your computer.

Font

A name given to a collection of text characters of a certain size, weight, and style. Font has become synonymous with typeface. Arial and Times New Roman are examples of font names.

Font size

The physical size of text, measured in points (pts), of which there are 72 per inch; the larger the point size, the taller the font.

Font style

Refers to whether text appears as bold, italicized, or underlined, or any combination of these formats.

Footer

Text that appears at the bottom of a printed document.

Footnote

In Word, the explanatory material, usually marked by a sequential number or letter, that appears at the bottom, or "foot," of a document; a footnote usually comments or expands upon the main text to which it refers (see Endnote).

Form

An Access database object that often serves as the main user interface for a database. It organizes records so that they are easy to work with.

Form View

In Access, the view in which you work with a form, entering and editing records.

Format

The layout of a document, worksheet, slide, or database, including elements like fonts, sizes, styles, and dimensions. It is changeable and affects the way the entire file appears, but does not change the file's content.

Format Bar

Toolbar that enables you to format text in a WordPad document.

Format Painter

A tool enabling you to copy many formatting settings from selected text to another section of text; it is especially useful in documents like flyers and newsletters where distinctive formatting is common, even essential, to the document's appearance.

Formatting toolbar

Used to change the appearance of text and/or data in a file; the formatting toolbar contains shortcuts to the most common formatting commands, e.g., Font Size, Bold, Increase Indent, and so on.

Formula

A mathematical expression that performs a calculation in a table or worksheet.

Formula bar

The area below the Formatting toolbar that displays cell contents whether they are labels, values, or formulas. You may enter and edit cell contents in the formula bar rather than in the cell itself.

Forward button

Allows you to revisit a Web page or system window after you have left it by clicking the back button.

Forward command

Used to pass a message you have received to another e-mail address.

Frame

An independent component of a Web page.

Full

A file-sharing setting that allows others to read and edit your shared files.

Function

A built-in formula included in Excel that makes it easy for you to perform common calculations.

g

Get External Data submenu

Appears on the Access File menu, and enables you to bring data from an external source into your Access database.

Global template

In Word, a template named NORMAL.DOT that contains default menus, AutoCorrect entries, styles and page setup settings. Documents use the global template unless a custom template is specified. See also template.

Go To

A useful command for moving great distances across a document, worksheet, or other file.

Graphical user interface (GUI)

An environment made up of meaningful symbols, icons, words, and windows that control the basic operation of a computer and the programs it runs.

Grid

A set of dotted horizontal and vertical lines for facilitating layout on a PowerPoint slide.

Gridlines

Vertical and horizontal lines on a table or chart that delineates cell boundaries; alternately, the dotted lines on a PowerPoint slide that facilitate formatting.

h

Hanging indent

A paragraph format in which the first line of a paragraph extends farther to the left than subsequent lines.

Hatchmarked border

Indicates that the selected object can be resized, and that its contents, such as text, can be edited.

Header

The summary information for an e-mail or newsgroup message. Also, the text that appears along the top of a printed page.

Header/footer

A header is an item or group of items that appears at the top of every page in a section. A footer appears at the bottom of every page. Headers and footers often contain page numbers, chapter titles, dates, and author names.

Help button

A button in a Help window that opens a dialog box or a program to provide an answer to your question.

Hidden text

A character format that enables you to show or hide designated text. Word indicates hidden text by underlining it with a dotted line. You can select or clear the Hidden Text option with the Options command on the Tools menu. Hidden text may be omitted when printing.

Hide/Unhide columns

An Access command that literally hides, or unhides, columns in Datasheet View. Hidden columns and the data contained in them are not seen in the datasheet.

Highlight

When an item is shaded to indicate that it has been selected.

History Explorer bar

In Windows 2000, it displays links for all of the drives and folders or Web pages you have visited recently.

Home page

The page to which your browser opens upon launch or clicking the Home button; also can refer to the main page of a particular Web site.

Horizontal ruler

A bar displayed across the top of the document window in all views. The ruler can be used to indent paragraphs, set tab stops, adjust left and right paragraph margins, and change column widths in a table. You can hide this ruler by clicking View, then clicking Ruler.

Horizontal scroll bar

Changes your view laterally when all of the information in a file does not fit in the window.

HTML

An acronym for HyperText Markup Language, the language that defines the way information is presented on a Web page. Office XP programs can automatically convert the formatting you have given a document into HTML, which functionally turns your document into a Web page.

HTTP

An acronym for HyperText Transfer Protocol; appears at the beginning of a URL to notify the browser that the following information is a hypertext Web document.

Hyperlink

Originated as an element of Web page design; usually text, clicking a hyperlink brings you directly to a predefined location within a document or to a specific page on the World Wide Web.

Hypermedia

Text, pictures, and other objects that are linked to files on the Web and will access those files when clicked. Also known as hyperlinks.

Icon

Pictorial representation of programs, files, and other screen elements such as command buttons.

Import

Allows you to select database objects from other databases and bring them into a new one.

Inbox

Holds the e-mail messages you have received in Outlook Express.

Inbox Assistant

In Windows 2000, creates filters that route incoming messages to a specific folder based on criteria you supply.

Indent

The distance between text boundaries and page margins. Positive indents make the text area narrower than the space between margins. Negative indents allow text to extend into the margins. A paragraph can have left, right, and first-line indents.

Index tab

The Microsoft Word Help tab that enables you to search the Help files using an alphabetical list of keywords.

Input

The data you enter into a worksheet and work with to produce results.

Input Mask Wizard

In Access, limits the type of data that users can into a field by automatically entering data into an easily readable and understandable format.

Insert Rows button

A command that enables you to insert a row into a table by clicking this button.

Insertion point

A vertical blinking line on-screen that indicates where text and graphics will be inserted. The insertion point also indicates where an action will begin.

Insertion point

A vertical blinking line on the Word screen that indicates where text and graphics will be inserted. The insertion point also determines where Word will begin an action.

Internet

A worldwide computer network made up of numerous smaller networks.

Internet Connection Wizard

Runs you through the process of setting up an Internet account.

Internet Explorer

Windows 2000's Web-browsing application.

Junction table

In Access, a table that has a one-to-many relationship with two other tables, it is required when creating a many-to-many relationship with a third table.

Keyboard shortcut

A keyboard equivalent of a menu command (e.g., [Ctrl]+[X] for Cut).

l

Label

A box describing the data of the text box attached to it.

Label

Text or numbers that describe the data you place in rows and columns. Labels should be entered in a worksheet first to define the rows and columns and are automatically left-aligned by Excel.

Label

In tables, data consisting of words (see also Value); in printing, a small, generally rectangular, adhesive-backed sheet of paper for printing folder captions, addresses, or similar data for mass printing

Label prefix

A typed character that marks an entry as a label. For example, if you type an apostrophe before a number, it will be treated as label rather than as a value.

Label Wizard

A set of dialog boxes that leads you through a series of steps ending in the creation of a prototypical label for your personal or business correspondence.

Landscape

A term used to refer to horizontal page orientation; opposite of "portrait," or vertical, orientation.

Launch

To start a program so you can work with it.

Legend

The section of a chart that details which colors or patterns on a chart represent which information.

Line break

A mark inserted where you want to end one line and start another without starting a new paragraph. A line break may be inserted by pressing [Shift]+[Return].

Line spacing

The height of a line of text, often measured in lines or points.

Link Tables

An Access command that enables you to create a link in your current database to a table in another database.

Linked object

Information contained in a source file and inserted in a destination file that maintains a connection between the two files; after linking, changes made in the source object will be reflected in the destination object (see "Embedded object").

Links toolbar

In Windows 2000, makes Favorites available as buttons in your browser window.

List box

A drop-down list of items. To choose an item, click the list box drop-down arrow, then click the desired item from the list.

Logical operators

Operators that allow you to connect multiple simple conditions in a select query.

Lookup Wizard

In Access, a way of creating a list box that enables you to look up the data that fits into the field you add the lookup list to.

Lurk

To read the messages on a newsgroup without participating in the discussion.

m

Macro

A set of instructions that automates a specific multi-step task that you perform frequently, reducing the process to one command.

Magnifying tool

Allows you to take a closer look at a page in Print Preview, it is controlled by the mouse and acts as the mouse pointer when in Print Preview mode.

Mail Merge

A tool enabling you to combine the fields and data from a datasource, worksheet, or database into a form document.

Make-Table query

An Access query that uses some of the records from one or more tables or queries to create a new table.

Map Network Drive

A Windows 2000 command that connects your computer to a remote shared folder as if it were a local drive.

Margin

The distance between the edge of the text in the document and the top, bottom, or side edges of the page.

Match Case

A command used during the Find command, forces the current application to match the capitalization of the specified search field.

Maximize

To enlarge a window to its largest size. Maximizing an application window causes it to fill the screen; maximizing a document, worksheet, presentation, or database window causes it to fill the application window.

Menu

A list of related application commands.

Menu bar

Lists the names of menus containing program commands. Click a menu name on the menu bar to display a list of commands.

Merge and Center command

In Excel, combines two or more adjacent cells into a single cell and places the contents of the upper left-most cell at the center of the new cell.

Merge cells

Command that combines two or more cells in a table into one cell.

Microsoft Design Gallery Live

A Microsoft Web page that provides additional clips and other graphics that you can download to your computer. Your computer must be connected to the Internet to access this gallery. The URL, or Web address, for this gallery as of July 2001 is dgl.microsoft.com.

Microsoft Graph Chart

A program that displays a chart created from a pre-existing table and a datasheet containing data related to the chart; you can directly access the chart and datasheet to change their contents and/or appearance.

Microsoft Organization Chart

The application you use to create an organization chart for a PowerPoint presentation slide.

Minimize

To shrink a window to its minimum size. Minimizing a window reduces it to a button on the Windows taskbar.

More Buttons arrow

Permits you to add buttons to a particular toolbar.

Mouse

A palm-sized, hand-operated input device that users roll on the desk to position the mouse pointer and click to select items and execute commands.

Mouse buttons

The two buttons on the mouse, or left and right mouse buttons, that you use to make selections and issue commands.

Mouse pointer

The usually arrow-shaped cursor on the screen that you control by guiding the mouse on your desk. You use the mouse pointer to select items, drag objects, choose commands, and start or exit programs. The appearance of the mouse pointer can change depending on the task being executed.

Move handle

In Access's Design View, the large black square in the upper-left corner of a selected item. Drag the move handle to place the object in a new location.

Multiple Pages display

A mode of Print Preview that enables you to view your document as it will be seen on multiple pages. You may decide to make changes and view the effect it will have on the way the document will appear on the pages when it is printed.

Multitasking

The ability to run several programs on your computer at once and easily switch among them.

My Computer

A Windows operating system utility that gives you access to the disk drives, files, folders, and other resources available to your computer; the default icon, a PC, appears on the Windows desktop.

My Network Places

In Windows 2000, allows you to view and access the computers that make up your network.

n

Name box

The box at the left end of the Excel Formula bar that displays the address of the active cell or the name of a selected range that has been defined and named. You can also use the drop-down arrow in the Name Box to select a named range.

Navigation buttons

The row of buttons at the bottom of a table or form used to move among records.

Network

Two or more computers linked together to allow for the sharing and exchanging of data.

New Toolbar command

Allows you to create a custom toolbar that can be placed on the taskbar or in its own window.

Newsgroup

An electronic bulletin board on the Internet used to post messages on a specific topic.

Nonprinting characters

In Word, the marks displayed on the screen to indicate characters that do not print, such as paragraph marks or spaces. You can control the display of these characters with the Options command on the Tools menu, and the Show/Hide ¶ button on the Standard toolbar.

Normal View

A tri-pane view that includes a left-hand window with an Outline tab and a Slides tab, a central area called the Slide pane, and below it a Notes pane, enabling you to work with different aspects of a presentation in the same window; in Normal view you can turn a task pane on or off and work with it while Normal view still displays.

Normal View

Used for most editing and formatting tasks. Normal View shows text formatting but simplifies the layout of the page so that you can type and edit quickly.

Note pane

A special window in which the text of all the footnotes in a document appears. The note pane can be accessed by double-clicking a note reference mark.

Notes Page View

A PowerPoint view option that enables you to insert reference notes that you can use during a presentation or print out for the audience.

Notes Pane

The horizontal pane below the main Slide pane in PowerPoint in which you can type speaker's notes to accompany the current slide on screen.

Object

A table, chart, graphic, equation, or other form of information you create and edit with a program other than Word, but whose data you insert and store in a Word document. In PowerPoint, the lines, shapes, text boxes, clips, drawings, and similar items you insert on a slide. In Access, one of six main components of a database: tables, queries, forms, reports, macros, modules, and pages.

Office Assistant

An animated representation of the Microsoft Office Help facility. The Office Assistant provides hints, instruction, and a convenient interface between the user and Access' various Help features.

Office Links submenu

Another Access command that enables you to publish parts of or whole database objects in MS Word; a Mail Merge may be created from this submenu.

Open

Command used to access a file that you already have created and saved.

Open Copy

Command that opens a copy of the presentation you want to work with instead of the original file.

Open in Browser

Command that enables you to open a presentation in your Web browser rather than in PowerPoint.

Open Read-Only

Command that enables you to view a presentation, but not to make any permanent changes to it.

Operating system

Controls the basic operation of your computer and the programs you run on it. Windows 2000 is an operating system.

Operators

In Access, the symbols and words used to express conditions for selection criteria in a query.

Option button

The small round button among a set thereof in a dialog box; when clicked, it dictates the exclusive choice of action for a feature; commonly called "radio button"; in Access, an object that facilitates adding a "yes" or "no" entry into a field.

Option group

In Access, an object that frames together several options for a particular field, used to limit the amount of options the user may choose from.

Options

The choices available in a dialog box.

Order command

Controls the order in which objects on the same PowerPoint slide are layered.

Order of operations

The order that a program follows when calculating formulas with multiple operations: (1) exponents, (2) multiplication and division from left to right, (3) addition and subtraction from left to right. In addition, operations inside parentheses are calculated first, using the above order.

Organization chart

A symbolic representation of a hierarchy or chain of command.

Organize Favorites command

Allows you to rename your Favorites and restructure your Favorites hierarchy.

Outbox

Stores e-mail messages you have composed in Outlook Express until you send them.

Outline tab

A PowerPoint tab available in Normal view that facilitates entering, editing, and arranging text that will appear on slides.

Outlining toolbar

The toolbar available on PowerPoint's Outline tab that contains commands for promoting and demoting lines of text as well as for controlling what is visible on the tab.

Outlook Express

E-mail software that comes with Windows 2000.

Output

The results produced by calculations done on the input data of a worksheet.

Overtype

In Word, an option for replacing existing characters one by one as you type. You can select overtype by selecting the Overtype option on the Edit tab with the Options command on the Tools menu. When you select the Overtype option, the letters "OVR" appear in the status bar at the bottom of the Word window. You can also double-click these letters in the status bar to activate or deactivate overtype mode.

p

Pack and Go Wizard

In PowerPoint, gathers all of the necessary elements of a presentation and compresses them so that they may be packaged onto a floppy disk for use elsewhere.

Page Break

The point at which one page ends and another begins. A break you insert is called a hard break; a break determined by the page layout is called a soft break. In Normal View, a hard break appears as a dotted line and is labeled Page Break, while a soft break appears as a dotted line without a label.

Page Breaks

A type of control that effects the way reports are printed, they may be placed anywhere in the report.

Page Setup

A dialog box allowing you to change the dimensions and the layout of what your database objects will look like on the printed page.

Paint

Windows 2000's built-in drawing program.

Pane

A sub-window in a program; some common panes in PowerPoint are the Slide pane, Notes pane, task pane, and Preview areas of dialog boxes.

Paragraph style

A stored set of paragraph format settings.

Parameter query

An Access query that is flexible and will prompt you to enter selection criteria every time the query is used.

Paste

To insert cut or copied text or objects into a document, worksheet, slide, or database from the Office Clipboard.

Paste Function command

Command that enables you to choose and perform a calculation without entering its formula on the keyboard.

Paste Options button

Appears when you execute the Paste command. Clicking the Paste Options button opens a menu of commands that enables you to determine what formatting will be used on the item you pasted.

Paste Special command

Allows you to paste the contents of a cell using formatting characteristics that you specify.

Path

See "file path."

Pattern

Used to fill in the area of the desktop that is not covered by wallpaper.

Personal Macro Workbook

Allows you to store macros so that they will be available to all Excel workbooks.

Personalized menus

Feature that permits the Start and Menu bar menus to adapt to your usage by temporarily hiding the commands you use infrequently so the others are more accessible.

Picture toolbar

Specialized toolbar for formatting Clip Art and other graphics; contains commands such as Insert Picture, Crop, and Format Object.

Placeholder

A dashed border on a PowerPoint slide that designates where to insert specific text or objects.

Point

To place the mouse pointer over an item on the desktop.

Point size

A measurement used for the size of text characters and row height. There are 72 points in 1 inch.

Pop-up menu

The menu that appears when you right-click selected places in the Windows environment.

Portrait orientation

A term used to refer to vertical page orientation; opposite of "landscape," or horizontal, orientation.

Position

The specific placement of graphics, tables, and paragraphs on a page. In Word, you can assign items to fixed positions on a page.

Post

To send a message to a newsgroup.

PowerPoint Viewer

A program that permits you to run a presentation on a computer that does not have PowerPoint installed.

PowerPoint window

The window that contains the open PowerPoint application, and displays the menus, toolbars, and presentation window.

Presentation window

The main area of the PowerPoint window where you create, view, and edit your presentation.

Preview area

A pane in a dialog box displaying formatting results, often of a graphical object, using the box's current settings.

Preview Diagram

A section of a dialog box that displays the results of formatting using the current settings of the dialog box and has additional tools surrounding the display to alter formatting.

Primary key

An Access field that contains a unique and constant value for each record and can therefore be used as the common field in linked tables.

Print Layout View

A view of a document as it will appear when you print it. Items such as headers, footnotes, and framed objects appear in their actual positions, and you can drag them to new positions.

Print Preview

Allows you to view how a document, worksheet, slide, or database will appear when printed. Includes a Magnifier tool, a text-editing tool, and the ability to view multiple pages at once. In the new PowerPoint 2002 Print Preview, the main command buttons include Previous Slide, Next Slide, Print, and Close.

Program

Computer software that performs specific tasks, such as Windows 2000 or Microsoft Word. Windows 2000, a utility program, enables you to use application programs. Microsoft Word, an applications program, performs more specialized tasks with specialized documents.

Program button

The button that appears on the taskbar to indicate that an application is open. The active program is represented by a highlighted (Office XP) or indented (Windows 2000) button.

Program window

A window that contains the running program. The window displays the menus and provides the workspace for any document used within the application. The application window shares its borders and title bar with maximized document windows.

Programs menu

A menu on the Windows 2000 Start menu that lists the applications on your computer such as Microsoft Excel.

Promote

To move a line of text up a level in an outline hierarchy.

Properties

The characteristics of a specific element (such as the mouse, keyboard, or desktop display) that you can change. Properties also can refer to characteristics of a file such as its name, type, size, and location.

Properties button

An Access button on the Formatting toolbar that opens the Properties dialog box, which enables you to change selected field or control properties

q

Query

An Access database object that uses a set of instructions you provide to retrieve and display specific data from tables and other queries.

r

Radio button

See "Option button."

RAM (random access memory)

The memory that programs use to function while the computer is on. When you shut down the computer, all information in RAM is lost.

Range

A group of two or more Excel worksheet cells, usually adjacent.

Range name

A name chosen for a selected group of Excel worksheet cells that describes the data they contain.

Read-only

A file setting enabling you to open and read a file, but not modify and then resave it.

Record

In Access, a row in a datasheet composed of all the field data for an individual entry.

Record selector

In Access, clicking this gray box at the left edge of a datasheet record highlights the entire record.

Recycle Bin

An icon on the desktop that represents a temporary storage area for deleted files. Files will remain in the Recycle Bin until you empty it, at which time they are permanently removed from your computer.

Redo command

Counteracts the Undo command by repeating previously reversed actions or changes, usually editing or formatting commands; only undone actions can be redone.

Relational database

A database that contains multiple tables that can be linked to one another.

Relationship

In Access, the join created between two or more tables using common fields.

Relative cell reference

Allows a formula to be moved to a new location on a worksheet. The formula will then follow the same directional instructions from the new starting point using new cell references.

Remove Filter button

In Access, undoes the filter that had previously been applied to your table, and shows all the records that appear in the table.

Repair

A function performed on a Access database when the database is damaged and is performing unpredictably.

Repeat

Command that performs your most recent operation again.

Reply to All

Allows you to send a direct response to an e-mail message that is also received by each recipient of the original message.

Reply to Author

Allows you to send a direct response to an e-mail message.

Report

An Access database object that arranges and formats data specifically for printing.

Resize

To change the size of an object (such as a text box or graphic) by dragging the sizing handles located on its border; you can also adjust the dimensions of many objects from a dialog box.

Resizing pointer

At the edges of windows the mouse pointer turns into a double-headed arrow that is used to change the size of the window by dragging it to the desired size.

Restore

To return a window to its previous size before it was resized (either maximized or minimized). A Restore button usually appears in the upper-right corner of a window, on the title bar.

Restore button

A button on the upper-right side of a window or box. Once you have maximized or minimized it, this button restores it to its original size.

Restore data

When data is lost, the data that comprises the backup copy, must be used to replace, or restore the lost data.

Reviewing toolbar

Contains commands for inserting, deleting, displaying, and navigating between comments.

Right-click

To click the right mouse button; often necessary to access specialized menus and shortcuts. The designated right and left mouse buttons may be reversed with the Mouse control panel to accommodate user preferences.

Rotate handle

The small green circle at the top of a newly inserted object enabling you to turn the object in continuous increments; holding [Shift] while turning an object enables you to move it in discrete increments.

Row

In tables, worksheets, or databases, a horizontally arranged collection of cells generally containing various categories of information related to a particular person, place, type of data, or topic.

Row height

The measurement of a cell from top to bottom.

Row selector button

The gray rectangle that appears to the left of each row and displays its row number.

Ruler

A horizontal or vertical bar marked with measurements such as inches or centimeters that displays, respectively, at the top or left edge of a document window.

Run

To start an application. Also refers to initiating the steps of a macro or activating an Access query.

S

Sans serif font

A font whose characters do not include serifs, the small strokes at the ends of the characters. Arial and Helvetica are sans serif fonts.

Save As

Command you use to save a new file for the first time, to save an existing file in a new location, with a different name, or as a different file type.

Save command

Stores changes you have made to a pre-existing file while maintaining its current location and name.

Screen saver

A moving or changing image that covers your screen when you are not working.

ScreenTip

A brief description of a button or other item that appears when the mouse pointer is paused over it. Other ScreenTips are accessed by using the What's This? feature on the Help menu or by clicking the question mark button in a dialog box.

Scroll arrows

Appear at either end of the scroll bar box. Click them to scroll the scroll bar up or down to view the database you are looking at.

Scroll bar

A graphical device for moving vertically or horizontally through a database object with the mouse. Scroll bars are located along the right and bottom edges of a window.

Scroll bar box

A small gray box located inside a scroll bar that indicates your current position relative to the rest of the document window. You can advance a scroll bar box by dragging it, clicking the scroll bar on either side of it, or clicking the scroll bar arrows.

Search and replace

See Find and replace.

Search command

Allows you to search for local or network files, other computers on your network, Internet addresses, and more.

Search engine

A Web site that generates Web links based on criteria you provide.

Search Explorer Bar

Permits you to keep an Internet search in the browser window and visit links at the same time. Also enables you to search local and network drives for files and folders.

Section

A part of a document separated from the rest of the document by a section break. By separating a document into sections, you can use different page and column formatting in different parts of the same document.

Select

Highlighting an item to indicate that it is the active object on the screen. Usually done in order to perform some operation on the item.

Select All button

The gray rectangle in the upper-left corner of the worksheet where the row and column headings meet. Clicking the Select All button highlights the entire worksheet.

Select query

The most common type of Access query, used to extract and associate fields from tables and other queries and present this data in datasheet form.

Selection bar

An blank column at the left edge of a column of text used to select text with the mouse. In a table, each cell has its own Selection bar at the left edge of the cell.

Sent Items folder

Folder that automatically stores a copy of each e-mail message you send in Outlook Express.

Series of labels

A range of incremental labels created by entering the first label in the series and then dragging the fill handle the number of cells desired. Excel automatically enters the remaining labels in order.

Serif font

A font that has small strokes at the ends of the characters. Times New Roman and Palatino are serif fonts.

Set as Wallpaper

Command that enables you to use an image as desktop wallpaper.

Shared folder

A folder that is accessible over a network to computers other than the one on which it is stored.

Sheet

The term Excel uses to refer to an individual worksheet (Sheet 1, Sheet 2, etc.).

Sheet tab scrolling buttons

Allow you to access Sheet tabs that are not visible in the window. An Excel workbook opens with only 3 worksheets, but you may use 255 per workbook.

Shortcut

A link that takes you directly to a particular file, folder, or program without having to pass through each item in its file hierarchy.

Shortcut key

A keyboard equivalent of a menu command such as [Ctrl]+[S] for Save.

Shortcut menu

A pop-up menu accessed by right-clicking the mouse. The contents of the menu depend on your current activity.

Show/Hide button

Turns on and off the display of nonprinting characters such as formatting, space, and paragraph marks.

Shut down

The process you go through to turn off your computer when you finish working. After you complete this action, it is safe to turn off your computer.

Simple Condition

In Access, a single selection criterion that is used to sort records in a query.

Simple Query Wizard

In Access, a wizard that enables you to create a simple, select query quickly and easily, by helping you through a series of dialog boxes.

Sizing handle

A small circle on the frame of an object (or square on the frame of a chart) that you can drag to resize the object. Sizing handles are generally located on the corners of a frame and at the midpoint of each of its sides.

Slide icon

A small rectangular symbol that rests next to the title of each presentation PowerPoint slide in Outline View.

Slide Navigator

Allows you to go to any PowerPoint slide in a presentation quickly during a slide show.

Slide pane

A sub-window in Normal View that facilitates creating, modifying, and enhancing individual PowerPoint slides.

Slide Show

Runs your PowerPoint slides as they would appear during a presentation.

Slide Show pop-up menu

Menu that offers commands for working with a PowerPoint slide show. Can be opened by clicking the Slide Show pop-up menu icon or by right-clicking a slide.

Slide Sorter View

A PowerPoint view option that displays all slides simultaneously in miniature form. In Slide Sorter View you can rearrange slide order by dragging the miniatures and apply special transition and/or animation effects to individual slides or groups of slides.

Slide Transition effect

A special effect that controls how a PowerPoint slide makes its appearance during a slide show. Slide transition timings can also be set.

Slide Transition icon

A small PowerPoint slide symbol that appears beneath a slide in Slide Sorter view to indicate that a slide transition has been applied to that slide. Clicking the icon runs a preview of the transition effect.

Slides tab

A tab in Normal View that displays miniature, or thumbnail, versions of PowerPoint slides in a presentation and that enables you to select or move PowerPoint slides easily.

Smart Tag

Enables you to perform external actions on types of data that Office XP programs recognize; for example, in Word you can perform actions on names, e-mail address, and so on; in PowerPoint you can perform tasks such as AutoCorrections, copying and pasting text, and so on.

Soft return

In Word, a line break created by pressing [Shift]+[Enter]. This creates a new line without creating a new paragraph.

Sort order

The sequence in which you arrange text or data in a table; ascending order arranges from the start to end of the alphabet, lowest to highest number, or earliest to latest date; descending order arranges in the opposite direction.

Sorting and Grouping dialog box

In Access, allows you to set the sorting order of fields and determine whether a field is used to group data in a report.

Sound Recorder

Windows application that lets you record and play audio.

Source file

A file that you transfer to a destination file—for example, a table from Excel or Access that you insert in a business report in Word.

Specific record box

In Access, the box in the bottom left corner of a datasheet or form that indicates the number of the active record.

Spreadsheet program

A software program used for calculations and financial analysis.

SQL query

In Access, a query created using the Structured Query Language, the basic programming language Access uses to create and perform queries.

Standard toolbar

The row of buttons just below the Menu bar that performs the most basic or commonly used commands in PowerPoint, e.g., Open, Save, and Print.

Standard toolbar

A row of buttons that perform some of the most frequently used commands, such as Open, Print and Save. Usually located under the menu bar.

Start

To open an application for use.

Start button

A button on the taskbar that accesses a special menu that you use to start programs, find files, access Windows Help and more.

Stationery

A picture used to enhance the appearance of an e-mail message.

Status bar

The gray bar at the bottom of an Office XP program window providing information about your current activity in that program. Word shows the current page number and section number, the total number of pages in the document, the vertical position of the insertion point, and whether certain options are active. Excel shows whether a cell is ready for editing and when the Number Lock key is active. PowerPoint information varies depending on which view users are in. The Access status bar displays the field descriptions you entered in Design View, etc.

Structured Query Language (SQL)

Programming language used by Access to create and execute queries.

Style

A group of formatting instructions that you name and store, and are able to modify. When you apply a style to selected characters and paragraphs, all the formatting instructions of that style are applied at once.

Style Checker

A PowerPoint feature that checks your presentation for visual clarity, case, and end punctuation.

Style dialog box

A feature that enables you to examine the overall formatting and styles used in a document template. You can also preview your document formatted in the styles from a selected template.

Subform

In Access, a way of embedding one form into another form, the subform displays related records to the main form.

Summary slide

A PowerPoint slide that summarizes an entire presentation by presenting all of the presentation's slide titles as a bulleted list.

Surfing

A synonym for browsing.

System Tray

The box at the right edge of the Windows 2000 taskbar that houses your system clock and various utility icons.

t

Tab Order

The direction in which the insertion point will move through the fields of an Access database object when hitting the Tab key.

Tab stop

A measured position for placing and aligning text at a specific distance along a line. Word has four kinds of tab stops, left-aligned (the default), centered, right-aligned, and decimal. Tab stops are shown on the horizontal ruler.

Table

One or more rows of cells commonly used to display numbers and other data for quick reference and analysis. Items in a table are organized into rows and columns.

Task Pane

A new feature to Office XP that organizes common tasks in one pane that is convenient to access on the screen. Word task panes include New Document, Basic Search, Clipboard, and Reveal Formatting; Excel includes New Workbook and Basic Search. PowerPoint includes New Presentations, Insert Clip Art, and Slide Layout; Access includes New File, Clipboard, and Search.

Task Scheduler

Allows you to automate Windows tasks.

Taskbar and Start menu command

Allows you to control the behavior and content of the taskbar and the Start menu.

Taskbar, Windows

A bar, usually located at the bottom of the screen, that contains the Start button, shows which programs are running by displaying their program buttons, and shows the current time.

Template

A preconstructed file containing default settings for data, format, and other common features of the file. Word templates exist for letters, memos, faxes, and the like. Excel templates exist for common financial documents. PowerPoint templates exist for various slide designs and layouts. Access templates exist for address books and so on.

Text box

A rectangular area in which text is added so that it may be manipulated independently; can also refer to a box inside a dialog box where you enter information necessary to execute a command.

Text label box

In PowerPoint, a text box created by clicking with the Text Box tool. Text in this type of box does not wrap to the next line when it reaches the edge of the box. Text label boxes are best used for single words or short phrases.

Thesaurus

An Office XP feature that supplies a list of synonyms (words with similar meanings) and antonyms (words with opposite meanings) for a word selected in a document.

Thumbnails View

Allows you to view previews of all image files in a folder rather than file icons.

Timing

The amount of time a PowerPoint slide remains in view before a slide show advances to the next slide. Animation effects also have timings to control when they occur.

Timing icon

In Slide Sorter View, displays the amount of time a PowerPoint slide will remain on the screen before the presentation advances to the next slide.

Title bar

In the default Windows settings, the blue bar at the top of a program window displaying the window sizing buttons, program name, and file name.

Title slide

A slide AutoLayout, generally used for the first PowerPoint slide in a presentation.

Toggle button

An object that simulates the pressing of a button, which may be used in Access for fields that have a "yes" or "no" type entry.

Toolbar

A graphical bar containing buttons that act as shortcuts for common application commands. A docked toolbar sits at the top, bottom, right, or left of the screen and does not block your view of the program window. A floating toolbar appears in its own pane rather than along the edge of the screen.

Toolbox

A set of buttons enabling you to format graphical objects such as dialog boxes, forms, and so on; for example, in Access, one toolbox contains items you can add to a form or report in Design View.

Triple-click

In some programs, performing this action is an easy way to select an entire line or block of text.

Undo command

Reverses the last action you performed. The Undo button includes a drop-down list of all your recent actions so that you may undo multiple operations.

Uniform Resource Locator (URL)

The address of a file on the Internet.

Update Query

An Access query that makes complete, uniform changes to records in one or more tables.

URL

An acronym for Uniform Resource Locator; an address specifying where a particular piece of information can be found. A Web address is a kind of URL.

Utility program

See "Program."

Validation Rule

A rule that determines the type of data that is acceptable in a database.

Validation Text

Lets the user know that the Validation Rule has been violated, and what type of data will be accepted into the database.

Value

The data that you place in the cell of a table, worksheet, or database; see also "Label."

Vertical alignment

The placement of text on a page in relation to the top, bottom, or center of the page.

Vertical ruler

A graphical bar displayed at the left edge of the document window in Print Layout view. You can use this ruler to adjust the top and bottom page margins, and change row height in a table.

Vertical scroll bar

Moves your view up and down through a window, allowing you to view portions of a document that are not currently visible.

View

A display that shows certain aspects of the respective Office XP file. Word includes Normal, Print Layout, Outline, and so on. Excel contains Normal and Page Break Preview. PowerPoint includes the Normal, Slide Sorter, Slide Show, and the like. Access has Database, Form, Report, and Design Views.

View buttons

In PowerPoint, the set of three buttons near the lower-left corner of the program window that take you to the three main program Views. In Word, the buttons in the lower-left corner take you to Normal View, Print Layout View, Web Layout View, or Outline View.

View Datasheet button

Toggles the Datasheet window on and off when you are working in Microsoft Graph.

Wait box

Determines how many idle minutes Windows will wait before initializing a screen saver.

Wallpaper

A picture you apply to your desktop.

Wave (.wav)

A Windows sound file.

Web

A subpart of the Internet that enables users to publish hyperlinked documents on special computers called servers so that others (clients) can access them.

Web browser

A computer application that enables you to view documents on the World Wide Web.

Web Style

A folder option that enables you to select an icon by pointing to it and open an icon with a single click.

Web tab

In the Display Properties dialog box, used to control Active Desktop content.

What's This?

A Help feature that enables you to click on a screen item in order to receive a ScreenTip that explains the item.

What-If analysis

Technique by which you change certain conditions in an Excel worksheet to see how the changes affect the results of your spreadsheet output.

Wildcard characters

Symbols that represent unknown letters or numbers when using the Find feature.

Window

A rectangular area on the screen in which you view and work on files.

Windows Explorer

A tool that allows you to view the hierarchy of folders on your computer and all the subfolders and files in a selected folder. Windows Explorer is very useful for moving and copying files among folders.

Windows Media Player

Windows 2000's audio and video player, capable of playing a variety of sound and movie formats including streaming media.

Winword.exe

The executable file stored on your hard drive or on a network server that actually runs Microsoft Word. When you launch Word from the Start menu, you are actually using a shortcut to this file.

Wizard

A series of specialized dialog boxes that takes you through the completion of certain tasks like creating a professional fax, developing a personal Web page, producing a topic-specific presentation, and so on.

Word processing program

Software used to create documents efficiently. Usually includes features beyond simple editing, such as formatting and arranging text and graphics to create attractive documents.

Word processing text box

A text box created by clicking and dragging with the Text Box tool. A word processing box allows text to wrap to the next line when it reaches the edge of the box and is useful for longer sentences and passages of text.

Word Wrap

Feature that allows text you are typing to continue on the next line when you run out of space on the current line.

WordArt

Text that is inserted as a drawing object, allowing it to be manipulated and formatted as an object rather than as standard text.

WordPad

Windows 2000's built-in word processing program.

Workbook

An Excel file made up of related worksheets. An individual workbook may contain up to 255 worksheets.

Workgroup

A group of computers that is a subdivision of a network.

Worksheet

The Excel workspace made up of columns and rows where you enter data to create an electronic spreadsheet.

Worksheet tab

The markers near the bottom of the Excel window that identify which worksheet is currently active. To open a different worksheet, click its tab. Worksheet tabs can be named to reflect their contents and colored for organizational purposes.

World Wide Web

A major component of the Internet, which is a vast global network of smaller networks and personal computers. Web pages include hyperlinks and present information in a graphical format that can incorporate text, graphics, sounds, and digital movies.

WYSIWYG

An acronym for What You See Is What You Get; indicates that a document will print out with the same formatting that is displayed in the document window.

X-axis label

A label summarizing the horizontal (x-axis) data on a chart.

Y-axis label

A label summarizing the vertical (y-axis) data on a chart.

Zoom

A command used in Print Preview mode while the cursor appears in the shape of a magnifying glass, allows you to take a closer look at the document in Print Preview mode.

Zoom box

The rightmost box on the Standard toolbar for setting the percentage of enlargement of an Office XP program file. Depending on the active program, the default range of enlargements may run from 10% to 500%.

index

The table below summarizes the external data files that have been provided for the student. Many of the exercises in this book cannot be completed without these files. The files are distributed as part of the Instructor's Resource Kit and are also available for download at http://www.mhhe.com/it/cit/index.mhtml. Please note that the table below only lists the raw files that are provided, not the versions students are instructed to save after making changes to the raw files or new files that the students create themselves.

Word 2002

Lesson	Skill Name/Page #	File Name	Introduced In
Lesson 1	Opening an Existing Document/WD 1.10	wddoit1-5.doc	do it! step 4
	Opening an Existing Document/WD 1.11	wdprac1-5.doc	Practice
	Deleting and Inserting Text/WD 1.12	wddoit1-6.doc	do it! step 1
	Deleting and Inserting Text/WD 1.13	wdprac1-6.doc	Practice
	Formatting Text/WD 1.14	wddoit1-7.doc	do it! step 1
	Formatting Text/WD 1.15	wdprac1-7.doc	Practice
	Previewing and Printing a Document/WD 1.16	wddoit1-8.doc	do it! step 1
	Previewing and Printing a Document/WD 1.17	wdprac1-8.doc	Practice
	Interactivity/WD 1.21	wdskills1.doc	Build Your Skills #2
Lesson 2	Searching for Files/WD 2.2	wddoit2-1.doc	do it! step 6
	Searching for Files/WD 2.3	wdprac2-1.doc	Practice
	Selecting Text and Undoing Actions/WD 2.4	wddoit2-2.doc	do it! step 1
	Selecting Text and Undoing Actions/WD 2.5	wdprac2-2.doc	Practice
	Cutting, Copying, and Moving Text/WD 2.6	wddoit2-3.doc	do it! step 1
	Cutting, Copying, and Moving Text/WD 2.7	wdprac2-3.doc	Practice
	Copying and Moving Text with the Mouse/WD 2.8	wddoit2-4.doc	do it! step 1
	Copying and Moving Text with the Mouse/WD 2.9	wdprac2-4.doc	Practice
	Interactivity/WD 2.25	wdskills2.doc	Build Your Skills #1
Lesson 3	Setting Up a Page/WD 3.2	wddoit3-1.doc	do it! step 1
	Setting Up a Page/WD 3.3	wdprac3-1.doc	Practice
	Inserting Page Numbers/WD 3.4	wddoit3-2.doc	do it! step 1
	Inserting Page Numbers/WD 3.5	wdprac3-2.doc	Practice
	Inserting Endnotes and Footnotes/WD 3.6	wddoit3-3.doc	do it! step 1
	Inserting Endnotes and Footnotes/WD 3.7	wdprac3-3.doc	Practice
	Applying Paragraph Indents/WD 3.8	wddoit3-4.doc	do it! step 1
	Applying Paragraph Indents/WD 3.9	wdprac3-4.doc	Practice
	Changing Line Spacing/WD 3.10	wddoit3-5.doc	do it! step 1
	Changing Line Spacing/WD 3.11	wdprac3-5.doc	Practice
	Inserting Page Breaks/WD 3.12	wddoit3-6.doc	do it! step 1
	Inserting Page Breaks/WD 3.13	wdprac3-6.doc	Practice
	Working with Multiple Documents/WD 3.14	wddoit3-7.doc	do it! step 1
	Working with Multiple Documents/WD 3.14	wddoit3-7a.doc	do it! step 1
	Working with Multiple Documents/WD 3.15	wdprac3-7.doc	Practice
	Working with Multiple Documents/WD 3.15	wdprac3-7a.doc	Practice
	Using the Format Painter/WD 3.16	wddoit3-8.doc	do it! step 1
	Using the Format Painter/WD 3.17	wdprac3-8.doc	Practice
	Checking Spelling and Grammar/WD 3.18	wddoit3-9.doc	do it! step 1
	Checking Spelling and Grammar/WD 3.19	wdprac3-9.doc	Practice
	Using AutoCorrect/WD 3.25	wdprac3-10.doc	Practice
	Inserting Frequently Used Text/WD 3.29	wdprac3-11.doc	Practice
	Using the Word Thesaurus/WD 3.30	wddoit3-12.doc	do it! step 1
	Using the Word Thesaurus/WD 3.31	wdprac3-12.doc	Practice
	Finding and Replacing Text/WD 3.32	wddoit3-13.doc	do it! step 1
	Finding and Replacing Text/WD 3.33	wdprac3-13.doc	Practice

Word 2002 (continued)

Lesson	Skill Name/Page #	File Name	Introduced In
Lesson 3	Interactivity/WD 3.37	wdskills3.doc	Build Your Skills #1
	Interactivity/WD 2.37	wdskills3a.doc	Build Your Skills #4
	Interactivity/WD 3.38	wdproblem3.doc	Problem Solving #1
	Interactivity/WD 3.38	wdproblem3a.doc	Problem Solving #1
Lesson 4	Creating and Modifying Tables/WD 4.2	wddoit4-1.doc	do it! step 1
	Creating and Modifying Tables/WD 4.5	wdprac4-1.doc	Practice
	Editing Tables/WD 4.6	wddoit4-2.doc	do it! step 1
	Editing Tables/WD 4.7	wdprac4-2.doc	Practice
	Inserting and Deleting Rows, Columns, and Cells/WD 4.8	wddoit4-3.doc	do it! step 1
	Inserting and Deleting Rows, Columns, and Cells/WD 4.9	wdprac4-3.doc	Practice
	Sorting Data in a Table/WD 4.10	wddoit4-4.doc	do it! step 1
	Sorting Data in a Table/WD 4.11	wdprac4-4.doc	Practice
	Calculating Data in a Table/WD 4.12	wddoit4-5.doc	do it! step 1
	Calculating Data in a Table/WD 4.15	wdprac4-5.doc	Practice
	Formatting a Table/WD 4.16	wddoit4-6.doc	do it! step 1
	Formatting a Table/WD 4.17	wdprac4-6.doc	Practice
	Creating a Chart/WD 4.18	wddoit4-7.doc	do it! step 1
	Creating a Chart/WD 4.19	wdprac4-7.doc	Practice
	Editing a Chart/WD 4.20	wddoit4-8.doc	do it! step 1
	Editing a Chart/WD 4.21	wdprac4-8.doc	Practice
	Adding Borders and Shading/WD 4.26	wddoit4-9.doc	do it! step 1
	Adding Borders and Shading/WD 4.29	mywdprac4-6.doc	Practice

Excel 2002

Lesson	Skill Name/Page #	File Name	Introduced In
Lesson 1	Opening a Workbook/EX 1.20	exdoit1-7.xls	do it! step 4
	Opening a Workbook/EX 1.21	exprac1-7.xls	Practice
	Editing a Cell's Information/EX 1.22	exdoit1-8.xls	do it! step 1
	Editing a Cell's Information/EX 1.23	exprac1-8.xls	Practice
Lesson 2	Cutting, Copying, and Pasting Labels/EX 2.2	exdoit2-1.xls	do it! step 1
	Cutting, Copying, and Pasting Labels/EX 2.3	exprac2.xls	Practice
	Entering Values/EX 2.4	exdoit2-2.xls	do it! step 1
	Entering Values/EX 2.5	exprac2.xls	Practice
	Entering Formulas/EX 2.6	exdoit2-3.xls	do it! step 1
	Entering Formulas/EX 2.7	exprac2.xls	Practice
	Using Functions/EX 2.8	exdoit2-4.xls	do it! step 1
	Using Functions/EX 2.9	exprac2.xls	Practice
	Using the Insert Function Feature/EX 2.10	exdoit2-5.xls	do it! step 1
	Using the Insert Function Feature/EX 2.11	exprac2.xls	Practice
	Copying and Pasting Formulas/EX 2.12	exdoit2-6.xls	do it! step 1
	Copying and Pasting Formulas/EX 2.15	exprac2.xls	Practice
	Using What-If Analysis/EX 2.16	exdoit2-7.xls	do it! step 1
	Using What-If Analysis/EX 2.19	exprac2.xls	Practice
	Previewing and Printing a Worksheet/EX 2.20	exdoit2-8.xls	do it! step 1
	Previewing and Printing a Worksheet/EX 2.21	exprac2.xls	Practice
	Interactivity/EX 2.25	exskills2.xls	Build Your Skills #1
	Interactivity/EX 2.26	exproblem2-1.xls	Problem Solving #1
	Interactivity/EX 2.26	exproblem2-2.xls	Problem Solving #2
Lesson 3	Merging and Splitting Cells/EX 3.2	exdoit3-1.xls	do it! step 1
	Merging and Splitting Cells/EX 3.3	exprac3.xls	Practice
	Formatting Cell Labels/EX 3.4	exdoit3-2.xls	do it! step 1
	Formatting Cell Labels/EX 3.5	exprac3.xls	Practice
	Formatting Cell Values/EX 3.6	exdoit3-3.xls	do it! step 1
	Formatting Cell Values/EX 3.7	exprac3.xls	Practice
	Formatting Rows and Columns/EX 3.8	exdoit3-4.xls	do it! step 1
	Formatting Rows and Columns/EX 3.9	exprac3.xls	Practice
	Inserting and Deleting Rows and Columns/EX 3.10	exdoit3-5.xls	do it! step 1
	Inserting and Deleting Rows and Columns/EX 3.11	exprac3.xls	Practice
	Hiding, Unhiding, and Protecting Cells/EX 3.12	exdoit3-6.xls	do it! step 1
	Hiding, Unhiding, and Protecting Cells/EX 3.15	exprac3.xls	Practice
	Defining and Naming Ranges/EX 3.16	exdoit3-7.xls	do it! step 1
	Defining and Naming Ranges/EX 3.17	exprac3.xls	Practice
	Filling a Cell Range with Labels/EX 3.18	exdoit3-8.xls	do it! step 1
	Filling a Cell Range with Labels/EX 3.19	exprac3.xls	Practice
	Applying Shading, Patterns, and Borders to Cells & Ranges/EX 3.20	exdoit3-9.xls	do it! step 1
	Applying Shading, Patterns, and Borders to Cells & Ranges/EX 3.21	exprac3.xls	Practice

cel 2002 (continued)

Lesson	Skill Name/Page #	File Name	Introduced In
Lesson 3	Applying AutoFormat to a Worksheet/EX 3.22	exdoit3-10.xls	do it! step 1
	Applying AutoFormat to a Worksheet/EX 3.23	exprac3.xls	Practice
	Interactivity/EX 3.27	exskills3.xls	Build Your Skills #1
	Interactivity/EX 3.28	exproblem3-1.xls	Problem Solving #3
Lesson 4	Inserting Text Objects/EX 4.2	exdoit4-1.xls	do it! step 1
	Inserting Text Objects/EX 4.3	exprac4.xls	Practice
	Enhancing Graphics/EX 4.4	exdoit4-2.xls	do it! step 1
	Enhancing Graphics/EX 4.5	exprac4.xls	Practice
	Adding and Editing Comments/EX 4.6	exdoit4-3.xls	do it! step 1
	Adding and Editing Comments/EX 4.7	exprac4.xls	Practice
	Creating a Chart/EX 4.10	exdoit4-5.xls	do it! step 1
	Creating a Chart/EX 4.13	exprac4.xls	Practice
	Moving and Resizing a Chart/EX 4.14	exdoit4-6.xls	do it! step 1
	Moving and Resizing a Chart/EX 4.15	exprac4.xls	Practice
	Formatting a Chart/EX 4.16	exdoit4-7.xls	do it! step 1
	Formatting a Chart/EX 4.17	exprac4.xls	Practice
	Changing a Chart's Type/EX 4.18	exdoit4-8.xls	do it! step 1
	Changing a Chart's Type/EX 4.19	exprac4.xls	Practice
	Using Advanced Printing Features/EX 4.20	exdoit4-9.xls	do it! step 1
	Using Advanced Printing Features/EX 4.21	exprac4.xls	Practice
	Interactivity/EX 4.25	exskills4.xls	Build Your Skills #1
	Interactivity/EX 4.26	exproblem4-2.xls	Problem Solving #2
	Interactivity/EX 4.26	exproblem4-3.xls	Problem Solving #3

Access 2002

Lesson	Skill Name/Page #	File Name	Introduced In
Lesson 1	Opening an Existing Database/AC 1.2	Office Furniture Inc	do it! step 4
	Opening an Existing Database/AC 1.3	Home Video Collection	Practice
	Editing Records in a Datasheet/AC 1.15	acprac1-7.doc	Practice
	Interactivity/AC 1.25	Recipes	Build Your Skills #1
	Interactivity/AC 1.26	Pepper Sirloin Steak.doc	Build Your Skills #5
	Interactivity/AC 1.26	Chocolate Turtle Cheesecake.doc	Build Your Skills #5
Lesson 2	Using the Table Wizard/AC 2.7	Tuning Tracker	Practice
	Establishing Table Relationships/AC 2.16	Employees 2	do it! step 1
Lesson 3	Creating an AutoForm/AC 3.3	Tuning Tracker 2	Practice
	Entering Records Using a Form/AC 3.21	acprac3-8.doc	Practice
Lesson 4	No new files		

owerPoint 2002

Lesson	Skill Name/Page #	File Name	Introduced In
Lesson 1	No pre-existing files		
Lesson 2	Opening an Existing PowerPoint File/PP 2.5	ppprac2-2.ppt	Practice
	Working with Text on the Outline Tab/PP 2.10	ppdoit2-5.ppt	doit! step 1
Lesson 3	Editing and Adding Text Boxes/PP 3.2	ppdoit3-1.ppt	doit! step 1
	Formatting Text/PP 3.9	ppprac3-2.ppt	Practice
	Moving Text Boxes and Aligning Text/PP 3.11	ppprac3-3.ppt	Practice
	Using Spell Check/PP 3.13	ppprac3-4.ppt	Practice
	Finding and Replacing Text/PP 3.15	ppprac3-5.ppt	Practice
	Drawing and Formatting Objects/PP 3.21	ppprac3-7.ppt	Practice
	Modifying and Enhancing Drawn Objects/PP 3.23	ppprac3-8.ppt	Practice
	Printing Audience Handouts/PP 3.25	ppprac3-9.ppt	Practice
	Saving Slide Presentations as RTF Files/PP 3.27	ppprac3-10.ppt	Practice
Lesson 4	Adding Clip Art/PP 4.2	ppdoit4-1.ppt	doit! step 1
	Adding Clip Art/PP 4.3	ppprac4-1.ppt	Practice
	Editing Clip Art/PP 4.7	ppprac4-2.ppt	Practice
	Inserting a Picture from a File/PP 4.8	ppcheckbox.bmp	doit! step 3
	Inserting a Picture from a File/PP 4.9	ppprac4-3.bmp	Practice
	Inserting a Chart/PP 4.10	ppprac4-4.ppt	Practice
	Customizing the Datasheet/PP 4.13	ppprac4-5.ppt	Practice
	Changing a Chart's Type/PP 4.15	ppprac4-6.ppt	Practice
	Setting Chart Options/PP 4.17	ppprac4-7.ppt	Practice
	Formatting Chart Elements/PP 4.21	ppprac4-8.ppt	Practice
	Adding Transition Effects/PP 4.25	ppprac4-9.ppt	Practice
	Navigating during a Slide Show/4.31	ppprac4-12.ppt	Practice
	Interactivity/PP 4.35	ppskills4-1.ppt	Build Your Skills #1
	Interactivity/PP 4.35	ppskillsimage4-1.bmp	Build Your Skills #1
	Interactivity/PP 4.35	ppskills4-5.ppt	Build Your Skills #5